Contemporary Authors®

Autobiography Series

ISSN 0748-0636

Contemporary Authors

Autobiography Series

Joyce Nakamura
Editor

Sheryl Ciccarelli
Motoko Fujishiro Huthwaite
Associate Editors

volume **29**

GALE

DETROIT · NEW YORK · TORONTO · LONDON

EDITORIAL STAFF

Joyce Nakamura, *Editor*
Sheryl Ciccarelli, Motoko Fujishiro Huthwaite,
Arlene Johnson, and Stephen Thor Tschirhart, *Associate Editors*
Marilyn O'Connell Allen, Melissa Hill, and Crystal Towns, *Assistant Editors*
Shelly Andrews, Cindy Buck, Charity Anne Dorgan, Mary Gillis,
Heidi Hagen, Carolyn C. March, and Adele Sarkissian, *Contributing Copyeditors*
Linda Andres, Kevin Hile, Tom McMahon, and Diane Telgen, *Contributing Editors*

Victoria B. Cariappa, *Research Manager*
Corporate Research Information Service

Hal May, *Publisher, Literature and Language Division*

Mary Beth Trimper, *Production Director*
Deborah Milliken, *Production Assistant*

Barbara Yarrow, *Graphic Services Manager*
Randy A. Bassett, *Image Database Supervisor*
Robert Duncan, *Imaging Specialist*
Pamela A. Reed, *Photography Coordinator*

Theresa Rocklin, *Manager, Technical Support Services*

Gale Research
835 Penobscot Building
645 Griswold Street
Detroit, MI 48226-4094

Library of Congress Catalog Card Number 86-641293
ISBN 0-7876-1974-4
ISSN 0748-0636

Printed in the United States of America

10   9   8   7   6   5   4   3   2   1

Contents

Preface   vii
Acknowledgments   xi

Preface

A Unique Collection of Essays

Each volume in the *Contemporary Authors Autobiography Series (CAAS)* presents an original collection of autobiographical essays written especially for the series by noted writers.

CA Autobiography Series is designed to be a meeting place for writers and readers—a place where writers can present themselves, on their own terms, to their audience; and a place where general readers, students of contemporary literature, teachers and librarians, even aspiring writers can become better acquainted with familiar authors and meet others for the first time.

This is an opportunity for writers who may never write a full-length autobiography to let their readers know how they see themselves and their work, what brought them to this time and place.

Even for those authors who have already published full-length autobiographies, there is the opportunity in *CAAS* to bring their readers "up to date" or perhaps to take a different approach in the essay format. In some instances, previously published material may be reprinted or expanded upon; this fact is always noted at the end of such an essay. Individually, the essays in this series can enhance the reader's understanding of a writer's work; collectively, they are lessons in the creative process and in the discovery of its roots.

CAAS makes no attempt to give a comprehensive overview of authors and their works. That outlook is already well represented in biographies, reviews, and critiques published in a wide variety of sources. Instead, *CAAS* complements that perspective and presents what no other ongoing reference source does: the view of contemporary writers that is shaped by their own choice of materials and their own manner of storytelling.

Who Is Covered?

Like its parent series, *Contemporary Authors,* the *CA Autobiography Series* sets out to meet the needs and interests of a wide range of readers. Each volume includes essays by writers in all genres whose work is being read today. We consider it extraordinary that so many busy authors from throughout the world are able to interrupt their existing writing, teaching, speaking, traveling, and other schedules to converge on a given deadline for any one volume. So it is not always possible that all genres can be equally and uniformly represented from volume to volume, although we strive to include writers working in a variety of categories, including fiction, nonfiction, and poetry. As only a few writers specialize in a single area, the breadth of writings by authors in this volume also encompasses drama, translation, and criticism as well as work for movies, television, radio, newspapers, and journals.

What Each Essay Includes

Authors who contribute to *CAAS* are invited to write a "mini-autobiography" of approximately 10,000 words. In order to give the writer's imagination free rein, we suggest no guidelines or pattern for the essay.

We only ask that each writer tell his or her story in the manner and to the extent that feels most natural and appropriate. In addition, writers are asked to supply a selection of personal photographs showing themselves at various ages, as well as important people and special moments in their lives. Our contributors have responded generously, sharing with us some of their most treasured mementoes. The result is a special blend of text and photographs that will attract even the casual browser. Other features include:

Bibliography at the end of each essay, listing book-length works in chronological order of publication. Each bibliography in this volume was compiled by members of the *CAAS* editorial staff and submitted to the author for review.

Cumulative index in each volume, which cites all the essayists in the series as well as the subjects presented in the essays: personal names, titles of works, geographical names, schools of writing, etc. To ensure ease of use for these cumulating references, the name of the essayist is given before the volume and page number(s) for every reference that appears in more than one essay. In the following example, the entry in the index allows the user to identify the essay writers by name:

> Auden, W.H.
> Allen   **6**:18, 24
> Ashby   **6**:36, 39
> Bowles   **1**:86
> etc.

For references that appear in only one essay, the volume and page number(s) are given but the name of the essayist is omitted. For example:

> Stieglitz, Alfred   **1**:104, 109, 110

CAAS is something more than the sum of its individual essays. At many points the essays touch common ground, and from these intersections emerge new patterns of information and impressions. The index is an important guide to these interconnections.

For Additional Information

For detailed information on awards won, adaptations of works, critical reviews of works, and more, readers are encouraged to consult Gale's *Contemporary Authors* cumulative index for authors' listings in other Gale sources. These include, among others, *Contemporary Authors*, *Contemporary Authors New Revision Series*, *Dictionary of Literary Biography,* and *Contemporary Literary Criticism*. For autobiographical entries written by children and young adult authors, see *Something about the Author Autobiography Series.*

Special Thanks

We wish to acknowledge our special gratitude to each of the authors in this volume.

They all have been most kind and cooperative in contributing not only their talents but their enthusiasm and encouragement to this project.

Contact the Editor

We encourage our readers to explore the whole *CAAS* series. Please write and tell us if we can make *CAAS* more helpful to you. Direct your comments and suggestions to the editor:

MAIL: Editor, *Contemporary Authors Autobiography Series*
Gale Research
835 Penobscot Bldg.
645 Griswold St.
Detroit, MI 48226-4094

TELEPHONE: (800) 347-GALE

FAX: (313) 961-6599

Acknowledgments

Grateful acknowledgment is made to those publishers, photographers, and artists whose works appear with these authors' essays.

Photographs/Art

Michael Basinski: p. 9, Nick Culkowski; p. 12, Ed Sobala.

Sven Birkerts: p. 17, S. Lippman.

Michael J. Bugeja: p. 50, Diane Bugeja.

Wanda Coleman: p. 53, Susan Carpendale; p. 68, George Evans; p. 73, Suzan Carson; p. 75, Terry Dorn; p. 76, Fred Burkhart.

Ann Erickson: pp. 101, 117, Nonie Mitchell.

Kaye McDonough: p. 212, Mark Green; p. 217, Mary Lucas; p. 218, John Geluardi.

Luis J. Rodriguez: p. 223, Mary Harrison; p. 228, *Los Angeles Times/Home Magazine.*

Gerald Rosen: p. 237, James Lerager; p. 242, Grant; p. 247, Sp4 Clark T. Bell/Post Signal Facility.

Ron Silliman: p. 340, Lennox Photo & Camera Shop.

Text

Michael J. Bugeja: Poems "J," "Hook, Line and Sinker," "Elegy: A Corrected Vision," "Art: A Possible Explanation," and "Re-Defining the Blues" from *What We Do for Music,* by Michael J. Bugeja. Amelia Press, 1990. Copyright © 1990 by Michael J. Bugeja.\ Poems "Song: To Ben," "Dr. Williams Calls," and "Bus Crash" from *Talk,* by Michael J. Bugeja. University of Arkansas Press, 1997. Copyright © 1997 by Michael J. Bugeja.\ Poem "HUNGER: Cafe Figaro" from *Flight from Valhalla: Poems,* by Michael J. Bugeja. Livingston University Press, 1993. Copyright © 1993 by Michael J. Bugeja. Reprinted by permission of Livingston University Press.\ Poem "Duty" from *The Visionary,* by Michael J. Bugega. Reprinted, Orchises Press, 1994. Copyright © 1994 by Michael J. Bugeja. Excerpt from "Adoption: The Fulfillment." Copyright © by Michael J. Bugeja. Both reprinted by permission of Orchises Press.\ Unpublished poem "Life's Ineffable Edge." Copyright © Michael J. Bugeja.

Wanda Coleman: All poems copyright © Wanda Coleman.\ Excerpts from "Hand Dance"

Michael Basinski

1950-

Michael Basinski, 1997

Ancient Factacy as a Form of Fictive Historical Memory

Eastern Slavs, at the beginning of their history, would cremate their dead, collect their ashes, and place them in urns. These urns would then be buried. The cinerary urns were sealed with a form of inverted dish. In very early burials a hole was carefully bored in the center of this dish. The hole was provided to permit the ghost to escape.

North and east of the Roman Empire, east of Teutonic Germania, in the forests surrounding the Elbe, Oder, and Vistula Rivers, was found the Lusatian Culture, the culture of the Slavs. In this territory lived the Venedian, a Proto-Slavic tribe. Because Venedian territory was a very long way from the Roman Empire, Rome's recorded history and the history of Western Europe, little is widely known in the west about this Slavic tribe.

The Venedian pantheon resembles that of other Indo-European tribes. Perun, Pron, Parom, or Perunder was their sky god. Perundan was Thursday. The Lithuanians called him Perkunas. The oak grove was his sacred place. Perun's name was used in the ritual of the rain charm. The Poles use the word *piorum* as an appellation for thunder and lightning. My grandfather would summon this god as an oath, a curse. "*Peruna!* May lightning strike you dead."

1

There was a goddess. Her name was Mokos, which means moist. She was the equivalent of the oriental Astarte or the Persian Anahita. She is personified as mother-moist-earth and survives outside the official pantheons in the imagination of the populace. Like a siren, she summons the Slav to earth and order.

The cult of Mary is preeminent in Poland.

A Legend: The Picture of Our Lady of Czestochowa

Prior to the year 1382, the history of the miraculous painting of Our Lady of Czestochowa rests in historical, shrouded desire. St. Luke painted the painting. He depicted the Holy Mother pensive in suffering, with deep sorrow reflected in her eyes and clouded brow. In 326 St. Helen, mother of Constantine the Great, moved the painting from Jerusalem to Constantinople. The painting found its way to southern Poland as part of a dowry. Ladislaus, prince of Opole and regent for Louis the Great in Poland, placed the image in Czestochowa, a small town in the middle of Poland. The Venerable Image was placed in the keep of members of the Order of St. Paul the First Hermit. It was 1382.

The painting is one of the oldest of the Blessed Virgin in the world. She is a Black Madonna. The scars on her face date from 1430, when a bandit struck the painting with a sword. The bandit fell dead. In 1656 the Blessed Virgin was declared Queen of Poland after the forty-day siege of Czestochowa by the invading Swedish army.

In each room of the house in which I lived as a child was the image of Mary. There were the many Marys of the kitchen and the many Marys of the dining room. There was the Mary of the bedroom, the parlor, and the hall. There was young Mary, Mary with the moon, Mary the Madonna, the Madonna and Child, and Mary with her naked foot on the neck of the snake.

The Fictorical Account Continues

The Slavs also venerated other beings of lesser orders. They all had supernatural powers. The world was populated by spirits, shadows, and pixies. There were familiars. Water

was alive. Stone was alive. A tree is a spirit being. A blade of grass can bless or harm. The darkness is the prankish time, thick with its own mischievous magic and impish dance. It is itself a spirit, and it lives. Pixies, *barstokai,* and duende live everywhere in the home, fields, in the forests, in the root cellar, mountains, in the swamps, streams, air, and orchards. Everything is alive, and each being can be playful and naughty. The line between realms does not exist. Stones talk. Water sings.

However, for the Slavs, the world was not simply bucolic or nasty. Death was everywhere. Cholera killed. My grandfather would summon the power of the disease with the most frightening of interjections: *O Cholera!* Or, *Idz do cholery.* The letter *c* is not pronounced in this interjection, which means very literally: "May cholera take you quickly." Or my grandfather would use the much more violent and mysterious interjection: *Psiakrew!* This powerful word is still very frightening to me. Literally the word means "dog's blood." Its power and impact, however, reside not in its meaning but in using the word at the height and heat of anger where meaning is meaningless and only the pure power of language magic is present. Magic was needed. Wolves killed. Romans murdered, as did the Huns, the Swedes, and the Rus. Barbaric, sub-human, Celtic idiots captured and ate Slavic children. Dark spirits, the undead, lurked. Bless yourself. Have the mark of the Three Kings above your door: K + M + B.

For me, Eastern Europe existed and did not exist. It was always, and still is for me, a place of shadow and sorcery and non-shadow. She is an elf princess dancing in the dusk or the movement you see in complete darkness. Out of the old European forests and dank swamps, bogs, and mountains, out of my mind, emerged a Poland—Poland, the Christ of nations, a country, a mystical location, an unknown place which is my ancestral nativity.

Ancestral Genealogy Recorded for the First Time Fresh from the Oral Narrative Tradition of a Kin-keeper

More to the fictive fact: sometime, so it was said, in 1878 or 1879, Michael and Rozalia (née Staniszewski) Rawski arrived in Buffalo, New York. They were Polish but Poland did not exist as a country. They were *Prusiks, Prusik*

Poles, as the story goes. In partitioned Poland my great-grandparents were the subjects of the Emperor of Germany. Their language was not permitted. Their culture was not permitted. In Buffalo, in 1882, the couple had a son (my grandfather). His name was Francis. He was baptized at St. Anne's Parish on Broadway, on the east side of Buffalo. The German Catholic priests misspelled his last name. They spelled it: R-A-F-S-K-Y. Since my host culture was never sensitive enough to spell Polish names correctly or pronounce them correctly, I've never felt an obligation to honor the spelling, grammar, or syntax of English.

America was, no doubt, better than life under the Germans, but it was not bucolic. Death, as in Europe, haunted the Polish immigrant community. In 1898 Michael Rawski fell to his death in a grain elevator. He left his wife and six children alone. Frank (my grandfather was never called Francis) went to work on the Buffalo docks. He was sixteen. He used the name Kelly. Probably, as the story goes, to please the Irish labor gang bosses. Frank was my mother's father. Alice Rawski was born in 1922.

In 1881, leaving German-occupied Poland, Michael and Jadwiga (née Bakos) emigrated to Buffalo. In all, they had six children that lived. One was a daughter, Anna, my grandmother. She and Frank married. She was eighteen and he was twenty-five. Each day to the docks she brought him lunch and a bucket of beer. They had nine children, eight that lived. Anna managed the family, obviously, and she worked in the Ellicott Square Building, then the largest office building in the world. She cleaned. One of the elevator operators was Joseph Basinski.

Joseph Basinski arrived at Ellis Island as a ten year old with his parents Anton and Maryjana Basinski. They took the train to Buffalo. Like other immigrant children on the east side, Joseph grew up in the bustling, expanding Polish neighborhoods. Rapidly constructed barracks housed new immigrants. German construction companies in league with powerful Polish priests built houses. To the west of this community was German-Catholic Buffalo. To the east was farmland. To the south were the Irish and the mills. The community was ruled by emperor priests that wielded huge economic, political, and spiritual power. The Reverend John Pitass was such a priest, and he ruled from St. Stanislaus Parish. He published the newspaper, intervened in labor disputes, and ran an immi-

grant bank. Volatile, energetic, and powerful, the communities fueled the factories of burgeoning Buffalo, New York. Buffalo was once the second- largest rail center in the nation and a leader in grain milling and steel manufacturing. Bethlehem Steel, in Lackawanna, employed twenty thousand workers. Republic Steel employed a work force of five thousand. After fighting in World War I, Joseph Basinski became a steel worker at the Republic plant.

During the same era, Michael and Maryanna Nowakowski arrived in Buffalo. Their daughter, Valaria, was born in 1902. She worked for her uncle Joseph Wysocki, a railroad worker and entrepreneur. He owned houses and a tavern near the tracks. Valaria cooked, waited on tables, washed dishes, and cleaned. She met Joseph Basinski. She was sixteen. He was twenty-six. They were married and lived in back of Wysocki's tavern. They had ten children. Their first son was born in 1920. His name was Michael, and he was my father.

These Polish immigrants and their children worked, slaved, and saved. The political system was rampant with corruption. Gerrymandering deprived the Poles in Buffalo of political clout. The Irish controlled the Catholic Church, and while Pitass was made Dean of all Polish parishes in Buffalo, the hierarchy of the Church remained Irish. Poles unloaded the grain boats. They made steel. They built cars and worked the coke ovens and forges. The women worked in silk mills (textile mills). Eugenic literature noted that Poles were only slightly more intelligent than Negroes. As Louis Adamic once wrote, "America is champagne served in a rusty can."

A Story

Frank Rawski, my grandfather, told me that he remembered the night that St. Adalbert's burned to the ground. The date was January 26, 1889. He said the entire community flocked to the site of the burning church. He also told me that as a boy he swam in a pond behind the church, the site of St. Adalbert's parish school (completed in 1887). In 1913, during a schismatic religious upsurge, parishioners broke with St. Adalbert's and the Catholic Church's allegiance to Rome. They marched down the block and founded a Polish National Church, the Holy Mother of the Rosary Parish, and built a cathedral. This became the parish of Joseph and Valaria Basinski and their children, including my father, Michael. The Polish Nationals could not pay their mortgage, and for a time the Catholic Church seized the cathedral. In court the Polish Nationals won their property back. The Catholics then moved across the street and built another parish, Queen of the Most Holy Rosary. My mother belonged to this parish. Hostilities between the two religious groups were high and remained high. When Michael and Alice were married in 1948 at Queen of the Most Holy Rosary Church, my grandmother did not attend the ceremony. She did, however, watch the bride and groom leave the church from her side of the street. My grandfather, Joseph, did attend the marriage ceremony, although he was dying of cancer. It was the last time he left his home. I was baptized at Queen of the Most Holy Rosary Church. In 1983, Eileen and I were married in St. Adalbert's Basilica. My father attended. Natalie was baptized at St. Adalbert's in 1985. The circle is complete.

Another Story

Joseph Basinski worked at Republic Steel. He worked with another man from the Walden/ Baily neighborhood named Tony Wojtan. Often they walked to the plant together to save the nickel trolley fare. Tony also worked at the mill, the bar mill, with my father Michael Basinski. Tony Wojtan's granddaughter, Eileen Kocieniewski, also worked in the bar mill with my father. Later, I met Eileen Kocieniewski, and we married. So, this is a tale of Republic Steel, urban community life, and old-time, working-class neighborhoods. The circle is complete.

Pa and Ma

My father, Michael Joseph Basinski, drove a truck before World War II. During the war he became a staff sergeant and won the Bronze Star. He fought in North Africa and Italy and was a member of the Blue Devils. He worked at Republic Steel his entire adult life. I am sure he would be alive and working to this day if Ronald Reagan and his Republican pirates hadn't sold the U.S. steel companies down the river and into Asia. He died in my arms after Christmas dinner six months after the plant

closed. Thanks, Ron, what a great presidency. My mother, Alice Basinski, worked in an airplane factory during World War II. Later, she worked packing tomatoes and then in a china factory. She wanted to be a secretary. But we all know how the rich help the poor achieve their goals in our society. Who would pack their tomatoes? Who would make their cups and plates? Who would make their war planes? Who would fight their wars? Alice Basinski was a factory worker all her life.

Rocks

During the Paleozoic era, 350 million years ago, western New York was under water. The area was covered by a great sea that blanketed most of the central United States. The layer of rock most often found in local digs dates from the Devonian period. Devonian invertebrate fossils abound. There are brachiopods, rugose horn corals, Bryozoa, crinoids, gastropods and cephalopods, and trilobites. This is my place. I was born on a Sunday night, at 10:00 P.M., on November 19, 1950.

First Memories

My first memory: Being carried. I am in arms. Someone. It is my father. And from above I see light pouring in, down. It is sunbeams. For years I did not know what the light was. But it was light pouring through stained-glass windows in an old, massive, Catholic church in Buffalo. I have an imagination that it was a baptism.

I have a memory of playing outside in the dirt. And I made a village, a Native American village. And again I recall going outside to play, and I went back to the place where I made my village. It was gone, removed or cleaned. Perhaps it was too close to some tomato plant? One knows how plants detest villages. But probably my play got dirt on the driveway. How appalling! Creation is like that, horrible. So it is with art. Art is dirt that gets on civilized sidewalks. Life instructs.

I have another memory. There was a man next door named Ray. He told me there was a bear loose in his house and that the bear lived in the basement. He wanted me to see the bear. I peered down his basement steps,

About 1955

and I saw the bear's paw prints leading to the coal bin. Forever, the prints of bears are there to be followed. There is a bear in every poet's house. I see bears everyday.

I have another memory. I built a farm on the floor with my blocks. There were corrals and stalls for my rubber animals, chickens, white calves, brown-and-white hogs and piglets. I went somewhere to visit a relative. When I returned my father was home, and we went into my bedroom. He told me how he had completed my zoo! I told him it was a beautiful zoo. Forever, creation will need precise definition. The obvious is never comprehensible.

I have another early memory. I was at the zoo, a place I very much loved. I loved all the animals. I was in the reptile house. At that point the reptile house was open to the public at feeding time. I remember in one enclosure, behind clear glass, a snake, a large snake. The snake was slowly and purposely slinking, with its tongue jutting in and out, towards a small flock of yellow chicks. The yellow chicks were peeping and peeping. I felt their fear and was

helpless. I was frozen with fear and outrage. I was helpless. I learned all about humanity.

My Education

I went to kindergarten at School 56. I magically adjusted rapidly and without much anxiety. I don't know why. This was a pattern I would not repeat often. I recall my mother asking me how I was doing. I remember telling her OK. And I remember telling her to leave. My first day at school I was assigned to play with clay. I built a clay corral and horses. I molded cactus and rattlesnakes. I made saddles and scenery. I recreated the entire Old West in gray clay. A boy that sat next to me was intrigued by my creativity and the direct channel I had with my imagination, and he played along, haphazardly. He spent all day working on a lame-looking cowboy that laid flat on the table! My creation was elaborate, and his was pitiful. When the teacher came around to inspect "OUR" work "WE" were praised elaborately and were allowed to display "OUR" work. But it was my work that was unique and intricate! His cowboy was simply a lump of lifeless mud. But we had worked, supposedly, together. We got equal credit. This was team work.

The bigger kids, the fifth graders or the sixth graders, told us little ones that School 56 was haunted. They said that a ghost lived on the upper floors of the school. During a fire drill, I saw the ghost peering down at me. I wasn't afraid.

My Education Continues

I was six. My mother sent me to parochial school. I was delivered into the clutches of the Felician nuns at Queen of the Most Holy Rosary School. These were among the most hideous and heinous years I was forced to endure. The Felicians were a barbarous community. Daily, we would be verbally intimidated, threatened with eternal life in Hell, stripped of grace, slapped and hit in class, beaten, insulted, and threatened with Sister Superior's office. And we would pray. And we would pray. We went to Mass each morning. We went to Mass in the afternoon. And more and more prayers were offered for our corrupt souls. The parish church and school were one large redbrick building. The grade school was on the first floor. There was a subterraneous chapel, and the main church was on the top floor of the building and the vaulted ceiling pushed its way up, a portal to the heavenly domain of Jesus, Mary, the saints, and God. Each day we school children filed by a mural on our way up to Mass. The mural depicted the Virgin Mary on a cloud pedestal. She was surrounded by suffering, screaming, pleading, naked people. They were modestly naked. Clouds covered their genitals. But the clouds did not shroud the suffering of these men and women. They were praying and pleading to the Holy Virgin for salvation. Sister told us these evil men and women were suffering in Purgatory. They were deprived of the sight of God in the hereafter. The expressions they wore revealed their frustration and agony. Actually, Purgatory didn't look too bad to me. There were no burning flames. Nevertheless, I learned. I understood that practicing religion was living in a self-imposed state of the most horrible agony imaginable. Why would people want this?

Mass was in Latin and Polish. Two languages which I did not understand. However, I did listen intently and hard. I could say the words perfectly, though they were void of meaning. The sounds and cadences ring and resound still clear in my head. In order to appear to be in the midst of worship, and to occupy myself, I learned to pray the rosary. I paced myself so that one cycle around the beads equaled the length of one Mass. Weeks, months of my life were wasted being penitent for sin and guilt that I never felt. Obviously, something was wrong with me. The entire world in which I lived felt self-loathing. I wanted to sin like everyone else. I prayed and prayed the rosary. I was sitting in Purgatory.

Each day, I was delivered into the hellish hands, each day again, given to Felician instruction. I remember squirming in my seat. I had to go to the bathroom. I held my body tight with all my might. I held back. And back. I made myself rigid. And I kept raising my hand and requesting a fast trip to the bathroom. My bowels were howling. I held on with all my might. The pressure increased. I was in deep pain. I was oblivious to the world. Each day one of us broke. Someone urinated. Someone soiled. You were punished for this. It was a sin. My body was a sin. Thank you, God. Thank you, Sister. I sinned. I had sin. God was on my side. I had a body I could not control. God loved me, and I owed it all to a Felician harpy.

A Story of Teaching Methods

I remember Neal. He was a riotous boy and full of energy. Once, he misbehaved. Probably he talked or looked out the window. Perhaps, he had impure thoughts. The entire class had to face forward while Sister beat him in the back of the classroom. The threat was that if anyone turned to look, they would be next. I faced forward. I fixed my eyes on the crucifix above the blackboard. Christ wore a crown of thorns. His chest was slashed and blood dripped from the gaping wound. I thought of his Sacred Heart. I thought of my sacred heart, bound in thorns, bleeding but aflame. I listened to the ferocity of each swing of the Felician's arm as she brought down the pointer on Neal's flesh. She flogged him. Neal's screams of pain and agony and sorrow and tears and pleas filled the room. She continued. The bride of Christ beating a seven year old. She beat Neal with such ferocity that she broke the pointer across his flesh.

My First Dream

I was six or seven. There was a factory and in the factory was a conveyer belt about two feet wide. The gray assembly line belt ran into a large complicated machine. Kids that were my age were on the belt. In the machine, I recall, were these rather large blades that came down and chopped up the kids. Somehow the kids were reassembled, and they came out perfect. Nuns ran the factory. My mother was in the factory. I was on the belt. I got off and begged and cried and pleaded. I promised I would change. They didn't believe me. I had to get back on the belt. I was afraid. I was more frightened than I had ever been before. I screamed and cried, and then I was very sad. I was headed for the machine. I was silent. I hoped they would like me after I was reassembled. I knew I had no hope.

Home

Home was a very strange place. My parents didn't live together. My father lived with his mother and some sisters on May Street, and I lived with my mother and her mother and father, my grandparents. We lived at 76 Harmonia Street. Since my mother had a large family, seven brothers and sisters, there were endless visits by aunts and uncles and cousins and combinations of the above. It was an onslaught. Visiting was relentless. They all had a rather small and narrow opinion of everything. Everything was stupid, and everything was somehow wrong, for instance, the rain: "That's not rain. You call that rain? When I was a boy, that was rain. It was wetter than this rain. It never rains now. This rain is too warm to be rain. Ten years ago, that was rain. There is never a good rain on Friday. Rain is stupid." It was difficult to live with people who were sealed emotionally and intellectually into a shell that existed at the brackish bottom of a dank, dark swamp in the unexplored reaches of the universe. I never missed home.

In the household in which I lived, I did everything wrong. I was in the way. I created a mess. Or I went to the bathroom. Or I was acting weird. Or I was humming. Or I ate supper. Or I took breath. "Look at him. He's breathing. Look at the way he takes breath into his body. Who does he think he is. He must get that from his father's side. Look at his nose. He's got the Basinski nose. He watches TV. Look he goes into that room! That's stupid. Can't he behave? Can't he be like everyone else? That's wrong. That's stupid. That's none of your business. You don't belong there. You don't belong here. That isn't yours. This isn't yours. You are a boy. He is always thinking. Must you always think!"

They were dust balls, sleeping for eternity deep under the sofa. They didn't bowl. They didn't go to union meetings. They looked at the Virgin Mary. They congratulated themselves on all the wonderful things they did. They walked to church. Life was small, ignorant, backwards, violent, repressive, insensitive, and cold. I learned that everything I did was wrong. I learned that I was to blame for everything. It was an emotionally sick and dysfunctional household. The seething illness often boiled over the sides of the pot and crackled in the flames. All life on earth was becoming extinct. Like some Jurassic mammal, I hid in the forest leaves. I escaped by blending in with the darkness in the moist mud under the rocks. I lived in constant emotional pain. Physical pain was a distraction.

Fragments Which Became Pieces of the Puzzle

I learned to be still. I lived in myself. I would have committed suicide, but I knew that no one would care. Being alone was very good. In some magazine I found a picture of a piece of strange art. It was a goat with a tire around it. The artist's name was Robert Rauschenberg. Someplace, out in some world far from Cheektowaga, somewhere, maybe Mars, far away, there was someone, at least someone, whose life was not controlled by snails. It made me thirsty. I imagined in that art place there was a company of people, and they were wild and free artists making the most stunning and strange art imaginable. My family would hate them completely and thoroughly. They would kill them if they could. I sat in my room and dreamed about conversation without punishment.

I was stupid for reading *Mad* magazine, and *Mad* magazine was stupid. I loved *Mad* magazine. Someplace in *Mad* magazine, in some parody article on pop culture, I came across the name Kerouac. I pronounced the name "Kurouch." Kerouac was, according to *Mad*, a beatnik writer. He was a bohemian. I wanted to be a beatnik. They were not normal, according to everyone. How splendid, I thought, if they weren't normal then I should fit in. They made art and slept on mattresses on the floor. They didn't wash. They liked and read poetry and made weird, unexplainable art. Beatnik life seemed so alien that I embraced its symbols as far as my little ability would allow. I ate plain yogurt. It was very sour. I read someplace, I think it was *Mad*, that beatniks ate yogurt and if eating yogurt was a measure of bohemianism, I would not be denied. Yogurt was sour against the middle of the road. I ate against the dull brutality of my life. I embraced the angelic sour. I loved its tart living sting. I loved Jack Kerouac before I ever read a word. It was clear to me that I was a poet.

Writing and reading were the things that created moonlight in the cell. I found that making little tiny words on paper made no noise. I could hide them. If they were found and exhibited, they would be meaningless. The meaninglessness of all words became friendly. No matter what I wrote it would be ridiculed so it didn't matter what I wrote. And reading also allowed me to be still and out of the way. Reading made no mess. It was not noisy. It

Age sixteen, masked as the Other

was a solitary act. Only prisoners know the true pleasure of reading. One of the first books I loved was *Cyrano de Bergerac.* I too was a freak and a poet, and I too loved but was unable to express my love because I was so grotesque. Decades of emotional abuse transformed me into a monster, a hideous, freakish beast. I was one with Franken-stein's monster, the monster who sat across from his bride and said, "We are the dead. We belong dead." Such frightening romance lived in my heart. Cyrano said, "Alone with glory flustering over me, alone as Lucifer at war with heaven." I was alone. I found that solitude did not hurt and wanted to be there for all time. Somewhere, I came across the poems of François Villon: "In my own country, I am in a far off land." He was a criminal. I was a criminal. I read all of Edgar Rice Burroughs's Tarzan novels. Tarzan was remarkably animal-like. I was an animal. While other people, boys and girls, teens, went to proms, basketball games, dinner, movies, shopping, talked, thought about pools and couches, I read Norse mythology, over and over again. Odin hung himself in a tree for nine days for knowledge, "myself for myself." I found I had a self. There is a tale of a Norse warrior who laughs while his enemies cut his living heart from his body. He laughs because he dies undefeated. Ha. Ha.

In the midst of the torture and violence of my life I found alcohol. The first beverage I fell in love with was hard cider. Hard cider cost one dollar a gallon and you could return the gallon jug for 10 cents. I drank gallons of cider and wrote thousands of poems, most of which went the way of most poems written in our society. They got thrown out. Trash collectors are the great receivers of creativity, art and literature. Anyway, if you drank half a gallon of cider, and then poured in a quart of beer, you concocted a substance called "cidie." It was a lantern in the abyss of home sweet home. I was never constipated. Cider was all important in the great scheme of things because cider was made from apples. The first cider was made from the apples of the tree of knowledge in the Garden of Eden. Cider is Eve.

Tribute: Shelley

Somebody's uncle brought some old anthology of poetry into the house. Someone, through oversight, gave this book to me. I think it was supposed that since it was a book of poetry it was a useless book, therefore, it should go to someone useless, like me. Someplace in this anthology I found a poem by Shelley, and I remember some lines like: "And the sunlight clasps the earth / And moonbeams kiss the sea / What are all these kissings worth, / If thou kiss not me?" My life had not been romantic. I was kissed by this romantic image, this notion, "What are all these kissings worth, if thou will not kiss me?" This was a reason to live. Odin!

Days of Wine and Carrots

I found out that night was kinder than day. My hands were fur covered. I was a forest thing. I found that drinking was kinder than sobriety. Shadows were friendly. The forest was mildly menacing, rabid and playful. If you were one with the forest and shadow, the fanged moonette would not bite. Darkness gave creatures a bit more space in which to stretch. At night the grief givers relinquished some of their collective power. What a relief. But, of course, there were the mentally ill who also found the night forest. And criminals also found it and a few drug addicts and alcoholics. But these dead souls were no more than a thorn in a sock. And, of course, there were the social outcasts and idiots who were fun to watch. There were the radioactive. There were the beaten and balding goddesses. There were broken pixies. It was like being on permanent vacation.

At some point sitting in a local tavern called Vincent's I made the acquaintance of a number of other young men and women equally, for whatever reasons, madness or pleasure, driven to engage the pathological society of night. The sorrow that is day made them lords of night. "Hell has no power over pagans," wrote Rimbaud, and it was so in those nights. I must honor these people for they were my company and my cosmology, universe and Communion of Saints. I honor my compatriots: Bob Boroszko, Tom Raczka, Peter Sloan, Nick Culkowski, Debbie Eckal, Brenda Feder, Dave Imeola, Wendy Imeola, and Paul Badura. Collectively, this was the Carrot Gang. The movable feast traveled from working-class tavern to working-class tavern in Buffalo at the end of post-World War II prosperity. The mills were closing. The city was degenerating. Flight to the suburbs was in full swing. Neighborhoods were in transition. It was a dance, a picnic for mischievous beings. Life was generally drinking and slight brawling and general disruption and noise. It was art and sarcastic and cynical nuisance. These Carrots were *The Wild One*, Lou Reed, John Cale, more motorcycles, a few guns, wine, mescal, some smoke, and a mythology which called on Odin, the Norse God of poetry, war, and knowledge, as guiding spirit and archetype. Often the Carrots would dance over the thin log of the bear pit. Sometimes you fell in. The Carrots never had a rule or a leader or a hierarchy or an agenda. The Carrots were a parody and mocked everything. The Carrot Gang was formed on the day Celine died. It existed, and it didn't. There were Carrot lampreys. A Carrot lamprey was a human (or almost human) parasite that attached itself to a Carrot. There were many who wanted to be Carrots that weren't and there were those who were Carrots that I haven't named. Such was the organic nature of Carrot-dom.

Carrot Games: Flushing

Invariably, mom-and-pop taverns would be populated by a few old factory workers with the mill dirt ground into each pore of their otherwise flesh leaving them gray as mice; a few greasy long-haired guys with bad tattoos who liked country music; overweight young women dreaming of honeymoon bowling and french fries; some of the insane, lost, discarded, and suicidal, and the primitive intellects who lived under stones, just a stone's throw from any tavern. Everyone smoked. Everyone drank draft beer, local stuff like Genesee or, back then, Simon Pure. President Kennedy's picture was behind every cash register. It always smelled. It was always dirty. It was never Sunday. It was always a dead-end street. Wanna be on the softball team?

Invariably, driving along in the city at night made the Carrots thirsty, so thirsty that the Carrots would have to stop frequently to quench that gnawing, horrible thirst. Spontaneously, the Carrots would descend on neighborhood tav-

At age twenty-eight: "Hell has no power over pagans," said Rimbaud

erns. The descent on the tavern was followed quickly by the flush. To flush, the Carrots needed to drink a lot, fast, and make a lot of crude noise and push each other around, play the same song over and over again on the jukebox, or play polka songs over and over again, break glass, scream, and monopolize the bartender. Shortly the patrons, the regulars, would disappear. They would leave. They would crawl back into the cracks in the plaster. Spineless and disinterested and fearful, they would climb back into their hollow existence. The bar would be flushed. It was almost a routine. The Carrots could flush an average-size bar in less then fifteen minutes. Life went on by, like some thin apparition unable and unwilling to locate its final rest. Time was to be wasted. Its passage was just a bit cruel. It was not as harsh and destructive as the hangover of daylight. Anyway, physical pain was a distraction. There seemed to be always another bottle of wine. If you lost your mind, you got a new one. Night was an intellectual property. Night was not evil, never criminal, and never organized or purposeful. What delight. What a forest for a shadowy forest thing like me. What an aurora. The Carrots were creatively malicious. It was a romper room. It was a wedding, a medieval street fair. It was an amusement park. "Hell has no power over pagans." Summon Odin. Odin!

Tribute: Beats

Kerouac was an inspiration but not a literary inspiration. The first thing I read by him was a prose excerpt called *Alone on a Mountain Top*. It was a sort of Zen thing. I wanted flames and rebellion and here was Kerouac meditating. Later, I read everything, after I learned to listen, be quiet, be off in the corner and listen, like Kerouac. I didn't want to write like Kerouac: I wanted to be Kerouac. I was his energy and his romanticism and his naivete and his working-class background and his suffering.

Like coming to the tip of the water mountain and breaking the meniscus and needing to breathe badly, I read everything in a great city gulp with roaring pleasure, despair, madness, and flowers. Beats, all of this poetry, silly poetry and poets drinking wine and writing poetry in cars and on roofs. Corso and Lenore Kendall, Diana Di Prima's *Loba*, Lew Welch, *Naked Lunch* took up my time. It was kissing, kissing me.

Once, one lost night, I read Ginsberg's *Howl*, after drinking wine, lots of it and deep in the darkness of the back of sock-drawer night; lost soul, I read *Howl* aloud to a young woman. I was bitterly young then. Holding hope, the poem, in my palm, I hoped my ragged and rugged and raging intelligent bohemianism would win this fair female heart. It didn't work.

Tribute: Poetry in the Schools

Somewhere in the night I worked at Buffalo China. I worked in the warehouse. I worked on the line. I would grind the bottoms of cups at a grinding wheel all day, millions of them: Jose cups, caprice cups, large-mark cups. I recall the patterns and colors: Newport gold, Oakwood green, Colonnade. Anyway, I decided to go to night school at the University of Buffalo. It had something to do with this growing, intense fascination I had with poetry. I signed up for a class in modern poetry and that night the rabbit got pulled out of the hat, Pandora's box spilled on the floor, and the doors of perception opened. In strolls Jack Clarke and asks what we should study. On the board he wrote Denise Levertov and *The Freeing of Dust*, Robert Duncan and *Bending the Bow*, Robert Creeley and *A Day Book*, and this big book *Archeologist of Morning* by Charles Olson. I was a cat with a can of tuna. I thought I made it. I was there. This was the company. Not too bad, I mused, a nowhere, working-class kid from east Buffalo and Cheektowaga sitting at the University of Buffalo and reading Ed Dorn. Clarke read us Olson's *O'Ryan* sequence and that was transportation way outa line. I had "It." The jams were unhinged from the doors.

As an assignment we had to attend a poetry reading. I had never been to a poetry reading. Clarke told us to get ready. He didn't have any specific instructions. He drank from his bottle of Red Barrel beer, which he often brought to class. He said we should find "It" and get ready for "It." "It" was a place where the poetry "Was," that space. I remember clearly this beginning. There was a lot of filing into what was then Norton Cafeteria, at the University of Buffalo. This lanky guy, the poet, Robert Creeley, took to the stage. The room was full for sure, packed in fact, like it was once for all the poets. He had on a ski cap, a kind of knitted pullover cap. I guess he had been away and had just returned to Buffalo after a year and a half or some such thing, and then there was his new book, and he read from *A Day Book*.

> Do you think that if
> you once do what you want
> to do you will want to do it?
> Do you think that if
> there's an apple on the table
> and somebody eats it, it
> won't be there anymore?

I fell like Icarus. I was burned by the poem, the poetry there in the room in person. And here was Robert Creeley writing a poem about thinking. I heard all the voices of the past: "He is always thinking. Thinking is stupid." They fell too, flat. I learned the song of the heart.

Olson's poems too flooded my world. I suppose it is all a cliché; however, Olson's poems did open a lot of avenues. All fact and history, which I had a lot of, were OK in the context of the poem. I became insane in the abstraction. Olson's neighborhood was like my neighborhood. There were buildings and stories and magic and myth. All things then were poetry, history, sociology, poetry all the same poetry. All words, real and not, were poetry. If it's "There" then it's "It." I wrote the word IT on a sheet of paper and hung it in my room. I was "There," and I wouldn't go back.

Shortly after reading *The Maximus Poems*, I would read one poem each day at lunch in the china factory. I made a pilgrimage to Gloucester, Massachusetts. I drank in Kelleher's, sat on Half-moon Beach, walked the Fort, gazed at Ten Pound, and celebrated with the Portuguese at the blessing of the fleet. I made other pilgrimages: the West End Bar across from Columbia University in New York City and to North Beach. I spent a New Year's Eve alone in the crowds of revelers in North Beach. I stood around in these places, but it didn't help the poetry.

But, I was Beat, I guess, I thought. I had it down to two pairs of pants. One was in the wash and the other on me. I was putting together the puzzle of myself. It was a ceremony. It still is. It is an attic, a lawn fate, a lost text, a new word, a spider web, a bottle of wine, an icon, an anarchism, a horned woman, the garden in spring, summer, fall, and winter. I read from poet to poet like Tarzan swinging in the jungle. I went to hear poets read. I

found the jewels of Opar. There were many poets visiting and teaching at the University of Buffalo at that time. One was John Logan. John could make words into music.

A Story

During Mardi Gras in New Orleans, in the early 1970s, it was a lion eating butterflies, with its twenty-four-hour bars and drinking sun up to sundown and sundown to moon up. It was a wonderful place to struggle with the roaring fire of an angry soul that refused to extinguish itself for the mundane mediocrity of life without art. I was getting pretty wild. I was walking through a French Quarter parking lot next to the abandoned Jax Brewery, a parking lot where hordes of hippies slept in vans and cars. Tom Raczka and I lived that Mardi Gras in my Pontiac Catalina. Anyway, we were walking in this parking lot, and this guy walks up to me and asks what time it was. I told him I didn't know and walked away and turned to Tom and said, "I think I know that guy. I think he is John Logan, a poet from Buffalo." So I went back and asked the guy, and it was Logan. John led us down Decatur Street towards the edge of the French Quarter to a bar called Jewel's. At that time, in 1973, Jewel was still running the place, and it was a wonderful run-down fellahin working-class tavern full of cockroaches, bums, French-speaking market men, battered women, broken men, the lost and dreamers, and saints, and those people attempting to hide from the world. It was a perfect sanctuary and drinks were way cheap. On subsequent journeys to the Mardi Gras, an event I made often in the 1970s, Jewel's was Carrot headquarters. There was an old lush named Bobo who would play this New Orleans cake walk on the jukebox over and over and dance in front of that jukebox over and over deep into the intoxicating forest of the night. There was a bartender named Larry and, of course, Jewel herself. If I could freeze life it would be in that bar. Later, I heard Jewel sold out or died. Jewel's became a gay bar. Things are not frozen, sadly. However, I must thank poet John Logan for his being, which was a great alcohol thirst and lust and passion for movement and his restless, guilty, wandering, grief-ridden soul, and for the momentary sanctuary that was that bar. Ah, yes, a bar where the bartender knows your name and what you are going to drink. And you know the people there and you can get a good, cheap, stiff drink. And people leave you alone to sit and drink and smoke and look out the window, sun up to sundown and sundown to moon down and rain down and listen to music which is words.

Salon

A salon is not a saloon, and that's too bad. About that same time in my puzzled life, which seemed to be falling to pieces but also falling together, I met and became friends with a musician-poet named Roger Kowerko, who at that point in my dance was a being that made poetry a community event. We had salon readings on Wednesday nights and Saturday nights at his house or the salon house of Richard Olson on Miami Street in Buffalo's first ward. These basement and living room salon readings were my first, so to speak, public poetry

events. Mostly, I was rather intoxicated when I read. Still, the event, now I understand, was the proper occasion for poetry. The alcohol was just a crow picking at my liver. Since then, twenty years ago, I have done hundreds of readings: salon readings, saloon readings, group readings, readings in more bars, coffeehouses, restaurants, schools, festivals, churches, art galleries, on radio, on video, on Donner and Dancer and Comet, and never mind. Artist Jeff Filipski said I do it for the high. I suppose so. It is some kind of a strange thing like finally being called on in class and having the correct answer. And maybe, it is like going home and not having to sit in my cell-self. Yes, it is escaping the self that I first tasted in Roger Kowerko's basement and Richie Olson's parlor.

Buk

At some counter-culture party, in around 1975, talking about anarchism, personal free-

The performance group EBMA (the East Buffalo Media Association), 1985: (right to left) John Toth, Don Metz, Jeff Filipski, Jeff Budzynski, Mary Ellen Halpin, Michael Basinski

dom, revolution, and David Bowie, this German guy asked me if I ever read Charles Bukowski. I said, no. And then later, my friend Paul Richmond lent me a copy of *Erections, Ejaculations, Exhibitions and General Tales of Ordinary Madness*, which I didn't read. But the name wouldn't go away. Believe it or not, one night, I was watching the box and on comes this special about L.A. poet Charles Bukowski. He was reading poems and drinking beer, saying the gods were good to him in his abrupt, sarcastic, wisdomic, cynical, rabid doglike tone, pulling and twisting each word to get its satirical and biting, sarcastic etymology banged out. He created each word new by breath and tone and sound. And the thought that every bar I had ever been in was a poem. And each demon was a poem. And each strange event, daily, was a poem. This made my entire strange life very much poetry. I didn't have to be rich. I didn't have to go to Harvard or Europe or Kentucky. I could just be a poet because there was poetry. And it didn't matter that my mother never took me to the art museum. And it didn't matter that my father only knew the words to polka songs and not the work of Beethoven, Bach, and Mozart. I certainly felt OK. Charles Bukowski set things in place, in order, things like beer bottles, satire, green Easter bunnies, and hyenas. My experience was as valid as any polo-playing rich kid's. I have in mind always a Charles Bukowski quote, which I have used often. And I will use it again. The story goes like this: Someone asked Bukowski why he was a writer and Bukowski, to paraphrase, replied, "I write not so much because I am so good, but the others are so bad."

Another Remembered Thing

The story goes like this: Someone walked up to Robert Graves and said, "Oh, you're a poet. There isn't much money in poetry, is there?"

And Graves said, "No, there isn't much money in poetry, but there is no poetry at all in money."

Metz

Someplace in the late 1970s, I met this musician named Don Metz. He had this group

Reading poems, 1980

called the EBMA (the East Buffalo Media Association). I started to write some way strange, I thought, experimental pieces for the performance group. I wrote time pieces, and pieces for time, experiments in form and sound, and sounding and with sound juxtaposition, shape writing fragmentation, constellations of text, all forms of text abstraction, and I have done it since then. Don said, "Here's some crayons. Have a blast." And whatever I came up with was OK. It went right into production. And then we would perform this stuff, new music and sound text and sculptures and slides, singing and screaming. It was a great amusement park of concerts. Sometimes we'd drive six hours with a ten-person ensemble, bring our own sets, transform a hall with John Toth's fabric sculpture, and no one would be in the audience. We were your avant-garde band. We came to your town but you were more interested in shoes under the front seat in your car. Fortunately, I didn't care. I liked empty ballrooms. I liked the Halloween. Ignorance and neglect were things I took for granted. We did gigantic shows with ten musicians and five voices and Ed Sobala running six projectors. And then we would do it again. And again.

Well, it went along and is still going for now almost twenty years. I do things called words and Don Metz does the music. We are the Rodgers and Hammerstein of the underground. Our productions are seemingly endless, and I guess I'll name some: *Marz, Homage to the Barbarians, Crash Test, SEA, Helicopter Obstacle Strike Tolerance, Gods, Conversations,* and *Elephants.* We recorded two LPs, *SEA* and *Enjambment.* And we still couldn't pay the bills. But Don always said, "So what." And then he said stuff like: "Well, we'd sit at home and do this stuff anyway, so why not perform." I couldn't think of any reason why not to perform. I liked the buzz. One of the best was when the Bethlehem Steel Corporation in Lackawanna, New York, gave us a building in the plant in which to perform a piece called *Magarac.* The ensemble was always organic. There are too many people to name, like Jeff Filipski, James Perone, John Neumann, Mary Ellen Halpin, and Michael Colquhoun. Once we were unplugged for presenting an obscene piece, so they imagined, set to music. And another time we were unplugged because the audience didn't understand what was happening and began to boo and freak out. We disturbed the entire bar full of dimwits. Their little minds and little worm worlds were shattered with bizarreness. It was great. I'm positive that they are shattered still, still sitting in a still tavern, with fruit in their drinks, listening to Three Dog Night and the pitifully commercial dullness of Guns n' Roses. Wanna play softball?

Success at Unsuccess

As a poet, literary artist, performance poet, sound poet, visual poet, fictioneer, and fragmental poet, I have had a lot of success at non-success. I believe, beyond any doubt, that poetry is a fluid and organic thing. And I guess that's a problem for the rigid world. "So what." I have changed forms, masters, and styles, and I have imitated Bukowski, Logan, Ginsberg, John Cage, and a lot of centrist narrative poets I don't know and I didn't know. I was doing lots of reading and concerts and it was all fun and somehow not the sun. I was still looking for a self as poetry. It was already, well, I was already knocking on the door of middle age. The poets in the *Norton Anthology* were born after me. The poets kept getting younger. And I keep getting older. I've had some literary despair here and there. I figured I lost it or didn't make it. In fact, mostly, I figured I sucked. The rejection slips read like this:

"Although the poems were interesting, and on occasion humorous, generally speaking I sorta find 'chance' type pieces impenetrable, i.e., not able to be understood."

"I don't publish pieces on creatures."

"Funny in a more oblique way."

"Your poems are bleak, emotionally claustrophobic and much too self-loathing. This reflects upon your point of view, your world view, which intellectually and spiritually paints you into a corner of a closet of dark cynicism, an unenigmatic uncharismatic inertia."

Oh well, I thought, like Nathaniel Hawthorne wrote in *The Scarlet Letter,* "Let the black flower blossom as it may." And so it did. When I started doing live performances the local paper said things like:

"Tasteless, if not outright sick."

"More monotonous than stirring."

"Sea sludge."

As narrated by Michael Basinski . . . the text sounds like the pitch of an old-fashioned snake oil salesman, with the dynamic level of his voice trailing off on virtually every word like W. C. Fields at his obscurantist best."

Oh well, I thought, no reason to believe the insights of reviewers who lived in a culture that created hair dryers. But not everyone was cruel. After reading a set of poems, John Montgomery (Henry Morely in Jack Kerouac's novel *The Dharma Bums*) said, "quotable and semiotically unstable."

And then Liz Was wrote me this in a letter about a non-existent book of mine that she read in a dream, "I picked it up and began

Mock wedding day, 1983: Eileen and Michael Basinski, in the middle, at the Ethnic Festival, Buffalo

reading: immediately I was sucked into the book in a very literal sense, I was in it, experiencing it, and what IT was was a moist vortex swirling around me clockwise in an oval about breast height. A whirlwind composed of all manner of small animals, birds, squirrels, rodents, etc., all moist and intense and flying, spinning, moving around in it but being it. I could see each of the animals' faces very clearly as they passed, and this was a frightening but exhilarating experience."

And then Jonathan Fernandez defined my work, or part of it, in print. He wrote this, "What is poetic in his published poetry is not poetic, and what is not poetic in his published poetry is."

It is kindness like all of this that makes the electric bills easier to pay. So, I forgot about the Left Bank, royalties, and being poetic royalty. Released into my own magic I meet many kind, lit spirits like Joel Kuszai and Bob Grumman. The list is too long. I'm sorry I can't name you all, pantheon of mischievous poets.

Tribute Some More

As hard as I thought I should try to be a plumber, work in a bank or sell car insurance, bag at a K-Mart or work in an auto factory, or load and unload trucks, count grapes, test mattresses, or be a monk, a bum, an alcoholic, a priest, whatever, I wasn't there. A forest creature just can't make pizza. One night, I was at a practice for this concert, and I did my piece, and I was listening to another piece being performed. There was Jackson Mac Low and Dick Higgins, and Don Metz and Ed Cardoni, Director of HallWalls Gallery, and Gary Barwin, Canadian poet, and then they were doing one of Jackson's pieces. And they were practicing one of Dick's pieces. And I said, well, these are my people. This is my company. I am the company too. This was the solve of the unsolved mystery. The truth is out there and that moment I found it. "It," get it. And the company was more than people and poets. It was poetry. Sounds pretty poetry corny, I guess, but, "So what." I was pretty relieved. I did not want to be a dentist. I didn't want to be a policeman or fix watches. I don't know about spark plugs. What does a forest creature know about cutting hair?

Daughter Natalie, "the Princess of Pixies," 1996

Hearth

Heart and hearth are order. Poetry demands its domestic rhyme and rhythm, which are the organic things and organic cycles of life. Eileen is Mokos, a jar of wild blackberry jam, sweet and full of seeds that get caught between your teeth. She's my purpose. Poetry happens less than an hour a day. Purpose is the cycle, the movement, the metamorphosis of life which is poetic, and this alone allows that hour each day to exist, like magic or it is the magic. In 1982 I was unbalanced. In 1983 Eileen and I married. In 1985 we had our child Natalie. This is a balance. Anubis, the weigher of hearts, sends approval. What are all these kissings worth? I never had a center of the world. And then I did. Sure as ghosts live in the garage, balance is not easy. The barge rocks on the Nile. But Eileen and Natalie make gravity. They revolve, sway, rock, rumble, and change in the most dynamic ways. The best thing I ever did for my poetry was to become a husband and a father.

It was hard for this forest moisture to make dill pickles and do dishes. But I learned that bedtime stories are poetic events. Being a soul mate and anchor and therapist, social worker and socialist, teacher, companion, and affectionate are the poetry in back of the poem. Shall I be poetic? Hearth life is the paper. Relationshipping and parenting are organic and poetry is the same, never in the same place twice. There is no poetry without a kitchen. There is no poetry without taking out the garbage or cutting the grass or paying the phone bill or waiting for the school bus. Once form is established it must change, if not, poetry becomes a poem, like a broken pocket fisherman or a black-and-white TV, and it is destined for the dump. Or worse, the voice of a poet becomes the poet's voice and not poetry. Someplace in *The Songs of Maximus* Olson wrote, "go contrary, go sing." I've tried.

Wendy Kramer recently taught me that walking in a supermarket was poetry. She said you can read a supermarket for hours and never get to the milk. That's what I mean, poetry demands a domesticity. Natalie is now twelve and the most beautiful girl in the world. She wears cool pants and writes stories about cats. She is water. I go to the store and buy a black pail. I read about the WNBA. The wild geese are headed for the Alabama swamps. I pick wild blackberries with Natalie. In summer we like corn. I write to Elizabeth Burns and Jeff Hansen. There is a humming bird in the bergamot. I dust. I trim the bushes. In fall we gather horse chestnuts and leaves. In winter it is cold. It is dark. I read a lot of books, and I don't have to work on the house. Eileen and I laugh. We have Christmas. We bring the ornaments down from the attic. They belonged to my grandmother. Pixies have taken my car keys. An elf hid the toe-nail clippers. Pixies tease the cat. Eileen and I have a glass of red wine. Our cat is named Scully. Natalie and I watch *The X-Files*. Gimli is our hamster. I write some poetry. Then I do the wash. And I write a little poetry. Pixies hid the gas bill. We make a shopping list. After shopping, before we watch monster movies, I write poetry.

BIBLIOGRAPHY

Poetry:

B (text broadside), Soft Dog Press, 1982.

The Wicked Old Woman (broadside), Textile Bridge Press, 1983.

The Women Are Called Girls, Textile Bridge Press, 1983.

A-Part (broadside), Score Sheet, 1991.

(With Barbara Tedlock) *Egyptian Gods 6* (broadside), Uprising Press, 1991.

Mooon Bok, Leave Books, 1992.

Red Rain Too, Run Away Spoon Press, 1992.

Her Roses (broadside), Uprising Press, 1992.

It Is an Open . . . (Christmas broadside; third series, number 4), The Poetry/Rare Books Collection of the University Libraries, SUNY at Buffalo, 1992.

Cnyttan, Meow Press, 1993.

Flight to the Moon, Run Away Spoon Press, 1993.

Vessels, Texture Press, 1993.

Worms, Veighsmere Series, 1993.

So Up, Buffalo Vortex, 1994.

SleVep, Tailspin Press, 1995.

Duende, Fubbles Press, 1995.

Catachresis Mum, Buffalo Vortex, 1995.

Odalisque, Word Outa Buffalo Press, 1995.

The Sink, Buffalo Vortex, 1995.

Coupid (broadside), Buffalo Vortex, 1996.

Barstokai, Meow Press, 1996.

Wen, Buffalo Vortex, 1996.

Empty Mirror, Non Compos Mentis Press, 1996.

Heebie-jeebies, Meow Press, 1996.

Idyll, Juxta Press, 1996.

Words, Buffalo Vortex, 1997.

Nome, Buffalo Vortex, 1997.

[Un Nome], Run Away Spoon Press, 1997.

Recordings:

Enjambment, EBMA, 1984.

SEA, EBMA, 1987.

Sven Birkerts

1951-

Sven Birkerts

I was born in Pontiac, Michigan, in 1951 and raised in a suburb of Detroit, but an enormous part of my growing up was wrestling with the ghosts of another culture.

My parents are both from Riga, Latvia, and they had not been in America long when they married and had their first child. I heard only Latvian spoken for my first few years; exposure to English did not come until I was in preschool.

But even then, the language and culture of their origins was dominant. Though this was likely not my parents' intention, I grew up believing that the real, the authentic, the *better* life had been then, in Latvia before the war, and that everything else—this, America—was an epilogue. A postscript. Granted, it was a postscript that threatened to far outgrow its preliminary text, but never mind.

Slowly, obscurely, this feeling changed. But it was there at the core of our family life for all the years of my childhood. My sister and I heard the stories, over and over, and we drank in the tones of reminiscence, the laugh or sigh that legitimated everything that was back then, conferred depth and resonance upon it.

Outside the door, everywhere around us, the shiny American 1950s were getting under way with the dream of the suburb, the new model car parked in the driveway, the ball game on the radio and, shortly, the astonishing fact of television. My parents lived at an angle to all of this—they worshipped European modernism, the sleek lines of Scandinavian furniture; they listened to classical music; they mocked the "idiot box," even though we eventually got one of our own. They still trailed the shadow of their vanished culture.

*

My father's parents were both literary people, but that which had brought them together was also what pulled them apart. When my grandmother, Merija, discovered that she was pregnant and announced her intention to have the baby, my grandfather, Peter, moved out. He set himself up in a small cottage on the Baltic shore near Riga and continued to write his books, including *The Psychology of Love,* which was published in 1925, the year my father was born. My father never met his father—not once—though they lived only a few kilometers apart. He was raised by his mother—and later a step-father—in an apartment in Riga. Family legend has it that when Peter came into town he would take his afternoon walk through the park where my father sometimes played, but if he ever saw his son, he never ventured closer.

My father's was a solitary childhood. As he tells it, he spent many hours in the apartment, drawing, building model airplanes, waiting for his mother to get home from her teaching job

*Paternal grandparents, Merija and
Peter Birkerts, 1922*

at the girls' gymnasium. Once, when our family visited Riga, he pointed out the window where he had sat and waited, and the patch of sidewalk on the corner where he would first see her.

Merija never aired criticisms of Peter, nor did she accuse him of desertion. To the contrary, my father grew up believing that Peter was a great man, a genius who had been called by his art to practice solitary devotion. My father now has a glass case in his studio at home in which he keeps his most valued things. There, arrayed neatly, are the thin-spired, fragile, paperbound copies of all of his father's books.

My mother, only a few years younger than my father, grew up in relative privilege. Also in Riga, but in a somewhat different milieu. Her father, Mike, had studied in Moscow to be a landscape painter, but made his living running a fairly prosperous photo studio. Her mother, Emilia, was the proprietress of an elegant hat salon—she had the adjacent storefront. In her heyday in the 1920s she traveled to Paris twice a year to attend the big fashion

shows. They lived elegantly, going every week to the opera and theater, and summering at the seashore. But all was not well between them.

As it emerged many years later, Mike had a second family in Riga, with a daughter just a few years younger than my mother. He went back and forth between households, and kept up the deception until the Germans invaded Latvia in 1944 and offered selective emigration to Bavaria. My mother's family left, Emilia and my mother sailing first, with Mike following several weeks later. In recent years, returning to visit Riga, my mother not only met her half-sister, but learned what had happened during those weeks. Mike had stayed behind in order to move his other family into the summer house on the shore. He thought they would be safer there—as very likely they were. Only then did he follow his wife and daughter.

Childhood photographs of my mother show a pretty and self-possessed girl. She always seemed to be posing—even in the most seemingly casual circumstances—and always smiling. To this day no photographer has captured her in a completely unguarded moment.

Emerson—so I learned recently from a biography—was reading at the age of three. I am astonished. I can scarcely remember being alive before the age of three, or four. How is it, I wonder, that my early life seems so diffuse to me? Is this semi-amnesia connected with language and culture, with the fact that I grew up in a primary environment that was somehow very different from the world I stepped into later?

My dim recollection of my earliest childhood: it is very much the feeling of a cave, of dark rooms and secure walls. I remember sitting on the carpet with my Tante Aija, looking on, enchanted, as she builds a house from playing cards. Or else I am sprawling in one of our deep butterfly chairs, watching my father bent over his drafting table.

Slightly older, walking, I venture out the screen door of our apartment in Pontiac, and then run shrieking back in when I spot a ladybug. It seems I had an irrational fear of spotted things and was truly terrified by cartoon drawings of dalmatian dogs on the endpapers of my Golden Books.

When my mother was very pregnant with my sister, she sent me down the basement stairs with a wastebasket. I fell, hitting my head on the concrete floor. My eye swelled up to grapefruit size and I was rushed to the hospital. Then, doubtless induced by the trauma, my mother went into labor. We ended up in two different area hospitals, and my father recalls several days during which he did nothing but drive back and forth between them. I was the first to be released. I remember standing on a patch of grass outside St. Joseph's Mercy Hospital (where I had been born, too) and waving up at the window where my mother held my baby sister, Andrea, aloft for me to see.

The nearness of things. How deeply we know our worlds when we are children! The hours spent at windowsills, slowly grating the teeth against some favored spot of wood. The understanding we possess of the undersides of coffee tables, the architecture of chairs, the weave of carpets and the grain of floorboards. For a year or two we lived in a little house in Birmingham, Michigan. I was more in the world then, allowed to venture short distances outside, but I still retain only the smallest cluster of recollected details. Sitting on my knees in the living room, pressing my ear against the speaker-cloth of our old radio, listening to "The Lone Ranger." Building an airplane on the sidewalk in front of our house, a magazine picture of a real plane set out nearby. And then, working with great application on the floor in the corner of the living room—I am trying to copy a dollar bill and am frankly amazed that no one has ever thought of this most obvious idea. Why earn money when you can just copy it?

I have a few friends in the neighborhood, including a boy with the wonderful name of Johnny Foreacre. One day we are all under a big tree across the street. Someone has an empty bottle and we decide we will try to melt it. I volunteer to get the matches. I remember sneaking into my parents' bedroom where my mother had matchbooks arrayed on strings. I am excited, aware of stealing, remorseless.

The same gang plays war games later. We drop clods of dirt on a little truck shouting: "Thirty seconds over Tokyo!" I run around gleefully, making eh-eh-eh-eh-eh machine-gun noises, full of the feeling that great important things are happening.

My grandparents Mike and Emilia now lived near us on the top floor of a small house on the Cranbrook estate. Cranbrook was, and remains, a complex of private institutions founded by the Booth family, Detroit's original newspa-

Maternal grandparents, Mikhail and Emilia Zvirbulis

per magnates. Mike had a job helping to mount exhibits at the Cranbrook Art Academy, and my grandmother worked for a time as a dorm mother at Kingswood, the private girls' school. The summer before I started first grade, while my parents were trying to sell one house and buy another, my sister and I were sent to live at Cranbrook for several weeks. For us, it was an idyll. Endless days—so it seemed—of roaming an enormous and beautifully landscaped estate. Exploring the vast gardens, the outdoor Greek theater, the fountains that were tucked away in strategic arbors. I made friends with Artie and Vince, sons of the garage-keeper who lived downstairs. They took me into the secret life of the place, into the dark garages where the busses were repaired, into the greenhouses;

they showed me the paths behind the tennis courts where we could always fill our shirtfronts with found tennis balls. Best, though, were the mornings when my grandfather turned to me at breakfast and said I could help him with his paintbox and easel.

My grandfather had rediscovered his original love for landscape painting, and on fine summer days he would take his easel and canvas down to the lakeshore. We would set out after breakfast, my grandfather walking ahead of me on the paths through the flower gardens, down through a long avenue of pines, pausing every so often to let me catch up. When we got to the lake I was free to roam. I would return when the bells rang the noon hour, often sneaking up slowly behind him, watching as he stood utterly oblivious, brush in hand, staring out over the water.

I had just turned six when we moved from Birmingham to a new house several miles away on Tahquamenon Street in Bloomfield Hills— my parents live there still. Now it looks like any other prosperous suburb, but then, back before everything changed, it seemed like the

Early reading, about 1954

fringe of the American wilderness. The roads were not yet paved, there were open lots, swamps, and near enough to walk to was the loose barbwire fence that marked the boundary of Cousins Farm, a great sprawling place that I never succeeded in exploring to the end. But from the first the name conjured a sense of intimacy, and when I was just a few years older, I went there almost every day.

I arrived several weeks late to first grade at Walnut Lake School, and for a very long time—years—I felt like a latecomer, felt that all the other kids, most of whom I would be in classes with for the next six years, shared some intimate bond that was denied to me.

I was still coming into English, so I am told. I only remember the sudden barriers to sense that would rear up. Someone would use a word—"starch" or "helmet"—and I would blink hard, startled at being on the outside of the word, denied the kernel of its meaning.

In the middle of the school year I fell from the merry-go-round at recess and broke my leg. I missed several days of school and then had to make my way about with crutches. My parents bought us a German shepherd puppy at about this time. There is a photograph in which I am hobbling along outside with a very small black and brown dog at my side. We named him Chipper, and he was the companion of my youth.

My first deep friendship began covertly. It was with a new boy who arrived when third grade was already under way. Murray Aiken. He had a large, closely shorn head ("Egghead" was his instant nickname) and a terrible temper. He could be goaded into tantrums, and so long as he was at Walnut Lake there were those who tried to get him going.

Murray lived nearby and we became afterschool friends. He seemed to understand that I did not want to declare a public bond with him—he was strangely attuned in that way. But when the school day ended we were inseparable.

I can't recall now what we talked about—it may not have been very important. But I do have a clear memory of the separate world we inhabited—a world that was utterly divorced from that of family life or even school life. We had projects and schemes; we explored. Cousins Farm, which could be glimpsed in the distance from Murray's front porch, was our special spot. We took our bows and arrows and stalked the cornfields, hoping to scare up pheasants or grouse; we fished in the cow pond for bluegills; we strapped on our hunting knives and roamed the deep interiors of the pine woods. We created the feeling of adventure, muttering words like "Hiawatha" and "Pathfinder." We convinced ourselves that small bands of renegade Indians still survived. We built forts in the woods, gathering deadwood and fresh pine boughs while Chipper rustled around after squirrels nearby.

At school, when other kids got after Murray, I stayed on the sidelines. I did not want to be identified as his friend. Even then I despised my own weakness.

I remember having a very highly developed sense of my own privacy, a psychological space that was apart from family and school friends, apart even from Murray. It was a space somehow defined by reading, by private ritual and fantasy, and it was a tremendous solace to think of it there, intact, to be repossessed as soon as I could be alone again. Later on, this sense of enclosed privacy would become more centered on books and reading, but when I was in the younger grades, fantasy prevailed. Most reliable—and memorable—were the rescue scenarios. I would be a resourceful hermit figure living in some very hidden but comfortable place—a cave or an elaborate tree house—when word would reach me of some threatening calamity. Silent, devious, I would slip into civilization long enough to save whomever was then the girl of my fancy. I would bear her away and she would then—and forever—share my perfectly appointed solitude.

This early world of fantasy was very nearly continuous with the rich atmospheres I discovered in reading. I don't have a clear memory of the first books I read, but I know that by third grade or so I was regularly bringing books home from the school library—biographies of Indians and Indian fighters, stories about explorers and inventors. They quickened the nerve of imagination and were easily carried over into my solitary play.

I did spend a good deal of time, much of my best time, pursuing projects on my own, building forts up in our wooded backyard or riding around the neighborhood on my bike. But absorbing as these thought-fugues were, they were nothing like what I found I could create with a book in my hand. For reading promised something that these other things did not—

it offered not only the experience, the story, but I could preserve it for myself as a kind of secret, as a reliable place to return to no matter what else was going on in the world around me.

This was essential, for the core feeling of being an outsider never changed much. Though I had long since stepped free of the language problem—had, indeed, created for myself an American childhood—I was reminded of differences every time I crossed back over the threshold. To slip back into Latvian, even if I was just telling my mother about my day, was to set my other life immediately at a distance. Nor was I ever comfortable bringing friends home. I felt uneasy, ashamed about being odd, on the one hand, but also proprietary, protective. I didn't want to risk any dissonance, wanted no quips or baffled looks from my friends. Nothing to interfere with my desire—to be accepted as a regular American kid.

My sense of being split between cultures intensified my desire to be alone reading or working on my projects. Only then did I feel entirely at ease—unconflicted, whole, free to dream my future.

School was very important to me in my younger years. I loved assignments, tasks, the feeling of mobilizing my energies on behalf of something. Intelligence was not then a liability—not like it would be in high school—and I was pleased about being known as one of the "smart" kids. But I was not a grind, and I was not much driven by parental expectation. I didn't have to be told to do my homework because I liked to. It meant that I could be in my room, on my own. And I enjoyed the feeling of things coming clear, horizons receding to disclose new horizons. I remember doing elaborate, time-consuming reports—on the human body, on the history of the Olympics, on Oregon, on Latvia. Each was an immersion, a long process of reading, copying out important information, drawing maps and charts and diagrams.

Outside of the classroom, on the playground, I was never more than a middling athlete. Decent at basketball and kickball, merely mediocre at baseball and football. I knew early on that there were kids who really could run, hit, catch, and who had the competitive thrust in them. Though I cared intensely about things like spelling bees and number games, I could never get myself to care about whether our side won or lost at some sport. I was tolerated by my peers—I gave things a good-natured go—but I was never brought into the inside circle, the first rehearsal for the cool crowd of junior high years. I didn't play Little League, didn't wear a team cap. My sports, which I only claimed later, were swimming and skiing—solo activities that I could carry on while listening to my own thoughts.

Maybe all children believe that childhood is eternal. They simply have no basis for thinking that they might ever feel any differently about things, or that life could present some other essential aspect. And then, with very little warning, comes the change.

I remember the dreadful melancholy that affected me during the last few months of the sixth grade. Suddenly I understood that we were all going to be leaving something, never to come back. The familiar terrain of Walnut Lake School started to seem strange. The low drinking fountains, the jungle gyms and swings, the presence of kids—little aliens—from the lower grades. As the snow melted our teachers began to talk to us about the fact that we were soon to leave, that we would all be in a big new school come fall. It seemed like we no longer had the heart for the old games. At recess boys would stand around in groups making brash wisecracks about the girls, who were standing around in groups of their own. We were all full of the new exclamation—"Gross!" Kids showed up with transistor radios and lip-synched to pop songs, strutting and acting strange. I had the feeling that my whole childhood had slipped its mooring and was starting to drift away from me. The sadness was cut through with flashes of giddy anticipation.

At the very end of sixth grade, Murray came over one afternoon and told me that his father had been transferred—they would be moving. I was overwhelmed, devastated. Everything familiar was being taken away at once. In the next weeks I watched as Murray's house was transformed. Toys were packed, carpets were rolled up. His room was stripped down to bare essentials. On the last day we walked around in his empty basement yelling and listening to our echoes. Then his mother called him upstairs. Letters and visits were promised, but the vacated rooms behind his back said otherwise. After we said our shrugging good-bye, I walked the familiar path home. I was normally not a crier, but I surprised myself with sobs. I couldn't

bear the feeling that my life had changed forever.

My early adolescence coincided with the explosion of British rock and roll, which became the intensifying backbeat behind every new awareness of self and world. Whatever else they were, those first teen years were a submerging of the private self of boyhood beneath a conflicted public persona that pursued the attitudes and accoutrements of "cool" even to the point of pretending a lack of interest in school. Reading saved me then—as it would in the future—by offering a place of refuge. When I read, that sense of dissonance I lived with was stilled. But my reading had changed significantly. I now buried myself in books about outsiders—Holden Caulfield in *Catcher in the Rye;* Finny in *A Separate Peace;* the disaffected young men in William Goldman's books, and Steinbeck's genial bums. Later I found Thomas Wolfe and Jack London. Somewhere in all of this confusion and immersion, between "hanging out" and the sanctuary of reading novels, a split self emerged. I felt myself playing at being one of the guys—shooting pool in Kim Swift's basement, learning to smoke and drink—and I also felt myself holding something back. I never would have told my high school friends that I enjoyed English class or had fantasies about writing. Any protrusion of intelligence or intellectual curiosity was immediately pruned back. Then came the news. Worried about what they were seeing, the emerging attitude problem, my parents decided to send me as a day student to Cranbrook, the all-boys private school down the road. I fought, cried, but to no avail.

Eleventh grade, my first Cranbrook year, was the loneliest year of my life. I was cut off from my old neighborhood friends and had not found a way into the brainier circles at my new school. At home my parents were fully absorbed by the demands of a new baby, my brother Erik, who filled his corner of the house with noises and routines. There was, strangely, freedom in this isolation. I drew more deeply into my privacy, listening to music, daydreaming, reading, learning guitar, and thinking about the girls at Kingswood, our sister school across the lake—girls who moved in the distance like mirages, playing field hockey in their green knee-sox or showing up at special school events.

With the beginning of my senior year at Cranbrook came an enormous transformation.

With sister, Andrea, at Tahquamenon Falls, Upper Peninsula, Michigan, about 1961

It was 1968, and the surrounding atmosphere was suddenly different. Martin Luther King and Robert Kennedy had been assassinated; the Democratic convention in Chicago had prompted the first real explosion of youth culture protest. We all felt a surge of generational solidarity: politics, music, a rage at the crewcut mentality that had brought things to this state. Long hair shocked and signified and anyone with any sense of independence started testing boundaries: home rules, curfews, school policies. Groups of furtive smokers gathered in select places on the grounds; we heard of "pot" parties in the darkroom. . . . Intelligence, nonconformity—a whole new demeanor surfaced. It was the times, and I felt, for the first time ever, a sense of arrival. Things fell into place. I found friends and, better still, a girlfriend. A group of us collaborated on publishing an alternative magazine. This put us in touch with the whole bourgeoning subculture: photographers, poets, Detroit's radical fringe. Before long we were seen as troublemakers, dissidents, and there were meetings with school officials, threats of disciplinary action. But this was all a great excitement. We were in accord with the times, on a mission, part of something that was just beginning to brew up in the culture. The other scheme of things just didn't matter like it was supposed to. My dissatisfaction extended to the supposedly make-it-or-break-it business of college applications. I was encouraged to apply to a range of colleges, but I took the easiest route— early acceptance from the University of Michigan. Adults still used phrases like "senior slump," but we knew better.

With the arrival of spring came trauma. I broke up with L., my dark and moody girlfriend, and for months could not see past the heartache. I wandered around the grounds, smoking cigarettes like a condemned prisoner. I wrote pastiches of Ferlinghetti and Rimbaud in my notebooks. Sartre's *Nausea* was the book for me, though in fact I could hardly decipher what the narrator, Roquentin, was saying. Kerouac and Hesse were more to my liking. Under their influence I began to have fantasies of becoming a vagabond, a lifelong wanderer. It sounds preposterous now, but this was, after all, the era of communes and lost children, of epical pilgrimages to Nepal. We were all desperate to connect with some deeper authenticity; we were at once romantic, disillusioned, and decadent. My parents watched me as if from a distance, shaking their heads, hoping that I would somehow snap out of it. More and more I kept to myself, had secrets, listened to the tom-tom messages coming through the airwaves on the new FM stations.

In the spring of 1969 there appeared in the *New York Times* the now-famous advertisement for the festival that would turn out to be Woodstock. My friends and I decided on the spot that we would go. We had no plan except to get there early, to find work if possible, somehow to be in on the ground floor of what was clearly the most exciting musical and countercultural event imaginable. We hitchhiked east several weeks before the concert, and by sheer dint of hanging around we fell in with some members of the Hog Farm, the West Coast commune that had been hired to get the site ready. For weeks, then, we camped with the Hog Farmers, waking early to do deepbreathing exercises with their yoga master, going out with various crews to dig latrines or hammer together rice kitchens. We were in awe of these California hippies, some of whom had been members of Ken Kesey's original Merry Pranksters (whose doings had been written up by Tom Wolfe in *Electric Acid Kool-Aid Test*). We sat around their campfires at night, sharing in whatever was being passed around, hearing the stories—the bus rides, the phenomenal "acid trips." But we held back, then. There was still a feeling of terrible consequentiality around hallucinogenic drugs. It was enough to watch the others—"Red Dog," "Wavy Gravey," a beautiful woman with a red dot on the tip of her nose. . . . An idyllic set of summer days, really. And then, abruptly, the sense of a great shadow sweeping toward us across the land. A generation arrived to party. Extraordinary excitement, mayhem, a grand seizing of liberties, a collective bravado, followed by an equally collapsing fatigue as a rainstorm drove everybody under plastic sheets or into the mud. My friend Marcus and I looked at each other the next morning—we knew that our Woodstock was over. We packed up our backpacks and started the long walk out, moving with a growing sense of liberation against the endless incoming tides.

I spent four years at the University of Michigan, majoring in English, taking my degree in 1973. But the whole college experience—dorm life, classes, papers and exams—was like a faintly indicated backdrop to the huge agitations of private life. First came the long misery, the crisis of relevance, when nothing seemed worth anything. The only thing that made sense was sitting around in various dorm rooms with my long-haired friends, listening to music. I dreamed of freedom, clarity, purpose. At one point, the summer after my freshman year, I hatched a plan to expatriate myself. But after a month of sleeping in fields and on beaches all over Europe, I felt my nerve fail me. I returned to school, but the funk continued. Nothing made sense, classes least of all. I worked a night job washing dishes and often stayed up until dawn, sleeping through school hours. On a final examination in Chinese literature I was in such a depression that I wrote a note wondering whether the professor might not be a butterfly dreaming he was a professor. I dropped the book on his desk and left. I collected incompletes as if a full set would win me a prize.

My father was worried. He talked to a friend of his, a client who knew some ranchers in Montana. Some strings were pulled and I ended up taking a job in Deer Lodge, at a place called the Tavenner Ranch. I wrestled with stacked bales of hay most mornings, then rode on the back of a long wagon, breaking those same bales to feed cows in various grazing areas. At night, bone-tired, I lay on my bunk in an authentic bunkhouse. I smoked, read, and tried to fend off melancholy. I had a calendar pinned to the wall by my window, and with the cheerless resolve of a convict, I x-ed out each day when it had passed. I felt utterly out of place—I had no interest in playing cards

with the old-timers—but I also felt strangely clarified. The hard work connected me to things; the ground felt near. And when I finally returned to Ann Arbor, I felt older, less vulnerable.

Late that fall, crossing campus at lunchtime, I encountered S., whom I had known first in my earliest Walnut Lake School days. S., who had bragged to me in the doorway of Miss Carpenter's class that she was already reading *The Wizard of Oz*. I had not seen her since early high school. Now, both of us remarking on the eerie familiarity of our reconnecting this way, we began to go out.

With the last year of college came the swerve into the world of books. Not school books, however, but the offbeat and often obscure books I dug up at the Wooden Spoon, a used bookshop in a rundown area away from campus. I went there daily, at first browsing, then selling and trading books I had picked up on bargain tables, and eventually working as a shelver in exchange for book credit. By the winter of that year I was far more interested in building a library in my room and hunting for first editions than I was by any subject I was taking. The one exception was a course in modern German literature, which I took with S. She and I competed in writing papers for our professor, each trying to be the more obscure and allusive. I was finally driven to the all-consuming expedient of writing a sixty-page essay on Thomas Mann's *Magic Mountain*, an essay which unexpectedly won a prize in that year's Hopwood Awards contest. I say "unexpectedly" because I had been working diligently on a group of interconnected short stories, and trusted that if anything scored with the judges it would be these. Tough, bittersweet, and, alas, owing their very spirit breath to Hemingway's "Nick Adams" stories. Instead of Nick, I had Peck. Peck lived in a college town not unlike Ann Arbor. He was a disaffected romantic, and there could not be a chilly rain falling but that he would have to be out in it, his collar up, his cigarette cupped. . . . He walked a hundred lonely sidewalks, even as his author, in the most anticlimatic way possible, was finishing school and looking for a job.

I stayed with what I knew—books. I found work as a clerk in the recently opened Borders Bookshop on State Street. Tom and Louis Borders were just beginning to branch out from secondhand books to new. I had been trading books with them for months. But this venture was different, felt marked by a distinct momentum. Something new was happening.

Nineteen seventy-three was a strange year. I was living in a small room above a delicatessen, hoarding and shelving my books, working for a small wage at Borders. If four years at one of our finest universities had left my mind slumbering, the daily handling of paperbacks in the receiving area sparked me off like nothing had before. I felt giddy. I brought books home every night and read until my eyes ached. Books on the mind, on structuralism, on Zen Buddhism and mysticism, novels by the wild new Latin American writers like Garcia-Marquez and Cortazar . . . I read, scanned, dipped, copied quotations; I had lists going of what I knew and what I needed to know. I didn't see how this project would ever come to an end. But at the same time—such inner splits are possible—I had started dreaming a new life for myself. S. and I had begun talking about leaving Michigan, heading to the East Coast, to the ocean. I would write, and she would paint. We would read and live simply. Through that winter, we saved our funds and gradually the plan took on life, became the thing we told

our friends. And in the spring of 1974 we left. I had packed my library and left it with my parents. I carried nothing but a folder of xeroxed passages—lines I deemed truly essential—and a few changes of clothes. S., flying separately, arrived at Logan Airport with only a suitcase. We went to stay with her sister and brother-in-law in New Hampshire while we looked around. A few weeks later we bought an old red SAAB for four hundred dollars and set off toward Maine. We got to the southern coast, landing on a spit of land called Biddeford Pool. An odd feeling, waking to find there is nothing to do but begin living your life.

Not knowing the shape or outcome of our lives, we often live as if the immediate moment were all that we should expect to have. Later, grown away from such intensity, we look back and wonder at ourselves, what we ventured, what we put up with, and what we imagined about ourselves. The two-year period when I lived in Maine with S. now appears, decades later, as a feast of isolation, solitude of the kind that I am not likely to find again. Conditions could not have been simpler. We lived first in a small cottage no more than a hundred yards from a long sickle-shaped Atlantic

With wife, Lynn, at the Massachusetts seashore, 1982

beach, then in a small apartment that looked out directly over a tidal inlet. Money was scarce—there were no pennies scattered on the windowsill or lodged in the crevices of the couch. We each had our few basic things, some books we had picked up—and time. Immensities of it. We knew only each other for at least the first year. A letter in our post-office box was something to look at and delay opening. Of this period I remember the hours and hours of walking: along the beach, along the roads, along the wild headland past the golf course where blueberries grew and a lighthouse could be seen in the distance. Over there, a faint shimmer, was Prout's Neck, where Winslow Homer had painted. And the ocean! We both made vows that we would never live away from the ocean again, come what may. At night the boom of the surf filled the bedroom. In the morning, weather permitting, we headed out to the beach as soon as we could. Not to swim or sunbathe, but to walk, to patrol, to see what had been left in the night. I would then head back and try to write—stories, poems, anything. But the feeling of inspiration I lived with far outstripped my abilities. I felt bottled up, stymied. The only thing that survived this whole long period was a small booklet of prose poems—passages about waves, rocks, and immensities of water and sky.

But I also read. I read with a patience and focus that I can now only dream about recapturing. It was possible, then, to inhabit a single powerful daydream continuously. Until circumstances eventually forced me to take jobs, I lived as if inside an unbroken thought. I would move from hours with a book to a long walk along the golf course, then back to the desk we had fixed up under the picture window. If I looked up I saw the inlet where the lobster boats came in at day's end. The fingers idled on the keys of my green Olivetti, occasionally constructing a sentence.

But such reveries cannot last forever. Our money ran out. S. and I both found work, and before long the dread rhythms of workaday life asserted themselves. Though neither of us admitted it—or even knew—our relationship was faltering. We had been fine so long as we naively shared a simple fantasy, but we were no good with adding up paychecks and arguing over what we could afford at the supermarket. I felt a pressure building up, a need to go back to Ann Arbor, to be with people, books,

and—as I fancied—in the midst of intellectual excitement. S. wanted to get married and start a family, begin building a life. We pretended around our differences for quite a long time, but when an Ann Arbor friend arrived for a visit I decided I would ride back with him. It was September, and the end of my second full summer by the ocean.

Leaving Maine to return, alone, to Ann Arbor felt like the right choice when I made it, but I was not prepared for the sadness, the feeling of "never again" that made getting through the days almost unbearable. I felt that I had left my younger, more vulnerable, *better* self behind. I missed S. fiercely. And when I learned, calling from a drugstore booth, that she was seeing someone else, the thin ledge I had been standing on broke away. I was back at Borders, selling remainders in their big new store,

The author's parents, Gunnar and Sylvia Birkerts,
about 1992

and I had the thought hourly—so it seemed—
that if something didn't happen soon I would
burst. But I didn't. Gradually, not right away
at all, my situation eased. I started having drinks
with P., a coworker, and by degrees we got
involved. The financial panic I had felt—I was
selling all my books just to make it to the
next paycheck—eased up. And then, an unexpected turn. Borders had a used and rare book
shop—Charing Cross—across the street from their
big new store, and they were looking for a co-
manager. They asked me if I had any interest
in the job. It was the right thing to come at
the right time. For after meeting my new partner, George, and seeing what disarray the previous manager had left, I understood that this
was a job that would take whatever I wanted
to give it. My energy, which had been pent,
turned in on brooding and regrets, was suddenly limitless. And if it is possible to experience great fulfillment while in the grip of despair, I did just that. George and I were at
the shop six days a week cleaning, organizing,
building, driving out to make bids on libraries,
studying catalogues and price lists—all of this
in preparation. And when the "opening soon
under new management" sign was finally taken
down, when the cash register was plugged in
and the music turned on, when the first customers came in to browse around, I was filled
with a sense of adult triumph. Able, somehow,
to bear the images of S. and our walks by the
ocean, memories which could still crowd me
with sadness.

Having a job to do, a store to run, made
Ann Arbor feel very different. Now I was on
the inside, closer to the principle of things
than I had been when I was a student. The
store did well. George and I were accepted by
the other business people on the street. We
dealt with books and intelligent people all day
long. There was, too, the perpetual thrill of
the chase, of arriving with our truck at the
home of someone who had called with "a basement full of old books" to sell. And for a long
time this was enough. But then, after a year, I
started having inklings. Even this level of daily
engagement was not enough, could not quite
dissipate the feeling that I ought to be writing, risking my soul somehow. I tried to get
back to the desk, but it was hard. I could not
slow myself down enough to reach what I thought
of as the writing state. It was during this long
period of frustration that I decided to audit

Joseph Brodsky's course in contemporary poetry. Brodsky, recently arrived from the Soviet
Union—he had been expelled for "parasitism"—
had never taught before. According to the customary standards, he was a terrible instructor.
His English was still rough, he often looked
depressed, and he would sit at the head of
the long seminar table waiting for students to
initiate conversation about poems that he had
assigned. Yet it was evident to all of us—we
were maybe a dozen—that our teacher was an
utterly unique individual. He had no small talk,
no interest at all in "making nice." He cared
for a handful of poets—Mandelstam, Montale,
Auden, Akhmatova—and for poetry; he spoke
of "the language itself" as if it were a deity.
And we started to get it, I think. We pushed
ourselves to get at the obscurity of some of
the lines he had us read. And when one of us
did connect, there was the sense that a victory
had been scored in the world, that universal
idiocy had been, if only for a moment, stayed.

Getting to know Brodsky was hugely, if sub-
liminally, influential. Though I continued to work
sixty hours a week at Charing Cross—continued to hoard books I would someday read, collecting first editions—a contrary itch had begun. Over and over, while I was driving to
some book sale, or working at the cash register, the realization would break over me: "This
is nothing, this is commerce, this is trading
on the soul-work of others." When would I write?
Would I ever? I was in my midtwenties and
my collected unpublished works would have fit
inside a flat briefcase. But while I was in my
book-dealer mode—consumed by finding and
selling the most unusual and interesting books—
I could not seem to switch to the other channel, the meditative place out of which writing
had to come. I saw, more and more, that though
I was busy, and on a surface level stimulated,
I was not satisfied. Many forces were in play,
though, and change began to seem possible.

P., with whom I was by then living, was
making plans of her own. She was applying to
graduate schools and thinking about moving to
Boston. I felt the temptation of change. I resisted for a time, even after she had gotten
her acceptance from Boston University. But then,
one afternoon, I was overcome. I had been
sitting on the bed in our apartment, looking
through a stack of books—again—when I suddenly knew. There was either selling books, or
writing books. If I did not now, very soon, try

my hand at writing, I would surely find myself living in regret. I told P. that I would join her in Boston later. First, I wanted to travel, to redirect my thinking. After I gave my notice and said my good-byes, I packed my things—by now my *thousands* of books—in boxes. My sister and I set off for an extended trip, visiting our grandmother Merija in Riga, and then traveling in Italy. My return ticket was to Boston.

I arrived in Boston in the fall of 1977, and P. picked me up at the airport in her huge red convertible. I felt like I was renewing my life again and wondered—as I still wonder—how many chances we are given. I intended to start up as I had a few years before, with just some clothes and a typewriter. I had a plan. Upon arriving and moving in with P., I contacted my parents and had them send me several specially marked boxes. These were filled with first editions I had collected while at Charing Cross. When they arrived I placed an ad in the *Bookman's Weekly,* listing titles and prices. A few days later I came in from a walk and found the mailbox jammed to the lid with responses—checks. My worries were over, I thought. I would set myself up as an independent book dealer. But as I began to scout the area, going to sales and bargain shops, I realized that my plan was not going to work. The scene was too competitive. There were too many dealers already working the area. I was going to have to find a job in a few months' time.

I smile now to remember how simple the financial calculations were. Two hundred for rent, thirty a week for food . . . I figured I had bought myself several months of writing. It was time to try once and for all. From early morning until midafternoon, I sat at a small table that I had set up in a walk-in closet. I drank coffee and typed. I had planned out a short novel about a young man who was trying to put his life together after a traumatic breakup. I wrote until the lights started flashing in my peripheral vision, and then I went into the streets and tried to walk myself back into calm. P. and I were living just outside the city and as I walked I saw the taller buildings looming up over the rooftops. It was an enormous, daunting city, I thought, and at times I fancied I was Rastignac taking on Paris. I loved the idea I had of density, of elaborately braided lives. I thrilled to ride the subway downtown and then

go walking the back streets of Beacon Hill. I roamed at will, half in the world, half in the story I was writing. I was doing it, I was finishing a book! And when I finally typed THE END after the last paragraph, I went to the corner market and bought a lottery ticket that encoded the numbers of my final page count. I waited for the daily number announcement after the news, then, honestly surprised, shredded my ticket. Nor did things go any better when I summoned P. and a friend of mine to a reading of my whole novella. They sat, dutifully, on the couch of our apartment. I was not far into the narrative before I knew, with a clotted feeling in my gut, that it was no good, that it was private business that could never be made public. Moreover, I heard the mannerisms, noted the pretenses. When I went to bed that night I felt that the central faith of my life—that I would one day be a writer—had been exposed as a vain illusion.

For a long time afterward I worked various low-level bookstore jobs. P. and I broke up and in desperation I answered a roommate ad in the paper. I ended up living with a poet more or less my age in a good-sized apartment in Cambridge. Neither Robert nor I had any furniture—or any heart for making a liveable space—so we left most of the rooms utterly empty and stayed in our respective bedrooms.

I was—I understand it now—depressed. Then it was just the way of things; it was my life, and the word "depression" never entered my mind. I shambled on. When I was not at my job—unpacking and shelving piles of books in one store or another—I sat in my room, reading. There is no magnet like a book when the soul feels empty, or underemployed.

It was at some point during this intense introversion that I first thought to try my hand at writing *about* a book. I had just finished Robert Musil's grand novel *The Man without Qualities.* Without really knowing what I was about, imitating the essayist mannerisms of George Steiner, Susan Sontag, and other admired critics, I started trying to make sense of the writer and his milieu and the world refracted in his novels. The task consumed me for weeks. I reread, marked, outlined, drafted, wrote, polished—and when I was finished I quite liked the way it sounded. I even liked how the typewritten words looked on the page. But what to do with it? I inspected the various journals on

With poet Steven Cramer, Cambridge, late 1980s

the newsstands in Harvard Square and decided to try a local literary paper called the *New Boston Review.* The piece was, to my delight, accepted, and another was commissioned, and with that began an epoch that has not, in some sense, ended. That is to say, never since agreeing to write that follow-up essay on the French modernist Blaise Cendrars, have I not been working at some review or essay. If I have rounded any corners in my life—and I certainly feel that I have—then this, the discovery of the clarifying pleasure of writing about books and ideas, has been one of the most crucial.

Writing, then, became the backdrop activity of my life. The work gave me a constant sense of direction, of mattering. I dreamed now of finding my way into that animated and high-level conversation that I was sure went on in the upper echelons of literary culture; indeed, the very thing that made that culture actual. I see from the vantage of the present, that this

may have been a great, if inspiring, illusion. Or else I am still in search.

In the meantime, though, there was ordinary life to be lived. And in that sphere a number of important things happened. One— the central one—was that I met Lynn, who is now my wife, and began to emerge from my long funk. We dated briefly, and then, as her roommate moved out, faced our first important decision: whether or not to live together. We decided to try, and before long I was carrying my few belongings from Robert's apartment to Lynn's, which was less than a mile away. A few tours back and forth were enough. I hung up my shirts and started my first enduring cohabitation.

Lynn and I lived together in that apartment for quite a few years; it became familiar as few things ever do: the hum of the heating plant attached to the hospital behind us, the long entry corridor where we put up postcards and drawings from our various artist friends; the scratchy stuffing sound when mail got pushed into the narrow chutes of the front boxes. . . .

Shortly after we moved in together I left my bookstore job in downtown Boston and began working at the Harvard Book Store in Harvard Square. I would remain there for the next five years, working with the most congenial and offbeat group of people I could have imagined. True book-lovers. I think back on this as a period of sustained happiness and productivity. I had made the connection to writing and now knew what I wanted. In many ways the bookstore job fed the writing. I could work all morning at the desk, knowing that at 1:00 P.M. I would be leaving my solitude to head in for the afternoon shift. This part of my life was very public, full of book conversations. There were duties, of course, but there was also a great deal of time for browsing and reading. I looked at books incessantly: while unpacking boxes, while shelving, when one of my coworkers brought something over. And we were, all of us, constantly filtering things to one another. I took books along on my lunchbreak, read at the counter when things got quiet, and carried different books home every night to read before sleep. I cannot imagine living at anything even approaching that level of immersion now. But that was another epoch: we were childless then, had little money, thought it bliss to be reading together in the same room, looking up every so often to let our adjacent solitudes connect.

Though a thousand things have happened since that time in the early 1980s, many of them of great private importance, my life loses narrative interest for me from the moment that I begin writing regularly. I don't know that I can explain this fully. Maybe it is a coincidence—when the writing begins the essential formation of character is complete. Or maybe the writing life has finally interposed a barrier between events and the acute focus on finding a way in the world, a path that feels like the intended one. In any event, there came a time when my life seemed less like a question waiting for an answer and more like something that I simply had to be getting on with.

I am struck now, looking back, by how easily a career did fall into place for me. Easily, that is, once the desire to be a novelist was exhausted, or suppressed, or transformed. The essays and reviews flowed one from the next. I was fortunate to find a number of journals—a number of individual editors—who encouraged my work. As it happened, I began to be identified with a certain kind of subject: the obscure novel, the work in translation. I began to accumulate clusters of what appeared to be related essays.

In the midst of this ongoing preoccupation came another key transition. I was offered the chance to teach a freshman composition course at Boston University—I, who had passively acquired a B.A. and had thereupon turned my back on any further contact with academe. I was hired, I suppose, on the assumption that as a writer I should be able to guide a group of utterly uninterested freshmen through the basic steps of producing readable work. I naively aspired to do more. I believed I could fill them with a love of the word. At this I failed miserably. But other classes were offered, other options arose. I taught summer school at Harvard, and then, through that, was taken on to teach expository writing, the required writing course for all Harvard underclassmen. I taught "expos" for seven years, and when that expired I picked up other courses at Emerson College, Simmons College, finally ending up with a position as a nonfiction instructor at the Bennington Writing Seminars.

The reviewing and essay writing had their own momentum, too. The topics—assignments—

Birkerts holding daughter, Mara, 1989

seemed to come in clusters. When I had amassed a great many essays on international writers, I was able to publish my first book, *An Artificial Wilderness: Essays on Twentieth-Century Literature.* Other collections eventually followed: *The Electric Life: Essays on Modern Poetry, American Energies: Essays on Fiction,* and then *The Gutenberg Elegies: The Fate of Reading in an Electronic Age.* But there was no thrill to match the first. When my editor at William Morrow called to say that she had just put a fresh finished copy of *An American Wilderness* in the mail, I felt an unbearable sense of urgency. I scarcely slept. All the next morning I hovered near the window to watch for the Federal Express truck. And there, at last, it was. I signed for the package, carried it into my study, and stared at the label. We were living in Arlington and I was home alone. I needed a ritual. So I paced up and down the hall, sat down and smoked a rationed cigarette with great delectation. Then, abruptly, I tore open the package. This was it, this was . . . and, full stop. There, bright red, so cruelly *not* the thing I was looking for, was a book on Ronald Reagan by Ronnie Dugger. . . .

A mistake, yes. The real book came the very next day, and I built myself back up, and it was delicious to walk around the thing, the shiny, hard volume-occupying object, looking away from it and then suddenly turning back, as if thereby impersonating the would-be customer who spots a catchy-looking cover and pauses to have a look.

*

Elsewhere, on the other track, the real life track that has become so hard to write about, Lynn and I had married; we had honeymooned, begun working steadier and more consequential jobs; we had moved from Cambridge to Arlington, had begun to anxiously discuss whether—then when—to have a child. And in 1988 our daughter, Mara Sophia, was born. The momentum of life doesn't seem to slacken, it now discharges itself through many circuits at once. As I write this, Mara is nine years old, we still live in Arlington, in a house that we bought the year after she was born. We have a three-year-old son, Liam Thomas. . . .

And in the telescoping of sentences the spirit slips away like quicksilver. This is an illusion. The days remain—dense, full, most of them with their embedded moments of repletion. I am at the desk, pen lifted off the page while the ear searches for a phrase; or we are all sitting outside in the bright tall afternoon, playing in the back near the basketball hoop; or Lynn and I are cooking together, drinking wine, talking; or I am hiding away on the couch with a novel that I want to be reading; or I have gotten up early to go swimming at the YMCA, am driving through the neighborhood in the near dark, watching the crows crisscrossing the road from their various outposts, catching a sudden glimpse of my life as if from the side, through another's eyes. . . .

BIBLIOGRAPHY

An Artificial Wilderness: Essays on Twentieth-Century Literature, Morrow, 1987.

The Electric Life: Essays on Modern Poetry, Morrow, 1989.

American Energies: Essays on Fiction, Morrow, 1992.

The Gutenberg Elegies: The Fate of Reading in an Electronic Age, Faber, 1994.

(Editor) *Tolstoy's Dictaphone: Technology and the Muse*, Greywolf Press, 1996.

Textbooks:

The Longwood Introduction to Fiction, Allyn & Bacon, 1991.

The Evolving Canon, Allyn & Bacon, 1993.

(With Donald Hall) *Writing Well*, 9th edition, Harper, 1997.

Contributing editor of *Boston Review*, 1988—, and *Agni Review*, 1988—. Regular contributor to *New Republic* and *New York Times Book Review*.

Michael J. Bugeja

1952-

AUTOBIOGRAPHIA POETICA

Michael J. Bugeja

In contemplating my autobiography for this series, I questioned whether I should focus on my life or my ars poetica. Then it occurred to me that this essay should be a "poetic autobiography," or a life told via poetic events, which herein will be divided into three sections: "The Juvenilia Years: An Awakening," recounting my earliest poetic memories through college; "The Apprentice Years: A Revival," covering poetic memories from young adulthood; and "The Pub-

lication Years: A Creation," summarizing poetic achievements from 1986 to present. Thus, this autobiographical triptych focuses primarily on the making of a poet, rather than the recognizing thereof, and so emphasizes the hitherto untold early experiences that urged me toward the poetic life. Also omitted are the politics of poetry—which, admittedly, make for "good" reading, name-dropping, and literary gossip. But politics can be mean-spirited, too, and mentioning incidents also revive them. Suffice to say that for every detractor I have enjoyed a dozen supporters who have helped me develop as a poet.

So I will be focusing on the latter in my "Autobiographia Poetica." That title contains Hellenic and Roman overtones, not so much to hearken the epics of Homer or odes of Ovid but to honor my own heritage, woven into so many of my poems. A first-generation American of Maltese extraction, my ancient maternal ancestors hailed from Greece and Sicily with surnames Apapolis and Aquilina. My father's name, Michael Carl Bugeja, dates back centuries to Gall and from there to the Templar Knights of Malta. Thus, if one must place me in an ethnic category to better explicate my writings, I prefer "Italian-American," joining ranks with my friend Dana Gioia and a favorite poet, John Ciardi. Both write in an easy, enlightening tone which I hope to emulate here, as if you were sitting across from me at my kitchen table, where conversation occurs in my house—in typical Italian-Maltese fashion.

For those of you unfamiliar with the Maltese archipelago in the Mediterranean, and its customs, I suggest you discover it for yourself on the Internet, using this link: http://www.fred.net/malta. The site is called Grazio's Virtual Malta after the distinguished scholar of Romance Languages and webmaster, Grazio Falzon, who has translated my poetic works for a Maltese audience (also available on line via this site). Grazio is another of those wonderful supporters who broadened my audience, in this case making it accessible worldwide in the language of my ancestors.

Growing up Maltese in America is difficult when no one can pronounce your name—even in my native Lyndhurst, New Jersey, a Silician enclave about five miles from New York City. The problem is the *j* because there is no *j* in the Italian alphabet. So I was shunned in my ethnic neighborhood where people made distinctions between those born in Palermo in western Sicily and those in Syracuse in eastern Sicily. So the *j* in my name was my scarlet letter, even though my mother's ancestors came from eastern Sicily. My teachers could pronounce names like Capicchioni, Pisciotta, and Sferruza but butchered mine, calling me "Boo-GAY-jah" or "BUG-a-jah" or even "BUGE-ah."

My name is pronounced "Boo-SHAY-ah" or, if you prefer a more Phoenician pronunciation, "Boo-JAY-ah," in keeping with the Semitic language of Malta, colonized first from the biblical Middle East out of what is now Syria. Bugeja is not nearly as melodious as the names with which we have come to associate American contemporary poetry: Dove, Merwin, Olds, et al. Nonetheless, how can you read my poetic autobiography if, as so many others, you cannot pronounce my name? Perhaps this poem will help, composed to introduce myself to admirers of my work who inevitably write and ask: What nationality is your name? And how do you pronounce it?

"J"

On the page, in the right font,
It resembles a jay,
Swoop of the serif like a tail
Guiding the ascender,

Quotations around the beak
Vibrating the backdrop
Of erasable bond, an endless
Expanse of sky. My name has

A history, thirty years' war
Fielding questions, teaching
Friend and foe how to call
Or curse me, lovers unable

To pronounce declarations,
Rivals, vows of vengeance.
Even my blood brother,
The serious Sicilian, disowns me,
No "J" in the alphabet, Giacomo,

A confused pigeon, as if paisan
Opened the wrong coop,
The homing sense lost,

So when I sing of myself,
Nobody joins the chorus,
Nobody hears the screech
Bluejays make as they sully

Line or limb, preen a feather
As I want to preen
The scarlet letter from my name,
Phoenician, phonetics of fate.

This poem symbolically captures the daily ritual of explaining myself, as if I have to account for being here in America. Explaining how I am and what I do are daily burdens that I have come to accept. In the coming sections, as I recount my life via poetic moments, I also will explain the impact of teachers, supporters, and others in the making of a poetic life, which happened for me via the less-traveled route of a reporter cum creative writer.

I. The Juvenilia Years: An Awakening

My mother Josephine was a powerful intellect with an imagination greater than my own. But she experienced insurmountable personal tragedies, as so many immigrant patriots did arriving in boatloads at Ellis Island earlier in this century. At age three Josephine left Marsa, Malta, for New York harbor, sailing with four brothers to settle eventually in Lyndhurst, New Jersey. She quickly established herself as one of the brightest pupils at Lincoln School on Ridge Road, about two miles from Rutherford, where the great poet William Carlos Williams practiced medicine. In the eighth grade, my mother's mother died, forcing her to drop out of school. Her beloved English teacher gave her two gifts: a blue spiral notebook with some of the teacher's favorite poems hand-copied inside, along with a first edition of *Best Loved Poems of the American People*, a 1936 Grove book whose reprints are still sold in bookstores everywhere. Josephine then sulked home to her father and brothers to cook, clean, and generally dedicate her life to their well-being and futures.

Josephine's future was bleak. She would marry young and lose her first husband in World War II and experience three stillborns with my own father; however, her most enduring pain was the end of her education in middle school. And yet that poetic notebook and little anthology led, in the tortuous way that life does sometimes, to my sitting here composing a poetic autobiography. As the great intellect Einstein put it, "Subtle is the Lord."

My mother would recite the Lord's Prayer with me before tucking me into bed. But she did not tiptoe into my bedroom toting a Bible; instead she carried her notebook or her anthology, depending on what she wanted to read to me that night, her long blue-black straight Sicilian hair spilling over the wool nightcoat that swept in behind her like a cape. By now the pages of the notebook needed paste-on re-enforcement stick-

"My mother, Josephine Bugeja, shortly after marrying my father," 1948

ers, and the anthology's book cover was as frayed as worn denim. At the time, I thought that she loved me deeply, my serious mother. I imagined, this is how children go to sleep in America, by the meter and melodies of Ben Jonson and Christopher Marlowe. Thinking of Josephine Bugeja now, I no longer envision a disenfranchised immigrant housewife but a discouraged graduate student trying out poems to a child to see how the child responds to tonalities of voice.

I responded.

In 1987, rummaging in my mother's basement for some lost item she needed in her kitchen, I came across the notebook. In it were poem upon poem by Ben Jonson, along with ones by Marlowe, Raleigh, Lovelace, Elizabeth Barrett Browning, and Shakespeare. My favorite poem was "Song: To Celia" because my mother would sing it in the cobalt shadows that the hall light cast upon my bed, as if a seraphim holding a holy book was lulling me to dream. My mother remains my dark angel who soars in my poetry and in my genes.

Case in point: Was it coincidence that Ben Jonson would become my major figure during my doctoral work, with essays about his poetry and plays published in an array of scholarly journals, including *Seventeenth Century News*? Or was it Ben Jonson's timeless verse? Or the power of a mother's imagination? Probably some of each. But my mother remains a central figure in my development as a poet, even in recent work like my sonnet crown, "The Influence of Lady Mary Wroth," one of my best works, requiring six months to complete. I hear echoes of my mother's tragic life and song, "Drink to me only with thine eyes," when I think of Wroth. Jonson dedicated his most famous play, *The Alchemist*, and three admiring poems to Wroth, born Mary Sidney (niece of Philip) in 1587. It can't be proved, but I always have believed Wroth is "Celia." By the way, a crown is a fourteen-sonnet cycle in which the last line of a sonnet becomes the first of the next—with the last line of the fourteenth the same as the first of the beginning sonnet. The form reminds me how history repeats itself, how all of us—especially mothers and sons—are connected poetically or otherwise in the life cycle. In "The Influence of Lady Mary Wroth," composed in the voice of a strong woman beset by miseries, much like my mother, I revisited the issue of Jonson and Wroth in several sonnets, including this one making reference to "Celia":

Song: To Ben

Drink to me only with thine eyes,
And I will pledge with mine
                    —*from Jonson's "Song: To Celia"*

Cups of ale and wine continue to blaspheme
My role at court. When drunken bouts begin
To undermine me, I can discipline
Crueler than a man. I'm not what I seem,
A widow in the Earl of Pembroke's home.
He talks of us at masques. The guise is thin,
Insiders say. You solicit him as patron,
But he suspects that "Celia" is my name.

Do not reveal my real one and sober up.
Cease using similes of drink and death
To symbolize the love you claim for me.
Stop looking for my kisses in a cup
And likening red roses to my breath.
I wouldn't get that close, Ben. Take pity.

Although my mother's influence on my verse is greater than any poet's, there is "an odd resident muse" in my canon, according to my friend and colleague, the poet Neal Bowers: William Carlos Williams. Williams's influence on me is odd, in as much as we employ two very different poetic styles—his being open and language based, and mine being fixed and formal (like Ciardi's). I don't know if Neal understands the irony of his term: resident poet. As mentioned earlier, I was reared in Lyndhurst, New Jersey, about one mile from Giants Stadium, which was a marsh when I was a boy, and about two and a half miles from where Dr. Williams lived on 9 Ridge Road in Rutherford. Lyndhurst has changed somewhat since I lived there through my high school years, with a greater ethnic diversity and more young professional New York commuters. In my day it was what a writer might call a "blue-collar enclave" of the Big Apple. In other words, nobody expected me to become a poet or go to college but to work in a factory at the local industrial complex.

Rutherford was the "socially acceptable" town across the tracks where Williams practiced medicine. In fact, Ridge Road runs through Lyndhurst and Rutherford. The thoroughfare is commercial in Lyndhurst—banks, bus stops, railroad station, tailors, apartments, delicatessens, auto parts, etc.—but residential in Rutherford, huge Victorian homes (still well kept) where families of prominence dwelled: bankers, businessmen, and Manhattan book editors with a twinge of British accent (à la

Michael, at age one and a half, with his mother, about 1953

Cary Grant). My family physician had a good Italian name, Candio, so I cannot claim that Williams was my pediatrician. But his very presence inspired me.

Williams's house, 9 Ridge Road, is the first dwelling on that famous street, a three-story Victorian house with fine woodwork around the windows. The house was situated across the street from a hardware-toy shop where my mother would take me to buy Lionel parts for my home set across the Erie Railroad tracks in Lyndhurst. When we would pass Williams's house, my mother would say, "A great poet lives there." I remember skipping down Ridge Road chanting, "A great poet lives there, a great poet lives there," without understanding the meaning of that ominous phrase. I would glance at the windows of that impressive house hoping to catch a glimpse of the good doctor dancing before the mirror in his north room and singing, "Who shall say I am not / the happy genius of my household?"

I never saw him. To live so close to such a master, to have his muse infiltrate your own as phantom resident, is to imagine yourself in shadows: his, of course, but your own poetic potential. I have composed several poems dedicated to WCW, including a rondeau redouble—"Dr. Williams

Calls," based on a real-life dream in which he opens the door of his estate to let me in—whose last stanza sums up my feelings:

> My poems lie in piles. The doctor states
> Prognoses candidly and puts the blame
> On too much Milton, far too little Yeats,
> On too much meter, an overdose of rhyme:
> He cannot help this time.

My greatest tribute to Dr. Williams is a contemporary ballad titled "Bus Crash: Rutherford, N.J." The poem is a true account of a bus crash in which my beloved third-grade teacher perished with others in Rutherford. For privacy reasons, I use only her first name—Lenore—poetic as the Lenore in Poe's "The Raven." My Lenore was the first woman besides my mother whom I loved. She could have stepped out of a television show in 1960; she was that glamorous and intelligent and shimmeringly young, a brunette with generous red lips who dressed for her third graders as if they were princes and princesses (and to her, we were). The references to Williams may or may not have occurred, although the crash did happen close to his home; moreover, I believe, he would have responded in the manner described in the ballad below, reprinted in its entirety:

Bus Crash: Rutherford, N.J.

> We will it so and so it is
> *past all accident*
> —*William Carlos Williams*

> Death has little meaning: at eight,
> I associate it with pets,
> Plants: the still and aquariumed
> Hamster, the Easter violets

> Wilting in the third grade window:
> Franklin School, 1960,
> My first beautiful teacher, young,
> Brunette, alive, a fantasy

> Transfiguring boys who fixate
> On her red lips and bosom,
> Punning her Poe-like name, Lenore,
> Smelling the pungent perfume

> She dabs on the nape between bells,
> The aroma of recess,
> Stirrings of sexuality:
> Thinking of her, embarrassed,
> I sample testers and buy Mother

> The same perfume at Rexall's,
> To wear on parent-teacher night
> Accompany her down the hall,

> My teacher greeting us, saying
> He's wonderful, wonderful,
> My mother greeting her, saying
> I know: Lenore in lambswool,

> Crinoline, her figure as full
> As the underside of moons
> Rising above me, her Avoned
> Lips as scintillant as spoons

> Laid atop each other: she tells
> Our parents that she's engaged,
> And because I don't yet know what
> The word means, I act my age,

> Bursting into the class to play
> With my mates while the hour
> Passes and the smell permeates
> The elements: wildflower:

> My only memory, her perfume:
> The rest I have imagined,
> Pushed out of me, pieced together
> Then as it might have happened:

> She boards the bus at the corner
> By the crossing guard, heading
> To Rutherford where she will live,
> Where she has planned a wedding:

> The bus barrels down Stuyvesant
> Avenue out of Lyndhurst
> To the intersected Ridge Road
> Where Dr. Williams, immersed

> In the sorry facts of his life,
> Composes mortal poems
> In the dim lamplight of his den:
> The clock ticks, a metronome

> In the moments before the crash,
> The bus outside his window
> Illuminating his north room
> A brighter shade of yellow:

> The broadsided hydraulic doors
> Unable to open, welded
> Shut as the metal shears like foil,
> Passengers trapped or propelled

> Out of seats to the curb, aflame,
> The doctor agape at his desk
> Witnessing the spectacle, horror,
> The aftermath, the grotesque
> Wailing of the dying and dead,

His appearing on the scene,
Perhaps trying to help Lenore
While the leaking gasoline

Ignites on the main boulevard,
Perhaps standing back, knowing
She's already beyond his help,
The inflammable world, blowing

Away like violets out a window:
The bridegroom weds another,
The boys burrow in the perfumed
Lambswool of weeping mothers,

And the sorrier Dr. Williams
Returns to his study alone
To record the causes of death,
Medical and melodic ones:

These, the desolate dark weeks
Of a suburban M.D.
Who saves some people twice: at birth
And middle age, with poetry,

So death still has little meaning:
I associate it with metaphor:
The canonized, the forgotten,
The still sweet scent of Lenore.

Nothing especially poetic happened to me after Lenore's death. My innocence blew out of that third-grade window like so many petals of violet. Dr. Williams was just another physician whose magic had limits. Curiously, however, it was another student teacher who revived my interest in poetry and who also lived on Ridge Road in Rutherford, Nancy Hutchinson, for whom I had a serious crush, as did about one hundred other boys in 1968. What distinguished me from them was the discovery that I could write poetry to relieve, well, hormonal rather than peer pressures associated with being in her class. She was slender as Lenore was voluptuous, had delicate but honed Scottish features and, unlike my black-haired third-grade teacher, wore her dark-blond hair cropped short in the style that many women still do in the 1990s. She wrote advertising copy when she wasn't writing creatively. Better still, she had a thrilling half-laugh giggle that appealed to seventeen-year-olds not quite ready to perish in Viet Nam.

That's not all she possessed, however. Nancy was married to an actual oh-my-God published poet, as handsome as she was beautiful, with long yellow locks and man-muscles who worked as a teacher in Newark school districts when build-ings in that city burned during the upheavals of that memorable year. He had courage and social commitment rather than acne and clumsiness. Nancy had a seventeen-year-old sister, as lovely as she, whose name was Kim, if I recall correctly, with whom my English teacher dutifully tried to fix me up. I took Kim to a few expensive dinners and theater shows in New York City to impress her, but I never did, and the dates fizzled as my infatuation for Nancy rose again to new heights. If I couldn't win her heart by composing poetry as powerful as her husband's, then I could memorize poetry to impress her, as this lyric rather accurately depicts:

Hook, Line and Sinker

To dazzle a student teacher
I memorized the Hamlet
"To be or not to be" soliloquy
Between home room and band.

I pondered a well-worn paperback
With the ken of an RCA Victor dog,
The master-voice waxing my ear.
I sullied the pretty pentameter—

The pangs of despised love,
The law's delay—and fancied
A firm on Main Street, pudgy men:
Quietus, Bodkins, and Fardels.

Then I happened on her, histrionic
In my passion, my iambs
Overstressed, and slug each arrow
From the malaprop of my heart:

Abuse the name of action—
Soft you are, the fair Ophelia.
Nymph in thy orifice,
Be all my sins remembered.

She paused, her lashes aflutter,
And said, "It needs some work.
Write it 100 times and leave
A copy each day on my desk."

I nailed it down. To this day
I hear the music in my skull
Thick as Yorick's, and think of her,
Who got me into this mess.

Such is the role of hormones and literature. If Nancy Hutchinson gave me motive, another English teacher, Angela Wisneski, gave me confidence to overcome my blue-collar background

"When I was nineteen"

and dream of one day becoming a published poet. Mrs. Wisneski was an elegant white-haired woman whose love of literature inspired everyone in honors English, where I ended up because of my crush on Mrs. Hutchinson. Mrs. Wisneski read us poetry in the plaintive voice of the creative writer on the circuit, seemingly ignoring the peeling green-painted walls of Lyndhurst High School. She reeked "The Village" and Edna St. Vincent Millay, one of her favorite poets. After hours, remembering Mrs. Wisneski's melodious voice—ideal for the stage, as she was, I later learned, an actress and playwright—we read poetry out of a thick anthology, featuring all the English masters with pictures and biographies on the left page and their works on the right and on subsequent pages. I do not know the name of the English text required in her class, but I do remember lapsing into a mystic state one day during her lecture, probably lulled by the penetrating yearning of her voice, the first yearning I associated with the metaphysical rather than physical. I had an epiphany. Two, actually. One was that I, too, might end up in an anthology as a poet, even though at the time my life goal was to join the navy as all obedient Maltese boys must; the second epiphany was that poetry filled the spirit because it communicated truth. Thus, Mrs. Wisneski gave me my life's gift that would set me on an irreversible course related to truth,

initially as a journalist, then as a poet, and finally as an ethicist.

Mrs. Wisneski knew that despite my aspirations, I was first and foremost a poet. No one would know this about me for years to come, nor would I know it, despite my epiphanies in her class, because my parents, guidance counselors, priests, and peers encouraged me to work at Hoffman-LaRouche, the major employer in the Lyndhurst area, which promised excellent fringe benefits, especially health care. So I focused on chemistry, scored one of the highest test scores on the specialized SAT in New Jersey, and learned German, the language of chemistry at the time. Science, after all, involved truth as much as poetry.

Mrs. Wisneski would remarry, after I left Lyndhurst High School, to a man whose last name was Brown, and she retired under that uninspired name, without knowing where I was or what I would be doing in life. My entry in the high school yearbook announced that I wanted to be a chemist, though she had scrawled over that depiction these words that would foretell my future: "You'll outdo Shakespeare, Shake-speare." Of course, I never will outdo Shakespeare or any other major poet anthologized in high school texts today. But I do credit Mrs. Wisneski with seeing into my soul and discovering it belonged to Will and poetry. A dozen years later, studying creative writing at Oklahoma State University, I realized that her prophesy had proved correct and tried to telephone her to share the news that, indeed, I was becoming a poet, specializing in Ben Jonson; but the principal at the high school informed me that she had passed away the year before. I immediately wrote this poem as a tribute:

Elegy: A Corrected Vision

To Miss Wisneski, English teacher

Paradise, of all places, is Penhurst mansion.
Chaucer greets you at the gates for a stroll
Under the chestnut trees. He speaks of Petrarch,
Their meeting in Italy. The Pearl Poet
Happens by, and he calls to her by name.

Inside, the sitting room glitters, a new
Set by Inigo Jones, Shakespeare,
Back from poaching, brings you a folio
While Jonson unfurls a map: he wants to prove,
In your presence, that Bohemia has no coast.

In the next room Milton has just realized
The meaning of Job and tells you in Aramaic.

You understand each syllable. Wordsworth writes
The last stanza to The Recluse, and Coleridge,
Reading over your shoulder, has an explanation!

All day this goes on! You overhear the voice
Dictating Blake's poems. Pope struggles
With a couplet and you provide the pentameter.
Emily Dickinson consults with you on a matter
Of punctuation, and you pinch yourself,

But there is no pain, only a groan of doors
Opening to the room of your deliverance, light
Bending over what must be a covey of angels,
Until you squint through all that glare to behold
The unborn masters waiting for your lecture.

Thanks to Nancy Hutchinson and Angela Wisneski, I was able to graduate twenty-seventh in my high school class whose senior enrollment was about seven hundred. Both teachers also encouraged my love of music, which they

The author, shortly after the death of his first daughter, 1982

saw as poetry's cousin; wanting to impress them, and learn better German in the process, I traveled at age seventeen to Salzburg, Austria, trying to enroll in the Mozarteum, one of Europe's best music conservatories. Again the dutiful Mediterranean boy, I had played organ in Sacred Heart Church for years but was no match for Salzburg native sons and daughters who auditioned that summer of 1969. I spent the rest of it working as an apprentice at a stonecutter factory, shaping and painting iron crosses for the grave. As I describe in an early poem, "Art: A Possible Explanation": "I twisted steel ribbons / Around the framework / Enameled to last a lifetime." That summer I also met a Swedish woman named Lena, who was on vacation in Salzburg and believed me to be in my early twenties rather than mid-teens, a lie I allowed because I was smitten with her Nordic good looks and compassionate nature. The Viet Nam War was intensifying at the time, and Lena asked me to stay in Europe so that I could escape the conflict when I graduated high school in less than a year. But I decided to return to Lyndhurst and attend college, avoiding the draft.

Two teachers at my high school helped me choose a college. Paul Contey, a passionate history instructor who would go on later to become principal of the high school, was an alumnus of Saint Peter's College in Jersey City. The brother of Laura Yanitelli, my home economics teacher, was president of that Jesuit institution. In the spring of my senior year I was accepted at that college with a full scholarship, based on my chemistry test scores, and began my studies in the fall of 1970, another volatile year of protest on campuses nationwide.

I excelled in the lab under the tutelage of one Father Saint George; but I became disillusioned with science in my sophomore year for three reasons:

> 1. I was living with housemates rumored to belong to Students for a Democratic Society, or SDS, and who took an interest in me because of my chemistry background, in some demand then, in an age of ROTC-building explosions.
> 2. I was dangerous to myself and others in the lab, using Mrs. Yanitelli's home economics skills—a dash of salt, a teaspoon of pepper—not really counting my drops but estimating them with fairly good accuracy, earning B's in my sophomore year. I knew sooner or later that I would not blow up an ROTC building but myself or Father St.

George in the lab. So I switched majors to German, the language I had learned in high school, with a minor in English literature, remembering Mrs. Wisneski's yearbook comment about my outdoing Shakespeare.

3. I read, for the first time, an issue of *Poetry* in the college library. The cover was yellow, and the featured poet was W. H. Auden whose diction reawakened the muse in me. Suddenly I remembered the epiphanies I experienced in Mrs. Wisneski's class, imagining my picture in a poetry anthology, and knew then what I would do with my life. Coming from a blue-collar family, however, I could not afford to switch majors to English, so I completed my degree in German while taking as many English electives as possible and, when not possible, journalism electives.

I was fortunate to have two newswriting classes with a great teacher who, at this writing, still edits a Sunday section of the *Newark Star Ledger*. Anthony Shannon, a 1958 Pulitzer Prize-winning reporter who had worked for the New York City dailies and at that time was public relations director of Conn Edison, the electric power company in the New York metropolitan area. He awakened a zeal in me to accompany my creative muse, a zeal that longed to end the Viet Nam War, or at least cover it as a combat correspondent. By now the Watergate break-in had occurred, and I read Woodward and Bernstein in *The Washington Post* each day, following the Nixon scandal.

My interest in truth and writing reached its zenith, and I discovered two ways of utilizing my zeal: poetry and journalism. I published a few poems in the college annual, *The Pavan*, and generally enjoyed my literature classes. I also published a few feature articles in the college newspaper. But my life then also had taken an unpoetic turn in as much as I fell in love with a fellow German major named Barbara, whom I married in my junior year abroad in Salzburg, Austria, where we had both enrolled for a semester's credit in a program sanctioned by Saint Peter's.

Salzburg was and remains important to me for reasons associated but not directly related to poetry, though one of my best collections—*Flight from Valhalla*—is set in that medieval city. This was a messy romantic time in my life during which I was torn between feelings for my first love (the Swedish woman Lena) and for Barbara, eventu-

ally choosing the latter more out of jealousy than real desire, as Barbara also had fallen for a foreigner, an Austrian native named Adi (short of Adolph). If I could break off my relationship with Lena, with whom I still correspond and luckily didn't marry—because I probably would have remained with her and not had the chance to meet my spouse of twenty years, Diane—then Barbara, I reasoned, could break off with Adi. Perhaps struck by the depth of my emotion, Barbara agreed to marry me in a storybook wedding at Mirabell Palace, where Mozart played or refused to play for his patron bishop. We were both still under age twenty-one and needed our parents' consent, which they gave freely, not angry with us for eloping abroad, but curiously supportive, as if we had spared them either money or pain. The whole episode is captured in this poem, a rare work that mentions my first wife, whom I would divorce a few years later after we returned to Lyndhurst.

HUNGER: Cafe Figaro

Salzburg, 1972

Sounds of music, sorrow. Mozart memorialized
A dozen houses down the block. Baker's
   dozen:

Bittersweet cocoa balls in a black Bavarian
Box. Pastries, too: Torten, Kuchen, forty odd

Schillings apiece, a thousand per rack,
More than I made in a week at the foundry.

An apprentice, I lived if you call it
Living above the cafe, two months

Into an unconsummated marriage, two more
To go. The Mozarteum doesn't want me,

My wife doesn't want me. Frau Mandel,
The maid down the hall, has not made

Up her mind. The end of a ten-hour day,
And I trudge to the room, inescapable

Scent of dough rising as I rise
Thinking of her clef-like form:

My hands have never touched the mysterious
Folds of a woman but can play the Steinway

Fantasias at the conservatory, innocent
Hands, Albrecht Duerer ones that pray

Or betray or do penance, gristle and bone:
Hunger. Ich habe Hunger. In German

You own the word. You have it
As a man has a woman. What did I want?

Food or fulfillment, co-habitating hungers
Slipknotting in the belly, the groin?

I live on potato and blood sausage.
Gluehwein, when I can get it. My own

Wife is pining for someone else, though
I don't know it. He loiters outside

By the street vendor who cries-a
Heisse Maronen!, Heisse Maronen!-a

As if her name is Hot Sweet Chestnut
And scowls as soon as she spots him.

Frau Mandel comes to console her, I think,
To ease her conscience. She has designs

On me. I hope she has designs on me.
Sometimes she brings us stale bread

From the cafe kitchen, and we steal
A moment to talk. Our eyes lock, of course:

Knowing, probing. Sure. Ich habe Hunger,
Frau Mandel. Bitte, Frau Mandel. "Please."

We have an understanding. She is going to
Relent, arrange a rendezvous. Arrive early,

She tells me—she is planning a surprise—
And I do, I do. I time it just right and run

Into the man at the window whose name
I know, or should know, he assures me: Adolph,

"Adi" for short. He is peeling one of
Several steaming chestnuts in his hand,

Which he offers. Take it, take it.
It burns but I take it, swallow each ember

Whole and then burst in on my wife:
The scene is wrong—she is wearing a gown—

Bed turned down, lights turned down,
The icebox door open, her arms open,

Awaiting me: hunger? How was I to know,
Frau Mandel? Thousand schillings a rack,

And there stood two of them. I thought
She spent the rent, I thought she was going

Crazy alone in the room. How was I to know
One hunger feeds upon the other until

The body consumes itself, the hands making
A clean slate of it, racks splattering on

The floor—Torten, Kuchen—apple, cherry,
Chestnut, mince. Someone is chanting

Heisse Maronen!, Heisse Maronen!, summoning
   her
To the window. She will perch there

Two days, the last trace of him. Of us,
Any semblance of a marriage as I kneel

Begging forgiveness, but also tasting
A piece of this, a piece of that. Frau Mandel

Raps on the door, wondering how we liked
Her incredible cache of perishable goods,

Compliments Cafe Figaro; opens up finally
To see for herself. She sees all right.

What rises in the room has shape,
Definition: hunger. Ich habe Hunger.

I own it, it is mine.

I wrote several poems, all juvenilia, about Salzburg during my painful years with Barbara, but do not have any to share here. The reason is ironic. Shortly after returning with Barbara to the States to live in an apartment two blocks from my parents in Lyndhurst, and to work at Blue Cross in Newark—finishing up my German degree at night at Saint Peter's—I sent a poem about my marriage at Mirabell Palace to the poetry columnist at *Writer's Digest,* Judson Jerome, who was critiquing poems for five dollars at a commune called Downhill Farm. Jud, whom I would come to know well later in life and whose cancerous death I still mourn, wrote me a harsh letter claiming I had no chance at success as a poet unless I understood the rigors of meter. The poem I sent was based on the alternating meter of "Sir Gawain and the Green Knight," which Mrs. Wisneski had drummed into my head, and like many of my own readers today, who await my pronouncement about their work, I waited for Jud to say I was talented; and when he implied virtually the opposite, I wrote an angry letter back demanding the return of my five dollars, which he sent, and an apology, which he didn't. Defeated, I decided that I would never be a poet, threw away my poems and college annuals, and embraced journalism to sustain the zeal I had felt in Anthony Shannon's class. Barbara, by now, had decided to leave me to pursue an engineering degree in Detroit. Before she left for Michigan she brought home *Editor & Publisher,* the trade magazine for journalists, and told me to look in the want ads. There was a notice for graduate assistants in the communication program at South Dakota State University in Brookings. Lacking a journalism degree, I enrolled to earn some credentials.

My life blossomed like poetry, although poetry was no longer the flower of my life. I excelled at journalism, having been trained at the undergraduate level by one of the world's premiere reporters; I divorced and lost track of Barbara; met and married Diane Sears, whose beauty

"My best friend in the English department of Oklahoma State University, Roger Jones, at a recent poetry reading in Texas"

rivaled Farrah Fawcett's—the pinup at the time; and upon graduation one year later, secured a position with United Press International, the famous wire service. Again success came easily. I broke one of the top news stories of 1975, reporting that the swine flu inoculation program caused temporary paralysis, and worked my way up the corporate ladder with assignments in Pierre, South Dakota; Lincoln, Nebraska; and Omaha, eventually returning to South Dakota as state editor in Sioux Falls.

The pressures and tragedies of daily journalism caught up with me after four years with UPI. My zeal evaporated. My spouse Diane and I moved thirteen times during my tenure with the wire service. I routinely put in sixty- to seventy hours per week and worked the major holidays. I saw the blood and gore of murder, assault, kidnap, child abuse, overdose deaths, traffic fatalities, prison riots, and myriad other calamities that occur daily in major cities and make cynical otherwise truth-seeking journalists. When one of my reporters investigated a drug-related story and received a death threat, as did I, I decided that I had had enough, looked at the want ads in *Editor & Publisher* again, and applied at Oklahoma State University, whose journalism school was seeking an adviser to the school newspaper, *The Daily O'Collegian.*

I got the position. Little did I know that within two years I would rekindle my love of literature, not to mention my zeal.

II. The Apprentice Years: A Revival

My first two years at Oklahoma State University were spent getting adjusted to the job. I excelled as a teacher and as a newspaper adviser, transforming the newsroom of *The Daily O'Collegian* into a student version of a United Press International bureau. But these successes had nothing to do with writing poetry or reading literature, which I did not contemplate then, focusing on the rigors of work-a-day journalism. Until, that is, I met a master's student majoring in creative writing who had joined the staff of the *O'Collegian.* Lisa Trow was an award-winning poet from Trinity, Texas, who saw how harried I was working with students from noon to midnight (when the paper went to press) and decided I should read some poetry during off hours to regain some perspective. She showed me some of her own work, which I immediately admired because her poems cut through surface truths of everyday human relations and contained epiphanies that revived my creative impulse. She struck a deal with me. If I would teach her newswriting, she would critique my poetry; but first, she implored, I would have to compose some. So once a week I would write a poem to give to Lisa, with whom I also would spend an hour or two editing her news copy, line by line.

We transferred our talents. In January 1981 I would enroll in the creative writing program at OSU to earn my doctorate, taking one or two English classes per semester and more during the summer. Lisa would go on to become managing editor of the *O'Collegian* and then graduate to begin a journalism career that included stints at newspapers in Huntsville and El Paso, Texas, where she reports today.

Entering the doctoral program would give me new direction and life goals. I had no doubt that I would continue to earn a living as a journalist, which I do still; but I also knew that poetry would become my life again as it once was in high school in Mrs. Wisneski's class. So with great anticipation in Morrill Hall on the OSU campus, I awaited my first poetry teacher who strolled into workshop a few minutes late, looking exactly like I had pictured a famous poet in a textbook anthology: trimmed beard; long black Aristotelian locks; and outdoor dress (jeans, flannel shirt, and boots). T. R. Hummer, whom we all knew as "Terry," entered and changed my life—one of the finest teachers an aspiring poet could have—who wrote passionate verse, slicing through surface truths or transforming them, just as Lisa had. In my class as well was Roger Jones, who would go on to become one of my best friends, godfather to a future child, and current colleague at Southwest Texas State University, where he teaches creative writing. The class also included poets who would become good friends during my time in Stillwater, including Philip Paradise and Melissa Harwood, both of whom still write and work in academe. All of us learned much from Terry Hummer, although I suspect I was his biggest challenge.

This was the early 1980s, and formal verse was not only rare but considered intellectually tacky. Not knowing the current trends, I composed a sestina for my first workshop assignment, sending Terry to the *Princeton Encyclopedia of Poetry and Poetics*. Terry was one of the few published poets writing occasionally in form at the time, mostly sonnets with a few terza rima narra-

tives thrown in for good measure. So Terry did not discourage me from composing traditional poetry and critiqued with insight and precision my sestina and other French forms to follow. Moreover, we shared other passions, including a love of music. After hours Terry would perform with a local jazz group at Stillwater honky tonks, playing sax. So in addition to reawakening my creative muse, he also did my musical one. I, too, played keyboards and a new instrument, mandolin, with local groups and even on occasion with Garth Brooks, an advertising student in the Journalism School whose best friend, Heidi Miller, was one of my advisees. Heidi would be killed in a car crash eleven days before graduation in 1985, and her memory would help launch Garth's superstardom as a country western singer, as his first hit—"If Tomorrow Never Comes"—is dedicated to her memory. Although I mourned Heidi at the time, especially her love of music, and wrote an elegy for her published in the *O'Collegian*, she passed from my own memory in a few years . . . only to return in a prophetic dream that I will describe later in its proper sequence.

In early 1981, before Diane conceived our first child, I was experiencing a musical revival. I had time to re-learn the clarinet and sax, which I studied in Lyndhurst as a child before taking up keyboards (which were cooler in the Beatles era). The saxophone was particularly appealing again, especially since my mentor Terry played it better than I, arousing a passion that I hitherto had associated only with poetry. Rather than compete with him, I celebrated Terry and his music in this poem:

Re-Defining the Blues

for Terry Hummer

Forget what you have heard, all those lyrics
Linking the sax to love. True, the noise
A horn makes in the blue smoke of the bar
Rises in couples like passion, the slur
Of Coltrane, Mingus, or Monk a mating call.
True, the position a player takes is exact
For romance, a slender woman aswoon
From the gentle caress. And true,
The undeniable shape of stem and mouthpiece,
The fitting of the parts, the moistening
Of the reed and subtle vibration at the lip.
Even the word—sax—so close, so close. . . .
But this is sleaze, and love has a higher
Range the player comes to know apart
From the jazz. The parting comes hard:

*Michael Bugeja with his wife Diane and daughter Erin Marie, together with
the judge (far left), at Erin Marie's adoption*

A jealous woman, a band gone bad, a habit
The pawn cures for a day. Give him a week,
And he'll complain about the tongue, as if salt
Of one tear were placed on the tip, jutting
Of the lower jaw and ache of the upper teeth,
The palsy of hands and fingers, yearning
For the god and pearl they once touched
So tenderly, we all mistook it for love.

By now, the end of my first semester in the
creative writing program, I was publishing poetry
regularly. My first acceptance letters came on the
same day from *Texas Review* and *Amelia*. Soon after I would place a poem with *Poets On:*, whose
editor Ruth Daigon would remain an avid sup-
porter of my work to this day. In a recent letter,
she writes me: "As editor of *Poets On:*, I can honestly say that when an envelope with the return
address, Michael J. Bugeja, arrived, I was delighted.
Your poetry was not only well crafted but had
such a distinctive voice, an emotional content and

appeal, a versatility that was quite unique." Ruth
was as encouraging early in my career as Angela
Wisneski was in high school. She continues in
her letter: "I love your sense of humor, the fun
you have with language and the way you can laugh
at yourself. But above all your integrity, your con-
viction and intelligence are evident throughout
all your fine work. With you, every word counts.
Every comma. Yet your poetry is seemingly simple,
unpretentious, which makes it even more powerful and gives it greater depth."

I don't know whether Ruth Daigon's words
about my work are true; I do know, however, that
every poet needs an editor like Ruth Daigon,
and I have had the pleasure of knowing several
who have sustained me throughout the years. To
list them would be to omit some; so I have chosen Ruth to stand in their stead, because she
has been there steadfastly urging me on during
dry periods when the words would not come, nor
acceptances.

"With our son Shane," 1991

One such time was during the loss of my firstborn, Erin Marie, who was delivered stillborn in November 1981 in Stillwater, Oklahoma. This whole episode is too painful yet for me to describe, because I blame myself for not chal-lenging the obstetrician's prognosis. On Friday of that fateful week, Diane and I had dinner at Terry Hummer's house. He made a wonderful Cajun meal and kept us laughing with his piercing Southern wit. At the time he was renting another writer's house, almost a mansion, and he showed us how he would mess a room with food cartons, newspapers, journals and the like, and simply close the door to begin messing yet another room. It was his way of housekeeping. Terry was the perfect host, and that night would be the last happy one for several years to come. The next day Diane said the baby was moving less, struggling almost; and she herself had broken out in cold sweats, as if there was a horrific problem. Worse, there was a small stain on the bedsheets indicating that her water had broken. I immediately telephoned our physician and scheduled an emergency appointment. Diane asked me to put my ear on her belly to listen for the baby; I could not hear anything but my own heartbeat. When we finally got to see the doctor, he did not do an exam but asked me how much

water would I estimate had leaked on the bedsheets. When I said a small shot glassful, he decided it was urine and said he would take the baby on Tuesday, when he routinely induced pregnancies artificially. I asked if he could take the baby immediately by Caesarian section, but he said that the Oklahoma State Cowboys were playing that day and that he had good tickets for the football game. He told us not to worry, and because I had been brought up to respect a doctor's authority, I did not challenge this pronouncement but led Diane away as if toward an execution. By Tuesday, she herself almost died because the baby had inside her and also had infected her. The entire episode is documented in my first book, *The Visionary,* from which this poem is taken:

Duty

I never guarded bodies or unloaded
Bags of black plastic
From a chopper. But I did my best
In your room with the ceiling fan
Hovered over the bed, the doctor
Ordering you to push, breathe.
I swear we were in a war.
There was blood, and in your belly

The shrapnel of stillborn
Pulled out piece by piece: a foot,
A leg, the tethered body finally
Cut from you. He put it on plastic,

On a table you couldn't see
With me standing there. No hero,
I wasn't the fighter who carries
His friend across front lines,
Who points a weapon at the medic
And says: Make her breathe.

I remember exiting the delivery room after that harrowing experience and seeing, in the waiting room, my poet-friends Terry Hummer, Roger Jones, and Melissa Harwood, along with other graduate students. They asked me if there was anything that they could do. I said there was. They could go to my house and put in the attic the baby crib and all newborn accoutrements so that when I brought Diane home she would not have to witness what we did not have: a baby. My friends did as requested. In retrospect, this denial was unhealthy, as was my urging Diane to conceive again, as if in doing so we could snatch from death our first daughter. We tried again in the year to follow and Diane conceived, only to lose the baby again, using the same physician. So young and naive were we! During this year I did not write any poems and confessed to Terry Hummer that I probably would never compose again. He doubted that would happen, predicting I would write fluently because of the depth of my experience and pain. His prognosis proved correct within a few years' time.

By 1983, Diane was teaching photojournalism as my colleague in the E. W. Scripps School of Journalism. The physician informed us that we probably would never be able to have children and should consider adoption. Diane, rushed prematurely into conceiving again, only to lose our second child whom we would have named Kelly Ann, rightly challenged my opinion that we should adopt. But she agreed to go through the application process because we were told the average waiting period for an infant was seven years. I wrote our family history in verse and Diane illustrated it with pictures. In sum, we had assembled a children's book that welcomed our unseen baby into our home, our history, and our hearts. The "Mommy Daddy Book" was the last document filed to complete our application and soon after we handed it in to an agency worker, I sensed that Diane was still hesitant about adopting a child. After all, her career had just begun in academe and the mere thought of babies brought sorrow. My stance seemed reasonable at the time. If we were to adopt, we had to be ready to receive a child at any moment, I argued. One night our views clashed in a terrible verbal fight in our bedroom; the confrontation went on for hours, with each casting blame on the other for the losses of our first two daughters. I made the point that we were bound, ethically, to adopt the child whenever it came but doubted that providence would move unless Diane made up her mind, then and there, to become a mother. Propped up against pillows, illuminated by lamplight, Diane sobbed that I was right and that she would change her mind because the Virgin Mary had brought her peace of mind, entering her being at that instant. We went to sleep feeling that the fight was important but not knowing why because the adoption process had only begun.

The next morning I was in Terry Hummer's office for our weekly critique of my poems. The telephone rang. "Yes," Terry replied, "he's here." Not wanting my session to be disturbed, I asked Terry if he could relay the message so I could determine whether the call was significant enough to take. Terry questioned the caller, and his face lit up. He repeated the message for me: "You're a papa." The words didn't register. Terry said them again and then handed over the phone. A journalism professor was at the other end. Diane had already gone home because a woman from the adoption agency was there making final arrangements for us to pick up our newborn whom we would name Erin Marie as if to resurrect our firstborn. In my poem "Adoption: The Fulfillment," I captured two moments when our first daughter died and the adoptive one entered our lives dramatically without warning, Erin's style to this day, celebrating her birthgiver and Diane—two courageous women—described in these ending lines:

So there are two women, both brave,
Two days that changed our lives,

And two babies who could be sisters,
Who even have the same name.

The adoption of Erin Marie marked the close of a life chapter. Diane and I were parents at last; however, in becoming so, we inherited problems that we never anticipated and that would nearly tear us apart in the next three years. We tried to juggle responsibilities that included child care, successful careers, and lingering pain from the losses of our earlier daughters. Worse, Erin Marie had medical problems that included skin disorders and asthma. Our poor baby was constantly scratching until she bled and cried, her skin so red and raw that she refused to be held most of the time, which increased her emotional discomfort. And the breathing problems sparked a combination of new and old anxieties; at any moment we might lose Erin Marie as we had two other children.

The stresses mounted for Diane and me. A grief counselor told us that 95 percent of couples who experience the loss of a child divorce within five years. We stayed together. Nonetheless, there is nothing poetic to report during this bleak period, other than the fact that Diane and I defied the odds. My predominant emotions then were anger and depression, which almost cost me my friendships with both Terry Hummer, who took a position at Kenyon College, and Roger Jones, who went to Texas to teach. In a last act of friendship and good faith, Terry nominated me to replace him as poetry editor of *Cimarron Review,* OSU's national literary magazine, which gave me solace because I could immerse myself in poetry after a long day at the Journalism School. I also developed lasting friendships and associations with a host of poets, including Miller Williams, Larry Lieberman, Sharon Olds, Neal Bowers, Diane Ackerman, Stan Lindberg, David Baker, Judith Kitchen, Steve Heller, Jonathan Holden, William Stafford, Fred Chappell, Jim Barnes, Walt McDonald, Ron Wallace and David Citino, to name a few and to apologize to others not included in this summary list. In retrospect, as I sank into and out of depression, poetry helped me survive, as I am sure it did others, including Sylvia Plath, whose verse probably added a decade to her life until life itself became unbearable. I would have a better fate, which included these poetic highlights: earning my doctorate with a 4.0 average, winning two Academy of American Poets university prizes, and graduating with more than one hundred published poems. To top off these successes in 1986, I applied for a professorship at the prestigious E. W. Scripps School of Journalism at Ohio University and, on a whim, entered a short fiction story in the *Writer's Digest* annual competition.

I got the job and won the *Writer's Digest* grand prize.

III. The Publication Years: A Creation

Poets tend to think that composition is creation. Of course it is. But for those who persist, who overcome the petty politics and continual rejections, and who go on to publish poems regularly in literary journals, there is the last, perhaps most difficult phase of literary life: the creation of an audience. Those interested in how I created my own should read *Poet's Guide* (Story Line Press), a small book that shares methods so that others may create audiences of their own. Briefly here, I will summarize the high points of the publication years and then focus on my most important creation with my spouse: the birth of a son who also defied the odds as I like to think I have as a spouse and a poet.

By 1988 I had published more than two hundred poems in some of the country's best journals—*The Kenyon Review, New England Review, Indiana Review, Quarterly West, The Georgia Review* and others—before placing my first collection, What We Do for Music, with Fred Raborg at Amelia Press. That same week I was notified by Rupert Loydell, editor of Taxus Press, a small house in Exeter, England, that he would be bringing out my dissertation, *The Visionary,* in a three-hundred-book limited edition. Coincidentally both books would be published in the early months of 1990 when Diane would give birth to a son, Shane Michael, whose conception merits some remarks, as I remember the night vividly.

Shortly after Diane and I had made love—a different kind of coupling that felt electric in a nonsexual way I find impossible to describe, appealing more to the brain than to the body—I drifted off in a half-sleep and had what best can be described as a dream-apparition. Immediately I recognized Heidi Miller, Garth Brooks's college friend and my former student advisee, who said she had good news: Diane and I would have a child despite what the medical establishment had said about our chances. Then she disappeared and I awoke, dismissing the experience as an imaginary figment. First of all, Diane had just been to a gynecologist who verified why we had lost babies in Stillwater and gave us little hope of ever having our own child. A bit disheartened, we had accepted the prognosis, happy to be adoptive parents and to rear Erin Marie, whose energy level was always twice that of other children—an exciting girl who to this day always seeks new thrills and freedoms and teaches us parenting skills we never knew existed (i.e. chat-room monitoring and shotput training).

And, of course, the dream-apparition was prophetic. I have no idea why Heidi Miller was the messenger. Up until that time I had been corresponding with Garth Brooks and confided in him, at which point he broke off communication with no explanation. Perhaps he felt I was trying to hitch my star on his success. Or maybe he was spooked. More likely he was busy catering to his global audience—in real life, Garth Brooks is a sensitive, caring, creative artist—and never even read the letter.

Nonetheless, the dream-apparition and subsequent pregnancy had a common denominator: grace. Although advised by her doctor to take a battery of tests, primarily to learn if the fetus had abnormalities (and so to encourage abortion), Diane refused, feeling that we would accept whatever we created, for better or worse. I should note that Diane and I had researched and carefully chosen this physician, a woman with a stellar reputation. Despite the advance preparation, Diane and I were still forced to face past fears and conquer them, opening up for me a new era of intellectual and spiritual growth, which naturally led later to poetic achievement.

Diane's pregnancy progressed normally until the final month. In April 1990, Diane began experiencing some of the same symptoms suffered when she bore our first daughter. As happened in Stillwater, her physician was reluctant to induce labor or take the baby by Caesarian section, claiming that Diane was experiencing psychological flashbacks—a seemingly valid medical explanation. By now, however, I was impressed neither by authority nor sound reasoning. As a poet and a parent, I had come to value intuition and a higher power. Thus, I did not allow the medical establishment to "call the shots," as it were, and that day scheduled an emergency appointment with a psychologist who dismissed the doctor's prognosis in a letter. Back we went to the hospital where the doctor gave Diane another cursory examination. The baby was fine, the physician said; no it wasn't, I asserted. Finally the doctor and I agreed to hook up Diane to a stress monitor for eight hours, during which time the physician agreed to induce labor if the baby showed any signs of distress. After seven and a half hours, the monitor lit up like a pinball machine and, within another thirty minutes, Shane Michael Bugeja was successfully delivered by Caesarian section.

The rest, as the saying goes, is history. When we brought Shane home from the hospital, I was notified that I had won a National Endowment for the Arts fellowship. The $20,000 grant allowed me to write poetry during a leave of absence. A year later, Judson Jerome—by now a friend and colleague—would pass away and pass on the poetic baton as columnist at *Writer's Digest,* another serendipity, as he was the critic who had dashed my poetic aspirations when I was in college and now had restored them, helping me create an audience: grace at work again. In the 1990s I was able to place collections with Orchises Press (*Platonic Love, After Oz,* and a reprint of *The Visionary*); with Livingston University Press (Flight from Valhalla); and with the University of Arkansas Press (*Talk*). In 1996 at Ohio University, I was appointed special assistant and ethics adviser to President Robert Glidden, a former band director and musician. A yet unpublished collection is dedicated to him and Miller Williams, both of whom share my zeal for art as a vehicle of

"Erin Marie Bugeja, age ten, waiting for her father to finish an autograph session," 1992

truth. Most recently I was selected as chancellor of the National Federation of State Poetry Societies, succeeding Tess Gallagher. My audience keeps growing, again I suspect because of grace (with a dash of perseverance). At this writing I am in the process of compiling a *New and Selected,* marking yet another phase of the poetic life: the gradual closing down of one's career.

And yet one truth remains, the thread of which I hope to have captured in my autobiographia poetica: that poetry, like life, comes full circle if you are patient and courageous enough, as I hope this final, most recent poem—dedicated to Diane—illustrates, an apt ending to this essay:

Life's Ineffable Edge

What came came at top speed into the dunce
Skull cap of fontanel, and suddenly
I understood the universe in pieces
As if the cerebellum had a circuit

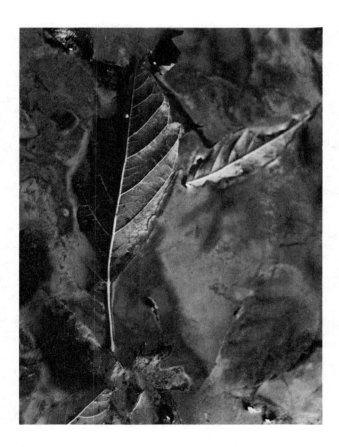

Photo used on the cover of Bugeja's first collection,
The Visionary, *taken by Diane Bugeja*

Hot-wiring my neurons. My new son
Whinnied when it happened and awoke
From half-sleep paradise of mother-suckle.

But this was not the fabled light of Christ
That comforts even at misfortune's edge.
For I had toed that precipice before
Beside two daughters lost in white-out
Pediatric wards. I could confront
The doppelganger light and still endure.
My son and wife beheld me eerily,

Silently, the way that pilgrims might,
Not at the phosphor-flick of seraphim
Nor at diffuse enlightenment of Zen
Nor at the near-death aftershock of being.
This light became a binary flash
Of terrifying cosines I could trace
With magic fingertips on moonlit walls,

Reciting quantum physics and equations
Easily as lullabies, emerging odds
Of origins on prebiotic Earth
Among a hundred billion bluer planets.
I know we're not alone and yet divine
A purpose in each quark and quandary,
Humbled by my nanosecond knowledge.

Why me? I ask my wife who buried babies
And nearing forty bore another one.
Why not the angel-aura of my daughters
Aflutter in the tunnels of transcendence?
My son is cooing, suckling her again.
"Because you're trusting nature," she replies,
"And nature knows that you can take it now."

BIBLIOGRAPHY

Poetry:

What We Do for Music (poetry chapbook), Amelia Press, 1990.

The Visionary, Taxus Press, 1990, reprinted, Orchises, 1994.

Platonic Love, Orchises, 1991.

After Oz, Orchises, 1993.

Flight from Valhalla: Poems, Livingston University Press, 1993.

Talk, University of Arkansas Press, 1997.

Fiction:

Little Dragons (short story collection), Negative Capability Press, 1996.

Family Values (novel), Sligo Press, 1997.

Nonfiction:

Culture's Sleeping Beauty: Essays on Poetry, Prejudice, and Belief, Whitston, 1992.

Academic Socialism: Merit and Morale in Higher Education, Orchises, 1994.

The Art and Craft of Poetry, Writer's Digest Books, 1994.

Poet's Guide: How to Publish and Perform Your Work, Story Line Press, 1995.

Living Ethics: Developing Values in Mass Communcation, Allyn and Bacon, 1996.

Guide to Writing Magazine Nonfiction, Allyn and Bacon, 1998.

Contributor of poems to numerous magazines and journals, including *Amelia, The Georgia Review, Harper's, Indiana Review, The Kenyon Review, Michigan Quarterly Review, New England Review, Poetry, Poets On:, Prairie Schooner, Quarterly West, Texas Review,* and *TriQuarterly.* Also former poetry editor of *Cimarron Review* and poetry columnist at *Writer's Digest.*

Wanda Coleman

1946-

DANCER ON A BLADE: DEEP TALK, REVISIONS, & RECONSIDERATIONS

Wanda Coleman

i take the eleven to San Pedro's exit on Gaffney
thru town to the cliffs the sand the sea
where palms bear witness this midnight
as i take this final drive
my dreams of water the roar the foam
played back against the violet vista
i find the unmarked gate and take the hidden road
i park at tide's edge and kill the headlights

(From "Death 101," May 1984)

There are moments I'm inclined to believe that defining poetry is as fruitful or as fruitless as talking about love. It eludes being gotten right. Experts and sources abound, yet the definitive definition remains elusive. As soon as a quorum is divined, a new sensibility emerges to throw all absolutes into disarray. Having spent considerable hot air on it myself, I've finally come to the momentary conclusion that the reader who appreciates a particular poet is drawn to that poet out of some profound and often indecipherable need. In this way the poem itself, with time, may transcend its author and all critics. But, for the sake of practicalities, circumscription continues, as it has since the Sophists.

What little I've been able to contribute to said ongoing discussion has taken place primarily during interviews, as opposed to any formal or informal essay on my favorite topic. When teaching, in workshops or in classrooms, I'm quick to point out that I'm a poetry bigot, believing it the highest form of human dialogue.

> hand story: once upon a time i laid hands in love
>   the sinister and the dexter
>   in the hope of a man. to give him
>   light by which to see me. once
>   upon a time i laid hands in love
>   to cure his flesh in the fire of
>   mine. burning together. once upon
>   a prayer
>
>   these hands

                (From "Hand Dance," August 1983)

My interviews, to the extent that I've had them, have rarely been dialogues. Rather, they have taken place under difficult and sometimes specious, or bloody odd circumstances. Sometimes, in the course of talking to me, interviewers discover they don't much care for me or what I have to present. More often the case, I had been up two or three nights working at one job, project, trauma, or another. I lived then, as I live now, in a rest-broken, sleep-deprived urban zone of endless stress and dissatisfaction. When the interviewer arrived, or when I arrived for the interview, he or she could not imagine the unsettling gyrations I had undergone mere minutes or seconds before at home, on the job, or outside on the streets en route as I bodaciously committed a score of traffic violations simply to arrive on time.

Yet now, I was expected to sit down, comfortably, and present myself, answering questions with as much bravado as I could muster in the manner expected from a "modern-day Langston Hughes" writing "movingly of the double oppression of being both a woman and an African American," endowed with those "straight-ahead, award-winning and powerful perceptions" torn from the guts of an "uncompromising" "skilled teller of tales," an "L.A. Blues Woman," the "Billie Holiday of Poetry."

> dense opal fog obscures her black os
> entry, a navigational feat
> strong persistent undertow
> distant cry. another ship anchors
> horn sounds, lights & beacons define a
> cool welcome. February and the end
> of a troubled voyage
>
> dock and the rank pungence of oil spillage
> San Pedro tourista traps, bars & Marineland
> the blemished old royal Dame Mary
> stars appear like teeth lost in a barroom brawl
> bleed on the floor of sky
>
> travel these streets more tortuous than Sargasso
> nor can one be more lost than drive her
>   uncharted promise
>
> home at last. for a price

              ("Port Angeles," May 1981)

Literary publications usually gave me the latitude to stretch, to say as much as I wanted in any fashion I or the interviewer desired because there was no hard cash exchanging hands. The disadvantage, I came to discover, was that sometimes these, occasionally unskilled, interviewers weren't always interested in my poetry per se; rather, they were more interested in *the music* they heard in my poetry—that "oral tradition"—and in my "electrifying" performance style. Or in rubbing elbows with someone considered a cult celebrity. What I didn't have the time, or ability, to do was convince them of the intimate relationship of my two disparate gifts—the writing and the presentation of the writing. Early on, I wasn't too certain of the distinction myself.

Mainstream and alternative publications either tried to protect me (from myself or the reader) or tried to fit me into their given agenda. Unlike other regions, serious American Black writers of African descent and of visible accomplishment have been a rarity in the western United States, countable on two hands and one big toe. Therefore, when budget and timing are major limitations (meaning they can't afford to fly in a big-name Black from the East), we test-proven issue-ready local spooks have to

Parents, George and Lewana Evans, 1943

absorbed and dismissed by a power structure no longer threatened by a passé '60s Black militancy, or any kind of American social militancy.

At some point during the mid-eighties, I began to tire of ostensibly talking about myself without talking about myself deeply; struggling to retain the grits and gravy of my existence for some imagined future memoir. Presenting myself in what I considered a recharged and powerful light became an unbearable pressure. Yet, I had convinced myself that I needed every modicum of attention I could garner because writers of all stripes who took root west of the Mississippi and south of the Sacramento were so terribly neglected by the rest of the English-speaking literary planet.

Poet's Blood, Poet's Blood Press, 1313 Ink Splatt, San
Francisco, New York. Aureate Poet Laureate, editor.
"Goddamn it, I'm going to discover the world's top notch
literati and my sweet buns are gonna go down in history
even if it does bankrupt the trust my parents set up . . ."
Poet must type poems . . . and then proceed to hitchhike across
country and deliver them in person on hands and knees. . . .
We publish what we like; mostly me and my friends publish
our own stuff. . . .

(From "Small Magazines Directory,
[A Listing]," June 1978)

By 1991, a little over twenty-one years after sending my fledgling manuscript to Black Sparrow Press, a deeply entrenched, unexorcised rage had "calderized" despite my having criss-crossed the nation doing over five hundred readings and having published more or as many poems, and having been blessed with a few honors along my circuitous route. The deep-rooted reasons for this anger were ensnared beyond unraveling, yet it persisted in the days that followed the fires in the name of Rodney G. King, up until and long after the sociopolitical eruptions died, burning as apparently cool as *pahoehoe* or liquid lava crusted over in volcanic ash.

This was in part, I began to realize, my long-festering subliminal response to a surface-addicted world in which any remnants of in-depth journalism and serious literature were being

suffice should a representative Black be mandatory. We come easily recyclable interchangeably without consideration of differences in national origin, style, content, or point of view. And whether we get along or not is irrelevant to those who view the Black subculture as monolithic.

But when someone was looking for a tough customer, particularly a "fearless womon poet" able to conduct a workshop in San Quentin, visit a skid row substance abuse rehab house, or read at an ill-reputed Youth Authority facility, someone who wouldn't wince when told her audience consisted largely of murderers and child molesters, Wanda Coleman was summoned. But this presumed toughness, rooted in a racist reality in which I too was stereotyped, was not the glamour stuff local newspapers wanted. Therefore, I was pushed, prodded, and spanked into either more "positive" postures or the acceptable kind of shock-value controversy easily rapidly subsumed by the cash-and-carry sensationalism of voracious tabloid exploitation driven by a new breed of pernicious corporate profiteers. I was not alone. The average citizen of fin-de-siècle U.S.A. was awash in a ceaseless flow of controversies, crises, catastrophes, and celebrity trials.

one day a sampling broke ground
grew high enuff to start to block the view
between my neighbor's terrace and my window
good. more privacy, i thought

four years later it matured and gave birth
sweet firm orangy apricots good to eat.
we picked them, me and my kids
sometimes neighbor kids stole them

but knowing nothing of trees
(and anyway, i didn't have time to know)
it went untended and grew wild while i enjoyed
the dance of leaves in late afternoon sun

my unkempt tree bears fruit less frequently
and what it bears is sharp tart pulpy

my fruit. stolen no more

(From "Tree of My Planting," May 1984)

By 1988, after a thirty-year struggle (my first poem published in 1959 at age thirteen), and having matured as writer and poet, it seemed that I had arrived when my first collection of stories, *A War of Eyes,* was favorably reviewed on page one of the *Los Angeles Times Book Review.* But I was just one hop ahead of the tsunami which had been building behind mainstream media's declaration of war against poetry, the quixotic charge led by the *Los Angeles Times Book Review* the year before. Although the then-editor provided evidence that poetry could and did make money, and an editorial stated, "Poetry is not naturally a nurturing pursuit. As an intense form of self-expression, it requires a professional attention to the self that is as far from conventional selfishness as a clown's attention to the red spot on his nose is far from conventional vanity." This lame defense did not alter policy and followed the announcement that the book review section would no longer review small-press volumes by contemporary and unknown authors. (Now, a decade later, that policy has been shelved. But the harm to notoriously frail literary careers can't be undone.)

This blatant and unfair reactionary censorship was more ice on the mushrooming cultural chill as states' arts funding collapsed nationwide, and a corresponding assault on the National Endowment for the Humanities and National Endowment for the Arts loomed on the sociopolitical horizon.

a cross red and gold with flame

a nation sleeps undisturbed beneath the bleeding moon where black flesh glistens, freshly hung

black & anguished

what would it have been like equal/free

a child whose mother's apron is the red white & blue
of a flag, her rhetoric of "wash those hands, your face and those dirty ears"

(From "All the Hate Hate Is," March 1981)

We southern Californian poets, a motley generation of Whitmans forced to toot our own leaves, already tremulously relied on local publications to, at minimum, mention our names. When the cultural war broke out, many were casualties; a handful of heavyweights who had breached the limits of regionalism were left standing. Fortunately, I was among the latter. But the weight of this stance had done damage, contributing to my complex rages made public; hurt and impotence long tempered to create the fabric from which I fashioned, and would continue to fashion, my poems—the good the bad and the rhetorical.

the walls sway and quiver
my pulse thumps at the lip of my left ear
i stare inward, mind focused
on everything i thot we shoulda woulda coulda
had love worked
i blame me i blame him i blame the world

(From "The Aftershock," October 1984)

In 1980, I was among the local literati invited to a salon at the West Los Angeles home of English drama critic Kenneth Tynan and wife Kathleen. That afternoon stands out in my memory as one of the rare times I've ever felt "in society." Mr. Tynan was ill at the time with the cancer that would subsequently end his life, and Kathleen was assisted by friends, one of whom took charge of introducing me around. I finally found myself face to face with gorgeous, olive-skinned, graying-haired P. Armando Fernandez, seemingly twenty years my senior, the cultural ambassador to Cuba. He promptly and scathingly asked, "Why is it they introduce you as a Black poet and not as a poet?"

Knocked speechless by his unexpected arrogance and his enormous question, I groped to recover my tongue. He abruptly turned and walked away. Greatly disturbed, I left early, barely able to concentrate on the drive home. I remember little about that afternoon, everyone and everything else blotted out by that man and that staggering, cruel question to which my very existence was the answer.

> we don't marry women like you
> your nappy head too dark skin
> even if in vogue
> turns us off
> and cookin' food an havin' babies is all
> we want you to do. and i can tell
> by lookin'
> you ain't ready for that

> (From "A Song for Some Sistuhs,"
> *Poems 1970–1972*)

In retrospect, I've speculated that Fernandez's infuriating question has been the subtext for my every interview since; therefore, in this literary moment, I've excerpted from some of my best interviews, selecting certain questions to be addressed in greater detail. As a result, I hope to make these moments re-speak me in a brighter and perhaps slightly less charring luciferosity.

Electrum

Interviewer's introduction: "Coleman's poetry is personal, written with an eye for detail. That's not to say, Wanda's not especially conscious of being Black and a woman and a poet in a world where none of these categories constitutes an occupational asset."

That is as true now as it was nearing the mid-eighties, when this quote appeared in an interview conducted by writer Ben Pesta for *Electrum*, now defunct, one of southern California's few maverick literary magazines to sustain any longevity short of support from a university or other patron. I had met Ben at a salon for the local Los Angeles literati, given by poet Nancy Schiffrin. The infinitesimal L.A. poetry scene that had cohered around the Beyond Baroque Literary Center in 1969 had mushroomed to teensy, and it was, and still remains, virtually impossible not to know or bump heads with everyone active. My answers for Ben, as they tend to be when face to face with the interviewer, depended on my mood and were pithy and to the apparent point.

"When I was in Diane Wakoski's workshop," I answered, "she used to say, 'I'm not a political poet. My poems are nonpolitical.' That's okay [for her]. Her history [as a White woman in America] validates that. But I can't be 'just a writer who [happens] to be Black.' Not in my lifetime, anyway. If I sneeze, it's political. If I breathe, it's political."

The specifics are vague, but I attended Diane Wakoski's 1972 poetry workshop at California Technical Institute in Pasadena. I had met Black Sparrow Press publisher John Martin that March, and he had strongly recommended I study with his "superstar" poet, author of *Motorcycle Betrayal Poems*. I was drawing unemployment insurance and had dropped college for the second time for obvious financial reasons, but primarily because I believed the department chair with whom had studied, a former Texan, was a racist. Unluckily, he taught every course critical to my cinema major.

> we don't hire black women as a rule
> especially with looks like yours
> skin flicks, maybe, TV rarely
> except when it's comedy haha
> unless you can coax the sex out of a note
> like Lena Horne or Billie Holiday

> (From "Song for Some Sistuhs")

In those days, I liked to considered myself a "jane of all trades," or "renaissance writer." I wanted to master all forms, from poetry to playwriting to scriptwriting, and to eventually go into filmmaking. In spite of my impoverished reality, that of a divorced mother with two children, I viewed the world through lenses tinted fire engine red. I had taken on a writing partner, actor and part-time preacher Christopher "Big Brutha" Joy, and we had enrolled together. However, Chris was not having the problems I was having with our professor. I pointed out to Chris that while we were both

*Wanda with her mother and brother, George,
about 1948*

Black, he was fair-skinned *and* male, and didn't stand out as much as I did among the forty-odd students.

In favorable contrast, Wakoski's workshop was minuscule, with rarely three to four students present at any one session. The benefits were greater intimacy, attention to detail, and in-depth analysis. The drawback was the increased intrinsic pressure to produce fresh poems.

During this time, I was still processing my feeling of being "left in the lurch" at the end of the civil rights, free love, and Black power movements. I had tried, repeatedly, to get my frustrated militancy into my work. I had learned to aptly mimic the strident Afro-American voices which had emerged during the Black Arts Movement, those of Ted Joans, Shirley Steele, and my favorite, Joe Goncalves. But less than a handful of these poems were ever published. After peaking at three thousand rejection slips by 1969, I had concluded that I was doing

something very wrong no matter how closely I followed *Writer's Digest* and other guides. I suspected that it had more to do with my approach to content than with style and form (not to mention bad spelling and poor grammar). John Martin had already forced me to begin examining this problem, passing along literature he considered excellent and literature he considered "drek," engaging me in arguments about my approach.

> we hire negresses like you to
> clean our bars at Sybil Brand or CIW
> try suicide again, it's one year in the slammer,
> said the White judge in Black robes

> (From "Song for Some Sistuhs")

Diane Wakoski took me steps further toward enlightenment, as I kicked and ranted, unable to fully articulate my point of view, stubborn in my stance, but absorbing as much information as she could supply, doing my own comparative analysis, going home nights to read and study as many of her books as I could obtain, as well as those by the authors (Robert Kelly, Garcia Lorca, Sylvia Plath) whose work she lectured on in class. Once I left Wakoski's workshop, our disagreements would continue to set the tone for each poem for a number of years. Eventually, maintaining Wakoski's posture in constructive opposition (if that makes sense), I began to fine-tune my side of the argument, distinguishing between mundane issue-oriented party politics and what I considered the higher political reality organic to the circumstances of my existence as an African American of slave descent.

Not least was an unexpected benefit from Wakoski's workshop, my friendship with poet Sylvia Rosen, a bond that's lasted over twenty-five years. The dark-haired wife and mother, a former New Yorker, drove into Pasadena from Canoga Park, a post-WWII suburban community twenty miles away in the west San Fernando Valley. Often, we arrived early, and as we sat alone, waiting for Wakoski and the rest of the class, we talked about our lives as girls, as women, and as mothers. With Sylvia I felt like a human being instead of a social problem. When Wakoski's workshop ended, we continued our friendship, made easier when I left the Watts I'd returned to in 1971, moving back to South Central in 1975 and then to Hollywood in 1976, communities well within Los Angeles proper. We continued to critique our poems, talked about our children, exchanged information about books (Kenneth Patchen, Adrienne Rich, William Carlos Williams, and Denise Levertov), joined other workshops, attended readings, and eventually shared the podium. Sylvia was my first poetry buddy and the only friend with whom I could share that part of my life devoted to literature.

Sylvia with shocking brown eyes
writes poems of dream worlds and weaves
purple platinum quilts of warm motherhood:
  inspiring

(From "Some Women," May 1975)

I had just wrapped up a divorce, finished a new book manuscript, and was in the throes of an intense new romance at the time of the Ben Pesta interview, working the usual two jobs to keep everything afloat. *Imagoes* was my watershed book in which I acknowledged my full womanhood and attempted to place childhood in perspective.

Ben asked: "When you were a kid down in South Central, did you want to be a writer?"

I grew up in the South Central of the Fabulous '50s, which was in constant flux as a steadily increasing Black population demanded more access to financial, health, and recreational facilities and an end to housing restricted along racial lines. My parents left Watts when they bought their first and only home in 1949, when I was three. We were the first Black family in the tiny working-class community where many of the streets remained unpaved, the rag man drove a horse-drawn cart, and a pushcart vendor hawked tacos for

"The John C. Fremont High School Championship Basketball Cee Team, fall, 1961. I was the team captain."
The author is pictured top row, far right.

ten cents. Milk was still delivered to the front or side porch doors, there was this new invention the neighbors had called a television, and when you made a 360-degree turn, you could see the tall buildings and trees miles away. No one was talking about smog, and evenings were spent snuggled up on the floor, near my parents' bed, listening to radio programs like *The Lone Ranger, Gangbusters,* and my favorite, *The Whistler.* There were two Spanish-speaking families on the block, and a family of Gypsies. But in time, these families disappeared, and the entire neighborhood became Black.

mass migration began in the 50s
we observed their withdrawal and kept note

we lived in their midst
the ones in the house on our left, a strange
  pair
they always crossed their yard on tiptoe
children, my brother and i watched them
through the thick barrier of morning glory vines
and peach trees
the female always wore an expression of dread
and kept peeking over her shoulders
in our direction
the male seemed less afraid but nevertheless
cautious. one time they saw us watching
and stood stark still, frozen
in the light of our
amazed inquiry

(From "Flight of the California Condor [2]",
September 1982)

One morning, during the fall of 1957, I gradually began to feel ill. But I didn't want to stay home that day and went on to school. It was a cold morning, but I was inordinately cold, and before class started, I developed the chills. I became so sick, the teacher became concerned and sent me home. After a few days I began to hallucinate, unable to distinguish between the real and unreal. Having developed myriad allergies after birth, I was prone to illnesses, particularly horrible skin rashes, coughing spells, bouts of hay fever and hives. An insect bite could swell as large as a saucer. But this was something new. Eventually, I would be hospitalized for what one doctor called "African sleeping sickness." At that time, children across the state were coming down with a mysterious type of encephalitis.

there was the county hospital. bars on the
  window
endless empty rows of beds
me under the yellow light bulb, tied down
unable to move. crying for Mama
three days of fever and drug illusion.
left a piece of me there . . .
woke in the dark, tied down
the doctor said i could swear like a sailor
but that couldn't be true. Pops had taught us
to never curse . . .
the doctor said i had bit him and
if i bit him again he'd knock my teeth out.
this a week before my 11th birthday
when i came out i was different

(From "Growing up Black," August 1974)

Once I recovered, I began to notice that my motor skills were slightly less, but my facility for language had increased. Always a poetry lover, writing in general began to dominate my interests. When answering Pesta's questions about being a writer, that seminal period was relived in a flash. I even remembered having left a Christmas gift, my leather-bound illustrated copy of *The Arabian Nights,* in the trunk of Pop's midnight-blue struggle buggy. He sold that old Plymouth while I was in the hospital. The loss was devastating. It came at a time when I had begun to regard books as friends.

summers long tedious
me into books comic and any kind
as long as i didn't have to be me
when relatives visited. always ashamed in the
sight of a camera. flashes going off. grotesque
  thing/me
jammed into the family photo album
cringing at all the things i had been taught to
  hate
and was: fat, black short nappy hair and ugly

(From "Growing up Black")

"I wanted to be a detective," I continued. I had read a lot of Agatha Christie (*And Then There Were None*) and Earl Derr Biggers (creator of Charlie Chan) on my way to Mickey Spillane (*Kiss Me, Deadly*) and Ian Fleming (creator of James Bond). My Uncle Kenneth, the perennial photographer at family affairs, had been a private detective before becoming a bridge champion. The fictional life of the gumshoe aroused in me a serious interest in crime fighting until I began to tackle science textbooks on

Wanda and her debate coach, Robert Bruce Newsom, hold the trophy she received as first-place winner in a statewide Negro history public-speaking competition, spring, 1964

criminology and its history, going all the way back to the days of the Inquisition and the Knights of the Templars.

"Then I wanted to be a musician. I played piano and violin. I was starting to get pretty good when I got encephalitis. . . . I was in bed for six or seven weeks and fell behind in my music lessons. Music requires a lot of physical discipline, and when I got well I just couldn't do it anymore." Although I didn't completely give it up until high school.

My childhood was a culturally rich palette of ballet lessons, piano lessons, and Jascha Heifetz–inspired violin studies at a storefront music school. My working-class parents scuffled to provide as many activities for their children as possible. I quickly abandoned ballet after sustaining several unsubtle insults about my body type and size, let alone my inability to pirouette. My father, a visual artist and advertising man, had long begun teaching me

drawing and graphics. "He carried a pad and pencil wherever he went. He drew caricatures in the doctor's waiting room . . . everywhere he had a minute and a place to sit down. Now, I carry a pad and pencil with me everywhere."

Time being so precious, I resented being forced to "hurry up and wait" endlessly at the post office, in supermarkets, at social services, at human resources, at gas stations during the gas crises of the seventies, on autoshop parking lots for inept or fake repairs made at a snail's pace, at the bank, in department stores, wherever consumers were predominately African American; and in heavy traffic during rush hour. Rather than succumb to numbness, I jotted down lines in a journal or on a steno pad, ideas for poems or stories, sometimes entire poems and bits of stories.

> eagle on my shoulder preening time to pay
> bills. figure out next week's budget
> same ol' story: broke on payday—never enuff
> kids watch TV, help when i need
> it's the weekend in Watts and i'm ready . . .
>
> i hit the hay cuttin' zees to the clatter of the
>   boob tube
> dreaming dreams of all the work waiting
>   unwritten . . .
>
> Monday a.m. it's go back to the factory
> eagle on my shoulder preens, flaps wings
> tells me, "kid, you don't need anyone to
>   make it
> jes your talent and ability—keep truckin'"
> same ol' story: barely have cash to pay the
>   baby sitter
> and buy gas. ahead, fifty miles of highway

(From "Friday Night Home from the Factory,"
June 1975)

Often my poems are literally quilted together as montages from dog-eared pages torn from various notebooks. Over the years, my demanding life ("under the gun," "on fast forward," and "seldom without a break," as per past descriptions) has denied me the contemplative time I've long coveted as my convolutions have invariably developed complications. This has caused me to make mistakes. But to the better, I've developed my signature version of a time-worn technique of weaving poetic strands into complete works, as if writing the one poem over years of fits and starts.

Caught between the inhumane circumstances of poverty and a poetic compulsion, I began keeping a book of lines which I've found invaluable when stuck or blocked. I kept notebooks of poems I'd be embarrassed to publish as initially written. I've come to regard such poems as "keys" which I use to unlock the finished publishable poem and/or story. Sometimes, the one key will unlock several poems yet remain unpublishable itself. Over time, I've noticed that I never actually lose a poetic idea and often unconsciously rewrite or revisit a poem written years earlier. Later, when editing it, a vague, disturbing familiarity sends me plowing through old notebooks to find the unsettling but unsuccessful predecessor. Thus, poetry, frequently assisted by music, has helped illuminate the workings of my memory.

> whispers
> voices in the radio that won't turn off, say
> "i'm lonely"
> music—i hate the music of lonely notes
> drip
> drip
> drip off the dial
>
> > (if i touch it i'll get burned
> > so i just listen)
>
> > (From "And You Say You Used to
> > Sing the Gospel," 1966–1970)

"Both my parents wanted to be poets," I continued in answer to Pesta's question. "So I am realizing some of their dreams. My father, in fact, wanted to start a magazine. He even taught me how to dummy . . . magazines [and newspapers]."

"A fairly esoteric skill to teach a little girl."

A boxer, an insurance salesman, a janitor, Pop worked tirelessly to keep his South Central print and sign shop open, in the garage if necessary, moving from location to location over the decades once Mom tired of the struggle and insisted he vacate the garage. She settled for the back- and eye-breaking dolor of a seamstress, exploited by sweatshops in exchange for the steady paychecks that would keep our household together.

> Mama
> don't shoot me down till you've heard the
>   whole story
>
> twenty years in the sweatshop, Mama
> thirty years unemployed, Papa . . .
>
> i watch my parents die
> twenty-three years watching my parents die
> can't do nuthin'
> Pops so old so old
> will lay down with sunset
> as cold as his god
> Mama will use the insurance money
> it will barely pay
> for the
>
> CENTRAL AVENUE SOUL TRAIN SHUFFLE
>
> daddy
> daddy
> i love you
>
> (a flower pressed between two dictionaries just
>   to say later)
>
> > (From "Sometimes I Have a Song for My Mommy
> > & Daddy," August 1972)

In his lion years, my father was in constant motion, always on the run, friends and associates coming by the house, men and women engaged in a ritual I've come to call scheming and dreaming. For many years there was always a printing press in the house or garage, an easel or drawing table set up, the rumblings of the airbrush motor drowning out the TV, my father under his visor, with his T-square, straight-edge, and X-acto knife, the air around him an aura of paint, ink, and rubber cement mingled with sweat and aftershave lotion. Me and my brother George were eager apprentices, quick on command to grab a giant eraser, roll of masking tape, or paintbrush.

> in a dream you came to me
> there in the sign shop, in the swivel chair
> you came silent smiling in a gold lamé
>   suit
> you were dead but everything was okay
> i woke sweating beside my lover
> cried into his arms
>
> > (From "My Years," January 1976)

My mother had a socialite's tastes and ambitions and supervised a roster of family activi-

High school graduate, summer, 1964

ties, including church socials, family picnics, and parties. She too had dreamed of being a journalist and a poet. But in the Los Angeles of their time, there was no place for my parents' creative talents.

Mom spent many long hours helping Pop chase his dream, accompanying him on interviews of Black celebrities, like Sarah Vaughan and Archie Moore, setting cold type, stapling endless brochures, booklets, and leaflets. I helped too, taught to handle the "ABC blocks" or ink the rollers on the old letterpress. Until his death in 1991, my father kept trying to get a Black this or a Bronze that going; he and his buddies invested in their professional mock-up of a Black *Esquire* magazine way back in the '50s. They had proved satisfactorily to themselves that they could produce a quality gentleman's product,

but would never convince a distributor. He died with his unrealized gospel intact—that forthright entrepreneurship was the key to the Black man's ultimate success. What I learned at my father's knees as he cut and pasted would sustain me when I entered the '70s California subculture of sex-oriented magazines as copywriter, proofreader, and editor; later still as a freelance editor of literary magazines and editorial consultant. His hard militaristic lessons on discipline resonate now.

Mom had a beautiful singing voice, sang in the church choir, and sang around the house constantly. An upright piano was always against the east wall of the living room. She played the piano, took lessons, and sometimes accompanied herself. She had a lilting way as she spoke, especially when her moon was right. She half-sung, half-talked stories on those rare nights when, still unable to read for ourselves, she read us to sleep. She listened to the radio while working around the house, sang along to her favorite songs. Years later, as I honed my performance style, I would unconsciously begin to borrow her style.

Around the age of thirteen, I had voice and pitch training. Over the decade that followed, I quietly built a repertoire of over a hundred songs to sing and was actually able to accompany myself on some of the gospel, Christmas, and folk songs, timidly thinking I might pursue a career as a latter-day chanteuse. But I had a problem. When listening to playback, I hated my recorded voice. I sounded more like a little girl than a woman, nothing throaty or smoky about it. My voice didn't sound as powerful as I felt I was becoming, and, at that point, I was unable to imbue it with the innate physical and inner personal power which was emerging on its own as I matured. Near the end of that decade, in 1968, I would find the answer to this problem in the world of experimental dance and theater.

Poison Ivy

thangs ain't changed in eight decades or eighty
or eight times eighty
so many 'illions have felt my identical pain
have moaned "why me" aloud alone at midnight
have wept shuddered and raged

(From "No Different Is No Different,"
November 1985)

"At home with my books," 1976

In the process of discovering or rediscovering Los Angeles, newcomers and visitors interested in poetry occasionally delight in discovering me as well. Twenty-eight-year-old Leslie Price seemed to fit that category. When she called, there was something in her manner that coaxed me into doing another (ugh) interview; although I was picky about who did the interviewing. The brown-haired, personable editor of the raw "grrrl zine" *Poison Ivy* finally opted to conduct it herself. It was February 1995, days shy of her birthday, when we met at the Chateau Marmont, legendary hotel of the stars, haunt of actor Christopher Walken, site of actor-comedian John Belushi's untimely exit.

"At what age do you feel your course of writing developed?" Leslie opened.

"I had my first breakthrough in [late] 1974. That was the year I lived or died, and I did both. After years and years of rejection and [mainly] bad work, the breakthrough came. I kept all of that work, by the way, and it's so bad that it's frightening."

"That will be encouraging to our readers."

"Nobody's ever seen it. I wouldn't dare show it to anybody. I keep it because it represents a period that was very important . . . the 70s were [my] big transition years . . . 1973 through 1976 were years when I began to know who I was . . . and say, this is it, this is me, I'm grown now, baby."

I was being cavalier with Leslie because the memories of those excruciating days were interred far deeper than I cared to delve. I was not only a poetry bigot in those days, but arrogant in my bigotry, often flaunting it to my detriment as by-product of my dissatisfaction with crummy jobs paying crummy wages, the long hours it took to earn bubkes.

Women's liberation and equality were on the lips of everyone except the Molochs who doled out the ducats, no matter how many bras were burned. And I was equally furious and disappointed that so many of my West Coast feminist literary peers apparently had a hidden agenda; seemed more interested in tête-à-têtes than profound social change for working-class women. All of the political correctness in the world could not prevent me from loudly expressing my disdain.

    when the door cracked open
    i thought there would be space
    enough for me
    prejudice is evident even though
    the faces lack five o'clock shadow
    and macho digs
    there's no doubt
    what their ideology is about
    but seems to me most sistuhs of the pen
    are not above the literary bullshit of their fellow
       men

           (From "The Feminist Press," August 1978)

When the Equal Rights Amendment went down for the count in 1982, my tongue bled profusely. And again, I found myself cramming my rhetoric into my verse, feeling hemmed in by the color-blind social myopia of the Fatuous 80s, a twisted rerun of the Fabulous 50s. (Off the record, I explain all of this to Leslie, wondering if and how much so-called Generation X women will profit from their foremothers' mistakes.) In expressing my rage poetically, eschewing the essay, which was the more appropriate expository form to contain it, I knew I was taking a risky short cut, placing broken prose in the stead of content more deeply considered and more skillfully crafted.

Clayton Eshleman had taken me to considerable task for exactly that kind of "easy, tossed-off" writing during the workshop sessions I attended in his home circa 1974. Again, at the behest of John Martin, I had enrolled in yet another workshop with one of my future literary siblings, determined to "get the poetry thang down cold."

My sessions with Eshleman would come near the end of a quest for the magic of language that had begun at age five, in kindergarten, when our teacher brought to class the first secular poems I'd ever seen. While I don't remember the poems themselves, I remember the 3-M paper they were printed on and the gooey purple ink they were printed with, and the chills that coursed over me as I held those pages, overcome by the power they transmitted. This, I knew absolutely, was the power I would seek to possess all the days of my life.

    the river
    opened
    his mouth
    to me
    today

           (Untitled fragment, April 1981)

Even as I vacillated between my other gifts, poetry was always with me in one form or another, and I always excelled when writing that Father's Day or Mother's Day poem, carrying it home proudly to show off.

My junior high school years, 1958–61, would be fairly unremarkable vis-à-vis poetry, except for two tremendously magnetic Black English teachers, the honey-toned fine-framed Mrs. Brewer, and umber-skinned hefty Mrs. Covington, the tough-love tag team of Gompers Junior High, which was, in that era, the most violent and dreaded coeducational campus of its grade level citywide. They were loved by the strivers, feared and hated by the slackers and not a few of the White faculty members. Armed with every American hero and heroine of African descent they could name, and a slew of rah-rah adages, they waged exceptional battles of inspiration yet conducted themselves as no-nonsense splendid Ladies of the Race, able to mow you down or build you up in an instant. Counting myself among the strivers, I was anxious to get into the class of Mrs. Brewer, the less intimidating of the two. But I wound up cowering two aisles away from my secret crush, Oscar Lopez, under Mrs. Covington's stern tutelage.

Mrs. Covington did not give out As. Students had to earn them by doing an assignment well within one evening. On the second evening you received a B, and so forth. I was eager to score one of her nearly extinct As and worked overtime at home, burning the midnight lightbulb, envying the perfectly composed Oscar, who never failed to turn in everything the first day, the only A student in class. But the most I could achieve was an A minus. The occasional B minus and rare C drove me to smoldering exasperation. Then came that part of the course devoted to poetry. Along with the poems of Paul Dunbar, Robert Frost, Langston Hughes, and Carl Sandburg, Mrs. Covington introduced us to William Ernest Henley's "Invictus." Cagily, she did not tell us the name of the author or mention his race, creed, or color, baiting us with supposition, inviting her dark-complexioned students to leap to the conclusion that "pole to pole," the author was likewise Black. I dove heart first into the gap.

This time, when Mrs. Covington asked who had memorized the poem in one night and was ready to get their A, my arm inched upward, trembling across the room from Oscar's confident salute. Surprised, Mrs. Covington gave me a skeptical look, but I reinforced my right arm at the elbow with my left hand. She called first on Oscar, who leapt to the front of the class and gave his usual sterling delivery while my pudgy knees knocked under my desk. Her soft officious summons by surname preceded by "Miss" made my stomach flip-flop. But I rose and faced my classmates, focusing on a point on the back wall, just above their heads—a

method I would rely on in the future to counteract butterflies and jitters. I started off with a bang, stumbled a bit during the third stanza at ". . . yet the menace of the years / Finds, and shall find me, unafraid," lifting my voice to compensate with a rousing finish. As the class applauded, I shyly shot Oscar a sidelong glance to catch his curt congratulatory nod. My A at last.

High school presented the first testing ground for what were becoming my two primary areas of interest, performance and poetry. Drama was one of the most popular classes offered at John C. Fremont when I enrolled in the fall of 1961. A school system that rigidly classified students by rather specious and stringent criteria, inadvertently promoting divisions, dissension, and

With husband, Austin Straus, at Whiskey A GoGo, Hollywood, 1986

low self-esteem, measured student intellects in tiers, which went something like this, if memory serves me right: triple X being genius, double X being gifted, X being superior, XY being above average, Y being average, YZ and Z being below average, and R standing for remedial, non-English-speaking, etc. Mixed classes were offered, but students were largely channeled into college preparatory or job-skill courses dependent upon ranking. These categories would eventually be phased out, but when I arrived I was promptly slotted as an X, and a math-science major. At that point, I had segued from action comic books to science fiction and fantasy, consuming as much Robert Heinlein, Isaac Asimov, E. E. Doc Smith, Arthur C. Clarke, et al., as I could access, to my parents' growing dismay. Yet I continued to gravitate to poetry and performance.

Unable to get drama for an elective, I opted for the next best thing, public speaking and debate, the Forensic League. There, I would come under the significant influence of my hawkish Irish debate coach, Mr. Robert Bruce Newsom. In my fledgling tournament, I entered the dramatic interpretation and impromptu competitions but didn't do very well. Studying the various categories, from humorous interpretation to dramatic monologues, I was thrilled to find "original oratory." As a debater I was only so-so, finding it difficult to organize my thoughts in a linear fashion, and unable to bombast my way through an argument, or destroy my opponent with rapier wit. When interpreting the words of others, I did fairly well, and that skill improved markedly with practice. But as writer and presenter of my own material, I began to take more and more first-place medals and trophies.

Recognizing my love of poetry, another English teacher, Mrs. Clark, took a personal interest in me and, with my mother's permission, took me on cultural excursions to museum openings and art galleries, and to my first poetry reading and book signing. To double the pleasure, the poet was Negro. Mrs. Clark was a member of the local chapter of Our Authors Study Club. I came away with the line "tongues of men and angels" thrilling my ears. I remember the heady air of expectancy and delight, the satisfied applause. As we descended the stairs, I stopped so Mrs. Clark could catch up to me, turning back to see the gathering around the poet as he stood poised, pen in hand. That, I decided, was the life.

Swing up, swing down
          no one swings here anymore.

Here lie naked ashen bones
mocking flesh,
          ah flesh
gold days of loving splendor.

Horrid holes
          of death once
sprang a kiss
          a loving gaze
          a breath.

Phalangeous scabs caressed,
dismembered ulnae held.
          Gone
          gone
          gone.

Memories of childhood
hang upon my bedroom wall.
No one loves here
anymore.

("Memories of My Childhood Hang
upon My Bedroom Wall," 1966–1970)

By the time I graduated from John C. Fremont High in the summer of 1964, I had decided I wanted to be a writer of poetry and fiction. Weeks before school ended, I was invited by a professor to share my latest work with her class of slow learners at California State University, East Los Angeles. She had seen me perform "The Epics of Infinity," my fledgling masterpiece, of which I was extremely proud. The class consisted entirely of Mexican Americans and Mexican immigrants. They listened respectfully as I was introduced and gave me a standing ovation when I took my bow, offering a hand here and there. One young man raised his hand, then rose to address me. His English was broken, but his message was clear. He wanted me to know that he believed I had a greater opportunity to realize my American dream than he, that my work was important to the world. I managed to contain my tears until I got home.

I took the words of this young man as my guide and enrolled as a journalism major on that same Cal State campus that fall. Of the five classes I would eventually drop out of, I managed to attend the poetry class of poet Dr. Henri Coulette the most faithfully.

During that first session, we sat there, terribly intimidated by this smoking wraith who was demanding that volunteers cough up their beginner's work for his critique. Supremely self-confident, I raised my hand. Dr. Coulette smiled wickedly as I handed over my barely typed reading copy of "Epics." Without missing a beat, he went to the blackboard and, as he read it aloud, began a scathing dissection of my grand clichés and aureate phrases. I sat there in the very front row, speechless with embarrassment. Every point he made was absolutely on target. Why had I never seen that myself?

I felt destroyed, yet illuminated. How could that be?

After the session, Dr. Coulette returned "Epics" and thanked me for being a volunteer victim. He studied me closely, a hint of concern in his voice telling me he was aware of his impact on my ego. He suggested I might consider revising it once I had absorbed the shock. When I got home, I looked it over, seeing it with a new and searing light. It didn't read the same anymore, and I would never read it aloud again.

Work had to be done. But what work, and how would I do it?

Slowly, steadily, I began writing the new poems as they began to come. They were slightly different, closer to the earth, less high-flown. But I was fated to leave Dr. Coulette's class and abandon college. In the interval between leaving Fremont and starting at Cal State, I had fallen in love.

In live performance at Whiskey A GoGo, Hollywood, 1986

> hold my hand
> it hurts
> i want it to come on
>
> taxi. night. the suitcase
> the doctor call the doctor
> i think so, babe, i want to be sure
> this time call the taxi
> help me get my shoes on
>
> contractions
> coming three minutes apart
> tell the doctor, babe. it hurts
> i know there's nothing you can do
> i'm crazy
> the pain makes me crazy out of my mind
> babe

(From "Giving Birth [2]," January 1979)

My new marriage and first pregnancy, however, did not deter my pursuit of The Muse. Blessed with more than enough spare time, I kept writing, typing up new poems on my old typewriter, a Christmas gift. But what was I going to do with these poems? Were they any good? Did they show any real potential? After days spent arguing with myself, I determined to send my fifty-odd pages of work to Dr. Coulette for his opinion. Mid-spring, an envelope arrived in the mail. After a long silence, Dr. Coulette returned my poems with a few comments and corrections but, to my disappointment, nothing more specific. Days later, I received my report card. Among the withdrawals and incompletes was a solitary grade glowing like a diamond in coal dust, my C in poetry.

> Give me a gun, I'll shoot to kill.
> I'm destitute, hungry and poor.
> I can't get a job, I've got no skill
> and I'm too old to learn anymore.
>
> Give me a match, I'll light a fire
> And burn this city down.
> Life in this world is no life at all
> when you live in Riot Town . . .

I'll take some loot, some lives to boot,
life's a meaningless thing
when you're cast on a reef of state relief
and each check adds to your shame.

Show me a place where bigots thrive
in the sweltering heat of hate,
where poverty, fear and unrest are alive
and negotiations too late.

(From "Riot Town," 1966–1970)

Watts burned that summer of 1965, the baby had arrived, and between motherly and wifely duties I harbored my writerly desires. When an article on the Budd Schulberg Writers' Workshop appeared, I knew I had to find it at all costs. Convincing my then-husband to babysit that evening, I left the house and took the bus down to 103rd Street. In my excitement, I had neglected to get an address. When I reached a crossroad, at Grandee, I didn't know whether to turn left or right. I turned right. Which was the wrong direction. But the steps I took would lead me to the next important stage of my development.

tremble before the weight
this life
the others
but this life especially
tremble before the weight
lovers piled up like bricks on the construction
  site
it's a heavy load for such a weak back
my hands tremble at the key
locking out the old. turning the key
in this new door
this life. . . .
such a tremendous weight
i tremble

(From "Watching My Hands Shake
at the Typewriter," April 1974)

My post-riot association with a Great Society–era teen canteen turned Watts creative arts center would lead me along three different paths in the same direction. Encouraged to write plays as well as poetry and short stories, I would be offered my first writers' workshop, become editor of the house newsletter, and participate in several other workshops at the site. During this time, I was introduced to Bliss Carnochan, professor of English at Stanford University. He took an interest in my short stories and offered to look at them. He was commuting between the

Bay Area and Los Angeles to conduct research at the USC library. On those Saturday mornings available, we would meet early for coffee, gingerly talking content and technique.

But as my sessions with Bliss were ending, my involvement with Anna Halprin's San Francisco Dancers' Workshop was beginning. In response to the riot, Anna had divined a project, a dance statement of racial harmony, "The Ceremony of Us." After an audition, I was selected to join the group of eleven Whites and eleven Blacks from whom the project would be culled. There would be two performances, one at the Mark Taper Forum and one at the workshop's 321 Divisadero address. I would come away from this experience with a profoundly new grasp of my physical and artistic strengths. When participating in forensics, I had glimpsed inklings of what I suspected was a subliminal *dialogue* between the performer and the audience. What had then seemed tenuous became a certainty with Anna's instruction. How one entered a space, where one stood, how one posed, these were a few of the vital elements of establishing one's authority. Listening to the audience was vital to receiving the audience. The information I came away with eventually provided the link I needed between my two gifts—those moments when writing itself became the performance and when the performance became the writing.

it comes. the sheaf of scrawlings
begging eye and ear
a cry. the long yowl of a two-legged critter
lost in the mean dark of unread pages

(From "A Literary Misunderstanding,"
October 1982

Bachy

I'm older than you were when you died by
  umpteen years.
It makes me wonder why I'm still alive, why
  any of us
are still alive. We should all be somewhere
  dying in
bloody beds or alleyways, all somewhere plot-
  ting against
racism, laying open our souls to the commitment that does
not stop at the grave.

(From "A Fan Letter to Fred Hampton,"
February 1972)

As the energy of the '60s Black Arts Movement waned, I had begun publishing in soon-to-be-defunct African American magazines, including the *Journal of Black Poetry* and *Body and Soul.* Simultaneously, I had begun submitting new work locally, and soon my poems were appearing in short-lived southern California literary magazines such as Michael C. Ford's *Sunset Palms Hotel* and the combination anthology and program for Jack Grapes's Alley Kat Reading series. By the end of the summer of 1979, I had published my second book, *Mad Dog Black Lady,* a chapbook, and established my reputation as a fiery performer, jokingly calling myself "the Sidney Poitier of the L.A. Poetry Scene."

Poet, actor, and typesetter Lee Hickman conducted his August 26, 1979, interview on the verandah of the tore-down Hollywood four-plex where I rented a unit on the upper floor, across the street from the Los Angeles City College parking lot. I had first spotted Hickman in 1969 at a Beyond Baroque reading, but we wouldn't meet face to face until the late summer of 1975, at a salon given by actor-poet Harry E. Northup to bring together the new generation of Venice Beach workshop writers orbiting the burgeoning literary center.

Lee had become the editor of *Bachy,* a hefty and substantial magazine published by poet John Harris out of Papa Bach, a West Los Angeles bookstore and counterculture hang. *Bachy* would lend cohesiveness and validation to the evolving mid-seventies scene of independent bookstores, poetry venues, and literary magazines that had begun to emerge. A small manuscript's worth of my poems had been rejected by *Bachy,* but my persistence to the tune of twenty submissions ultimately paid off, and I became an occasional contributor. By the time Lee and I sat down to laugh and gab over coffee, my poems had begun appearing in small magazines nationally and overseas.

"So you published your first poems around the age of thirteen?"

"I was a kid—yeah."

"How about your first stories?"

My summary was fast and loose: "I didn't publish my first stories. They were really never publishable. I started getting away from writing when I got married. About 1966, I decided I wanted to go back to it. I really wanted to accomplish something in that area. And the Movement was . . . building . . . momentum at that time, and I said, 'I want to write for the Movement, man. I want to get out there, and I want to write propaganda. You know, do the thang.'"

(Actually, I published "Watching the Sunset," one of my fledgling stories, in *Negro Digest* in 1969, the last issue before Hoyt Fuller rechristened it *Black World.* Excited by the more militant change in tone, I was confident that more of my work, particularly my poetry, would be accepted. But my poems were returned so rapidly, and without comment, that I began to suspect they weren't read, merely opened and placed in the return self-addressed stamped envelope [SASE]. Confounded, I retired my efforts and sent my work elsewhere.)

But the thang was over by the end of 1969, before I was out of the box. The post-riot enthusiasm for revitalizing Watts and all of Black Los Angeles had collapsed in a morass of false economic starts and empty social promises. As the urban madness returned to usual, Black gradually went back to being unbeautiful.

> He came to me
> whispering how together a sister
> I was; how deeply right-on
> in my philosophy
> how my mind was superior to
> any other woman he'd ever met.
> But all he wanted was . . .
>
> He talked to me
> radical ideas on how to change The System
> theories on the ultimate
> defeat of the White Race
> on where and how he'd initiate
> the Black takeover
> but all he wanted was . . .
>
> He cried with me—the pain
> of 400 years in wine-red eyes
> quoting from Fanon and Malcolm X
> speaking Black words
> making Black promises of
> our fighting the revolution side by side
> but all he wanted was . . .

(From "Soul Sister Supporting the Black Revolution Laying Prone," 1966–1970)

I divided my time between the Watts arts workshop and a drama class at Mafundi Institute further down 103rd Street. Within days of my fateful bus ride, I met members of the Budd Schulberg Writers' Workshop who invited me to attend. But after a handful of sessions at The House of Respect, I was stymied and disappointed by the blatant bullcorn and boisterous cronyism that dominated the sessions and promptly took a powder. I was too serious to high-sign, and while I didn't mind the hang with the gang, I had no patience for posturing and pretense. Dr. Coulette was the standard by which I was coming to judge all mentors. I wanted nothing short of the difficult but informative criticism he had offered. I did not need to be coddled or to have my ego stroked. L.A. had neither a solid Black community nor a solid core of Black literati with whom I believed I could constructively interact. I was as angry as the next militant over, but my parents had provided me with an unshakable sense of self-worth long before Watts burned.

My involvement with Anna Halprin demanded so much time, including considerable travel between San Francisco and L.A., that I was forced to drop the Mafundi workshop. Once "The Ceremony of Us" ended, I again began to seek mentors, to cruise through intermittent evening workshop sessions at Beyond Baroque's 1969 location, to drive across town to attend other workshops, like the minority Open Door workshops at the Writers' Guild of America West. Ever eager to enhance my writing skills, my chance would come when my brother George left home to attend art school. When he rented a basement room from one of his professors, I went out to visit and stumbled into the gritlicious reality of writer Charles Bukowski.

> . . . he was fat and old and white with an
>   elephant's guffaw
> and me sitting on the floor near his knee,
>   stars in my eyes,
> dreams between my teeth. And he kinda
>   laughed at me and
> said, "There's two ways to die, young and
>   old. And dying
> young is the worst possible way. . . . I like
>   your spunk, kid . . .
> try hard not to die young."

(From "How Not to Die Young," 1976)

"How did you find out about the L.A. poetry scene?"

My answer, in retrospect, should've been, "But, Lee, *we* are the Los Angeles poetry scene." But I hadn't yet come to that realization. Who came to mind were poet-in-exile Tom McGrath,

the late Stuart Perkoff, and the holdovers from L.A.'s Beatnik and coffeehouse era. Between that generation and the post-WWII Baby Boomers loomed one figure all by his lonesome, Hank a.k.a. Charles a.k.a. "The Buk" Bukowski, whose alter ego, Henry Chinaski, had made Black Sparrow Press one of the top alternative presses in the country.

One summer afternoon in 1970, I braved one of those steep hills off Alvarado Boulevard in Echo Park to visit George. I was curious to meet this "strange White dude" he kept telling me about, Bukowski's friend, a poet and calligrapher who actually made his living ripping off corporations for free goods, from fur coats to stereo equipment. When George tried to describe his new whereabouts, words failed. "Doi-Doi, you have to *see* this to believe it." When I arrived, George gleefully led me upstairs to meet poet John Thomas. I could hardly contain my amazed shock. The hillside hideaway was a riot of photographs (the only one I remember, Lenny Bruce, slacks-down on a toilet), paintings, rare books, knickknacks, and a simply staggering amount of well-organized stuff.

On subsequent visits, sometimes with my first husband in tow, we'd wave a brief hello at Thomas as he watched us from an upstairs window. We'd then go down and around to George's basement door, which was occasionally left unlocked. One night when I dropped in, George was gone and the door was locked. I vaguely recall a sense of urgency. I was upset and had to see him, so I decided to wait outside on the grounds. After a few minutes, the door opened behind me. Rose, George's teacher and John's wife, invited me inside. Sensing that something was wrong, Thomas tried to amuse me with small talk. Drawn out of myself, I was fascinated by the huge man with the Orson Welles' voice, particularly when we got around to our mutual interest, poetry.

Within weeks, I was returning on a regular basis, on my own, not to visit George but to brainstorm with Thomas. Eventually, he grew to trust me enough to lend me rare books from his collection of Ezra Pound, T. S. Eliot, Charles Olson, et al. Finally, I worked up enough nerve to ask him to review my freshly typed manuscript of poems. Thomas was reluctant, but I reassured him that I wanted the absolute truth and that he was not to spare my feelings. He took me at my word. Excited, I took the marked manuscript home and began pouring over each precious page.

Barely nineteen but passing for twenty-one, George went "carousing" with the considerably older Thomas, hanging with "these crazy old White guys," and filling me in on their anarchistic shenanigans. The wildest of the bunch was this Charles Bukowski. Suddenly, I was hearing Bukowski's name on the lips of all my peers. His controversial stories were starting to appear in the underground, alternative, and European press. Everyone had something to say about Mr. Bukowski, most of it negative.

After I separated from my first husband, I continued to drive up from South Central or Watts to frequent Hollywood rock, soul, and folk clubs. I was particularly keen on the impromptu performances that occurred during an open mike session before the main audience had arrived or after it had gone home. One of my favorites was a bookstore and headshop performance venue called The Bridge. The young owner, declaring "it was no longer happening in L.A.," had sold The Bridge to Peter, a German-born tool-and-die maker, and taken off for Boulder, Colorado, "where all the Hippies are going." As the story went, Peter was one of Charles Bukowski's drinking buddies. However, my attraction to The Bridge was Peter's Black girlfriend, a singer-songwriter, and the handful of women who stayed after-hours to share their musical gifts: singer-songwriter Judy Sill, an amazing auburn-haired singer named Natasha, and Shurli, who, six years later, would become my mother-in-law when her son became my second husband.

Buying books was a great luxury in those days. What I couldn't borrow and return, or obtain from the public library, I read straight off bookstore shelves. I took every opportunity to study the numerous small-press magazines I couldn't afford to buy, and jotted down the addresses of potential places to send poems. Most of the presses that had produced the beautiful limited editions Thomas lent me were either defunct or published by invitation only. Of all the writers Thomas and I had shared, I gravitated toward Bukowski most. (Black Sparrow's Diane Wakoski, Jack Spicer, Sherril Jaffe, Paul Bowles, and Fielding Dawson would come later.) Peter carried an ample sampling of Black Sparrow books, especially Bukowski, at The Bridge. Eager to read more, I'd stand around the stacks, to Peter's annoyance, gingerly devouring the

wonderfully printed Bukowski, trying not to break the spine, as per Peter's exasperated instructions, because, as he knew, I couldn't afford to pay for them.

> i am trapped in the office
> the Xerox has broken down
> my nails have been chewed off one by one
> by the IBM. the artificial air has given me the
>   flu
> my legs cramp from filing charts
> this special art of the clerical drone
>
> what union do i organize
> with what time with what army
> and in the meantime, who will clothe my back
> and feed my brood?
>
> who will hold me close, say "it's all right"
> i'm alone and scared
> and my horoscope has been voided
>
> what union?
> except the soft firm joining
> hands and thighs

(From "Dear Sergeant Jack," March 1981)

The more I read, the more excited I became. Dare I wonder if the publisher who likes Charles Bukowski would like me? I dared, and mailed my painfully retyped manuscript to Black Sparrow Press with an SASE. In March 1972, the manuscript was returned. Disappointed, I set it aside. Days later, an unsigned postcard arrived at my mother's address. It read simply: "Please call me right away [phone number]." After vacillating back and forth and consulting with several friends, I decided I had nothing to lose, and the call was local.

Thus began my twenty-six-year association with Black Sparrow Press. Responding to my eagerness to learn, publisher John Martin steered me first to Wakoski, and months later to Clayton Eshleman. In the meantime, I had become a Bukowski fan, trying to imitate his style, going to his readings, and hanging out at the infamous Bukowski parties, invited along by Peter's girlfriend.

But it didn't take long to realize that my approach to language was, at root, radically different from Bukowski's. I had no qualms about his fast-paced bare-bone prose. But it lacked music. Bukowski was tone-deaf. And I loved the musical lyricism of writers like Neruda, Robert Louis Stevenson, and Brother Antoninus, a.k.a.

"With the lead singer of L.A.'s premier rock band of the 1980s,
Exene Cervenka, of X," 1985

William Everson (who would eventually displace Bukowski as my favorite). I was also enthralled with the plays and poetry of Amiri Baraka (LeRoi Jones). Bukowski was no stranger to poverty and class arrogance, and I related to that aspect of his writing psyche well. But as a Black woman, I had a perspective Bukowski couldn't fathom, and I was starved to articulate it. I was extremely self-critical and knew I was still far from my goal.

Apparently sympathetic, John Martin encouraged me to join yet another workshop, handing me a copy of Clayton Eshleman's just-published *Coils*. I liked what I read and agreed to join Eshleman's workshop.

Off and on the record, I've explained to interviewers that my cultivated public persona of an "imposing," "outspoken," "uncompromising" Black poet has its disadvantages and contradicts my private nature as a rather inarticulate introvert. Over the years, I've come to refer to myself as a "functional extrovert," driven out of shyness in pursuit of life's necessities.

My major peeve has been my failure to bust through the going dominant culture stereotypes others use to define me. These days I'm instantly a Whoopi Toni Maya Oprah, ready to hug at the drop of a tear. But this is a major improvement over my '70s image as dopefiend prostitute gangster thief. Poet and intellectual was never the assumption. And this was often the sorry case in workshop settings.

> classy, pretty, hot sexy mama
> chocolate bar, black cow, righteous sistuh
> domineering, independent, Friday night fool
> wench, wonderful, dynamite broad
> reserved, more women like you in New York
> "baby i swear you've got ten personalities
>   and one of 'em is a man"

(From "Description of Self by Others,"
November 1974)

In Halprin's dance workshop, I had learned how to get in touch with my feelings and release them. But once they were released, I couldn't get them into my work satisfactorily. The few instances that worked were accidents. I wanted control. I wanted my internal rages to snatch readers into the page and never let them go. I wanted my anguish to move readers so greatly that they had to close the book and rest. I wanted my readers to *experience* my text viscerally. I wanted to wring the blood out of language. Clayton Eshleman was the answer. It was during his workshop that I would discover the rage beneath my rage.

In his kitchen or dining room, over gourmet freshly ground coffee, the sizable workshop, divided nearly equally between men and women (usually women dominated poetry workshops and readings), gathered to read and critique their work. I had more on the romantic front than I could handle and was not looking for a man. But I found one, Wilhelm Reich, the Austrian psychiatrist. At that time, Eshleman was an enthusiast of Reichian therapy. I got myself to a library and began reading Reich. Eshleman's cathartic approach to discussing one's "material" was valid. But I was not equipped to share the machinations of Black urban ghetto life with my workshop fellows, some of whom were snidely racist. During one meeting, I was flat out called a liar.

After that particularly nasty episode, I decided to leave the workshop. I had tired of struggling to conceal how shaken Eshleman's sessions left me. Sometimes I became so upset I could barely make the long drive home. I would pull off the freeway and park until I could get myself together. Yes, I had to acknowledge, I'm angry about the indignities my people have sustained. And yes, I'm terribly enraged that racism still stymies our best and cripples our brightest. But the subtext to all of this was the hell my life became the day I entered the Los Angeles school system. I may have developed a love for poetry at the age of five, but I also developed a profound hatred for racism (and anyone of any stripe who perpetuates it).

So I dropped out of Eshleman's workshop. I was becoming afraid of what it would mean if, as I was encouraged to do, I actually vented my hatred. This is an easier assessment in hindsight, but at that time, all I had to offer the perplexed Eshleman was confusion tantamount to no explanation. I had yet to develop the means to express my truth.

What I had learned about myself is exemplified in this incident, coincidentally from my kindergarten year.

In the Los Angeles of 1951, the African American population was so insignificant that classroom integration seemed more or less an organic process. Even Watts was a largely White community. If you lived in a certain neighborhood, you went to the neighborhood school. Whenever my parents needed time alone, George and I were taken to stay, sometimes for a weekend, sometimes for weeks, at the central-city home of my grand-aunt and -uncle Douglas. When I became school-aged, my mother enrolled me in the elementary school nearby. The measure was stopgap. She found a babysitter and housekeeper through our church, a matronly woman who agreed to visit our home during work hours. Mom then had me transferred to the school within walking distance from our new South Central home.

At first, Mom would drive me to school, dropping me off at the entrance. But when she changed jobs, that became a luxury. She took me by the hand and walked me along the strict route I was to take each day, cautioning me to look both ways when crossing intersections and to never speak to strangers. I was not to stray, tarry over a candy counter or comic-book rack, or visit the homes of new friends without her permission. If someone tried to kidnap me, I was to run into the nearest open door and scream for help. And if a strange man in a car offered me candy, I was to keep walking, looking straight ahead as if no one had spoken. I was to do the same with barking dogs.

But I was a stubborn study. When the first day came for me to walk the route alone, I refused to leave our front porch. Infuriated, Mom resorted to the peach limb and drove me off the porch into the driveway. But once she went back inside, I followed. She locked the screen door and would not open it, staring stonily at me through the smoky grid. Then she closed the big door. I had no choice and started walking.

My kindergarten class was mixed, boys and girls, Blacks and Whites. The girls were separated from the boys on the playground during recess and tended by monitors on the lookout for scraped knees, thumbs with splinters, and precocious expressions of puppy love. Anyone had access to the monkey bars, slides, and swings

The author at home in her Hollywood apartment, with her husband (far upper right corner), 1987

in the giant sandbox. The younger boys played truncated, supervised versions of baseball (catch) and football (tackle). The girls were relegated primarily to hopscotch, jumping jacks, and jump rope. But everybody played dodgeball and four-square, a forerunner to basketball. To play four-square, each player stood within one quadrant of an orange square. Your partner stood in the opposite quadrant. Each player had a turn to start a round and pass the ball. The object of the game was to get the ball to your partner without stepping on a line or having it stolen by the opposing team. It was my favorite game.

Shortly into the term, Gail, whose Catholic family had moved to Los Angeles from Texas, was solicitously introduced to the class as "the new girl." Ours was a prim lace-shod teacher, a rigid, thick-bodied, and grimly distant White woman. Watching Gail turn her into gushing smiling jelly quickly caught our attention. Mrs. So-and-So's harsh milky hands, infamous for pinching ears, actually *touched* this newcomer

with affection! We were impressed right out of our little ribbed cotton socks. Her parents drove a sleek new convertible, and Gail loved to flaunt it by tossing her head as she climbed into it every day after school. Gail had status.

Gail also had what was called a peaches-and-cream complexion. On extremely hot days, Gail and the other fairer-skinned White girls inclined to faint or blister were given bench privileges, the best seats in the shade reserved to protect them from the sun's rays. We tougher, dark-skinned girls were allowed to play on. Gail's skin was flawless, and she flushed at the neck when angry. Her effusive mop of sable hair was, for a few weeks, a beautifully coifed mass of Shirley Temple curls. Before bangs and ponytails became the rage, Gail would sport them.

While there were several girls and boys I gravitated to, everyone got along as children do, with the usual childish territorial conflicts. The coyly manipulative and beautiful Gail, self-confident beyond her years, was about to change all of that.

Within days of her arrival, the boys, who had seemed indifferent about sex, began fighting among themselves about who would be Gail's partner during coed games. One boy was injured so seriously he was taken away by the school nurse to the rarely seen school doctor. Gail also seemed capable of likewise upsetting the girls and pitting them against one another. When a commandment failed, Gail was not above lying and cheating to get her way. Wary, I kept my distance, watching these jealousy-inspired skirmishes wax and wane. When she had dispatched everyone of even vague interest, Gail turned her attention to me. Before the entire group, I was drafted as her Truly Best Friend. So friend it was. When Gail discovered I could match her brain power, we became inseparable. And when it came to the boys, I had dibs on her castoffs.

Our bond, though, would come to an inauspicious end over a game of foursquare.

Always the center of attention, Gail had managed to likewise seduce tall lanky Susan and round-faced Italian American Maria. These two dark-haired women, barely in their twenties, aspired to be full-time elementary school teachers. They devoted an inordinate amount of time catering to Gail's needs, and I got the spillover. But that morning, Gail and I ended up on opposite teams on the foursquare court. And my team was winning.

Wanda Coleman, with poets John Giorno and Amiri Baraka (LeRoi Jones), Chicago, 1994

Before the game was over, Gail began her game of distraction and threw a temper tantrum, seizing the ball out of turn at every opportunity. Thoroughly intimidated, the other girls let her have it. But when my turn came, I refused to give up the ball. Screamingly ugly, Gail stomped and instructed the other players to take the ball away from me. They obliged, but I wouldn't let go. As they backed off, I stood mid-square, the ball tucked at my waist, impervious to threats. Gail gathered the other two girls into a huddle. Monitor Susan was standing nearby, saw trouble, but assumed our tiff would resolve itself. Gail altered her body language for a fresh approach. I was a head taller, but she put on a smile and, on tiptoes, put her face so close to mine we were nose to nose.

Surprised at this dramatic change, I assumed that Gail had decided to apologize.

"Are you sorry?" I asked.

"Yes," she lied sweetly, but I saw the glint in her eye.

"No."

Instantly livid, she hissed, then stammered, searching her vocabulary for an epithet strong enough to hurt me. "You-you're nothing butta-buttabutta nigger!"

I bounced the ball in her face and caught it again.

Furious, Gail dashed after Susan, who was trying to recover from her shock. She had heard Gail call me "nigger" and, her illusion of Gail shattered, was reluctant to come to Gail's defense. Sensing a fight, the other girls stopped playing and circled our square. Gail begged the reluctant Susan to make me give up the ball. Maria joined Susan and took over the situation, coaxing me to give up the ball. I refused. One girl leapt at me, attempting to knock the ball away. I held it fast. While Susan stood back with arms folded, Maria grabbed me. We struggled for the ball. I curled my body around it and weighted it against the ground.

Worried that they'd attract the displeasure of the school's vice principal, Maria and Susan tried reasoning with me. I insisted that it was my turn and that I was being treated unfairly. Maria turned my own word against me, pointing out that it was unfair of me to prevent the other girls from playing by keeping the ball. I looked at their faces. The girls agreed. Fair or not, I was now the bad guy. I gave the ball to Susan. As the crowd dispersed, Susan gave the ball to Gail, who promptly turned to me and stuck out her tongue.

I was left standing alone in the middle of an empty square.

At some point, I had repressed my childhood rage which had begun with Gail. But in Clayton Eshleman's workshop, I rediscovered it. Nearly two years would pass before I would succeed in channeling it into my poems. Now that I had tapped into the source of my rage, all I needed was the discipline.

Midway through our *Bachy* interview, Lee quoted a review of my first book, *Mad Dog Black Lady:* "'Whoever would rather not walk in the predawn ghetto, or live there daily, faced with a sordid ferocious reality, might look into this book for a painful amazingly spirited glimpse of an underside of our culture seldom addressed in polished/published verse, much less in terms so mercilessly lucid. . . .' Many of your poems take place in the ghetto. They seem to be in contemporary times, not out of your childhood. Is this you or a dream of you?"

"This is me. . . ."

"Do you use personae in your work?"

"Yeah."

"How much would you feel that the reader should have to work to be able to distinguish between the fantasy and the reality?"

"They shouldn't, because it's insignificant. I use other voices, but they're not fictions. Most of the dialogue I use is verbatim. I . . . pride myself on having an ear for dialogue. That's why I like scriptwriting. . . . I have a memory for what people say and how they say it."

The last element needed for my poetic breakthrough came as a direct result of work as part of the writing staff for the daytime drama *Days of Our Lives.* I had met scriptwriter Pat Falken-Smith circa 1969 while she was engaged in a movie project with Howard Hughes. Six years later, she would lift me from the morass of men's magazine editing and take me on staff. The world of television moved at ten times the pace. Deadlines were mercilessly final. I was placed on a work cycle of ten days on and four days off. Nearly a generation younger than my fellow writers, and Black, I had no choice but to drop my literary pretensions in the name of bread and butter. The poetry I was forcing myself to write during this eighteen-month period was the worst I had ever written. Stubbornly, I insisted. When Falken-Smith lost her contract as head writer, her staff was let go, one by one, during contract negotiations. Last hired, I was the first fired.

Prior to my days with *Days,* I had written my poems, draft after draft, in longhand. Now that my soap-opera script career had ended, the poetry returned. But with a major difference. *I could now compose on the typewriter.* All those painful, handwritten drafts suddenly disappeared from my life. The hours and days it had once taken me to write a poem were reduced to minutes; within an hour I could write several poems, most of them excellent.

It had all come together. At last.

this is the ritual of the hand becoming
the whole. a body of itself
the gesture that allows
possession

    if i am not all, who am i
    if i am not i how am i all?

at the tip of each finger a separate universe

    if i am you
    then why aren't you me
    and if you are me
    then why the deep silence

this is the ritual of the whole becoming the
  hand
shaping a certainty . . .

i am rooted in a tree of hands where i nest
give birth. stretch my arms to take the wind

here. a forest of hands where the only fauna
are my eyes

          (From "Hand Dance," title poem
          Hand Dance, 1993)

BIBLIOGRAPHY

Fiction:

Art in the Court of the Blue Fag (poetry), Black Sparrow Press, 1977.

Mad Dog Black Lady (poetry), Black Sparrow Press, 1979.

Imagoes (poetry), Black Sparrow Press, 1983, reissued 1991.

Heavy Daughter Blues (poetry and fiction), Black Sparrow Press, 1987.

A War of Eyes and Other Stories, Black Sparrow Press, 1988.

Dicksboro Hotel & Other Travels (poetry), Ambrosia Press, 1989.

African Sleeping Sickness: Stories & Poems, Black Sparrow Press, 1990.

Hand Dance: New Poems, Black Sparrow Press, 1993.

American Sonnets: 1 through 24 (chapbook), Woodland Pattern Book Center/Light & Dust Books, 1994.

Bathwater Wine (poetry), Black Sparrow Press, 1998.

Nonfiction:

(With Jeff Spurrier) *24 Hours in the Life of Los Angeles,* edited by Carol Schwalberg, Klaus Fabricius, and Red Saunders, Alfred Van Der Marck Editions, 1984.

Native in a Strange Land: Trials & Tremors, Black Sparrow Press, 1996.

Contributor to more than thirty anthologies published in the United States and abroad, including *Breaking Ice: Contemporary African American Fiction,* Penguin, 1990; *High Risk: Forbidden Writings,* Penguin, 1991; *Lure and Loathing: Essays on Race,* Penguin, 1993; *ALOUD: Voices from the Nuyorican Poets Cafe,* Holt, 1994; *Postmodern American Poetry,* Norton, 1994; *Grand Passion: The Poets of Los Angeles and Beyond,* Red Wind Books, 1995; *United States of Poetry,* Abrams, 1995; *Best American Poetry,* Scribner/Simon & Schuster, 1996; *African American Literature,* Norton, 1997; *Trouble the Waters: 250 Years of African-American Poetry,* Penguin, 1997.

Spoken-word performer on nine recordings, including *Twin Sisters,* with Exene Cervenka, live at McCabe's, Rhino Records, 1985, reissued on New Alliance Records, 1991; *Black Angeles,* with Michelle Clinton, New Alliance, 1988; *Nation of Poets,* National Black Arts Festival, 1990; *High Priestess of Word,* Idiot Savant/New Alliance, 1991; *Berserk on Hollywood Blvd.,* Idiot Savant/New Alliance, 1992.

Contributor of poems and fiction to more than seventy literary magazines and periodicals, including *African American Review, Another Chicago Magazine, Bathos, The Black Scholar, Bombay Gin: The Naropa Institute Literary Magazine, Caliban, Callaloo, Different Homeland, Epoch, Everyman, Greenfield Review, Hyena, Lingo, Michigan Quarterly Review, Obsidian II: Black Literature in Review, Partisan Review, Phoebe, Poetry/LA, Poison Ivy, The Progressive, Prosoda, River Rat Review, VOLT: A Magazine of the Arts, Urbanus,* and *Zyzzyva.*

Paul Di Filippo

1954-

TWENTY-ONE SCENES UNTIL AGE TWENTY-ONE

A review of life is not an orderly account from conception to death. Rather it's fragments from here and there. A telephone call. A message, my eyeglasses are ready. "You can keep quite comfortable on codeine." A comment. "He looks like a sheep-killing dog." Said about me by Pollet Elvins, Kell's father, who later went nuts from paresis.

(William Burroughs, journal entry)

Preface

In 1976, some months before my twenty-second birthday, two things happened to me that proved in hindsight to be determinants of my entire subsequent life.

While attending Rhode Island College I met, fell in love with, and set up housekeeping with Deborah Newton, my incalculably essential helpmeet, guide, and inspiration ever since.

And I wrote and sold my first story, "Falling Expectations." (Appearing in the short-lived magazine *UnEarth,* the story was a parody of the work of noted science fiction author Barry Malzberg. Curiously, Malzberg—who was gentlemanly enough to forgive this youthful indiscretion when we later became friends—had once propounded the theory that a writer's first sale could be retroactively unpacked to reveal his entire career: a notion my own humor-filled, homage-laden body of work indeed supports.)

The two decades (and a year) that followed this egocentrically epochal moment in time were for me and Deborah as full of events and characters as the lives of most people. Travel and tragedy, moments of quotidian glory and exceptional if hard-won vocational triumphs. A succession of day jobs, the reluctant abandonment of some old pleasures and a few old friends, the acquisition of new. A strengthening of talents, a pruning of possibilities. Ac-

Paul Di Filippo

ceptance of limits—and even an inviting new green prospect or three. In twenty-one years (as I write, it is still, barely, 1997) I have, I think, matured considerably, learned much, and been disabused of certain hindering misconceptions about myself, others, and life in general.

And yet this second half of my life so far seems—in certain lights, on certain days—some-

Paternal grandparents, Paolo and Maria Di Filippo

how paler and more compressed than my fading first two decades (and a year). Nothing new in this observation, I suppose. One needn't be Ray Bradbury or Thomas Wolfe or William Wordsworth to identify this feeling. As often noted, the days of our youthfulness frequently seem in retrospect more elastic than those of our adulthood, more capacious of both joy and sorrow, more vibrantly colored and exciting. It is hard sometimes, in a self-pitying mood, not to view one's adulthood as anticlimax, or as a second-act scenario less capably scripted than the first.

Without falling, nostalgia-blinded, into that nowness-denying trap, though, one must still affirm, I think, that by the age when the state in its practical wisdom grants you drinking privileges (odd, that you're encouraged to begin consuming muzzy-making alcohol just then!), your character is pretty much fully formed, all the primal shaping events having burned their unfading white-hot ideograms into your cortex. Predilections and prejudices, capacities for pleasure and pain, paths and potentials—even if yet partially unplumbed—are all present by then, later life only multiple permutations of the primal puzzle pieces.

This essay, then, is an attempt to sketch in a handful of representative moments that time-lost boy I once was, before he took a series of discrete steps, each seemingly inconsequential yet compoundedly irreversible, and walked across a threshold into a new world, all unwitting that he was even moving, or shedding selves as he moved.

One

The light inside the Lister Worsted Mills was heavy with cotton motes, as if the very photons had swelled to macroscopic dimensions. The smell of hot oil and chemical dyes and finishing solutions permeated the air. Machinery clattered and hummed with a merged mechanical voice that nearly drowned mere human speech. The constant traffic through the aisles of hand trucks, pushed by utility boys trundling down the stained floorboards, supplemented the noise. Lung and ear problems were consequences of this environment. The actual tedious, backbreaking work extracted its own physical toll, both cumulative and occasionally calamitous. Yet the jobs offered by this Rhode Island factory, along with others of its kind across New England, still lured many working-class men and women, immigrants and native-born alike. Training was provided to novices, overtime was plentiful: families could be supported. The wave of closings and relocations that would shutter Lister Worsted and nearly all its kin in the region were yet to come, unforeseen in this year 1949.

Two women worked side by side in the twisting department, where single threads (always breaking, always to be spliced) drawn from ranked hanging bobbins were cunningly plied onto new cones: Catherine St. Amant and Maria Phillips.

Catherine was the daughter of Pasquale and Mary Moulica, immigrants from Italy. One of seven kids, she had grown up on the family farm in North Smithfield, Rhode Island. The rural life lacked all appeal for the adult Catherine, and she had willingly entered the mills at the first opportunity. Married to Clair Edward "Bob" St. Amant (a city boy, raised by his sister, Mabel, in nearby Woonsocket and environs), Catherine had two children: Eddie and Louise.

Maria Phillips, nee Di Christofaro, had been born in Providence, Rhode Island's capital. She had married Paolo "Paul" Di Filippo, a newcomer to this country. Somewhere along the line, matriarch Maria had thought it a smart move to Anglicize the family name to Phillips. She had borne eight children, five boys and three girls. The youngest boy was named Frank. The family now lived in North Providence, a municipality separate from its neighbor and boasting less congested conditions than the capital. Number 24 Marconi Street, a house built by the family, offered more land and living space than the former Dante Street establishment.

The demands of the incessant machinery and the production quotas afforded little time for chatter during the hours of work. Lunch, though, when an eerie partial silence of idling motors descended, opened up a small space for conversation. Flocked with airborne waste, sitting on makeshift wooden benches within sight of their machines, eating their home-packed lunches, the aproned women could catch up on matters of real interest: family, hearth, and friends.

"Catherine, you come to my house later. I have some nice homemade pasta for you."

"Thank you, Maria. I'll send Bob."

The whistle sounded, and they returned to the glimmering threads.

Two

Bob St. Amant drove south to the Phillips home. Although only a short trip across tiny Rhode Island, the journey represented a significant chunk of his limited free time. (Provincial to the bone, used to compact villages that offered everything they needed, most Rhode Islanders saw any trip longer than half an hour as monumental.) Working himself in the mills, at Slatersville Finishing, Bob was also a part-time policeman, employed mostly to direct traffic at nighttime social events. His fun consisted of a beer or two after work with cronies at a local social club.

Beside him in the car was his daughter, Louise. Pudgy as a child, Louise had slimmed down to an attractive girl with thick waves of chestnut hair. Still in high school, Louise loved to pal with her big brother Eddie and his friends. Some of them had motorcycles, mammoth In-

dian and Harley models, and she would ride behind the owners joyously, even driving when allowed. A good student, she read omnivorously for pleasure; Donald Henderson Clarke was a racy author she had sampled. Her favorite uncle, Raymond—her father's brother—had lived in a small cabin behind their house at Primrose Pond until recently. An amiable and talkative retired veteran who spent each month's pension check on liquor and books, he shared many volumes with her.

The St. Amant car reached Marconi Street. A short dead-end paved lane with a pronounced slope, the street held only three or four scattered houses separated by undeveloped lots. Number 24 was a brick Cape, four rooms on the first floor, two double-sized, slant-ceilinged ones above.

Louise and Bob climbed the back porch—cloaked in wisteria—and used the rear door, the entrance most favored by the family themselves. A tiny hall gave way directly onto the kitchen, the center of the Phillips family life.

At the sink, bent forward from the waist, a shirtless young man was soaping his dark hair.

Francis John "Frank" Phillips, Maria and Paul's youngest son (a sister, Agnes, had followed him), still lived with his parents. His childhood on Dante Street had included helping his mother make wine and sausages. (Despite having lost several fingers on one hand from a fireworks accident in her youth, Maria was deft and craftwise, even crocheting with ease.) Once as a child, while swimming alone at a local pond, Frank had suffered a burst appendix, somehow dragging himself home despite the pain, luckily in time for treatment. He had spent the years 1944 to 1946 in the navy, finishing his service on the gunboat USS *PGM-26* shepherding minesweepers. (A brother, William, serving in the army, had not returned from the conflict.) Postwar, still disposed not to stray too far from home, Frank too entered the network of local textile mills, working first for Steere Mills, then for Foley and Smith in Centredale. He passed his check each week directly to Maria, who allotted him a few dollars back for himself.

When Frank finally straightened, Louise saw a handsome, tall, well-muscled man with a big smile.

They were married three years later, in 1952.

Their first child, Paul, was born on October 29, 1954.

Three

From his upper bunk he could see something new in the weak predawn light filtering through the curtains of the Millville, Massachusetts, house: a couple of small objects placed on the floor not far from where he and his younger sister, Cathy, slept. The tantalizingly vague objects had not been there last night, when the two children went to sleep. Their presence could mean only one thing.

"Cathy—are you awake?"

From the lower bunk came the reply: "Yes."

"Look—do you see two presents?"

"I do."

"I guess Santa came then."

"He must have. Can we get up now?"

As the big brother, Paul set the rules.

"No. Not till Mom and Dad come."

They lay there not speaking, ecstatic tension in their very bones, as the light strengthened and conferred substance on the familiar furnishings of the room. The boy saw the innovative desk his father had made: a board hinged to the wall and, when not in use, secured flat against the wall with a hook and eye. It let down for activities and was supported by two ropes. There were storage chests full of their toys, Mother-Goose-decal-decorated dressers, a big gaudy lamp (he had once dreamed it talked to him), the trickily casement-hidden sliding doors that led to the rear of the second floor of the old house. In those rooms he and Cathy frequently played, lying on their stomachs on the floor, coloring pictures while from the radio issued "Hound Dog" and "Love Me Tender." Beyond the frequented rooms, there was a separate staircase that led from the second floor directly outside to the ground. The family never used it, but sometimes the boy would open the second-floor door and peer down the well's musty windowless vertiginous depths. The "secret" exit gave him an excited feeling.

Outside was a large yard. A towering pine strewed the ground with needles. Under it one year, his father had built him a real igloo, using just snow and his hands. In the summer, the sandbox offered lots of fun. Once, however, Cathy, running, had tripped and whacked her forehead on the sandbox's wooden corner. Bleeding heavily, she had had to be rushed to the hospital, where doctors sewed up her cut. The best feature of the yard was a large thicket of lilacs. In the summer, you

could worm your way to the lush green center, where the decaying stump of a tree was concealed, and become completely invisible.

There were a couple of kids on dead-end Miller Street to play with. A scary neighbor named Mrs. Crow lived in a dilapidated spook house. A small grassy hill at the end of the pavement provided sledding and a tumbling spot.

Hours must be passing! thought the boy in the upper bunk. Slowly, colors leaked back into the world as the sunlight asserted its solstice-weakened self. What *were* those toys, the opening notes in a Christmas symphony? Some kind of stuffed animals, maybe. . . .

Soon the house would be full of relatives, mostly Mom's. Uncle Eddie and Aunt Lucy, Nana and Papa Bob, Nana's sisters, Aunt Jenny and Aunt Fannie. There would be so much good food even the plump little boy in his flannel-lined Husky-sized jeans would be satisfied. Perhaps they would drive to North Providence later in the day and visit Papa Paul, the grandfather he was named after. Papa Paul must be very lonely, with nobody to keep him company at Marconi Street.

Cathy called out excitedly: "I can see what they are, Paul!"

He could, too. "I think we can get up now, Cathy. But be quiet."

And they played quietly with the new toys until their parents came, but then they shouted and yelled and raced downstairs and everything was even better than they had imagined.

Four

The detached wing of the school that held his first-grade classroom was what people called "modern." One-story high, oddly angled beams, flat roof, and lots of glass. Once while the teacher was talking, a bird had flown straight into their classroom window, causing a huge boom before it fell dead to the ground. Everyone jumped, even the teacher, and the girls had screamed.

He walked to school on his own each morning. At first, it had been hard to remember the way, but after a while it became easy, and he even tried shortcuts. In the block just before the school—which sat in the center of Millville amidst a small assortment of stores—a bridge spanned the Blackstone River. It was fun to pause on the bridge and throw stones and sticks into the frothing water. In the afternoon, Mom would often come to meet him, holding Cathy's hand and pushing the carriage holding their new little brother, Francis John.

Once a week after school he would walk a couple of blocks further away from home, up a steep hill to their church for his catechism class. In the depths of winter by the time class ended it would be too dark to walk home, so his father would be waiting to drive him back to Miller Street. (His father went to work at the mill very early but was home by midafternoon.)

Somehow recently he had learned to read. It hadn't been very hard, more like being reminded of something he had once known well and saying, "Oh, yeah." The things he liked to read best were comics. His favorite right now was one about Mighty Mouse, whom you could also see on TV. In this story, Mighty Mouse had to fly through space, the whole universe in fact, in quest of something. The huge distances, the planets floating in blackness, the strangeness of the kinds of life that existed on other worlds—Paul wasn't sure if it was frightening or wonderful. But he couldn't stop reading the comic.

Today, said the teacher, they were going to see a film. So at the proper time they lined up and marched across the recess-yard and into the older part of the school. They sat on folding chairs in a windowless room. An angular projector hulked on a table at the rear of the room. They had a small version of this machine at home. Paul watched the teacher thread the film, and he felt he could do that, too. Maybe even faster.

The lights went out, and the black-and-white film clattered through the radiant mechanical labyrinth and flared onto the tripod-balanced screen.

The film showed a barefoot boy in cutoff pants walking down a dusty country road. A fishing pole was balanced on his shoulder; his dog pranced alongside.

Somehow he was in the film then, a part of the everyday magic on the screen. He was the boy, and that was his dog. And he knew exactly where they were going. The rest of the film was less revelation than confirmation.

When the lights came back up, he couldn't remember for a few moments who he even really was.

*Maternal grandparents, Catherine and
Clair Edward St. Amant*

Five

During the summer of 1961, they lived for a few marvelous weeks in a cottage on a lake in Greenville, Rhode Island, the house on Miller Street left behind forever. There Paul learned to swim, by jumping off the dock and doing what he had to do to stay afloat. In the lake was a big fish with several hooks lodged in its jaw, painful souvenirs of narrow escapes. The tough survivor could sometimes be lured to the dock by sprinkling crumbs on the water.

By this time, his parents had enrolled him in a book club: every month, to his delight, a new Happy Hollisters book arrived. The first one told how the Hollister family had to move to a new home, and he felt its relevance keenly. It helped that the new home the Hollister children occupied was full of pleasant surprises, such as secret passages.

When September rolled around, he had to start second grade with Mrs. Sharp at his new school, Stephen Olney Elementary, even though he didn't actually live in the proper town yet. So every day his mother would drive him there, picking him up in the afternoon. On the way home, they would often stop for a soft-serve ice-cream cone at a seasonally transgressing Dairy Queen.

But now the lake and the daily drives were, like Millville, things of the past, for the Phillips family was moving into 24 Marconi Street with Papa Paul. Paul's grandfather would only be with them for a short time, however, just until Dad's sister, Aunt Lillian, finished converting her garage into an apartment for the widower. Then no longer would Papa Paul sit solemnly in his sleeveless T-shirt in the kitchen, jug of zinfandel at hand, offering advice to "Louisa" on preparing the tomato sauce and cooking the pasta.

The brick house, one chimneyed wall covered with ivy, was perfect. Paul's bedroom, shared with Francis, was huge! (The brothers slept in one double bed, no bunks.) Cathy got a room the same size all to herself—but only until their new brother arrived. (His crib already shared the space.) They were going to name the new baby Robert, after Papa Bob.

Paul saw Nana and Papa Bob a lot. Many weekends Paul would pack his suitcase (really the carrier for Mom's big manual typewriter,

that intriguing object removable with the pinch of two clamps), and his grandparents would take him home with them. He had a pink-plastic-handled jackknife Papa Bob had given him that he carried everywhere.

Living in North Providence, he resumed walking to school, Cathy accompanying him now, two grades behind him. In short order, he began to explore his new town. Parts of it featured stores and sidewalks—yet it wasn't quite a city. Parts of it featured acres of woods, a pond for swimming, and even working farms—yet it wasn't quite the country. There were planned housing tracts, still a-building—but it wasn't quite the suburbs. What it was, was a perfect amalgam of alluring features, a little of everything an adventurous boy could want.

Getting to know the new kids was hard. One dark-haired, dark-eyed boy seemed approachable, though—intelligent and interesting to boot. His name was Stephen Antoniou.

"What kind of name is 'Antoniou?'"

"It's Greek. We even go to a Greek church."

Stephen liked a lot of the things Paul liked. Before long, they became best friends. Paul had never really had a best friend before. He and Stephen were such good friends, they even shared comics.

"Look," suggested Stephen one day outside Douglas Drugs, where they purchased their comics, "if I buy all the Marvel comics, and you buy all the DC ones, we can read twice as much!"

"That's a great idea!"

Comics having risen in price from ten cents to twelve while allowances remained fixed, it took a lot of such ingenious scheming to keep up. Especially when the nickel cost of nougaty Zero bars and limeades from the soda fountain inside Fotarsky's Market were factored in.

Six

The darkened gymnasium rumbled with laughter, rocked with shrieks. Crumpled paper balls and small hard candies flew through the damp-wool-fragrant air. It was a December Saturday, a day of license, and the handful of supervisory teachers could barely control the kids. Anarchy flowed from the makeshift bed sheet movie screen into the crowd. It was the annual Christmas film party, and the Little Rascals and Three Stooges reigned.

Mother, Louise St. Amant, about 1949

Paul roared and stomped his feet along with the others, lost in the Stooges' antics. When the lights came on, he and Cathy got in line to see Santa, who occupied a chair in the milk room. Santa gave you a trinket and some candy. Then it was time to don coats and mittens and vulcanized black rubber boots with gussets and buckles and go home.

On the walk, Paul thought about how great the Stooges were, whether on the movie screen or on TV. There was so much wonderful stuff on TV for kids. The Mouseketeers, Captain Kangaroo, Boomtown, Gumby, Davey and Goliath, Looney Toons. He could lie for hours on the floor before the set. And not just during the day. The adult shows at night captivated, too: Perry Mason and the Rifleman, the Real McCoys and Red Skelton, Paladin and Jackie Gleason. Endless variety, a richness of scene and situation.

He recalled some of his favorite episodes. The time Gumby and Pokey had met the spirit of the Indian Thunderbird, for instance. What made them so compelling? Stories and characters, dialogue and simple tricks of tale-telling he had noticed swirled in his brain. *This* frequently joined to *that.* *A* was likely to cause *B.* Push *here* and it popped out *there.*

Stories—even wild Stooges episodes—had a logic, whether dreamlike or scientific. This he could see now.

But how you could start from nothing and build a story—that remained a mystery.

Seven

When Paul and Stephen weren't cloistered in Stephen's basement (mixing chemicals from his Gilbert set, smashing handfuls of loose transistors with a hammer to see what they were made of, stealing gunpowder from Mr. Antoniou's cache of shotgun shells for "experiments"), they were either off exploring or playing at Marconi Street.

North Providence offered more excitement than local amusement park Rocky Point. There were streams to ford in summer and ponds to slide on in winter. There were forest-wrapped historical cemeteries and senile houses rotting unattended. (The newly framed unfinished homes on Brook Farm Road functioned as pine-scented gym sets and castles.) Footpaths and untraveled dirt roads—parallel ruts separated by a

grassy, wildflower-dotted hump—laced the land. A bus graveyard offered more modern thrills. Stephen and Paul clambered in and out of the weather-exposed interiors, redolent of moldering vinyl, sitting behind the driving wheels and steering the ghost buses to unknown destinations. A lone caretaker sat like a spider in his shack at the center of the automotive mausoleum but was easily avoided, even when deliberately taunted.

At the farthest corner of Notarantonio's car dealership, where pavement gave way to grass, sat a black Lincoln Continental, the growth of saplings around it sign of its abandonment. The key was still in the ignition, and although they never dared start the engine, they sparingly used all the electrical apparatus until the battery died, powering the windows up and down and listening to the radio.

"This is just like the car the president was shot in," one of the boys observed.

They built a network of rafts in a swamp, setting up cast-off furniture on the sodden floats, and cooked wild onions in tin cans full of marsh water set over a candle's flame, daring each other to eat some.

Marconi Street held lots of children, often found gathered under the hickory tree that dropped its tasty nuts in the fall. Paul hung out with the Leonardo boys and the Delfino

Father, Frank Phillips (Di Filippo), 1951

girl, and of course the Mignellis. The extensive Mignelli clan, unsupervised—in fact often locked out—by a negligent TV-watching mother, wandered snot-nosed and improperly dressed for the weather. The "retarded" brother, Eugene, could often be persuaded to eat a banana peel for a penny or to foil a dare. Cathy became best friends with Cindy Mignelli and got ringworm from the Mignelli wading pool.

Ambered in summer noons, floating in autumnal dusks, exploding with spring nights, crunching through winter mornings, Paul and the other children never lacked for excitement. Sledding or playing war (with "dirtbomb" grenades), riding bikes or building forts, they roamed in a world mainly free of adults and their senseless constraints.

Stephen and his father had built a clubhouse in the backyard: four plywood walls and a flat roof that slanted from front to back. The enormous interior held tons of useful junk, mainly TV and radio chassis whose miraculous guts Stephen could somehow decipher. In the tree next to the clubhouse, Stephen himself built a lofty platform. There were rungs nailed to the tree, but the first one was deliberately placed so as to be reachable only by chinning yourself on a limb.

"Stephen, I can't do it!"

"You're too fat! You'll have to stay down there."

Paul went home instead.

Across the street from his house were a couple of acres of brambles, rock moraines, and a burbling spring. He could climb one of the oak trees there just fine, because its branches were lower. He could sit in it alone and think.

Eight

His parents assembled the three children in Paul's bedroom. Baby Bob was safe in his crib. Sitting on the edge of the bed in a row, the children were delivered the news.

"Papa Bob is gone now. He died yesterday."

One of them—hard to say who—began sniffling, then crying fully. Then they all cried, really comprehending only that an immense sadness had come to dwell where before there had been none.

Later that day Paul recalled what he had seen one morning on the way to school not

long before. A little girl's foot had gotten run over by a car as she was crossing the road. Wailing, she had been comforted by the crossing guard until an ambulance had come. Afterwards, everyone thought there was blood on the road, but it wouldn't wash away. The red rubber and fabric of the injured girl's sneaker had been ground into the pavement, and the slowly fading stain remained for weeks. He saw it every day.

Some months after they lost Papa Bob—perhaps lost only in the same way Paul himself had seemed lost, when, angered, he hid in a utility closet amid the furniture-polish-scented mops, causing an hours-long manhunt for him?—his mother told a story.

"Papa Bob was visiting us the day before he died. You kids were eating your supper, and you wouldn't finish your vegetables, Paul. Remember? While he thought I couldn't see him, Papa Bob ate them for you, so you could have dessert. I almost yelled at him, but something inside told me not to. And that night he died. So I'm glad I didn't."

Paul was glad, too.

Really, nobody deserved getting yelled at.

Nine

His father had switched to second shift, leaving the house in the afternoon and arriving back after they were asleep. They sent him off to work each day with a chant: "Good night, sleep tight! See you in the morning, don't forget to call!" His mother, once Bob could be placed in nursery school, had taken a daytime waitress job. That meant that Paul and Cathy and Francis, home for lunch, had free rein. Mostly they were good, but, as in the astonishingly irreverent *Cat in the Hat,* there could be trouble. That time with the can of whipped cream, for instance. . . .

Nana had moved alone to an apartment just a few blocks away from Stephen Olney School. She had had to learn to drive, even though she was an incredibly ancient age, fifty-five. Now after school Paul often went to Nana's for a snack.

Sadly, Papa Paul was gone, too. He hadn't lasted long at Aunt Lillian's. The healthy regimen the old man's daughter imposed hadn't suited him. "Louisa," he told Paul's mother, "she won't even let me eat what I want."

Paul's Aunt Lillian owned a cabana at a private beach, Cold Springs. In the summer she would often let the Di Filippos use it. (Mom, reversing Maria's old decision, had, despite the confusion caused at school, changed their name back to the one she preferred.) Beach roses twined the boardwalk linking the cabanas; horseshoe crabs scrawled messages in the sand. His father taught Paul how to bodysurf.

He had a dog now, Tippy: half poodle, half unknown breed. He had a massive rolltop desk, bought from the Leonardos, with a million niches and drawers, where he could sit and draw comics. Beside the desk was a green vinyl chair with chrome legs and arms, his favorite place to read.

Every week Mom took all of them to one, or two, or even three libraries: the Veazie Street or Union Free branches, or the central Providence location. They all had their own cards and could take out whatever books they pleased. Paul read the Hardy Boys and Tom Swift, Eleanor Cameron's Mushroom Planet series. Emily Neville's *It's Like This, Cat* made him think how great it would be to live in exciting New York City, like the boy in that book. Michel Rouze's *The Mystery of Mont Saint-Michel*, with its French schoolchums wandering in a secret labyrinth beneath a cathedral, tinged his own adventures.

His fifth-grade classroom was in the old part of the school: tall windows that never opened properly and had to be propped up when they did, dingy plaster walls and dark panelling. One day the teacher said, "Would anyone like to volunteer to organize the books out in the hall?"

Paul's hand shot up. "I would!"

For several days after class he alphabetized the motley collection, assorted fiction and non-fiction, and made cards for each item. A notebook would record borrowings. And he would be the first patron. He knew which book he was going to take out, too. *The Year When Stardust Fell* by Raymond Jones. He had never seen anything like this book, with its endpapers featuring a collage of strange images: rockets and robots and men in space suits.

When he finished the book, he was hooked. This science fiction stuff beat the Hardy Boys by a mile! If only he could find more! Could the real libraries possibly stock this stuff?

They sure did.

Ten

Nineteen sixty-five was some kind of miracle year.

The absolute best show of television history, *The Man from U.N.C.L.E.*, ruled the airwaves. He and Stephen and Gary Dicasparro had purchased all the toys that went with it: guns and badges and radios. Fully equipped to emulate their heroes, they had only to assign roles.

"I want to be Illya Kuryakin," said Stephen.

"And I'll be Napolean Solo," said Gary.

Well, that left Paul little choice. "I guess I'll be Mr. Waverly then." The dour old head spy, played by Leo G. Carroll, who always stayed back at the HQ.

But as soon as he said it, he realized it was the best choice for himself. You got to give all the orders.

They joined the Boy Scouts that year, too, at the prompting of Stephen's older brother, also named Paul. It was okay, except for the rigid nature of the activities. They all went to camp that summer, and Paul hated being told how to spend his time. The woods and lake at Camp Yawgoo beckoned, alluring acres of adventure, but you were marched around and forced to participate in dumb things you had no interest in. He ended up spending a lot of time in the camp library.

Nothing got his goat more than being told what to do. Feeling he knew how best to run his own life, he demanded a free hand, resented any authority. Last year he had gotten into trouble for this. Mrs. Tondreau had told him he could be in charge of the hallway display case. So he had tracked down the school custodian and soon had the man removing and adding shelves. Mrs. Tondreau had gone bananas, and his parents had heard about it. Why had she told him he was in charge if he wasn't?

His mom's typewriter (the one whose case had once carried his clothes on overnight trips) now helped him compose a newspaper detailing events on Marconi Street. He sold the hand-illustrated sheet for a nickel from door to door. The typewriter helped in another area. He subscribed to the official *Man from U.N.C.L.E.* magazine, but it wasn't enough, so he wrote his own story about the secret agents: two-and-a-half single-spaced pages, mounted on a cardboard backing.

Stephen had slot cars to race. When they tired of that, they decided to build a computer. The big cardboard box that had held the Antonious' new refrigerator sat out in the driveway. They studded it with flashing lights, dials, and buttons, and cut a narrow slot in the front. Then Paul climbed inside with his typewriter. Soon, with Stephen as showman, they had a horde of kids flocking around, asking the computer questions and receiving typed answers.

Paul's mom bought him a transistor radio from Sears, big as a canned ham. All summer he lay on a green-cushioned lawn chair, listening to the radio and reading. Ray Bradbury and the Beach Boys, Andre Norton and the Beatles, Robert Heinlein and the Rolling Stones, Isaac Asimov and the Kinks.

He and Stephen got their haircuts at Norm's, right next to the school. Norm was cool, the only unmarried guy they knew. He drove a sporty car and wore gold jewelry. He kept *Playboy* for his adult customers, but Paul and Stephen stole looks whenever they could. One day they were so enraptured by the sight of a naked Ursula Andress bathing in a rushing torrent that they lost all awareness of the need for stealth, and so of course Norm caught them.

"Hey, gimme that! You know you kids aren't supposed to be looking at that! Gedouta here now, or I'll tell your folks!"

They walked slowly toward no particular destination.

"Holy cow, did you see those boobs?"

"I couldn't believe my eyes!"

Paul thought then of Donna Delfino, who lived diagonally across from him. Once she had written graffiti—placed where he was certain to see it—saying she loved him. The notion had made him nervous, and he had started seeing less of her.

If she loved him, though, would she take off her clothes?

Even so, he doubted she would resemble Ursula Andress in the least.

Eleven

Paul and Stephen sat side by side on the swings of the playset in Stephen's yard. Really, they were too big to be using the old childish toy. Just starting eighth grade now they were, having survived Mr. Albanese's seventh grade,

where all the boys had been forced to wear neckties each day. (Paul's dad had taught him how to knot his tie, but Paul had picked out which tie of his dad's would best match his polka-dotted Carnaby Street shirt.) But the familiar apparatus—rusted poles planted in foot-grooved earth—had seemed a safe and reassuring place to discuss the disturbing news Paul had brought.

"So, you're really moving then," Stephen said.

"Yes. In just a week or two. To Lincoln. It's so my grandmother can live with us. She doesn't like being alone anymore. This new house is so big, it's got a separate apartment for her."

Stephen was silent for a time. "Lincoln. That's not so far. Just the next town over. I bet we could bike it easy. You coming back here, me visiting you. Remember that hike to the quarry?"

"I sure do." Stephen's brother Paul, as an advanced Scout, had taken their troop on a long autumn tramp to the lime rock quarry in Lincoln, in search of some mysterious caves

Paul and his sister, Cathy

reputed to exist there. It had begun to snow unexpectedly, trapping the unprepared Scouts far from home without proper jackets or footgear, and they had had ignominiously to phone for rescue.

"What a joke that was," Stephen continued. "Almost as bad as the time my dad caught us riding to Providence."

Paul laughed. Forbidden when younger to cycle into the city, they had tried just that and been nabbed. Now, of course, they were allowed to ride the Douglas Avenue bus into Providence any time they wished to visit the bookstores and Woolworth's, Shepard's Department Store and the Outlet.

"Guess you won't be coming to Lee's farm this year then," added Stephen.

Their classmate, Nancy Lee, lived on the last operational farm in the town. Each spring for years now, she had brought their entire class there on a weekday field trip to observe the cows and horses and cornfields. You could pull crayfish from the brook and drop them onto the electrified cattle fence to hear them sizzle.

"No, I guess not."

Stephen suddenly grew upset. "Damn! There's gonna be so much we can't do together now! What good is that new record player if I've got no one to listen to records with me? And what about high school? We were all set to go to high school together next year!"

Losing the sense of anticipation that had been present along with his sadness, Paul felt his eyes fill with tears. He didn't look, but he suspected Stephen was crying too.

"No, no, Stephen, it's okay. Don't worry. Nothing's gonna change."

"It's all gonna change. Just wait and see."

He couldn't admit it, couldn't affirm his friend's sad diagnosis, but he knew it was true. Everything *was* going to change.

Twelve

It was October of 1967. New boy coming into a semester already begun, Paul sat in the principal's office at Lincoln Middle School, waiting for someone to show him to his class while fuming over this latest instance of adult stupidity.

"We're putting you into the highest division," the principal had told him. "But you'll

have to take remedial reading."

"Remedial reading! How come?"

"Because of your grades in that subject."

How could he tell her that the marks on paper lied, that he was just so bored by the school primers that he refused to participate? Obviously nothing he said would change her ignorant adult mind. He would just have to put up with this nonsense.

A stout boy with a wing of wavy black hair across his brow entered. His name was Michael Coletta, and he would be in all of Paul's classes (except for remedial reading, of course). Together, they walked to the class already in session.

The middle school was a big transition. Your classmates came not just from your part of town, but from all over. You had homeroom in the mornings and a locker for your stuff. (Hell! what was that combination?) Classes changed hourly, each one in a different hard-to-find room. There was dreaded phys-ed to contend with (blue shorts, red shirt, both with the school name emblazoned; uniforms were another thing he hated!). But once he got into the groove, he began to like the schedule and varying pace.

Except for remedial reading.

The dullards were sentenced daily to the farthest classroom on the bottom floor, as if they might be contagious. Given color-coded texts and workbooks (you hoped to graduate to lilac), they had to write answers to simplistic questions meant to gauge their comprehension of the banal stories presented.

Paul held up his hand on the first day. "If we finish before the time is over, can we read something else?"

"Of course."

Fifteen minutes into the first class, he was done with the assignment. From his ring binder he pulled out the latest issue of *Natural History*. He had first seen the magazine in a doctor's waiting room, and his mother had gotten him a subscription. He thought he'd like to be an archaeologist when he grew up. Reading Michener's *The Source* had confirmed this.

The teacher looked oddly at him, but he just ignored her.

A couple of weeks later, he was out of remedial reading for good, shifting over to music class.

The house at 124 Old River Road, set on a whole acre of land, was much bigger than their previous one. Still, there were only two bedrooms for four kids. So Paul and his brothers shared one (back to bunk beds!), while Cathy had the other all to herself. He didn't mind, since he was the boss of the boys' room, enforcing discipline by such measures as tossing objects not stored in their proper place out the second-floor window, clothes and toys sailing through the air to serve as odd lawn ornaments. For the first time he had several built-in shelves on which to display his growing collection of paperback books. Often he would sit on the floor before the small library, handling individual volumes and recalling the stories they contained with a sense of ownership.

Lincoln had it all over North Providence. Bucolic, relatively unspoiled, bigger by many square miles, it offered, along with adjoining Cumberland, a wealth of snarled woods and stonewall-bordered roads, burred fields and muck-bottomed ponds, pebble-bedded streams and storied ruins.

The houses were farther apart than in North Providence, and there was no focal point for hanging out. Michael Coletta, for instance, lived miles away. But with the attractions of the landscape and his books, Paul found he didn't miss other kids so much. In fact, he *liked* being alone. Alone was dreaming, alone was roaming, alone was sovereignty over his own soul and destiny. Stephen paid him a visit or two, and Paul returned several times to North Providence. But things weren't the same between the boys. New names and incidents, known only to one or the other but not to both, surfaced in their conversation, necessitating explanations where before none were ever needed.

By the end of the school year, they barely saw each other anymore.

Thirteen

Tippy died, hit by a motorcyclist; they buried him beneath a tree out back. After two unsuccessful successors—a murderous German shepherd and an imbecilic Irish setter—they lucked upon a mixed-breed puppy, mostly golden retriever. Named Cicero, intelligent and possessing a mild temperament, he proved a fine companion for Paul's long walks.

Over the course of twenty years his father had become a boss at Worcester Textile, formerly Foley and Smith, putting in twelve hours a day. And he brought work home, too, huge

complex spreadsheets of numbers charting input and output. For many years now, on the occasional Saturday, his father would take Paul into work with him, and the boy would roam the industrial Gormenghast, familiar as the creases of his own loam-caked work shoes, his preferred tramping gear.

Although his mother was waitressing at night now, at Johnny Shadow's, she still found time to take the children regularly to a new library, in the Saylesville portion of town. Dark and cluttered, staffed by two ancient ladies (one short and round, the other tall and gangly, as if members of a comedy team), this new resource held a long shelf of science fiction paperbacks. He stole a few when he realized no one ever checked them out, rationalizing that he was giving them a better home.

With neither parent home in time to cook, with Nana working too, it fell to Paul to have supper ready for Dad and his siblings. Meat loaf, pork chops, canned beef stew and egg noodles, shepherd's pie. He liked planning what to cook. Oh, and the laundry needed doing too, please. No problem, he could handle any chore.

Plump and self-conscious, he adopted a fairly consistent outfit of flannel shirts (left untucked) and carpenter's pants (the tool pocket on the right leg was perfect for holding a pen), never thinking it was a uniform in its own way.

His ninth-grade classmates baffled him. For the most part they were utterly bland and boring, preoccupied with trivial interests and flighty affections, uninterested in exercising their minds. The realms of learning to which they were being offered the keys by a faculty of dedicated and competent teachers (with exceptions, of course: the unintelligible doddering chemistry teacher, the football coach forced to sketch history) were terra incognita to them, and would plainly always remain so.

Still, on some level he longed to join his peers, to be accepted into their cliques and circles. Maybe the lure was simply to be near the girls. God, they were beautiful, with their miniskirts and windowpane stockings! But he talked to them hardly at all.

One morning in Paul's homeroom the students stood for the anthem piped in over the PA system. He set down the book he had been reading: Harlan Ellison's *Earthman, Go Home!* It had a great cover by Jack Gaughan (already he had a sense of cover artists and even pub-

Paul, Cathy, and their brother Francis, 1963

lishing imprints as individuals). In the foreground, a red-suited spaceman; behind the dauntless explorer, one of his fellows was turning into a plant while a bird-faced monster roared. Spaceships dotted an apricot sky.

The girl standing next to him caught a glimpse of the book and began to snicker. Uncomprehending, he took a while to realize what had provoked her laughter. Soon the laughter spread, until a knot of sniggering gigglers surrounded him, as if he were a bedlamite on exhibition.

Red-faced, he flipped the book over.

He made sure no member of the unthinking herd ever saw what he was reading again.

Fourteen

He walked into the designated room one afternoon in 1969 after classes had ended, and his quiet high school existence immediately shifted gears.

Paul had decided to join the school paper, about to be reorganized under English teacher Robert Welch. Fencepost-thin and beaky nosed, a kind of drily sardonic Lincoln figure in wool vest and sport coat and cords, probably only in his midtwenties, Mr. Welch seemed the epitome of adult wit and sophistication. (Soon met, his beautiful wife, Linda—who looked just like folk singer Mary Travers!—added her charm to her husband's. And they lived in exotic Providence! Maybe someday he'd live there himself.)

The room was full of unfamiliar faces. But unlike so many of his peers, they seemed somehow sympathetic. Paul sat down.

"Okay, kids, the first thing we've got to do is come up with a new name for our paper to reflect the big changes we're going to make. Any suggestions?"

No one offered anything really vital. So Mr. Welch said, "Okay, you've heard the phrase 'paper tiger,' right? What if we call our newspaper 'The Paper Lion?'" The lion was the symbol of the school's athletic teams.

It sounded hip. A vote clinched the new name. *The Paper Lion.* Groovy! Paul liked it, and that was good: because for the next three years his life would revolve around the newspaper. And a nucleus of people in that room would become his new best friends.

There was upperclassman Bob Oster, first editor, chunky black-framed glasses setting off the sparkle in his eyes when he launched a particularly wry comment. There was blonde-maned Susan Kippax, second to hold the editor's post, a *wunderkind* who was to skip a grade and graduate a year early with a full Radcliffe scholarship. There was Doris Ripley and her youngest brother Donnie. Their father was a minister, but the five Ripleys (add David, Denise, and Dawn) were hardly angels. Each was certifiably *out there* in his or her own way. Lorraine Choiniere, doomed by plain looks and unfeminine quick-witted acerbity always to be "one of the guys," remained unfailingly cheerful and witty nonetheless. Suzanne "Soodi" Laughlin, short and possessed of a waterfall of midnight hair, could draw comics better than the artists of *Mad!* The craggy-faced Wynne brothers, Mike and Chris, both well over six feet tall, were a contrasting pair: Mike, fond of Zappa, manic and impulsive; Chris, Laura Nyro fan, reserved and deliberate.

Others there were, too, in this self-selected lot of agitators and artists, the unsatisfied and engaged ones. Under the umbrella of the newspaper, they would mount a naively ethical, easily outraged, Zeitgeist-tinged, three-year battle against the Establishment, personified in their hated principal (buzzcut and bow tie, natch!), bringing untold grief on the head of their advisor (who never backed down).

As that first meeting broke up, seed of all that was to sprout (friendships and teapot tempests, betrayals and battles, exaltation and drudgery), Paul approached the teacher.

"Mr. Welch, I want to write some kind of satire."

"Sounds great. Have you ever read *Gulliver's Travels,* Paul?"

"No. Should I?"

"Absolutely."

"What else do you suggest?"

Mr. Welch cupped his chin. "There's a lot of great satirical science fiction out there. That's really the kind of stuff I enjoy."

Heaven was born in an instant.

Fifteen

Cathy had begun to date. Her first boyfriend had a motorcycle (her mother's daughter, for sure!). Francis loved sports: wielding a hockey stick, he'd hit a rubber ball for hours, then shoot baskets for just as long. He began to caddy at Kirkbrae Country Club. Still the runty baby of the closely bound quartet, Bob found two friends close by: a boy named Loring, his own age, and the elderly next-door

"Up a tree," 1968

widow, Mrs. Robideau, who practically adopted him.

This was Paul's nightly ambition: to write something for the newspaper if the deadline was near, first in longhand, then pecking it out on his new typewriter (a manual portable from Sears encased in its streamlined lime-green case); afterwards or instead, to gulp down two or three books.

If he started the evening with a science fiction novel half-read, he could usually finish by nine or so, then pick up a second. If he got all the way through *that* one by midnight, no matter how scratchy his eyes were he'd try to read a few pages of a third, just to have the pleasure of inserting his bookmark in it. (He had a subscription to *The Magazine of Fantasy and Science Fiction* now and was a member of the Science Fiction Book Club.)

He liked some of the other kinds of reading assigned in class. Hesse's *Demian* and *Siddhartha,* for instance, or *Catch-22.* But science fiction was the only *real* literature. Not everyone dug that, though. Mentioning Zelazny's *Lord of Light* for its Hindu themes in world history class had fallen flat. Well, their loss.

About the only other activity as enjoyable as reading was walking.

He could stay out for hours at a stretch, reeling the miles in like thread on a spool. Down winding Great Road, the old thoroughfare between Providence and Worcester, Massachusetts, or on the paths beneath the high-voltage towers—or on no paths at all, crashing through undergrowth to discover an uncharted pond or spring or swamp. Once trolley-car tracks had radiated from Providence, and a long stretch of right-of-way (no rails or sleepers, but still cindered) offered an artificial treed arcade, startling in the midst of nature's splendid spendthrift chaos. The Blackstone River (were any of those sticks afloat the same ones he had tossed in from the bridge in Millville so many years ago?) was paralleled by a crumbling canal and towpath. He could hear the ghostly hoofsteps and the cries of the bargemen still.

Every weather and season beckoned, but autumn, his natal time, remained his favorite. Woodsmoke-scented air juicy and tart as a slice of lemon, windfall apples exuding sweet rot, maple and oak leaves crushed fragrant by the handful, bare tree limbs etched against a sunset sky.

Standing on a hill, looking into a shadow-patched valley, he coined a definition for glory: the exaltation of the self in harmony with the outer world. Then, like Florian in James Branch Cabell's *The High Place,* he descended. (Always, you had to come down.)

Certain times of day and special weathers and places became inextricably bound with whatever he chanced to be reading just then. Here came a rainy afternoon that conjured up Brian Aldiss's *Greybeard.* This tangle of pines evoked *Lord of the Rings.* A gravel pit recalled Edgar Pangborn's postapocalyptic *Davy.* This evening hour when colors bled out of things meant Jack Vance's *The Dying Earth.*

He loved walking so much that when he turned sixteen, he disdained driving lessons. Cars were evil.

Of course, not everyone thought so.

"Hello, Paul? It's Stephen. Stephen Antoniou, you idiot! Stay home, I'm coming to show you something."

Stephen arrived driving a fire engine. An actual, full-sized, ladder- and hose-hung 1940-vintage fire engine!

"You know I've been volunteering at the fire station, right? Well, they were getting rid of this baby, and I bought it. Want a ride?"

Cars were evil. But fire engines, now *they* were another story!

Sixteen

What he wrote for *The Paper Lion* were mock-anthropological essays poking fun at the customs of the inhabitants of "Nlocnil" (Swift had colonized the virgin territory of his mind without resistance); parodies of all the useless tests they were subjected to, with foolish multiple choices; and rhetoric-laden editorials. "If you're not part of the solution. . . ." Challenging as the student paper was, others demanded escalation. David Tierney stole a mimeograph machine from the school and did one issue of an underground, bong diagram prominent on the front page. Paul helped distribute it, was soon busted by The Man, ratted, and got off. He felt sick about it, but hell, he had never told Dave to *steal* the damn machine!

Firesign Theater was scripting their lives: "Shoes for industry, shoes for the dead!" The *National Lampoon* replaced *Mad* in his heart: "The Vietnamese Souvenir Baby Book: place infant's stump-

print here." He encountered a collection of Paul Krassner's writings from the *Realist:* What really happened on Air Force One! Even science fiction was mutating: Delany, Malzberg, Brunner. *England Swings SF!* Call it "speculative fiction," if you had made it to the other side.

They wore their black arm bands for Cambodia and Kent State, wove dandelion diadems and, crowned with peace, defiantly flaunted their integrity all day till the blossoms withered. Not their only actions, however.

Lincoln High School boasted a central grassy courtyard, accessible only during the day. Unless you went over the roof at night. Which they did with a couple of gallon-cans of gasoline to kill a giant peace sign into the turf. (Ecology hadn't been invented yet.) Lawn jockeys across the town greeted the dawn with painted white faces in place of subservient black. They rode buses into downtown Providence to march on the army recruiting office and the State House. (Introduced by Mr. Welch to Conley's, a great secondhand bookstore on the east side of the city, Paul would, with half his heart, rather have been there than marching.)

Somebody invented dope. Maybe it was roguish rebel ex-politician Norman Jacques, who lived in a ramshackle, coal-stove-heated cabin and who was their own combination of Timothy Leary and Tom Hayden. Maybe it was the wrong-side-of-the-tracks boys from poorer Manville. Once the cloud was out of whoever's magic lamp, it colored everything.

Here's how you make a "zilch": take one dry-cleaner's bag, twist and knot at intervals. Suspend over a pan of water, then set aflame. Watch the sizzle-plop display while stoned. Far out! Homegrown *2001* trip scene, man!

"Paul, you should run for student council president on, like, a Yippie platform."

"Yeah, sure, why not?"

He worked on his speech harder than anything he had ever written, honing it, sharpening its barbs, alternating guaranteed laugh-getting lines with rabble-rousing sentiments. Came the day he was to step before the entire assembled student body and faculty, he was knock-kneed nervous. But once behind the podium, intoxicated by his own words and the attention of an audience, he turned in a performance worthy of Abbie Hoffman.

His parents heard about it later in a conference with Principal Brod: "That son of yours nearly caused a riot!" When his father saw Paul later, he shook his head and smiled, saying, "Boy, you must have really said some wild things. That Brod is a whining shifty bastard, isn't he?" And he clapped him on the back.

Columbia University sponsored a yearly conference on high school newspapers: awards, panels, seminars. Mr. Welch said they were going to go, and he got the school to fund the trip.

They stayed in a Times Square Howard Johnson's Motor Lodge, rode the subway uptown. *It's Like This, Cat.* "Hey, we're in *Harlem!*" (There wasn't a single black face in Lincoln High. He recalled now with new understanding the confusing moment in 1965—it must have been during the Watts riots!—when his mother had called them inside from their play, saying a horde of nonexistent rioters was marching from Providence.) SDS and imagined whiffs of tear gas. Skipping with arms linked down the sidewalks, chanting a silly improvised song with the refrain "I see subway steam!"

All work and no play it wasn't. Even The Movement had to rest.

The eight-track in Mike Wynne's van blared Little Feat: "If you be my Dixie Chicken, I'll be your Tennessee Lamb. . . ." They pulled up in front of the old Loew's State Theater in downtown Providence and tumbled out laughing. It was 99-cents movie night. The rococo interior of the thirties-era movie palace was all sooty gilt and ripped upholstery, grotty floors and threadbare carpets. You could have dropped two of the smaller Newport Mansions into its balconied maw. Clouds of dope smoke produced an atmosphere like a burning rain forest. Every seat was filled with screaming hippies and teenyboppers.

They settled in, and the show began. Old Batman and Flash Gordon serials and the Marx Brothers. Mick Jagger in *Performance.* The advent of images failed to diminish the noise. But Paul was swept up and lost.

Barefoot boy going fishing with his dog. The Rascals and Stooges cavorting on a suspended bed sheet.

Surely this moment was eternal.

Seventeen

By graduation day, his hair had hit his shoulders, and he was ready for a change of scenery. But first, let's celebrate!

Lorraine Choiniere's parents, thanks to the savvy of her contractor dad, had managed to build an inground pool on their extensive property, despite not being rich. Paul had swum there many times. But tonight was going to provide a watery experience like no other.

The graduation party began at dusk and only took a couple of hours to spin out of control. Visible from the road, the gathering attracted every cruising teenager within miles. Soon the lawn and pool were thronged with elbow-to-elbow revelers, noisy as Armageddon. Music blasted from speakers. Lorraine loved Traffic: "It's only the low spark of high-heeled boys. . . ." They had seen the group play the Providence Civic Center, caught Alice Cooper elsewhere.

Lorraine wanted to be his girlfriend, had invited him to dances for years now, invitations he refused with disingenuous excuses: "You know I don't do dances, Lorraine. That's for jocks and cheerleaders." Really, though, he didn't fancy Lorraine in particular—or having a girlfriend in general. The thought of a romantic relationship frightened the pudgy lad. Although he did have a crush on Sherry Mowbray. There she was now, strolling barefoot beneath the tree-strung fairy lights, bell-bottoms sweeping the turf, arm in arm with some lucky guy.

Michael Coletta was going to Providence College. Mike Wynne was joining the navy! (Paul's draft lottery number had come up reassuringly high.) Doris Ripley and Chris Wynne, both a year older than Paul, had already been away from the scene for some time.

Paul Tondreau—a late-blooming friend recently transferred from Cumberland—passed him a joint (the air was thick with cannabis fireflies) and asked, "What are you doing next year? College?"

"No way. I'm going to Hawaii. The Sandwich Islands, man."

"Hawaii? How come?"

"It's as far as you can go without a passport. I wanna see something of the world besides Rhode Island."

"Cool."

By midnight's tolling, Paul had smoked more pot than John Lennon. Large gaps separated events. He found himself wobbling at the edge of the pool's deep end with a nearly empty pint of Southern Comfort in his lax grip. Joplin was *dead*, man, *dead!* Can you believe it—

Someone maliciously pushed him in.

The water closed over him like a caul. Fully clothed and sneakered, he sank. Directions disappeared and time melted. Elemental voices spoke secrets in his ear. Jellied blue light surrounded him. Reborn a merman, he moved his arms with languid unconcern.

Somehow he was breathing air again. He clambered out and made his way home on foot. Dripping and angry at first, he soon found laughter overtaking him.

He was *going* places—places none of his other peers were going, or even knew about. And he didn't mean just Hawaii! By summer's end he would be far, far away from this scene.

Eighteen

Each weekday morning that postgraduation summer he rose at 5:30. Quick cup of coffee, cereal or toast, then off to the mill with his father. They had fun in the car, cracking jokes, talking about characters at the mill. He recalled many rides with his father when they

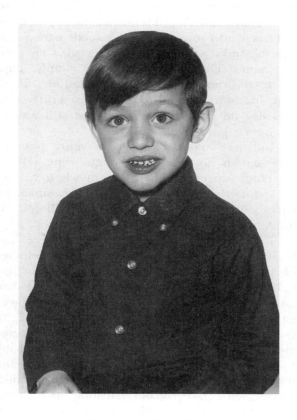

Youngest brother, Robert

both were younger. Dad had liked to sing: "Mairzy Doats," "Funiculi, Funicula," "Love Letters in the Sand." At Marconi Street Dad had lodged hi-fi speakers right into the wall, opening the plaster he and Papa Paul and his brothers had once laid. As a family then, they had sat around the dining room table and sung along to Mitch Miller records. Paul still knew all those lyrics, but now he preferred Neil Young. "Don't let it bring you down, it's only castles burning. . . ."

At Worcester Textile his dad went to his office, and Paul clocked into the Roving Department. The roving machines were an early stage in the process of sheep to cloth. The input yarn was still wispy, long hanks thick as a woman's wrist, comprised of easily separated fibers. The hanks were piled like soft-serve ice cream in pressed-cardboard, metal-rimmed, open-topped barrels big enough to hold an adult. These barrels had to be muscled into place behind the roving machine, the hanks drawn out and over a rack and fed into the machine, which tightened the yarn into greater coherence and deposited it on upright spinning plastic bobbins big as cylindrical bowling pins. These serried bobbins filled in minutes, and then had to be "doffed" into utility trucks.

For eight hours a day Paul fed two machines and doffed them. The work was more or less continuous: something was always either full or empty. The women who actually ran the machines treated him like a favorite nephew, and he suspected they would've even if he weren't the boss's son. He got hooked on the salt tablets provided to compensate for the sweaty heat of the mill. He popped the crumbly evil-tasting pink lozenges continuously.

He understood all his fellow workers deeply and instinctively, these honest, hard-working parents and their already mill-enthralled children. Were their roots and his not identical? But at the same time he knew he was no longer one of them, if he ever had been.

He rode home with Bobby Biagetti, a Manville guy in his twenties Paul had vaguely known before this period. Once home, he changed his clothes, shrugged off the day's labors as easily as if they had been a few flakes of dandruff, and roamed the landscape before supper, his energy and spirits inexhaustible.

Let's see: banking every check till September, he'd have—wow, almost a thousand bucks! That should last him a long time in Hawaii.

Although the ticket cost alone *would* eat up a significant chunk of his savings. . . .

A week or two before he planned to leave, his parents approached him. Smiling, his mother handed him an envelope.

"What's this? A plane ticket! You didn't buy my plane ticket, did you?"

"It's an early birthday present. We'll miss you, but we know you really want to go."

On a swingset, tearful yet excited.

Nineteen

His army-surplus green duffel was packed halfway full with unread science fiction paperbacks, minimal clothing in the rest. His carry-on luggage was his green portable typewriter and a copy of Norman Spinrad's *The Iron Dream.* He was heading off to see the world and to turn himself into a writer. More details than these his plans did not exhibit. Go with the flow, man.

The flight, his first, was uneventful. In Honolulu he rode a bus downtown, found the local YMCA, and rented a room. He read a whole Jack Williamson book before he could fall asleep.

It took a few days, but he lucked onto a furnished studio apartment not far from Waikiki Beach. Boy, was it expensive, couple of hundred a month! His money wouldn't last long at this rate. He'd either have to find some kind of grunt job or earn money from writing. There were only two catches to this latter strategy.

He didn't know what he wanted to write, or how to sell what he had written.

Oh, sure, he knew he wanted to write science fiction, but exactly what *kind?* Liking everyone from Asimov to Ballard, van Vogt to Disch, he couldn't settle on one style or topic.

Sitting patiently on his kitchen table, his typewriter reproached him each morning he opened his eyes not ten feet away from it. He'd lift its lid, thread in some paper, poise his fingers over the keys—but nothing would come. Nothing, that is, except chatty letters home.

After a week or so of this frustration, all sense of remorse suddenly lifted. Hell, he was only eighteen! He had his whole life before him! And here he was on an adventure! Screw writing! (At least for now.)

He began to explore, as he once had explored Millville, North Providence, Lincoln. Renting a bike, he cycled all over his island. (He couldn't afford to visit any others.) He swam and lay on the beach a lot, hiked Diamond Head one glorious (by his definition) day. There was a great library a few blocks away from his place, and that was where he read Jack Finney's *Time and Again.* Victorian New York and coconut palms made a weird mix.

Before Christmas, having made no friends, money dwindling, he called home. "Mom, Dad, I think I'm coming back."

And of course they said he could.

Twenty

One Thanksgiving he ate so much he got physically and spiritually sick. Under the lash of his own burdensome appetite, he resolved to change. A notebook (large, not one of the small ones he now carried in his rear pocket to go along with his side-pocketed pen) became a meal diary. Writing down what he ate proved extremely educational. He began to pare away. And he discovered fasting. (Mom had been into yoga and health foods back when only beatniks were.) Every Wednesday he took only water. On Thursdays he ate simply, hoping to disorient his body's expectations, hoodwink his own metabolism. Then on Friday and Saturday he drank only juices, but still walked for hours, giddy with hunger.

In three months he lost seventy pounds, entering his normal height-weight zone (always a territory to evoke chastisement when visiting the pediatrician) for the first time since he was about three years old. But he still felt fat inside.

Every Sunday for his whole life there had been some sort of family dinner, vast helpings of pasta and roasted meats prepared by his father. Visiting relatives always appeared. Uncle Louie, one of Nana's brothers, was a frequent guest since the death of his wife, Aunt Trip. Louie was the most silent person Paul had ever met. He'd sit wordlessly for hours in the living room of Nana's attached apartment, rocking and digesting his meal, the weight of the familial and personal past palpably radiating off his dour countenance. Paul could feel that weight often enough himself.

The author's parents (right) with Cathy and her husband, Tony Fratus, 1974

But such familiar figures as Uncle Louie were now supplanted at the Sunday meals by an "outsider." Cathy had a new boyfriend, Tony Fratus. Tony had graduated from Lincoln High a year or two before Paul. With a luxuriously cultivated beard like Karl Marx's, Tony was big and hairy everywhere except atop his prematurely balding head. "I shaved my skull on a dare, and it never grew back!" Jovial and devil-may-care, loud and harmlessly wild, he drove an old convertible MG. "I was raised by Gypsies, man. They stole me from my family when I was real small."

Cathy and Tony had become Jesus Freaks. They attended a local evangelical church, and Cathy got into arguments with Mom about whether drinking a glass of wine at meals, as Mom did, was proper Christian behavior.

One Sunday, as Mom was washing dishes after the big meal, Tony climbed the cellar bulkhead outside the screened kitchen window, placing his face on a level with Mom's, and told Mom he and Cathy were getting married.

The wedding took place in the big backyard of the Lincoln home. Francis, a lanky teenager, and Bobby, finally shooting up tall, would now share the bedroom formerly shared by three, while Paul moved into Cathy's space. More room to display his books.

Lots of friends Paul hadn't seen in a while showed up. The Wynne brothers, Lorraine, the Ripleys.

"Hey, Mike, remember when we all drove to the beach and stayed up all night and then at dawn I did that great rap about worshipping the sun?"

Doris Ripley was almost finished with college. (Paul himself had just begun.) Lorraine had her own apartment now. When he visited later with Doris driving, he smiled to see a Traffic record cued up on the turntable.

The ceremony was conducted by the Jesus Freak preacher. It was quickly over, and Cathy and Tony were now married.

*As a tutor for remedial English students,
Rhode Island College, 1976*

At one point in the day, Paul noticed the dim scar centered in his sister's brow.

Two children running across the lawn, sandbox waiting with cruel gouging corner.

Twenty-one

He had made contact with science fiction fandom in a roundabout way, riding a Greyhound bus to Toronto to attend a convention in 1973. On the ride home he met an affable fellow named Mike Blake, who told him there were a bunch of fans right in Rhode Island.

"Come to Don D'Ammassa's house. We're going to start a club."

They called it RISFA, the Rhode Island Science Fiction Association. The only rule was that there were no rules. No officers or manifestos, no dues or group publications. All they did was gather every Friday at Don and Sheila D'Ammassa's hospitable home in East Providence to talk about science fiction, watch Monty Py-

thon on PBS, and play Risk. Real good times, if occasionally the arguments got intense.

"You really *like* that Perry Rhodan shit?"

"No, but I have to buy it so my collection's complete."

But science fiction itself was retreating from the center of his literary perceptions, if only by an inch or two.

Rhode Island College was for most of its students a commuter school. Paul rode two buses there, one from Lincoln to downtown Providence, and another outbound to the Mount Pleasant section of the city where the campus sat. If he had a class at an awkward hour, he might drop Mom off at work (she was co-owner of a machine shop now, managing the books and the office) and he'd take the car, popping Yes into the eight-track. "I'll be the roundabout, the words will make you out and out . . ."

His major was English, natch, his undeclared minor history.

Emerson and Hemingway. Whitman and Faulkner. Dickens and Donleavy. Thoreau and Pynchon. Shelley and Wolfe. Dickinson and Waugh. Chaucer and Gaddis. Byron and Nabokov. Man, these guys could write rings around most science fiction writers! Ahem. Uh, Professor? 'Pears I mighta been a little hasty in my, er, critical disdain, if it's not too late to register my new approval, sir . . . ?

He wrote a few funny essays for Rhode Island College's the *Anchor,* without really connecting with the anonymous staff. No *Paper Lion* rerun there. But most of his efforts went to producing a column for Don D'Ammassa's fanzine, *Mythologies.* "Arrant Nonsense" his column was called, and the pieces certainly lived up to the title. But the writing served sufficiently to scratch a slumbering itch.

The self-exculpatory feeling that had freed him from reproach in Hawaii still lingered. What he was doing now—learning, living—was enough. God, he was just ready to turn twenty-one! Practically the whole of his life still stretched ahead of him.

Down this chalk-dusted corridor or before this particular library shelf, across this quad on a *Greybeard* day or in this fusty classroom, from his typewriter or out from under a stack of used books, out of the mouth of this teacher or in the gaze of this girl—

Who could say what miracles would come?

BIBLIOGRAPHY

Science fiction:

The Steampunk Trilogy, Four Walls Eight Windows (New York City), 1995.

Ribofunk, Four Walls Eight Windows, 1996.

Destroy All Brains!, Pirate Writings (Brightwaters, New York), 1996.

Ciphers, Permeable (San Francisco), 1997.

Fractal Paisleys, Four Walls Eight Windows, 1997.

Lost Pages, Four Walls Eight Windows, forthcoming.

Joe's Liver, Cambrian (Campbell, California), forthcoming.

Contributor of nearly one hundred short stories to publications, including *Amazing, The Edge, Interzone, Pirate Writings,* and *Science Fiction Age.*

Ann Erickson

1943-

Ann Erickson, 1997

Elongated Buzz of Model Airplanes, Late Summer

I played on the concrete back steps of our brick house in Gary, Indiana, with airplanes: a hard rubber black B-52 bomber, a large metal passenger propeller plane with a turquoise fuselage and copper wings, and a wooden model Piper cub I'd glued and painted myself. I'd throw them off the steps to fly nose down into the grass. I myself jumped off the top steps over and over again for hours, flapping my arms as hard as I could, landing with a thud on the hard packed sand and grass.

I climbed the sour cherry trees and swung around the green painted metal pipe laundry poles, played football with little boys in vacant lots, knelt with marbles on concrete in brick housing complexes, roller-skated (lock-on metal skates) on clicking sidewalks, hid in laundry rooms to play slave girls and pirates, bought nickel candy bars and boxes of pumpkin seeds, passed the ominous small windows of local bars, and ran down alleys and green lawns until the late summer sun went down.

*

"It's too bad that you had to be alone so much when you were little," my mother sighs now.
"What about the twelve Finnertys?" I ask.
"Who are the twelve Finnertys?" she asks.

Kathy and Richard and I go to the quonset hut movie theater in Monte Rio.

The walls are decorated on one side with World War II murals painted by Art Longoria, including "Quonset Hut Village" and a tribute to the "We Can Do It" poster of a woman factory worker flexing her biceps.

Kathy comments, "You know, the 'We Can Do It' woman died last week."

"My mother," I begin to reminisce, "worked in a war plant."

"Well, my mom didn't, but my grandmother did." Kathy retells her grandmother's story about the women who worked with her, becoming her grandmother, doing her grandmother's voice. I can see it and hear it.

I'm not able to "do" my mother's stories. I have images in my mind: Mother taking buses through Baltimore at night and the woman working with her who got rubbery gunk in her long hair. "There weren't a lot of women where my mom worked. She was part of an emergency crew that fixed breakdowns at Western Electric on the East Coast."

Kathy remembers her father, "He said, 'every generation has its war.' But he didn't serve in 'his' war, the Korean War."

"Well, my father wasn't 'into' the military. He didn't go overseas, thank God, but he traveled all over the United States in the army, and Mom followed him with me. I was a baby. She could do that because he was an officer. We traveled on trains all the time. I must have been in twenty-five states by the time I was two, a lot of them in the Deep South because he was in charge of black troops."

"Trains," Kathy muses, "you must love trains."

"Trains are like my mom. My folks used to let me travel by train alone to my grandparents. The stewards and porters were so nice, I wanted to work as a train stewardess when I grew up. It was safe then, just like you and the kids in Japan. My parents' lives only got hard after they settled down, some little basement apartment in Ohio in the winter. Mom was isolated with me. Dad resisted going into engineering for years. He was a writer, wrote

"I'm six and my cat Fido and I are in front of our house," Gary, Indiana, 1949

plays, comedies—always wanted to be a lawyer, a minister, an actor. They finally got a house in Gary. When they had my sister in 1950, my dad went back into engineering, only he was years behind in his career. My mom wasn't able to get back into being a speech therapist until I was twelve and Nancy was six; I could help her a little with the housework and Nancy then. She'd been a substitute teacher and was into the American Association of University Women and theater groups, so she didn't go nuts. She hated being a housewife."

The house lights dim and the movie starts. . . .

*

We moved to Fort Wayne, Indiana, in the late '50s, which made survival sense for us as a family, but was kind of hard on me as a kid.

In Gary, the kids had giggled, "You talk like a book," but they liked me and wanted me to make up stories and jokes. In Fort Wayne I was going into miserable preadolescence; the only kids who wanted me to design play fantasies ("Wounded World War II Paratrooper" or "Wild Stallions") were my younger sister's friends, six years younger. My junior high school peers baited me into describing my hilarious (to them) dreams of romance and touched me with an American origami cootie catcher which inevitably came away from me covered with pencil-drawn cooties.

The library is polished linoleum primarily, and there is an occasional blue light here and there, reflected on the waves of the old waxed linoleum. Thinking of the original library, I believe there is some sort of dome and occasionally I believe that the color scheme is really kind of mostly tan and dark red, maybe with blond wood. Back in the old days wood was really used frequently for banisters and practical purposes like railings and tables, often polished and amazingly fat, I mean large round hunks of wood, worn by hands and finished to a sheen. I'm thinking of the Fort Wayne library where the librarian tells my father and me that there is no copy of Joyce's *Ulysses* in the library, much less one available to a ten-year-old girl. Daddy thinks this is funny, just like when I try to buy a graveyard plot.

I'm looking at a copy of *The Beacon*, the Harrison Hill School newsletter, dated December 18, 1956. My poem "Fireside Fantasy" is featured on the front page with a block print illustration, a rhymed, alliterative Christmas poem:

The snow whirls at my windows;
The wind bays at my door;
But the warmth of my hearth
Is firing and gilding my cold gray floor.

However, another poem, "Wild Ride," in the same grade school newsletter, is more vivid:

Through the frosted silence,
     against the copper sky,
Through the twisted thickets,
     with the wind whipping by

In spite of the fact that there was no sleigh ride in my life experience, and, in fact, no hearth in the house I was living in, I did manage to express the Midwestern winter in the "frosted silence" and "copper sky." I created a cross pattern of sound, beyond rhyming and alliteration, and used inner language, a language which of course still came in part out of books, stories by Poe, Conan Doyle, and Galsworthy.

I open a high school yearbook, *Totem 1958*. There's that brick building with Ionic columns and busy '50s sedans; a man in a hat and overcoat; girls in socks, saddle shoes, camel coats, straight skirts, and scarves; boys in windbreakers and chinos: "To a real swell gal in my algebra and English classes. You've suffered through Mr. Coats and flunked algebra with me (just kidding)."

Thirty of us out of a class of two hundred were Sputniked into accelerated classes. Mr. Coats actually taught me to outline and to write serviceable prose; he introduced us to a surprising range of anthologized literature. In return, we tortured Mr. Coats in every conceivable fashion.

Years later I go back to tell Mr. Coats that he has taught me more than the Swarthmorians. He nervously chats, his blue eyes darting back and forth behind heavy glasses. My vision suddenly opens up to take in, behind him, the increasingly disruptive class of current high school students, grimacing, climbing on desks, setting up pranks as we speak, with the expressions of devils in hell.

I also had physics; four years of mathematics, with the Robert Stack look-alike; four years of Latin, with the crusty older teacher who insisted that we study mythology and Latinate English in depth—but allowed us Roman banquets in costume; and economics, with the wizened man who endured my defenses of Goldwater free enterprise economics and my falling asleep in class. I tended to make B+s; I had my own interests. I stayed up to watch late movies on the TV we finally got in 1959, sometimes getting to hear my dad's wisecracks about the actors and the filming; I read my short stories to my dad, or listened to him read his comic plays—or I stayed up all night with my best friend Plogsterth to discuss religion, sex (*The Call Girl* by Dr. Harold Greenwald), and our labyrinthine interests in Russian opera and Sherlock Holmes.

My poetry accommodated classic forms and played with language, including poetry which I wrote in Latin:

Mare albens, albens	the white white sea
In retibus habeo	I have in the net
Retes rosae albentum;	white roses in the net
Mare cedit	the sea ebbs
Et nunc est nullo.	and now is nothing.

I also referred to art objects I'd seen on my trip to Europe, when I had joined my French professor grandfather and my gay, temperamental Nana on their sabbatical in the summer of 1958. I'd stepped out of my ugly-duck self into a swan suit and had been thenceforth insufferable, according to Plogsterth.

My poetry combined my natural bent for minimalist concrete images with my passion for Anglican liturgy and biblical imagery. I loved poetry by Sappho, Catullus, François Villon (in translation), John Donne, Shakespeare, Swinburne, and—of course—T. S. Eliot. Something in me must have resisted Eliot, however, because I wrote a satire of "The Love Song of J. Alfred Prufrock" which featured Millicent the Librarian. The poems I like best now from then evoked the bleak Midwest itself:

> The sky like smoke, the slowly-streaking rain,
> Roll behind the trees in timeless hours,
> From the dull light of the city
> To the dark of the clustered houses.

I also wrote short stories with predictable O. Henry endings and most of the editorials for the high school paper. I was the editorial editor, but it was easier to write the editorials and do the cartoons myself than to ask my peers for writing. The high school literary magazine used six of my poems in 1961 without printing my name with them, although other students' names appeared with their poetry. I was furious, but I was afraid to say anything to anyone.

When the SATs rolled around, I got the highest score in the high school and won the Midwest Scholarship to Swarthmore College— my ticket out. Later, while I was at college, my family moved to South Bend, Indiana, near Notre Dame University. No more Fort Wayne.

*

I spend four years in the Swarthmore College library, a lot of them in the stacks, some

With the boys in the high school physics lab, 1959

of the time in the women's bathroom where I can lie on the couch and smoke and take a break when my friends come in, some of the time in the smoking basement where the sleaziest students, including myself, hang out—but another library is the one I want.

To proceed to this library, I advise you to go into my memory midwinter in the highest tower of the old, the oldest, Parrish dormitory which is a four-story stone-faced building with a pillared porch and dormers, endless central stairways, irregular rooms and attics, large fat railings and linoleum floors, window sills where girls freeze cider for hard cider, and terrible four-story brambled black trees outside, which crook in the howling hard nights against jagged stars—through which the moon shines down onto Parrish's dark shiny surfaces

—the wind is howling—a student is boiling water on a hotplate for Knorr's vegetable soup—

In the central tower of Parrish is a room which does not have many windows, but a high pitched ceiling, dim-lit by electric yellow lights in low lamps, and high bookcases, filled with yellowing copies of science fiction magazines. I crawl from my room, wrapped in blankets, to write papers at 2 A.M., 4 A.M., 5 A.M., sick with exhaustion and procrastination, to read notes, spew and forget intricate argument, outline, write implausible sentences and meaningless development—until I run, stinking of late nights and deadlines, arrive in seminar in a dress, nylons and high heels, unwashed and uncombed—my papers also arriving in a mess, barely making it through the mimeo shop for my fellow seminarians.

*

At college, I was a Midwestern girl who drank and danced, in the context of students from New York City whose parents sang Spanish civil war songs (the SATs were prominent in Swarthmore admissions policies in those years) and upper middle class students from East Coast prep schools. After I saw a slide show about Hiroshima, my politics switched 180 degrees, and I marched with Quaker and New York students (in my suit and nylons) in nonviolent antiwar marches in Philadelphia.

In spite of trips to the Peppermint Lounge in Manhattan, I managed to read and love Spinoza—and to get enough As and Bs to take aesthetics with Monroe C. Beardsley and American literature and modern poetry with poet Daniel G. Hoffman. I remember arriving for seminar—Mr. Hoffman was playing jazz clarinet in his elegant living room—his bright dark eyes and slender fingers alight. In a kind of rapture of the deep, I wrote weekly papers, on Ezra Pound's ideas on cadence, on W. B. Yeats, Robert Graves, or Wallace Stevens. In all those years I don't remember studying any female writers—although it seems to me that Mr. Hoffman himself bucked the tide of those times by suggesting that his seminarians read Ralph Ellison's book of essays, *Shadow and Act.* Except for poet John Oliver Simon, I don't recall any of my fellow students taking my self-definition as a writer seriously—even my wise and wryly ironic roommate, Laura. I wrote a few painful lyric poems and some experimental poems:

> As I see you savage now
> And then emerging from your
> Opaque eyes
> The egg round smoothness
> White ideas.
>
> The vast idea of boundless
> To some is spheric
> And to some symbolic
> And to you is boundless

*

I'm looking at an old picture. I am standing at Clothier—the students are gone—my mother takes pictures. I have graduated with honors, but I have no place to go.

In writing this, I'm beginning to get the feeling: *what a moron*—"There's another authority figure. There's another brick wall. Let's see if we can smash ourselves into it!" *The same thing over and over again. Duh.*

My friend Kathy says, "Well, if it wasn't for adolescents, the world would never change." That's writers, then, the perennial adolescents.

Today I am blathering on to Kathy and her sixteen-year-old son, Will's friend Travis, about what silly crazy rascals Roger and I were when we were young. I don't know how I get onto this—yes I do—a kid is about to jump off the railing of the Hacienda Bridge into the Russian River, the way that hundreds of kids have gotten broken arms and head injuries. I start out that Roger and I were such fools, often fueled by a bunch of hard liquor, how we used to go out on the trestle bridge in South Bend, Indiana, where trains actually did go—such fools—how we tried some of his Italian grandpa's grappa (like grain alcohol, but smooth as silk, I say) and within fifteen minutes waltzed right past Roger's staid law professor father, who was watering the lawn, to go out to the boat dock and sink Roger's old wooden rowboat right out in the St. Joe River in front of the house.

"But later things got bad," I go on. "We never should have gotten married. It would be like your pals W. H. and Jose marrying each other!"

I can remember a good time in the center of it all—times skinny-dipping at Pinhook in the hot summer nights when we were first together, sensuous delight and freedom.

"Those were wild times," I tell Kathy and Travis, using the movie *Austin Powers* as an inadequate metaphor, "but we made a lot of mistakes, as Austin Powers says."

*

We kind of bumbled into our marriage. He had plans to go into the Peace Corps, possibly eventually into politics. I had no plans at all, so I just fell in with Roger's plans. This snowballed into a great formal wedding, preceded by chaotic prenuptial quarrels between me and Roger and the hand construction of a beautiful lace dress by Plogsterth and followed by a limbo in Chicago with no money to live on while we waited for our Peace Corps training.

I got my first job working in the claims department in the sub-basement of Marshall Fields' department store. Roger began to teach me how to cook and to clean with unfamiliar equipment. He had lived on his own and partially worked his way through his undergraduate years at the University of Chicago; I had moved into Roger's world.

In Chicago, I wrote a small collection of taut, concrete poems—which I am able to publish in today's journals, even "experimental magazines," thirty years later (and Roger says he still has his copy)—but in 1965 I felt embarrassed giving my mother a hand-lettered and illustrated version, feeling it was "homemade" and weird. I experienced life in a momentary

and perceptual fashion. The poems were an effort to catch the "dictation" of thoughts, sounds, visual images, and kinesthetic sensation as I experienced them in combination:

> pattering of feet
>   falling
>   with
>   the
>   fragments of the tickets
>
> through the glitter
> of the station
> of the pavement
> the glitter of the steps
>
> glitter through the ribbon feet

My poetry and journals tracked our Peace Corps travels from our training in San Francisco and St. Thomas in the Virgin Islands—to Liberia in West Africa. I have published some of this material in my chapbooks, *The Book of Hours of Jeanne de l'avenier* (1991) and *TraduXion* (1995).

"The Funeral Party in Dark Night" appears in both collections. This poem embodied the spiritual and physical experience of time eating itself in Africa. The physical details named in the poem came from two funeral ceremonies I heard and saw in Monrovia, Liberia. One funeral was a West African ceremony at night—I could hear the drums—and the other was an AmericoLiberian march down the main streets of Monrovia, dignitaries in black top hats and black coats with tails, with plants ritualistically tucked in their pockets:

The Funeral Party in Dark Night

The funeral party in dark night
passing in and out of doors

the funeral march in day
at night like shadows in white sleeves

at day in black, black hats, glasses black, black
  suits,
black jackets dusted shoulders red

a plant in each pocket
in each straight printed black suit
frail vine snatched out of the moldering earth

out of the smell of mold and smoke

out of the vision wavering in heat
kaleidoscopic patterns retinal cones and rods
shimmering points of color growing
creeping earth all growing
in around the pillars of cement crumbling
dust of wood in a year/ mold of book in a
   week
and even the mold itself
and the leaves and earth here are rotting
giving giving away
to new leaves new
vines, crawlers, upspringing
trees, new mold
new dust, new burnings
a land where no
landmark is

                    sane same same sane
and out of it every
man snatched
each out of it
out of it

a pale green withers
on a black suit chest

Today, in 1997, my fears and fury concerning the role of the United States in Liberia—my feeling that the United States was a giant leech on the blood of the Third World—does not sound so radical or unique. Yet today, Americans might not know that Liberia was once,

"In my graduation cap and gown," Swarthmore College, 1965

before so much American involvement, a peaceful backwater with no real tribal tradition of war—today, when Americans read newspaper accounts of Liberians starving to death in the embargo of Monrovia, or hacking each other to pieces with machetes.

However, when I was twenty-two years old, in 1966, and living in Liberia and writing these poems and journal entries, my ideas and feelings made me seem like a strange woman to Peace Corps and AID personnel:

The Liberian Forest is Numbered

as a truck throws up red dust
on the road, past the shadows,
the slim trees slashed,
past the sudden black of a woman's eyes
stepping aside with her heavy load
the truck passes also white signs with small
   neat numbers.

Number 45 is the store of number 45
and other sections.
In it white solid fat buys
white solid fat.
Some 50 dollars worth of charming
European jams and jellies
frozen steak and peas.
Outside, little boys sell huge bananas,
pineapple and avocado
for pennies.
Women sell ground nuts and old chewing gum.
Men beg.

This was a pretty matter-of-fact description of the trip to the store near the Firestone rubber plantation. Line breaks and sound pauses were used for drama and contrast.

February 17, 1966: Packing all morning, arrangements for photos, kitten. Pick up a small grey and white kitten at AID home, unsuspecting then cries for mother. Sleeps in a washpan in jeep. Up Bensenville Road, stop to see friends in small village, further up road, washed out bridge. To Kakata, trailer. Dinner with PCVs. Cat cries all night.

February 18, 1966: Go into Kakata to buy curtain material from Lebanese. Lebanese very affable; one offers us cigarettes (Roger to go hunting), one gives us chairs and Fanta. Walk home through rubber trees, tribal homes. Make curtains; living room not yet partitioned from bedroom on porch. Dinner sardines. Cat bounces around a little more, still frightened.

February 19, 1966: Conversation with Giant Beetle. Power off, refrigerator defrosting—I finish the job. Curtains for living room. Cat—Neutrino, particle without mass or charge, Roger says, only angular motion. Cat plays on bed, shadowboxes—we have to put him in trailer.

February 20, 1966: At sunset, soccer game at BWI (little boys have little soccer game)—players rugged, tremendous struggle—comes right up to our feet—cheerleaders in tribal full length dresses in school team colors. Evening—candles, radio Senegal, Neutrino.

February 25, 1966: More housework. Pineapple and oranges prepared. Attempt to think about teaching. Slow evening. Make bread. Bug-a-bugs cover walls, attracted by spotlight on trailer. Roger shoots out spotlight. We sweep bugs off walls and out of trailer.

February 26, 1966: Morning—walls covered with striped sessee bugs come to eat bug-a-bugs. New houseboy—Albert Gibson—appears. Taught him the floors. Roger and Albert putty windows. I write course description and ideas for library and book use. Albert and I see man squatting in back scooping sessee bugs into can. (People eat them.) Five or six children come by to collect them in bowls. Albert pauses to refresh, read comic books (*The Silver Surfer*). Asks me why don't we paint our rock candleholders? Albert discusses Vietnam with Roger. Walk through woods to movies—see country devil in straw skirt dance to drums. Stop at green fluorescent lighted bar.

February 28, 1966: Morning, wind, rain—flock of cowbirds going "gock—gock" on front lawn. Rice birds in back. Roger and kitten play. Rain continues on roof.

March 8, 1966: Attempt to begin History of Science class. Spent whole class explaining vocabulary: "system," "classify," "speculate," "observe," "equate"—trying to get class to see likenesses and distinctions. Am I wasting time? Fear that director will take away my science class and give it to gym instructor. Children's Lit—spoke of teaching path from child's world to adult's. Bead story and introduction.

Library work with Mr. Sprague—in conversation he turns out to be teacher and friend to Ralph Ellison. We speak of Tuskeegee Institute, Peace Corps, Ellison. I invite him to dinner. He comes. Henry Notuway visits: Henry knows how to make rice bird slings out of raffa. After Henry leaves, we have steak, green beans and bread. Roger and Mr. Sprague talk long

of Chicago, Negro in U.S., Cassius Clay (perhaps not so much loved by Southern Negroes?), Tuskeegee Institute at Kakata Teacher Training Institute, AmericoLiberians, education, the old days. Neutrino falls asleep on Mr. Sprague's shoulder, then goes outside for the first time to investigate MYSTERIOUS NIGHT. Mr. Sprague is a magnificent man.

March 15, 1966: I develop homesickness hysteria—the weeps. At just the wrong moment Albert arrives—mind snapper. Roger throws out cat—water is off—gas is off. Albert works grimly (lets in cat?). I stare at stony wasteland and jungle in back of house.

March 21, 1966: Newton—what is science? Dolly comes through with Wittgenstein-like science, not closed fact. Neutrino asleep on my lap while I write diary in the john—Neutrino is larger and cattier, has begun adolescence, likes "chop" best of all foods. Nurses on towel, afraid to go outside in daytime. . . . Afternoon arts and crafts, fan, baskets of double palm leaves. Mr. Sprague for dinner—discuss Baldwin, James Brown, old-time entertainers—reads my poetry and enjoys it.

Faculty Meeting

solemn granite move surely
up out of the cave into mirage

      (audio-visual aids)
    we also offer them white gloves
      and flowered hats

the great ambition is to go to the U. S.
there the cars, soap, clothes, canned foods
are for real, firsthand
this is the dumping ground for old goods

almost all the students ask how they can get a
  job
when they get there.

What Mr. Sprague really said was, "When are you going to publish?"

The African trunk: the Peace Corps provides us with a trunk of books to keep us busy. The books I like best include *The Alexandria Quartet* by Lawrence Durrell, *Wand of Noble Wood* by Onuora Nzekwu, *Teacher* by Sylvia Ashton-Warner, *Invisible Man* by Ralph Ellison, *King Solomon's Ring* by Konrad Lorenz, *The Silent Language* by Edward T. Hall, and *Black English* by J. L. Dillard. I've also picked up a copy of James Baldwin's *Giovanni's Room* and William Burrough's *Nova Express* in New York City and a copy of *On the Road* by Jack Kerouac, with a lurid fifties-style paperback book cover, at a Monrovian bookstore.

Sometime near the end of May 1966, I took 40 micrograms of LSD (this sounds like a small dose, but this was Sandoz). I was frightened—and then frightened of subsequent mental sensations that must have been "flashbacks" in weeks following, so frightened that I went to see the Peace Corps doctors in Monrovia. They gave me temporary doses of phenothiazines and shipped me back with Roger to Washington, D.C. I had to leave everything in Kakata behind—worst of all, Albert and Neutrino.

> morning this morning
> came to me with fear
> then I heard
> the voices of people
> drinking coffee together

I was in George Washington University Hospital, in an acute ward with other government employees. Over time I made friends with other patients and was, of course, the editor of the ward 6-B newsletter, publishing patient poetry and prose. The staff didn't know what to do with me because I didn't seem to want to leave. They finally dosed me with phenothiazine on a steady basis, enough I say nowadays "to drop an elephant in its tracks," and sent me back to the Midwest with my mother, to rejoin Roger.

From 1966 to 1969, Roger and I lived in Sarasota, Florida, while Roger taught many of the basic science courses at New College, a new, expensive private liberal arts college where Roger's brother John was a student. Roger had only a B.A., so he was a "tutor," but his lectures (his performance, for example, of the "mating dance of the crickets") were famous and we always had a gang of students at our house, eating spaghetti and fixing motorcycles.

Readings for the New College English seminar they let me sit in on: *A Clockwork Orange* by Anthony Burgess, *The Medium Is the Message* by Marshall McLuhan, and *Magister Ludi* by Hermann Hesse (although I was not really able to read that one until decades later). I was also interested in *Women and Madness* by Phyllis Chesler, *The Bell Jar* by Sylvia Plath, *Asylums* by Erving Goffman, and *The Golden Notebook* by Doris Lessing.

Psychiatrists continued to prescribe phenothiazine for me and prognosticated a dim future for me apart from Roger. I couldn't smile or walk very well and found it difficult to read as a result of the medications. I tended to sleep a lot and had a hard time keeping any job I got. However, I continued to write—to examine metaphysical and personal issues—even though one of my doctors decided my writing was a "symptom of mental illness."

We first lived in a little house on the main drag of Sarasota, across from a glass-blowing shop and a little restaurant called the Mecca—vision of the little spun glass figures in the window and the miniaturized mosque against the iridescent shell-blue sky. Later we moved out onto a key to live in an old estate owned by the college. I loved swimming in the light green water and waking up to the hiss of the dolphins following the fishing boats between the Bay and the Gulf.

My poems were often short portraits of friends, sketches of instants, occasionally metaphysical riddles or succinct metaphors. I wrote "White" when the buildings on the estate were being painted:

White

> the painters paint everything white
> the garage, the outbuildings, the house,
> the compressor inflates the landscape
> like a livid frost and wind
> household periwinkles bow their heads
> to flat scatterings of snow
> silvered leaves like old ladies'
> arrangements of flowers and hair
> But stop them. They are painting the palms
> the grass the sand opaque white
> we move in a world of still white
> and they are painting the sky with the lie

I finally was able to hold a position as a dry cleaner's clerk—then, miraculously, I was able to teach fourth grade successfully in a small Catholic grade school. The principal and other Franciscan teaching sisters were kind and supportive: "I don't care how noisy your room gets. Just shut your classroom door."

My class did well on the general tests at the end of the year, and I had saved enough money to leave my marriage. The school was consolidated into a larger school, making it easier for me to decide to leave Florida for California.

I told my family that I was going into a teacher's credential program at University of California, Berkeley. However, looking back, I see that I never completed the applications. My sister Nancy went out to Berkeley with me, both of us exhilarated—by the intense blue California sky, Tibetan stores, Mexican and Chinese restaurants, hippies, Telegraph Avenue, the Bones Sisters camping on the Navarro River in Mendocino—until she went back to University of Wisconsin, Madison, in the fall of 1969.

By 1970, I was working as a biller and invoicer for wholesalers—by day printing hundreds of invoices, and a few poems, on an IBM 632, by night living in a two-bedroom crash pad in an old house at Shattuck and Ashby. The house had a little yard and trees, rickety stairs, high ceilings, curious wood-framed closets and cupboards (my first room was a large closet with a window and mattress), and odd partitioning of apartments. As many as fifty people moved in and out of our apartment: young drifters from New York and Wisconsin, a few returning veterans of Vietnam. The core group was me, an intellectual hippie man, a visionary woman, and a Mexican-Cherokee man who owned an old school bus. We painted the school bus, of course, and rode in it to Marin County, eating peaches and granola on the bluffs overlooking the Pacific Ocean. At home we shared brown rice and veggies, occasionally with cheese or bacon—the others panhandled for food money while I worked for the rent—and we had family meetings around a circular table in the kitchen. I was older than the others and drank wine and took phenothiazines instead of using psychedelics; I tended to be the person who wiped the honey, orange peels, and Bull Durham off the circular table in the morning.

The crash pad people followed the visionary woman to Maui, so I was left with two puppies and the shambles of the apartment. I put the word out for a "nice couple who weren't into drugs"—a young couple turned up. It turned out that this fifteen-year-old boy and nineteen-year-old girl were not into drugs, because they were on the run and she was expecting a baby. We became a little family and lived with, or near, each other for several years—changing diapers and bottles, picking up toys, working stupid jobs, watching Creature Features and TV reruns, eating licorice and New England boiled dinners, and drinking cola.

Tranquilizers

> tranquil like a ghost of glass
> a single finger of smoke ascending
> she thought about and wrote the past
> what came alive beneath her fingers
> hurt too much. She ripped it up
> and sat again not living
> tranquil like a ghost of glass

I had found a psychiatrist, formerly associated with my Peace Corps training group, who felt that the Peace Corps had been so eager to get me out of Africa that they might have been a bit overzealous in my psychiatric diagnosis and treatment. I asked him to supervise me while I stopped taking phenothiazine and he agreed. I had no psychotic symptoms when I quit; instead, I had energy and could read and move easily again.

I hated being trapped behind a billing machine in fluorescent-lit offices—so I dreamed up a new way to make a living. I advertised as a cleaning woman in the paper and began working, most often for computer analysts and mathematicians—sometimes for disabled persons—and I became a janitor for shops that I picked walking past because I liked their businesses, a health food store, a handmade dress shop. I became a novice gardener with Jim. Jim was a master "organic landscaper gardener"—a big, kind, dark, handsome and spacey older man, who would fix dinner from his garden for me at the end of our work days.

> we sat in the garden's
> sour clover sting
> apple blossom
> in a heart's second stopped
> against blue sky
>
> in memory's next moment
> the grass moved
> the sun slipped
> the stream ran
> by time's run down shack
> I ran
> down childhood's road

However, Jim was in his forties and did not want to live with me or to have more children. At twenty-eight, I was beginning to want my own children and to live with a man again.

I worked for an older woman, Joan, who had raised two children as a working single parent, but was now disabled by spinal disease and struggling to recover her own life from isolation and depression. After I cleaned her house, Joan often fixed steak with Bernaise sauce, and we sat up drinking wine and smoking cigarettes, talking movies, books, politics, men—she'd goad me to find a husband and have kids, publish my writing, teach. . . .

I opened the door of Joan's apartment one afternoon to see Peter slouching in a T-shirt in the hall, cigarette dangling, French gangster style. He was one of Joan's son's pals and "business partners," so I was wary of his interest.

However, one evening, a year later, I was going to hide out baby-sitting my teenaged-mom-friend's baby—but she decided to turn the tables on me, pushing me out of the cozy milk-smelling house to go out myself. Peter was sitting in LaVal's on the north side of Berkeley, blearily drunk, with the saddest and oldest of eyes. When he recognized me and realized I was talking to him, he shook himself into sobriety and went to get cigarettes, wondering, he said later, if I would be gone when he got back.

We drove around for hours in the '59 Jaguar roadster he was restoring—and talked for hours in an all-night restaurant in San Francisco. Peter had one last poker game with his business partners the next day, and we moved in together the following night, buying each other a coffee cup (for him) and a plant (for me).

Peter was an Austrian Canadian, whose father had moved the large family from an endless struggle with poverty in Manitoba to Berkeley in 1960. Peter had gone to Catholic schools, making good grades at first—and had helped his father build houses in Berkeley for sale—but then he had gotten into going to rock concerts at the Fillmore and Winterland and into hustling small business and small cons on the tough edge of west Berkeley.

A frost had killed the eucalyptus trees in the Berkeley Hills in 1972, so Peter and his partners had put together a tree cutting business which was making him $45,000 a year at the age of twenty-three, when I met him. He and I spent money wildly, driving in his Jaguar roadster and going to the most expensive restaurants—he bought me a white fur coat for our first Christmas. I was afraid to suggest buying a house, because he pulled back from marriage. I was thirty; his family, the Schicks, tried to accept Peter living with an older woman.

He liked my age. He liked to chaff me about our first date being the movie *Harold and Maude,* me dressed in Pointer-sister-style thrift store finery and him in sleek polyester slacks and long-sleeved shirt, player-style. I pressured him to stop gambling and to call me if he was out late; he wanted me to stop drinking, to work, and to do a lot of cooking and house-work—he coaxed me to approximate the food in restaurants he liked. Peter was more social than I was, so we had lots of bright, interesting people who hung out at our house for dinner, penny poker, and TV—most especially the young students, Brian and Marilyn.

I wasn't afraid to let Peter read my writing, except that sometimes it would make him cry. My writing opened up and became much more experimental, open, and direct. I wrote more—and longer pieces.

In 1973 we both wanted to move where there were "trees and birdies." We'd had the habit of jumping into the roadster in the middle of the night, driving north and waking up in the Sierras—or in Lake County. We moved to the very small, funky town of Guerneville, where one of his best friends had moved. We found a little group of cottages and swept in, me in my fur coat and Peter with his cars. Glenda and Frank, old river hippies, were watching, heehawing with laughter, from the window of their front cabin.

The little group of cottages had been put together by two old Russian brothers near the Russian church on Orchard Avenue—small, irregular little wooden cabins, sleepy in the mist and late sun. We began to slow our pace, sitting with Glenda and Frank watching the sun set behind the redwood-covered hills—waking up to apple blossoms outside the tiny windows of our cabin in spring, opening our door to little trick-or-treaters, coming home to Christmas lights twinkling in fog.

But there were few jobs there then. Peter and his buddy couldn't establish a business hustle, although they struggled and argued constantly.

October Wind

> the bird is gone
> one cat brought it in
> one cat took it under the house

he is gone suddenly to doctor
an old GTO dead on the road
like Lazarus struck dead twice
he leaves bedazzled in his red cap
carrying a tool case lightly as a
    lunch box
[I like cat bereft or bird bereft be
    back be back]

I tried to stop them with the miracle of the
    voices of the birds
all crying one voice to the other
finches starlings blackbirds
it was not the cats but the hunters
I heard their guns all afternoon
& each race of birds
sings the hunted's song doppled stricken
    screaming

each feather catches me
I sweep along the floor
my broom does not direct it
it flies & catches me
my mind stopped in its
    floating
given over to the wind
I do not stop the present's
    screaming

In 1975, I had to have six uterine fibroids removed, and the doctor warned me, "If you want kids, you better have them now." I got home from applying for General Assistance after the surgery to find Peter sitting in a dark, wrecked cabin, his face beaten in. Peter had gotten beaten up by a truckful of country men because he sold their seventeen-year-old girl cousin a car with an oil leak—it had blown a head gasket in a few miles. We went to the city on the bus and stayed with our friends, Brian and Marilyn, feeling despair.

After I'd run off to Los Angeles—showing a little independence—Peter arranged for us to go back to the river and eventually agreed that we could try to get me pregnant, although he felt hesitant.

His face was suffused with joy, however, when I finally got pregnant a year later. Brian and Marilyn let us camp at their house again, so that I could be near my magic doctor in Berkeley and feel safer about a possible high-risk delivery. I tore trying to push Lani out quickly because her heartbeat had slowed—then I was looking into the most intense bright little eyes I had ever seen—seeming to come from the far end of the universe. Peter drove us north

as I nursed her, lying in the back of a station wagon full of flowers.

Glenda said that when we brought the baby home to the river, we "acted like animals, snarling and keeping everybody away." We had no money for food or laundry, and I had a hard time sitting up to nurse her—she seemed to eat every twenty minutes, twenty-four hours a day.

morning noon and night
(lying in my arms a sense of death diminished)

on my shoulder
forehead wrinkled, her eyes
seem sunken, button bright
she hangs upon my pockets
and my hair, scuffles up my body
in the bed till she has overshot
the mark and cries

Peter held her to comfort her, did laundry, cooked, and sold his restored '59 silver Alfa for a third of its value. He would tease her into "talking" by spinning the pinwheel on her basinette only if she "talked." But he could not make enough money hustling cars. He got his father to buy us a house, but then I was isolated from my friends because I still could not drive.

Peter and I spent all our days together, working, laughing, arguing—drying apples from the trees at the new house. He planted a huge vegetable garden, grapes, herbs, berries, put in a lawn by hand, repaired the house, played with Lani and the neighborhood children, letting them mess with his tools and wonderful junk that he collected, building Lani a slide. . . .

But Peter was beginning to have serious drug problems, staying up all night, sleeping for days, sometimes depressed or enraged. I was turning into a shrew. I began to try to leave Peter, but it took years—going away and coming back.

In 1981, we had our big beautiful son Will ("the Potato," Lani called him, "Why does everyone want to see this Potato?"). I had ruptured a disc in my back during the pregnancy; but, by the time Will was born—I was working in the kitchen until I was ready to have him—the hospital wanted to release us the morning of the birth.

When Will was still a baby, the night of the full lunar eclipse, my father called to tell me that he had gotten a diagnosis of lung cancer. I quit smoking immediately—but this did nothing to help my poor parents. Within a few years, in spite of a valiant struggle, my father was dead.

The children and I often stayed at the cabins near Frank and Glenda during these hard times:

observation on time

in the silence
I heard knocking
I rushed outside
there were apples dropping
on the roof

While my world with Peter was collapsing in on itself, my contacts with other people were beginning to expand and my ideas about myself were changing.

Around 1979, while walking Lani in her stroller in Peter's neighborhood, I'd met a group of artists, musicians, and writers who congregated in a house down the street. I published

a poem and an essay, my first adult publications, in their journal *Metalink*. Two poets in the group, Jennie Orvino and Wiley Jadavega, asked me to read with them in the "Garbo's" poetry series. It was the first time I read in public: my arms were shaking so that I could barely see the pages.

I had also gotten more involved with the town of Guerneville when Lani and Will were babies and small children: going to an infant development class; playing with the River Childcare moms and kids and Activities Director Michael Fisher at Kindergym; going to the Parent Rap Group; and participating in a co-operative parent nursery school. We had played with Deborah and her kids Aura, Elijah, and Mosie in Peter's neighborhood, and with Timi and Lilia in Glenda and Frank's neighborhood. Now we got to know Nonie and her kids Lee, Nova, Spartacus, and Homer—and Kathy and her kids Travis and Melissa—families we would be close to for the next twenty years, women who would be my friends for the next twenty years.

*

Erickson with second husband, Peter Schick,
Christmas, 1974

January 19, 1983: The Parent Rap group people are going to keep journals. Well, my sister coughed up my diaphragm, a lot of important children's clothes, sox, nail scissors, and new Chinese gifts, including this terrific journal. The faint suggested pictures on the pages of flounders, ships, wild birds suggest to me beyond the dull journal assignment the voyage of fairy tales and imagination. No reason my journal can't cover a few extra trips. . . .

March 28, 1983: First poetry reading with Simone O. and Joanne Kyger. Bob Kaufman recites "Kingfishers" and "Alfred Prufrock"— "Kingfishers" croak, wonderful diction. The "c" sound ("k") becomes rocks in river. Lynne Wildey, his old lady, reads feathery endless tumbles of mind-wandering Zen and psychedelphia.

April 11, 1983: Second time. Howard Hart— old-timer, jazz, eclectic—asks me to read short poem again:

I am satisfied silent
but I am filled by storymakers
I laugh at chanting bells
they paint on trees and hills
to shake them off, shake them off
I walk alone

Maureen Hurley (California Poets in Schools), Pat Nolan (male ego humor), Bob Jones (clear imagistic poetry), Lynne Wildey. . . .

Peter arrives to hold baby. Later, makes a perfect sandwich. Peter gets finewise burned-out, good a hair too long.

February 1, 1984: Pat Nolan's class is scrubbed.

> the movement
> in the crystal ball
> clock bell
> imperceptible
> the glacier
> the ticking

*

I had made a commitment to try to read at open mike at every poetry reading. I'd had singing lessons in high school and had sung folk songs and Bach at Swarthmore, which had taught me to "open my throat in public." Now I tuned in on the silent reaction of the audience (I told a friend that poetry readings were like auctions) and the way that my work sounded and felt aloud. I could use tone, depth, cadence, pauses, and silence. I thought about how I looked and moved, wearing slacks and white shirts to be dramatic and slightly masculinized, to be taken more seriously. I rehearsed at home, even using a tape recorder.

In the '80s, I trained with California Poets in the Schools poets Maureen Hurley, Mike Tuggle, and Susan Kennedy, watching them

"With my baby daughter, Lani," 1978

present workshops in the schools and eventually presenting my own series of grade school workshops. Maureen had a firecracker string of techniques to set off student writing, mixing in calligraphy and photographic images. She was eager to initiate projects and bring people together, as well as to promote herself, spending years building California Poets in the Schools and the Russian River Writers' Guild in Sonoma County.

When Pat Nolan's "modern poetry class" folded, Maureen thought that I should ask him to teach a smaller class. I didn't understand then the "significance" of his background with the New York poets in the St. Mark's Poetry Project, or with the Iowa writers, or with Andrei Codrescu on the river, as Maureen did, but I recognized something in his writing akin to mine.

Pat ended up teaching a very small class—me. I hadn't read anything more modern than Auden, except for black and feminist poets. Now Pat and I were discussing Donald Allen and George F. Butterick's anthology, *The Postmoderns*, while Will sat on my lap clinging to me.

*

Pat Nolan's original syllabus: field trips to small press and used bookstores.

I carry this out geometrically. Wherever I go, I go directly to the local Twice Told Books/ Cody's/ Copperfield's/ Treehorn/ Small Press Traffic/ Small Press Distribution/ Salvation Army/ Goodwill/ Flea Market/ Friends of the Library booksale—poetry reading—and spend my last $3/ $15/ twenty-five cents on the thinnest and most homemade book I can find. My favorite scores are Kathy Acker's *Empire of the Senseless* in a free box and "uncorrected galley proofs" of Haruki Murakami's *Wild Sheep Chase* at a thrift store.

As years go by, and I become editor of *tight*, poets send me copies of their latest chapbooks and journals—or favorite books and journals—and I become librarian to hundreds of skinny books, occasionally dropping some off at a coffee house near Santa Rosa Junior College.

*

Pat took a look at my work, griping that it wasn't typed, but not about the fact that the poems were embedded in raging journals. He said that he himself ranted on in his journals until eventually something useable appeared. He gave me a few "assignments"—such as list poems, or poems in columns showing simultaneous levels of experience and consciousness. He wanted me to try a "cut up" poem—I responded with a "flip book" poem, generated by watching a Nova TV program on the nature of time. Each line of the poem was in flip-book style, repeating layers of the whole poem:

After Hours

In timelessness
    a memory
In empty space
    a radiance
    remembering
    the tapestry
    of eons' light

Pat: "Well, you can write, but you sure can't cut with scissors."

He was also assistant teacher at Will's nursery school then (much cutting with scissors). Soon, however, Pat left to work for the forestry service. He had already let go of my classes. He didn't feel that I needed more skill in reading or writing poetry, but in the years that followed, he's told me about new bookstores, photocopying establishments, good places to publish, possible contacts, special readings, poetry world gossip. He's never let me retreat from the feudal warring society of poets: "You haven't gotten *Poetry Flash* yet?" "That always happens—forget it." "You don't have to let them change a poem."

      the library
where
the spirits live in leaves
where
the field rumbles with that golden dust
where
children play

where

In 1985, the kids and I were living in a cabin in downtown Guerneville, across from the mortuary and next to a resort, down the hill from St. Elizabeth's, the fire station, and the library. I began to take meals over to our ninety-six-year-old neighbor, Grover Kohler, who became "my job" and kind of part of our family. My friend Nonie taught me to drive my old Datsun 510 so I could get to Russian River Writers' Guild poetry readings and so I could chauffeur Grover in "my machine."

There were other kids in the neighborhood, and Tom Printy and Tony Garcia opened Coffee Bazaar a few blocks away. I felt a sense of the physical world layered over the spirit world in Guerneville:

Sidhe

a mask on midnight
colors bright
blond iceland pony mane

the children ride
3 on a bike
blond/black headed

the sunset tunnels down the darkened hills
like wheat

hot
the wind feels like the ocean
cold

weave for me these daisies
cafe flowers
clever
how clever I was

to find a little village near cafe society
when winter drags in
trailing skirts of ghosts in trees

the harvest trails along the road
black walnuts hulled in green
apples yellow leaves
they drop their apronfuls

& we've kept earth's keep a century
the sweetest kiss I tasted

the old old man sits at my gate in terror
separated from the world
surrounded by a fire he says

      Sidhe
they are coming up yes
from the west
sky like sapphire
light bells ringing
& the drumming horses
like the sun
they're black

I'll deck my doorway & my children with red
  thread

On February 17, 1986, Peter called from Santa Rosa to wake us. The Russian River was lapping at our front steps. I had to scramble to get the kids and car up the hill, to have a neighbor carry Grover out, to wade in after the pet rat, to canoe in after the cat. Lani at first thought it would be like other floods we had been through; then, she wept bitterly in St. Hubert's Hall up the hill, watching chemically toxic, septic, whirling brown water filling her loft upstairs in our cabin, knowing all her toys were going under. We were homeless for months, with hundreds of other river people, until our property manager found us a rental. Peter washed the teddy bears and Grover's paintings, but I hadn't had the stamina to clean or save our stuff, our photos, my books—except that I stood out on the deck of our rental cottage and ironed each page of my writing to dry and disinfect it, the blurred pages fed to the fireplace.

We were able to return to our homes downtown, but I was afraid of the next rainy season:

the cards and the coins foretell
their futurism seems short
I can't remember yesterday
except to sit in the same room
or unsolicited memory a slide movement clarity

meanwhile
my daughter is watering
the garden in her leotard
the pale rat rides on her shoulder looking back
the rat's nose is
high and quivers in the air
the rat's eyes have
a personal expression
the rat's whiskers
vibrissae
the rat's mouth

a dismayed moue

My mother was able and willing to buy a house for us above flood line. I found one on the border of the Monte Rio and Guerneville school districts, on the margin between the redwoods and oak scrub hills. I had to leave Grover and the easy sociability of being downtown, but we were secure and safe.

My poetry was taking different forms: condensed, concrete capsules; fragmented stream of consciousness; parallel thought and experience; and the mythologizing of personal experience, cutting connective syntax:

The author with her children, Will and Lani, about 1989

"Discussing a 'cover shoot' with 'cover girl' sculptress Abigail Swaim," 1992

I'm also your midnight fool fatality
the hanged man fool devil
in the dark hour while you are working
pentacostal
my body slung like low moans
the bags of great desire
the sobs of softening flesh
lays on the bed
the fruit unwanted in the orchard

but the bees that eat out the eyes of the
   mortality
and the ants that harvest the overweening syrup
honey gold the lion the ass
the Samson brought low
I my chariot is down
and I bend my knee
to my useless courses

When I read at the California Poets in the
Schools conference at Asilomar in October 1986,
I felt blank air. I needed to work for a more
"experimental" audience. My work was starting
to be published, in Ralph Smith's *Greenfuse,* in
the Santa Rosa Junior College *First Leaves,* and
in Sonoma State University's *Mandala.* Using

the newsletter *Poetry Flash* and Len Fulton's
*International Directory of Little Magazines and Small
Presses,* I soon sent work to small press magazines all over the United States and began to
have the private excitement of acceptances in
my post office box.

In February 1988, I self-published my first
small chapbook, *Queen of Diamonds,* using the
book design and stitching methods I'd learned
in Maureen's workshops, compiling a few older
poems and a few new ones. I also began working as an aide at the Writing Lab in Santa
Rosa Junior College's English Department. I had
contact with many instructors and students and
was very glad, but this semester was interrupted
by surgery. I had neglected a large uterine fi-
broid until it was so large there was danger of
malignancy. I was lucky; the tumor was benign:

souvenir

ovary hung in the no space
of the abdomen
like the star
alone in the sky

dust of the exploded galaxy
gone.

            the quazar
            on the tv set
            in the silent room
is that whisper
after

is that color
of the window
when the first birds'

            song

In the year that followed, I graded high
school and junior college papers, worked at a
Guerneville daycare, and wrote the poems I
included in my second chapbook, *Defense of Rose
of Sharon:*

In Defense of Rose of Sharon

I work at the daycare where daffodils stand
    like thoughts
or telephones, my father said

what in the name of the devil is the purpose
of this family that lets its babies die?

she wants to start something new apart from
    this family
looking inward she feels a liquid

5 high school girls compared the characters
    of Ma to Rose of Sharon
in exactly the same words   noble//to
    selfish
Rose of Sharon had the temerity to want milk
for herself and her baby

I brought the high school teacher these
    papers and my comments
he blinked and said "well just what is the
    trouble?"
I had stayed up all night grading 60 papers
    so I burst out
"they seem to think she was a selfish twit"
he said, "well we did discuss it in class"
"and after all she did change"
apologetically   for this selfish twit
but after all   she did change   she did
    change   she did change
so that her milk did not go for that selfish
    baby
but was poured back into that starving man
that America that eats her bones her dreams
    her babies

and she Rose of Sharon has passed the first
    test   the first exam
in the school of Ma
whose hazel eyes must have seen a hundred
    dead babies
the family that she's saving is her sons, her
    men,
her starving men, her imprisoned men, her
    crazy runoff men
her men who unionize, her men who prove
    they help by
doing women's work   they salt the meat

Rose of Sharon never asks again for milk
and I am working at the daycare
I graded this man's papers for 60 dollars
I am watching 12 children for the mothers
    that work
the children are picked up by Ma and Rose
    of Sharon

Pat thought the content might be too political for the times, but the thin book was a
finalist in University of California Berkeley's
Occident Press competition.

At the Santa Rosa Junior College, I was
stimulated by working in the classroom with
two writer-teachers: Kay Renz, who employed a
vast array of techniques to help specifically learning disabled adults make a transition into the
mainstream English program—and Joyce Griffin,
who used creative writing to teach language skills.
Both Joyce and Kay let me participate fully in
their classrooms. I wrote constantly now, in the
margins of textbooks, on envelopes—when the
students were writing. Kay complained to the
students, "She writes poems right here in class
and then she goes and gets them published!"

"twing'kel" was based on board work Kay
was doing on short vowel sounds—the class was
suggesting words and sentences—I had brought
up the issue of "sentence fragments" with "After running out into the street." My later arrangement of the words and phrases followed
an inner associative pattern—and was published
eventually in John Bennett's *Lost and Found Times:*

twing'kel twing'kel

hat eggs pit ox gut//embryo gym sky

voluptuous
woman
                              I ate.

gangly
boy
                              he walked.

After running out into the street.

sky sky sky// voluptuous
falling down

I   he walked
gangly boy   eggs pit
ox gut

embryo

sky.

Pat wanted me to start a magazine, to get connected with other writers, and to establish credibility as a writer. I started *tight* magazine with a pilot issue in 1989: local writers, Santa Rosa Junior College students, and one young poet from my grade school CPITS workshop.

Within months I met a dynamic young performance poet and nationally published illustrator, Mark Neville. I sent copies of the second issue of *tight,* bound with Mark's cover, to poet-editors on both Mark's and Pat's mailing lists. *tight* was off the ground.

Starting in 1990, Mark and I often performed together and went to poetry readings in the Bay Area and Sonoma County—readings for Richard Benbrooke's magazine, *Tomcat,* for William Talcott's magazine, *Carbuncle,* as well as Douglas Powell's sophisticated Sweetlife Cafe series in Santa Rosa. We read my poems "Baruch Spinoza meets the cat goddess" and "wall of sound" as duets:

Baruch Spinoza meets the Cat Goddess

    Dei
amor intellectualis   disappointed in love,
don't make me laugh   his sour quips already
                        suggested
the kisses of the kitten a tender heart
bright eyes like dawn   that reaches out
                           to God
voices of the plant and   through the mediaeval
                       guise of
        animal   Folly, Passion,
                       Maya,
and also the   known as darkened
                       death
    wonderful void   and the dusky raiment
that the stars   of the skeleton
    exploding pass into who comes to visit all
the shimmering black

When Mark would arrive at our house with deli sandwiches, it meant the fun started. I had a houseful of artists and performers. My thirteen-year-old daughter Lani was already producing a series of covers for *tight,* the "tight" women—tough comix-style women who wrapped around the cover so that it looked good open or closed—some readers expected refined "arty" covers, but I noticed that the "tight" women always sold magazines.

I began to work and play with text and graphics, page and book design. Nonie, a gifted painter and photographer, was willing to do several "cover shoots" for *tight.* She designed a computer-melted-photograph cover with me as the "cover girl" and also produced a beautiful true cover shoot with my sculptor and writer friend Abigail Swaim as the "cover girl."

I had met Edward Mycue at a Carbuncle reading; I was honored when Ed asked me to publish a book in his Norton Coker Press poetry series—and then delighted when I realized I could design the book myself. I already had a project in mind. I had seen a Book of Hours when I was fourteen in France. I wanted to use that structure to fix the spiritual in the cycle of the seasons and life. I asked Mark to design the cover (referring him to Hieronymus Bosch), some illustrations, and illuminations of some of the letters in poems. I also asked Lani to try for some illustrations. I organized the book after the traditional model: the first section was a calendar of seasonal poems; the second section presented "women's concerns" in a parallel to the "prayers to the Virgin"; and the final section related to death, as the traditional Book of Hours closed with "prayers for the dead." The project was ambitious, but I felt that the book finally gave a good sampling of vivid short work and longer poems; that it addressed important concerns, including the war in Iraq; and that it showcased Lani's and Mark's art as well.

"it's the magic spell" from *Book of Hours* was a collage of sense experience in an afternoon at the daycare where I worked. The children were playing with sand and a hose—and theirs are the voices in this opening excerpt:

(1) it's the magic spell (I think it already
    broke
but they did not break it) granular/ leaf/ not
    magic/
dormers above the/ ding/ dong/ dong/ sthat's
    too
much sand wind who put the wet sand in/
    can't

get magic/ I put the wet sand in/ airplane
   drone//
rusk rusk// cicada// wet godderly sand/ wet
gobbly sand/ wet gobbly sand/ / I get magic
   you
guys just get the dirt// I get magic too// just
   us 2
get magic// ding dong ding ding// rumble
         look up purple morning glories collect
            & the
bees & butterflies return the hose is gone
put in all the gobbly sand we're gonna make
magic cause we're mean witches no we're good
witches but we teach magic

Both *tight* and the *Book of Hours* got strong
reviews in *Factsheet 5*. Mark had subscribed to
a sampling of magazines and to *Factsheet 5* for
me for my birthday—but, sadly, I was still getting the magazines after we had parted the
ways, our strong wills in conflict.

There were islands of tranquility in the disturbance. I was braver in writing longer, looser
poems—hearing and seeing what Jack and Adele
Foley were doing, as well as reading sequences
by John M. Bennett, Jake Berry, and Jim Leftwich.
My post office box was full of hundreds of
other poets' new works for *tight,* month after
month. I was researching Japanese linked verse,
renga—getting notions about associative word
values and "movement" in larger writing structures. One evening I got to collaborate with
old *renga*-by-mail hands Tundra Wind and Pat
Nolan in composing the "Plum Blossom Renga"—
kind of a six-hour mind-meld experience—around
Tundra's dining room table.

I didn't have the energy for the Poetry
Marathons in my backyard and driving to endless readings anymore. My kids were beginning
to grow up—Lani was a little defiant; Will was
a little clownish. In 1992 and 1993, I worked
in the English Department and the Learning
Skills Department at the junior college, as well
as grading papers for four instructors. I was
passing out at night coming home, blood pressure elevated. Because of delayed paychecks,
part of the time I couldn't even afford lunch
at work and part of the time we had more
money than ever before. I was a good untrained
tutor with learning disabled adults, but I found
interaction with all these instructors and spe-
cialists very stressful. I finally ended up having
an accident with Will in the car. I decided
not to drive any more and not to carry such a
heavy workload. Now I was going to have to

give up sodium, exercise, and struggle to lose
weight.

*

March 17, 1994: Tim the Invisible Goat's
Birthday. I'm thinking of Mom baking the cake
with the green frosting and coconut icing for
Tim the Invisible Goat's Birthday long ago.

I now understand that teenaged children
are the ones who change their minds about
major life decisions every two days and take
such long showers that the breadwinner of the
family has to take martial arts and assertiveness
training to get into the shower for two minutes at 6:15 A.M. when said breadwinner's bus
is leaving down the hill at 6:45. This is the
case unless said children are out and about
with their buddies making tree forts in other
people's yards, concocting gunpowder, picking
fights with Santa Rosa police over food giveaways (punk sponsored food giveaways are always illegal), watching screaming musicians till
wee hours or being screaming musicians till
the wee hours, sitting up and talking in laundry rooms with dear buddies, smoking cigarettes
and drinking endless cups of coffee, having fights
with best friends, cutting classes, riding their
bikes late at night and trying not to wear bike
helmets and getting spotted by Mom riding home
from work on the bus, getting detentions—if
children are engaged in these activities, they
need not bathe for days ("crusty").

Meantime, I've graded five zillion trillion
journals, quizzes, and papers, written an NEA
grant proposal, and produced the Brownstein
book and another *tight.*

*

I was becoming more aware of the impact
of "language" poetry on modern poetry. I became friends with the major poet David Bromige,
making a special effort to get to his readings
and ones that he recommended, tickled by his
professionalism in performance and his trick-
ster wit in language. Hanging out with Steve
Tills and David Bromige, I got to see and hear
major "language" and "postlanguage" poets. My
favorite of all these sophisticated writers has always been Cydney Chadwick, the satiny-dark-subtle
writer of prose poems and editor of Avec Press.

*"Clowning around with Lani and Will
at a wedding," 1995*

*

I begin to read Charles Bernstein's *Content's Dream*—then, Chomsky, Lenneberg, Lakoff. I call my first husband, Roger Peters, who suggests Donald Griffin. I read Roger's *Mammalian Communication, Animal Thinking and Animal Minds* by Donald Griffin, *Origins Reconsidered* by Richard Leakey, *Left brain, right brain* by Sally P. Springer and Georg Deutsch, and *The Chemistry of Conscious States* by J. Allan Hobson. I get to try a family "experimental writing workshop" as a means of developing language skills for one of the kids, and I continue to work with college students with specific learning disabilities. I must continue to think of poetry as "transmission of global brain experience" rather than as play with syntax. I publish reviews in *Taproot Reviews* and short essays on documentary and the poetics in *Chain* and *Juxta*.

*

Edward Mycue encouraged me to design more books for Norton Coker Press. In 1995, I made a retrospective collection of my work which responded to myth, folktale, other cultures, and other artists' works: African experi-

ences, Lebanese folktale, the Arabian Nights, haiku, Shakespeare, Greek myth, Kurosawa, Baudelaire, and de Nerval. The book's title *TraduXion* was a word in my mind for crossing/translations. The poem I liked best in the collection was the most direct transmission of mental experience—a walk down my street—my neighbor's tree blossoming, a bell hanging in it—the osprey climbing in the sky above—the spirit of the tree (the Japanese folktale "tree spirit" of my childhood)—the myth of Orpheus and his dead Eurydice—the association of the dead and forget-me-nots—the effort to communicate thought progression:

orfeo

axis   upright   overblown
skin envelope   breathing in & out
waking   contiguous sense
convey parallelograms   shifting solutions
choice of step
bargain with antiquity

                              animalism forgotten
& the rest forgetting
can I show you   forward lineaments
cannot draw   secondary motion
through the darkness   million striking leaves
          spears of bay
to where the trees break   to the vista
          sky
                    of sun
the fish hawk
          climbs

from   the tumbling mountain
dishevelled earth
          the ranks of the dead
spectral forget-me-nots   out of
compost   flesh moldering
cold breath
     electric

shattering flowers   below
a tree of flowers   light dim
stillness in the cone of petals
                         bell
                              hanging
silent white green light
                              a bee
              spirit canopy
the girl of the tree   puts her finger to
her lips

Now I was ready to present an entire chapbook in this direct way—and to allow it to move in an integrated progression. In 1997,

Norton Coker published my third chapbook, *Jane Eyre in the Forest*. *Jane Eyre in the Forest* was written entirely in 1996 and 1997, in the atmosphere of Bronte's *Jane Eyre* and films such as Rappeneau's version of *Horseman on the Roof*. The poems used pattern and space on the page to set patterns of thought and sound—the experiences move through a casual beginning, daily experiences at home, on the bus, at the junior college—through disturbance and nightmare, walking in the mountains near my house in the fire season—to some quieter resolution:

                          house on fire

transfiguration   trans
            substantiation

behind   the windows an
                    inconsequential
                    sudden
                    instantaneous
        the whole house goes   up
        in an instant
            liquefaction   sil
                    houette   the frame
            pelvis   contains
            fire in   window frame
            dark walls   & shutters
            melting   furnishings
        the screen   the bones
        of thighs   a tripod
        of fire we
                are alike &
                unlikeable   arrogant
        we ride like
        aristocrats   lost souls
        who have not forgotten

            the bones   the frame
                in overeating calm
                in placidity   we
            are the wind
                    we burn
                    cold streaks out in
                    the high trees   &
            we are that which
                looks   through
            the occurrence

                    I think
                the feminist necessities
                have become   my life &
            freedom   but what makes
        me dangerous   is
        you who

        I burn &
        I live with a strength
    that supersedes
            a mark   on the landscape
                a will
                    that will   suddenly
            make nakedness
        the opening   eyes
                    reveal a melting hell
            an explosion

                    what's natural
                eats   the furnishings
            the bell &   the fabrics
        fall away   in a river

1997: Will is now an actor and musician and in high school. Lani is at Reed College. I'm a shelver at the library and an aide in the junior college English Department. I'm starting to think about writing prose.

"My Joan Wilder fantasy," I say to Will.

"I'm scared," says Will.

BIBLIOGRAPHY

Poetry:

Queen of Diamonds (self-published), 1988.

Defense of Rose of Sharon, Occident Press, 1989.

Book of Hours of Jeanne de l'avenier, Norton Coker, 1991.

TraduXion, Norton Coker, 1995.

Jane Eyre in the Forest, Norton Coker, 1997.

Contributor of poems and short prose works to numerous periodicals, including *Anomaly 4* (an audio magazine), *Chain, East and West Literary Quarterly, First Leaves, Juxta, Poetry USA, Sonoma Mandala Literary Review, Taproot Reviews* (essays), *Texture, Women's Voices,* and the e-mail publication *The Experioddicist.* Contributor of poetry to anthologies *A Stone's Throw* and *Sonoma County Poets Collection II.* Founder and editor of *tight* magazine.

Mary Fabilli

1914-

A LITERARY LIFE

My last name in Italian is spelled Fabiilli (pronounced Fa-BYI-li). I was baptized Amalia Elisa Fabiilli, but we children dropped an "i" from the middle so that in the United States we became Fabilli.

Pacentro (center of peace) is a little village in the mountains of Abruzzo in Italy, east of Rome. The village lies opposite the Maiella in the Apennines and not far from the Gran Sasso, a high peak in Italy. I think Christ had the Gran Sasso in mind when He said to Peter, "Thou art rock and on this rock I will build my church," for, of course, Gran Sasso means Great Rock. Besides it's not far from Rome, and that's where Peter established his See, the Papal Court.

I believe that Italy was the original Garden of Eden (and still is), until Satan tempted Eve and she tempted Adam, and they disobeyed God, and He chased them out of Italy (to North Africa probably), where they had to practice agriculture by the sweat of their brows, and it must have been quite an effort being, as they were, so close to the Sahara desert. This is all speculation to which I am entitled, for I am a poet, though very minor I confess, and I stick to the truth as much as possible even as I roam through the volcanic, limitless Apennines.

There my parents were born and both in the same village. My father belonged to the land-owning peasant class, and my mother to the artisan class. Her father made useful and ornamental things out of copper and iron. He did not make gold jewelry. It was in Sulmona nearby that the goldsmiths practiced this art. The Roman poet Ovid came from Sulmona in the valley, and he must have taken long walks up the mountain to Pacentro when he wanted to write about nymphs or minor goddesses. My cousin, Mario Fabiilli, born in Pacentro, also writes about mythical and attractive young women, for he too is a poet. At other times he writes religious poems or those about being far from his native land when he

Mary Fabilli, 1997

was trying to earn a living in Canada. He quickly returned to Italy, and now lives in Chieti with his wife. They go to Pacentro in the summer for it's much cooler in the mountains, and his four grown children join them for their August vacation.

My father used to tell us about the "iena" which came down from the higher peaks to eat little children who had disobeyed their parents and wandered far from home. In the morning nothing was left of them except the little feet in their shoes. The lesson was to stick close to home, especially when it got dark outside. Since then I haven't strayed far from home wherever it might be. I never did find out what kind of animal the "iena" was (not a hyena—more like a tiger), something quite hungry and ferocious. It's too late to ask my father now. He is buried in the cemetery near Delano, California, which is a long way from Pacentro.

I do know that there is a big national park in Abruzzo full of wild animals and lots of "ienas" no doubt. Tourists are beginning to explore the region, but I would not advise it. My father was a great storyteller and all his stories were convincing.

He also taught me to read Italian, when we were living in Jeanette, Pennsylvania, and I was about three years old. He was reading *Les Miserables* by Victor Hugo and pointed out the words as he read them. I became very depressed when we learned about Cossette hoisting a bucket of water according to the illustration. I can still see her big eyes and curly hair, her cap, the thin arms, and the huge bucket. She had a very pathetic expression on her face. That's how I learned to read Italian and not French. I don't remember how I learned to read English, maybe my sister Josephine taught me before I entered the first grade. She knew everything but was not always eager for my company, sometimes not at all, especially when she was with her next-door neighbor, Josephine Everly.

Father, Vincenzo Fabiilli, 1930

They were great friends and of the same age, and corresponded when we landed on a farm near Delano, at which time she sent Jo a subscription to the *Ladies' Home Journal* where we learned more about the Protestant view of life, quite different from that of Italian Catholics. My parents didn't know we were acquiring heretical ideas along with American popular culture.

When my father was a young man in Italy, he and two of his brothers came to the United States to earn money so they could acquire more bits of land in the Pacentro countryside. They were what you would call today legal immigrants, recruited by Rockefeller agents in Italy to work in the coal mines of Colorado or the coke ovens of northern New Mexico. They preferred laboring above ground, so chose the coke ovens of Gardiner, not far from Raton. They made coke out of coal, lived frugally and saved their money and went back to Italy, maybe going back and forth several times across the continent and the Atlantic Ocean. When my father had earned enough money, he married my mother and left her in Pacentro when he returned to work in New Mexico. He then went back and brought her with him, and they lived in the company town of Gardiner, where I and my sister Lili were born about three years apart. Josephine had been born in Italy. When she was about one year old, my mother had a son whom she named Louis, but he died soon after. When I was about one, she had another son also named Louis, but he too died. They had been baptized soon after their birth and went straight to heaven. It's strange to think that two family members whom I can't see are disembodied sinless souls enjoying the Beatific Vision these many years; while we, sin-soiled, struggle here below, not knowing what the future will be, but hoping to rejoin them, if not immediately after our deaths, hopefully through the purgatorial fires. What are they like, I wonder, these two souls with the same name?

St. Catherine of Siena used to talk about the beauty of souls in the state of grace, so they must be resplendent as well as much aware of us; watching over us, praying for us. My father and mother are both dead and united in heaven with them. It will not be long before we five, Josephine, Lili, Virginia, Albert, and I, follow them, and hopefully enjoy the same perfect peace.

At the Last Judgment our souls will be united to our bodies and I will be able to see my brothers with my own eyes and they will see us with bodily eyes, while now they see us in God. It is all very wonderful to think about and to believe while still wandering in the dark night of faith.

My father's name was Vincenzo Fabiilli, and my mother's name was Giacinta Pone. They both had Christian first names, those of saints, for that was then the custom with Roman Catholics. In those days they did not use first names like Butch or Tiffany. I don't know what is the style since Vatican II and the new regulations regarding baptism.

It was only recently that I read the life of St. Hyacinth, after whom my mother was named. What a very remarkable evangelist, of whom the Fundamentalists of this country would be proud! He was called the Apostle of the North (north of Rome, not north of Berkeley), and he preached the gospel in Poland, Prussia, Lithuania, Scandinavia, the Balkans, and Russia, and died peacefully in 1257 at the age of seventy-two.

My father was named after Vincent of Saragossa, or Vincent de Paul, or Vincent Ferrer, or Vincent Palotti or Vincent Strambi—all saints who protected him throughout his life. Vincent must have been a popular name in Italy, France, Spain, and the Spanish dominions. One of my University of California-Berkeley friends is named Vincent. His father was from Sweden and his mother from Latin America. He spells his name Vicente.

After I was born on February 16, 1914, I was named Amalia in honor of an obscure Spanish saint whom I haven't found in a dictionary of saints. As I grew up I came to the conclusion that Amalia was not a suitable name in America because people pronounced it "Amollya," quite disgusting, so I told my sister Jo I wanted another name. This was in Colorado, long before I went to school. She said, "What do you want, Angelina or Mary?" After a bit of reflection I chose Mary, thank goodness, so I have been Mary ever since. Years later, when I was confirmed, I chose this name. This was in Delano, California.

My sister Virginia was born in Sopris, Colorado, the site of which town is now at the bottom of a lake, where a dominating rooster tried to climb our backs and crow. He was an unholy terror. We also had mild-mannered chickens and mice. After Virginia grew up, she became a Sister of Social Service and now lives in a convent in Oakland, not far from Berkeley.

It was after Colorado that we moved to Jeanette, Pennsylvania, where my father worked in a glass factory with Italian and Polish immigrants, and where my brother Albert was born in 1920. He

survived and turned out to be a saint on earth, looking after my mother in her old age until she died in 1977. He now, with Lili, supervises the care of my sister Josephine, who lives in Santa Clara, California. She can't remember the title of her own Ph.D. thesis. When she left Dominican College and University of California-Berkeley (U.C.Berkeley) as a librarian, she spent many years working for the State Department and the Pan American Union establishing libraries in Latin America. It was after this that she got her Ph.D. at the University of Southern California, then taught Spanish and French in Dominican College in San Rafael, and finally retired. I found out from a friend of hers, who also studied at USC, that her thesis was on the subject of Baltasar Gracian, S.J., who wrote *El Criticon*. Another good friend, Camille, is going to try and borrow this thesis so we can read it. Josephine was born in 1910. She turned out to be the scholar in the family.

In Jeanette we children used to go to a yard near the factory and look for fireflies. Once we

Mother, Giacinta Pone Fabiilli, 1930

"My sisters Lili (left) and Josephine," 1938

found violets. One spring there was a flood which ruined the contents of a store nearby and the owner committed suicide. Another time some boys were trying to drown a cat in a rain barrel and it swam on the surface round and round. They wouldn't stop, so I fled the scene.

There I went to the first, second, and third grades. Every morning we saluted the flag and recited the Twenty-third Psalm, "The Lord is my shepherd," which I liked. It must have been the King James version. I developed an ear for English poetry.

Other poems I heard were Latin hymns and sequences which my mother sang or recited. She had a beautiful contralto voice and also sang Italian folk songs, some in the Pacentro dialect. There was also the poetry of the Mass, in Latin and English, and the slow dance of the priest as he moved back and forth in front of the altar, and occasionally turned to face the congregation and say two words in Latin. The scene is still in my mind, so I must have been drawn by the drama and sacred mystery of the action.

Nowadays, after Vatican II, the priest faces the people and they stare or glare at each other, and

there is no mystery and no Latin. The English translations are neither accurate nor beautiful—just a pedestrian variety of the American language. Even Cardinal Ratzinger is dismayed at the way the liturgy has been manufactured by Pope Paul VI and his advisors and the modern liturgical committees which proliferate endlessly. Whatever possessed Pope Paul VI to destroy the Roman Rite is the only mystery there is. It's called the new Mass or the *novus ordo* and, between you and me, it's a hackneyed version of the Mass and the sooner it's forgotten the better. Not to mention the havoc played by some women in religious orders who intimidated their bishops with demands for ordination to the priesthood and inclusive language. There are a great variety of feminists, including me, but I'm not one to say "Abbe, Mamma" in addressing the First Person of the Blessed Trinity. If my readers don't know what I'm talking about, it's no wonder. All I'm trying to do is explain how I became a poet through the various experiences of my life. They are not the same as purely Wasp experiences, though I was affected by some of those too. Here I'm trying to tell the truth about the development of a writer, and I don't have time to compose a bilingual or trilingual encyclopedia or dictionary. The reader will have to do his own research or skip this part.[1]

Even in England the onslaughts of some women have prevailed, and heaven only knows what's going on in the Episcopalian Church and the Queen's English. She is head of that church. Some Anglo Catholics have slipped into the Roman Catholic Church to escape the changes that have taken place in regards to the ordination of women.

As I write this I am listening to a tape of Gregorian chant to preserve my sanity. The languages I was brought up with were Pacentrano dialect, Italian, Latin, and English, including Italianized English and vice versa. Nowadays I write in American English, and that's what I speak, when I have a chance to say anything. Much of the time I'm drowned out by other people, and since I have become hard of hearing, my utterances are few and far between. But with pen and paper there's a free flow of words and how I

---

[1]When I say "he" in this context I mean "she" too—as well as eunuchs and castrati. It's no good to mess up the English language with "he, she and it," when "he" takes care of the whole lot. Anybody that objects should take lessons in the King's English.

love them! Especially the Latin words of Gregorian chant which I hear as music.

We children were taught to say our basic prayers in Latin, long before we learned the English versions of the Our Father, Hail Mary, Glory Be, and Eternal Rest. This last prayer has to do with people who have died. "Eternal rest grant unto them, oh Lord, and let perpetual light shine upon them." We were very much aware of the souls in purgatory and how we must help them with our prayers. One never prayed for the damned. We never knew how many people were in hell or who they were, but we knew once in they couldn't get out. So that's how it is being brought up an Italian Catholic in the United States. I lived in two worlds—that of Pacentro, that of America, and because of the recollections of my mother, Pacentro was more populated and vivid: a foundation of Italian Catholicism with a plastering of Americanism on top.

The Pacentro of my parents' remembrances no longer exists, except in the minds of us children and as we reconstruct it from bits and pieces. For example, my mother used to sing about "il cacciatore," the hunter, and how he wooed Nina by singing about the life she would lead if she married him. It's a lovely song and has many verses and we were all intrigued by the life of the hunter and his faithful dogs, especially when the snow fell and they all gathered around the "focolare" or fireplace. We never did find out if Nina accepted him after such a splendid serenade. My sister Lili remembers some of the verses and sings them when she feels like it—sometimes during the long drive to Cupertino to visit Albert. I decided to ask my cousin Mario in Italy, also a poet, if he could send me the verses of this song. His reply was that he had never heard of it. So we in California are the keepers of the music and the words, those in Italian and those in dialect, such as this one my sister remembers, of which Mario is ignorant:

"And you who sleep on that mattress
here I am outside going mad."
"E tu che durme n'stu mattarazze
stenghe cha fore, mo iesce pazze. . ."

When things were going badly, my mother recited the psalm "De Profundis" and spoke earnestly to God. When things were going well, she sang the "Salve Regina" or the "Te Deum." As time went on we became familiar with the "Dies irae," sung at funerals, and with "O Salutaris,"

sung at Benediction, and with the "Stabat Mater," sung on Good Friday, and other hymns and sequences or chants such as "Pange lingua."[2]

Because of my father we learned ancient folk tales and true stories of brigands who lived in the caves of the mountains and preyed on travelers and honest folk. These caves were also used by Italian men in World War II when the Germans occupied Pacentro and the surrounding country. They did not want to be sent to labor camps. Some German officers were billeted in Aunt Annie's house and, when one of them learned that one of my cousins was dying of malnutrition, he brought special food and medication for her and saved her life. She is still living, but who knows if he is.

Because of my mother our lives were full of poetry and music. After the daily Rosary in the evening, the Litany to the Blessed Virgin was recited, full of marvelous images: Turris Davidica, Turris eburnea, Domus aurea, Foederis aurea, and so on. This litany is to be found in the missal mentioned above. There was also the lovely "Adoro Te" by Aquinas, which was sometimes sung at Benediction. If today I want to hear the singing of "O Salutaris" and "Tantum Ergo" I go to the 5:15 p.m., Tuesday Mass at St. Patrick's in San Francisco where prayers to Our Lady are said after Mass, and then the Benediction or the Blessed Sacrament with the Latin hymns by St. Thomas Aquinas. This church was built for the Irish in San Francisco, but now is used mostly by Filippinos or people like me, neither one nor the other. The last time I went to this Mass, only "O Salutaris" was sung during Benediction. I wonder why. Are they going to discard the Latin altogether?

It was in the state of Pennsylvania, no less, that I learned I was a wop, a dago, a ghinny, or all three put together: terms of contempt or derision uttered by various children, and no doubt

---

[2]Anyone who wishes to look up these Latin songs can find them in *Saint Andrew's Daily Missal*, 1937, or in the *Dominican Missal in Latin and English*, 1948, that is, if one can find copies of these missals which were discarded after Vatican II and the new Mass. I still have my two copies, quite well worn, and full of holy cards, including one of Our Lady of Pompeii on the back of which, in Italian, is "The prayer of immigrants," asking Jesus to remember that He and Mary and Joseph were once immigrants in Egypt, and beseeching Him to turn His attention to those who leave their homelands out of necessity to earn a living. Pope Pius XI on October 30, 1921, granted an indulgence of 330 days to whoever said this prayer. These two books are real treasures and also contain many Latin-English litanies.

by adults, otherwise how did the children learn them? This form of verbal persecution continued in Columbine School near our farm in California, and in the grammar school in Delano, until one day a teacher in the fifth or sixth grade became aware of the situation and told the whole class that she was proud to be an American, but if she wanted to claim another country it would be Italy with its history of great art and music.

After this things went more or less racially peaceful until I entered the University of California at Berkeley in February of 1937. The verbal persecution had to do *not* with my nationality but with my Roman Catholic religion, and this continues to this day.[3]

The contempt for Italian-Americans surfaced again when I went to work in the new Public Museum in Oakland, California. Because I was in favor of labor unions, some of the ignorant young men staff members came to the conclusion that I belonged to the Mafia. This identification with the Mafia is fostered by movies and by Italian or Sicilian-Americans in the ghettos of New York. They paint all Italian-Americans with the same brush in order to make money and become famous in Hollywood. Just the other day one of them received some kind of an award in that film city and it was televised. Italian-American actors spoke up in admiration of this Sicilian-American director and producer.[4]

So now that this is all brought up, let us forget it and return to the story of my life in the small factory town near Pittsburgh, Pennsylvania.

After the birth of my brother Albert in Jeanette on October 3, 1920, my father decided that we should all go to Italy and live there, while he would return to America and work, and travel back and forth. My mother agreed to this plan, and in June of 1922 we took a ship (third class) and off we went, landing in Naples. Monsignor Cercone, a relative of my father, met us, and as we disembarked we saw some men fighting on the docks. My father asked, why were they fight-

---

[3]For confirmation one can read *The Persistent Prejudice* by Michael Schwartz, Indiana, 1984, or *The Catholic League for Religious and Civil Rights (The Catalyst)*, a current newsletter by William A. Donohue, New York, New York.

[4]Anyone interested in reading about the smearing of Italian-Americans should read a reprint of a talk by Geraldine Ferraro, in *Growing Up Italian* by Linda Brandi Cateura, New York, 1987, p. 263.

ing? Monsignor replied, "Take no notice, they are Black Shirts or Fascists." It was about this time that Mussolini was coming into power, and he accomplished this on October 31, 1922.

I remember the carriage ride, winding up the mountains from Sulmona to Pacentro. It was at night and the air was fragrant.

When we got to the village and settled in Father's house overlooking the Maiella, we learned that the local Fascists had been dosing their opponents forcibly with castor oil. One of them was the Archpriest who became very ill as a result.

We spent six months in Italy and I was very happy there. We would go with Father to his apple orchard and sample the apples until we were scolded and told to eat only one at a time. He had other pieces of land here and there which we would explore, as well as the cobbled streets of the town. I learned how to carry a small copper amphora of water on the top of my head under a round piece of twisted cloth. Water was fetched from the public fountain near our house. Our mattresses were stuffed with dry corn shucks or straw and rustled when we slept on them. Toilet facilities were indoors, the urine and excrement falling in a pit below, and later used as manure.

Jo, Lili, and I, and possibly Virginia, went to school for a few hours a day, learning the 3 R's and how to speak and write the standard Italian language. We had a woman teacher and she was very likable and skilled in the art.

We visited relations on both sides of the family and especially my mother's mother and her two daughters, Aunt Annie and Aunt Mary. The latter was married and the other engaged to be married. Aunt Annie had a cat which slept at night at the foot of her bed. If Grandmother fried little octopi in olive oil and garlic, all the cats in the neighborhood would come to the door because of the pungent and zesty aroma.

Alas, my mother found it was difficult to get cow's milk for Albert, and had to rely on expensive goat's milk. In fact, everything she needed was expensive. She wanted to keep Albert in good health and was worried lest he should sicken and die like the other two little babies named Louis. He did not die but prospered, and now lives in Cupertino. Mother lived with him after my father's death, and she died at the age of ninety in 1977.

One morning in late October when we children were staying overnight with Grandmother and Aunt Annie, the church bells rang as usual but no longer with a clear tone, but a muffled tang, tang, tang. We looked out of the window and saw snow had fallen during the night and transformed everything.

Grandmother and Aunt Annie always went to early morning daily Mass. The main church was near their home, and that's where we went on Sundays. The men and teen-aged boys would stay out of the church and look at everybody going in until just before the Mass started, then they too would troop in.

When my mother was a girl she attended daily Mass and also all the funerals and weddings and baptisms and all kinds of festivities. When a person was dying, it was customary for people to go and pray at the bedside, and to comfort the family. Mother kept busy doing housework, caring for her younger siblings, sewing, spinning and weaving, and washing clothes—these were washed in the "canali" where there was flowing water and flat stones. Soap and cold water were used and sometimes the water was freezing. My mother's life was a happy one as a child and young woman. Her sorrows began when she married and had children and left Italy, family and friends, for a bleak mining town in New Mexico. No wonder she kept remembering her life in Pacentro, telling us about it over and over again, all the things she did, the dramatic events that happened, and about her parents and dear Uncle Pepe who lived with them and was a priest, and finally died at home and went to heaven. She had three sisters and a brother. He was the youngest and at times would be very annoying. She and her sisters went to school and learned the 3 R's. Her brother, after he finished grammar school, was apprenticed to a tailor, and later studied music in Pacentro, Sulmona, and L'Aquila. He eventually came to the United States, earning a living playing the clarinet and saxophone in movie houses. Many years later he taught tailoring to convicts in San Quentin, and much later taught music in a grammar school in the peninsula after taking education courses at San Francisco State College. When he died, he left some of his property to this university.

Because of the political situation in Italy and the high cost of living, my mother thought it would be better for all of us to return en masse to the States, especially since we children would get a better education there. She convinced my father and again we took a ship, third class, and crossed a stormy Atlantic to New York in December of 1922. We had to go through immigration at Ellis Island and we all passed the health test

except Lili who had a sty in one eye. This was enough to send her back to Italy, and if she went we would all go. We were grieved about her, for Lili had been segregated, until my father got in touch with an uncle in New Mexico and it was proven that Lili was born there and hence an American citizen. If Josephine had had the same problem, she would not have been allowed to stay since she was not yet a citizen. A little thing like a sty could change the history of a family Lili got well, grew up, and became a teacher of special children in Redwood City until she retired. She has two sons and some grandchildren. Her husband died some years ago. Her name is Lili Fabilli Osborne.

My father had heard that California was a land where agriculture thrived and all kinds of fruits and vegetables were produced, as well as grapes and oranges. He wanted to farm, not work in factories anymore.

After leaving Ellis Island we went by train to Raton, New Mexico, and stayed with our aunt and uncle and their children whom we met for the first time. Meanwhile Father went to California to look for a farm. One of the things I remember of life with my cousins is that some of us would jump up and down on Mike's bed, one of the family, while he was at work. This was in January in 1923.

In February Father called us to Los Angeles where we lived for a month in a cottage on a hill with a yard full of roses. He went to the San Joaquin Valley and selected a small plot of land—twelve acres—and called us to join him, which we did in March in 1923. What I remember vividly were the golden-orange poppies growing everywhere. Our land was in the middle of a section, and we lived in two box cars until our house was built—four rooms.

One room was a bedroom for Mother and Father, one room was a bedroom for five children. One room we called Father's undressing room where he changed clothes after work, stiff with dust and perspiration. We also used this room for taking baths in a wash tub, and later for a kerosene stove in summer. It also had shelves for dishes and crockery. Some shelves were empty so we used them for a game called "peoples." We made little figures of men and women and little pieces of furniture and composed dramas as we moved them around. There was a sewing machine opposite the shelves. Josephine and Mother sewed our dresses. Albert's and Father's clothes were store-bought or from the Sears catalog.

The other room was the kitchen, dining, and living room. It had a coal stove for cooking and heat in winter, a dining table for seven people, a kitchen table for making pasta, shelving for buckets of water brought in from the stand-pipe outside, and a bench for washing and rinsing dishes.

We had an outhouse for a toilet, but usually we used a chamber pot and dumped the contents through the holes. Father used the outdoor toilet always. Once he was bitten there by a black widow spider, was violently ill for a week, and felt the effects like arthritis long afterwards.

Both bedrooms had large closets for dressing rooms and for the use of the chamber pots, two large beds for us girls, and a cot for Albert. We always dressed or undressed in the closet and were very modest. There were large trunks in both bedrooms.

For illumination we kept kerosene lamps. Much later we had Flamo, a kind of canned gas for lights, also a kerosene stove in the all-purpose room when it was too hot to use the coal stove.

Why Father chose those few acres from the land agents, DeVenney and Turner, in such a desolate spot, with no running water, no indoor plumbing, no electricity, and no clear title to the land is a mystery. Maybe it was all he could afford for a down payment, but considering the fact that a home had to be built made it that much more expensive. He said the soil was good. Eventually during the Depression he lost the land and went to work in other peoples' vineyards to support himself and my mother. By that time we had all left home and had a hard time supporting ourselves.

But to go back to the early days, Mother was completely isolated from her family and friends, and very much alone when we went to school and my father worked on his farm. He planted a vineyard, umbrella and cottonwood trees for shade, pomegranate trees, ground fruits like cantaloupe, casaba, and watermelon; a vegetable garden, tomatoes, bell peppers, cucumbers, and lettuce. There was a cellar to store food, and he made wine each year for home consumption. Then too he bought two cows, two mules, and some chickens.

The house faced east, with the Sierra Nevada mountains in the distance and wheat fields in between. In winter the tops of the mountains were snow covered. The west was behind the house and provided glorious, flaming sunsets. To the north was the dry bed of the White River, full of tumbleweeds, jackrabbits, cottontails, and rattlesnakes. We would make forts out of the tumbleweeds and play games, and avoid the snakes. At times Father and Albert would go hunting for rabbits and bring one back to skin and roast and eat. A Basque shepherd taught my father how to cook them in the ground, wrapped in burlap over live coals, and covered with earth until they were done.

To the south and west was our vineyard and a dirt road leading to a paved one, half a mile away, where we walked to pick up the bus for school in Delano about twelve miles distant. This was after one year of education in Columbine School, which was not as far. Father bought a Model-T Ford, and on Saturday we drove to Delano to buy staples or what was most needed, and also to get books from the public library. On Sundays we went to Mass at St. Mary's Church where Father Benoit was pastor and had supervised the building of the church. I used to look at the statues of angels with their pretty faces and wonder why I was not pretty, and why didn't they have statues of sunburnt homely angels. Father Benoit preached wonderful sermons about Catholic doctrine and often quoted St. Thomas Aquinas. Once when I went to confession (I was about fourteen), he asked me if I wanted to be a nun. I said no. Did I want to get married? Again, I said no. He asked no more questions. I suppose he was trying to find out if I had a vocation to the religious life. I assumed one had to be holy to become a nun, and I was often losing my temper, and being disobedient, and having uncharitable thoughts. How could I possibly be a nun? As for marriage—it made me sick.

One evening when it was my turn to do the dinner dishes, I delayed and delayed. It's not that I refused, I just wanted to do them in my own time, when I felt like it. This irritated Father to such an extent that he gave me a powerful slap on the face which either broke my nose or dislocated it. After that I no longer sat near him at the table, so as to avoid more tremendous slaps. You can very well imagine the uncharitable thoughts I entertained about my father, their intensity and duration. And how difficult to feel contrition!

He and my mother quarreled frequently, especially when things went wrong from an economic point of view, for it was the Depression,

Mary Fabilli, about 1940

Because we had access to the public library we became voracious readers. It was in this library that I discovered Emily Dickinson and immediately liked her short terse lines of poetry. Novels were our fare as well as poetry; the Brontë sisters, Charles Dickens, Louisa May Alcott; the Russians, especially Dostoyevsky and Tolstoy. Dickens was my most favorite, and eventually I read all his novels except for the last unfinished one. We liked mystery stories too, Agatha Christie, Josephine Tey, and later Michael Innes. We didn't like the hard-boiled novels or the ones about sex. Romantic love was OK, but not sex, which was disgusting.

Our parish priest, Father Benoit, French-Canadian, told the parishioners that every home should have a picture of the Sacred Heart and two books, *The Question Box* and the Bible. Father acquired all three. The Bible was the Douay-Challoner version. I began to read it starting with Genesis. By the time I had left the farm, I had read it two or three times. Later I found that Byron too was a great reader of the Bible. One of my favorite poems is about the Assyrian. I was inspired to write psalms, which I did, but after a batch of them I realized they were phony, and the Holy Ghost had not cooperated. So I gave them up and tried to write like Emily Dickinson, and again failed.

The most notable event occurred when, on a trip to San Francisco for medical help for my mother, I found a copy of *The Golden Treasury* by Palgrave in a secondhand bookstore for fifty cents on September 1, 1930. I was sixteen years old. I still have it.

I began to read this studiously and, by the time I had pondered over the poems, I acquired a knowledge of what poetry was all about—especially lyrics. On reading "Winter" by William Shakespeare, I learned one could write about disagreeable mundane things such as Greasy Joan and Marian's nose and still make a thing of beauty. What a blessing! That's how I learned to write the kind of poetry that didn't embarrass me and that I could show to others for comment. From studying Shakespeare's sonnets, I tried my hand at these and eventually with much effort produced eight or ten, some of which I later destroyed. I made no effort to publish my work. I was never capable of profound thoughts like Shakespeare's.

and there was no prosperity around the corner, as Herbert Hoover kept predicting in years to come.

During one such quarrel my mother, in her recriminations, went too far and so enraged my father that she had to escape out our bedroom door. I had been sitting on the doorstep staring into space when she came rushing out; at the same time I heard a crash. When I went in to examine the cause, I learned that Father had hurled a chair at her and one of the legs had broken the plaster board of the wall. If he had aimed a little to the right, he would have broken a window also. We remonstrated with Father, pointing out that if he had hit Mother he would have made a hole in her back. He shrugged and went off to do his chores. After all, he didn't want to maim her, he merely wanted to kill her. She had hit a very raw nerve.

No wonder we children came to appreciate the Russian novelists, for they wrote about life as it really was, "full of sound and fury."

After grammar school in Delano, east and west sides, we went on to Delano Joint Union

High School on the east side, and again were transported by a bus.

I hated sports. The only one I played was volleyball, and once a stout female athlete punched me in the stomach with the ball to get me out of the way. This experience diminished what little interest I may have had in the game. Some of those San Joaquin Valley girls were ruthless sports enthusiasts and jumped around like jackrabbits. My strategy was to keep out of their way and dodge any ball that came flying by.

What I did like was the English class and the teacher, Miss Salber. Lili had her too later on and profited from her talents. My Latin class was taught by a dreamy-eyed man who loved to talk about Spinoza, and now and then would plunge reluctantly into Latin grammar. Algebra and geometry were a mystery to me and I was glad when those courses were over. I managed to get a "C" in both, much to my surprise.

The first personal friend in my life (aside from family members) was a girl I met in high school, probably after the summer vacation of the first year. One day someone came up behind me and put her hands over my eyes and said "Guess who?" I turned around and saw a cheerful face with brown eyes, curly hair, and a freckled skin. We became fast friends and discovered we had similar tastes and wanted to become writers or artists or both. It became our custom to eat our bag lunches under the mulberry trees in an adjacent park, and to talk about everything of mutual interest. At the end of the sophomore year she and her mother moved to Los Angeles, but we corresponded faithfully until one day, about eight or ten years later, she wrote to announce that she was going to get married and was very happy and very much in love. This was a shock to me—how could she be a writer or an artist and get married? After that our correspondence dwindled and finally ceased. Her maiden name was Katharine Ames. I will never forget the cool hands over my eyes and her merry voice saying, "Guess who?" I have often wondered about her life. Could she be like me, an old lady of eighty-three with arthritis, living alone, or unlike me surrounded by children and grandchildren and an aging husband? I have forgotten her married name and have lost her letters, but I keep her in my prayers just the same. Katharine was the only close friend I made in four years of high school.

When Josephine graduated, my parents were able to send her to Dominican College and then to the University of California, Berkeley for the rest of her college career. She became a librarian and started looking for work but couldn't find any because of the general unemployment.

When I graduated from high school, I went to live for one year with my mother's brother and wife in San Francisco, Paul and Edith Pone. I entered San Francisco State College, not too far from their home on Baker Street. One of my professors claimed he couldn't spell, but this did not prevent him from knowing the subject matter of the course, English or history.

My small room was at the back of the apartment, and through the window I could see the fog racing across the night sky, and all the phases of the moon, and listen to the fog horns, a mournful sound.

My aunt was a very good cook but she was not happy. She suspected my uncle was having an affair with a blonde, for she found hairs on his coat. I tried to reassure her of Paul's love, but wasn't able to relieve her anxiety. If there was an affair, nothing came of it, for they lived together the rest of their lives. Paul really did love and appreciate her. She was from Oklahoma, Protestant, prejudiced against Catholics and immigrants; a true blue American. But she was madly in love with Paul, a Catholic who didn't go to church, and an Italian immigrant who had become anglicized. She made wonderful flaky biscuits! After that year I returned home, far from the scudding clouds, the fog horns, and the blonde hairs on Paul's clothing. Uncle Paul was very handsome, but in his old age he looked like Pope Paul the Sixth. I don't think Pope Paul liked Italians either. He preferred the French.

Josephine had not yet found work when I returned from San Francisco. One day she heard of an opening at the Tulare County Library in Visalia. My father drove us there to be interviewed by Miss Gretchen Flower, the librarian in charge. When she examined Jo's papers she regretted that there was no job for a professional librarian, only one for a book-mender—clerical work. I applied for this and mentioned I was very fond of the Russian novelists. This must have intrigued her, and after reviewing my credentials, she gave me the job. Because of this, I had access to a greater variety of books and availed myself of the privilege. I remember reading Gertrude Stein and looking at the paintings of Salvador Dali in one of the art books. I had been writing poetry habitually and now began to experiment, imitating Dali to create surrealistic images in words and

Gertrude Stein for stream of consciousness. In between mending books, I would jot down phrases, take them home, and continue experimenting with words and images.

Miss Flower supervised my work and tried to teach me how to mend books efficiently, using the Stakhanovich method. This I did not like at all, so when alone I would wave my arms around and exercise my hands as I worked. Since I wasn't fired, I must have mended the requisite number of books.

For two months in Visalia I had room and board with a Protestant minister and his family. Then Miss Clare Rolfs, the children's librarian, asked if I would like to rent a room in her large two-bedroom apartment, and I could also have kitchen privileges. I was happy to accept this proposal. Her apartment was on the second floor of a spacious colonial house with green lawns, shade trees, and flowering bushes. Miss Flower didn't approve of this arrangement. She believed that librarians and clerical workers should not fraternize. But we didn't care. Miss Rolfs was a Catholic and so was I, and we went to Mass on Sundays to a nearby church. She had a large friendly dog named Jiggs, and he slept beside her bed at night. My room had a double bed and was big enough to serve as a studio, for I was learning to paint in oils. I also became acquainted with another staff member, Ida Mae Johnson, a petite young blonde always neatly and attractively dressed. We often ate together in local restaurants or coffee shops. She had a little car and lived out in the country. Once I spent a night in her home and noted that some of the walls were lined with newspaper, so I knew her family was not well off. At least they had newspapers! The only paper we had at home was an Italian weekly containing a romantic serial novel which Mother would read aloud to Father in the evening. Then one was left in suspense until next week!

My father could read and write in Italian, and had studied up to the third grade and was later in the peacetime army, the Bersaglieri or sharpshooters, before he went to work in America. These soldiers wore cock-feather plumes in their hats and were all good-looking. Father learned to speak English passably well, but my mother refused. She thought the language was barbarous, full of thick staccato sounds cut short. Nothing mellifluous about it! Not musical like Italian. She did pick up enough to shop and to make friends at church and to talk with and confess her sins to

a succession of Irish priests after Father Benoit left.

Miss Flower periodically visited the branch libraries in Tulare County. One day she returned from such an expedition in a great state of agitation, mixed with tears and anger, because of the poverty she had witnessed in the Okie camps. She hurried to the Welfare Department in the same building and demanded that something be done to relieve their suffering. On top of the Depression there was also the Dust Bowl tragedy and the frantic escape to California. I earned sixty-two dollars a month, and when Father was hospitalized with cancer I was able to contribute ten dollars a month toward his care. He recovered for the time being.

My sister Lili had graduated from high school and was marooned on the farm. I asked Clare Rolfs if she could come and live with me and share my room while she went to junior college. Clare consented and Lili enrolled in the local college. She was very popular there, as she had been in high school, and good at sports. She also took part in a play, and we rehearsed the role. Although I had never acted in a play, I was full of advice on how to interpret her character. The play was a big success, and the actors had many curtain calls.

I do not remember the name of the play or her part in it. It is strange what one remembers and what one forgets. The Christmas play in which she acted at church in Delano when she was nine or ten, I do remember. She played the part of King Herod and was a very convincing tyrant. During the two summers she lived with me in Visalia, she worked in a cannery.

The owner of the cannery, on learning that she wanted to continue her education, offered her a room-and-board job in his home in Berkeley so she could enroll in UC, Berkeley. She accepted and entered in the fall of 1936. We corresponded, and she urged me to come up because there were plenty of room-and-board jobs available. In the spring of 1937 I too enrolled at UC, with a major in art and a minor in English. I found a room-and-board job in the home of a woman professor of education, who had a lovely and thoughtful young daughter who tried to make me feel at home. My room was in the basement, damp and cold and heated with a kerosene heater. I was sickened by the fumes and in despair until my sister Jo came to the rescue. She at last had found a library job in Marysville and sent me ten dollars a month so I could rent a room near campus. I was extremely grateful and moved into an upstairs room on Benvenue Avenue. I got an NYA job (National Youth Administration), which consisted of working several hours a day in the Institute of Child Welfare near the campus. I was to observe children from a screened area and write down what they said and did. They couldn't see me. I found this literary work congenial. The head of the project asked me to copy some Navajo Indian paintings when I had time at home, and gave me five dollars for each. I liked this work too. When I ran out of money for food at the end of the month, Lili would share hers with me.

She introduced me to her friend, Cecily Kramer, a philosophy major. She had perfect complexion, dark eyes, black glossy hair, and was a vibrant person interested in all the arts. She had met Robert Duncan in one of her classes, found him impressive and remarkable, and arranged for us to meet him on campus, which we did in the fall of 1937. Poetry was his major interest but he also loved painting, drama, the dance, and was in a continual dialogue, mostly with himself, carrying on with great animation, with constant arm and hand gestures. I noted that his hands were large and hairy. He declaimed his opinions and ideas in a loud voice and looked about to see who else might be listening. He had black unruly hair and dark eyes which sometimes looked in different directions—the popular term is wall-eyed. He seemed to be searching for perfect understanding and hence needed a very large audience. A poem that best describes the person I knew in those days, he wrote much later and titled "Despair in Being Tedious," published in *Ground Work*. In this he describes his spasm of talk to which he too listens.

We three became fast friends and often met on campus or in our rented rooms. Both he and I had poems published in *Occident,* the UC Berkeley literary magazine. He showed us his current poems and asked to see ours. I don't remember if Lili or Cecily wrote poems, but I did. Lili and Cecily wrote prose pieces which Robert greatly admired.

It must have been in 1938 that I met Virginia Admiral, who was studying art and admired some of the line drawings I made in a class by Ray Boynton. She was slender, diminutive, pretty, but very serious as to aspect, and had long blonde hair piled on the top of her head. She told me she was a Trotskyite. What's that? I asked. It was

a purer form of Communism, she said. Stalin had betrayed the Revolution, whatever that was, but Trotsky had not. Later I found out Trotsky was as ruthless as Stalin, if not more so. Virginia called the Russian communists Stalinists, and despised them. When he was in Mexico, Trotsky had an affair with Frieda Kahlo, who was married to a communist painter whose name was Diego Rivera, and who painted big lumpy people and machinery. I like her paintings very much—they are about human beings—but her husband's work is cold and doctrinaire. Trotsky was murdered in Mexico in 1940, but by this time Virginia had found art and creative writing much more interesting than politics. As for the Marxist slogan "Workers of the World unite, you have nothing to lose but your chains," well, I thought, you have to work in the first place, and if you didn't have to work you probably didn't own any chains either. You were cast adrift in unemployment and hunger as in many cases in the United States. I thought this was distressing and something should be done about it or else people would really revolt. Roosevelt understood this, which Hoover did not, and started the Works Progress Administration (WPA). As for free love, part of the Marxist moral code, I came to the conclusion that men could abandon their wives and children when they fell in love with someone else, as Shelley did when he fell in love with Mary Godwin and left Harriet and children to their own devices. Her device was to commit suicide. Shelley knew nothing about Marxism but a lot about free love and finally drowned off the coast of Italy after being agitated by dreams.

Virginia, like Shelley, was proud of the fact that she was an atheist and had been one from an early age. But this did not get her expelled from UC, Berkeley as Shelley was from Oxford when he propounded that creed. Virginia and I have been friends for many years even until today, and she is still an atheist, and still thinks I'm crazy for being a Catholic. But I pray for her just the same, especially when she lands in the hospital due to smoking, which she has at last given up. When she was going through this struggle several years ago, to console her I wrote a prose poem called "The Last Cigarettes of Aurora Bligh." She liked it.

I never did find out what Robert believed, but I did realize that he had graduated from communism and Trotskyism, and was more or less a homosexual anarchist, poet, and a host of other mysterious things. Some beliefs were quite con-

Poet Robert Duncan, about 1940

tradictory and, if you questioned him, he didn't stop to listen but went on with his own spiel. He was a comfortable friend and we became fond of him. He told us that he was homosexual and didn't want to change. He was the first one I ever met. Not long after, I met another one who was a Catholic who didn't like Robert and considered him uncouth. He and Robert rented rooms in the same house for a while, and he was shocked and horrified when Robert pulled crab lice from his body and burnt them in a candle flame. He had told us he had crabs. We didn't know what they were, and when he described them and the constant itch they caused, we advised him to go to the college hospital quickly and get help. I presume he did because the itching stopped. He never told us about his sexual adventures of which we mercifully remained ignorant, for we girls were not really interested in sex, only in romantic love. Virginia was mourning the death of her boyfriend

who was a Trotskyite from the Mormons of Utah. Several of these ex-Mormon students at U.C. Berkeley were Trotskyites. One of them, Kenneth, once invited a group of us to dinner and cooked a very interesting dish of macaroni with tomato sauce, melted cheese, black olives, and corn kernels which he had learned from a Mexican family in Salt Lake City. It was really delicious and I often use his recipe. He should have been a chef, for he loved to cook and entertain.

Sometimes I wondered if I would ever meet a heterosexual man who would find me attractive. Eventually I did and married him, but we did not have any poetry in common, and this union ended by mutual agreement, and he went his own way. We had been married by a priest to please my parents. He was not a Catholic.

To go back to our college years, it was probably in the fall semester of 1938 that Virginia Admiral and I became destitute. We told Ray Boynton, our art professor, that we would not be able to continue our studies because of our desperate plight. He suggested we go to work in the Oakland Art Project. So we did manage to get a job in the WPA, which was an education in itself. We worked on dry point, etchings, mosaics, wood sculpture, stained glass, and I designed a small mural for the Institute of Child Welfare at UC, Berkeley. We probably remained there for two years, at which time Virginia went to study under Hans Hoffman in New York City, and I continued my studies at UC, Berkeley graduating in the fall of 1941. In the summer vacations I worked in Ball Cannery in Oakland and wrote a prose poem about the experience. The Japanese attacked Pearl Harbor on December 7, 1941. We were astonished and dismayed. The United States entered World War II—a time of blackouts and rationing and of mighty war efforts.

I got a job in the Richmond Kaiser Shipyards and helped build Liberty and Victory ships in bits and pieces, which were later welded together and set afloat. First I worked as a steel checker and belonged to the Shipfitters' Union. We women workers demanded the same pay as men and got it. After I hurt my back lifting up some iron parts, I stayed home to recover for several weeks, and then worked indoors as a secretary-artist and helped to design launching programs. When I made the drawing for the S.S. *Loyola Victory,* I read about St. Ignatius and other saints and began to study seriously the teachings of the Catholic Church, which I had not done in the past. I had gone through a somewhat agnostic phase for a number of years and had even stopped going to Sunday Mass at Newman Hall because the saintly, aged parish priest had no solutions for an unemployed student which I was. When I told him of my economic straits, he advised me to go home, but things at home were as bad as things in Berkeley. He didn't seem to know what was going on in the world. I didn't want to upset him with my angry ideas about the state of general poverty and despair. I just gave up on him and his Hall, which was for the benefit of middle-class kids and not for us rebels from the fringes of society. Now I began to realize there were very good reasons for believing in the teachings of the church, whether one was rich or poor, so I continued to study the subject and to go to Mass again when I felt like it. I liked especially the writings of St. Teresa of Avila, St. John of the Cross, and Dorothy Day in the Catholic Worker paper. Much later I had the chance to meet her.

When the war came to an end, I made a short visit to New York to see Virginia Admiral and her husband and baby. When I returned to Berkeley, I left the shipyards and got part-time work teaching art at the YWCA in Oakland and a private school in Berkeley. During the war Lili had helped to build airplanes; my sister Virginia had joined a religious order; Albert was rejected by the army because he was deaf in one ear and had returned to Delano to work in a vineyard with Father and help support my mother.

Robert had come back to the Bay Area after some years spent in the eastern states where he met many artists and writers, and had kept in touch with Virginia Admiral in New York. He had been inducted in the army, didn't like it at all, confessed to a doctor he was homosexual, and was released with a 4F. He returned somewhat chastened because of a failed marriage to Margy and the abortion of their child. I never met his wife. She was a close friend of Virginia Admiral and also an artist. She is still living at this time (August 1997).

It was through Robert Duncan that I met William Everson, the pacifist poet and printer. We fell in love and decided to collaborate as artists—he to print his poems on a handpress, and I to decorate them with linoleum block prints. We were legally married on June 12, 1948, but I had explained to Bill that we would have to separate eventually, since I wanted to return to the sacraments and the practice of my religion. This caught his attention, and he wanted to know why separate? I said it was because we both had been formerly married, and I was sure the church would consider these marriages valid, since our former mates were still living. He found this disconcerting. I gave him a copy of the *Confessions* of St. Augustine, and spent a lot of time explaining to him the teachings of the church. I was going to Sunday Mass so he came with me and felt confused and out of place. Finally during a midnight Mass at St. Mary's Cathedral in San Francisco on Van Ness Avenue, he received the gift of faith and wanted to become a Roman Catholic too. We separated so that he could be baptized, receive two other sacraments, and so I could at last go to confession and receive communion. The separation was agonizing for we really loved each other and were truly compatible, but it turned out to be a blessing in disguise.

Before all this took place, Robert Duncan published *Heavenly City, Earthly City,* for which I made line drawings. The book was financed by Bern Porter, who is still living at this time in Maine. I liked the poems in this book and was happy to do the art work. As payment I received copies.

Several years later, after I had returned to the church, Robert wanted me to make drawings for *Medieval Scenes,* but I refused after reading the poems, some of which were misogynist and bigoted. Robert was hurt and so was I, and we stopped seeing each other. He met Jess Collins, an artist, and they began to live together and continued to do so until Robert's death.

Bill Everson went to live in Maurin House, a Catholic Worker House of Hospitality. Dorothy Day, who had published some of Bill's religious poetry in her paper, came to visit the House. I met her and invited her to stay with me, which she did for about a week. She was a large impressive woman, and I considered her to be a saint. When she left me, she gave me a relic of St. Maria Goretti which a priest had given her and which she always carried. I still have it.

Carroll McCool was put in charge of Maurin House by the pastor of St. Mary's Church. He was a Catholic who had been a sergeant in the medical corps in the U.S. Army during World War II and had gone through Africa, Italy, France, and Germany, and all the horrors of war, and seen the concentration camps and their starving emaciated prisoners. When he returned to the States after receiving a wound, he entered the Trappist Order. However, his health failed and he was told the regime was too harsh for him, so he returned to California to take care of his mother and engage in works of charity. He had a small pension because of his wound. He and Bill became great friends, and he taught Bill how to pray the Rosary, and how to persevere in prayer—without ceasing.

Carroll became my friend too, and we have kept in touch all these years.

Once when I went to visit Maurin House, I met Ruth Hallisy, a devout Catholic and college teacher. She was an attractive young woman, tall, slender, and graceful, and dressed beautifully. She introduced Bill to Father Osborne, a Dominican priest who taught at St. Albert's College in Oakland. He became Bill's spiritual director. Ruth urged me to go to Sunday Mass at St. Albert's, a Dominican house of studies for the training of seminarians. So I went and found that the Mass said there was very beautiful, and the sermons doctrinal.

Bill entered the Dominican Order as a lay brother. The friars had voted to accept him, but not Father Zammit O.P. He was certain that Bill as a poet and printer would become frustrated, because the duties of a lay brother were taxing and various. He must be a handyman able and willing to clean and polish, have carpentry and plumbing skills, chauffeur and care for the cars, and handle many other duties that the choir brothers had no time to do. He might be required to cook, wash dishes, launder, mend furniture, and polish floors. Most of the time cooking and laundry were done by Dominican Sisters in a convent attached to the college. It may be that lay brothers also did gardening, although I'm not sure about this. Father Zammit thought Bill was more fitted for the Benedictine Order. However, the majority approved on the recommendation of Father Osborne, Ruth Hallisy, and the pastor of St. Mary's Church. Carroll however did not approve—he probably knew more about Bill's inner life and interests than the Dominicans did. When Bill finally chose to leave Maurin House, Carroll and I accompanied him to the door of St. Albert's College (now a priory). He vanished into the cloister accompanied by his new friends. This was in 1951, and he remained there for almost nineteen years.

I continued to work part-time but then applied for a full-time job at the Oakland Public Museum and was accepted. I resumed the writing of poetry, which had been interrupted by my marriage to Bill. Linoleum block printing had taken its place. I also began to paint pictures, mostly in opaque watercolor.

My evenings were devoted to religious studies, the life of Christ, the history of the church, and the Bible, which I had always kept with me.

I learned that Christ had a sense of humor. He told the apostles not to fear those who opposed their teaching, who kill the body and can't kill the soul. If God had care for sparrows, two of which could be sold for a penny, would He not take care of them too? They were worth more than many sparrows.

I figured out that if "many" equalled at least a hundred, then at two sparrows sold for a penny, the apostles would be worth more than fifty pennies. No wonder I loved Jesus, He was my kind of a poet, someone I could really trust and worship. Since God took care of sparrows and apostles, He would take care of me too, however insignificant.

"My husband, the pacifist poet and printer, William Everson," about 1948

At St. Albert's, classes were taught for lay people by Father Paul N. Zammit O.P., Father Starrs O.P., Father Fulton O.P., and others. The first two are dead, but Father Fulton is still living. He was a convert from the Methodist church and loved the color purple and Brooklyn, New York. Under him we followed the journeys of St. Paul. Father Zammit taught Christian doctrine, and so did Father Starrs, who also explained the rule of the Third Order which I had joined. It is now called the Dominican Laity. Ruth Hallisy helped me to love and understand the liturgy and to use St. Andrew's Daily Missal. She died of cancer of the throat on May 10, 1989.

Work at the Oakland Public Musem was varied and interesting. The building was located near Lake Merritt and catty-corner from the main library. The elderly man who helped me with my duties was a devout Baptist, a gentle and saintly soul whom I liked and respected. He was fond of me but, convinced that all Catholics go to hell, tried valiantly to turn me into a Baptist without

Albert Fabilli, the author's brother, 1980

success. I had no time at work to explain the teachings of the Catholic church, so I gave him a copy of *The City of God* by St. Augustine. This he read with intense pleasure and satisfaction and stopped trying to convert me. He too is dead. I will never forget his kindness, his cheerful smile, and the light that shone from his blue eyes as he thanked me for *The City of God.* When the new museum was built in Oakland, not far from the old one, but not as close to Lake Merritt, we staff members were transferred there, and I became associate curator of history, in charge of exhibits relating to the Spanish and Mexican periods of California history, as well as those about war, peace, labor, and politics in the twentieth century.

I carried on research at the Bancroft Library of UC, Berkeley, the Oakland Library, and other institutions. In reading about Hernán Cortés, I was reminded that my first husband had greatly enjoyed Prescott's *Conquest of Mexico.* I too found this period absorbing. The best biography of Cortés, in my opinion, is the one by Salvador de Madariaga, the best on the conquest was by Bernal Diaz del Castillo. *Cortés,* by his secretary, Francisco Lopez de Gamara, was also important.

The history of Doña Marina especially interested me. She had been given away by her Aztec mother and stepfather to prevent her from inheriting lands and peoples destined for their newborn son. This is according to Bernal Diaz del Castillo. The Indians who acquired her gave or sold her to the Tabascans, who in turn donated her to Cortés. She knew two Indian languages and with Aguilar, who knew one, she became Cortés's translator and secretary. She was one of the first persons in Mexico to become a Christian, and remained Cortés's faithful friend and ally, and never betrayed him as she easily might have done. It is partly because of her and Aguilar that the Conquest succeeded, and that Christianity was brought to Mexico.

The women of Mexico should raise a statue in her honor and place it in the center of the capitol, for she helped free the people from the horrors of Aztec sacrifice and slavery, and also their contempt for women. It was the hearts of slaves or captives that were torn out and offered to the Aztec gods, while their bodies were rolled down the pyramids and became the food of zoo animals.

When Cortés witnessed those idols stinking and encrusted with blood and jewels, and with the unpronounceable names, he was so sickened and outraged by the scene and the practice of human sacrifice that he struck them with his sword and tried to cast them out of the temple, to the horror of Montezuma and his priests.

I suppose our present Pope, John Paul II, would not approve of this action. Even the Catholic priest who had accompanied Cortés in the visit to the temple told him this was not the time to destroy statues. The people must first be convinced of the truths of Christianity.

I for one say a "requiem aeternam" for Cortés because of this noble deed which actually threatened the success of his conquest. Besides which he made a speech to Montezuma and his nobles and priests about the futile worship of false gods, a copy of which he sent to the King of Spain. This should be published in the daily papers of Mexico and the U.S.A. Instead he and Doña Marina have become anathema to the people of Mexico, and I don't know if they are even aware of Aguilar; may he, too, rest in peace.

In one of the Mexican codices Doña Marina is portrayed wearing a long white tunic and has long, black wavy hair. She stands beside Cortés and is larger than he, indicating her importance in the eyes of the Indian artist.

"My sister Virginia," 1980

To return now to the subject of writing, Robert Duncan had always been interested in my literary work and tried to get it published. Bill Everson, on the other hand, was *then* of the opinion that women couldn't write poetry, not the real genuine stuff. He did like my artistic abilities and the lino block prints I made for two of his poetry books, and for a broadside. These are now collector's items, as is also *Heavenly City, Earthly City* by Duncan.

Bill was a master at handpress printing and a perfectionist as well. It was fascinating to watch him at work and the care with which he pulled off a perfect page.

He liked to read his current poems aloud to me. Some of them were long and lugubrious. I preferred his nature poems to the lengthy, rhetorical, philosophical ones. He admired Walt Whitman. I couldn't stand his bloated pomposity, though I admit he has written some good poems. I liked Emily Dickinson, hence the difference in tastes. Duncan liked everyone. At any rate his interests were broader than Bill's and included women and Dante.

In regards to music, Bill loved Wagner, whereas I preferred Mozart. As for movies he never wanted to see them, though I did. If he did go, the

images would not fade from his memory, and he would become agitated for days afterwards. Duncan enjoyed them and at one time hoped to become a movie star himself. Bill did not like to travel far from home. We went to Santa Cruz one weekend, but I don't remember how we got there. We had no car. He could drive but I couldn't, except for the Model-T Ford my father had on the farm.

We both came from the San Joaquin Valley and this created a real bond—the memory of the flat lands, the flourishing vineyards, orchards and cotton fields, the sunsets and the Sierra Nevada mountains, the sound of distant trains and infrequent airplanes, the hot summers, the Tule fogs. We were hicks from the same farmlands. Robert Duncan came from Bakersfield, a biggish town or small city, and from a more elevated class structure. His father was an architect, and his mother was very refined and wanted her son to become the same. Maybe that's why I never met her. Robert met my mother, and we all met Virginia Admiral's mother, a modest little schoolteacher with winning ways. But where was Robert's mother? He complained about her disapproval of him, his ways, his friends. But which of his friends did she meet?

Bill was deathly afraid and in awe of Kenneth Rexroth. He feared he might say or publish something derogatory about his poetry. I was amazed at this dread of offending a literary despot—narcissistic, opinionated, abrasive; a self-educated man and abstract artist who held court in San Francisco and tried to crush anyone who didn't meet with his approval. (Before Rexroth died in 1982 at age seventy-seven, he was received into the Catholic Church by a Jesuit priest.) I didn't like his poetry or his paintings. I lost respect for Bill's judgment because of this numbing fear, and realized he had no real confidence in his own literary efforts. This may have shown a certain amount of discernment. When Bill read his poems to me and I suggested improvements or showed mild discontent, he became annoyed and had no respect for my criticisms. So what was the use of listening to his poems if I couldn't comment? A form of torture! I used to think, is this how I will spend the rest of my life?

When Duncan read his poems aloud, I could drift off into dreamland, and he wouldn't care. Not so with Bill, he wanted perfect attention.

Carroll McCool of Maurin House said he liked poetry that rhymed. He didn't understand Bill's poems. So Bill had used him as a sounding board too.

I never read my poems aloud. I hear them in my mind, not with my ears. I never go to poetry readings. I prefer to read a poem slowly if I like it, and not at all if I don't. You can usually tell right away, after a line or two. Anyway, now I have become hard of hearing.

The last poem in *Aurora Bligh,* "An Hour or Two of Quiet Talk," is based on a literary evening in Rexroth's home, though it strays far afield and is not historically accurate.

After Bill entered the Dominican Order, circa 1952, he told me he planned to write an account of his conversion to the Catholic church. I assumed he would take St. Augustine as a guide and encouraged him in this project. When several more years had passed peacefully, maybe in 1955 or 1956, he phoned me and said Sheed and Ward were anxious to publish his story but could not do so unless I read it and gave my consent. I asked why, and he said because he had written about me. I was alarmed and phoned St. Albert's and talked with Father Meagher O.P. I asked him if it was really necessary for me to read Bill's book. He explained that Bill had discussed my sins. The Dominican Order as well as

the Catholic publishing house needed my permission before publication.

Full of dismay and apprehension, I agreed to read the book. When I did so, I was appalled and horrified to realize that Bill was willing to reveal the most intimate details of our life together. It seemed to me that if a man loved a woman, he would keep such intimacies secret, especially if they involved actual sins.

The answer to this was that Bill did *not* love me and perhaps had never loved me at all. He had used me to satisfy his emotional and physical needs, he had *used* my house as a home for himself and his handpress, he had used my talents to decorate his two books of poetry, and now he was using his memory of me for the sake of literary fame.

When we were living together, I wasn't exactly sure what sin we were committing: if our former marriages were valid, then the sin was adultery; if they were not valid, the sin was fornication. Or if, on the other hand, we were living a common law and legal marriage, such a union needed to be blessed by the church before we could receive the Sacraments. In Bill's book we were committing adultery. He had come to this conclusion because we had not been able to prove that our former marriages were invalid.

A human being who sins should repent and confess his sins to God and endeavor to amend his life and habits. If he is a Catholic, he must also confess his sins to a priest, receive spiritual counsel, absolution, and a penance. Bill and I had done this when I returned to the church and he became a Catholic.

It was not required that we publish our sins for the world to read and relish. In fact, this could be a source of scandal rather than edification. After her conversion, St. Margaret of Cortona would shout from the housetops in the dead of night that she was a sinner! Her confessor told her not to do that anymore for reasons mentioned above.

But Bill was anxious to wallow in a detailed description of his sins and mine too, mostly mine! Of course there were exaggerations and factual errors, but these were minor. Most of the story was true enough.

If the book were published, my family and I would be exposed to notoriety, contempt, and curiosity. My mother and sisters and brother had accepted Bill as a member of the family and had prayed for his conversion, and had rejoiced when it happened. He, on the other hand, would repay them by publishing this outrageous account. He would be safe enough in the Cloister of St. Albert's, where no one could enter, but we would all be exposed to the eyes of the public.

Would I be able to earn a living under such circumstances? Would I be able to retain my sanity if the book was published? How would it affect my old and ailing mother and my sisters and brother?

I had to think about all these things, and I decided that I could not consent to the publication of the book, not unless every mention of me was expunged! The rest of the book could stand on its own. I found no fault in it except for his idea that marriage was a cure for homosexuality. Nor did I accept his version of Original Sin, in which Eve is the chief culprit. The church teaches otherwise.

St. Augustine had written about his conversion and barely mentioned his mistress. He had not accused her of sin, nor discussed the details of their relationship. Even so, and perhaps because of this, his book is a masterpiece and will endure until the end of time. For Bill to write a work of art, it was not necessary for him to mention me at all. His own life was rich enough to engage the attention of the reader.

I realized Bill would hate me if I withheld my consent. But since he did not love me or care what happened to me, what difference did it make if he hated me? So I gave him my verdict: leave me out of the book entirely. He was beside himself with fury, and sent Frank Sheed of Sheed and Ward to see me and convince me otherwise. Frank Sheed was a neat and dapper little man. He reminded me of Hercule Poirot. I gave him my reasons, and he accepted them without question. He said he would publish Bill's book by editing it so that there would be no mention of me.

This he did, but Bill rejected the edited version of the book, so it was not published— though I understand that many people have read the original anyhow, and Oyez published a chunk without my knowledge or permission.

Bill wrote me several angry letters in which he psychoanalyzed me according to Jung, but since I didn't understand them and had no confidence in Freud, Jung, or Everson, I tore them up and burned them in the fireplace. I felt that after some years had elapsed, Bill would come to an understanding of my point of view and would regret having sent the letters. He wouldn't want posterity to read them. I was mistaken.

There is a large fireplace in my house capable of burning any number of literary masterpieces! My home is not a Maybeck House as some people have surmised, it is described architecturally as "California Craftsman." It was built for a wealthy woman after the San Francisco fire and earthquake. She needed a cottage for her piano and for her furs. That's why it has such a large front door and deep built-in storage drawers.

Bill's friends were angry with me because of my refusal to consent to the publication of his conversion story. I felt sorry for him and for them too. But I did not apologize.

About two years later Robert Hawley, a bosom friend of Bill, offered to publish and print a collection of my poems. This is how the book *Aurora Bligh and Early Poems* came into being in 1968. He published two more of my books: *The Old Ones*, Oyez, 1966, and *The Animal Kingdom*, 1975. (Oyez is the name of Hawley's publishing house.)

I also sent poems to poetry magazines and would wait for weeks or months for acceptance or rejection. This was most tedious and time-consuming. I decided to publish my own work to give to family, friends, and libraries. In this way I put out four pamphlets of twenty-four pages, each illustrated or decorated with my line drawings. They are *Poems 1976-1981*, Kentucky, 1981; *Winter Poems,* Berkeley, 1983; *Pilgrimage,* Berkeley, 1985; and *Shingles and other poems,* Berkeley, 1990.

When I was asked to contribute to an anthology or magazine, I would comply.

The three books published by Oyez, much to my regret, did not sell well. I do feel greatly indebted to Robert and Dorothy Hawley for bringing them out.

One day in December of 1969 as I rode on the 40 Telegraph bus to my job at the museum I glanced at the newspaper a woman in front of me was reading. It had a headline to the effect that Brother Antoninus (Bill Everson) had removed his Dominican habit at a poetry reading. I couldn't read the small print, so at lunch time went out and bought a newspaper. Sure enough, Bill had indeed removed his robes and gone off to Stinson Beach with a woman thirty years younger than himself, and who already had a baby.

The impression I received was that he had renounced his religion and all his Catholic friends. Why?

That night Father Zammit O.P. phoned me and asked if I had read the newspapers. I said yes. He said, "Do not be distressed. It is good that he left. He should have gone long ago." And he hung up. I felt relieved.

About a week later I received a letter from Bill saying that, regardless of what I read in the papers, "Christ was still the lodestar of his heart."

I phoned Carroll McCool and told him about this message. So we decided to pray for Bill and we continued to do so until his death.

Bill married Susanna and adopted her son Jude. He taught for a number of years at UC, Santa Clara. His subjects were poetry and printing on the handpress. He had a successful career as a teacher and maker of books, and was an inspiration to many of his students.

In 1977 John Knight, one of Everson's intimate friends and admirers, told me that Bill had Parkinson's disease. This eventually made it difficult for him to teach; however, he continued to give poetry readings. His wife became a nurse and supported the family.

Longtime friend Virginia Admiral, 1980

When he was eighty years old, he and Susanna separated and divorced. He died in his home on June 2, 1994, age eighty-two.

I was able to attend vespers for his death at St. Albert's Priory, the funeral Mass next day, and his burial at the Dominican cemetery in Benicia.

All this I reported to Carroll McCool over the phone. He is now living at Emanuel Convalescent Hospital in Alameda. On September 6 this year (1997) he will be ninety years old. I visit him when my sister Lili is able to give me a ride.

After Robert Duncan and I hurt each other's feelings in regards to his book *Medieval Scenes,* we saw each other rarely, except when he needed something. He asked me to cooperate with Ekbert Faas who was writing his biography. He introduced me to Robert Bertholf, a friend from the Lockwood Library of the University of New York in Buffalo. He also wanted me to meet Eloyde Tovey who was then employed by the Rare Books Department of the Bancroft Library and had worked on his oral history. She and I became friends. She lived in Berkeley and we saw each other frequently.

When Robert was very ill in San Francisco, she suggested that I phone him. I did twice, and we had the same cordial and amusing interchange of words as in the old days. Shortly afterwards he died February 3, 1988, age sixty-nine. My sister Lili and I visited Jess Collins and expressed our sympathy for the loss of his long-time companion.

I admire much of Robert's poetry and respond to its music and mysterious meanings. We really cared for each other and had many productive hours together. This is also true of my friendship with Virginia Admiral, who lives most of the time in her home in New York City. We communicate by letters or by telephone.

It was a strange coincidence that Adrian Wilson died on the same day and year as Robert Duncan. He and Bill had been colleagues and both practiced the art of fine printing.

Some of my poetry is formal and straightforward and rational, not deranged like the other stuff (language poetry) out of a dream world. One such poem was published recently (1997) in a Bristol Banner Book. It is entitled "The Woman, The Man, The Disembodied Soul." I like it because it expresses my convictions in a few words without ornament.[5]

---

[5]This poem was inspired in part by meditation on the lives of *Women of the Beat Generation* by Brenda Knight, Conari Press, Berkeley, 1996.

Some of my poems are included in this book, though I am not a Beat poet. I was invited to contribute because I belonged to the "generation" like Josephine Miles and others, also because of my friendship with Bill Everson and Robert Duncan. This book is often a sad and mournful account of the literature and lives of women associated with Beat poets and their attempts to live the same life-style. The poem "Howl" by Allen Ginsberg is a sentimental account of the sad fate of disordered young men, but without a thought to the lives of their women friends. What is also strange and scary are accounts of abortions performed like pulling out weeds with no awareness of the human being, male or female, whose life is suddenly truncated, no mention at all of this fatal issue.

The life of Elise Cowen is perhaps the most tragic. She loved Allen Ginsberg. She met her death by jumping out of a closed window in the house of her parents.

Recently I received my copy of *Bombay Gin,* the annual literary magazine of the Jack Kerouac School of Disembodied Poetics, Vol. V, No. 1, 1997. It contains a poem in memory of Elise by Janine Pomy Vega, one of the writers featured in *Women of the Beat Generation.*

My poem in this magazine is entitled "The Concert." It is about the tango and very brief.

The Beat book reminded me of the failure of my first marriage. I was involved in art and poetry, and we both had to earn a living; we were not really happy together. Hence, separation and divorce.

I had not then read the chapter on "Holy Purity" in *The Way* by Josemaria Escriva. I am reading it now in my old age with much pleasure because of his psychological insights and sometimes sharp words, like a slap on the face, not to punish, but to awaken.

The Way was published in 1939, but I doubt that it had become well known or translated into English until much later. It is never too late to read a good book. This one is very much like reading poetry. A little at a time goes a long way. One does not want it to come to an end, like a mystery story.

Yesterday a book arrived which I had ordered by mail. It's about St. Michael the Archangel. I look forward to reading it.

Most of my reading material now comes through the mail from catalogs.

Recently I received *The Book of Durrow* from Daedalus. I already have a copy of the *Book of*

Fabilli with her mother, 1971

Kells. Years ago when I was studying art at UC, the art historian, Dr. Horn, praised these volumes for their Celtic beauty, especially *Kells.* I saw this one in Dublin many years ago when I was young enough to travel and to walk in guided tours.

It seems to me that I should end this account by reporting my own death.

I am still glad to be alive and no longer young. Old age can be a blessing: a serene existence, going to daily Mass when possible and reading the lives of the saints. Even if I don't like the novus ordo Mass, I still attend, because of the Eucharist, and my hope for the future of the liturgy. Not in my time, but for others. I'm in no hurry. One at last learns patience.

My friend, Miné Okubo, writes from her studio in New York that all her friends have died, the last two in December of 1996.

We first met when we studied art at UC, Berkeley, but she was three years ahead of me. We met again in July of 1972 when she had a one-man show at the Oakland Museum. Since then we have exchanged Christmas cards on my part, and Japanese New Year greetings on hers.

She is now eighty-five years old and is preparing for an exhibition of her paintings in the fall and winter of 1997. She writes that she must finish her life's work. There is so much to do and so little time left. I can hardly read her handwriting, she is in such a rush, that I must guess at some of the words.

It is comforting to have a friend near one's own age who is still devoted to her art and pursues it with steadfast determination; who "does not follow anyone," but is true to her private vision. It is necessary, she says, to leave my work in a finished state so that it will talk for me.

BIBLIOGRAPHY

Poetry:

The Old Ones, Oyez, 1966.

Aurora Bligh and Early Poems, Oyez, 1968.

The Animal Kingdom, Oyez, 1975.

Author of self-illustrated and self-published poetry, including *Poems 1976-1981,* 1981; *Winter Poems,* 1983; *Pilgrimage,* 1985; and *Shingles and other poems,* 1990.

Also illustrator of *Heavenly City, Earthly City,* by Robert Duncan, and of two poetry books and a broadside by William Everson. "Mary Fabilli: A Selection from Her Works," by Drew Gardner, appeared in *Talisman,* No. 13, Fall, 1994, Winter, 1995, edited by Edward Foster and including three new Aurora Bligh stories. Contributor of poems to magazines and anthologies, including the poem "The Woman, the Man, the Disembodied Soul," in a Bristol Banner Book, 1997, and "The Concert," in *Bombay Gin,* Jack Kerouac School of Disembodied Poetics, 1997.

Judy Grahn

1940-

RIDING THE DRAGON'S BREATH

Identities

Two gifts my mother gave me before we left Chicago. She took me to an exhibit hall at the Field Museum (I believe) that was filled with wax sculptures of all the peoples of the earth (done by a woman whose name I cannot recall), so that my first impression of world humanity is just how stunningly luminous and beautiful and varied we all are.

Her second gift was to take me to the Brookfield Zoo, where I witnessed Sinbad, the world's largest gorilla, hanging upside down eating a bunch of grapes with such delicacy and finesse that I ever look again and yet again at animals, revising my perceptions and prejudices, knowing there is always more to know.

The facts of my life are simple enough: born early on a hot morning at Evergreen Park, Illinois, in Cook County Hospital, to Vera Doris and Elmer August Grahn, who lived with two children in a one-bedroom apartment in Chicago. Odd to be born in Evergreen—as that is what the family name means, "evergreen"—originally it was Grahnquist—branch of the evergreen. July 28, 1940. Sun sign Leo. Fire. Expression. Lionhearted.

My father was born in 1898 in Motala, Sweden. He was four when his parents immigrated to Galesburg, Illinois, and he did not speak English when he entered the first grade. My grandfather (August) worked for the railroad; my grandmother Frida bore nine children and cooked six meals a day after what I assume is a rural Swedish custom. What my parents said of her is that she never left the kitchen except to go to childbed.

Nineteen forty is the Year of the Dragon in the Chinese system. I am not Chinese but there is hardly any form of divination I have not used to try to understand my life. My astrological chart was revealing, as it showed a

Judy Grahn at age six, 1946

dramatic red line cutting through it. "You'll be going along on a course and then whoosh, all at once everything will change—everything in your life, all at one time." That red line, that's the dragon's breath—a wave of fire that periodically reaches out, transforms me. Shifts me into some other space. I was the youngest of the cousins on both sides of my family. My mother's sister Sybil had four children—I recall that side of the family only vaguely. A grown divorced man desperate for attention groping my twelve-year-old body in a cemetery; my uncle giving me a shot of whiskey behind the barn.

Being startled into sentiment when my aunt announced at dinner that we were eating the family's beloved cow.

On my father's side there was a klatch of cousins—nine or so. I don't know if I always felt estranged from them or if this disengagement occurred gradually as a result of my father moving my mother and me to New Mexico in 1949. Recently my mother divulged that "one day he came home and said 'Get packed, we're moving.' And so we moved." A red line day. I was eight. My sister had gotten married a few weeks before, and continued to live in Chicago. I would see her for an evening (across a table, looking so strange and tense) once again when I was twelve and my mother and I came back on the train for a brief visit. And not again until I was forty-four.

The reunion programs on television show happy people clambering into each other's arms—orphans reunited at last. The announcer rubs tears under his eyelids, the program ends.

The reunion of Judy Grahn (left), her brother Rodney, and her sister Joan McKay, about 1984

In real life the reconnection is not that easy, maybe barely happens. Maybe not at all.

"You were my baby sis, and you will always be," my sister insists as I sit looking at her, wondering what ties us. "I practically raised you. I'm the one who took care of you, day in and day out. Mom certainly didn't—she refused to take care of you." I search my memory for my sister's care taking, find only a matte-black space. To her, to my cousins, there was family reality. There was Michigan Avenue. There were aunts and uncles, Christmases, the look and smell of each other's houses, the chitchat and rivalries and shared secrets and hurt feelings and hugs. To me, there is a blank wall, ash.

A dragon's breath has wiped out everything, except my mother, my father, and me. We three left Chicago and intensified, moved into a bright-colored painting with animation, memory, vivacity. In my inner album of pictures of the past, I was born at a moment in May 1949 when I walked out into the intense continual flash of New Mexico sun, gasping with wonder at a horned toad sitting under a tall-leafed century plant. Laughed long and again. Cradled its fantastic body in my heated hand, shared the wonder with two friendly neighbor children.

That's the story I remember, and my conscious memory forms around the axis of that sunshine flash. The time before that moment is a pictureless, formless history guarded by watchdogs of grief.

The Blessing of Smallpox

My mother had smallpox when she was born, defining moment, that disease the fire that would sear her life and mine, fuse them together and apart, into their peculiar, particular directions. Last year in India as I filmed my colleague Dianne interviewing women of the religion of the goddess Bhagavathi, the discussion about smallpox particularly riveted me. She might send you a disease, the women said, and it might blight your life and luck. Then again, they said, it might be a blessing, something you had been needing or exactly what you wanted. That is a pendulum I swing in as well.

The first time my mother tried to kill me I was probably only a few weeks old. (This is a recovered memory.) When I said to my sister, "I think our mother is schizophrenic, brought on by the smallpox," she said, "No, that isn't true. I asked a doctor once. She just doesn't do what is right. You can't count on her for anything. She drives me crazy, the way she is."

Unlike my sister, I assimilated "crazy" as one of the attributes of artist. I found that the non-materialism of my parents' lives gave me certain adaptabilities, and that the pressure of tensions under their roof gave me astounding powers of concentration.

One of my first memories of New Mexico was of the leaking roof.

Ping! ping! ping! I awakened to water falling on my face. The New Mexico August monsoon had come, and my mother was crying out in distress to find me soaking wet. Water was pouring through the thin corrugated tin roof as she rushed to put pots and bowls under the leaks; at leak thirteen she ran out of vessels. She was completely distressed by this, shamed and upset. Why couldn't he provide a decent roof over our heads. But I remember the thrill of it, the coldness of the water, chasing the falling drops with the pots, how the streaming water was an artist staining the white tiles of the ceiling a particular red-brown color, how the ceiling retained the unmistakable signs of a leaking roof. The sky could not be kept out; here in this place, the sky WOULD come in to us. I was nine. We were out of Chicago, running free. We were in Her hands now.

My father had rented to house us a structure he always afterwards referred to as a cinder block shack, a garage apartment built with very little exact measurement, and out of odds and ends. The cinder block did not keep out the extremes of weather as it didn't line up at the corners and on a bright day you could see light in the cracks. In a spring dust storm we would get the broom to sweep the piles that pyramided up from the floor under the windows. The west wall was adobe with its natural insulation, defeated by the other three porous walls. The roof of corrugated tin and full of nail holes was "roof" in name only; the windows did not open, nor fit snugly; the floor of the tiny kitchen sloped, and the only doors hung uneasily to shield a single closet and the minuscule bathroom. A curtain divided the bedroom from the greasy little kitchen. The whole thing was maybe four hundred twenty square feet, an oven in the summer and a drafty freezer in the winter. Much of the time there was not enough water pressure, and my mother, her face tense with rage and shame, would send

me out with the kettle to the big yard and the spigot outside Miss Welsheimer's basement apartment to draw water for dinner.

My father's hope for a white-collar job quickly deteriorated, and he was forced back into cooking. New Mexico, 1949. A nonunion state, he complained with understandable bitterness, as, having spent his young adulthood fighting for decent wages, he was now situated near the bottom again. He would remain there until he was able to draw Social Security at the age of sixty-five—fourteen years later.

In the total of his work life my father made "good money" for only perhaps six to eight years of his life, when he worked for a steel mill in Chicago. He gambled that away in card games on Saturday nights. While other men in his family bought homes for their families, he kept his three children in a one-bedroom apartment, near Michigan Avenue. He was constantly jailed for drunk and disorderly conduct, and frequently driven home by the police, to whom he inevitably referred as "po' lice," that is to say, parasites living on the misfortunate.

Even in New Mexico working as a fry cook at the bottom of the (industrialized) world, he made twice as much money as my mother, though unlike her not always able to get it home and spent on socially relevant matters, such as food and clothing for his family. Struggling to justify this iniquity, and to establish the falsehood of his supremacy over her femaleness, he resorted to verbal abuse. She was stupid, he asserted, her way of thinking was not real thought; only his memorized lists of facts and his well-told anecdotes constituted intelligence. *(She was defective, then.)*

Using these methods and a broad, tiresome assortment of racial jokes, he asserted the major teachings of western culture, from Darwin to Genesis, from Frances Bacon to the Monroe Doctrine. I would struggle half my life to get out from under my identification with his maleness and his false sense of superiority, and his racialized class shame.

Sacred Connections

My life alone with my parents in New Mexico perfectly prepared me to be a poet and prophet, if that is what I am. In the absence of material clutter, real life bumps against you; the elements are right there with you, in relation. New Mexico in 1949, when we moved there from Chicago, was the Mississippi of the Southwest. A generally poor state, whose kindnesses are immediate in both the people and the desert, and whose cruelties are sporadic and just as likely to come from the fierce plants and insects. The land is still talkative, as no one has come with cement and petrochemical noise to tell her to shut up. (The land that I grew up on is a rock, and the rock is an ideal powerful mother, interactive, vibrant, just-as-she-is.) The riches of beauty and abundant life forms surrounded me, and gave me a great knowledge of the sources of happiness, love, passion, and death.

My mother and I hardly spent a single day without commenting on the beauty of the Organ Mountains, a nine-thousand-feet-high formation strung along the eastern rim of the Mesilla Valley. The mountains' light-and-shadow-struck surfaces created such vivid pictures that we turned toward their living faces several times a day, as intently as we might have—in different circum-stances—turned to Mecca or the colorful meaningful statue in the plaster grotto. My parents stayed home on Sunday, my father's only sober day, and sent me to the Methodist Sunday school, where I experienced none of the mystery or beauty of our elemental mountain veneration. Still, I was a spiritual child, full of wonder and curiosity, trying to find a place in middle-class Protestantism. At thirteen I brought home a three-dimensional wall hanging with a miniature painting of the Organ Mountains. My mother hung this on the west wall of the narrow living room, between the air-conditioner and the window permanently painted shut, replacing the dime-store depiction of Jesus. It's like we couldn't get enough of those fine mountains, and when I was sixteen I climbed their needle-point peaks.

The history of Las Cruces is one of revolution, as the name "The Crosses" refers to a pueblo rebellion against Spanish colonization in the seventeenth century. During the Indian overthrow, three of the oppressive (I assume) padres were crucified upside down on a hill outside of what was then still a village on the Rio Grande River. Or that is the lore I was told as a child. The Tortugas (Turtle) Indians were very present in my grade school, and the first Christmas season we were there I saw the lights of their torchlight procession winding up Tortugas Mountain, west of Las Cruces. They went up at night, probably near or on December solstice, and barefoot. Later when I went to the college that the Anglos built near Tortugas Mountain, the freshman class was required to carry buckets of whitewash up to paint the football letter "A" on the side. Then I would feel with my own feet just how sharp the rocks are and how prevalent the sprawling prickly pear plants with their long curved spikes, and I would marvel again at the lives and spirit of indigenous peoples and their relation to the land of their (our—everyone's) being.

At school an event concerning a Tortugas girl would give me my first understanding of the word "poor" when a middle-class Anglo boy stuck a mocking finger into a hole in her skirt, over her hip. I was standing near her, talking to her in the schoolyard, and he reached between us, giggling, his finger lightning, a red line. My astonishment at his action was followed by a new sense of shame. I loved her, especially her serene energy and her intelligence, and though it is forty-five years ago I remember her name—Julia Gonzales—may she be blessed—and the pain on her face and in my heart. I had never known she had a hole in her clothes. I had holes in my clothes. I had never known they mattered. But now after this I suddenly noticed my companions, the other Anglo girls I grouped with for lunch. I saw us from outside ourselves. We were the only girls who frequently brought money (25 cents) instead of a homemade lunch, and went off the schoolyard around the corner to stand in line, surrounded by delicious greasy, pickley smells, to buy hot hamburgers with shining moisture dots on the brown buns. I found this exciting to do because it made me feel important that I could use money just like some of the boys did. (Our mothers worked and were too tired to make us lunch.) But now since the white boy Gary giggled as he stuck his finger into Julia's skirt, I looked again at the girls and realized we were all "ranked" together. The nice girls sat in their clothes perfectly clinging to them and ate healthy sandwiches from neatly, almost ironed, brown bags. They did not speak loudly. Did not stand in line with the boys to put on boxing gloves. I saw that Charlotte had crusty elbows and red, open "poor sores" on her legs and that both her clothes and mine were held together with pins and didn't fit exactly. She was mean, too, meaner than I. I didn't want to be considered mean,

Father, Elmer August Grahn, about 1983

but I was clumsy and aggressive and full of wild energy. I stepped on Priscilla's ingrown toenail and hurt her; I chased the boys and held them down and kissed them so they hated me; I teased the other girls and made them mad; I stood in line with the boys to put on boxing gloves. I wanted everything, and had no idea how to get it.

Going home with bony Charlotte to see how she lived, my newly categorizing eyes witnessed that she and her mother lived in a single adobe room with a dirt floor. *(They were poorer, then.)* Her mother sat on the bed where there were no sheets; there was no couch or chair. The big orange-and-black box of Tide stood outstandingly like a little American god on the chipped off-yellow sink as the only thing colorful; there were no cupboards. The room was naked; there was no modesty or subtlety, no nuance or mystery, no way to hide anything. No picture of Jesus or of the Organ Mountains. There was no decoration, as though they had fallen out of beauty and symmetry. How deeply sad and defeated the woman looked. I understood their poverty as absolute.

I took Charlotte home, and my mother was appalled. "Don't bring her back," she said,

which made me angry, and so began my horrified comprehension of the class distinctions that were separating all the children I knew. As I turned twelve and thirteen I would try to make friends with the Spanish-speaking girls, but they rejected me socially. While I comprehend the colonial reasons, my hurt was also real. As I turned thirteen and fourteen I tried to make friends with the middle-class Anglo girls, and one by one they would be forced by their mothers to reject me. Their lives weren't any less mean: C's mother was vicious in disciplining her to line up the hangers correctly in the large closet in her personal bedroom *(they were richer, then)*; and J who talked with only a trace of her mother's deep Virginia accent would aim a pistol at me point-blank, trying very seriously to kill me. *(Another Mother Tongue:* "Romeo and Juliet, Revisited.")

Carrying this further, I was still eleven when I rode my bicycle around town examining how everyone lived. I saw that the range of Spanish-speaking kids was from unplastered adobe houses to great tiled mansions with hundreds of acres of farmland, and that this continuum also lined up on a basis of lightness and darkness of skin color and degree of identification with "Indian." *(This had something to do with "race," then.)* I came one day on a street that held only black-skinned people, and I saw that the street had no sidewalks. *(These people were "poor" and treated as a group category, then.)*

At thirteen under pressure to find a man to support them and their future children, the girls obeyed the patriarchal myth of female inferiority as a prerequisite to "desirability" and began to turn from their intelligence, their ambitions, and their arts. They applied for jobs with the boys as girlfriends. *(They were heterosexual, then.* At fourteen and again when I was fifteen I knew that I was a lesbian. I told no one.) From eleven through sixteen I spent much time on a footbridge over the twelve-foot-wide irrigation canal a mile from my house, studying the water as it was siphoned off the Rio Grande, gazing at the waters from the river, smelling Her restless motions and talking to Her noises as she rustled in muddy rivulets over the wooden dam. This was the only place in my life where I was *reflected*—my face down there along with the trees, the sky, sparkling lights, the bodies of dead puppies, and old rubber boots. *(I was not really all the way in society, then.)* I was something wild and apart.

At fourteen I had lost all the class, race, and sex wars and was alone. *(The poet accommodated easily to this and decided to be a philosopher as well.)*

I was a spiritual child and despite being a "good girl" always revolutionary—in certain ways. My mother recalled once that I ran outside at the age of three to tell her that "church music!" was playing on the radio. Around age eleven I brought home a picture of Jesus in a glass frame from the five-and-dime; I was drawn to the pretty man with the soft eyes and the touchable lush brown hair. I wrote poems that the lady had me read aloud in Sunday school. Everyone thought I was religious, though it turns out "spiritual" describes me more accurately—a love of lightning storms and black widow spiders, knowledge that trees can kiss you back and the moon comfort.

Despite the fact I usually wore boys' clothing, never married, became a lesbian, and God knows what-all, I was the one who inherited the family Bible, a tome, written in Swedish, with a worn matte black cover, dating from the nineteenth century, full of pressed flowers. My parents gave me a big, expensive, special edition of a Bible in English when I was ten or so—with red ink passages and supplementary texts and color photos. I read it, some. Felt guilty whenever I lost interest. In June of 1987 I was the one who orchestrated my father's memorial service.

Yet at thirteen I conjured Jesus and then sent him away. The occasion was one of blood, lots of it; I awoke saturated, pillow soaked and getting sticky. From habit I rolled over to let the hot relentless stream go down my throat so I could preserve the precious stuff. Economy. (I imagined that I would re-digest and so retain it.) Smell of iron thick and musky as calf's liver, pajamas caked and shiny. Big crusting plug starting at the left nostril, the clot stringing down the nose passage, delicate and rubbery as a sea animal. Don't pester it or you'll die. Pulse a natural pump. Chance the flow will stop (if you do something right). Right nostril streaming away, salt-rubbing throat, grinding in to the tissue, intolerable AAAAARRRRRGGGGGHHHH rawness. Heart hammering. Lost cause. Turning over to escape the salt wash. Flush of blood pouring out, out to freedom, free flow. The towel my mother brought a red towel now. Red Sea. Panic, crying, "No! Stop," and "God, why don't you help me," clawing at the swollen,

With Wendy Cadden (left), about 1975

drowning nose. Both nostrils streaming. My mother went to call the doctor, first getting dressed, putting on her coat. She had to walk ten blocks to the phone booth. A cold night, windy.

Would Jesus help me? Despite Sunday school and my attempts, I had never had a vision of him. I had been baptized in the summer at a friend's Baptist church. (My parents sent me to the Methodist Sunday school, where St. Paul reigned.) I had written poems that became prayers, and all summer had sat in the useless car my father brought home, painstakingly flattening and squaring big nails with a metal file, and then using wire to make them into crosses, one of which I hung around my neck. The others I put in tiny boxes and gave to our neighbors as presents. "Irene, Good Night," playing on the radio.

When he arrived, I stared at him. Was dizzy, weak, panicky. Figured I had lost almost as much blood as he had. He looked like his picture, and I sympathized. But I needed someone more robust, someone who would not succumb to blood. Wouldn't die when it relentlessly streamed out. The blond god who appeared in my vision was nice; a nice fellow. I bowed my head in appreciation, met his kindly eye. He and I are friends. Then I sent him away. Aware I needed someone else, someone bigger, older, formless at that time. I felt the emptiness as a surprise and then shouldered it. I could wait.

After, as the years of possibility separated into shards of reality, I was willing to go on bleeding, and to give up any notion of religion—to let structures such as place, meaning, family—fall away utterly in order to follow a path (a verb) named only poetry. And to follow it as myself—female, daughter of a cook, lesbian, nomad American, shard of my mother's broken pot.

I needed something that could contain the paradox of my life.

Defining Moments—Definitions

What are defining moments in an artist's life? What can I say has influenced the courses of my work—begin with the work itself?

My approach to art is through the scrim of *use*. What is its purpose? Will people use it? Does it further society? Wendy Cadden first asked me this question about my poetry shortly after I had gone to live with her. I was twenty-seven. Her question remains a central organizing principle of everything I do. I'm not advocating any kind of utilitarianism; few modern poets pay more attention to form and musicality in their work than I do. The question "what is its use" has the effect of bringing my view outside myself, so I am never doing "self-expression," for instance. I am always on a mission.

Use in poetry begins with the aesthetics of beauty, grace, rhythm, image, passion, spacing (silence), and something like an altered-state-impelling-wave. No wave, no poem.

My father was a woodcarver. He sat in the cinder block apartment with a cardboard box of tiny tools, making ships out of orange crates and string.

This art of his taught me where everything creative comes from; how simple and complex it is to make something meaningful and beautiful from meaningless materials and some wave that exists inside the artist. He used no blueprints, maybe two lines on paper describing the maximum size and lines of the mid-hull. Shipness lived in his mind and emerged from his hands.

Everyone we knew loved his carvings, and I still have some of them. I love them, treasure them. But they are of little or no use, in and of themselves. My friend Dianne wrote me from France that she and Peg and Valerie (doing Valerie's research) came upon ship models hung in an old chapel—carved by sailors who had survived shipwrecks at sea, and submitted in grateful thanks to St. Anne, for their lives. That is what I mean by *use*. Given to a place where members of a community would come, and take heart or other memories, resolutions. A complete connection. An offering.

When I was old enough he left parts of the ship making for me to do—the painting, then the making of details like cannons and rowboats, then the rigging, the "rope ladders" patiently tied using waxed heavy string. Poems and great stories have this open relationship: they leave a part for you, so the minds blend. My mind blended with my father's mind as I worked on "our ships."

My father gave me a love for poetry, and then he expected me to write as though I were Rudyard Kipling and Alfred Lord Tennyson, to write of wars and brave men and colonial battles. He taught me much about form, not about content.

My mother gave me a love of scientific method and explorations, and her tragedy and how others helped me gave me a compassionate love for people—and especially women—and a desire for justice that is central to all my work.

The trick is to broaden *use* so it includes beauty, love, stillness, nothing, self-revelation, philosophy, what everybody around is saying, revolutionary politics, mysticism, whole communities of connectedness.

What people tell me about my poetry is of its use to them: "Took me through my mother's death." "Changed my life, so I changed direction—ran for president." "Took me through my stay in the mental hospital." "Got me through graduate school." "Reunited me with my wife." "Introduced me to my lesbian love." "Saved my life." "Got me through my jail term." "Explained me for the first time." "Told me what to write my novel about." And so on.

To accomplish poetry of use like this, I think, the poet must learn how to use herself perfectly—without being centered in either autobiography or self-expression, or, for that matter, a particular myth.

Definitions have always been difficult for me; that's why I constructed "the goddess" as a verb in my first understandings of Her, in *She Who*. I never wanted to have to choose butch or femme, and during the 1980 years when I slid into a very butch public image I

With Paula Gunn Allen (left), 1983

hated it as I hate all boxes. My handwriting could never stay on the lines in my notebooks, could never stay a single size or shape. Sometimes my own lover cannot recognize my handwriting; some days I cannot properly spell my name. Sometimes the face in the mirror is not "mine." This is so reassuring—that we can be in transition; we can transit; we do not have to be caught in a trap of identity.

Spirits

I was forty-three or a year older when I finally sent my mother a book to show her she had borne and raised a successful writer. Prior to this I lied. I told her I worked in a bookstore, yet millions already knew my poetry. The reason I lied to her is that in particular my audience knew a poem—the seventh of *The Common Woman Poems*—that I had written to her. It is called "Vera, from my childhood." The poem says a number of things I believe she would hate—that my father was a drunk. ("Promise me you will never tell anyone," she urged me when I was nine.) And secondly it uses the word "bastard." ("Never use foul language like your father does.") Thirdly the poem blames my mother's boss for oppressing her, as that was my childhood memory—my mother tired from work, tricks he played on her, how he insisted on calling her "Jean."

Once I brought up with her how much I had disliked him. She got her little brown change purse and snapped it open. Inside were two or three dollar bills and some quarters. "He *hired* me," she said, "when no one else in town would. And the thing I am most grateful for in my life is that finally, at forty-eight years old, I had money of my own. It wasn't *much* money. It doesn't *take* much money. It was *enough* money, to pay for food, and the gas bills. That made all the difference in my life." She looked me in the eyes *(my eyes astonished and ashamed, realizing I knew nothing about her.)* "I'll always be grateful. To *him.*"

So I never sent her that poem. The little red-and-white book I sent her was *The Queen of Wands*, a book of linked poems whose main character is Helen—Greek Helen, of Troy—and of European folklore—and of American workforce—of Hollywood, of my imagination. Helen the weaver, the worker, the stolen Shakti fire of objectification, and also the burning or flowering wand, the "flower rod" of HD, the Sacred Tree of Life . . . the one who is "most beautiful," "most valuable," and "most likely to be lost." (For those interested in psychology it is worth noting that my sister's name is Helen. She was named Helen Joan Grahn, though always called "Joan," and that the name is most often used of any, in my extended family of birth.) I tried to suggest that Helen could be any (western) background, any version of "beauty," and that she had lived century following century, as far back as the Greek overthrow of the matrilineal Trojans.

My mother said to me on my first visit after this event, "This is my book," and she embraced it against her heart. She read it until the pages frayed, and it remained on her bookshelf fourteen or fifteen years later. The book broke through my mother's shell, and she came out to play with me at last. By shell, I mean there is simply no one home. The eyes are—if not totally blank always—at least unresponsive. Or the response comes much later, after you have forgotten the referent. Or something appears out of the blue and has no context, so you can't respond. But there is no dancing between your two faces. There is no interaction or reflection.

By the time I was writing this poem I was in my early forties. My mother had withdrawn increasingly for decades behind layers of deafness, my father shouting, calling her stupid.

Our voice contact consisted of two or three phone calls she made to me every year, each lasting exactly three minutes. That was the amount of change she took with her to the phone booth. She refused to allow installation of a phone in her apartment until after my father's death.

But suddenly on the heels of sending her my poems, my yearly visits to Las Cruces contained a new dimension: my mother wanted to take me aside and talk to me. She gestured for me to follow her into the kitchen or bedroom where we huddled together knee to knee, my sweat pants against her frayed dress hem, her eyes and eagerness and terror mixing into a vortex that both thrilled and exhausted. My mother was talking to me! That great taken-for-granted privilege others had, that lush mother money they spent so easily, they took so completely for granted—of hours on the phone with "my mom," of discussions with Mother; the casual way they mentioned spending an afternoon with their Mama, of having an argument with her, of going shopping, being visited by her, hurry to clean the house, the rolling of eyes, "Oh God, Mom came to see me," being given unwanted advice, feeling she was interfering, meddling again, "her taste in clothes," going out to lunch (*going out to lunch together seemed to summarize what I wanted from her*), driving in the car together, all the myriad ways daughters describe the difficult and necessary and obvious web with their mothers.

None of this applied to me. For me the triumph was, "My mother heard a sentence I said to her; she asked me a question; she met me eye to eye." Somebody was home, for once. Somebody responded to my knock on her face. The expression matched—to some extent—the subject at hand.

The promise of normalcy, a relationship, a conversation, I surged forward to take the offering. What was it? More interesting than I could have imagined—and less normal. "Do you think I've lived before?" she asked, and a few other similar questions. Did I know about her past lives? Who might she have been? She wanted me to explain her—in terms of spirituality. "Sometimes I feel I've lived before," she explained. Her inner life. In her stuttering evasiveness, what I've just described took several visits to elicit. Over a year passed while we negotiated this early narrow passage. Then I began answering with more than nods and shakings of the head. (She could hear nothing of what I said aloud.) I began writing short answers, first on my own initiative, then on her insistence. The only paper she would accept at first were matchbook covers—on which I scribbled such wisdoms as "I think so, too," "maybe," and "I don't know, ask again."

In fear, she tore up these scraps before we completed our sessions, not allowing me to take them with me. During this first year or so I visited two, three times a year. I stayed two days. Our "talks" lasted about two hours at a time and were directed entirely by her. They followed an exact formula. First we repeated what we had done last time, then she added a bit more. A new question, an additional revelation about her wondering. The sessions completely exhausted me, so much so I could hardly think by the end and was grateful to quit, to get away from her relentless impossible quest, to replenish myself. I couldn't bear more than two sessions a visit. Yet this was the closest I had gotten to my mother since I was a child—that dangerous, treacherous terrain.

While filming her mother, 1996

She expressed extreme eagerness. She'd saved up questions between my visits, she said, and then it took great effort to get her to recall them. I studied patience—she was *there*—we were "talking"—sort of—she was in dialogue with me! I was ecstatic—flooded with love for her. She too was delighted with our newfound reach across.

"This book," she clutched the little red volume, "meant so much to me . . . everything." Long pause, deep look. "You can't know how much."

"I think I do," I say. She doesn't hear, but follows my eyes, clutches my hand in her dry fingers. Child brightness flows across her face. Surprise. "You *do* know!" Laughs. I follow suit. I do know and what I don't I can wait to learn. Maybe she'll deliver it to me . . . maybe not.

From three minutes a year on the phone we have graduated to two, then four, five hours of "conversation" each visit, twice a year. Slowly deciphering the cryptic script of her secret mind. After two years or so the matchbooks give way to sheets of paper. Then, she pulls a sheet of paper out of her apron. "I wrote some questions down." Trust. Trust is growing. So is my frustration at being unable to speak with her. I had tried to persuade her to write me, to write something besides the relentless cheery three sentence nonrevealing notes that arrived about once a month.

Her fears at first she articulated in the generic "them." We must tear up my matchbook notes because "they might read them." She refused my scribbled suggestion that she write her questions to me and mail them: "They might take the letter from the mailbox and read it." No response to questions of who "they" might be—why "they" might be interested.

I decided to try a different tactic on a visit. I began to shout, "I love you," as I sat knee to knee with her. Because of the soft expression on my face she grew curious. "What is it?"

I would repeat, several times, then give her a tight, long hug. After a few visits with this included, she began to hear me. At first just a few words, then a sentence, then two. Then she would hug me. Then once she looked me in the eyes for a while. "You and I are more than mother and daughter," she said. "You and I are friends. I feel that you are my friend."

My therapist, Mary, said to me of this: "Do you know how many women long to hear those words? Do you know how fortunate you are?"

This is only one example why, I say, while it is difficult for me to tell my life stories because people frequently project their own pain

Mother, Vera Doris Grahn, at the age of ninety-four, 1996

into them, but listen to this: I am a daughter whose mother came to think of her as a friend, and anyone who feels sorry for me—is—missing—the—point.

Going out to lunch with her seemed to summarize what I thought I wanted from her; in the long run I have acquired so much, much more.

The Queen of Wands

Wands refers to a tarot suit, fire, and the flowering rod of creativity, work. Some of the content of *The Queen of Wands* grew from a dialogue engaging Paula Gunn Allen and myself during the early eighties, some of it is from a theory that a Stanford University- educated scholar (Bella Zweig Debrida) had that Helen of Troy had once been a goddess. Some of the content developed from thinking about fragments of Sumerian poetry that I later learned to credit to a priestess of the goddess Inanna. Much of it is from various folk sources, and a certain amount derives from my own life experience. I say "derived" as nothing seems more futile than our attempts to put our lives into poetry without using myth, and myth is like a mold into which you pour everything following the experience of the furnace, the dragon breath that produces the melting that blends the minerals to produce the metal. And if it wasn't formed with one mold, it certainly was formed by another.

That is to say, I've never written "free" verse or "real" life that doesn't use myth, form, rhythm, and so on. And I live them, these crucibles. They are how I make sense of life, as though we can only "remember" parts of life that we can tell a meaningful story about. This applies collectively as well as individually, socially as well as psychologically. And like Helen in Wands, *my mother too had "fallen out of her own story" and, therefore, of social existence.*

Following her reading of *The Queen of Wands* and our decade of haltingly reaching across the abyss of silence between us, my mother frequently could carry on a complete coherent conversation with me, particularly if my partner Kris Brandenburger (who has a special way with children) was also present. Finally, when she was eighty-nine, she went to lunch with me. This was an exultant day for me—to go to lunch with my mom! I loved it, and so did

*Judy (right) and her partner,
Kris Brandenburger, 1995*

she. We talked, just like mothers and daughters. She told stories and heard my questions. She asked me questions about myself. (I don't tell her stories as she cannot listen to that much of me. She listens to me one sentence at a time.) At this one lunch we were remarkably normal. (I wanted to stand up and announce to everyone else, "Look, we are having lunch!") Afterward, she remembered it and remarked on it as a good time. After this Kris and I always take her out to eat, though it is not the same as that day. That day was very special because it was just the two of us, and she talked to me.

The Queen of Wands contains only one poem that is explicitly about my mother. *I used my feelings to encapsulate a thought about the self-betrayal, how the patriarchy seduces our attention away from the molten core of the feminine. As a child, I didn't ever want my father to think of me as "stupid" and inconsequential, like her.*

The land that I grew up on is a rock

I

From my mother, a rock,
I have learned that rocks give
most of all.
What do rocks do? They hold the
forces of the earth together and
give direction. They interrupt
the mindless sky in its total
free fall.
Rocks turn the monotonous winds
from their courses and bring down rain

before the all-collecting sea
reclaims it—so you and your friends
can have some, too.
A rock is a slow, slow
cooled-off flame, and a cradle, both.

They are like bone, the rocks. They frame.
They remain. They hold you.
They grind together to make digestible dirt.
Because of their slow lasting
nature, they are said
not to feel tangible hurt.
We were star-struck, my father and I.
We ate fast intellectual pie.
And we made fun of her, my mother;
she made material, actual pie.

But once, in a flash of insight,
he said of my mother: "Without her,
people like you and I would fly
right off the earth."

He made a gesture of his hand helplessly
sucked into the sky (like a navigationless bird).
He knew she was a rock
and so did I. He knew the worth
of gravity and certain repetition,
the safety of enclosure.
I knew the mute, the flame-charred
female wall, the dam
of granite rock between one's child self
and the molten family core,
the hell of terror, the inner and the outer
fire: my father's ire.

II

"You never listened to me."
Unexpectedly my mother weeps, recalling
how we never took her on our flights of thought
or left her, her own falling-out time.
How we locked her from our patch of
significant sky (that she was holding still for us)
my father and I,
as though she were a sheer wall of will
to be mined
to mill
and to grind and to be there
with or without our care.
It is so shocking for us
to see her now, a rock
weeping.

She is rocking
in her rocking chair
a little madly, deliberately deaf
to our star-struck talk.
She is chalk.

III

This lasts only a moment, a few years,
for my mother's tears
quickly evaporate and
return to their own mother, the sky
who weeps intermittently over everything,
renewing
without care,
and with the greatest care,
especially over the rocks,
bathing and cooling them
who by their basalt nature
cradle their feelings for the
longest time and most profoundly,
taking continuous
though sometimes secret, pride
in what they give
and giving the most of all.

Whether we (sky divers) care to learn
how to share this treasure,
my mother's spirit will return and return
teaching us. Whether my father and I
will learn, or not.

"Your mother is a saint," he says.
He means,
the center of a rock, particularly
the one we live on,
is molten like a star, the core
is light,
enlightening, giving of
intelligence.

Stretched far into the cold unwieldy sky
my father and I
in reaching for a star,
we nearly overlooked the one
that pulsed, all that time,
there (beneath us)
under our floating feet, and *in* us,
in the person of my mother,
rocking sometimes somewhat madly
in her brilliance-giving vision
as the earth,
a rock, a star.

My mother's characterization in "The land that I grew up on is a rock" is curiously bland relative to the incident it revolves around: the "breakdown." In my mid-adolescence one day my mother sat down in a wooden rocking chair, and stayed there. Didn't go to work, didn't go to the store, didn't cook, rarely spoke to us, didn't comb her hair. Her eyes withdrew to the point that she evidently could not recognize us. Nervous and restless, she paced the living room all day long, six steps up, six back. She continued in this state for a year. A red line moment.

I remember the terror on my father's face, how small he suddenly looked. My comprehension of his dependence on her. The poet has condensed this experience into a single image of a rock, rocking. Of both the hard mineral crust, "the mute wall" and the moving act of swinging, verb and noun, particle and wave, the paradox embodied.

I see that my father's analysis of my mother in this poem really falls short—to say that my mother is a saint is a bit like saying the earth is a saint. The earth might swallow your village in mud or knock your house down around your ears. Vast intelligence she may be, full of lightning and lava—and giving of everything. But everything is everything. Saint she ain't.

As I said earlier, the first time my mother tried to kill me I was a few weeks old. Perhaps brought on by her infant bout with smallpox, she was completely oversensitive and given to hallucinations and visions—which late in life she told me a little about, once she began to trust me.

She had not wanted a third baby, and certainly not in that period of time when she had no money of her own to feed me, not enough money to buy milk. A husband who believed independence from the nagging of womankind meant spending his salary on the boys at the bar and the quicksilver goddess named Lady Luck.

I can say that I believe I am the only person who ever got into my mother's mind, and the tool that enabled it was the one my father gave me: poetry. Recovered memory is shaky ground, and I find I constantly seek clues as to its accuracy. My mother has never been able to endure the least hint that she ever did anything harmful to anyone. Her neighbors think of her as someone who would not harm a fly. The story she told inside the family was that we must be wary of my *father's* violence. My father's power.

My recovered memories tell a different myth, one I continue to explore. In this, her ninety-fourth year, she has stopped the "reach-across" between us, no more talk of spirits or visions, no more questions to me about her inner life, no more revelations about her interior experiences. She has settled for one or two stock

In Kerala, India, 1997

stories of her girlhood, and can no longer make her way through to the point of them. She continues to say fragmentary things she has said for decades: "Do you remember Chicago? Were you there? Awful things happened there." I've never been able to get her to suggest what awful things these might have been.

Yet a month ago when I visited her with my partner, Kris, we took her to a café. During dinner, which she ordered for all of us, demanding that we eat the same thing she wanted, she turned to me. "Do you remember Chicago? Awful things happened to you there when you were a child. The lady came to visit. A lady came."

In my memory I recall a lady too, a concerned person who was worried about how they were treating me—and who came to talk to them about it.

Surprisingly now my mother continued, "You cried and cried when you were born." Her face changed; she looked up at the corner of the ceiling and imitated another woman's voice: "'*Why is your child crying?*'"

Turned to me again, "Do you have a memory of—now I can't remember. . . ." And she lost the thread. *And I will pick it up, and go on with it, drawing that red line.*

BIBLIOGRAPHY

Poetry:

The Common Woman Poems, Women's Press Collective, 1970.

Edward the Dyke and Other Poems, Women's Press Collective, 1971.

She Who, Women's Press Collective, 1973.

A Woman Is Talking to Death, Women's Press Collective, 1974.

The Work of a Common Woman, Diana Press, 1978.

The Queen of Wands, The Crossing Press, 1982.

Descent to the Roses of the Family, Iowa City Women's Press, 1986.

The Queen of Swords, Beacon Press, 1987.

Plays:

The Cell, first produced at Antioch College, Ohio, 1968.

She Who, first produced in California, 1974.

Queen of Wands, first produced in Ithaca, New York, 1985.

Queen of Swords, first produced in San Francisco, California, 1989.

March to the Mother Sea, first produced at the Michigan Womyn's Music Festival, 1990.

Nonfiction:

Another Mother Tongue: Gay Words, Gay Worlds, Beacon Press, 1983.

The Highest Apple: Sappho and the Lesbian Poetic Tradition, Spinster's Ink, 1985.

Really Reading Gertrude Stein, The Crossing Press, 1989.

Blood, Bread, and Roses: How Menstruation Created the World, Beacon Press, 1993.

Other:

Mundane's World (novel), The Crossing Press, 1989.

The Woman Whose Head Is on Fire (collection), St. Martin's Press, 1998.

Grahn's work appears on recordings, including *Where Would I Be without You: The Poetry of Pat Parker and Judy Grahn* (vinyl recording), Olivia Records, 1975; *March to the Mother Sea: Healing Poems for Baby Girls Raped at Home* (cassette recording), LavenderRose Productions, 1990; and *A Woman Is Talking to Death and Other Poems by Judy Grahn* (cassette recording), Watershed, 1991, as well as on video anthologies and in documentaries. Also contributor of short stories to *HIS/HERS* anthology and *ZYZZYVA Magazine* and of articles and essays to collections, journals, books, and magazines.

Crag Hill

1957-

LIVING A LIFE THROUGH LANGUAGE

for Laurie, who has always been there

My fortieth birthday approaching, I look back at the young man I was twenty years ago. Timid yet reckless, I swerved out of the path of things I knew I had to do, avoided many of the people I needed to meet, craved and shunned community, pushed aside the responsibilities that wouldn't leave me alone, and hurt those who loved me.

I've come a long way as a human being and as a writer. Teacher, father, husband, poet, my body of work, which perhaps at first glance seems scattershot, undeveloped, from this perspective unfolds in a logical way: raw, eager, imitative writing transformed through experimentation, through experience and industry, into writing that knows what words can do, that knows where they can go and lets them go with as little interference as possible.

I decided to become a writer for two reasons. Desperate for clarity, for balance, I learned in a high school creative-writing class that putting words on paper, however clumsily, focused the swirl of my life. I also wanted to do something my parents could be proud of, that I could be proud of, after quitting in high school most of the things that had mattered—playing baseball, attending classes, making popular friends, polite conversation. Writing, creation out of chaos, words summoning a definable, palpable world, would bring me out of the turbulence I flung up, arms and legs flailing, around me.

That creative-writing class saved my life. Self-destructive, a heavy drinker, taking any drug that came into my hands, I might not have lived until twenty, let alone forty, without the largess of poetry: bountiful meaning in a seemingly meaningless world. I cannot count the mornings I woke up in bed or on some floor not knowing how I got there, wondering how my face got cut up or where I left my shoes

Crag Hill, in the ruins of a monastery in County Wicklow, Ireland, 1985

or jacket. Presumably my generation had nothing to live for, our society shredded by its involvement in the Vietnam War, so we spent an inordinate amount of time taunting death. That creative writing class my senior year showed me I had something to live for.

I do not remember individual poems—I have them buried in an unmarked box in the basement—but I can recall their gist: tirades, self-doubting pleas for personal and universal sanity, or observations of the natural world, poems about trees with roots, the sturdy base I was missing. None of them were artful—flat, flaccid, overgeneralized, too earnest, awkward—not even the ones the *Green Bay Press Gazette* published under the pseudonym Ernst Winkler, but their value was incalculable. Or, more precisely, the process of writing those poems was priceless: writing them forced me to jump out of my careening personal life to look at what the hell I was doing, to construct something solid I could stand on. In searching for the right words, I began to find myself.

Our first poems are literally written for ourselves. We may write them with a friend or sweetheart in mind, and some of us may even think of publication as we write, but ultimately we whelp those poems into shape to give form to our incipient selves. As the poems form, however tenuously, so do we. As we write about birdsong in the morning, or a homeless woman whose amputated leg bleeds through its dirty bandage, or as we articulate those feelings we soon begin to recognize as love, we build ourselves. Those first words help us to unveil the person we are, word by word, layer by layer.

My first poems were more about the world outside than my interior life. I sang about sunrises on Lake Michigan, great blue herons defying gravity, leaves moving gracefully from green to red and brown, or I screamed about the poverty I saw in Chicago or Milwaukee or reported in magazines and on television. I raged at the inequality between rich and poor, between whites and blacks, fumed at how adults misunderstood their children. Unable to genuinely connect with my parents and friends, my first poems were all I had. They were my best friends, my family.

Uncomfortable as troubled son, juvenile delinquent, dropout, burnout, I reveled in what I perceived to be the dual role of the poet: observer of beauty and critic of ugliness. I imagined nothing more important to do with my life. If poetry could save my life, it could save others. I had a raison d'être.

A reason for living, however, may not be enough to make one. I couldn't eat poetry. Nor could I stay home. I had to find something to do so that I could be self-reliant. I

chose what other young men with a 1.79 high school GPA have chosen: military service. I could get away, as far away as I would want to go, to the four far-flung corners of the world, in the navy.

Fortunately, I avoided that exotic but dubious route at the last minute, saved not by poetry this time but by physical injury. The night before I took the navy physical, at which time I would be effectively enlisted, I popped my elbow in a softball game. Playing second base, I took a throw from left field and leaped toward the base to tag a runner who had taken too wide of a turn. We hit the bag simultaneously, runner crashing on top of my arms, on top of my glove with the ball.

I dropped my glove, ball stuck in the webbing. Dazed, in too much pain to argue the call, I straggled off the field. Everyone stood around and watched, unaware of the extent of my injury. Finally one of our players left the field, took a look at my elbow, two bones at odds with each other, crisscrossing, and took me to the hospital.

By the time my elbow had healed, I had changed my mind about military service. Working at Manitowoc Engineering or Mirro Aluminum had to be better, I thought, than six years enlistment in the navy, better than what would seem like an eternity taking orders from strangers. Besides, what could the navy do for me in terms of poetry?

I really just wanted to read and write. I wanted to sift the shelves of the public library, inhaling the poetry of William Wordsworth, Emily Dickinson, Ezra Pound, e. e. cummings, William Carlos Williams, Walt Whitman, all names resonating with poetry. Reading and writing would be a way to get out on my own, to make a world for myself out of words. I could do that anywhere.

When I started to read poetry that summer, I found models for the poetry I was trying to write. Robert Frost taught me how to hold still long enough to spot the human in the natural world, to listen closely to the way people talk; Allen Ginsberg helped me channel my rage, long lines acting as whiplashes; Anne Sexton showed that my day-to-day life, my stumbling, temperamental interactions with people I loved, could be the stuff of poems.

I made my way through the shelves of poetry in the balcony of the Manitowoc Public Library, an excellent collection of poetry for a beginning reader and writer. Ginsberg and Gary Snyder were mixed in with Frost, Wallace Stevens, and Carl Sandburg. William Wordsworth, William Carlos Williams, and Walt Whitman leaned up against each other. Stupefied by Stevens's *The Aurora of Autumn*, awed by Alfred Tennyson's long poems, by the stateliness of his language, amused by Ogden Nash, dumbfounded by Emily Dickinson, enamored of Theodore Roethke's imagery, all my reading was new and knew no bounds, articulating a world I could thrive in.

I read insatiably for the first time in my life. Skipping parties, I often read through the night until I turned off artificial light to let in the morning sun. I began to keep a notebook I flooded with beginnings of stories and drafts of poems, with groping annotations of my life. Imitating the writers I was reading, so powerful their voices to someone whose own voice wavered between a tremulous whisper and a red-faced shout, I was nevertheless forging a way of life, a clearer sense of what I could do.

For six months, I worked at Mirro Aluminum as a trucker. Shuttling crates of handles, screws, and unassembled pans between the warehouse and the assembly lines, I stole time to write. Carrying paper and pen in my work shirt, I scribbled away behind stacks of crates or hidden in a bathroom stall. I hated what I was doing for pay, but writing on the job was some consolation. I was making something then that I cared about, and, I snickered, I was getting paid for it, if indirectly.

I survived for half a year as a trucker. Promoted to forklift operator, I dumped a stack of crates—carrying four when I should have been carrying two—coming around a corner on my first day. The toppled crates smashed the glass out of a vending machine and almost crunched one of my supervisors. Demoted to trucker again, I walked out of the factory and out of the job before the end of the shift.

I had saved a thousand bucks though. After a few months in which I did nothing but read, write, and party, I heard that Mike Peltier, a high school acquaintance, was taking off for California and needed a traveling partner. This was my chance to pull up the stakes I felt were pinning me down, to get away from who I had been to find out who I could be.

We took a ride share to Seattle from Madison with no plan of action for our arrival, but the not-so-simple act of going out into the world on our own was strong enough motivation to go—the pull of the West Coast, the frightening allure of the big city, out muscled the pull of Manitowoc, the stifling familiar.

The theme for this trip surfaced in a poem I wrote the first night before we slept in a field strewn with cow chips above the Missouri River:

> A bed of sticks
> Can suffice when serenity overwhelms.
> On the road through Welcome and Free Born
> Means loving the simple joys we have.
>
> As wide as the world may be
> People are as wide with friendship.
> I mourn having to take a trip
> To realize people are not cruel.

We lasted a week in Seattle, holed up in Green Lake Motel, venturing out during the day to explore the city aimlessly, returning to our rented refuge at night to drink beer or watch TV. The extent of our job search was one trip downtown to Job Service, where we took a series of tests to ascertain our vocational abilities. I completed one test but, true to form, I walked out after we were directed to a room to take a typing test, something I knew I couldn't do. Our hearts weren't into finding a job. Procrastination took enough of our time and required no prerequisite skills. With nothing better to do, we decided to hitch to California, hoping some golden opportunity there would fall in our laps.

Before leaving Seattle, I read Jack Kerouac's *On the Road*, a book someone in Madison recommended when they heard we were hitting the road. The novel provided a model I tried to match: "I envy the adventurers and their escapades," I wrote of the book in my journal. "All they need is an ocean to travel to and a road to travel on. The only purpose for them is to meet people. And with people have a life without worries. Only an occasional need for food. Being poor is as far from their mind as a permanent home is."

After hitching and busing to the Los Angeles suburb of Van Nuys, we again did nothing to find work, and we did very little to explore the area and its people. The farther we got from home, it became clear, the greater its emotional tug. Spending our savings down to our last sixty dollars, we decided to turn back to Wisconsin. After a night trying to sleep poolside at Travel Lodge motel in Blyth, and waiting for a bus in 114-degree Arizona the next day, we made it as far as Las Vegas, where Peltier's parents bailed us out, wiring us bus and food money.

I had had a taste of being on my own. I hadn't stuck my neck out too far, hadn't done much to remain independent, but I knew I was going to get out of Manitowoc again soon. I was going to find a way to get into college to study literature, to learn how to teach, to do what I could to become a better writer.

I will never forget how overwhelmed I was on my first day at the University of Wisconsin-Stevens Point, how intimidated. Though I had bulked up intellectually, read shelves of books, perhaps many more than my fellow freshmen, my intellectual activity had been solitary. I did not know how to relate to other students, never having been one, at least not seriously.

I was taciturn in class and a hermit at night, missing the many lectures and readings that occurred on and off campus. I confessed my desire to be a poet to my friends and roommate, yet I didn't seek out the literary community active on campus I so desperately wanted. Much to my dismay, I learned later, I missed Gary Snyder reading on campus that first semester.

After a summer in Wisconsin Rapids, living with Michael Anderson (now known as Miekal And), I became more involved. Miekal was inspiring, the most knowledgeable and ambitious young writer I had met. Familiar with my beloved Beats, he also was tapped into the thriving small press community in the Midwest. I quickly learned that places like Milwaukee, Madison, Oshkosh, and Minneapolis teemed with poets.

I gave my first public reading that summer, participating in an event Miekal organized at the Wisconsin Rapids library. I read a long blank verse poem I wrote especially for the occasion that recounted a dream in which I glimpsed a tombstone inscribed with the year of my death, 1983. I remember dreading the reading, counting down the days as if my universe was doomed to explode on that very date.

The following school year, with Miekal as my role model, I joined the University Writers, took a creative writing class with Dave Engel, finally became a part of a community of writers. It was not easy, though, to lay open my writing, especially to people who I felt had more talent, more polish, but who did not work as diligently as I did, who may not have needed poetry as badly as I.

I attended every reading of many, one every other week or so—Midwestern poets such as Doug Flaherty, Philip Dacey, Michael Tarachow, and James Hazard. The mother of all readings, however, was Allen Ginsberg's. For three hours, he rocked gently in a rocking chair, reading an elegy for his father or singing Blake to the accompaniment of a harmonium. He mesmerized the audience by intoning long, sonorous lines in a deep, confident voice.

After the reading I was pleased to find the guts to approach Ginsberg. My burning question, an issue I had struggled with in my poetry, something I had argued about with Miekal and other poets, was about mixing politics and poetry. We didn't talk for more than a few minutes but he reinforced what I thought: find the emotion boiling under the surface of political issues, not the rhetoric. That emotion, Ginsberg said, our human drive to have fairness and sanity in our world, is universal.

I immersed myself in the Stevens Point writing community for a year and a half, studying with Mary Shumway and Rich Behm, getting to know Anthony Oldknow and Tom McKeown and many other student writers trying to create poems they could call their own. Poets became less intimidating, the gap between their abilities and mine less daunting. I learned how to revise, working the following poem, the first I published under my own name, through more than a dozen drafts:

Shoveling Snow

The clouds are dirty napkins
tossed in the branches of trees.
Crystals of light
sting my eyes,
break my rhythm.
Suddenly, the tree,

the shaking branches of the oak,
swoop down,
stumble on air,
fingers break,
fingers fall.

I scoop them up with footprints,
throw them over my shoulder.
The last words of old friends
grow harder and harder to hear.

Then I dropped out. I stopped going to readings and classes, took failing grades in all my courses except one. I had to get out of Stevens Point. The college gave me what I asked for—experience as a student of literature—but it didn't feed the fire of life that was smoldering within me. Academic routines didn't seem authentic, cut off from the delights and concerns of daily life most people experience. I had to hit the road again.

As a teenager in the 1970s, I was mad for the madness of the Beats—Ginsberg, Snyder, Phillip Whalen, Lew Welch, Lawrence Ferlinghetti, and, of course, The God, Jack Kerouac. Beat writing fed both my adolescent disdain for many things humans have done and do—their frenetic pages mirrored my rages—and my pleasure in the natural world.

In 1980, without job prospects, never having lived in a city larger than 150,000 people, with $450 dollars to my name, I rode Greyhound to San Francisco to gorge on the manic energy of the Beats, to pursue their lifestyle (or what I imagined it to be), drinking, smoking, staying up all night, rushing toward ecstasy or insanity. I was primed to howl at city lights.

Attending a poetry reading at the Grand Piano coffeehouse on Haight Street the very night I arrived at grimy Seventh and Market, I knew I was in the right place. Words were thick in the air everywhere, emitting the passionate, expressive potential of language.

Always hungry in mind and stomach (my Tenderloin hotel room lacked a kitchen among other amenities), even if I had to beg to get past the cover charge, I attended readings virtually every night, including Beat legends Gregory Corso, Bob Kaufman, Michael McClure, Philip Lamantia, and Jack Micheline, and I haunted the basement of City Lights where poetries large and small bulged from shelves and magazine racks.

My knowledge of poetry expanded exponentially. As it grew, I soured on Beat writing. Their work seemed clumsy, wordy, obvious, self-centered; it no longer crackled with urgency. One evening Laurie Schneider and I stormed out of a Corso/Kaufman reading at the Art Institute. Mugging for the audience's adulation, Corso was silly, his poems trivial, and Kaufman's mumbling irked us.

Despite the disappointment in that event, I didn't stop going to poetry readings, nor did I stop reading and writing. Within a year, in an issue of *Soup*, edited by a generous angel of poetry, Steve Abbott, I stumbled upon examples of a poetry that sent me reeling again, that radically shifted my way of looking at writing.

Earlier Abbott had shown interest in the following poem, "Blue Heron," which he said he would try to publish in *Poetry Flash*, the monthly poetry news/calendar he coedited with Joyce Jenkins:

Blue Heron

by swift of stream
at its mouth, its kiss
the source lips strength, consequent song
takes wing in wind

and tributary
many thoughts, trout
silverflesh of stars, stones
dance in the snag

the pike
as river's arrow
teeth to the current
the sway of lily
the skulls of shore, that earth may speak
many-tongued, many whispering
ripples through reeds

and these heard
the blue heron and the breath
of wings

But he either didn't find a place for it in *Poetry Flash* or he forgot about the poem. And so did I after reading *Soup*. I did not write a similar poem for over ten years.

The eclectic second issue of *Soup* included two essays, "Language Writing: The Pluses and Minuses of the New Formalism" by Bruce Boone and "Modes of Autobiography" by Ron Silliman, a discussion of books by Ted Berrigan, David Bromige, and Lyn Hejinian, and it included a curious poem, the first in the issue, "China," by Bob Perelman. I was delightfully perplexed, never having read anything like it before (or never having been ready to read anything like it). It resisted paraphrase and exploded the notion of coherence as I knew it (or as I thought I needed it in poetry). "China" made my thoughts run. I wanted to write such plain yet enigmatic lines. The two essays gave me some insight into Perelman's poem, increased my appetite for more poetry like that, and pointed the way to the plenitude of language-centered writing.

I didn't have to go far: San Francisco was one of the loci for Language poetry. Silliman, Perelman, Carla Harryman, Barrett Watten, Michael Palmer, Lyn Hejinian, Robert Grenier, Kit Robinson, Leslie Scalapino, Steve Benson, David Bromige, and many others lumped under the L=a=n=g=u=a=g=e coin lived in the Bay Area. Busier than bees, these writers organized countless readings and discussions ("talks") about language-centered writing and related literary and philosophical issues. New Langton Arts, Intersection, New College, San Francisco State Poetry Center, Minna Street Gallery, Tassajara Bakery, Larry Blake's, and other coffeehouses, bookstores, lofts, and galleries hosted these paradigm-shifting events.

An accompanying print explosion dated from the 1970s: Perelman published *Hills,* Silliman *Tottel's,* Watten *This,* Jerry Estrin edited *Vanishing Cab,* David Levi Strauss brought out *Acts,* Hejinian produced Tuumba chapbooks, exquisite letter-press collections, and Watten and Hejinian edited the provocative *Poetics Journal.* The ideas of language-centered writing seemed omnipresent.

Writing in San Francisco—writing in America—was clearly undergoing a revolution equal to if not greater than the Beat literary renaissance of the 1950s. Everyone seemed to be talking about Language poetry. People loved it, grabbed onto the movement's coattails, or hated it, attacking its obscurity, its aloofness, accusing it of stripping writing of its humanity.

I had only peripheral contact with these writers but I was intimate with their ideas, their intense analysis of written language, especially its social/political functions. Prolific essay writers, they critiqued the conventions and clichés of contemporary poetry (particularly the Iowa workshop style), arguing that the potential of written language cannot be realized until it is first liberated from the expressive mode. Published in journals and/or collected in anthologies such as the *L=A=N=G=U=A=G=E Book* and *The Politics of Poetic Form,* these essays forced me to look at language under a microscope, to consider all its constituent parts. Feeling as if I were looking at writing for the first time, my writing changed course. Previously a writer of lyric poems, I learned other ways to put words around the world.

I started writing cut-up poems, cutting words, phrases, sentences, and lines out of magazines, newspapers, instruction manuals, poems by other poets, whatever print material I thought might yield a poem. I hunted the world for meaning with a pair of flexing scissors. Rather than searching for ways to express myself, I sought the means through which language could express itself. Some of these cut-up poems still surprise me, including the following poem, published in my first collection *I Chings and Prototypes:*

Postmodernism

The big new flower on diction's dung
cause even the strongest among us to run up
  the white
body of work—one that extends from paint

This is therefore a textbook case of the way
  in which
no limits need be set.

Even those who cannot name a great painter,
go to pieces—and neither should we—when
  new names
design to music, dance, poetry and the science

And there were signs
many years ago—that "There are few things
  not purely
the work of others,"

These are the achievements that never give up
  their last
brows, he thought.

edged, modernism made us.

It can be applied to a tall public building
to change our lives for the better.

Not always knowing what some of these poems meant exactly, I learned to be comfortable with not being in full control. The cut-up process released language from my self-centered grip so it could speak for and of itself, so it could generate its own web of significations. By choosing materials, of course, I had my hand in the poems, but they had their own impetus along the way, suggesting options at each crucial instant of choice. These were not poems as I had once known poems—vehicles of self-expression, not *my* poems.

In practice, there was nothing I could not try with words, no experiment invalid—"no limits

Hill, exploring Mexican poetry, in Puerto Vallarta, 1984

need be set." Though the process took precedence, the results still had to please. The answer to one question determined whether a piece of writing was pleasurable: Does the work spark new ways of thinking? As a writer and a reader, I sought such pleasure in many different forms, found it in many different sources.

Mixing details about San Francisco life, mundane and extraordinary, with reflections on the process of writing, Ron Silliman's *Tjanting* showed how to build a text, one discrete sentence at a time. Thought sentences rubbed shoulders in paragraphs, no sentence was dependent upon the preceding or subsequent sentences to define its meaning—they each spoke for themselves. Utilizing the Fibonacci sequence (1,1,2, 3,5,8,13,21 . . .) to organize the sentences into paragraphs of one sentence, one sentence, two sentences, and so on, *Tjanting* was a marvel on the micro- and macro-level. The transformations each sentence underwent from paragraph to paragraph turned them inside out in revealing ways, and the unabashed wordplay was delightful, yet the inclusiveness of the writing

particularly appealed to me. Silliman was willing, it seemed, to write about anything. He described things he witnessed without embellishment: "A pile of old clothes discarded in the weeds of a vacant lot . . . In the plastic blue dish sat old soap silvers . . . An odor specific to porn shops . . . Storefront sounds of butcher paper & windows covered with buzzsaw hammer . . ."

I realized things weren't inherently poetic, that there weren't absolute subjects for poems— roses, bones, sunrise gradually illuminating green hills, death of a loved one. The overlooked minutia of our lives also overflow with meaning. Paying attention to the inconsequential, I no longer had to experience extreme emotional states—achieved either through alcohol, drugs, sleepless nights, or volatile personal relationships—to write. Writing could be generative, not simply descriptive.

I wrote a couple of short works to practice writing what Silliman called the "New Sentence," including a piece entitled "In One's Own Calligraphy," which began, "The beginning is self-evident. The sound of water in a sink. Dawn. The self is evidence. Hands shuffle bowls. This open book, brown page." Written in a twenty-four-hour period, the piece described everything around me as I wrote and did not conceal the act of writing, a valid subject in itself.

Then I undertook my first book-length project, *Prospectus.* Written over a period of months, one sentence at a time, it loosely borrowed the structure of *Tjanting,* its progressively longer paragraphs, sentences from earlier paragraphs transformed in later paragraphs to anchor the new, discrete sentences in place. The first two paragraphs go as follows:

> Funny, but I've never been here before. These spaces. Dew on the sliding glass. There was sun today, sky a certain blue only proximity to the sea could give it. Very little wind. I read to listen. Look at the music.
>
> These spaces have never been here before. This floor. The moon is full, morning now. Funny. The brush, books, coffee cup, within reach. Sliding on glass, dew. A spoon in a bowl, a photostat, a piece of thread. The walls shake with a neighbor's waking. Hard core. I took the bus home. Who started it is not the same. Watch. Very little wind. To look. Listen at the music. I read.

The piece continues for eighty-two pages, the last paragraph running fifty-six pages in length. I remember being so obsessed with writing sentences, writing about what I saw or heard on the bus, or walking on Market Street, or sitting in The Owl and The Monkey coffeehouse, that I was afraid I couldn't stop. Even when I decided to put my pen down, put it out of my reach, my brain continued to construct sentences.

If Silliman demonstrated the potential of autonomous sentences, Bruce Andrews, in *Praxis,* liberated and empowered phrases. I don't know how many times I read the first page of *Praxis.* Language had never seemed so abstract, yet so resonant, so open-ended.

Though many of these phrases connected in striking, often disconcerting ways, I was also pleased by the phrases that didn't, that hung in the air, steadfast in their separateness. My first book-length poem, *Sixixsix,* used *Praxis* as a springboard. Collecting phrases from various sources (newspapers, magazines, my own writing), I constructed a poem consisting of 666 phrases in each of three sections. Recording

them in chronological order as I found them, connections between phrases were accidental, created out of the process rather than my intentions, what was missing as important as what was included. The poem begins:

> the exercise
> you would think
> the elemental
> too nearly
> rudimentary
> aperture
> an unusual effort
> her guise
> on the water as if it were
> kissed each toe
> caused a series of depressions
> such scenarios
> another pass through
> quality of being real
> fragments
> manipulate
> enough's enough
> there ever being more to come
> lines of a buttock
> after shutting off all nights
> could scarcely be more timely
> it would be many years before
> the color blue underneath
> we each have our days
> another is there later to drink from
> swinging door of the kitchen where other
> thereof
> vivisection

The number of phrases for each section was fortuitous. "Off the Line," the poem's first section, was transcribed into a booklet of paper I had sewn together, but not yet used, for watercolors. Before beginning the next two parts, each one drawing from different source material, I counted phrases in "Off the Line." When the count totaled 666, I mischievously chose to use the same number in the other sections of the poem.

The number of lines in *Sixixsix* was unplanned, yet the poem's implication, at least for my work, echoes the biblical meaning: The book does not mark the beast or foretell the ending of the world, but it does delineate the end of the world of my writing as I had known it.

Robert Grenier and Clark Coolidge, both associated with language-centered writing (though quite independent of it as well), pulled me deeper into the body of language, pointed out how to activate the heretofore unknown or

Crag Hill (right) and Bill DiMichele,
cofounders of Score *magazine,*
Oakland, California, 1985

neglected meanings of words and how to burrow below them into letters, phonemes, and the spaces between them—no part of our language is devoid of meaning.

Grenier's *Oakland* and *Series* pulse with the power of individual words. Each word, freed from its confining role as a link in larger discourses, resounds with its own infinity of connotations. Grenier's poems demand as much, if not more, exploratory, constructive reading as Robert Frost's "Stopping by Woods on a Snowy Evening" and other canonized poems. Grenier simply took out many of the things readers depend on to help them make meaning. By expecting that readers supply the missing pieces out of their own reading, out of their own linguistic imagination, Grenier emancipated them.

Coolidge's *Space,* a mind-boggling book I found at San Francisco's public library, hinted at the untapped meaning behind and/or below words, a notion I had never even considered. How to make sense of "is so/of/I/from"?

Coolidge may not have intended to spotlight the dust-mice crevices under words, yet the seemingly random chain of verbs, pronouns, and prepositions forced one to look into those dark spaces. I had to enter to see what I could see.

Silliman, Andrews, Grenier, Coolidge, and others helped reform my thinking. Through them, I finally caught on to the concrete/visual poetry that had previously befuddled me. Having thumbed the Emmett Williams's *An Anthology of Concrete Poems* for years—one could find it in so many used book stores—I could not figure out how Aram Saroyan's "eyeye" or "lighght" was poetry.

A poem by Claus Bremer provided one of the "aha" moments that helped me break the cognitive barrier. The poem starts and ends with illegible lines, all eight words of the sentence "participate in a process rather than confront results" typed on top of each other. In the next seven lines, the sentence is systematically revealed, pulled out of the mush of typeovers, and the last seven syllables push it back into illegibility.

That line became my manifesto. Mapping out the process of writing, language forming thought and revealing feeling, was more important than the finished product. The final form had to display the process in such a way that other readers could experience the process and product simultaneously.

I leaped into concrete poetry, exulting in its ability to tease meaning out of the bodies of words and punctuation, even in the parts of letters—those meaningful humps in the letters s and b, in the upward curve of the letter c, in the angles of ts and ks.

The concrete poems I published in the inaugural issue of *Score,* the magazine of visual poetry I started with Bill DiMichele and Laurie Schneider in 1983, included blow-ups of typewriter correction tapes. White letters in a black field, the phrase "father had," the words "air" and "just" flirt with coherence. The emphasis in these found poems was not the denotative or connotative meanings of words; the visual had to vibrate, had to engage the spatial intelligence of readers first as paintings do.

I also "wrote" poems that could be readily paraphrased, including the following dissection of the attitude of many Americans:

A r
me i can

"With my wife, Laurie Schneider,"
London, England, 1985

Score and other literary magazines with the mettle to include visual poetry in its pages also published a type of poem I explored for several years in which one word, such as "spirit," is transformed into another word, such as "poet."

When I began the poem by systematically degenerating the word "spirit," I had no idea where it was leading. Midway through I saw hints of the word "poet" and then cruised through the process of regeneration from "Poml" to "Pomt" to "PoEt." The poem spoke of my belief that my spirit, my spiritual life, was intertwined with my practice as a poet.

As I was gaining a reputation as a visual poet, I continued to produce verbal poetry. In 1986, I began a series of pieces in which I systematically "edited" classic texts such as George Orwell's *1984,* James Joyce's *Ulysses,* and Ron Silliman's *Tjanting.* Using their words as base material, I processed works such as *1 Than, Yes James, Yes Joyce,* and *Reading His Margins.*

The book that remains my favorite, *Dict,* was derived from a reading of Webster's New Collegiate Dictionary. Reading the dictionary from cover to cover, or at least the left half of every definition, I wrote down the poems I found hidden in the dense text. The methodical selection process of *Dict,* a book of "creation by discovery," as Jack Foley wrote in the introduction, dislodged poems that I could not have consciously composed.

The process of discovery, of leaving things out, covered some poems that were similar to concrete or sound poems:

ar

ar

Ar

AR

ar

or

is a poem whose meaning is only fully revealed when read aloud, repetitively, as the documentation of the rise and fall of an episode of laughter.

1. OWNLR
2. daeh
3. overshld
4. iswat
5. ebda nelis
6. ob was ound
7. ilp
8. outmh
9. lapcper

is either a list of words that were, meanings and uses now extinct, or a list of words that will never be, words that failed to attach to things, words that remained empty.

Dict spawned an ongoing interest in short poems, especially poems less than six lines in length. One collection, *American Standard,* includes many that butt up against the boundaries of concrete and verbal poetry, often with a quick sense of humor I found hard to infuse into other forms.

I held two jobs in San Francisco from 1980 to 1990, including nearly six years of full-time at Graphic Reproduction, a business that specialized in reprographics for engineers and architects. Hired as a bike messenger, which I did with less joie d'vivre than many of my rambunctious cohorts on two wheels, I worked in the photo department when pickups and deliveries were slow. After a few weeks, trained to do contact printing, to opaque negatives, to trim, clean, and wrap finished orders, I became the night shift, working solo in the basement of an old building near First and Mission from 11 P.M. until 7 A.M.

For the first couple of years, I enjoyed the work, took pride in making sharp, dense negatives and clear, clean prints. Working a shift without a supervisor also gave me the chance to explore the art of photography at no personal expense. Many a night I finished my work in a few hours. If I didn't nap on the balcony couch until rats scratching in the garbage cans woke me up, I filled the rest of the time playing around with different photographic papers and chemicals and different techniques.

The job, in fact, was ideal for a visual poet and publisher of visual poetry. I could do costly enlargements and reductions for no cost; I could try multiple exposures without planning; I could wash exposed paper with random splashes of developer and not have to clean up the mess. The enlargements of typewriter correction tabs, printed in the first *Score*, would not have been done—*Score* itself would not have been published—had I not worked at Graphic Reproduction.

But I also despised the job. The business had a lot of disgruntled employees, a lot of turnover, demoralizing conditions that made it difficult to punch in. I survived as long as I did because I quit several times too, sometimes for longer than a month. I came back, however, usually after a Greyhound ride back to Wisconsin to visit Miekal and Elizabeth Was at Xexoxial Endarchy in Madison. I returned again and again because the perks of the job, its free materials, were hard to pass up. I also still hated to look for other jobs.

Thinking I wanted to stay in the field of photography, I switched to another company, shooting photostats for advertising firms. A hectic marathon of working on orders overdue before they even came in the door, that job burned me out. Desperate to work a job I liked, I decided to reroute my life out of the darkroom. Ten years after first attending UW-Stevens Point, I returned to college to get the teaching credential I said always I would get.

My transition from photo technician to teacher paralleled a transition in my writing. I circled back to the idea that I could teach as I circled back to the lyric poem. But by no means was I writing the same kind of lyric poem that I wrote as a teenager, however much skill I might have acquired in the intervening years. My concept of what a lyric poem could be had been transmogrified.

The first booklet I published after returning to college, *Trains Slay Huns*, took one element of lyric poems, sound, and amplified it so that it was the driving force of poems. "Translating" English poems into English, I attempted

to "retain as much of the sound of the original as possible, without the constraints of literal semantics," I wrote in the introduction. Translating Robert Frost, William Butler Yeats, Larry Eigner, William Carlos Williams, Wallace Stevens, David Bromige, and others, I tried to write poems whose sounds compelled, trusting that meaning would bubble up from the stew of assonance and alliteration.

One of the first translations I completed is the most successful. Rising above the exercise of homolinguistic translation, it is a poem whose sound and sense feed off each other:

Adapted from a poem by Tu Fu
translated by Arthur Sze

The nation has spoken, yet hills and rivers
   survive.
A spring is in the city, but there is no bounce.
Touched by the hard lines, flowers breed tears.
Conceived by preparations, birds are frightened
   in the heart.

The beacon fires turned for three consecutive
   months.
A flutter from home would be worth ten
   thousand pieces of old.
As I catch my white head, the stairs became
   fewer;
So scarce that I cry in vain to hasten them
   with an end.

When a fifteen-credit class load and over twenty-five hours of work chomped into my writing time, I had to adapt if I were to continue to write daily. I had to find some way to sustain a project over time. Still fascinated with the concept of the new sentence, I hatched a project in which I would collect sentences organized around the days of the week. Hypothesizing that what I wrote about on Mondays would be different from what I wrote on Saturdays, I collected sentences for over a year.

Though the form is different, *The Week* is similar in content to *Prospectus*. I was again inclusive, writing about anything I could fit a sentence around. As with *Prospectus*, writing itself was an important subject: "Each sentence is a/new day." Or: "The object of/representation is the existence of/occasion." Again I did not shy away from puns and other kinds of wordplay: "The motion/over there creates emotion over here." Or: "He is my inspiration, but not my breath." Or: "Sitting too/close to the news one could go blond."

The Week, unlike *Prospectus,* went through dozens of revisions—first thought was not best thought. Paring down flabby sentences, rewriting those that never got off the ground, *The Week* is a more sinewy piece of writing. The raw material—one attentive sentence at a time—was similar, but my willingness to reshape it changed the end result.

Though the page I kept for sentences written on Sunday, a day I caught up on correspondence and personal projects, was filled quickly, it took me months to fill the page for Saturday.

As I turned the corner from student to teacher, time to write became scarce. I had to choose between the many activities I was involved in. Publication of *Score* and its series of booklets, mail-art, The Outpatients, a poetry performance group/garage band I played with, and much of my correspondence had to be shelved. Writing, the one activity I was unwilling to give up, was still creating many of the moments in which I felt most alive.

The author with his mother in the California redwoods, 1986

Teaching high school in Berkeley was intensive. Prepping for three different classes and grading papers until ten o'clock at night, I did not write every day. When I found the time to write, I couldn't pick up the energy of something I wrote days before, couldn't get into the kind of longer projects I love to do. I decided to go back to the lyric poem, something I could hammer into shape in one sitting. But when I sat down to write, whatever quiet I could fit into was quickly assaulted with images of lessons gone awry, conflicts with students, doubts about my ability to teach, ideas for future lessons—I could not turn off the teacher.

Not until I devised a chance/composition method. I wrote down words I randomly chose out of magazines or the first words that popped into my mind, scattering them on the page one line at a time. Speed writing between these key words, I joined them together as unconsciously as I could, allowing each word to nudge the flow in its direction, not worrying about what lay behind or ahead. With the next draft, I would break up the chunk of prose into lines of verse, then cut and rearrange that material until I thought the poem had said what it wanted to say. Unlike many of my earlier works, I consciously entered into the process. After the initial rush of random composition, nothing was sacrosanct, all open to revision. The results were the kind of elusive poems I could not have written earlier, such as the opening poem to *Another Switch:*

The Stuff of Rough Houses

Filling in one side as the other stares bare,
the first row rose in a pause.
Posture is the only requirement.

His mind, the product of modern times,
builds the parts, then the heart.
It just wanted to be known.

Unfounded criticism found its mark,
scraping paint off bone,
the made thing all space thrilled.

The landscape grows on him.
Different colors activate stairs peaking.
Render it absolute.

aspirated, exasperated, exaggerated.
Flow becomes wolf,
first in order, then in horror.

I had found a way to play, to make improbable connections, to surprise myself with what words did on the page. Often I did not know what I wrote until long after I had "finished" a poem.

Many of the poems in *Another Switch* critiqued the society we try to function in, echoing my first poems written in the 1970s:

Hounding Numbers for a Reason

Present shadowed by the future,
the plane shakes off a crowded street.
What a day to be a lie.

Sexuality spawns whole industries,
the occasion of existence,
the same mindless mall.

The whole night is suffused by waste,
the heart to tell, the mouth to beat.
Now they get their time.

War begins to divide the people.
Excitement turns to incitement.
The possibility of two words infecting each other

chases tomorrow from today.
Sometimes fantasies are forthcoming,
time a curve as well as a line.

Population oozes
from every point in the room.
Soldiers take the promised land.

One of the motivations for getting a teaching certificate was so that my wife, Laurie Schneider, and I could move out of the Bay Area to one of the places we traveled to each summer in Idaho, Wyoming, or Montana. I dragged my feet, however, holding tenaciously to a challenging position teaching English to both Ivy League-bound and at-risk students at Berkeley High School, not inquiring about job openings elsewhere. Finally, when Laurie herself decided to go to graduate school at Washington State University a decade after finishing her undergraduate degree, we moved to Pullman, a small town nestled in the wheat-producing Palouse, a distinctive geographical region in the little-known corner of southeastern Washington.

Having to adjust the speed of my life from frenzied city to unhurried college town, my writing has evolved apace. Living in a town I am happy to call home, I write more about the place I live in, feeling less compulsion to experiment. Perhaps writing the kinds of poems I wanted to write as an eighteen year old, I meet the world with more delight than fury:

We Saw the Sound

we never saw the meadowlark
who rolled its melodic flute
through brush above Lyon's ferry

but a few miles down the road
we saw Palouse Falls, much larger than we
  expected—
loud and brown, full of winter run-off

it drowned almost all sound around it
but itself
      and the memory of meadowlark melody

Laurie and I had our first child, Liam Orion, on January 25, 1996, a momentous, life-transforming event. As he started to grow up, growing from baby blob to crawling infant to toddler always on the go, he entered my writing:

Look, Liam
there's light, isn't there?
Not much but it's all so even
it casts everything in the same tone

Look at the leaves there on the grass, wet
and not in the trees, stripped bare
just one mountain ash left with red berries

Look, Liam, can you see the hawk
on top of that tall pine? Now chased off
by magpies, its tail steadies its flight

Look, here, at your tiny handprints
pressed in the dew on the window

I want to hold those forever

As poetry helped me find my identity as a teenager and a young man, prose writing is now helping me find out who I am as a teacher and resident of the Palouse. Writing essays on educational issues, reviews of books by writers who have taught me much about the Inland Northwest—Kim Stafford, David James Duncan, Mary Clearman Blew, and others, I have also written about this region that surrounds me, that rounds my rough edges:

Hill's latest inspiration: Liam Orion Hill, born January 25, 1996

Finding Home in the Palouse

I've acquired a new home, one that dived deep within me without my knowing it. It's called the Palouse, a funny name, starting "puh" on the lips, ending "loose" on the tip of the tongue. Maybe that's what caught my attention, that insistent sibilant at the end of the word, a sound that got me to stop: "Sst . . . sst . . . come here. Take a look at this."

Scouting a place to live three years ago, I was amazed the first time I saw the Palouse, never having seen anything like its golden roller-coaster hills. For two years then I drove 195 south to Lewiston, Idaho in the morning to teach and back to Pullman at night. Small pieces began to accumulate from this commute, slowly added up to something I could hold on to.

I was never bored on that drive, often soothed, succored by the softest hills I've ever laid eyes on. I've floated with hawks, watched cottonwoods snow, their seeds bil-

lowing through Uniontown, soaked my feet with blue herons in Upper Flat Creek, and shuffled in underbrush with ring-necked pheasants.

Weeks of rain and melting snow taxing the watershed, I've watched ditches and culverts become creeks, creeks become rivers, and rivers spawn lakes. I've watched mallards float these seasonal lakes until water percolated into earth. I was no longer passing through.

This landscape never shows the same face twice. The waves of seasons mold its moods: expectant, somber, fuming, exuberant, satiated. Dominated by wheat, it may first appear to have a sameness to it, yet if you're looking, it's easy to pick out something different: coyote slinking away from the highway, redwing blackbird swaying at the tip of a cat-tail, a slump of waterlogged grass and clay on a road cut. Sometimes things shock: dead doe on the highway shoulder, neck snapped, or a red-tailed hawk, pulverized on the pavement, only its fluttering tail-feathers left to identify it.

How can anyone love this landscape whose native habitats survive only in fragments, many smaller than a single acre, land untouched because it's too steep to plow. How can we not? We have to love its colors, gliding from green to gold to brown to green with the grace of a symphony, one movement to the next.

You've got to pull your car to the side of the road to let the wind touch you, to inhale the smells it carries: overturned earth, dew on pea shoots, rain soaking dry wheat husks after harvest, muddy creeks bubbling through thick grasses. If you don't, you'll pass right through.

After my first reading in the area at which I read selections from the various phases of my writing journey, ending with the essay above, one of my teaching colleagues remarked that my poetry has improved. His comment, meant as praise, rankled me.

I do not think my earlier writing begged for improvement. I think my colleague would have been more accurate had he observed that the motivation for my writing has changed. My experimental writing had been seeking out a space in which to exercise my imagination, attempting to build it from scratch, separate from my day-to-day life. Now perhaps my writing and my daily life have fused: my writing explores the space I live within.

I may have taken many roads less traveled than other writers, but I've picked up a lot as a writer from the stops and detours along the way. I would not be the writer that I am today, the teacher of writing that I am today—allowing students not only to express themselves but to experiment with the kinds of forms I have experimented with—had I not written what I have written. Those writings are not my family, but they sure are some damn fine old friends.

BIBLIOGRAPHY

Poetry:

I Chings and Prototypes, Xerox Sutra, 1983.

1 Than, Xerox Sutra, 1983.

Sixixsix, Xerox Sutra, 1983.

American Standard, Runaway Spoon, 1989.

Dict, Xexoxial Editions, 1989.

Trans-Forms, Score, 1989.

Trains Sl-ay Huns, Generator, 1990.

The Week, Runaway Spoon, 1991.

Reading His Margins, dbqp, 1991.

Yes, James, Yes Joyce & Other Poems, Loose Gravel, 1994.

Another Switch, Coker, 1994.

Editor:

(With John Byrum) *Core: A Symposium on Contemporary Visual Poetry,* GENERATORSCORE Press, 1993.

(With Bob Grumman) *Vispo Auf Deutsch: An Anthology of Verbo-Visual Art in German,* Runaway Spoon, 1995.

Also founded *Score,* a magazine of visual poetry, with Bill DiMichele and Laurie Schneider in 1983, wrote and served as editor through fourteen issues.

José Kozer

1940-

(Translated from the Spanish by Jorge Guitart)

If I am José Kozer, then I have written some thirty-five hundred poems to date.

If it is true that I am José Kozer, then I am the best Cuban poet of Jewish extraction in the world. Apparently, in the whole world, there is only one Cuban poet of Jewish extraction, but that is of no concern to me.

In poems and interviews I have said more than once that I was born in Old Havana next door to a brothel and as a child I spoke fourteen languages fluently. I also said that in my presence a woman I once loved made love to several young men under a grand piano in a mental institution in New York. And I also said that my father told me he had a long conversation with Trotsky one afternoon in a village in Bessarabia. All lies, or maybe not. In any case, all literature.

José Kozer, b. (Old) Havana, Cuba, 28 March 1940, the son of Jewish immigrants from Poland (David) and Czechoslovakia (Ana); paternal grandparents: Leizer and Sara, killed in the Warsaw ghetto (or not); maternal grandparents: Isaac and Elena, who settled in Cuba circa 1919, Orthodox Jews of the purest strain, shaven heads, strictly kosher, horrendous Spanish—a mixture of Yiddish and Cuban slang.

He has lived in New York since 1960. Since 1965 he has taught Spanish and Hispanic literature at Queens College. He'll be living permanently in Torrox, Malaga Province, Spain, beginning in 1997 and till death do them part. He holds a B.A. from New York University (1965) and an M.A. from Queens College (1971). He refused to finish his doctorate in Luso-Brazilian literature. Instead he wrote (to date) some thirty-five hundred poems. There will be more.

His poetry has been published in magazines and literary supplements in Latin America, Spain, Canada, and the United

José Kozer, Yegen, Spain, 1991

States. He has been translated partially (very partially) into English, Portuguese, Greek, German, Hebrew, and French. He received the Cintas Foundation Fellowship in 1964 and the Julio Tovar Literary Prize (Canary Islands, Spain) in 1974. He is the author of more than twenty books and chapbooks. There are several master's theses and doctoral dissertations about his work. He has translated several books of fiction and poetry into Spanish. His work is represented in several anthologies brought out by prestigious publishing houses in Spain and Latin America, and blah, blah, blah.

Let us recast all this information, starting with an epigraph from Franz Kafka: "A writer who does not write is like a monster prowling madness" (*Letters*).

Literature Emerges

It must have been at the house on Estrada Palma Street, in Havana: 515 Estrada Palma Street, second floor. I must have been eight. It was summer. The torrid summer of insinuations: heat, monotony, heat, endless moments in a darkened room.

And it must have been at nap time, when I, full of pep and restless, was forced to lie down and rest. The day before I probably had gone shopping with my mother, which was something we did on Fridays. We went downtown, to the fine department stores in Havana: El Encanto, Fin de Siglo, Los Precios Fijos. We were going by the bookstore in the basement of El Encanto and she must have stopped and said, "It is time for you to read, time for you to start reading on your own." It must have been that way, for now I am lying in bed in the room at the farthest end of the endless house. I am about to read. I open the book my mother gave me the day before. It is wrapped in the finest tissue paper and has the seal of El Encanto. I don't tear up the wrapping. Rather, I open the package with the greatest care. The caution of first experiences. First I remove the seal (which I was to use as a bookmark) and then undo the wrapping and flatten the tissue paper carefully. (I must have kept it as a souvenir. I wonder where it is now.) I touch lightly the cover of that book (it must have happened that way) and finally I hear it creak when I open it. I feel the emotion of the first pages, so easy, so devoid of any import, just the title and the author, just a few strange words, probably the address of the publishing company and information about copyright and the like. "Printed in . . ." Title: *Robinson Crusoe*. Author: Daniel Defoe.

De-*fwah*. That's the way I pronounced it then, and De-*fwah* it has been a lifetime. And was it not because of this book—it sure was—that years later when I had a wife and daughters I thought that if I were to have a son I would call him Daniel? I said to myself, I will name him after the Daniel of the Bible, the forsaken one, in grave danger of death in the lions' pit or the fiery oven. But underneath the biblical Daniel

Havana, 1942

there must have been the other Daniel, the forsaken De-*fwah*, and I in danger of being in real danger for the very first time: *Robinson Crusoe*.

I lay down to read: another era, another place. I could see that it was not of the here and now. Because it did not deal exclusively with the present, it had to be interesting. But I wasn't getting hooked: it was not that interesting. It dealt with this guy who left his country on one of those tall ships with great sails—a ship that set sail. What words! And the words went around talking about the same things, like moths circling a lamp at night and hitting the lightbulb. The ship was sailing, it had set sail, it glided across the ocean, there were top sails and mainmasts and rigging (what words!), gale winds (what things!). And then the ship was wrecked. Did it make an impact on me? No. Such a mishap was of no interest because I knew that nothing bad could befall Robinson Crusoe: the book was just starting.

And of course he was spared. Even I could have written that. It was clear that the author wasn't going to kill the main character right at the beginning.

He was now on the island, The Island. And over there, not too far, was the ship, broken to pieces, on the spot where it had run aground. And the adventure began, the adventure of days, of all days, the small daily struggle, the true adventure of the myriad problems that had to be solved to survive and later to just live, every day. I liked that. It was like my daily nap, the obligation of hours and schedules, the sensation of life that comes from what happens again and again: another day, another page, another problem to solve, another matter to take care of, another life to live, and everything somehow preordained by a greater hand, invisible (invincible?), always there, a hand or a mother or a place, a creation or a place, an orb, round, infinite, always present. Or something like that. I was only eight. What do you want?

And I loved that book intensely, not for the danger signaled by the footsteps of cannibals or the adventures into the unknown, but for those things which, when they became known, governed daily existence, put everything in order, allowed living, filled life with its frugal abundance, defined it as a series of small lovely moments that were in themselves sufficient. It was sufficient and more than sufficient to lie in bed all afternoon and later lie awake undetected in the wee hours (those first wee hours) reading about how Robinson Crusoe discovered the turtle eggs that nourished him and how he brought from the wreck a case of rum or some such alcoholic beverage, which, like the good Puritan he was, he never touched except to cure some tropical fever that was consuming him and almost killed him. And he made, or brought from the wreck, utensils. He brought tobacco (I think) and yarn and knitting needles (as I recall) and I am not sure what else since at that point I took his place.

I was Robinson Crusoe. And I woke up everyday at the crack of dawn. I read a little from a huge book (it was the first ritual in the morning) and then I washed in the ocean or in some stream and I fixed myself breakfast. I planted things, made them grow, kept the fire lit (this was crucial). I would stretch my arm and the tree would yield a piece of fruit. Frugality. I had a notebook where I recorded routine happenings and some matters of the heart but also apparently unmanageable matters and how my intelligence conquered them. I recorded data about my body, which was not like that of a warrior, just healthy, and accus-

tomed to the sun and the ocean spray and the winds. I was the tree that bore fruit and the arm that moved toward the tree (I was the fruit). I was the fishing tackle and the fish that I baked over odorous logs from tropical trees. I was the hand that shot the arrow toward the bird of my hunger and plucked its feathers and roasted it slowly on a bamboo spit. Bow, bird, fire, hunger, I was all this. I did not distinguish between goat and goatherd, vessel and goat milk, milk and lips, palate and lips. I was alone on the island, The Island, without a woman or parents or friends or company. It was never Friday or Monday. I never went out, I never came in. It was never summer and the short cold spells of Cuban winter never came. I was just living. There were not two of us, we were not two. There were no changes or distances or separations. Time was indivisible. There was only one character, singular and alone. It was the true story of a hand doing things, of the eye in its travels from one line to the next, one page to the next, the book. My mother had given it to me. She had said, "Read!" I read it. I obeyed.

There I lay, day and night, forever reading, forever hidden, dark, dark and protected. There is nothing else, books, books, the Book. Make it, read it, devour it, give it, return it to the Indivisible. In the dark of that second-floor room I read *Robinson Crusoe* incessantly and deeply, unable to leave it one single moment. I read it (in a room, on a second floor, in the city of Havana, in the Santos Suárez district, circa 1948) without being able again to breathe in a different way. I read it from cover to cover, and when I finished reading it, when I turned the last page and closed it, I took a deep breath and opened it again (I breathed again) and I read it again in its entirety.

As an adult, as late as my mid-thirties, I was not able to fall asleep at night unless I imagined that I was lost on an island—The Island—and I was Robinson Crusoe.

This (Too) Is Cuba, My Friend: A Family Album

Tío (Uncle): a biography

But why Cuba, Tío? My uncle's voice, round, paused, slowly rabbinical, explains: a place to wait before you got a visa to El Norte, the

United States. But why did you stay? Well, the papers were taking a long time, and I was taking a liking to this place, and I was making headway. Besides (he lowers his voice), I am a sensualist.

Nineteen twenty-nine, summer, the SS *Bremen,* docked at the San Francisco pier in Havana harbor, the cardboard suitcase, courage, courage, he walks down the plank, walks onto Avenida del Puerto—Port Avenue. Age, seventeen; height, five seven; weight, one hundred twenty pounds (how come they called him Beer Barrel some years later?). Pinstriped black suit (a bit short on him), overcoat (tight), worn-out shoes, polka-dot tie. On his head he wears the yarmulke (the Jewish beanie, the Jewish equivalent to the skullcap of popes and cardinals), earlocks curling down over his rounded ears. There is a note in his pocket, the address of a friend of a friend from his shtetl (village, hamlet) in Hungary, from which he came a week ago. In his head, his large intellectual head, he is carrying a few Spanish words already, and he thinks he can pronounce them without a Jewish accent, without those guttural R's that Jews make, those R's that stay in the back of your throat a long time. He knows how to say San Rafael, a street in Havana, though he thinks it means "street." *Dónde?* Where? He knows how to say that, as he extends the ancestral short arm of the Jew, as if searching for a horizon (always new, always a diaspora: to leave, travel, change, become transformed, wander). And, of course, he has learned to say *gracias,* thanks, *de nada,* you are welcome. *Gratzias, gratzias.* He'll manage.

Tío Max, Uncle Max, the argonaut, arrived in Havana in July 1929. He was frightened by the sight of so many people of color in the port area. He almost dropped his huge suitcase when he saw his first black person. His sensualist eyes almost left its sockets when he saw his first black woman, walking by, so bountiful and desirable in her tight dress ("your buttocks move so nicely / from Camagüey to Santiago / Santiago to Camagüey"). This is for me, he said, and the next day he got rid of his earlocks.

The friend of his friend welcomed him at his home. They drank schnapps. The afternoon heat had begun to make him dizzy. He was ravenous. He was asked to lunch at the rickety table with two rickety chairs in the rented room of the immigrant. And the friend of his friend served him a plate, a single plate but a plate-

ful. Tío Max was startled. What is this? he asked in his guttural Yiddish and asked again in Hungarian, his second language. And the friend of his friend explained, laughing. These are called *frijoles negros,* black beans. And my uncle repeated in his heavy accent, *frrijjoles neggrros.* And then he said to the friend of his friend, in Yiddish: Say, is everything black in this place?

The next day, his earlocks already off, he started doing business, buying and selling. From what he sold he bought and what he bought he resold. A year later he had a watch-repair shop. And he went to the Sunday dances at the Israelite Center. Dancing the *danzon*—the slow solemn Cuban dance—and the bolero—the love ballad—he began to socialize with the local young women, the *Polaquitas*—Polish girls. In Cuba they referred to all Jews as *Polacos,* Poles. And he made friends among young men who, like him, had cut off their earlocks not too long ago and had resurfaced looking modern.

Israelite Center, Sunday, dances. Tío Max quotes Buber (now I know he had not read him), whole passages of the Torah (the Pentateuch, the word of God in the original). As a child I thought that the Torah was the wife of the Toro, the bull. My father, who longs for something else, refutes him. They are, grudgingly, friends. In the end their political leanings and their interests are incompatible. My uncle attacks like an Isaiah. My father quotes Marx. Tío Max raises his (short) prophetic arm; his is the voice in the wilderness. He points the way, just as Jeremiah, Job, and Ezekiel did thousands of years ago. My father counter-attacks with quotes from Engels and Utopian summaries. He tells of Kropotkin's dream, of the ideals of Owen and Cabet, of Fourier's wonderfully crazy phalanstery, of Anarchism and Cooperativism. Goy stuff, says Tío Max: things Kristlejers—Christians—do. They understand nothing. In reply, my father invokes the gigantic bearded figure of Bakunin (come on, he was impotent! screams Tío Max), and excitedly he harangues, makes pronouncements, contradicts himself, describes libertarian societies. And if it weren't for the fact that the orchestra suddenly started playing one of those admirable stately *danzones* there would have been war and bloodshed and my father would have broken into the "The International" at the top of his lungs.

They have quarreled again. Tío Max says religion. Papá says revolution. Tío Max says Zion,

Zionism. Papá says 1917, Lenin, Trotsky, the October Revolution, Red Square. And my uncle silences him suddenly when he reminds him how Stalin, Comrade Stalin, is acquiring more and more dictatorial powers.

And they are having words, half in Yiddish with touches of Russian, Polish, Hungarian (the thick language), half in broken Spanish. But Tío Max's Spanish improves quite rapidly. Papá, however, gets stuck forever. My father will never lose his thick Jewish accent, his Polish accent. He will fall in love with Cuba and Spanish but will never be able to express his love correctly. He will open his mouth and his native tongue will stubbornly make his new language atrophy.

Papá's Grammar

You had to see this immigrant babbling
　　verbs from Yiddish into Spanish,
you had to see him among death notices,
　　headlines and Bolshevik stories, stumbling
　　before his children.
His embarrassment on the street took
　　cover behind the dialect of Galicians and
　　the merchandise of Catalans.
He fell flat decisively among the tatters of
　　his misplaced conjugations.
He said va for voy, ponga for pongo, he
　　slaughtered his prepositions.
He said foi for fui, joives he said for
　　jueves and the street was slippery.
Fate was fatal and despotic with him.
　　There was a wealth of jeers on every
　　corner.
And he would get entangled in his own
　　verbs, there was a furious accumulation
　　of obstacles in the penury of his tongue
　　twisters.
Cornered by the numbered shelves, he
　　begat poetic children and a
　　disenchantment with haggling.
And now his children were leaving him as
　　if he were a Wednesday death of ashes.
His children were leaving him as they put
　　Spanish words together most
　　competently.
Rapidly his children were coming out with
　　the purest syntax, from father to child
　　there was a great widening of the
　　supreme exaltation of words.
This immigrant, damp, was shrinking in
　　the latest wreckage of his red vocabulary.
Last he was suffering, forever handicapped
　　in the tears of the Niemen, the end of
　　Poland.

(From *Bajo este cien*)

Papá: a biography

David, Duvidl, Duftche, a Polish Jew, twenty years old, arrives in Havana, in 1927. An idealist. He supports the Bund, later Trotsky, the Bolsheviks. He suffers imprisonment for being an ideologist, a promoter of revolt, a rebel, and a revolutionary. In prison he studies, dedicates long hours to learn to read and write Polish (in his shtetl children are taught to read and write only Yiddish; the *cheder* is the only school, a religious school). After certain readings and certain experiences he considers himself a Marxist. A Marxist of the first era, before Stalin: a democrat, free, a libertarian, participating in an open society, a just society, Utopia.

He arrives in Cuba in 1927. Why did you leave, Papá? I couldn't stand my old man, he says, he was a fanatic, and besides he starved us to death, he was a miser, I was sorry for my mama, poor woman, small and alone, tiny and alone among five hefty guys that only thought of eating, shouting, working, making love. I had to leave, I had other ideas, I didn't want to go to the cheder, didn't want to be sent to a yeshiva, I wanted to speak Polish, read and write Polish, I was Polish, that's why I left. But, why Cuba? Son, like everybody else, to wait for my papers, to go to El Norte, but I fell in love with all this, just like the others.

My father buys and sells, resells, saves, and waits. He embraces Cuban culture. He becomes assimilated, integrated. The Pole becomes a Cuban. The Jew becomes a real Cuban. He is Cubanized. I am just like any other Cuban, this is my pueblo, my people, except he says *poiblo;* whenever he opens his mouth, whenever he speaks Spanish, the whole thing crumbles. Damn tongue, damn tongue-twisting language: *no puedo!*, I can't do it (except he says *no poide*). And when he writes Spanish he is not understood. What awful handwriting, what gibberish his written word. He speaks and writes perfectly in Yiddish, beautiful. In Spanish, he can't. That hurts him. It's logical. It renders him helpless, it holds him, it leads him to seclusion (more and more, as time passes), he speaks less and less, becomes mute. His pores exude silence. The old man feels like a failure. The language fails him, ideas fail him, the International fails him, the Utopian dream, the myth of peace. Comrade Stalin triumphs. Trotsky is expelled. Red treason. The flag of peace turns into a flag of war, a pact with the enemy. Stalin sells out the motherland. Stalin sells out the International. Stalin plays Hitler's game. Unforgivable.

My Father, Who Is Still Alive

My father, who's still alive,
—I haven't seen him but I know he's
    shrunk—
has a family of brothers dead in the ovens in
    Poland.
He never saw them, learned of his mother's
    death
by wire, inherited nothing from his father,
not even a button. Who knows if he inherited
his father's ways.
My father, who was a tailor and a communist,
my father who wouldn't talk, sat on the
    terrace
to no longer believe in God
and have nothing to do again with people,

hating Hitler, hating Stalin,
my father who once a year had a shot of
    whiskey,
my father up on the neighbor's apple tree
eating the neighbor's apples
the day the Reds entered his village,
and made my grandfather dance like a bear
    on the Sabbath,
light up a cigarette and smoke it on the
    Sabbath.
And my father left the village for good.
He left swearing forever against the October
    Revolution,
insisting forever that Trotsky was a dreamer
and Beria a criminal,
shunning books forever, he sat a small man
    on the terrace
and told me that the dreams of men are
but a phony literature,
that history books can lie because paper
can hold anything, my father
who was a tailor and a communist.

(From *Bajo este cien*)

"The whole family," Havana, 1950 (Kozer is in the back row, second from right, next to his father at the end, behind his mother and grandmother, who sits next to his grandfather, and his sister on the floor between their maternal grandparents)

The mythomaniac is born. The inventor. One foot in reality, in the facts, in what happened; the other foot in the air, in what should have happened. The mythomaniac tells me things, he asks me to listen, wants me to listen to him (this is constant). At home he repeats, retells, enlarges, and magnifies the same anecdote. And with his old Jewish accent he goes over events again and again. Are they real? Is he twisting things around? We start for La Concha Beach Club and as soon as we leave home he goes into action: his Tale.

The Tale (of my father, the mythomaniac): he saw Trotsky, he was a friend of Fabio Grobart, founder of the Cuban Communist Party (whose real name is . . .). He was in the underground against the Machado dictatorship. He was with Mella, he and Marinello. He didn't join the Cuban Communist Party but he was as Marxist as the best Marxist. He knew how to save himself and wait for the moment to gamble everything when the cause, the true cause. . . . And he told me he was a tailor in the Polish army, made caps for the lieutenants, the proud lieutenants of Polish cavalry, who ended up in the common grave dug in the ground in the forest near Katyn. It was the Bolsheviks that murdered them, threw the flower of Polish cavalry into a huge open grave. And he told me about horses, about the house where he was born (in Chekhonov, near the Ukranian border), about the cellar of the house filled with charcoal and sacks of potatoes (here in Cuba you buy potatoes by the pound at the grocery store, unheard of, he'd say); he told me about his own father (a fanatic and a miser) and his mother (a cooking angel, day and night in the kitchen); his brothers, five mastodons, five huge human fortresses, who died in Nazi concentration camps.

Abuela: a biography

And I see that grandmother, that abuela. I cannot tell her apart from my maternal abuela, the one I knew. I see them as a single person, single, yet double, but inseparable, in the kitchen, by the charcoal stove in the shtetl, by the charcoal stove in the house in Old Havana, the house across the street from the market, the market infested with flies, across the street from the Cuban grocery of Abuelo, my grandfather.

Abuela at Home: A Remembrance

Abuela, her fermented urine, like that of a
   mare, the
juniper twigs to sweeten the embers in the
   charcoal stove. You
smell strongly of smoke, of cockles and tiny
   little fishes,
the whiting in its tray
you knead
the dough, then go from smells to migraines,
   bride's tulle
decomposing
if you lean your disordered shadow against a
   birch tree
and you love your rolling pin
your two-tone apron with deep pockets
and you are held up by the aroma of white
   lilies that you distill
with both hands and gather like a basket
   with puff pastries and
unleavened bread
a Sunday
of great ladles and tureens; the zephyr blew
   in and your throat
opens to a voice in the taverns; you were the
   joyful walnut that
sprouted like the issue of David, you regaled
   us with the insipid
operetta of your dead, remember? the flowery
   patina of the
scarves with which you covered your shaven
   head
and on the sly
at dusk on Passover you gave us the shape of
   the herring in its
cream, the whiteness of chard soup, and your
   fate
intoxicated us
with its raspberry odors, and for us your
   pulpit was your oven
with its new flan that smelled of an arbor
   and you feasted us,
old figure of Israel in a zither.

(From Bajo este cien)

Papá: more biography

The mythomaniac speaks and invents. I listen and reinvent. The link has been made, a pact of blood ("in order to learn you must bleed," the old saying). I am his diaspora, his errancy, his disillusionment. I am his voice, his inadequate, impossible, incommunicable word. I am his nervousness at the time of speaking. And I control myself so he can speak. So that his Spirit can speak through me.

*Wife Guadalupe with daughter Susana,
Spain, 1979*

And he tells me: Lenin spoke calmly, Trotsky
was fiery. Did he see them? Where did he get
that? Where did Papá-Hero and Papá-TallTale
come from? I write. Out of the jumble of his
biography I make poems. Out of his linguistic
jumble I get a diction, a body of writing: letters, words, sentences.

I saw Kornilov, I saw Trotsky harangue the
Red Army, I conspired with Grobart Simkhovich.
No, I do not know the date of my birth. I do
not know how old I am. My birth was not
recorded, I do not exist, I do not have a language, I do not have words to retell my stories, I have a few old words, jumbled, backwards, useless in these tropics, speak for me.
And he married my mother.

He married Ana, Hana, Hanele, eldest daughter of Abuelo Katz, the one who had the Cuban grocery store, a founding member of Adath
Israel, the first synagogue in Cuba. The kind
grandfather whose bones repose in the old Jewish
cemetery in Guanabacoa, one of five Jewish cemeteries in Cuba.

Abuelo: a biography

I Have Come to Call Thirteen Men

I have come to call thirteen men to come
 bury my Abuelo.
I mean, dress him in the long robe of the
 splendor of the Jews.
Yea, let them lift him as ash, this milky
 lamb, let his white
flesh crumble in the urn.
And all the Jews from Ostrava, from Zvolen,
 from Ternava and from
Bratislava
come to Prague to see how the elders lament
 the expulsion,
get out the squared leather boxes and bind
 his arms
so that he roams through the alphabet of
 Deuteronomy,
so that he roams with his great boxes of
 lima beans among
men of business.

(From *Bajo este cien*)

Tío César and my aunts; Mamá: a biogra-
phy

My maternal grandfather arrived in Cuba
in 1919. Five years later he sent for his big
family. Three daughters and a son. The three
little girls: my mother and my two aunts (Tía
Perla, Perl, Tía Perica; and Esther, Queen Esther,
Esther Amalque) came down the eternal plank
of immigrants, the plank of the SS *Hamburg*,
docked (eternally) in the old pier in Havana.
Dumbfounded, the two little ones, my future
aunts (one five, the other three), approached
a black man (a vegetable peddler? a longshore-
man?) and they tried to rub off the strange
soot that covered his skin, they tried to remove this pitch that covered him. They had
never seen anything like it. The feeling of
strangeness in the newcomer, another culture,
another language, another (mental) architecture, a different type of food. Emotions in the
face of so much unfamiliarity.

And the son? Well, that's quite a story. He
was something. He arrived in caftan with orthodox earlocks, with the Bible in his heart,
his light blue eyes filled with the voice of Yahweh,
the voice in the wilderness, and matzo, Exo-
dus and manna. But a week later you could
see him on the corner of Acosta and Cuba,
playing a mean game of dominoes with the

guys in the neighborhood. He didn't know a word of Spanish but he beat them. I killed them, he would say. And his R's glided perfectly, round, clear, and Cubanized. Barely a week later! And of course no more earlocks, no more overt signs. Gone was the yellowish mien of Eastern European Jews. He felt like eating sancocho (Cuban stew), or salcocho, as we call it. He felt quite amorous (his wife, my aunt, a lot of fun and quite stunning: dark and wonderful, a local beauty). Grandfather had a hard time with this son of his. To put it bluntly, he was a debit to his race. He doesn't want anything to do with *shul* (school) or the synagogue. From work he goes to the baseball game and on Sundays it's more baseball, then dominoes. And any free time is devoted to the dark beauty, my future aunt. For this is Cuba, my friend.

It was quite different with the daughters. Demure, very proper, good girls, the Katz girls.

Abuela is wearing her cheap wooden slippers. She is walking around the house like a ghost. I hear the faint echo of her wooden slippers, I hear her cracked voice, full of guttural R's. I wonder what she is saying. She smells of kitchen, of charcoal. Abuela is a smell. She smells of Old Havana, of potato fritters (latkes), of a head scarf (babushka). The babushka of my babushke; my grandmother's scarf. She smells of orthodoxy (she is more fanatic than Abuelo, I have been told, believes more deeply, if such a thing is possible). She smells of rancid grease.

The three daughters. Mamá goes to school. She learns to speak properly, a nice Cuban accent, a real Cuban tone. A Havana accent. I hear her nice voice, very Havana, soft, coaxing. Her sweet diction. She is careful with her S's (she doesn't drop a single one). She speaks slowly, properly, how sweetly she speaks. She is bourgeois. After school she helps Grandfather at the grocery store. She is the cashier. And for her excellent work she receives a little bag of imported cherries (a reward). Just for her, the eldest daughter.

And from her mouth to me, language. From Abuela's palate to me, a pluralistic stew. From Mamá's vocal cords to me, a pluralistic language. Her language becomes embedded in me.

Mamá's Grammar

In May, what bird was it
mother loved; or she spoke of mimosas.
She says she doesn't remember the name of
    the rivers that set the boundaries of her
    birthplace,
even though in summer
a male and a female would drown, a male
    and a female in summer. She mentions
a crucial
conversation with her sisters; they are like
    friends, their little pinkies intertwined.
    They will leave. How depressing, even
    though in every cabin on
the ship there is a centerpiece filled with
    tropical fruits; on deck gorgeous courtesans
    speak some guttural tongue; they are not
    astonished by aviation
or the transatlantic cable (letters) attacked
    by open-mouthed sparrows
or they send out night moths. They'll arrive
among powdered boys with aromatic earlocks
    who'll spread out on the streets: Apodaca,
    Teniente Rey, Acosta. They'll end up
buying a mahogany wardrobe (tepid initials
    in their underwear) to be used also
as a safe. They'll take up residence. Soon
    they'll call everyone by their first name at
    the Zionist seminars, Mamá
in her faultless Spanish.

(From *Bajo este cien*)

This is what she (Mamá) gives me: honeycomb, corn custard, flan, tamale. She is her cornstarch, the thickness of her flan. Mamá, the tool that will make transmission possible; transmission of the gesture, the heroic act (Papá). The double gift: from Papá the anecdote, the thrill of happenings remote and heroic. From Mamá the tools, the surgical equipment, the farming implements to execute, transform, reinvent. I am made of both, I plagiarize both. I listen. I am no one: I am them. Their own reinvention. They give me an anecdote, I transform it. They give me the word. ("And God said: Let there be light, and there was light." "In the beginning was the Word and the Word was with God.") I perpetuate them. I am that. I write: I am the continuity. The word is the link with all; that is why there are no languages, only the word (the Word). To continue, to break. Papá, the Marxist, breaks. He is looking for Utopia. Mamá, the bourgeois, carries on: her perfect Yiddish matches her perfect Spanish, she'll always call it *castellano* rather than *español*. She is the dictionary, perfect. And I can still hear her asking, Son, do you speak *castellano* perfectly?

José Kozer: a biography

Here is where I come in, 28 March 1940. Havana: a house next to a brothel, a little whorehouse in Old Havana. Everything is set for a spectacular leap, ladies and gentlemen. Here is the new generation, those who assimilated. I am Cuban (it was only much later that I discovered and accepted that I could be that without having to stop being that other thing, Jewish). A Jew from the other side of the Jordan. (Let us remember that Hebrew means he who comes from the other side of the river.) I am here already, I can perform. My language performance. That's my show. To make poems. To make things up, be the poet. I have the anecdotes, I have the implements. It's just a matter of becoming obsessed and creating. A clear situation: a room, a table, a chair, a window, or rather the inner image of all that. And start reinventing because paper "can hold anything."

Here I am, in fiction, in the fiction of a room ("A Room of One's Own"). I can stay here and resist death, madness, and the cataclysms of history: Let there be a Diaspora and There Was One.

But change is no breakup, for poetry provides links, it is the continuator and the wound healer. It helps you to be well again, to survive, to keep your sanity. (How many mental patients does each immigration wave create?) Well, I can resist. Resist Papá who invents me, who tells me things and counts on me to resist. Resist Mamá who imposes her own language, soft and polished. I write. Is it because I yearn for notice, or notoriety? Or is it because I cannot find myself and am looking to be another, dissatisfied? I am looking to be my grandfather in the Warsaw ghetto or my grandfather in the Cuban *shul*, the synagogue in Old Havana.

I am Abuela who dies in the ghetto. I am Abuela of the wooden slippers and the smell of charcoal. I am three sisters arriving at the San Francisco pier, coming into the heat, eyeing the bundles, the deformed shapes of fruits, the tubers. *Wos is ñame, tate?*, What is name, Papa?, to which my grandfather replied: *a zaje me este in Kuba,* a thing they eat in Cuba. I am two languages.

There is a table. It is lunch time. Food is served on each plate in an impeccable order imposed by Mamá, by the impeccable figure of my father at the head of the table. He would come home at noon, come in, deliver the loaf of black bread or rye bread he was carrying under his arm, and go straight to his room. From the bedroom to the bathroom. You could hear the water running. He shaved and showered. The ritual lasted forty-five minutes. At one o'clock the four of us sat at the table. Silence! *Scwaig schtill!* Be quiet! When one eats, one does not talk. Papá came out of the bathroom, clean, immaculate, impeccable. I hear him in the bathroom, the shower running and him singing something heroic and strange. Years later I would learn that it was "The International," first in Russian, then in Polish. And he would follow it with the Polish national anthem, in the original.

We are having lunch, at 515 Estrada Palma Street, between Goicuría and Juan Delgado Streets. (It is 1 P.M.) The dishes, the table, the kitchen door that opens and closes so that lunch dishes come in, go out. The facts of lunch, of variation. Variability. There is gefilte fish with chrein (fish stuffed with horseradish) and there is ropavieja (shredded beef with tomato sauce, Cuban style). There is ropavieja and the tray with the latkes appears. Each dish is one more possibility; multiplications. A parable: from one loaf many loaves, from one fish many fishes. Wealth. Spiritual wealth; of the welcoming country, the redemptor, and of the country of origin, ancient, wandering. Each dish, each person, each member of this family constitutes another possibility, another shade of Havana heat, another perspective from heat to cold and from cold to heat (a diaspora, isn't it?). Each one of them an anecdote, a tool, a vehicle of communication (towards the others, for the others), another basting, for endurance, survival, continuity. They are not going to break. They (we) are going to die but they (we) are not going to break. We are tied to one another, linked. Spun and strung, the one and the host. One is all. Cuba turned, it is Jewish, it is Eastern Europe. Well, like them, we Cubans divided and scattered ourselves all over the world. The Wandering Cuban. That's it.

Kozer and Guadalupe in Madrid, 1989

My Motherland Is Cuba Also

My motherland is Cuba also,
since my father the Pole moved there in 1927
paid his blood coin in clandestine Marxist
    evenings
a tailor shop on Villegas Street
I, too, Cuban patriots, captains, dictators,
was born next door to a corrupt brothel
my eyes watered thinking of Martí,
I placed my hopes on the mountains.
Today I accept the upheavals of history.

(From *De Chepén a La Habana*)

It seems that way: there was an upheaval. There have always been upheavals. Except that this time it was our turn, that's all.

It happened to us. We were internationalized, we lost our identity, we mixed with others more and more. Is this a new history? Or is it the same old Yiddishe Geschichte? The same Jewish history that the *lererque* Bertha, Bertha the teacher, taught me at home, on

Estrada Palma Street. Did everything change? I don't know.

I only know that this (too) is Cuba, my friend.

José Kozer: A String of Dates

1958: Leaves Cuba. May 1959: Returns.

He works three years (1960-63) on Wall Street: coat and tie and long hair (pre-Beatles). Creates a commotion on elevators and on the Street. Export manager of a company that sells small airplanes, airplane radios, and automatic pilots. He makes money. He is not happy.

Marries Sheila Isaac (1962). In 1966 they have a daughter Mía (Milonga). Great immaturity. Fights. Drunken bouts. Poker games that last three days and three nights and end at dawn. A B-movie hero. Experiments with drugs. No money. He is not happy.

He finishes a B.A. at New York University (1965). The same day he picks up his diploma he runs into a professor of Spanish on the elevator who invites him to study and teach at a place called Queens College ("whose name I do not wish to remember"). He starts graduate studies, teaches as part-time lecturer (or swineherd—my translation).

1967: Promoted to full-time lecturer (major swineherd—still my translation) in the Department of Romance Languages, Queens College.

1968: He finally separates from his first wife. Takes full custody of his two-year-old daughter. Her mother has to be hospitalized for problems with her nerves (bluntly, she is nuts).

1968-70: Drunk as a skunk day and night.

1970: After not having finished a single poem in almost a decade he returns to writing and during several decades he is unstoppable, does not leave any statues untoppled or any poems unfinished. Ergo, if he were José Kozer, he would have thirty-five hundred poems to his credit to date.

1971: Receives the Master of Arts degree in Luso-Brazilian Literature from Queens College. He decides not to continue for the doctorate and to devote himself fully to poetry. He is able to do it. Poetry will be his new way of getting drunk. He smokes, stops drinking. He buys a house in Spain (in Nerja, Malaga Province). He smokes. He meets the woman who will become his second and present wife, his mate forever after; he begins to be happy.

1974: Routine. He marries Guadalupe, née Barrenechea. His wife begins to learn English and can't tell the difference between "guerilla" and "gorilla." They laugh. Everything is in good order.

1976: Suffers from depression, spends a month in a semi-catatonic state: a good item for the biography of a poet, isn't it? Susana Kozer is born (Susa or La Niña), the spitting image of her mother with her Spanish face and "the most beautiful eyes that human islands have seen."

1977: Stops smoking. Publishes more and more. Starts speaking (and writing) Spanish again. His English gets worse.

1978: A sweet moderation in every aspect of daily life, nothing in excess, except in the writing of poetry, in the excesses of which he is immersed. He gets to write 365 poems that year. He seldom drinks. He goes back to smoking but with admirable moderation.

1978-83: He is still 155 pounds, exactly what he weighed when he left Cuba. He is promoted to assistant professor (inspector of swineherds— my translation). There are two constants: his happy marriage and his creation (no adjectives). Let us say that his life is *Liebe und Arbeit,* as Herr Freud said.

1983-84: A new promotion at Queens College (associate professor, or director of swineherds). Coinciding with this promotion he sees his life as entering its final stretch. He starts writing fewer poems per year.

1984 to date: writing. His diaries. Some creative prose and, as always, poetry, poetry. His life will be that: to write poetry "and the rest is silence."

1985: Final promotion at Queens College: full professor (governor general of swineherds). Mamá is proud.

His, then, a biography, one more biography. Thus:
Name: José (which in Hebrew means the one who is one too many, the added one, the superfluous one.

With Spanish critic Jorge Rodríguez-Padrón (left), New York, 1980

Last Name: Kozer (which does not mean "kosher" but rather— as far as we know— the Caspian Sea, or cossack, or frankly, nothing.

The person who writes about himself here is the author of numerous books and chapbooks of poems, published in the United States, Mexico, Argentina, the Dominican Republic, and Spain. His work has been translated, partially (I repeat again), into English, Portuguese, Italian, French, and Hebrew. And it has appeared in more than 250 literary magazines and supplements (mostly) in Spanish-speaking countries. The Mexican publishing house Verdehalago was planning to bring out several volumes of his published work in 1997. (We shall see.)

Thus, a trivial life, that of José Kozer. The anodyne as the center of his creation. To awaken the poetic animal by giving it the slightest attention, dissembling. Nothing goes on, nothing obstructs. This dissembling is at the center of his poetic activity. Thus, he gets up every morning at the crack of dawn: he washes, has breakfast, sits down to work. He engages in translation, writes in his diary, reads. And from there (though not always, not always) a new poem emerges.

He goes to work, to the university, teaches his classes, comes home—or rather escapes from the university—to eat lunch at home. Generally and as a rule, during lunch he has long intense conversations with Guadalupe; the sweetness of these conversations. They share Guadalupe's excellent cooking, the good wines of sweet France, and words in their obsessiveness. They understand each other very well, know how to leave plenty of room for each other and not to get in each other's way (or be against each other): a good couple.

They love each other.

The poet and his beloved: the corrosive poet and the innocent beloved. The innocent beloved purifies the corrosive poet, frees him from the three *asavas:* that of sensual desire, that of the desire to exist, and that of ignorance; a good thing is the Beloved.

In the evening the poet reads in his room on the second floor, lies in his bed for hours (as Valle-Inclán and Proust did, and works there as they did). To read lying down, to read for death, the way you read Bernard Berenson, so admired, and D'Annunzio, so little admired.

He reads. At nine he turns off the light.

Poetics

If it is true that Paul Celan said, "Poetry does not impose, it exposes," then he spoke well. Paraphrasing Celan I can say, "Poetry imposes itself on me and I expose it."

I don't know where it comes from; in any case I could say it comes from everywhere, which is to say anywhere. And since it exposes itself, it is abrupt, unexpected. You are expecting it all the time but it comes out unexpectedly. How? Through a stutter, a trivial image, words that join one another strangely and resemble an arbitrary dictation. Gathered in your head by your voice.

Actually, we are all always immersed in poetry: day and night (particularly night). But with poetry it is the same as with the music of the spheres: it is constantly in tune, which is why we can't hear it. Poetry is making sounds all the time and in order to hear it we have to stop listening. Result? A poem (another one), of whose gestation we are hardly aware; another poem extracted imperfectly from the perfection of poetry (Poetry?) that is with us day and night.

The imperfect poem (and its sensation of unreality and indeterminacy), a source of insatiability, a goad to create.

During gestation everything is marvelous. However, the finished poem makes us feel that there is something imponderable in it that doesn't work. Something has failed, it doesn't move, something (once more) has not been made round. You can't put your finger on it, can't tell exactly what has failed, yet the result is opaque when aspiration was transparent and global. The result? An antsy sensation of dissatisfaction, perhaps puerile but ever present, which assaults us and makes us uneasy as soon as the poem is finished, an imperceptible (but constant) itch that provokes us into trying another poem.

That is to say, the need to expect once more the unexpected: poetry, poems.

Poetry returns. And the instant it returns, tranquility (but of the type induced by threats) and nervousness, a horror and a great joy, all diluted in an invisible smile. It returns, and from its bounty we know that the language we use to make the poem is inadequate, as inadequate as dictionaries, taxonomies, tropes, and figures, not to mention accursed grammar, reverent and logical, which rejects the disorderly order demanded by the poetic.

A poem, then, is always a residual incorporation, the incorporation of fecal matter into a sacred center.

Oh beautiful fecal matter! as Rabelais said.

One Time Only

On August 18, 1960, I left Cuba and was left out. I was left out of language and speech, out of the one (but not unique) place one generally goes back to. I never went back.

I am first- and last-generation Cuban. My parents, Jews from Eastern Europe, went to Cuba as immigrants, became Cuban citizens (legally and spiritually). They loved Cuba. I was born there, in Havana, 1940, and one day I left. Flew to Miami on Cubana Airlines. Went from Miami to New York by Greyhound. Blacks had to sit at the back of the bus still.

Since I think that my daughters, born and raised in the United States, are American (legally and spiritually), my death will put an end to my Cuban generation, a brief lineage.

No big deal. It is not a tragedy or a melodrama or a soap opera. It is rather the norm of the world we live in. We all are first and last generation of something in a changing world that evaporates very fast, in the same way that Cuba evaporated for me in 1960.

Thus, perhaps, for several decades, to be Cuban and specifically to be a Cuban poet, has meant to be last, or, let us say, at the head of the rear, let the paradox stand, always standing on line, rather far from the entrance.

This being in last place implies a diaspora I am very familiar with, archetypically as well as ancestrally. Diaspora is *atopos* (No-place): nowhere and everywhere; not of a nationality but of a global nation. You are included in it; there is a free and open center which, if you listen carefully, fills your pockets with poems. Diaspora, then, is a center in flux and at the same time a flux without a center.

To be last, to be in the caboose of the train: that's what it is to be a Cuban and to be a Cuban poet. We are the whole world, we are all *Polacos* (Poles), which is what they called Jews in Cuba. We are no one, like Ulysses responding to horrible Polyphemus with his brutal eye and terrifying beard. Like Ulysses we

respond, I AM NO ONE. It is Rimbaud's "I is another."

Our mother tongue, all the same, is a nowhere space, foreign and marginal, speaking in many voices with multiple meanings. Though we Cubans continue to speak and write a Cuban language, we have undergone multinational contamination. Our new writing is full of Peruvianisms, Colombianisms, Anglicisms, Spanglicisms, echoes of the Slavic logos, and touches of the variety used in Spain as the standard. And we are Polacos; we are adaptable (in the best sense of the word); and we are, well, tradespeople, in the best sense of the word, for trading is a noble occupation, and it can even be the world's salvation, against all rhetoric and ideology, since it is through trading that humans best understand one another.

And we live in an outer region, thinking and speaking and writing a marginal language made of defective bits and pieces, surrounded as we are by strange islands speaking alien languages from which we Cubans take. On the other hand it is no longer painful and we do not take it personally. Rather, we are revived by the infusion.

For a romantic poet in the first half of the nineteenth century, it would have been a sign of marginality, but for us Cubans this being last is the norm and a normality that we accept. It allows us to be NO ONE; it allows us to be diurnal but full of shadows, and to be nocturnal when the rooster signals dawn. There is a plain fact that rules us and guides and seduces us: we are a mélange and a porous receptacle, as if the place we lived were Cuba/Kuba, a country of great wines and huge snowstorms, where we mutter in Spanglish while we gather the fruit of the royal palm at twenty degrees below zero: a new manna for a new poetry.

The Cuban poet of today, always last, is a pilgrim from the Alps walking around Machu Picchu. He enters the promised land (anyland), which is by the Urals or by Cuba's Turquino Peak. He speaks of Tibet or of the High Pyrenees. For we are the whole of the dictionary: we welcome it, negotiate with it, absorb it, and regurgitate it in the (new) splendor of poems.

Poems of the promised place, postponed and perpetual, the no-place of always. With that poetry we are finally American, we are Spanish, Tibetan, African; we are the children of the old caftan and the *kipá;* we smell of the ammonia of tabernacles and synagogues, we smell of strong smelling salts and of *guarapo*— sugar cane juice—with a touch of lime juice; we squeezed the lime three times. With this language we have been speaking our poems for the last thirty-eight years: speaking and speaking, which means writing and writing, living at different centers from the same center, dispersed, a mixed breed, getting rid, little by little, of false limitations and false categories of identity, nationality, and profession. We change the shape of the Caiman (meaning Cuba—shaped like a crocodile) this way or that, we stretch it one way, the others stretch it the other way. It does not have a unique shape and it lengthens and lengthens towards its final shape, which is that of an island that has no representation.

A Catechism: Q & A's Attempting to Explain the Poems of José Kozer

There are seven days in a week, seven days to write poems. Seven days to ask questions and to try to reply. Here is a questionnaire on the matter of my poetry: questions have been invented so that I can attempt to explain an inventory, an invention. There are eight questions (inventions) and eight replies (inversions).

Q 1: Though it is possible to detect your latest themes in your early books, it is obvious that the emphasis was on something else then. When did the change occur? How did you shift from epigram and antipoem to narrative and metonymy?

A: When I write I am not aware that I am writing. At the earliest stage I was burdened by an awareness that I wanted to write, I was overly aware of that want, and, to make things worse, I thought that writing poetry was important. For the last twenty years or so I've been writing and writing as in a trance. Transit and moment: the poem occurs and recurs. It is an occurrence: it explodes. I then forget. I know I write poems, and I know they are not epigrammatical or antipoetical but are instead anecdotal and metonymic; I know it. And yet I am not aware of it. Everything is imprecise, unreal, indeterminate. A music. The words evoked gather in chains and form clots. Something like that. I don't know exactly at what point a poem lengthens, changes shape, gets entangled, gets bogged down, goes against me, branches out, becoming two, becoming three, filling the page with tributaries. The development of my work, from one stage to the next, has been organic, it has just happened and it has been as natural as breathing or waking or stumbling. A natural development, except it has been propelled by a feverish drive that feeds on itself, the drive to write poems, the more the better.

Q 2: In your book, *et mutabile* (and mutable), one can see a return to the poetry of memory, to evocations that are genealogical incantations. It is also evident that you have assumed the body and language as the locus where traditions, stories, and diverse memories converge. It is not by chance that the poet asserts several times, "I am my father."

A: My body does not matter, or rather, it can only matter to me. That is to say, the ego that suffers because it is dying (an anticipation) knows itself to be surrounded by ephemeral flesh that no one is interested in. Then, that deficiency, that unease felt by the disappointed body, a body that knows how useless it is to cling to anything, leads to the intuition that one must move into a greater body, a less ephemeral one (if it exists).

That greater body is in the history of the family, the living record of any individual who descends from others, and it is also in the language that links individuals and families with a tradition, a community. That community, with its history, its memory, its archetypes, its breathing, sometimes finds a point of reunion, of convergence, in creation. A poem can be (it has been many times for me) a site, a date, a convocation, a summons that has been accepted. In a poem family records, anecdotes, fictions, and recastings fuse with things seen and lived, with readings, with the imagined. That whole, that momentary globalization taking place in the text, forms a body greater than my body, which is that of the family, coming to life as language, as logos, as a gasp, a gasp setting in, trying: a poem. The son is father; the gatherer of the crumbs of others creates a "new" crumb for the others, and escapes, vanishes, forgets. The poem (the result) perhaps touches lightly something even greater, beyond years and the mourning of the dead and the closed planet. Does it touch God ever lightly, or eternity? I do not know. I write poems not to know but from the obscure belief in a language that wants to live, manifest itself and live, there, above, above all language.

Q 3: In *et mutabile* the love theme reappears though closely related to a certain lewdness that is nonetheless not devoid of tenderness. For example, when you say: "O plump woman of mine, I love you. Here, wipe off my slobber; that's what they used to call soul. A matter of words."

A: It is well known that it is hardly possible anymore to write love poems "in all seriousness." I mean, in the twentieth century. In the Renaissance, the Spanish poet Garcilaso was lucky to find the territory of Eros still virginal for poetry, a territory that he could contemplate through a rhetorical language that falsified nothing since it was new and recent and still fresh. Paradoxically, his language was natural but highly rhetorical at the same time. This allowed him to write love poems without renouncing his Provencal and Petrarchist aura and without repudiating for the sake of rhetoric any part of the amorous intensity he felt, which he effectively transmitted (transmuted), while successfully shunning the facile and the tired. But in the twentieth century, how could we write about love except through irony or even lewdness? I can speak about love to that plump woman I love only by avoiding the declamatory. I can only sing to her if I renounce grandiloquence, that is to say, if I use irony to mask or supersede the hackneyed rhetoric of love. Harlequin romances and soap operas on TV are very serious but poets "joke" about love, play with it. Only in this way can they nourish it back to life. You can't take love seriously, you have to undermine it, undermine any serious erotic language, make it vulnerable by kidding and sneering and being sarcastic about it. Serious sarcasm, serious sneering, serious love. Slobber as a reflex of the soul. Or is not my slobber my glory?

Q 4: In your poetry, particularly in your book *Trazas del lirondo* (Traces of the man rendered bare), one can find frequent references to bad odors, pubic hair, flatulence, as well as remarks about how the body of the poet is not ideal but quite the opposite: something wasted and deplorable.

A: A poem of mine is not an ideal opportunity for a biographer; a poem of mine is never me in the morning, clean-shaven and fresh from the shower. In my poems I am not necessarily clean, young, new, or renewed. Any poem finds me almost bald and stinky. Any poem contains a diction that has been devalued, a contaminated ecology, the body as waste dump. Body and text are joined, and their union contains virtue and vice, sin and salvation, degradation and loftiness ("loftiness and hairs," to cite Vallejo). The body lethal, the text that dreams it is an idea, and vice versa. How could I not listen to my intestinal rumbles? How could I not point to the presence of that primordial muck that is part of me? Artisans start out with dung and when they are done they should always have traces of filth under their fingernails. Bakhtin rebelled against the idiotic separation of the body into two regions: high (aristocratic, spiritual, sanctified, the better region) and low (plebeian, materialistic, where carnival-like pudenda are located and point to the putrefaction underneath). We are living matter, a text simultaneously in a state of putrefaction and beatific iridescence. We are violence and meekness, a mix of vitriol and virtue without a categorical top or down. We are mixed breeds, growing roots above ground and branches and leaves below ground. We are a paralogical language that seeks a "miscegenation," a crossbreeding involving varied languages and varied literatures and continually on the verge of prostitution. Today the poet has no choice but to carry with him or her all poets (that is to say, all languages: that of Villon, that of Juan Ramón Jiménez). Poets must carry on their backs every tradition and everything that has been done. And they must know it all. It is a gigantic task, complex and multiple, as it comprises and encircles everything. There is always something stuck in the poet's throat; our voice is a hoarse, broken sound—a whimper. The poet expectorates: not everything that comes out is crystalline.

Some time ago, feeling childish pains and having childish concerns, I wrote:

"I am not Federico García Lorca"
"I am not Nicanor Parra"
"I am not César Vallejo"

Today I would write that I am all of them because I am none of them. Because I am Ulysses and Noone. JK is John Keats. Joseph K. found his Kafka. Did he find him? It's just a saying.

Q 5: It has caught my eye that you never ignore how things taste, as if knowing that were

The author and his mother, about 1988

a kind of wisdom. I mean, in your poetry there are frequent references to music and the plastic arts but just as frequently you talk about the things people eat and drink (including wine and bread). Your love for the way things are prepared or the way a table is set goes well with the medieval atmosphere that is so noticeable in your poetry.

A: Actually, there is no wisdom, only taste, a taste that is not a knowledge but rather a reception of surfaces. Cioran writes that the wise person does not produce anything; he writes that to say that he is not wise. But, who is wise? To say anything contradicts wisdom; to say nothing, to forget that we live by saying and writing things nullifies, our record, the mark of our wisdom. A creator, then, can never be wise (Socrates, Buddha, and Jesus did not write anything). Therefore I don't have to know anything; I am left with a taste. "A taste of you," as a Cuban bolero says, or a taste of a meal shared with family, of wine being poured rapidly, of bread in a full mouth that is laughing irrepressibly. The glory of the sun: bread is noon, wine is summer, a table is agape, friendship. All of a sudden we are not alone but are intertextual; an affinity in the finite, between body and moment, poem and company. A solitude shared with others, the joy of being in the company of others, the nourishing laughter of friends in summer, the joy of the text: *a moveable feast*. I write, I am at a feast. A poem comes out. We were many. The table is set; I milk it. There is no other fact, no other text, no other need. We laugh and time does not

exist. We chew and nothing dies. I open my mouth and a fish gets its food. I cough up words and the text laughs. The poem grows wider because I chew, swallow, drink, ingest (ingurgitate, as Lezama used to say) wine-words, corn-words, the word corn itself filling your mouth as you utter it as part of a poem and are in awe of its roundness.

Q 6: I see your poetry as an attempt to turn reality into something static. Instead of giving us motion as in a film, you give us snapshots. This forces the reader to stop and see life, not as a story but as a series of detached incidents, an aggregate of motionless moments.

A: The ultimate truth, if it exists, is static. Poetry looks for truth in beauty and in the good, though the good may be "flowers of evil." Truth, beauty, the good: the way they sound; the sound of words such as kindness and blessedness. It all adds up to something static which moves me, physically and emotionally. To retain (I am anal), detain, contemplate. To stay more than to be, perhaps having a foreboding of a union between staying and being: a becoming static, a staying, the room where one stays in ordinary life, the anteroom of the future and at the same time it is the future itself, one site, immutable, an established site, a place of joy because it is invariable and together.

Besides, I make my poems static because, frankly, that is the only technique I have at my disposal. I don't have the fluidity of the novelist but the static flexibility of the poet who grabs language by the neck before it crumbles. Before language crumbles on me, the poem is done: a piece, a yoke, a link. I see it through a crack, quickly. I capture it quickly and then forget. It is the quickness of Sterne, Stendhal, Diderot. I make a spark static, or rather the spark becomes static instantly in my presence. It is something similar to what Sterne is doing in his *Tristram Shandy* when he says,

"Who are you, Sir?
"You puzzle me."

It is a leap, an unexpected move, very fast. A spark has been captured. And a vision is rendered static and is perhaps closer to truth, to the beautiful and good static truth of blessedness.

Q 7: A sort of crossbreeding is noticeable in your poetry, an effort not to heed limits.

To the chronological swings in your poetry one would have to add the marriage between colloquial language and the lyrical tradition, between painting and narrative, all of it sprinkled generously with a sort of ecumenical Spanish, filled with Cubanisms, Mexicanisms, and Peruvianisms.

A: I live today, I am an echo of that today: the resonances in the cavern of the day-to-day go out in concentric echoes, compounded, a composition of babels, techniques, media, instrumentations, races, diversity. A metal strip being bent sends out particles and a poet grabs them and gathers them, puts them in, begging the blindness of execution and language for substance. The poet is not given that substance, but if the poet is Cuban the mouth fills with gofio—roasted cornmeal; and if the poet is Jewish, it fills with matzo, the Jewish gofio, an ancestral, Judaic gofio, which is at the same time current and Peruvian, current and Mexican. Mexico, Mejico, with an x or a j, an emblem of the double, of an American Europe, the breakup of the one, disunion and expansion, modernity and infuriating tradition. We are stuck in a dead infuriating tradition, wishing to recover a new serene tradition to go with a happy, diverse, laughing, and iconoclastic modernity. In our era there are hardly any "isms"; there aren't any left. It seems as if we were waiting for the good news of the recovery of a stable tradition, alive, open to change, which needs no categories, which doesn't have to be called anything; it does not have to be Stridentism, or the Generation of '98, or of '27, or Dadaism, Expressionism, or Surrealism. For we aspire to a modernity that is a liquid melting pot, tranquil and serene, filled with humble items, within limits. I know I am aiming at Utopia and therefore not telling it quite straight. Everything is wrong: we are end-of-the-century people close to the second millennium, open as never before to apocalypse, and we are quite far away from serenity. But modern poetry does not cease to propose for itself, and struggle for, a serene, ecumenical, distributive, plural serenity. With each poem I write I sort of pray that our disorderly pluralistic excesses will not lead to the chaos of new and more terrible ideologies but rather to the embracing of all peoples and all words.

Q 8: How did your interest in Oriental poetry and in Zen affect your own poetry? The mysticism in them is not in contradiction with that in your Jewish ancestry. This is visible in your latest books, particularly in *De dónde oscilan los seres en sus proporciones* (From which beings oscillate in their proportions) and *El carillón de los muertos* (The Carillon of the Dead), and most especially in *Carece de causa* (It lacks a cause). There is an enormous presence of the religious and the melancholy in them, as well as a sense of blessedness, a sort of covenant between humans and the hostile world they inhabit, a sacred pact.

A: Consider the Old Testament. How terrible is the God of Israel (the Father)? And what about the Mother, soft, serving as mediator? For me the latter is Cuba, the New Testament, Mary: a fire that splits (the Cuban writer Lydia Cabrera says "fire is sacred") and once it splits it calms down, it turns into embers and then into the warmth of a nice tropical evening. But Cuba abandoned me. She cast me out when I was twenty. The outcast began to look for her, recover her in every form possible, searching for the soft mother that Cuba represented (for him), the mother who soothes the stern God, Jehovah the Just, the Implacable One who hands out absolutely no deferments. A Cuba that in poems fuses with, and becomes diffused in, Zen; an Orientalism of soft severity, concise and *satorial,* a religious Orientalism that has helped me balance my Jewish origins and the heartbreak of exile, as if the Burning Bush took on the shape of the Caiman and the latter in turn adopted the Lotus Position. There is the ruby, the small jewel of tranquility, its place at the center of a fragile flower. Four are the Vedas, and the fourth one, the Atarva-Veda, is signaled by fire (Atarva is the fire priest), a fire which is Jehovah, which is the Cuba that expelled me, though it is a fire that the mantric repetition of the sacred syllable (OM) softens, seduces, reduces, and controls. That fire becomes baked bread, a crackling log, a hearth. From the hearth, the home, come bread and poems, by the light of a lamp that brightens a table, ancestral and Cuban, traditional and modern, around which once sat sixteen of my people sharing a meal for my sake.

More Catechism: Two More Questions, and That's It

Q 1: would like to explore music and painting in your poetry. How do they work?

A: I was raised in a house where no music was played, classic or popular. At some point I discovered music and took an interest in classical music, especially baroque, and religious music, Gregorian chants, oratorios, romantic music. Around 1970, and as part of the process of freeing myself from alcohol, I started to dance with myself and to listen to a great deal of music. I began to write with music playing constantly in the background. Incidentally, it is something I have not been able to do in the last four or five years.

Listening to music I become loose. Words themselves become loose and burst out of me. They are like the splinters of some metallic object blown up with explosives, as if the explosives had lain unused inside of me for a very long time. The levity of a Mozart, the possibility of *divertimenti,* and of making a poem while dancing to it I find quite liberating. I experience two interconnected types of freedom, one created by music and the other by oriental repose. This serves to relax the tension of exile, the tension of having to live in two languages. It helped also in dealing with tensions created by a number of situations: my failed marriage, my having to raise my daughter as a single parent, my having to earn a living while not giving up on writing, and everything connected with our diaspora. Whenever I let music lead me, I was able to create poems. For the first time in my life I felt adventurous, not only in the streets of New York or the brothels and tough neighborhoods of Havana, but on the streets and brothels of language, which is like a tough neighborhood.

My language comprises all. Its dictionary is unlike anything: it never ends and it regenerates itself. The dictionary is the true phoenix. And so today I can write a divertimento-like poem and tomorrow a painful requiem that wishes to touch the unknowable. My work is an open text. There is another element to it and that is writing provoked by looking at paintings. But I am no longer in the East Village in New York City, sharing my bohemian life with painters but in the solitude of my room where before a painting I play the game of solitaire known as "writing a poem." Who may the painter be? Van Gogh, Picasso, Soutine, Vermeer, Poussin, and Bacon. Gauguin to a certain extent; then Klee. I look intently and I do recombinations. I am looking at a reproduction of a Klee and next to me is Velázquez's

Kozer's daughters, Susana (left) and Mia, about 1992

Venus (which has always intrigued me). And so from here I take a scrap, from there a fragment, a remnant, a residue; I extract a color, a tone, an image, a move. Using something that is fixed and static, a laminated surface, a center within a motionless frame, I manufacture my poem. You could say that I base myself both on the dynamics of music and on the tendency toward the static in painting. Two centers, two references, two different types of stimuli get together and somehow, through a multifarious diction, gradually become baroque, creating poems that mix languages and feature cross-eyed images and ambidextrous movements. A few years ago, at a party, a certain individual (actually a twerp who thought of himself as a great intellectual) had this to say about me: "Kozer is a rogue who may be talking to you about God one instant and in the next he is uttering the lewdest and most vulgar things. He is telling you about the ineffable and without missing a beat he starts scratching his balls." This was said with the worst of intentions but

Guadalupe and José Kozer, Southampton, Long Island, New York, 1992

it did not bother me too much, on the one hand because it came from him and on the other because in the end it was a compliment. It was something that could have been said of Joyce or Rabelais or Villon or the Archpriest of Hita. For to use two languages effectively is not a perversion. What is a perversion is not to be able to use two languages effectively.

After all, I write poetry by superimposing languages. You could say that to a Yiddish base I tend to superimpose a Cuban reality. Because my texts combine such disparate elements they end up looking baroque or rather neo-baroque, which is unavoidable because of what I am. Living in the era I live in, I have no choice but to take part in the general disorientation that is perhaps the product of too much information and of an overabundance of referentiality. So many things can happen and so many things can be done now at millennium's end that we have become disoriented. Besides, we have lost our roots, our center, our base, our foundations. The disorganization and superimposition

of planes in my texts is nothing but the reflection of the historical moment we live in. I start to write a poem impelled by some stimulus: a red on the rug, the cry of a bird that just went by my window, the book that is open on my desk, a leaf falling. Whenever Bécquer saw a leaf falling, it reminded him of his beloved, whom he lost. This memory motivated a poem: it is now a beloved leaf in a text. In Bécquer's case, the correspondence was symmetrical: vertical or perpendicular. I see a leaf fall and it becomes a paper leaf, a leaf in the natural world, a leaf that would not have fallen in Cuba (a tropical country), a leaf that reminds me of the shape of a birthmark on a concealed part of my anatomy; a leaf that is the razor's edge, one cut and you are dead. And so everything forks and forks again into many paths of signification. The poem so created looks like a spider with eight legs, as Vallejo said, moving awkwardly all over the page, losing its contours, getting lost, recovering: poems with too many legs, moving coarsely and changing direction suddenly and unpredictably, many different things happening at once. It is as if you were trying to watch eight TV channels at the same time.

Q. 2: In your book *Bajo este cien* (Under this hundred) there is a poem that strikes me as fundamental, "San Francisco de Asís," your Saint Francis of Assisi. Isn't this poem an attempt to find what we could call the spirituality of surface? Your writing it here, isn't it attempting to find things that escape dogma? In the poem we are told:

> Through his eyes he loves the things of the
> world:
> > the girls at the bottom of the pond,
> > the fish astonished
> > over the surface of the miracle of the
> > seas, the devout
> > scene of the crucifixion itself.

Later it adds:

> He loves it more—it's known—than the skin
> of the wild ass
> > or the pristine tapestry with unicorns or
> > the too obligatory gospel.
> Poor Francis: in a sienna solitude he worships
> bugs
> > over the scourge of a scale.

(From *Bajo este cien*)

This referential multiplicity, isn't it trying to extract a spirituality from that surface constituted by all events and all things?

A: Yes, clearly. And such a process involves a concept that I would summarize by saying that a saint is a person who lives in the present. Few people are able to live in the present. The present is eternity; the present is, furthermore, the future that is God. Those who live in the present live in God. They live in a state of enthusiasm (a word whose etymological meaning is "to be in God") and of a quiet holiness. That is perhaps what this poem attempts. Saint Francis is blind and from his blindness he contemplates the world. What does it reflect? His inner self? No: it reflects the world, for world and inner self are one thing: a surface. Let us remember *Heart of Darkness* when Marlow says that the only way one can survive is by being on the surface. We never accept this surface; I think only saints recognize it and accept it. Medieval people want a divine depth, romantics a dreamy other-world, and Cubans look for themselves outside the island. And they end up not seeing the island or God or anything. In poetry you have to learn to sing what is: the poetic function is that of immediacy: the rose becomes a poem, the vase becomes a poem. Before my eyes I now have an ink bottle. This actual ink bottle is lost to the eye without ceasing to be real when it becomes the tomb of the Pharaoh, an Egyptian cat, a sarcophagus; that is to say, a poem. You have to look at the bottle, touch its surface lightly with blind eyes for what is final, sticking to the present, cleansing ourselves (for the poem) of dogmas, conventions, and the institution of poetry, the child of the most deplorable romanticism.

If you sit up straight in a chair and you observe your body, you will discover its tension: a tension in the navel, in your creating hands, in your knees and thighs. If now you center your inner eye on your anus and distend it, you'll see how your whole body relaxes and distends automatically. This example illustrates that an awareness of the physical, of what is most palpable, allows us to jump into the spiritual and serene. By becoming aware of the material we can access the incorporeal. But you cannot aspire to float weightlessly if you have not stepped on the ground first. "Saint Francis of Assisi" (the final poem, the hundredth poem of my book with a hundred poems) is an attempt to naturalize the body (or any object) in the face of fallacious dimensionality. It is an attempt, let's say, to purify the body through the word. And I say body because I do not dare, in poetry, to say soul. I never use major words in my poems: I never say time, love, soul, death. I float apart from so much depth, so much metaphysicality. My poetry is music flush with the surface. The poem is a moment: haiku, quickness, instantaneousness, *satori* (enlightening) of a surface. This, deep inside, is the only thing that I barely find; a poor find. I am poor.

BIBLIOGRAPHY

Books:

Padres y otras profesiones (title means "Parents and Other Professions"), Editorial Villa Miseria (New York), 1972.

(With Isaac Goldenberg) *De Chepén a La Habana,* Editorial Bayú-Menoráh, 1973.

Este judío de números y letras (title means "This Jew of Numbers and Letters"), Editorial Católica, Ediciones Nuestro Arte (Tenerife, Canary Islands, Spain), 1975.

Y así tomaron posesión en las ciudades (title means "And Thus They Took Possession in the Cities"), Editorial Ámbito Literario (Barcelona), 1978.

Jarrón de las abreviaturas (title means "Ideogram's Vase"), Editorial Premiá, S.A. (México, DF), 1980.

La rueca de los semblantes (title means "The Wheels of Countenance"), Editorial Instituto Fray Bernardino de Sahagún (Colección Provincia), (León, Spain), 1980.

Antología breve (title means "A Short Anthology"), Editorial Luna Cabeza Caliente (Santo Domingo, Dominican Republic), 1981.

Bajo este cien (title means "Under This Hundred"), Editorial Fondo de Cultura Económica (Col. Tierra Firme), [México, DF]), 1983.

La garza sin sombras (title means "Heron without Shadows"), Ediciones Libres del Mall (Serie Ibérica, Barcelona), 1985.

El carillón de los muertos (title means "Death's Carillon"), Ediciones Último Reino (Buenos Aires), 1987.

Carece de causa (title means "It Lacks a Cause"), Ediciones Último Reino (Buenos Aires), 1988.

De donde oscilan los seres en sus proporciones (title means "From Which Beings Oscillate in Their Proportions"), H.A. editor (Tenerife, Canary Islands, Spain), 1990.

(by Aida Heredia) *La poesía de José Kozer: de la recta a las cajas chinas* (title means "The Poetry of José Kozer: From a Straight Line to Chinese Boxes"), Editorial Verbum (Madrid), 1994.

et mutabile (title means "And Mutable"), Editorial Graffiti (México, DF), 1995.

Los paréntesis (title means "The Parenthesis"), selected and with a prologue by Roberto Echavarren, Editorial El Tucán de Virginia (México, DF), 1995.

AAA1144, Editorial VAM/VERDEHALAGO (México, DF), 1997.

Chapbooks:

Por la libre (title means "Off the Books"), Bayú-Menorah, 1973.

Poemas de Guadalupe (title means "Poems by Guadalupe"), Editorial Por la poesía (Buenos Aires), 1974.

Nueve láminas (glorieta) (title means "Nine Plates"), Editorial La máquina de escribir (México, DF), 1980.

Nueve láminas (glorieta) y otros poemas (title means "Nine Plates and Other Poems"), UAM-Iztapalapa (Correo Menor, México, DF), 1984.

Díptico de la restitución (title means "Dyptic of Restoration"), Ediciones del Tapir (Madrid), 1986.

Somero animal de la especie (title means "Shallow Animal of the Species"), no. 6, Ediciones delanada Universidad Nacional del Litoral de Santa Fe (Santa Fe, Argentina), 1988.

The Ark upon the Number: Latin-American (Cuban) Poetry (bilingual edition, Spanish/English,

translated by Ammiel Alcalay), Cross Culture Press (New York), 1989.

Verdehalago, Verdehalago, Un acercamiento a la poesía (México, DF), 1990.

Prójimos (title means "Intimates"), no. 1, Editorial Carrer Ausías (with English translation by Ammiel Alcalay), (Barcelona), 1991.

Trazas del lirondo (title means "Simple Traces"), (Separata No. 16 de la revista Casa del Tiempo), Editorial de la UAM (México), 1993.

una índole (title means "A Sort of"), Editorial Pequeña Venecia (Caracas, Venezuela), 1993.

José Kozer, selección de su poesía, no. 173, Material de Lectura de la UNAM, selected and with an introductory note by Jacobo Sefamí, (México, DF), 1993.

a Caná, Las Hojas del Diluvio (Barcelona), 1995.

La maquinaria ilimitada (title means "The Unlimited Machinery"), Editorial Cantus Firmus, Colección Orbe Novo (No. 1), (New York), 1996.

Translator:

(And author of prologue) Lafcadio Hearn, *Kokoro,* Ediciones Miraguano Libros de los Malos Tiempos (Madrid), 1986.

Akutagawa Ryunosuke, *Rashomon and Other Stories by Ryunosuke Akutagawa* (short stories), Ediciones Miraguano, Libros de los Malos Tiempos (Madrid), 1987.

(And author of prologue) Saigo, *Mirror of the Moon* (poetry), Ediciones Miraguano, Libros de los Malos Tiempos (Madrid), 1989.

(And author of prologue) Natsume Soseki, *Mon, the Gate,* Miraguano Ediciones, Libros de los Malos Tiempos, No. 39 (Madrid), 1991.

(And author of prologue) Nathaniel Hawthorne, *Libro de las maravillas para chicos y chicas* (short stories) Miraguano Ediciones, Serie La Cuna de Ulises, No. 18 (Madrid), 1992.

(And author of prologue) *Seurat's Sunday Afternoon Along the Seine,* Fondo Editorial Pequeña Venecia (Caracas), 1992.

(And author of prologue) Saito Mokichi, *Shin-itamau Haha (Mother Dies),* Editorial Ver-dehalago (México, DF), 1994.

Nathaniel Hawthorne, *Leyendas del bosque frondoso* (short stories), Ediciones Miraguano, Serie La Cuna de Ulises, No. 21 (Madrid), 1995.

Contributor of poems, short stories, and essays to more than 250 literary magazines through-out the world. Poetry is represented in more than 18 anthologies.

Kaye McDonough

1943-

Born August 8, 1943, to Lucille Bechman McDonough and Edward Arthur McDonough in Pittsburgh, Pennsylvania. Like the lives of other "nice girls" raised in this era, mine has been the story of other people. The wider backdrop for my '40s-'50s childhood was the Pittsburgh described so well by Annie Dillard—or Ann Doak, as I knew her—in her memoir *An American Childhood*. We grew up in the same neighborhoods, even lived on the same streets, went to the same dancing school, attended one of the same schools, country clubs rolling in the background, with the crucial twist that I was raised Catholic. My parents knew her parents, her mother receiving my mother's tribute: "Pammie Doak's a smart cookie, and she looks like a million bucks." My mother detested the company of "wives." "All these gals ever want to talk about is how they're going to change the draperies in the living room." The first through sixth grades I attended Saint Bede's, a parochial school taught by nuns, the ones Ann Doak heard had tails. Egalitarian Pittsburgh was somewhat *more* egalitarian for the Scottish Presbyterians than it was for the Catholics. Let's not even think about the "kikes," "coons," and "hunkies." The swimming pool on Washington Boulevard used by the "jigaboos" was referred to as "the inkwell." Pittsburgh did not stand at the vanguard of a Free Society.

I like to think about the gentleman poet-publisher James Laughlin making his escape from Pittsburgh with his Laughlin Steel fortune long before I was born. The Laughlin mills were among the many that lined the Three Rivers area, dumping their slag and spewing emissions with no compunction. The city was divided among those who ran the mills and those who worked in them. Bankers, lawyers, brokers (of which my father was one) followed hard on their heels. I loved to drive at night along the Allegheny River lit by the orange firestorms of the mills. My cousin Bob, a lawyer and art collector now living in Santa Fe, has told me that, like myself, he admired the painting of this sight that

Kaye McDonough with her son, Nile Corso, 1996

hung on the wall of the PAA (Pittsburgh Athletic Association), a more pleasurable activity than working in the mill itself. One of my teenage crushes who had worked in a mill one summer, as did a few other sons of executives, talked about the discomfort and dangers of the great boiling pots of fiery ore. My growing up was studded with headlines and photographs in the *Sun Telegraph* and *Pittsburgh Press* of steel strikes, the "evil" unions, "corrupt" union bosses, workers being injured and killed in strikes. After all, it was at Andrew Carnegie's Homestead plant that Frick had given the order to the Pinkertons to fire on the steelworkers. David McCullough, the author of *Truman*, whose family lived just up the street from my grandparents on Glen Arden Drive, recently ran an exposé on his PBS series concerning the negligence of some of these old Pittsburgh families, a negligence that resulted in mass deaths in the Johnstown Flood. Frick Park, Mellon Park, the Carnegie

199

Library, and the Carnegie Museum number among the more positive legacies of these robber baron scions. Like my favorite heroine, Nancy Drew, I explored these parks and much else of Pittsburgh, only I did it by bicycle without Ned Nickerson, heading to the two Berger's soda fountains, to the Beacon and Manor Theaters for seventeen cartoons or serials plus a double feature, to the Phipps Conservatory, even to a *Mystery of the Moss-Covered Mansion* I had discovered off Homewood Avenue, always making tracks for home afterwards like Lad, a heroic dog from the stories of Albert Payson Terhune, a favorite writer of my childhood.

I always had loads of friends, even in Somerset, sixty miles or so out of Pittsburgh, where we moved when my father tried to make a go of a lumber business, the MacLamb Company (named for himself and his partner, Mr. Lambert). I was an early reader. My mother taught me to type, so by four or five I was writing plays for the neighborhood. We had a cornfield in back of us and a forest lay beyond. I have a fine memory of the smell of new-mown grass and an even better one of my friend Ronnie's dead dog stuffed by a taxidermist. Another friend, Richard, had a Lionel train with operating cattle cars that I lusted after. Girls didn't have such things. By first grade, we'd moved to Worth Street and then to Bucknell Street in third grade, right across from Saint Bede's and just a block from the convent that housed my teachers, the Sisters of Saint Joseph. They passed our house morning and evening, no matter what the weather, in their long black robes with white starched bibs, wooden rosaries hanging from their cinctures. "Good morning, Sister Mary Alacocque." "Good morning, Kathryn." (No "Kaye." Saints' names only, no nicknames please.) "Good afternoon, Sister Mary Ida." "Good evening, Kathryn." "Good evening, Sister Maristella." Sometimes at school we'd practice for the atomic bomb by hiding under our desks (the desktop to catch fallout, I'm guessing?) or by flattening ourselves against the corridor walls. In those days, you went home from school for lunch. We had to deliver "speeches" based on books we'd read, memorize poems over our bologna sandwiches.

Sometimes we'd have a theological "mystery" to cogitate, such as the matter of Mary Magdalene's redemption. Who in the heck understood that? What had she done wrong exactly anyway? Always, every morning, every day, the catechism. *Who made you?* "God made me." *Why did God make you?* "God made me to know, love, and serve Him in this world." We learned the intricacies of sin, both mortal and venial, the Seven Deadly Sins, sins of thought, word, and deed, though what they meant by "impurity" was never completely spelled out. By my first confession in second grade, I had amassed thousands of misdeeds, "through my fault, through my fault, through my most grievous fault." I liked the lives of the saints, especially Saint Francis with his love of the poor. My friend George Scrivani, raised Catholic as well, recently reminded me of Kerouac's preference for Saint Joseph, the workingman's saint. Francis was for the bourgeois, like me, I suppose. The Seven Corporal Works of Mercy have to be for everybody: feed the hungry, give drink to the thirsty, clothe the naked, visit the imprisoned, shelter the homeless, visit the sick, bury the dead. (Someone should send them to Newt Gingrich.) On Easter Sunday, we'd wear all new clothes, symbolic of Christ's resurrection, while my father attended the "Golfer's Mass" on the nineteenth hole, a joke I didn't get for years. During Lent, I'd try to go to mass every day. Nothing will ever be as otherworldly as those early morning masses, the melancholy Gregorian chants and incense floating into my newly awakened consciousness. When the monstrance holding the host was removed from the tabernacle for "adoration," I became transfixed. I would stare until it was iridescent, shimmering, hoping for the highest of the high, a transcendent vision. Transubstantiation was not merely symbolic. This little wafer was God, *"patrem omnipotentem, factorem coeli et terrae."* When I finally got in to see Bernini's Saint Teresa in Ecstasy in Rome many years later, the emotion expressed in this voluptuous sculpture was completely familiar to me.

I loved my world of plaster saints, as the poet Gregory Corso calls them. Saint Anthony of Padua, Mary in blue, radiating light, her foot casually crushing the serpent, that schlemiel Saint Joseph, the noble Sacred Heart of Jesus holding his radiant heart in his hand, the Little Infant of Prague. These were all smaller than life-size, accessible. However, even by third grade, some cracks were starting to show in my Catholicism. I knew the Church had made a mistake about divorce. It should be allowed. I would go into the empty church to say the Stations of the Cross on my knees, even prostrating myself, begging that Mother and I could leave my father. Christ betrayed, dragging his cross, Veronica with her veil taking the imprint of Christ's face, these are the images that have stayed with me. The new, bigger, and better Saint Bede's they built, with its streamlined Mary, et al., was never as inviting as the old one. The sculptures, the long, low, intimate architecture of the old Saint Bede's, the chanting, the Latin mass we learned by heart, were the power of my childhood Catholicism. I've held on to some of that early awe through the arts.

The Episcopalians and Presbyterians belonged to Fox Chapel, the Catholics to the Field Club, and the Fox Chapel wanna-bes to Longue Vue, a beautiful club my great-grandfather helped found. I suppose with his "brogue," as my grandmother called his thick German accent, he was not Field Club material. I don't know. My grandparents, Aunt Lihi and her husband, Uncle Joe and Aunt Virginia, my parents, all "belonged" to Longue Vue. My family never talked about any of this ethnic, religious, social hierarchy. I

grew up eating fish on Fridays, going to confession and to mass on Sundays and Holy Days of Obligation, keeping Lent in a big way, and never thought anything about it. When I changed from Saint Bede's to Ellis, a private girls' school with a few token Jews and Catholics, I gradually became aware of being "Catholic." For example, I said the Our Father, they said the Lord's Prayer; in retrospect, even their name for it sounds hierarchical. It *would* be the *Lord's* Prayer. Wondering what in this world I was doing among them, I kept my mouth closed for their grandiose finale, ". . . for thine is the kingdom and the power and the glory . . .," and turned red with embarrassment. For them or for me? I guess they knew what *they* were about, even in prayer. The extent of prejudice against Catholics took me a long time to realize.

My mother, superficially the dutiful daughter, the wronged wife, was at heart a deeply rebellious, independent spirit who thought

"At the Sphinx: Pa Heidenkamp, my great-grandfather, and Aunt Lihi, are seated on camels, directly to the left of the Sphinx; other parties unidentified," 1920s

"My first birthday celebration, with Ma (my grandmother), and Aunt Lihi," August 1944

nothing of flicking the nonfiltered butts of her Lucky Strike and Pall Mall cigarettes into my grandmother's rhododendrons while drinking Four Roses on the rocks before dinner, or Canadian Club and soda afterwards. "I use lots of ice," she always said, as if that somehow cut the effect of the alcohol. "I have to have *some* fun." She preferred the company of men and enjoyed nothing better than staying up till the wee hours baiting my uncles, or her father, or her husband, always playing the devil's advocate, just, as she put it, "to get a rise out of them." She enjoyed penetrating the good-humored veneers of her sister and brother, until they were red in the face with rage. She had a gut instinct regarding vulnerabilities and sacred cows and loved to pooh-pooh the goody-two-shoes remarks of lesser spirits—her mother ("Lu-*cille!*"), her sister, her husband, me, anyone in her swath. She didn't stand around and wash the dishes. "Hell, no!" (with the emphasis on "Hell") "I'll do them tomorrow." A striking 5'10", 112-pound beauty along the lines of a Lauren Bacall or a Rita Hayworth, for whom she was sometimes mistaken, she roared through life, oblivious to the fact that she was hell on wheels. She must have taken to heart one of the many roles she played in high school, that of "Kay Dixon, the girl who upsets things," from *Hurricane Hal.* "You are as dull as doughnuts," she chided me. "At your age . . ." She used to get up, roll out the tennis courts, play three

sets of tennis with her father before breakfast, swim across the Allegheny River and back (it wasn't polluted in those days), then hang around in the rooms over the stables with the grooms snorting snuff. She was proud that she'd played hooky from school. "She's full of the devil," or, "He looks like he could raise some hell," was her idea of a compliment. She never mentioned that at Springdale High she was Most Popular Girl, vice president of her class, captain of the basketball team, and predicted "to win first prize in a beauty contest." Maybe her bad girl pose was the only way she knew to register her objection to a stultifying life of caretaker to her mother, Aunt Lihi, Uncle Joe, Uncle Bill, her father, her father's business, her child, her husband, and half the town of Springdale.

In that preconfessional era (a "confessional" was the box you went into in church to confess your sins), before the daily gut-spilling of talk show TV, it was "put up and shut up." The world was a safe place. Americans were a wonderful, beloved people who had helped save Europe from Hitler and the Germans. (Wasn't our family originally German? Mom could speak and understand German from hearing it in the home—oh, well, "keep it under your hat.") "Tramps" and "bums" were okay if you saw them sleeping on the railroad trestle as you crossed to go to the Homewood Library. Alcoholics, on the other hand, were unspeakable creatures, rolling in the gutter, not, as it turned out, most of your family, friends, and neighbors. "Depression" and "dysfunction" were not in the lexicon. What else was left but to be happy? "For chrissake, would you quit your bellyaching?" was my father's frequent request to my mother. His golf and cocktail buddies had given him the nickname Si, for Silent, a true man of the '50s. To everyone else he was Ted. He was what they call "Black Irish," black hair combed back flat to the head, white skin, and an urbane William Powell country club demeanor. His dry humor kept him and his friends entertained through innumerable holes of golf and cocktails. My mother claimed she had never loved him, but he certainly was handsome, funny, and smart. His family, Catholic like my mother's, lived in Winchester, Massachusetts. He met my mother while he was studying engineering at Carnegie Tech. No question existed about his love for her. He had even threatened suicide if she wouldn't marry him. He was "the best thing to come along" to get her away from her quarreling parents. My mother not only wanted to get out of her family, she wanted to get out of Springdale, Rachel Carson's hometown, "that goddamned, stinking, little town," as she called it, where she was born and raised, where she went to school, ran her father's business (Bechman Real Estate and Insurance) when he was incapacitated, sometimes hospitalized, from a series of what were euphemistically called "nervous breakdowns" (he drank), making her the only woman realtor in the Allegheny Valley, the town where she was known everywhere as the granddaughter of Joseph Heidenkamp, Springdale's richest man. She never got very far. I always wanted my mother to have one of those *It's a Wonderful Life* revelations, her own life so much mirrored Jimmy Stewart's, even down to the Building and Loan, but this never happened. She loved Springdale, but could never admit it.

Joseph Heidenkamp, or Pa Heidenkamp, as he was called in my family, was born near Essen, Germany, the youngest of a large family. He did not want to join the German army, so he left Germany with the proverbial ten cents in his pocket for Creighton, Pennsylvania, where the German glassmakers had settled. Vowing to show the disapproving family of Louisa Baldus that he was worthy of her, he developed and patented a special process for making thick, high-quality plate glass, the type used in department store windows. I grew up with a piece of it covering our dining room table. Eventually he made a fortune. They married and had six children responsible for my "cast of thousands" childhood. The five girls were sent to Saint Aloysius' Academy, a convent school. The oldest, Aunt Anna, known as Mother Cecilia in the order of the Sisters of Saint Francis of Penance and Christian Charity, died before I was born of an "enlarged heart," which, from what I've heard about her, sounds appropriate. Like all her siblings, she had a sharp mind, so in this pre–women's lib period, she became mother superior of her convent rather than heir to Pa Heidenkamp's glass plant, handling its legal matters regarding adoption. The second child, Teresa, my grandmother, the artist of the family, painted vases with fluid drawings, a skill inherited by her daughter Vera and Vera's son, my favorite cousin, Jack. My mother and I couldn't draw for beans. My grandmother remembered silvering and drawing on

mirrors in their kitchen during Pa and Ma Heidenkamp's leaner years. The rest were: Mary Heidenkamp Dwyer, who, when I was a teenager, unexpectedly choked to death on shish kebab at Sanremy's in front of a full table of startled relatives; my favorite relative of all, Elizabeth Heidenkamp Thomas (Aunt Lihi); Louise Heidenkamp Westermann, the glamorous one who lived on Park Avenue in New York City (the only one to move away from Pittsburgh); and my uncle Joe, Joseph Heidenkamp Jr., who refused to take over the plant, preferring to set up his camera early in the morning at Frick Park to photograph birds feeding their young or flowers blooming. Some of his work was bought by Walt Disney for use in his nature films.

Pa Heidenkamp was struck by a car and killed one rainy evening as he was leaving the PAA. The story in the paper read, in part, that he was "the founder and president of the Heidenkamp Plate Glass Company . . . that merged with the Standard Plate Glass Company. . . . [He] became chairman of the board. He also was president of the Springdale National Bank, but since his retirement more than eight years ago he had little to do with its business. [He] was a member of the Keystone Athletic Club, the Pittsburgh Athletic Association, Duquesne Club, and was a charter member of the Longue Vue Country Club."

I loved all the stories my mother told me about him. When he opened his glass plant in Springdale, no housing existed for his workers, so instead of having cheap row housing built, Pa Heidenkamp had each house designed individually, despite the expense. My mother used to drive me by to admire them (the key words here are "drive by"). He paid the highest wages in the area to his workers. He would take his entire family by carriage down to the Park Schenley Hotel in Oakland so they could attend the opera. Every night after dinner, he and his wife listened to classical music, read classics of German literature, studied books of prints, and looked through the stereopticon at foreign lands they planned to visit. She died of cancer before this was possible, an event my mother couldn't mention without sobbing. He felt the money he'd earned was not worth anything if he couldn't enjoy it with those he loved, so he retired early and took family members on cruises and trips around the world. He and his wife were loved and respected, especially for their playfulness and kindness to children. I was told by Aunt Lihi that they never quarreled and never raised their voices. He provided for three generations of his family through hard work, careful planning, and his wits. Self-made, self-educated, fair to the people he worked with, generous, this lover of the arts was my ideal of what a man should be. I hope we don't one day find out that his plant was partly responsible for polluting the Allegheny River. My son Nile's middle name is Joseph, after him, or at least after all he represented in our family.

My mother would sit up late at night, often school nights, till one or two telling me this family history while she cried and drank. When my mother went to the parish priest for advice on my father's drinking, she had been told that her husband would spend less time in bars if she would drink with him at home. Such was the advice of the Catholic Church on alcoholism in the '50s. Unfortunately, my mother took it. "Do you know what it's like to grow up in the biggest house in town?" (Sad). "My father wouldn't let me go out with anyone. No one was good enough for me." (Boohoo). Her peculiar self-image was the gawky, small-town "hick," as she referred to herself, with a bad complexion and a bad education. She veered from self-pity to being her Royal Imperial Majesty. "All I ever wanted was a family," she'd cry, as if we weren't smothering from the plethora of aunts, uncles, cousins, and grandparents living up and down every street in our neighborhood. She meant "nuclear" family, in our case like a nuclear bomb. Despite everything, I adored my mother. She was my hero. Bigger than life. She had guts. She was generous to a fault. A good-hearted person, she once even purchased a house for a family of seven that was in financial trouble. I bought her entire tragedy, hook, line, and sinker.

My parents' early marriage transpired during the black-and-white era of Sam Spade and Richard Diamond. I could hear their radio from my room. No need to go to the movies, though we did. My parents *were* film noir. They read Erle Stanley Gardner, Raymond Chandler, and my father's favorite, Mickey Spillane. Maybe he read one too many. I can't watch a detective movie from that era without thinking of them. Bogey and Lauren Bacall. Watch your back, here comes Lizabeth Scott. My parents

were well into their nightmare by the time I was born, the year *Casablanca* won Best Picture. My father suffered from debilitating episodic depressions alleviated by martini after martini, Gibson after Gibson. You knew he'd had too many when this mild-mannered, elegant, amused, and amusing person let his pain be known. I don't need to drag my parents through the mud here. I loved them both. Suffice it to say that while most families had the Cauley Detective Agency protect their house from burglars, we had them to protect my mother from my father. As far back as I can remember, I'd make my escape by myself to my grandparents' house out the back door with my suitcase, always at night. In Somerset, when I was small, I'd go to the bus station alone. My mother would follow as soon as she could. She would never have jeopardized my father's job by call-

"Daddy at Longue Vue, 1950"

ing the police, though what difference would it have made? No matter how much money he made, he gambled it away. My saddest memory is the least violent: my mother, tall and beautiful in a new formal gown bought especially for the New Year's Eve dance at Longue Vue, wearing a corsage. I can picture her reflection in the full-length mirror of my parents' bedroom. Midnight. Daddy at the club, having forgotten to pick her up.

He liked to talk to himself in the bathroom mirror, holding cryptic conversations that struck him funny: "Hi, Casio. How's Fyke?" You were never quite sure what would set him off. My cousins Joe and Jack, who were like brothers to me, called him Dr. Jekyll and Mr. Hyde. My mother's sarcastic humor probably didn't help.

During World War II, my father worked for Dravoe Steel, a war-related industry rendering him ineligible for service. Since Aunt Lihi's husband was at war, my parents lived with her to keep her company in her house on Beechwood Boulevard, the one she had inherited when Pa Heidenkamp was killed. I was born at Mercy Hospital during that period. Aunt Lihi was something of a dreamer and a romantic. I was told that when she was a baby, a premature infant, they kept her in a shoebox on the mantel to keep her warm, she was that small. When she died at age ninety-five, she weighed seventy-five pounds or so and still had all her wits about her. She was a great golfer. We have photos of her taking lessons from Sam Snead in Colorado Springs. She was always pointing out a lush display of spring flowers, the vista from the Pink Terrace at Longue Vue, the view from her apartment window, the moon. "Oh, Kathy," as she liked to call me, "would you look at that! I've been all over the world, and I can tell you, you're never going to see anything more beautiful than that." When I was little, she liked to carry me around to look at her wonderful paintings and take me to Mellon Park. As I grew older, she'd take me to the Phipps Conservatory for the flower shows and to the Carnegie Museum. When I was twelve, she took me on a tour of Europe, first-class on the *Queen Mary* and *Queen Elizabeth,* to the British Isles, France, Germany, Switzerland, and Scandinavia, a trip that gave me a window to another, better world of art and beauty. Aunt Lihi treated me like a daughter and never made one single derogatory remark about my father.

"He always behaved like a gentleman around me, Kathy." The autumn after that trip, the final horror show occurred. My mother's face was a sheet of blood. The rest of her life she had nightmares about the chase to my grandparents' house. That was the end, Catholic Church or no. Mother and I never went back. We lived with my grandparents on Glen Arden for good.

If there are better people in the world than my grandmother and Aunt Lihi, I haven't met them. My grandmother, like Aunt Lihi, was unfailingly polite, interested, and kind to every person she came in contact with. She ran her home with an order and regularity I appreciated and wouldn't go to bed until absolutely every plate and glass, knife and spoon, had been inspected for spots, cleaned thoroughly, and put in its place. She was sweet and petite, less than five feet tall, and walked on her tippy toes when she took off her shoes. Though she'd raised three children already, she never made me feel anything but at home. My grandfather, known to like a drink, enjoyed singing barbershop quartets with his son Harry and Aunt Vera's husband, Joe. Their house embodied safety and security. The day I put it on the market in the '80s after my mother had died, I curled up on the sofa for hours. I had to leave the closing. My uncle's wife said, "Oh, you're all alike," meaning my mother, grandmother, Aunt Lihi, and me. "You're so dramatic. It's just a house." She didn't know she'd given us a compliment, my three mothers and me.

Not long after we'd moved in, my grandfather developed cancer. For three years he lost weight and deteriorated. In the end, he roamed the streets in the middle of the night, thinking he was back on the farm of his childhood calling the cows. You didn't know whether to laugh or to cry. My mother took his death hard. I can picture the room at Ellis where I first read Emily Dickinson, just about this time. "Because I could not stop for Death, / He kindly stopped for me, . . ."

At my grandparents' we watched Bishop Sheen's weekly TV show. Who knew he was a hard-nosed right-winger? Wasn't the '50s the McCarthy era (I watched the hearings on TV), with Herb Filbrick's *I Led Three Lives* on TV as well, the story of life in a Communist cell block? Where were all these Communists? The Ethel Walker School, an all-girls Connecticut boarding school I attended my junior and senior years, had Cuban girls from families that I now realize probably supported the dictator Batista. Walker's had secret clubs and hazing. I am ashamed to say I was a participant. My fascination with the McCarthy era dates from these experiences. The great Clifford Odets of *Waiting for Lefty*, a fink? Elia Kazan? Arthur Miller kept his integrity, spelling it out in *After the Fall*, as did Dashiell Hammett, who went to jail rather than name names. What kind of code do you live by in real life?

Walker's was not my happiest experience, but I did enjoy writing skits for the many theatricals they had, particularly the Dial Senior Play that Kim, Leine, and I collaborated on. At Walker's, I first read the plays of Eugene O'Neill, who became a lifelong hero. The English Department head, Miss Hunt, unjustly accused me of cheating on an O'Neill paper. She didn't realize *Long Day's Journey into Night* was for me an all-too-familiar personal hell. At Walker's, I walked out of one of her classes because she was ruining Byron, making fun of him, the way small souls laugh at those with the courage to be big. I loved all the Romantic poets, Shelley, Keats. I watched the inaugural of John F. Kennedy—his elegant morning coat and top hat—in the main living room of Walker's. "Ask not what your country can do for you . . ." Walker's felt minuscule and confined. The national debate over whether a Catholic should hold the highest office had set off much confusion within my family. I had never realized that a Catholic *couldn't* be president, so I found the whole matter puzzling, but began to follow the politics of this handsome new president with interest, even met him once, just like Forrest Gump, in Hyannisport.

Young women of that era must have been thought to be colorful and amusing edible treats. I knew a Cuppy (Cupcake), Candy, Cooky, Muffy (Muffin), and Pinky. The young men's names were a bit more dynamic: two Bings and a Biff (I don't mean Cooper's cousin here). Women today can't know what you're talking about concerning life for women in this era. Sometimes I feel like a relic. I never did figure out why my mother wanted me to have a deb party. I always felt awkward about it, as if we had no business in that world. My family weren't social climbers—they were happy with each other— nor were they Blue Book types. We weren't in the Social Register. The rest of the Catholics went their own ways. Why didn't we? As it turned

out, the deb parties were a lot of fun; with their dancing and drinking, they were a great training ground for the more hedonistic aspects of the '60s, only they had Lester Lanin instead of the Jefferson Airplane. All the outrage over drugs in the '60s is almost comical. What hypocrisy. These people were on a bender that wouldn't quit. Their kids were drinking at age twelve. Many died in alcohol-related car crashes. *Lost Weekend* in evening dress. You'd even fly east for parties in Greenwich or Long Island. I was too airheaded to realize that these costly events and the lifestyle that went with them were staged at someone else's expense. Once when the steelworkers went on strike, they threw blood on the door of the Shadyside Presbyterian Church where my best friend, Cuppy, and my former boyfriend, Gordon, were married. People laugh at political correctness, but the '50s and early '60s could have used a big helping. I didn't get the drift that you were supposed to marry one of these people. My mother was in no hurry to see me enter the contract that had wrecked her life. The Catholic Church did not treat my mother well.

My family was Republican. Who had ever questioned it? Everyone we knew was a Republican, so I was a Republican too, though the first time I voted it was for Lyndon Johnson, not Barry Goldwater, whose views conflicted with my early religious principles. However, I was oblivious to my own anti-Semitism, racism, classism, you name it: a typical '50s young American. We all needed to have our consciousness raised. Luckily for me, I was accepted on early admissions to Vassar, then an all-girls college (sort of sister school to all-male Yale), for the fall of 1961. I had attended Carnegie School of Drama the previous summer in lieu of summer stock at the Pittsburgh Playhouse (my mother had objected). I suppose most people think of Vassar as snotty rich girls simping about. My mother thought it was a "hole in the ground" in a "godforsaken area." My father thought I should have gone to the secretarial school Katie Gibbs. For me, it was a series of discoveries: we read about Leftist political activity at Vassar during the '30s, the radical theater of Hallie Flanagan, who had been called before HUAC, Napoleon and the French Revolution, the great Marat and Danton (at the time, I preferred Robespierre), drama, art history. For a History 105 course, I wrote a paper on Edith Wharton.

Koestler, Silone, Isherwood, Auden, Hemingway, Eliot, Joyce. I didn't just read *A Portrait of the Artist as a Young Man,* I memorized it. "The soul . . . has a slow and dark birth, more mysterious than the birth of the body." Literature was replacing my crumbling Catholicism. The power of the Vivien Leigh portrayal in *A Streetcar Named Desire* at the Juliet Theater in Poughkeepsie stays with me, the beginning of my deep affinity for the theater of Tennessee Williams. Through it all, Miss Mercer, chairman of the English Department, encouraged me to become a writer. She also suggested I see the school psychiatrist for my ongoing family difficulties. I was grateful to her for her support, but I thought the psychiatrist was a jerk. College women are in the cocoon waiting to be butterflies? Come on. Women I knew were reading *The Bell Jar* and making suicide attempts. Sylvia Plath, her book *Ariel* not yet published, was still very much alive (at least until February of my sophomore year). A Wellesley graduate, she had taught at nearby Smith, in the not-too-distant past. The plan was for me to write stories my sophomore year, plays my junior year, and a publishable novel my senior year. What would I have to do? Go insane or kill myself was the message. I was sure I wouldn't live past thirty, a belief I held till age thirty-one.

F. Scott Fitzgerald was from a background like mine. His daughter, Scottie, went to Walker's and Vassar just the way I did. "Peck and Peck and peck and peck" was still there. He understood the world of the parvenu midwesterner. How had he managed? I was reading *The Crack-Up,* Fitzgerald's account of hitting the skids on alcoholism, just about the time I drank my father under the table when he visited for a parents' weekend. Fitzgerald's imaginative world seemed to parallel mine, complete with his ambivalent indictment of the moral negligence of the rich in *Gatsby.* In the Trumbull biography (new in 1962, no Nancy Milford yet), I discovered Fitzgerald's beautiful and strange wife, Zelda, whose tragedy has haunted me all my life, perhaps because she was a woman on the literary scene, albeit playing a peripheral role, very different from the old warhorses, George Eliot, Willa Cather and the rest. I may never fully understand what hits me so hard about Zelda Fitzgerald.

Vassar had its share of stupid preppy types like me, but it also had intellectuals, Leftists,

and scholars. I was lucky to know Susanna Margolis. She was raised in a town called Roosevelt, in New Jersey, after the president my father had said "ruined the country." Susanna began the one-step-forward-two-steps-back task of educating me politically and intellectually. The great movements of the '60s hadn't quite hit yet in 1962. The "keep your feet on the floor, girls" speech delivered by Vassar President Sarah Gibson Blanding during my freshman year gives some indication of the archaic world that still existed for women at that time, even privileged women. Many went to mixers and to Yale for weekends. Dates were spent drinking as fast as you could get it down. Bo Diddley, the Twist, beer kegs, more car accidents. When one blind date at Yale introduced me as his "cheese," I made my escape by jumping out a bathroom window. I was at Vassar when the Cuban Missile Crisis occurred. We talked long into the night about what we'd do for our last twenty-four hours, what to take to the shelters? Wait a minute . . . *what* shelters? Several women wanted to lose their virginity immediately. Who to call? The limitations and closed-boxed-ness of our lives stood in relief. The unspoken imperative was to get out there as fast as possible and, like the Legion of Decency–condemned Auntie Mame, *live, live, live.*

I was having some problems. Sometimes I would sleep twenty-three hours a day, several days running. A friend across the hall told me they used to wonder if I were dead. Then I'd be unable to sleep, sometimes for five days at a time. I was drinking too much at the Dutch, an off-campus watering hole. Summer after freshman year, I traveled with three other young women on a month-long car tour of the United States that culminated in a visit to the Seattle World's Fair. While we were in Palo Alto, I fell in love at first sight. I was eighteen: his name was Hutch, his nickname was Ishi, after the last California Yaqui Indian described by the anthropologist Kroeber. Indians, to me, were the Lone Ranger's faithful Indian companion, Tonto, or in display cases at the Carnegie Museum. I'd never heard of Kroeber. Hutch and his brother were radicals. Their hair was long (for that period), they had mustaches, and they'd been to Cuba and to the Helsinki Convention. My Lord! Communists! They had a huge Cuban flag hanging on their wall. I didn't want to leave. I had met the enemy, and they were fabulous!

"With my mother," about 1964

My mother encouraged me to leave Vassar at the end of my sophomore year when two of my closest friends, Connie McGraw and Elizabeth Hudgins, were leaving to travel in Europe. She had thought I was getting "too serious" at Vassar and still wondered why I hadn't gone to Briar Cliff instead, where I could have learned to play a good game of bridge. Spent that summer in New York with Susanna and others in an apartment full of pop art on the Upper West Side. That fall of 1963, briefly attended *"La Cours de la civilization française pour étrangers"* at the Sorbonne in Paris. I'd arrive at school to see students wearing red sashes. Political protest was so unfamiliar to me at that time, I thought they were having a party until I saw the French police turn hoses on the protesters, blowing them across the street. At the Paris movie houses, the French, outraged by the actions of the southern police, ran newsreels of the dogs loosed on southern "Negroes." We were as shocked as they were, especially Hudgins, who was from North Carolina. We read Camus, Genêt, Baudelaire, went to Ionesco plays. Discovered Van Gogh's "Dear Theo" letters and *The Autobiography of Alice B. Toklas.* I carried around a copy of the vitriolic *A Moveable Feast,* which had just come out, hoping to find ghosts of the writers whom Hemingway wronged. The cafés we frequented in the Latin Quarter were filled with students from all over the world, including Northern Africa, not the only place where French colonial policies were running aground. Some African blacks and French spat at us or got into angry conversations, holding

us personally responsible for all that was going on in our country. From Apple Pie Pittsburgh, I had never dreamed that anyone could find fault with an American. I didn't have a clue what was going on in the South and felt stunned by the level of anger directed at us. More shocks were ahead. I was staying at the Hotel Recamier on Place Saint Sulpice, then a quiet square with religious shops—I felt right at home—not the busy designer boutique area it is today. One of the hotel residents, a professor from the Sorbonne, knocked on my door to tell me: "Your president has been assassinated." That was the Thanksgiving weekend Kennedy was killed. The world as we knew it seemed to be falling apart.

Hudgins was a rare bird. She combined a Southern literary sensibility with a razor-sharp mind that did not suffer fools gladly. At Vassar, she had been a classics major. I had turned to art history after some disagreeable experiences in the English Department so nasty I didn't show my writing to anyone for the next ten years. With our mutual interests in Greek and Roman culture, archaeology, Italian Renaissance history and art, we planned a trip that turned out to be one of the great formative adventures of my life. Hudgins was game to go anywhere: the pensione in Taormina where D. H. Lawrence and Frieda had stayed, the Delphic Oracle, the lair of the Cumean Sibyl, Lake Avernus, the mythological Gate of Hell. Siracusa, Agrigento, Knossos, Mycenae, Tiryns. Greeks spat at us in the streets of Athens. The American Express office was bombed. We stayed up late at night talking and arguing about Dostoyevsky, the Brontës, life, love, our futures. We were all set to walk into Paris of the '20s. Where was it? (The foreign edition of *Time* was full of photos of the free speech movement. Though I thought they should dress better and not *swear,* I was definitely attracted to it and applied to Berkeley. They turned me down.) I remember on Mykonos, the American students singing "We Shall Overcome," with their arms linked. Our big claim to fame was meeting the Beatles in Paris before their trip to the States (more Gump). John Lennon talked to me for several hours about his writings and drawings. I felt I had met a real artist. He, I suppose, a real piece of ass, though not much happened other than talk. I guess Hudgins and I were groupies, but virginal ones. We were only twenty, and this was 1964.

When I returned to Pittsburgh that summer, some of my friends were already engaged, even married. Instead of wanting to settle down, I felt uneasy. Hudgins and I had read most of E. M. Forster, including *Howard's End*—"Only connect." Back home now in North Carolina, she wrote about the future taking shape for us: country clubs, bridge, golf, tennis, luncheons, parties. I couldn't even play golf or tennis. Our letters expressed anxieties about the tightening of the noose. Why I didn't go back to Vassar at this point, I'll never know. I hadn't flunked out, but somehow I felt that bridge had been burned. Spent a solitary year of misery at Boston University, relieved only by reading about the Bloomsbury Circle and seeing young Rudolf Nureyev fly through the air for three nights running at the ballet in Boston. Developed bronchial pneumonia and nearly died. My father finally decided to visit me from Manhattan, where he was now living, a visit that coincided with the arrival of my worried mother, who had come to take care of me. She ended up downstairs at a bar consoling Daddy, who was threatening suicide again. My junior year was drawing to a close, senior year for most of my friends. BU had been a mistake. I was twenty-one years old. What did a young woman do who didn't get married? Hmmmmm . . . a tough question in 1965. This one went to California. It was supposed to be for just the summer. I stayed for twenty years.

I'd been accepted as a transfer student in art history at NYU, but first, one last visit to California. I landed in Palo Alto, Stanford Summer School, June of 1965, smack dab in the middle of the '60s. David Harris, president of the student body, had just had his head shaved by more conservative students for being a peace activist. Norman Mailer had just delivered his famous flag-upside-down speech on a visit to Stanford. Ken Kesey, Hells Angels, et al., were in high gear in back of the campus. The Gandhian pacifist philosophy of nonviolence in the growing Vietnam War protests had an immediate appeal to me. Down south in the Salinas Valley, Hutch and his friends at the Salud Clinic were deeply involved in the farmworkers' movement led by Cesar Chavez. When I went to Berkeley on a visit to Hutch's friend, Butch Leslie, I was introduced to its utopian community in this pre-hippie era. No paisley, rock and roll, drug culture yet. These were the political activists and idealists who wanted to change

American society, not drop out of it. The bus rolled past windows hung with Leftist slogans, great open cafés up and down Telegraph, students in Levis and blue work shirts, all engaged in dialogue. Here the Seven Corporal Works of Mercy meant something. This was the living community that the calcified Catholic Church had failed to create. One of my first visits to San Francisco, with a Chinese guy I'd met at Stanford (in his escape from China he'd survived by eating frogs), was to North Beach. Topless clubs. The Actors' Workshop. The Jazz Workshop, Finnochio's, Vesuvio's, Spec's, and the cornerstone of it all, poet Lawrence Ferlinghetti's bookstore, City Lights.

Wow.

Let them get married there in Pittsburgh.

"Our summer made her light escape / Into the beautiful" (Emily Dickinson).

Up to her death, my mother would repeat, "You kicked it all in the teeth, you kicked it all in the teeth," as if I'd done some incomprehensible thing staying in California. That fall, living platonically with Butch and another guy in San Francisco on Noe and 18th, a working-class neighborhood, I spent three months at Brandon's Secretarial School. This provided me with a livelihood for life, first as a secretary, later as a typesetter. Fred, a composer I'd met at Stanford, and I met every day over drinks at the Sea Witch or Buena Vista. Fred's roommate, Leon Katz, director, playwright, and teacher at Carnegie Tech and Vassar, had known Alice B. Toklas while he was working on his thesis and had sampled her brownies. In exchange for typing up such scripts as Gorky's "The Lower Depths," he would take Fred and me out for dinner and conversation.

I arrived at Berkeley, where I'd finally been admitted, early in 1966 and quickly ended up at the farmworkers' table, where I began meeting all sorts of "outside agitators," aka "nonstudents," some from the PLP (Progressive Labor Party) table. One of them, Jerry Rubin, looked like Hutch, with his big mustache and dark swept-back hair. "I'm reading books like this," he said, indicating *The Mandarins* by Simone de Beauvoir. Aux Deux Magots and the Flore sprang to mind. The day he and other activists were subpoenaed to appear before HUAC, he dressed in a Revolutionary War uniform. Usually more of an observer than a doer, I had my *Lad: A Dog* moment when, as the only student available that day, I signed for the campus anti-HUAC rally. The oratory at Berkeley was an education in itself: Bettina Aptheker, daughter of the Leftist professor, even the legendary Mario Savio occasionally spoke. Ronald Reagan was governor and Ed Meese, Reagan's future attorney general, was in charge of the tactical squad which he sent to demonstrations on campus. I recall my first sight of the squad with their helmets, crossed nightsticks, legs spread apart in a solid line so close to where we were sitting in at Sproul Hall we could almost touch them. Did they have guns? So many marches, demonstrations, speeches, sit-ins. Tear gas. Sometimes panic. These went on and on for years. Your standard '60s fare. I lived on Dwight Way near Telegraph Avenue, so I always had a lot of people staying with me, sleeping bags all over the living room, big spaghetti dinners. My neighbor Gary, a self-described White Magician (thank God, think about self-styled Black Magicians such as Charles Manson), talked to the parking meters in front of our house on acid. The casualties of the '60s were starting to roll in. I took a number of friends to psychiatric emergency at Alta Bates and Highland Hospitals.

At a party down the street I met Frank Sears. Tall, twenty-seven years old, yet another with a mustache, the first person I'd ever met to call himself a poet. We stayed up talking all night, on into the following day and the next and the next. Raised in an army family, he had left home in seventh grade. He had worked in the tobacco fields in Canada, lived by his wits, and was self-educated. My self-made man, just like my great-grandfather . . . well, not exactly. Frank had just escaped from a mental institution in Mobile, Alabama, where his wife had committed him. I thought she didn't understand his poet nature. Leaving his wife and newborn son, he returned to Berkeley, where he had first met her at a poetry reading. With his photographic memory, Frank could recite Yeats and Dylan Thomas by heart and would sit up all night with a fellow poet gauging the validity of poem after poem, weighing every word in every line, discussing how a poet ought to live. Frank took me to Oakland to all-black bars to hear blues. I'd listen to him talk to "the wise, old heads" at the pool tables all night long.

"Can You Pass the Acid Test?" I flunked. Later on in Marin, my daily mescaline trips concluded badly as well. Casteneda I am not.

I never did like drugs very much, pot included. Preferred my familiar alcohol. I knew Frank was experimenting with LSD, then legal. I didn't know that he was involved with speed—methedrine, amphetamine, whatever. I'd never heard of any of it, didn't know what it was. With my high energy, everyone assumed I was on speed as well. The only time I ever tried it, I felt no effect. But I fit right in. I liked their mental showdowns, with the emphasis on honesty. (Not total honesty. My art and poetry books were disappearing at an alarming rate. Moe's on Telegraph is the bookstore built by junkies.) I was having problems again. Type in my textbooks liquefied and ran in streams off the page. I couldn't read my assignments. My depressions and excitability seemed worse, with paranoia added. Sitting on too much anger as well, I thought of drinking as my only safety valve.

Amid all the psychedelic posters for every conceivable event, political and musical, was something unusual. Billed as a Gathering of the Tribes, predating Woodstock, it was the single greatest "happening" from that period. Every person who had the least counterculture spirit attended the Human Be-In in Golden Gate Park. I am still meeting people who were there on that day. Frank and I went with poet Jonathan Durfee and his sister, who brought a big basket of tangerines to hand out. Presided over by Allen Ginsberg, Gary Snyder, Suzuki-roshi, Ferlinghetti, Lenore Kandel, and I don't know who all, it was a magical day of music, poetry, and brotherhood unmatched for me since, the pinnacle of the '60s. The downhill trajectory that followed began that evening when police bashed heads on Haight Street.

Frank took me to readings at the Steppenwolf, Blind Lemon, the Albatross in Berkeley, to the Committee, North Beach, and the Haight. Through him I met a group of poets that included Don Hutton, Jack Thibeau (member of the Mabou Mines and actor in the early Sam Shepard plays), Gene Ruggles, and a "patron of the arts," as Frank called her, Alix Geluardi. The daughter of a Canadian wildcat oilman and a beautiful invalid mother, she had gone to Marymount, followed by a brief marriage that produced her wonderful son, John. Her father had taken her on his forays to Las Vegas, where she developed a taste for risk. She once saw him bet a million dollars on a roll of the dice. She loved artists and poets and ended up giving away a fortune.

When I asked my mother if I could bring Frank home to "meet the family," she cut me off without a cent, as they say. "Your great-grandfather would turn over in his grave. He wouldn't want one penny to go to you for what you are doing." I had made the mistake of telling her Frank and I were living together: a mortal sin, the least of my worries at that time. "Never darken this door again." She actually said that. I surprised her, and maybe myself, by getting a job. Frank and I moved to the city as I finished my incompletes and graduated while working. Earning a living for both Frank and me gave me a sense of independence I'd never had, even if I didn't make a lot of money. (Luckily, Frank, being a speed freak, didn't eat much.) In a show of thriftiness, I took to carrying a little thirty-five cent bottle of port in my pocketbook that quickly took me where I wanted to go. Your typical '60s Dream Couple. Within my family was another: back East, my father had re-married. At his wedding, which I attended, his old friend, a handsome advertising executive, passed right out, face down on the floor. Daddy and his bride (addicted to barbiturates) left by helicopter. Soon she was calling from behind the barricaded door of her bedroom, nailed shut to protect herself from him. Why hadn't I told her? she demanded to know. Within three months, the marriage was over. Daddy called me wanting to visit. I told him no.

Drugs were not understood at that time, at least not by me, and were thought of in terms of religious/mystical experience rather than chemical dependency. I had no idea of what to do to help Frank. We moved to an apartment on California Street in San Francisco with a poet friend of his, "Paul X," next to a complex of apartments in a rambling condemned building, each unit holding people in their twenties in every conceivable grouping. Ingrid, the Raffel sisters, Desmond, Dennis, Jilly and Rick, John . . . a cast of thousands. Everyone had doors open and circulated freely, frequently gathering in the backyard. Butch was living with a group of people on the second floor. When Paul X painted our windows one day while I was at work, we were instantly evicted, our belongings set on the sidewalk in the rain. We moved to Pearl Street, where the freeway crosses Market. My jewelry showed up at Abe Cohn's pawnshop. Frank's eyes turned yellow. He had developed serum hepatitis, another ailment I'd never heard of. I came home from work one day to find my mother seated on our "couch" (a board supported by two concrete blocks) listening to Frank talk about Yeats. "The look in his eyes scares me," she confided. She had a point. Her verdict: "You must be out of your mind." She had come all the way from Pittsburgh to put Frank away and take me to a clinic in Boston. Now we had war. I was twenty-three and no longer a minor. Most importantly, I was financially independent. She went home with her mission a failure. Frank and I had wanted to marry but our friends were telling me that while I was asleep, he was breaking into apartments. We put off the ceremony. Who knows, maybe he wasn't divorced. There he'd be in the morning, rocking away in the ten-dollar chair we'd bought at a thrift shop. (I still have it. It's all refinished and fixed up now, just like me.) When he broke into his friends' apartment in the Fillmore, ruining some paintings, I moved out. We could reunite and marry when he got himself together. I went to live with Desmond and the Raffel sisters on California Street, he moved in with Butch upstairs. When this arrangement began to sour, Frank decided to go to Mendocino to clean up and to write. I always saw Frank as a poet, not as an addict.

I got home from work one day to see a note from the police department tacked to my door. What now? A robbery? An accident. What happened? The driver of the van Frank was in had gone off the road and run into a tree somewhere on the road to Ukiah. Frank's friend had died on impact. Frank was thrown from the vehicle. He had survived for a week in a coma, then died without regaining consciousness. Frank was dead? Because he carried no identification, no one but his wife had been notified. Somehow they'd gotten hold of her in Mobile. She had asked that I not attend the funeral. The Roving Rat Fink's column in the *Berkeley Barb* ran a tribute to Frank. By coincidence, it appeared in the issue that featured a "Funeral for Hip" held on Haight Street. Now my mother was happy and reinstated me on her payroll. Her words of wisdom? "It's all for the best." She even bought me a new car. And that was supposed to be the end of that. Things were never the same between my Mother and me after Frank's death. I've never been to Frank's grave (nor my father's, come to think

*"Folsom Street, San Francisco—*Lovelights *and* Micheline *drawing on the wall," about 1972*

of it). "Wear me from in, / so you may keep me longer" (Frank Sears). He is me now.

I went to work at San Francisco State for a well-meaning professor of international relations whose office was, unfortunately, in the Administration Building. This was the period of escalating demonstrations, including bomb threats. We would frequently have to draw our blinds and sit under our office desks. Just like Saint Bede's. I wasn't worried, but the professor was terrified, I think. In the meantime, the ghettoes had blown up. Since our first-floor apartment was right on the border of San Francisco's black neighborhood, the Fillmore, we watched army tanks literally roll by our window. The extent of the show of force was awesome for '50s folk like me who had been raised waving the flag at Memorial Day parades. This was frightening. The double assassinations of Robert Kennedy and Martin Luther King occurred one after the other. I'd go out to the car in the mornings to find its windows smashed.

I moved back to Berkeley. The lid was being closed on the '60s.

Butch had been working for an Upward Bound program at SF State. He was also in an army reserve unit stationed in Berkeley and didn't want to be called to police student demonstrations as some units were. He went to Canada. Another major loss for me. My Berkeley neighbors and I watched the Chicago riots on TV together. Our initial exhilaration at seeing the massive demonstration quickly turned to horror as the police went wild. When Butch snuck down over the border to visit, Berkeley was an armed camp. You couldn't come or go off the freeway without presenting identification. Dancing to the Doors at parties was all well and good, but Butch returned to Canada saying that America had become a police state.

A radical professor came through the window of the SF State president's office, up the hall from where I worked, followed by a group of students who staged days of sit-ins. Some of them I knew from Berkeley. The police became a permanent fixture guarding the doors of the Administration Building. Some doors were chained shut. The mood was dark and oppressive. Continuing to work there seemed totally wrong. I quit and went on a camping trip up the coast to Vancouver, where Butch was living in a Canadian park in a tent. I joined him for a few days and will never forget all the deserters we talked to who were living there as well, among them guys who had watched their army buddies push Vietnamese out of helicopters to their deaths. One horror after another from the disastrous war in Vietnam. It poured rain.

One ray of light: Hudgins had come to visit me in Berkeley and liked it so well she returned with her boyfriend, her childhood friend, Anne, and Anne's brother, Chris. I showed them Mill Valley, which was then a reasonably priced place to live. They liked it and moved there. My old friend Connie soon followed. She and Anne bought a house that was a second home to me for many years. I got a small apartment in nearby Tam Valley, and Anne and I went to work for one of Hutch's friends who was starting a small migrant health consulting firm and educational products office down by the Gates, where the houseboats were moored in Sausalito. On my lunch hour, I'd roll posters at East Totem West. When hard drugs had come into the San Francisco scene, many people evacuated to communes, the "country," "back to nature." Mill Valley attracted artists and musicians. Gates Five and Six had an anarchic, artist/hippie communal spirit at that time. Rock and roll blasted from the heliport. Janis Joplin would show up at the No Name Bar or the Trident in Sausalito. If anyone would stare, she'd say, "Hey, man, this is San Francisco. I thought everyone was supposed to be cool." The painter Jean Varda with retinue had a houseboat at Gate Six where he and everyone else would throw parties.

Do you really need to hear about my problems at this time? Marin General Hospital, Gestalt therapy, my mystery "rash." Let's just say that I laid the cards on the table with my family, signing back stocks and the like. The sky did not cave in. Mother and Aunt Lihi did, however, cut me out of their wills. (Aunt Lihi thought I was a Communist.) Frank was dead. I couldn't fix it. I didn't go back to Pittsburgh for five years. Ripped up my mother's checks and mailed them back.

Glide Memorial Church in the city held wildly joyous services that I sometimes attended. Gene Ruggles made sure I went there to his benefit for the Alcatraz Indians: young Michael McClure in black motorcycle duds, as handsome as Brando in *The Wild Ones,* Joanne Kyger pacing in a raincoat delivering quirky poems, the memorable moment of Robert Duncan's entrance in his long black cape and wayward, visionary eye. The San Francisco poetry scene in all its glory, theatrical, anarchist, with its heart in the right place. On the ferry to Marin, string quartet playing, the commuters, of whom I was one (working in the city at Youth For Service, an agency that offered job training to delinquent kids), passed Alcatraz on the way. We'd wave to the Indians who were occupying it and flip them the V sign.

The first real poem I wrote followed Frank's death. Alix offered to publish it as the cornerstone of a memorial to Frank in her anthology of '60s poetry and artwork, *185.* Through Alix I got to know the poet Bob Kaufman and his wife, Eileen, who were reconciling at that time. They even had a wedding on Mount Tam. I was about twenty-six. Spent lots of time with Gene Ruggles, who had known Frank. Gene introduced me to the poetry of James Wright, Robert Bly, Vallejo, Neruda. Got to know the photographer Mark Green, the poet Jack Wilkins aka John Breen, novelist Jerry Kamstra, poet and publisher Al Winans, and many other remarkable and colorful people.

Alix encouraged me to show some of my poems. She sent me to an open reading at Minnie's Can Do in the Fillmore run by her friend, poet and filmmaker Ruth Weiss. Ruthie welcomed me the way she did everyone else, with total acceptance. The East Coast may turn up its nose at West Coast poetry, but the poetry scene, like San Francisco itself, is international, inclusive, and supremely tolerant. I read at least twice a week for the next year at Minnie's and the Coffee Gallery Open readings run by Tom Cuson with this nucleus of poets: Marty Matz, Danny Propper, David Plumb, George Tsongas, Janice Blue, and Wayne Miller. David Plumb, originally from the East, was reassuringly familiar. Because Wayne had known Frank, I felt connected to him and fell in love. Blue? Won't go into that. David Moe had *Lovelights,* a poetry newspaper that looked like a pornie rag he sold in newsstands all over the city. My favorite person to read with was Jack Micheline.

He gave Lawrence Ferlinghetti a poem I'd written about Bob Kaufman which was my first published by City Lights. Jack's been a great friend to me over the years.

Went to visit my father just before I turned thirty. He woke up one morning in the late '60s to find himself in a hotel in Nassau in the Bahamas, with no idea of how he got there. He had apparently been there for days. This prolonged alcoholic blackout, not his first, finally scared him. He dried out for nearly a year. A friend got him to AA, where he centered the rest of his life, visiting hospitals in Harlem, running meetings in the Bowery area, attending his homebase meetings in the Murray Hill area of the Upper East Side, where he felt most comfortable. On my last visit to Butch in Vancouver, following that summer at my father's in New York, I had my last drink just after my thirtieth birthday. I feel lucky to have bottomed out early. I was already having blackouts at age twenty-one and was throwing up blood the last year I drank. The depressions gradually lessened, I got trained as a typesetter, a trade I enjoyed, one that was related to my writing and afforded me a comfortable enough living. Worked as a typesetter with poet-publisher George Mattingly and others at the West Coast Print Center run by Jack Shoemaker, founder of North Point Press, later with friends Kim Dunster and Kina Sullivan. Somewhere in here, went on a Pushkin, Tolstoy, Lermentov, Conrad kick.

The first few years I could barely speak, I was so used to relying on alcohol; my sex life was certainly affected, but overall I was in much better condition. Thibeau helped me out at this time, and the poet Tony Dingman. Began writing what I thought of as a long poem in speaking parts called *The Reminiscences of Zelda Sayre Fitzgerald* in an effort to figure out the continuing sadness and outrage I felt about Zelda Fitzgerald's life, as well as to create a contemporary mythology, one of my driving forces as a writer. Far from being unable to write sober, as I'd feared, I kept on going, full hog into 250–300 or so notebooks I've kept over the years, a practice that has kept me sane. Doing a reading was another story. It was Jack Micheline who came to get me to read with him in Berkeley at a benefit run by Andy Clausen and Michael Wozcjuk for the Rainbow House. With Jack, I was able to read without getting a buzz

"Old friends Alix Geluardi and poet Gene Ruggles," Marin County, California, early 1970s

on. He helped me carry my press to the car when I bought it in Palo Alto and gave me the first story I printed on it: *Purple Submarine,* reviewed by Charlie Plymell as an "instant classic." He did a recording of some of his poems that we inserted in the letterpress book, an idea we'd gotten from a magazine of poet Kell Robertson's. Under the imprint of Greenlight Press, I did letterpress and offset editions of poetry by a mixed bag of North Beach poets and artists, Moe, Patricia Ross, Jackie Baks, Judith Faust, Blue, Neeli Cherkovski, Jack Mueller, and Kirby Doyle. Some books I never got to: poet Ken Wainio's, woodcuts by Kristen Wetterhahn, a translation of the Radiguet book, *Le Bal du Comte d'Orgel,* by poet-novelist Rod Iverson, and *The Frog Symphony* of old friend Jim Nisbet, poet and novelist.

In the mid-'70s, a new crowd had come into North Beach, among them poets Jack Hirschman and Neeli Cherkovski from Los Angeles. With a teacherly empathy for any sort of artist, Jack brought a warm and open spirit of internationalism and community to North Beach and an anti-drug message. The new scene attracted bibliophiles and poets with a more aesthetic, intellectual approach than the macho, two-fisted-drinking, pot-smoking ethic of the previous bohemians. Though San Francisco had Allen Ginsberg and its Polk Street, the gay movement (pre-AIDS) was now felt all over the city. Giant poetry festivals, readings, readings, readings everywhere dwarfed the former scene. I loved all of it. My dear friend, former rabbinical student Neeli Cherkovski, with whom I've taken many a turn on many a San Francisco street, was from a family of bohemians, his uncle, Herman Cherry, an expressionist painter of some repute. Neeli, like Ginsberg, was openly gay. I liked it that he didn't drink much and that he had a wonderful sense of humor. I always think of the "poet's menus" he liked to invent featuring Twice-Tortured Breast of Chicken and Potatoes Browning. He did funny imitations of Ferlinghetti, Gregory Corso. Neeli's been "a mover and a shaker" (as Peg Biderman would say) since his first arrival in North Beach. The reaction of some of the more entrenched bohemian types was to punch him in the nose. He survived the whole thing, writing biographies, essays, and poetry. Gerry Nicosia, poet and author of *Memory Babe,* with his familiar midwestern ethic and sensibility, became a lifelong friend. Through Neeli, I got to know Bobby Sharrard, who went to work at City Lights. Bobby and I met Allen Ginsberg and Peter Orlovsky together at the end of a magical day in 1976 spent in Berkeley at a KPFA benefit reading, a meeting that led to friendships for us both. Poet and scribe George Scrivani, maker of mythic environments and intricate, colorful notebooks from his stays in India, had lived in monasteries in Europe, studying Gregorian chant. He, too, had been to the Cumean Sibyl, loved the classics, music. A Renaissance man and fellow traveler, George now does his "service" by helping AIDS victims. East Coast poet fresh from Naropa, John Landry, was writing an epic poem on the early New England Indians, an unusual subject at that time. The Winged Wondrous Wainio. Raymond Foye, precocious whiz kid, quickly made tracks for New York. Philip and Susan Suntree, Tom Dawson. Poet Stewart Lindh traveled between North Beach and Paris. Lisa Brinker, later Gregory Corso's wife, bravely entered the scene when she was just eighteen. Poet Tisa Walden (Deep Forest Press) published and cared for many local poets. Kristen. Blue. Poet Jack Mueller (Peace Corps vet [India], playful, erudite like his theologian father) and his wife, Judith Faust, a photographer, got me an apartment across the hall from theirs. I used to pass Jim Hartz's apartment on the way up Green Street, the apartment that looked so safe and secure with its grandfather clock and books. (Who knew?) He had once lived at the monastery of Gethsemani, helping Thomas Merton organize his library as well as living and working at several Buddhist monasteries. Underground poet heroes Kirby Doyle and Howard Hart resurfaced in North Beach; Harold Norse, Beat poet with European literary roots. An occasional Andrei Codrescu. The Mission poets, like Alejandro Murgia and Roberto Vargas. The prison poets. The surrealist contingent headed by Philip Lamantia. Philip's wife, Nancy Peters, poet and editor at City Lights. And please, don't forget Shigeyoshi Murao, Ferlinghetti's former partner at City Lights. What a great scene. Too many stories to begin to tell. I can't manage to cram in even the highlights. Too many people. All the artists and poets and friends.

Somewhere in the early part of this, Naropa, the Jack Kerouac School of Disembodied Poetics, founded by Allen Ginsberg with Anne Waldman, opened in Boulder, Colorado, opening a flow of poets from both the East and West Coasts. It was through this Naropa connection that Gregory Corso, with his year-and-a-half-old son Max, came to San Francisco in the fall of 1977 to stay with Andy Clausen, then something of a protégé of Allen's, and his family in Oakland. Neeli and I were standing in front of City Lights when I met him. You can't imagine Gregory's force in real life, his intensity, his wild appearance. He honed in on you like Saint John the Baptist coming out of the wilderness, his eyes laserbeaming straight through the window of your soul. "Shove a rose up your hah-ah-t (heart)" were his first words to me that I took to have deep personal, symbolic, sexual significance. (He was trying this line on everyone at the time.) Where Allen and Peter had glowed like angels on the midnight streetcorner of Columbus and Broadway, listening to Bobby Seider's horn blow out the long notes, Gregory was something else again. Lautreamont? Villon? A big pussycat? Who in the heck was this guy? When Gregory first met my friend Alix walking down Grant, he slapped her face just like a Zen master. "Wake up!" Apparently at Naropa, he'd thrown firecrackers into Rinpoche Trungpa's meditation room. Gregory's humor went through the spiritual roof: The Master comes in disguised as a beggar to test you.

When Lawrence asked me for "any hot new poems?" for a new City Lights journal, I told him all I had was the Zelda stuff I'd been working on, which I didn't think would be his cup of tea. The Fitzgeralds, Virginia Woolf, were far from being central figures for the Beats. Though the material was definitely true to who I am, it had very little to do, I thought, with the kind of populist, political, and social-change message that Lawrence has always championed. (I had first heard him read in Berkeley with Adrienne Rich at a benefit for the farmworkers in the '60s, as I remember.) Surprisingly, he was amused by the prologue and published it, but felt I would get no publisher until the play was produced. To me it wasn't a play but rather a long poem in speaking parts. (An obvious influence: Michael McClure's "Jean Harlowe and Billy the Kid." A remote influence: Ed Dorn's "Gunslinger.") My friend Kaye Cofini brought Elizabeth Warner, an editor at Frontier Press, to hear a reading of mine. Elizabeth told me they had been looking for an interesting manuscript by a woman for a long time, and she liked my Zelda business. Frontier Press applied for a grant to do a Hunke Manuscript and my "Zelda," to be printed by Alaister Johnston, illustrated by Frances Butler, a publication beyond my wildest dreams. When they failed to get their funding, I remembered what Lawrence had told me and mailed out what was now my "play," the genesis of years of legal difficulties with the Fitzgerald estate. Saint Clement's Theater in New York, which had done a Kenneth Koch play and other poets' theater, accepted "Zelda." In the course of several readings given it there, Nancy persuaded Lawrence to publish it. My friends were stunned. I was stunned. Lawrence insisted on the title *Zelda*, one already used by Nancy Milford in her biography. I was so happy to be published by City Lights, I was ready to go along with anything he wanted, but I'm glad I insisted on a subtitle or I would have had even worse legal problems. *Zelda: Frontier Life in America*, an edition of three thousand copies, came out toward the end of 1978. City Lights had a Books in Print list of sixty-eight authors. Of these, seven were women, only four not co-written with men: myself, Anne Waldman, Diane diPrima and Isabelle Eberhardt. Pretty good company.

On a cross-country bus trip in the early '70s (I used to like to take the bus back and forth across the country talking to people), I had visited Santa Fe, which was then a homey, funky place. In 1978, on the way to New York to work on *Zelda* with a group of actors at Saint Clement's, I decided to stop there again. Stayed at a slightly seedy hotel where you could pay by the week, full of singers and musicians who had come to work at the Santa Fe Opera. Spent day after day in the Santa Fe book and photo libraries studying the Pueblo Indians, in particular the Hopi. Nancy Peters had described visits she and Philip took to the Bean Ceremony, as well as some of their other Southwest adventures, no doubt following the lead of their surrealist predecessors Max Ernst and Dorothea Tanning. I had no car (had sold it to finance my upcoming trip to Europe), so took a bus up to Taos and walked several miles out to the Taos Pueblo to attend a Corn Dance. There I had the good fortune to meet Leo Garen. He knew many San Francisco poets who had lived in Los Angeles, where he worked part of the year as a screenwriter. His mother had died when he was young, so he was on his own at an early age. I do like these self-made guys, I must say. Leo had worked in Provincetown, directed the first Genêt plays in America, the early Le Roi Jones (Amiri Baraka) plays, and he'd directed a feature-length film released in Europe. He took me out to his little rented adobe a few miles from town, horses, sheep on the road, a Spanish family and old-style potter hippies next door, the Sangre de Cristos Mountains blood-red against an India-inkblot sky. He encouraged me to move to Taos, which he was certain I'd prefer to Santa Fe. I could live with him. Who ever wanted to go anywhere else?

I moved up to Taos to Leo's a few days later for what was supposed to have been a few weeks. The reading at Saint Clement's was postponed till later in the year, so I stayed, the first of two six-month attempts to make a go of it there (1978 and 1979–80). It turned out that Leo had interesting friends and took me along on his visits to the novelist John Nichols, to Stephanie, a principal in John's *The Magic Journey* and co-owner, with Maggie Kress, of one of the many galleries there, to Noel Ferrand, who ran the Music Festival, to the painters Louis Ribak and Bea Mandelbaum. Many artists and writers I never met, but it was fun to see them come and go. For instance, when Seymour Krim visited Tally Richards at her gallery, he could be seen in afternoon-long conversations with John at Dori's Café. The painter Andrew Dasburg was still alive and occasionally attended art openings. The actor Dean Stockwell appeared one day at the Kachina Lodge making a film. Crazy man Dennis Hopper, a friend of Leo's, blew through; his brother had a wild jewelry store there. Leo knew the Southwest well. He took me to a Buffalo Dance at San Juan Pueblo, to San Geronimo Day at Taos Pueblo, to the D. H. Lawrence Ranch, all sorts of places. Pueblo Indians swathed in blankets sat next to you at Michael's Kitchen, appeared all over town, right out of the otherworldly, mystical literature of local legends Mabel Dodge Luhan, D. H. Lawrence, Frank Waters. Poets Andy and Linda Clausen, and Michael and Niko Wojczuk had rented the Dorothy Brett House. A poet friend of theirs, Janet Cannon, who ran a local radio poetry program, clued me in on the job market. The art openings, the painters and writers, the film people, the Pueblo, the Spanish culture (New Mexico was Tijerina coun-

try—remember the documents laid on the courthouse steps in the '60s?) made Taos unique. I spent nearly every day in the old Harwood Library, where I got to know the librarians, Tracey McCallum, a poet (now director of the Harwood), and John Flexner. I recently learned that John and his wife Carolyn, a Peace Corps veteran and one of my closest friends, spent several years in South America on the trail of the Yage Letters before the birth of their children. Taos was full of wonderful people like them.

By 1978 I had made it my mission to travel to every Indian ruin or pueblo I had read about, and nearly succeeded. I drove a rental car out the half-ruined road leading to Chaco Canyon, gunned it over a collapsed bridge, Navajo horses running across the road, the Red Rock at sunset, and camped there, before the "improvements" of asphalt and numbered parking spaces. Huddled in my rental car with two Navajo girls selling jewelry while a sudden thunderstorm pelted us at Canyon de Chelly. Camped at Betatakin, ancient site sacred to the Hopis. Visited

At the Caffe Trieste, San Francisco, 1985: the author is holding son Nile, with (from left) poets Neeli Cherkovski, Gregory Corso, George Tsongas, and Jack Micheline

With Gregory Corso at the Cathedral of Notre Dame, Paris, 1983

the Hopi Reservation during the Jemis Kachina ceremonies, young eagles tied to rooftops at Shungopovi. I'd found the Living Sacred.

Leo and I felt sad parting when I left for Europe, even though we were not "in love" with each other. I liked Leo a lot. Spent seven months in Europe (London, Paris, Italy). Read at a Jean Jacques Lebel Poetry Festival there, Shakespeare and Company, La Pensée sauvage, met all sorts of interesting people. I just can't go into everything here—plays in London, travel in the south of Spain, the Italian fresco towns of Arezzo, Perugia, Padova, Mantova, San Gimignano, the crazy Italian Poetry Festival at Ostia, poet Ted Joans, who was kind to me, English surrealist poet David Gascoyne and his wife Judy, French poet Jean Pierre Faye, who took me to meet the novelist Alberto Moravia, my friends Idi, Reiner and Jeff Gould, Wainio in Paris, and on and on.

In the course of this period in Taos and Europe, Saint Clement's did my play two times as a reading with two different casts and then as part of a poetry festival in what is called a

"preview" for parties who might be interested in mounting a New York production. When City Lights published my book, they, of course, displayed it in their window. Tennessee Williams, my hero, who happened to be in San Francisco at that time, had purchased a copy—City Lights book clerks can attest to this—saying: "What a great idea for a play!" and proceeded to write his play *Clothes for a Summer Hotel* using the Fitzgeralds as "ghosts," much as I had done. I have never seen or read it, but I am assuming that with his genius, Williams surpassed anything I could ever think about doing in the theater. I don't want to know. His play, directed by José Quintero, starring Jason Robards, another hero, opened several months after the Saint Clement's *Zelda* preview was shut down. Lawyers from two top gun New York literary law firms, one representing Scottie Fitzgerald and her parents' estate, the other from an agency representing a Lane York, supposedly possessing the sole authority from the Fitzgerald estate to write a play on Zelda, threatened an injunction. The latter work has never appeared, leading me to conclude Lane York was a red herring. The grounds were alleged "copyright infringement." None existed, but the threat alone was enough to clobber any hope of a New York production. I went to Lawrence for legal help. He wished me luck. I didn't know who to phone. My mother wondered how I ever "got away with writing about those people in the first place," and I began to worry that the Fitzgerald estate might be capable of wiping out every nickel she had, making me reluctant to pursue litigation too actively. Because the Saint Clement's pro bono law firm was also the Lane York law firm—a conflict of interest—the theater was left without legal representation. I went to BALA (Bay Area Legal Aid for the Arts). By the time the paperwork cleared and a young, inexperienced lawyer was retained months later, all the damage had been done. My play was marginal to begin with, the Williams play had opened with full-page interviews and articles in the *New York Times*. To all appearances, I had plagiarized his idea. I decided to forget the whole thing and return to Taos.

Out of nowhere, while I was in Taos, came a standing-room-only production of *Zelda* in Salt Lake City, where no one had heard of my legal problems. A young African American woman, a professor of drama at the university there, named Charlene Bletson, originally from Watts, had come across the script while she was teaching at Smith one summer. A lesbian group in New Haven, the Theater of Light and Sound, wanted to do a black *Zelda* with all the characters in drag wearing stacked shoes. That never happened. A half-completed documentary based on the play never came off. *Zelda* was produced at the University of Cambridge in, of all places, New Zealand. I can't complain—that's Katherine Mansfield country. *Zelda* made the semi-finals of the Eugene O'Neill Theatre Awards, under Artistic Director Lloyd Richards. No production in New York ever came through, though I was told several women's groups were interested. I was lucky to have gotten City Lights. Thank you, Lawrence. What do you want, egg in your beer? The book has gone out of print but City Lights has published my poems over the years in addition to my book, so I have no complaints in their regard.

Discouraged by my inability to earn a living in Taos, I returned to San Francisco. I soon got involved with Gregory, whose marriage to Lisa Brinker had run into difficulty. I had always liked Gregory, my lover and friend with whom I had my only child, Nile. He moved in with me in 1981. That's been it for me. I have felt married to him in a funny way ever since, though we haven't lived together since 1985 when Nile was eight months old. Loyalty? Catholic guilt? Nile? For whatever reason, Gregory's been as close to a husband as I've ever gotten. How he has felt about the whole thing remains his business. He's had five children in all (Max, twenty-one, and Nile, thirteen, played computer games and hung out together in San Francisco this past summer), relationships beyond number, and has lived at least twenty lives to my one. It would be my guess that he has been a much more important figure in my life than I have been in his. Gregory was my chance to right all the wrongs that had happened with Frank.

I had my poet again. "I am your Humphrey Bogart," he used to say to me, "I am your Keats," but he didn't have to. I knew he was. Was I his Emily Dickinson, his Lauren Bacall? No, that was Hope Savage. He painted "Rarely, rarely comest thou Spirit of Delight," a portrait of Keats and "Percy Bysshe" (as Gregory likes to refer to Shelley), when we were together, so I like to think he was often happy, at any rate. In poetry, as in our backgrounds, we came from different ends of the spectrum, but I think we were trying to accomplish a similar thing (or am I dreaming here?): classicism, mytholgy and the Romantic vision stood on their heads, with a streetwise, political edge. My slant is feminist independence, his the poet as unacknowledged legislator. He's just better at it than I am. A lot better. I like it that he is better. As a joke, the poet Jack Mueller once said we were like the Good Girl/Bad Boy Catholics, but I know Gregory is the true one, the real human being, from seeing him respond time after time to people, news, situations of all types. He laughs about going to the "Bad Boys' Home" run by Catholic priests when he was young, attending the "School of Hard Knocks." For me, he is a bellwether of morality. Some people don't understand what we were ever doing together. (We both liked Piero della Francesca and the Met's *Sarpedon*? He smelled good?) I don't know what his reasons were (he is funny—he once said, "You had food—it was known," making me laugh). He will find the self-deception or pretense and annihilate it with his "Divine Butcher" humor. For me he is the genuine article, the real thing. I have been very much in love with Mr. Corso. My "Crazy Jane and Jack the Journeyman." My wayward priest.

Recently he said, "I didn't know it was faith all the time." Aunt Lihi would have liked this. Pretty game at ninety-two, she found out Gregory was a poet and wanted to read something of his. What I had on hand was *Herald of the Autochthonic Spirit* with its drug dilemma poem. Aunt Lihi, obsessed with God and the Spirit much the same as Gregory, said she liked and understood his book, even though she felt he was "on the wrong track." Here my two worlds meet.

Gregory and I had our son, Nile Joseph Corso, August 11, 1984. Gregory was fifty-four, I had just turned forty-one. My father died unexpectedly on New Year's Eve that same year, eerily fitting, I thought. Gregory and I split up the following April after a four-year effort. With a possible view to relocating on the East Coast in Lenox or Amherst, I visited my mother in Pittsburgh. While Nile and I were there, she was diagnosed with terminal lung and bone cancer and given one year to live. We stayed in Pittsburgh with her. Just before my mother died, Aunt Lihi asked, "You aren't going to leave me, are you, Kathy?" We stayed. Aunt Lihi had a stroke and died two years later at the age of ninety-five, same as my grandmother. I said good-bye. Too many memories, too many deaths—the '80s and '90s full of them. Right here, right now, Gregory is close by in Greenwich Village, where Nile and I sometimes visit him at Roger and Irvyne's. In true spontaneous Gregory fashion, he had Nile read with him at the Smithsonian Portrait Gallery in Washington, D.C., two Aprils ago while Allen was still alive, initiating his son into the world of poetry. For me, there's not all that much time left. At fifty-four, I've got 250-plus notebooks to make something of, a bunch of poems that I suppose I should put together in a book or two. But right now I have Nile to raise. He's just thirteen.

Last year I worked at Manuscripts and Archives, Sterling Library at Yale, in a queer kind of attempt to reconfigure pieces of my life. At the moment, I'm in Tom Lux's poetry seminar at Sarah Lawrence College, where Grace Paley and Joseph Campbell once roamed, trying to get on get an M.F.A. so that I can teach and be home with Nile for his summers and vaca-

Nile Corso just before his thirteenth birthday, Andover Street, San Francisco, 1997

tions while he still lives at home. I don't want to hire someone else to be there the way my mother had to. On a recent trip to Paris, I showed Nile the Latin Quarter hotel where Gregory and I stayed when I got pregnant. It's become a Best Western. Just this summer, Nile and I drove down the California coast and up again inland through miles of farm country. There were the migrants, as they've been all along, broiling in the sun, no shelter anywhere in sight.

Nile and I live in "white bread" near New Haven with its troubled ghetto, shootings, and panhandlers. My three mothers, who forgave me, are posthumously picking up the tab. We have two fish, two dogs, and four cats. Helping me get through life here are my friends, Roy and Mary, the kind of people I admired when I first went to Berkeley. A year or so ago, I was invited to visit a graduate seminar at Brown taught by George Montero on "Paris in the Twenties." They'd read what you would expect: Djuna Barnes, Hemingway, Gertrude Stein, Fitzgerald, and then two modern takes on the

'20s: Tennessee Williams's *Clothes for a Summer Hotel* and my *Zelda*. For that one time and place, I was exactly where I always wanted to be. I've been lucky enough to have had my comradeship of writers in real life even if it was something quite different from what I expected. The '20s, Bloomsbury, Mabel Dodge Luhan's Taos lie there in the books. The Beats, with North Beach in tow, are in the process of joining them. Lost worlds, maybe as lost as Chaco Canyon, Betatakin. Chips and shards to sort through. In the end you have to put them together for yourself—or maybe, like Robespierre, just blow that sucker up.

Epilogue: San Francisco—Summer 1997

Jack Micheline's room at the Abandoned Planet bookstore on Valencia just around the corner from the Roxie Theater where Kush had his old Cloud House. All the walls and ceiling are painted bottom to top in surrounding color. Micheline's funny men, the azure blues, pinks, yellows, Jenny, one-armed Ed Balchowsky, the pimps, the hustlers, the "whoors," and the floating babies, pink, blue with aureoles of color wafting up and down one wall, white words of a Jack-type poem imprinting another. "Mene Mene Tekel Upharsin." Jack's somewhere in his sixties now. Like Gregory, he doesn't like his false teeth, so he's dispensed with them. Like Neeli, he has diabetes. "It's for the children, the children," he intones as he sits in a small chair. That and a small table are the only furniture in the little room, yet it's as splendid as any Provence chapel. Cocteau, Matisse. Rich joyous color towers to the ceiling window lit by hard San Francisco light. Nile is amazed, speechless, never seen anything like it. Lisa, as always, appreciates the moment, smiles. "They didn't know I was a religious poet," Jack says to nobody. *"I'm nobody! Who are you?"* (Emily Dickinson).

*

The Four Directions are running out. Catch what you can.

BIBLIOGRAPHY

Play:

Zelda: Frontier Life in America, edited by Lawrence Ferlinghetti, City Lights Press, 1978.

Poems have appeared in anthologies (*City Lights Anthology, The Stiffest of the Corpse: An Exquisite Corpse Reader, San Francisco Poets Anthology, California Bicentennial Poets Anthology*) and in journals such as *Ahem, Beatitude* (nos. 21–34), *Café Society, Cenizas, City Lights Review, City Lights Journal, Exquisite Corpse, The Holy Earth Megascene, Manroot, Phoenix, Poetry San Francisco, San Francisco Gallery, Umbra,* and *Would You Wear My Eyes?*

Luis J. Rodriguez

1954-

*Luis Rodriguez with wife Trini and son Ruben, St. Norbert College,
De Pere, Wisconsin, 1994*

One

Birth is an ignition. From the chaos. Where a word sparks the creation. A great eloquence to open the door. So I was born. Earth womb to mother womb. July 9, 1954, about 6 A.M., according to the modern calendar system. Under the Mexica Sun Stone system (the so-called Aztec calendar), the year was 7-*Tochtli* (Rabbit), within the thirteen-day period of 1-*Tecpatl* (Obsidian Knife), in the day of 13-*Itzcuintli* (Dog). I was born on a wound, on the border between the United States and Mexico. "The Fron-

tier," they call it. El Paso, Texas. The pass. An entering along a journey. Moments after I emerged from my mother, the nurse dropped me. Shocked into reality. I've lived my life like this. Shocked into motion. Shocked into the rivers of my life. Shocked into the depths. Wake up! Wake up! I fell into awareness. My mother had babies as if she were on an assembly line—a "Mexican factory." The undocumented women gave birth, then were pushed out the door. "Next!" a doctor might say. The women came to give light. *Dar luz.* Birth. A spark. A flame. Or a raging blaze.

One-year-old Luis in the arms of half-brother Alberto with (from left) brother Jose Rene and half-sister Seni holding sister Ana Virginia, "one year before we left Chihuahua, Mexico, to move to South Central Los Angeles," 1955

Two

My brother Jose Rene, three years older than I, and my sister Ana Virginia, a year younger, were also born in *el chuco,* as El Paso is known. When I was two years old, my parents took their three small children from our home in Ciudad Juarez, Chihuahua, to one of the most imaginal cities on the continent: Los Angeles. A splendid place; splendid with images. An imagined place. For too many people, this town was the end of the line, where the railroads stopped and the ocean stood like the hand of God to contain our exile. My mother worked in the city's garment industry; she also cleaned homes as a domestic worker on the days she wasn't trying to raise her children. My father, although a former high-school principal and biologist in Mexico, never had his credentials recognized in the new country. He worked in dog food factories, paint factories, in construction, and as a door-to-door salesman of pots and pans, Bibles, and insurance. He sacrificed everything to make it in America. This was his dream. This was also the gateway to our nightmare.

> Strange voices
> whisper behind garbage cans,
> beneath freeway underpasses,
> next to broken bottles.
> The spatter of words,
> textured and multi-colored,
> invoke demons.
>
> They must run to America.
>
> Their skin,
> color of earth,
> is a brand
> for all the great ranchers,
> for the killing floors
> on Soto Street,
> and as slaughter
> for the garment row.
> Still they come:
> A hungry people
> have no country.

(From "Running to America" in *Poems across the Pavement*)

Three

South Central L.A. Watts. Ghetto/barrio. 105th Street. My first home of remembrance. My older half sister, Seni, had already found an apartment there with her husband, Diego, and their two small daughters. She invited the family to come on over. In those days, there were only certain places for Mexicans to live. East L.A. for sure. Nothing but Mexicans (across the Los Angeles River—another wound). And South Central L.A.: Mexicans, Africans. Poor people. Small wood-frame homes, stuccoed duplexes. And government housing projects. Africans. Mexicans. We lived next to each other; too many times we didn't know each other. My first memories were of being alone. Of having no voice. Of living in my head. I fantasized a world not of this world. In silence, I played with my toys: my battered trucks, chewed-on army men, and chipped marbles. A dirt mound in the alley behind our home was my favorite spot. Alone. I was not prepared for the world. I entered school afraid. I refused to speak. I only knew Spanish, and this provoked disdain. One teacher told me to sit in the back of the room—which I did, without doing anything but play with blocks for a year. Don't speak Spanish! Kids punished and swatted for speaking Spanish. Two generations before, my people were punished for speaking their indigenous tongues in Mexico. It keeps going on. Language is the first door to close.

> There is a sense of having possessed
> a deep something,
> a beautiful something,
> and having it stolen.
> As a child I felt spent, useless.
> But beneath all this, I had it.
> Somewhere, sometime. . . .
> I can't escape the thought: it lingers
> around, itching behind my skull,
> this inescapable awareness that I had it once
> and it was taken away.

> (From "Notes of a Bad Cricket" in
> *Trochemoche: New Poems*)

Four

Tortures. Big brother to little brother. Anger in his eyes. In the mouth that spat out my name. Why did he hate me so much? I loved my brother. But he only wanted to hurt me. I remember being thrown off rooftops. I remember having a rope tied around my neck and being dragged across the front yard. I remember beatings and threats and bops in the head. My mother, who didn't know because I couldn't tell her, would force me to play with him. Sometimes she'd whip me for hiding in a closet. She was a good mother. She cared. She cried at every indiscretion. She punished and she wiped the tears. But she didn't understand why I didn't want to play with my brother. My sisters couldn't help (my youngest sister, Gloria Estela, was born at the General Hospital in East L.A.); they too were brutalized. My father didn't pay attention. He had other interests. I remember him coming home, and I would want to be held. This wanting to be held! This didn't last long. My father struggled not to show an emotion. He did, however, give the children new names. Animal names. Jose was *el rano*, the frog; Ana was *la pata*, the duck; Gloria was *la cucaracha*, the cockroach. I was *el grillo*, the cricket. (My brother-in-law Diego later changed this to *el grillo pélon*: the bald cricket). But to say I love you?

> Where have you been, my father?
> You were always escaping,
> always a faint memory of fire,
> a rumor of ardor;
> sentenced to leaving
> but never gone.
>
> . . . For years your silence
> was greeting and departure,
> a vocal disengagement.
> I see you now, walking around in rags,
> your eyes glued to Spanish-language
>   telenovelas
> keen to every nuance of voice and
>   movement,
> what you rarely gave to me.
> This silence is now comfort.
>
> We almost made it, eh Pop?
> From the times when you came home late
> and gathered up children in both arms
> as wide as a gentle wind
> to this old guy, visited by police and
>   social workers,
> talking to air, accused of lunacy.
> I never knew you.
> Losing you was all there was.

> (From "Death Watch" in *The Concrete River*)

Five

South San Gabriel. The Hills. Dirt roads. Just outside of East L.A. Chickens, roosters, and mangy dogs in the backyards. It was poor county territory, like Watts. We moved to the flat area of South San Gabriel. I was nine when we got there. By then we had already moved around several places in South Central L.A., to Reseda in the San Fernando Valley (one of the first Mexican families to set foot there), to Monterey Park, then to South San Gabriel. Maybe seven homes by then. For a short time before landing there, we were homeless after my father lost a substitute teaching position in the San Fernando Valley. We lost our house, our car, our furniture, and much dignity. We ended up sleeping in the living rooms of *comadres*. Or at my sister's home. There were no family shelters then. I remember cold baths. Nights of corn-flake dinners. The yelling. One night my sister stabbed her husband with a nail file. I remember blood. Soon after that, we got evicted.

In South San Gabriel, we finally found a small, one-bedroom, wood-shingled home with a large dirt backyard. Rented through a poverty agency that pushed us this way. I saw Watts burn on TV in 1965; the fire singeing the edges of my soul. Then later my father obtained a job as a laboratory custodian for a community college in the San Fernando Valley. He made about fourteen thousand dollars a year for a family of six. Poor, but not homeless, not starving. Poor but proud. By the time I was thirteen, our family had bought a two-bedroom home in San Gabriel for twelve thousand five hundred dollars—more than sixty miles from my father's job, but he managed to make it to work and back every day until he retired. It was 1967. The house wasn't much, but it gave my father's dream a shape. Our own home. (The bank's home?) This is what America was all about, right? My father wanted this. To be part of America. To believe we could belong. We never did. But we bought a house. We tried . . . I tried everything to get out of it.

Six

Gangs. Tattoos. Drugs. Sniffing aerosol sprays and glue. Streets. Vacant lots. Guns. Skipping school. Jails. Courts. From age eleven until eighteen, I immersed myself into *La Vida Loca,* the crazy life. I became part of Las Lomas barrio of South San Gabriel. I shot and got shot at. I OD'd and helped others who did the same. Weed. Pills—downers, uppers, mescaline. Alcohol. Heroin. PCP. . . . But I also read books: at age ten I ruptured myself and had to be hospitalized. I read a score of illustrated Bible stories for children. I shouldn't have wanted this; like so many Mexicans, I had fallen through the cracks of two languages. But these books engaged my imagination. I awoke to the power of words. Of story. After that, I read all the time. I also discovered the opposite sex: my first sexual encounter was at age twelve inside the dugout of a makeshift baseball field. I became socially active: I walked out of my school at age thirteen during the East L.A. Blowouts of 1968. Only two of us made it out the gate, but by age seventeen I had led three walkouts with hundreds of students. I took part in other civil disturbances, including the 1970 Chicano Moratorium against the Vietnam War. I participated in revolutionary study groups and dabbled with amateur boxing, martial arts, work (warehouse, janitorial, lawn maintenance, car washes, taco stands), as well as painting murals, writing po-

ems, and Mexican (Aztec) dancing. I dropped out of school at fifteen; a year or so later I went back and eventually received my diploma. I would fall, stoned on chemicals, on top of a torn sofa in an empty, graffiti-filled lot in the Hills . . . and I would spend hours in libraries. I would battle in the streets . . . and I would practice intricate dance steps. Enigmatic. Chromatic. Perhaps psychosomatic. Walking between two worlds. Inside two skins. Something had to give. Something had to die. Something had to live.

> when the wasted poems become dawn and
>   are not gray-speckled haze
> when the upholding structures collapse
>   from their perjuries
> when the money-system no longer
>   determines worth
> and purgatory is no longer your driveway
> when the factory-spawn stops lactating
>   'burbs,
> whose milk is dioxin, drying up earth's
>   blood
> when all value is inside of you
> when the wasteland's raped-terrain bursts
>   green
> when the creative heart is the only
>   blossoming

(From "Notes of a Bald Cricket" in
Trochemoche: New Poems)

Seven

Laguna Park. East L.A. August 29, 1970. Thousands from all over the United States, Mexico, and other places gathered here to protest the Vietnam War. In the biggest barrio of the country. I participated, drawn by a call to struggle. I was sixteen. Tired of the streets. Looking for a way out that connected to the fire within. Few things could get close. The sheriffs arrived, ready to riot. They came with helmets, tear gas guns, shotguns, and batons. I was one of the first to fall, struck on the head and then wrested to the ground. I went from jail to jail, ending up in the old Hall of Justice jailhouse, called the "Glasshouse." I had been arrested before, but now it wasn't about stealing, fights, or being stupid. I felt a sense of purpose, that I was part of something bigger. They put me on murderer's row, next to a cell that contained Charles Manson. The tier consisted of mostly Africans and Mexicans. I held my own, considering that the first

"At age thirteen in South San Gabriel I was already into the gang life—that I got into at age eleven—which we called 'La Vida Loca' ('The Crazy Life')"

night I had a razor blade placed to my neck. But I wouldn't back down. For some, we were heroes to be part of the so-called East L.A. riot. Whittier Boulevard burned. Parts of other barrios burned. *¡Ajua!* we yelled from behind iron bars. Chicano journalist Ruben Salazar was killed, and we tore up the cells on the tier. *¡Ajua!* We had a cause. We fought for justice. I found a reason to exist.

> Soon I sit battered, humiliated
> in the dankness of a jail cell;
> officers wallow around
> contemplating my "suicide."
>
> But this time
> they will have to kill me.
> Each time a fist smashes
> across my belly, pommels my face,
> I reach out
> to the cries of the curb,
> the ballads out of broken brick,
> and the smoky outline of a woman's face
> burned onto a cell wall.
>
> They will have to kill me!

(From "Chota" in *The Concrete River*)

Eight

Life was breaking out of me. I didn't want to end it anymore. Before this, I did everything I could to die—drugs, standing on the street

corners in the path of bullets, even suicide attempts. I had a near-death experience sniffing aerosol sprays combined with pills and whiskey. Once I almost slashed my wrists. But I didn't die. I found my poetry and somehow my life. I survived other arrests: for attempted murder, for fighting with police. For disorderly conduct. But by age eighteen, I had joined a revolutionary cadre organization after a couple of years of studying, organizing, and waking up to a new consciousness. Another awakening. I became a student of American revolutionary Nelson Peery. I won my first writing contest and attended my first poetry reading in Berkeley, California. I flew on my first airplane to get there. I started to breathe again. Mentors arose to meet me. I arose to meet them. A hero of going down was now going up. A turnaround. Full of motion and intent. It worked for me. Notwithstanding the fact I often wanted to run away, to give up. Or that there were setbacks, emotional and psychological as well as physical. I kept going. Kept getting stronger. I gave up the drugs and spray after seven hard years of ingesting them. I gave up the violence and jails. By age twenty, I felt ready to start a family, to obtain steady work. In August 1974, I married Camila Martinez, Mexicali-born and lifelong East L.A. resident, at the Guadalupe Church on Hazard Street. She was just two months out of Garfield High School. I was working the night shift at a paper mill. Although I tried college for a few months, I didn't finish my courses. Work. Politics. Marriage. This was my life now.

> There comes a moment when one faces
> the fresh features of an inner face;
> a time of conscious rebirth, when
> the accounting's done, the weave in its
>   final
> flourish, a time when a man stands before
> the world—vulnerable, nothing-owed—and
> considers his place in it.

(From *Always Running: La Vida Loca, Gang Days in L.A.*)

Nine

Paper-mill utility man. Truck driver. Bus driver. Foundry worker. Smelter operator. Steel mill worker. Construction apprentice. Carpenter. Millwright. Welder. Pipe fitter. For seven more years, I worked it. I gained skills. I rode hard the concrete streets through L.A. industry. It helped keep me out of prison. I had two children: Ramiro Daniel was born in June of 1975; Andrea Victoria in April of 1977. I saw their births—powerful ignitions. We lived in Florencia/South Central, in Pasadena, and back in Watts. Most of this time, I also worked with youth, many of whom were hurting like I had been hurting. I gained greater political and organizational clarity through intense commitment, work, and dialogue. But there were also unemployment lines. Welfare. Arguments with Camila. Drunken bouts. Affairs. And treachery. In early 1978, Camila and I broke up. Later that year I quit the Bethlehem Steel Mill, where I had worked on a repair crew for four years. I moved back to East L.A. I wanted to become a writer. But I didn't know what to do. So early in the morning or late at night, I wrote. I took night classes. I read all the time. And I kept working, visiting my kids on weekends. But my focus was on writing. One instructor at East Los Angeles College stuck it out with me once a week, even though I ended up being his only student. "If you're serious, I'll come to class," he said. I agreed to show up. He did, too, and I learned. Unfortunately, I didn't always pay attention to when my children needed me. When Camila's

"A piece of one of the murals I painted at age seventeen, trying to get out of the violence and drugs through art," 1972

new boyfriends and new husband would physically abuse her and sometimes the kids. I kept trying to work and get my writing together. I kept drinking. I kept forgetting. I just wasn't there.

> The blast furnace spews a lava of insipid
>   dreams,
>   a deathly swirl of screams; of late night
>   wars
> with a woman, a child's book of fear,
> a hunger of touch, a hunger of poetry,
> a daughter's hunger for laughter.
> It is the sweat of running, of making love,
> a penitence pouring into ladles of slag.
> It is falling through the eyes of a whore,
> a red-core bowel of rot,
> a red-eyed train of refugees,
> a red-scarred hand of unforgiveness,
> a red-smeared face of spit.
> It is blasting a bullet through your brain,
> the last dying echo of one who enters
> the volcano's mouth to melt.

(From "The Blast Furnace" in
The Concrete River)

Ten

In early 1980, after getting fired from a chemical refinery in East L.A. as a pipe fitter/welder/mechanic, I got a job at a chain of weekly East L.A. newspapers—including the *Eastside Sun* and *Mexican American Sun*. I had entered a threshold, this time as a writer. That summer I was accepted into the Summer Program for Minority Journalists at the University of California, Berkeley—one of a few to ever do so without any college degrees. An eleven-week intensive on-the-job training program. In the fall of that year they provided me my first daily newspaper job at the *San Bernardino Sun*. I started out as a crime and disaster beat reporter. I worked from 4:30 P.M. until 12:30 A.M. I had a forty-channel radio to pick up police, fire, and other emergency frequencies. I had seen death and destruction in Las Lomas. But now I witnessed the results on a daily basis. I saw bodies shot. Cut up. Electrocuted. Mangled in car wrecks. Burned to a crisp. I covered prostitution stings, drug raids, and SWAT battles. I dealt with double murders, love triangles, gang retaliations, suicides, accidents, robberies, and corruption. I interviewed many people. I drank a lot. I wrote a lot. I ignored my babies a lot. In 1981, I returned to L.A. on weekends, some sixty miles away, to get involved in the Latino Writers Association, mentored by such writers as Victor Valle, Helena Viramontes and Manual "Manazar" Gamboa. We organized barrio workshops, a reading series, and the publication of our own literary arts magazine, *Chismearte*. We visited prisons and brought some of the best Chicano writers to East L.A.

In mid-1982, I moved back to East L.A., this time in the basement of my brother's house in Boyle Heights. I met Paulette Donalson, beautiful African-American journalist and aspiring actress. We married in November of 1982. Around that time, I got hired by the American Federation of State, County, and Municipal Employees (AFL-CIO) during the largest union representation campaign in U.S. history—some sixty thousand University of California clerical and blue-collar employees. I did their publicity and worked on their newspapers. I freelanced for the *L.A. Weekly* and *Nation*, among others. I covered events in local communities, particularly around the rights of undocumented people, but also in Mexico, Nicaragua, and southern Honduras. I did radio programming at KPFK-FM. Unfortunately, I tried to work in L.A. as a professional journalist but found out later that the editor of the *San Bernardino Sun* had blocked me from working in the newspapers I applied to. (He told prospective employers I was an "advocate," the death knell for many a good journalist!) But I also worked on poetry, short stories, and novels. Included was a fiction version of my gang days that I called "Mi Vida Loca." I received twenty-two rejections from major U.S. publishers on this book. I would have gotten more, I'm sure, but I stopped after that. None told me why they rejected the book, except one. In a letter, this publishing house stated they had published an "Hispanic" novel ten years before—and they felt they had done enough as far as "Hispanic" literature was concerned! I knew then that my work was being judged, not on its literary merits, but on the name, on my culture. I kept freelancing. I couldn't stop believing that my writing would finally amount to something. I had given up so much for this to happen. But I had also sabotaged many things that had come my way.

Wading through the lush of memory,
  through speechless seconds,
seeing myself on the backhand of past
  lives, crumbling emotions

surround me, as this obsessive and
  irresponsible poetry man beckons
to writer. To tell truths. Oh such a liar!
  I'm just a sleeveless
jacket in a closet of worn clothes; I'm the
  incision of scarring verbs
across the faces of all my loves. This
  Mexican who is a stranger in Mexico,
this pocho who hates milk with his coffee,
  juice with his vodka, who speaks
English with an East L.A. accent and
  Spanish with an East L.A. accent.
This Tarahumara's lost son, this graveled
  tongue, this ghost
beneath every ruin, rising like jaguar's
  breath in a tropical storm.

(From "Notes of a Bald Cricket" in
Trochemoche: New Poems)

Eleven

Drinking and depression. I felt lonely most of the time. My kids came and I tried to show them a good time. But they weren't the center of my life. They knew it. I acted as if I didn't. Was I becoming my father? Still, I refused to go back to industry. To go back to crime or jail. Or to drugs. I couldn't go back. Drinking, unfortunately, kept me going. When Camila and I broke up, I fell deeper into the bottle. In the early 1980s, I had moved in with Diana, and we drank all the time. I had partnerships with women, but drink was what linked us. Paulette was not about that—and this was good. But we didn't last long. In the winter of 1983, I left Paulette and moved in with Susana Gil, a Mexican-Colombian friend of mine who was also going through a separation. I recall a night in which Susana sang songs on the floor of her home, with a guitar across her lap, and both of us reached unconsciousness with a bottle of tequila. When I awoke, I saw Susana asleep, her head toward the floor and the guitar on her lap.

For a long time I tried to keep the alcohol out of the house, but not out of my life. I worked in Denver, Washington, D.C., Salem, Austin, Portland, San Francisco/Oakland, San Diego, and Miami as a troubleshooter for AFSCME. Every day, I ended up at a local bar. The Bethlehem Steel Mill had closed down in the early 1980s; whole communities were affected. There was a twenty-percent rise in alcoholism and eight suicides the

*My daughter, Andrea Victoria, at age sixteen,
Los Angeles, 1993*

first year after the closing. The United Steelworkers Union, Local 1845, set up one of the largest food banks in the country, feeding four thousand to six thousand families a week. I ended up participating in the theater/poetry workshops set up by Local 1845. The union hall sponsored The TheaterWorkers Project, created by Susan Franklin Tanner, which involved former steelworkers telling their stories on stage. It received support from people like Bruce Springsteen, and the project traveled all over the country. By early 1985, Susana and I had broken up, even though we had bought a house together. I still raged. I still felt the emptiness. I felt alone and scared. Again. I drank to ease it all. Again. I didn't know what to do but run. And run. Drink. And run.

> I ran across bridges, beneath overhead
>   passes,
> and then back alongside the infested walls
> of the concrete river,
> splashing rainwater as I treaded,
> my heels colliding against the pavement.

So much energy propelled my legs
and, like the river,
it went on for miles.

When all was gone,
the concrete river
was always there
and me, always running.

> (From "Always Running" in
> *The Concrete River*)

Twelve

I received a phone call: Camila's husband had beaten her up. This wasn't the first time. Once, in Denver, Camila called to request money from me when I was working on the newspaper. I asked her if she and the kids were okay. She said fine. I found out later from a mutual friend that she had called from a battered women's shelter. Now another friend called to say my children were safe at her house. But she didn't know where Camila or her husband were. I got into my car and drove from San Bernardino to L.A. to get the kids. When I got there, they were already at Camila's house: that night, I slept curled up next to my young son and daughter. Then her husband came. He was drunk. He threatened to kill Camila. He heard I was there and threatened me. I got up. We had a confrontation. The dude pulled out a large knife. I looked at him and told him to go ahead and stab me. I wasn't scared. But I also told him that none of this was worth killing anyone for, that he had to hang on to his dignity, that it was all going to be okay. At one point, Ramiro, about four years old, walked into the room and asked what was going on, a frightened look on his face. The dude then sat down on the bed and cried. I didn't take my kids away from Camila, although I almost did then. Camila and her husband eventually broke up. I just knew that I couldn't raise my children the way she could. Camila was a good mother, but she had rotten relationships with men (once I was one). I hoped she would finally find her peace and a decent guy, too.

> Outside the Bull's Eye Inn
> the hurting never stopped.
>
> Outside the Bull's Eye Inn
> we locked into hate
> shrouded in the lips of love.

Outside the Bull's Eye Inn
we had two children
who witnessed our drunken brawls—
my boy once entered our room,
and danced and laughed with tears in his
  eyes
to get us to stop.

But inside, beside the blaze of bar lights,
she was the one who stole into my sleep,
the one who fondled my fears,
the one who inspired
the lust of honeyed remembrance.

She was the song of regret behind a
  sudden smile.

(From "The Bull's Eye Inn" in
The Concrete River)

Thirteen

I moved to Chicago in May of 1985. To get away. To begin anew. Stepping onto another threshold. I became editor of the *People's Tribune* weekly newspaper, a small political publication. I felt I could make an impact. I covered strikes, civil rights battles, homeless organizing. I went to the South, to Appalachia, to cities in struggle. Although I had undermined so many things over the years, including my relationships, I continued in the direction of my aims, determined by my wounds. Wound to a womb. Chicago was as different from L.A. as any city could be. I needed this. I also got involved in the struggles there. Among the homeless. The urban youth. And the poets. In 1988, I became active in the growing and vibrant poetry scene in the city's bars, cafes, libraries, and theaters. I worked with such poets as Michael Warr, Patricia Smith, David Hernandez, Carlos Cumpian, and Marc Smith. By then I stopped editing the newspaper. I began work as a freelance computer typesetter, writer, and editor. I was also employed weekends at WMAQ-AM, all news radio in Chicago, as a newswriter and reporter. I was on the board and staff of *Letter eX*, Chicago's poetry news magazine.

I married Maria Trinidad Cardenas, "Trini," in March of 1988 in Kenosha, Wisconsin. She had been part of a large Mexican migrant family in California, eleven brothers and sisters; they eventually settled in Pacoima, where she went to school and grew up. Three years before I showed up, she landed in Chicago to edit and write for the bilingual revolutionary newspaper *Tribuno del Pueblo*. Our son Ruben Joaquin was born in September. I read poetry in many venues by then: bars, schools, cafes, prisons. I began poetry workshops in public schools, juvenile facilities, and homeless shelters. (I ended up facilitating weekly workshops at one women's shelter, Irene's Place, for four years.) Poetry swirled in and around me. My oldest son, Ramiro, also came to live with us that year; he was getting into a lot of trouble in L.A. and Camila wanted me to start raising him. He was thirteen, angry and resentful toward me.

In late 1989, I published my first poetry collection, *Poems across the Pavement*, under the imprint I started, Tia Chucha Press, which I named after my favorite aunt: Tía Chucha. I volunteered for the Guild Complex, which would become the largest and best literary arts organization in the city. In 1991, my second book of poetry, *The Concrete River*, was published by Curbstone Press in Connecticut. I did readings in Toronto, Montreal, Puerto Rico, Paris, and London. By then, Ramiro had joined a local Chicago gang. I decided to rewrite *Mi Vida Loca* and do it the way it was

*My sons, Ruben, Luisito ("Chito"),
and Ramiro, 1995*

originally intended, as a nonfiction memoir. For Ramiro; for all young people. In early 1993, Curbstone Press issued a hardcover version of the book called *Always Running: La Vida Loca, Gang Days in L.A.*

Fourteen

I again traveled across the United States. When *Always Running* first came out, I went to thirty cities in three months. Ramiro went with me for the first ten days and five cities. We spoke on the *Oprah Winfrey Show, Good Morning America,* CNN's *Sonya Live,* and National Public Radio as well as local TV, radio, and print media. We read at bookstores, schools, conferences, and gatherings. This was one of only a few books on gang life ever written by a former participant. Ramiro talked about what it was like to be in a gang during the present. We made a powerful team. We may have reached some seventy million people with our media and community presentations. After my son returned home, I continued to spread the message of justice, of peace, of being there for our youth, and of stopping the growing imprisonment rate. I imagined another world: abundant, just, and equitable. I began to engage the greater imagination among people for the same things. But back home, Ramiro got into more trouble. He seemed to be imbalanced without me. I got accolades. Fellowships. Awards. Once, on the brink of my own bankruptcy, with thirty thousand dollars in debt, I received a fellowship that allowed me to pay our bills. An advance from Touchstone Books/Simon and Schuster for the paperback rights of *Always Running* helped Trini and me make a down payment on our first home. The person working the bidding with the eight New York City publishers vying for the rights asked me what I thought I should get. "I don't know," I said, "but whatever you do, make them pay."

Any good craftsman carries his tools.
Years ago, they were always at the ready.
In the car. In a knapsack.
Claw hammers, crisscrossed heads,
32 ouncers. Wrenches in all sizes,
sometimes with oil caked on the teeth.
Screwdrivers with multicolored plastic
    handles . . .
Nowadays, I don't haul these mechanical
    implements.
But I still make sure to carry the tools
of my trade: Words and ideas,

the kind no one can take away.
So there may not be any work today,
but when there is, I'll be ready.
I got my tools.

(From "Carrying My Tools" in
The Concrete River)

Fifteen

I stopped drinking in early 1993. I had to be there for Ramiro. For my daughter, Andrea, who by then had moved in with us. I had to be there for Ruben and Trini. My father and brother-in-law had died of cancer within three weeks of each other the previous year. My health was not going to hold either if I didn't take care of myself. By that time, I worked with gang youth in predominantly Puerto Rican Humboldt Park. Most of them were friends of Ramiro. We con-

Closeup of a mural with an exerpt from Rodriguez's "City of Angels," International Youth Arts Festival, Rome, Italy, 1995

nected with youth in the Mexican community of Pilsen, collaborating with youth organizer Patricia Zamora. I didn't need any more excuses. Ramiro was getting kicked out of schools. Landing in jail. Getting beaten up by police. Getting shot at by rival gangs—and shooting back. I had to be there. I had to be sober. To write. To be father. To be companion. To mentor, organize, and teach. I also did workshops in homeless shelters, in schools, in juvenile facilities. To keep money coming in, I kept traveling. By then I had quit all my other jobs, including WMAQ, a CNN radio station, after I refused to reconcile myself as a journalist with the one-sided and distorted coverage of the Persian Gulf War. I ended up going to Europe again, on a tour of seven German cities, one Austrian city, and Amsterdam with six American poets. I had a relapse in June with drinking, chugging down about twenty-five large, dark German beers. I felt like dying. My body reacted badly; alcohol was toxic to my system. It was the last time I ever drank.

In mid-1993, photographer Donna DeCesare and I received a grant from the Center for Documentary Studies out of Duke University to photograph and interview Salvadoran gang youth in L.A. and San Salvador. Donna and I went to L.A. for several weeks in the summer and to San Salvador in December. The Zapatistas started their armed struggle in Chiapas, Mexico, on January 1, 1994, when we were still in El Salvador. Soon after, the paperback version of *Always Running* appeared through Touchstone Books. I went to fifteen cities in one-and-a-half months. I did residencies in Pennsylvania, Berkeley, Chicago, Connecticut, and other places. I visited prisons, juvenile facilities, and schools, including the most violent, most crowded, poorest, and even some of the richest. From East L.A to Brooklyn. From Miami to Seattle. I received hundreds of letters from youth, teachers, parents, and organizers. The youth in Chicago I was working with, along with Ramiro and Andrea, started Youth Struggling for Survival in August of 1994 at the University of Illinois, Chicago. Although mostly Mexican and Puerto Rican, the group also consisted of African and European-descended youth; they all came together to change themselves and their environment. Camila had by then traveled to Chicago from East L.A. to help with Ramiro; she also got active in YSS.

In January of 1994, I participated for the first time with the Mosaic Multicultural Foundation's Men's Conferences, run by renowned storyteller

Michael Meade, along with teacher-elders such as Malidoma Somé, originally from the Dagara tribe of West Africa, and Jack Cornfield, a leading American Buddhist. I also moved toward understanding my indigenous roots, working with tribal elders in the Lakota, Navajo, Quinault, and Creek nations. A circle was being completed—a circle I began in my late teens trying to break out of the crazy life. In late June of 1994, my fourth child, Luis Jacinto, was born.

> I'm dawdling on the edge of this sea in a
>   glass, this last vestige
> of my mother's fears, this grandfather
>   poison that poisoned
> my grandfather, this nectar of dried
>   screams, this bruised cant,
> this woman who presses her nipples to my
>   cheek, whose chatter
> cannot be climbed, whose kisses are
>   stained lullabies, who tells me
> I belong although I cannot fit, who dares
>   the fool's lament;
> the call-and-response of night crawlers, the
>   tones beneath my rambling,
> who has become the last shriek of tequila
>   dreaming,
> whom I now grieve, ambling to the funeral
>   tune of a child's cry
> pulsing silent yet determined within me.
> O for beauty's fist to pommel this mask
>   into itself,
> for taste that is candy and not porcelain,
> for wisps of saliva to wither on my hair
>   and chin,
> for words to nuzzle and soak my tongue,
> for language's naked prowlness to enter
>   these shoes;
> for a bald cricket's lyrical death on a
>   dance floor.

(From "Notes of a Bad Cricket" in *Trochemoche: New Poems*)

Sixteen

In 1995, Moira Productions, working for the Independent Television Service, followed me and Ramiro, as well as YSS, for about a year. They were filming a series called *Making Peace* for PBS-TV. Unfortunately, three of our YSS leaders—Marcos Cordova, Eric Arellano, and Eddie Ramos—were killed during that time. I also did videos for "The United States of Poetry" (never used), the Lannan Foundation, Noetic Sciences, and the

Poetry Center of San Francisco State University; CDs and tapes for Tia Chucha Press (*A Snake in the Heart: Poetry and Music by Chicago's Spoken Word Performers*) and Rhino Records (*In Their Own Voices: A Century of Recorded Poetry*), among others. I did recordings for Folkways Records and Oral Tradition Archives that have yet to be released. I helped found Rock-A-Mole! Music and Festival Productions in L.A. with Lee Balinger, Ernie Perez, and David Sandoval. My poetry, essays, reviews, and stories have been published in magazines and anthologies, including *Los Angeles Times, Nation, U.S. News and World Report, Utne Reader, Prison Life, Philadelphia Inquirer Magazine, Grand Street, TriQuarterly, Chicago Reporter,* and *Hungry Mind Review.*

I returned to El Salvador with Donna to do major presentations at government and nongovernmental agency gatherings, as well as at an exhibit of Donna's work in the capital. Donna and I also did similar presentations in Raleigh, North Carolina, and in Paris, France. I went to Mexico to do talks and a reading at a gathering in Taxco, Guerrero, Mexico, on the same issues of L.A. gang youth being exported to Mexico and Central America. In late 1996 (and again in 1997), I traveled to the Navajo Reservation to speak at schools, at conferences, and among elders. In early 1997, YSS, with the help of Frank and Louise Blazquez, caravaned to the Pine Ridge Reservation in South Dakota; we also established regular sweat lodge ceremonies, while learning more about our indigenous roots, with YSS youth and adults. By then, I had attended multicultural men's conferences in Los Angeles, San Francisco, Chicago, Atlanta, and Seattle. YSS connected with Barrios Unidos, a mostly Chicano urban peace organization based in northern California, as well as other similar organizations. Andrea was in college, working and trying to survive as a single mother. (Her courage and leadership has continued to amaze me.) I had four grandchildren by then—Ricardo, Anastasia, and Amanda (from Ramiro) and Catalina (from Andrea).

Another poetry collection, *Trochemoche,* and a children's illustrated and bilingual book, *América Is Her Name,* are scheduled for publication in 1998 by Curbstone Press; I also have a book of essays, a short story collection, a handbook on youth and violence, and another nonfiction work on contemporary gang life in process. I had won fellowships and awards from the Lila-Wallace/Reader's Digest Fund, the Lannan Foundation, the National Association for Poetry Therapy, PEN Oakland, San Francisco State University's

Poetry Center, and the *Chicago Sun-Times,* among others. I had finally united with family. I had finally begun to recover from my worst addictions. I had found respect and a vital place within my community and in the political struggle. There was much to be grateful for, much to feel accomplished about. But not all was well.

Seventeen

In January of 1997, Ramiro was arrested, beaten, and charged with allegedly shooting at two police officers, and for shooting a truck driver at a Chicago intersection. He was taken to the new maximum security section of the Cook County Jail. Bail eventually ended up at $1,250,000. If convicted, Ramiro could get twenty years to life. We got the news while YSS held a ritual retreat at the Jane Addams Community Center. My eight-year-old son Ruben, Andrea, and Camila were there, and it affected everyone at the retreat. This had happened before in 1996. Ramiro had other attempted murder charges dropped to two counts of a felony discharge of a weapon. He was sentenced to four months at a Department of Corrections boot camp and several months of house arrest. He went through all that just fine. He had started attending college, working, and trying to be present for his daughter, Anastasia. He had, in effect, stopped being active in gang life. But he was still troubled. A moment of rage led to the incident for which he is now incarcerated. I see part of my rage in him. I see him on a similar suicide path. But much has changed in twenty years. There are fewer resources, less compassion, less tolerance, and fewer incentives to help young people like Ramiro. He is a leader, a poet, and a caring person who also has many problems and could use proper help and guidance. However, the county jail is not a facility for such help to occur. As a family, and as friends in YSS and everywhere, we are not giving up on him. We will stand by him and assist him where we can. But we know we can't save him. This is another personal ordeal he will have to get through and, hopefully, overcome.

I intensified my own spiritual quest, particularly in the traditions of my people, the indigenous peoples of this continent: I have participated in ceremonies, sweat lodges, and prayer meetings with my Native American relatives on both sides of the border. But I have an open and expansive view of such things. I have also

Speaking to an overflow crowd of high school and college students at Black Hawk College in East Moline, Illinois, 1995—"in a scene similar to talks and readings I've done all over the country since Always Running *first came out in 1993"*

participated in a Buddhist meditation retreat, worked with Christians in rites of passage training and sanctuary work, and read and learned about spiritual paths from all over the world, including Africa, India, Asia, and Europe. I also maintained my revolutionary vision and commitment. My writing, my work with youth and the abandoned, my resolve to be father, mentor, teacher, and poet has all been healing for me. My aims are now to stay sober, sane, and structured. I went through too many relationships, too many jobs, too many interests, too many potholes—but it was all good if I make something of all this. With Trini (we've become loving and supportive companions), with my children and grandchildren, with my writing and the various institutions I have helped create, I have contributed to my world, my community, and my history.

I've reconciled with my mother, who I realize was trying her best against great odds. I've reconciled with my sisters and my brother, who despite his rage against me as a child turned out to be a decent person. I am presently on a

path—at forty-three years of age—that will have to traverse even more bumpy terrain. But I'm going into it with an engaged imagination, with deep and clear intention, and with all my creative faculties in gear. Revolution is now more real than ever. My struggle is part of a larger one— the way an individual's personal aspirations connect to and intersect with those of his community. For me, any personal healing is linked to helping heal our society, presently fractured and imbal-anced. Conscious life activity. Deliberate and open. This is how I must live in this great period of momentous global transformations.

I write this having completed a number of circles in my life, but also with a heavy heart for Ramiro and others like him, many who have already been abandoned by an economy and the previous social compact. But my resolve has only strengthened. My vision has only sharpened. There are difficult roads ahead; if anything, I'm more prepared for them than I have ever been. According to the ancient Mexican people, we are living under the Fifth Sun. *Nahui Ollin.* A time

of change. Of movement. From the heart of a
person to the heart of the universe.

> There is a mixology of brews within me; I've
>   tasted them all, still fermenting
> as grass-high anxieties. I am rebel's pen, rebel's
>   son, father of revolution in verse.
> I am capitalism's angry Christ, techno
>   Quetzalcoatl, toppling the temples
> of modern thievery, of surplus value in word-art
> —exploited, anointed and perhaps double-
>   jointed. . . .
> I am disciple and elder; I am rockero and hip
>   hop bandit,
> rapping Aztlanese in-between brick-lined texts.
>   What do I know?
> What blazing knowledge can I spear? Who can
>   burn with me and not get burned?
> Violence used to be great solace; alcohol my
>   faithful collaborator,
> scratching dank words from stale corners. Now
>   there are whole cities
> in my gardens. Neo-Azteca drums pulsing from
>   my temples. Saxophone riffs
> streaming from the sky like a waterfall into the
>   canyons of my body.
> Walls carry my name, walls and their luminant
>   fractures.
> Walk with me to the Maya. Walk with me along
>   headstones of past loves,
> past plans, long-gone junctures. Walk with me
>   through the forest
> of collective remembering, shamed and honored
>   by the trees. I'm the holy villain,
> the outlawed saint. The most Godless and
>   therefore dearest to the mystery.
> Where suicide is not solution. Where poems no
>   longer puncture the phantoms.
> Where walking with me is to become brethren
>   to rain and night sweats and the betrayed.

(From "Notes of a Bad Cricket" in
Trochemoche: New Poems)

BIBLIOGRAPHY

Poetry:

Poems across the Pavement, Tia Chucha Press (Chicago), 1989.

The Concrete River, Curbstone (Willimantic, Connecticut), 1991.

Trochemoche: New Poems, Curbstone, 1998.

Nonfiction:

Always Running: La Vida Loca, Gang Days in L.A. (memoir), Curbstone, 1993.

Fiction:

América Is Her Name (for children), Curbstone, 1998.

Contributor of poetry, articles, and essays to numerous periodicals, including *American Book Review, Chicago Review, Crossroads, Letter eX, Los Angeles Times Book Review, Nation, National Catholic Reporter, Poets and Writers,* and *U.S. News and World Report.*

Contributor to anthologies and textbooks, including *Risking Contact: Readings to Challenge Our Thinking,* edited by W. Royce Adams, Houghton Mifflin, 1997; *Lives in the Balance: Youth, Poverty and Education in Watts* by Ann C. Diver-Stamnes, State University of New York Press, 1997; and *Elements of Literature, Grade 10,* Holt, Rinehart and Winston, 1997.

Audio recordings include poems "Tia Chucha Press" and "The Concrete River" on *In Their Own Voices: A Century of Recorded Poetry,* Rhino Records, 1996; and poem "Palmas" on *A Snake in the Heart: Poems and Music by Chicago's Spoken Word Performers,* Tia Chucha Press, 1994.

Video recordings include author profile in *Making Peace,* a four-part PBS-TV series, Independent Television Service and Moira Productions, 1996; and interview and poem "Bethlehem No More" in "Social Workers and the Challenge of Violence Worldwide," University of North Carolina Center for Public Television, 1996.

Gerald Rosen

1938-

Gerald Rosen, 1984

When I was growing up in the Bronx, I never imagined that I might one day become a novelist. Novelists lived in Manhattan. They summered in the Hamptons and studied abroad and spoke French. We had no books in our house. We summered at HaYa bungalows, forty shacks on two acres of land in Nyack. My grandparents were illiterate Jewish immigrants from "Austria," which was a euphemism for Poland. My father's parents had come from Russia but were already dead when I was born. No one would tell me exactly which town any of my ancestors came from. I guess their history was too dreadful to be remembered.

My father had a high IQ and skipped a year in school, but he had to leave in the tenth grade when his father died. He never read a book in his life. I think he felt he got too late a start and could never catch up with those who had already been reading. My mother graduated from high school, worked in the Woolworth's briefly, and took a short fling at dancing in a nightclub in Boston. She idolized Ruby Keeler. She took great pride in the fact that her father, an illiterate former baker, owned half of three apartment houses, including the large apartment house in which we lived.

My family was ambitious to succeed in America, as I was myself; that I was born in the Royal Hospital on the Grand Concourse was not insignificant in regard to my family's hopes. As my mother always said, "My father is a landlord, and remember, a landlord is the lord of the land."

I was born on December 24, 1938, at the node where the Depression met World War II. My father's family, eight orphans from the Lower East Side, actually feared starving to death, which was why my father hoarded food in the basement during the war. The Nazis might come and put us in boxcars, but we would not go to our deaths hungry.

The war made a powerful impression on me. I couldn't imagine how the world had gotten into such a chaotic state. Nor why someone would want to come across the sea and kill half the people in our neighborhood, including me. (The other half were Irish.) I told my father at about the age of five that I wanted to get everyone to sign a treaty when I grew up so there would be no more wars. I remember very well the rationing, the patriotic songs in school, the celebrations at the end of the war, the sadness for Mrs. Diamond, a poor, widowed dressmaker across the street whose only son had been killed, and especially the films of the Holocaust. I had not known any time of peace until I was almost seven years old.

Everyone in our neighborhood—six-story apartment houses glaring back at each other across a

Maternal grandfather, Sam Berger

imity to Yankee Stadium, which housed the greatest baseball team of all time and brought many celebrities and world leaders to our neighborhood. We were not the Jews who formed socialist parties and reading groups like the family of another Bronx writer, Grace Paley, whose father was a physician. We were *New York Daily News* Jews, but we had driving energy and a fierce desire for any learning that was useful in getting ahead.

I attended the local public schools, but I chose to go to De Witt Clinton High School in the North Bronx on the edge of Van Cortland Park. Clinton held thirty-five hundred boys, tough guys from the South Bronx, Italians from the East Bronx, and Blacks from Harlem. I saw it as a step away from my former world, a combination prep school and blackboard jungle, and I enjoyed the thrill of being part of its athletic, macho reputation since I was not very tough myself, although I did manage to play on the Bronx championship basketball team. High school players were not allowed in this league, and we lost the city championship to a team from Manhattan that had more ringers than we did.

When it came time to go to college, I wanted to go out of town, to meet Protestants and learn their manners and ways. My family supported me in this desire, but what was I to study? It had to be something which led immediately to a career, or the people on the block would kid my father for wasting his money. I chose Rensselaer Polytechnic Institute to study engineering. I had never met an engineer and had no idea what one did except that it involved math and science, at which I excelled. I liked liberal arts, but I would have been afraid to major in it alongside rich and cultured people even if my parents had permitted me to.

I had begun to read books on my own at the Highbridge Public Library when I was about fifteen. The first book I really liked was *Catcher in the Rye;* it had never occurred to me before that literature could be about someone like me, and that there might be people in the world, authors, who could understand me and might be able to advise me. I never lacked friends in the Bronx, but I was always somewhat the outsider. There were two brothers on my block who were also outsiders, Marty and Irwin Licker, both of whom were serious druggers and died young (Marty at thirty-seven, Irwin at twenty-nine). Irwin was my younger brother's age, but Marty, who was a year older than I and two years ahead in school, became my tutor in the

narrow blank street with no trees—knew each other. Because of rent control and housing shortages, no one ever moved. My mother had been a teenager on the block, and my grandparents were well known in the neighborhood and at the old storefront synagogue. The fact that I was the landlord's grandson gave me some prestige on the block. At five years old, I would "produce" shows on the staircase inside our hallway. I would choose the talent, decide who would sit on the steps to watch, and announce the acts. Everyone saw this as my right since it was "my grandfather's building."

Yet this was about the only advantage I had in life. I knew no one who had gone to college or educated himself. The only professional I knew was my uncle Ben, who lived upstairs and was an armed robber. My mother believed in education and would pay for anything I desired as long as it was "educational." Yet we had no real culture in my family, few public institutions of culture in the Bronx, and little beauty. (Perhaps this was why the residents burned down the South Bronx in the 1970s.) Our sole source of pride was our prox-

Greenwich Village–Harlem–Times Square axis, which became an important shadow to the world in which I was a good student and "a nice boy."

We were both present at the birth of rhythm and blues in the hallways and bathrooms of Clinton among the kids from Harlem who had formed vocal groups and were creating their own music or covering the songs we, in the advanced underground of New York City high school students, were listening to each night on Alan Freed after we returned from playing basketball or stickball or touch football. I loved this music: it touched my heart, it mystified my parents, it ennobled the kids who sang it in the toilets. It was something that was mine, far from the sentimental gop that my parents' generation called popular music. It was also black, which was very far from the white art I had been raised on, and it spoke from an alienated, outside, down-and-out, non-middle-class stance, which spoke for my feelings as well.

It was a small step to jazz, just a walk of a couple blocks after a Knicks game at the old Garden to Basin Street one night, led by my pal Marty, to see Clifford Brown/Max Roach and to pass through a door from which I would never exit. I had not imagined adults could behave like this, poor people from the streets, like myself, creating a new and sophisticated art form for the world right in front of my eyes. I would talk to them (Coltrane, Basie, Brubeck, Ornette Coleman). They were nice to me. Once (age sixteen) I bought a drink for Ella Fitzgerald and thus was able to purchase one for myself, and Ella, wise to what was happening, laughed warmly like the parent (or God) I always wanted. I had never seen men creating beauty, poor men. Later, much later, when I was thirty, these experiences would make it finally seem possible that even I might create art myself. But not until I had an Ivy League Ph.D., and the small measure of self-confidence that came with it, and, having become an antiwar rioter, I burned with things I wanted and needed to say.

The writers I found for myself and liked as a teenager included Hemingway, Fitzgerald, Virginia Woolf, Thomas Wolfe, Kerouac, Dylan Thomas, Camus, Dostoyevsky, and the musicians Miles, Brubeck, Desmond, Shearing, Cannonball, Bird, Monk, Coltrane, Eric Dolphy, Dizzy, Oscar, Errol, Sarah, Billie, Anita, June, Chris, and dozens of others. In some ways, I think I was

Maternal grandmother, Minnie Berger

more influenced in the meaning and style of what it means to be an artist by jazz musicians than by writers.

I wrote about these Bronx years in my fifth book, *Growing up Bronx,* a novel which I tell people is about two-thirds true (except for the parts in which I behave courageously). I did not write much about my brother, Mark, four years my junior, in this book because a major theme of the book is failure in America and Mark was a great success. He was a good kid, putting up with all my elder brother impositions. Each fall, he would good-naturedly run down the street again and again as I practiced passing a football to him; in the spring, he would don his catcher's mask so I could practice my pitching. He followed me to De Witt Clinton and then to my fraternity, Phi Sigma Delta, but at the University of Vermont he met a fellow sixteen-year-old, Lucy Blau, whom he married and had three nice kids with, Lauren, Pam, and David. He died of cancer at the age of forty-eight while heading a Wall Street law firm that had grown from 65 to 250 employees under his three years of stewardship. He was a tough, excellent lawyer who argued important cases like Dalkon Shield and Love Canal. He was loved by his kids and their friends and respected by his employees, who hired a bus to come to his funeral, which was also attended by a huge crowd of kids whom he had helped in Westchester County.

We drifted apart somewhat during my most radical and "hippy" years when I moved to northern California, but we continued to hold an unspoken affection for each other which I am happy to say surfaced and flowered again during the final months of his illness.

At Rensselaer I majored in electrical engineering and drinking, not necessarily in that order. I did well enough in my studies, as I was good in math and that carried me through most exams, but I had no real aptitude or background in the technical, material side of engineering. I had never fixed a car, or anything else for that matter, and after two years I realized I was not cut out for engineering, but what could I do? Beneath it all nagged the nightmare of winding up back in the Bronx in a boring job that would stifle my growth and probably kill me. RPI was a difficult school, on a par with MIT for undergraduates, and no one could coast through; thus I began a life of cramming for exams which didn't interest me and then getting completely drunk immediately afterwards. We had our desperate fun, but I was pretty miserable—lost and directionless and yet afraid of leaving or of disappointing my parents, who had sacrificed to send me to RPI. I washed dishes and refereed basketball games, but this came nowhere near paying for my tuition.

During my senior year, I decided to continue on to Wharton to study for my MBA. I felt that undergraduate school was all I was entitled to from my parents, but my mother talked my father into helping me to pay for Wharton, the renowned business school of the Ivy League University of Pennsylvania. I graduated in the top quarter of my class at RPI, but I am probably most proud of the fact that some friends and I began to hire black R & B and jazz bands from the red-light district on Green Street in Albany, and thus we were among the people who changed the face of American college life forever.

When I had arrived at RPI, the typical party consisted of students playing bridge with their dates and then drinking beer and singing slightly risqué traditional fraternity songs, or else dancing the Charleston to white, college boy, Dixieland bands. After my high school experiences and my times in Harlem when I went to the Apollo Theater and haunted record shops where the clerks taught me how to listen to jazz chord changes, I could not pretend to inhabit a straight white sensibility anymore, and thus spent much time on Green Street, listening to great jazz with the African American prostitutes and dancing to Bill Gory and the Meadowlarks. When we hired these people to come to Troy to play at our fraternity, two formerly separate worlds began to intermingle, and it was my impression that the musicians liked coming into a college atmosphere. I certainly enjoyed having them there, and once, after I was drinking with the Trinidad Steel Band during the afternoon before their performance at RPI, they strapped a large steel drum to my waist and taught me a few licks, and when the band was introduced to great applause I appeared on the stage and played a couple songs with them, to the great astonishment of the students in the audience.

A great disappointment to me occurred when I rushed several fraternities and learned that I could only join one of the three Jewish fraternities on campus. After all, hadn't I come to RPI to leave my roots behind me and become a kind of "real American" (i.e., a Protestant)? I had always harbored the notion that life was sad and lonely only because I was in the Bronx among immigrants and their children, and that there was a clean and reasonable world out there in America, a world like the one I saw on TV with Fred MacMurray and General Eisenhower, a world of people I could think highly of since I had never met them. I found at RPI that I could begin to eat unfamiliar foods like squash and zucchini, but I was not ready to swear allegiance to Jesus Christ in order to be allowed to join a fraternity. This experience was one of the reasons why my friends and I were motivated to win the sports championship of the twenty-eight fraternities during my senior year, and I was proud to have starred at quarterback, as captain of the basketball team, shortstop, and starter on the volleyball team, even though it was all only on an intramural level.

At Wharton I began at a distinct disadvantage because most of the other students were business or economic majors from fine schools, but I worked extremely hard to win a scholarship for my second year so I would be less dependent on my parents. As soon as I caught up to the others, I found the work much easier than engineering and quickly became one of the handful of top students, graduating with honors. At the same time, I continued to live a double life, drinking heavily at down-and-out boisterous bars, dating wild girls from the Art Institute, and spending much time at the black jazz clubs in South Philly such as Pep's and the Showboat in the Negro Douglas Hotel. I felt more at home in these clubs than in the social activities at Wharton. I was finally banned from a couple of the local women's colleges for harmless but admittedly inappropriate behavior, such as jumping onto the stage after a Brendan Behan lecture at Bryn Mawr, and sitting Buddha-like in the center of a nursing school dance I disliked which resulted in police intervention.

It seemed that the closer I came to success in America, the more I was haunted by the transience of things. My basic stance at this time was that life was meaningless anyhow, so one might as well earn a decent living and live in a civilized manner, buying the best seats for concerts. (I had found wonderful cheap seats for the Philadelphia Orchestra, in the opera orchestra pit at the feet of Eugene Ormandy. You could see only the first row of musicians, but when that big sound rolled over you, you didn't care.)

Still, I was in my familiar position of having some friends I liked but of feeling lost and lonely. I kept thinking about how my grandfather, Sam Berger, had died suddenly when I was in the second grade and how the family disintegrated after this, with my grandmother, Minnie, collapsing and never really coming back to life. When she died, my aunt Helen, my mother's younger sister who lived with her parents, began to deteriorate, and then she died while the nominal head of the family, my mother's older brother Mac, who had always entertained us by telling jokes and playing the piano on the black keys and singing to his ukulele, descended into drunkenness.

What was the point of all my studying and success? Where was it leading? One place it led was the Boeing Airplane Company in Seattle, which hired me in its "Executives of the Future" program after my first year at Wharton, one of the most desirable summer jobs in the United States. Now I was really on my way, but I wasn't sure to where.

I tell the story of that remarkable summer in my most autobiographical book, *Mahatma Gandhi in a Cadillac,* so there is no need to repeat it here, but in summary, it was the summer when I met my first wife, Charlotte Mayer of Lewiston, Idaho, and decided not to be an engineer or businessman but to become a teacher as a way of working against my ego and moving onto a spiritual path which I felt would finally extend to me a hope of getting somewhere that made sense to me in my life. Of course, I continued to drink and party. I was not, after all, going into a monastery. That was where Charlotte had just been thrown out of.

Well, a nunnery, to be precise. Charlotte, a year younger than I, had begun as a premed major at the University of Washington, but a spiritual crisis had led her to join a convent in Kansas. She was really a kind of Beat Catholic, like Jack Kerouac, and the sisters threw her out soon after for reading Bertrand Russell and Jean-Paul Sartre. She showed up back in Seattle on a freight train, and we met on the first day at work at Boeing.

Looking back, I see that in Charlotte I had found the one young woman in all America whom it would be most difficult for my parents to accept. Not merely a Christian, but a practicing Catholic, a *German Catholic,* a poor peasant farmer's daughter from a nowhere town in Idaho, a former would-be nun, now studying theology at a Jesuit university (Seattle University), a girl without social graces who loved Negro music and was terrified and thus rejecting of the demands of good society.

Her foreignness and unacceptability were attractive to me since I wanted a different life than the one in which I had been raised. Not just the Bronx, but my home life had been difficult for me. My family existed on a kind of San Andreas fault that kept moving. They had built their life on a fatal contradiction. To maintain their place as the landlord's children, they had to keep spending money. But to establish themselves permanently on that level, they had to invest every penny they had and borrow against and mortgage all they owned. Besides the mortgage on the building my grandfather had taken my father in on, there was also the unimaginably large debt on our half of the liquor store, which sucked our cash for ten years until my father had finally barely paid it, and then, after a couple months to catch his breath, he went into punishing debt again to buy out his partner. Thus there was continual insecurity about cash and the consequent fights and tensions, and then the final and fatal tragedy when, shortly after my father managed to pay off his second crushing debt and the store became fully his, Governor Rockefeller, to avoid a political embarrassment concerning payoffs for a liquor license, came out as a champion of the people and did away with the fixed pricing and the monopoly of liquor licenses, thereby wiping out in one day most of what my father had struggled over for more than twenty years, and sealing his sad fate. My father would fall over dead on the cash register shortly thereafter.

In *Growing up Bronx*, I portray the violent, more colorful side of my father's life. Earthquakes, riots, floods, hurricanes, these are the stuff of memory and good drama, and they naturally come to the fore in a memoir. This is not to say that the stories of my father's trying to run over people with his car or fiercely beating me up are not true. My father would undergo these outbursts, but about once a year. When they are selected and joined together in a narrative they create a memorable character, but I did not have space to record the many sober and good qualities my father showed much of the time. He was liked on the block and known as a man who kept his word; a hard worker, to say the least, and sober, he took very little for himself, preferring to invest every penny he could lay his hands on.

My mother was in a difficult position: her status as landlord's daughter drew forth much jealousy from the neighbors, as did the fact that she had married beneath her class. I see now that her status was shaky. Was she the pretty princess of the block, with her photo in the papers on the rail of a ship as "show-biz hopeful," or merely the daughter of an illiterate Polish baker with a husband who had gone only through the ninth grade? Added to this was the fact that my father seemed addicted to the excitement of stress, of living at 299 of a possible 300 stress points before he snapped, and when the stress slackened he would bet money he couldn't afford on ball games to move himself back to the edge.

This helped me greatly as a novelist, as my survival depended on reading my father's moods instantly. Was he at 295 points, or 299? Could I ask him for a dollar, or would that set him off and result in his attacking me? He couldn't attack my mother, not when they shared the same dream and his future depended on the goodwill of her father, who had taken him into the

real estate business. This resulted in my mother's tendency to explain her spending (which my father felt threatened his life, and my mother felt sustained the only thing worth living for) by pointing to my "needs," and when I would deny this, my father, if their fight had progressed far enough or if he had lost on a bet that day, would flail after me, beating me until I cried in pain and terror and then beating me for crying.

Yet I'm sure these traumatic memories were far less frequent than I recall. For the most part, my parents somehow managed to make it through some very difficult years for the world and for the Jews in particular. They never came close to divorcing, they sent two sons to expensive colleges and graduate schools, they were there for us in sickness, and they made a home where people felt welcome and enjoyed the jokes and music and life spirit. I am most grateful for their giving me the chance to get the kind of education I needed to feel secure enough to make something of myself in the larger world.

The author at his bar-mitzvah, standing between parents Eve and Sol Rosen, with brother, Mark, 1951

I have always feared debt and dreaded being tied to people who feel they must spend their way to an identity. This was one attraction of Charlotte. She never believed she could become middle-class; she had had that dream beaten out of her by the citizens of Lewiston when she was young and the daughter of "Hog Joe." She was defined as "bad," in contradistinction to her mathematician brother, Rod, eleven months older, the "good one," a nice guy whom she felt she could never compete with in the town or her family, so she became the "bad girl" and spent some time in a reformatory before becoming valedictorian of her high school and taking off for Seattle on her own to put herself through college.

I think *Mahatma Gandhi* gives a fair picture of that summer of 1961 in Seattle, but when I finished the manuscript, which was originally about six hundred pages long, I found it lacked conflict, so I had to make the relationship between the protagonists more stormy. Leslie is more unstable than Charlotte was at that time; as in *Growing up Bronx,* I invented and compressed incidents to bring out the dramatic value—for example, like Leslie, Charlotte once threatened to jump out of a moving car during an argument, but this occurred a couple of years later in Boston. To the degree I made Leslie unstable, I had to make her parents more intrusive to justify her volatility. I also enlarged Leslie's stature at times to make her a kind of beacon from where Danny might want to go. An example of this is in the scene where Leslie takes the boys to Seattle's Birdland, the all-night African American dance hall. In real life, we guys took Charlotte there.

The figures of both my roommates are also changed, especially Hal, whom I made into a kind of Jewish foil for Danny to heighten the conflict, to bring out Danny's values, and to clarify what was at stake for him from the traditional point of view.

When I returned to Wharton for my second year, I began to explore paths to a career other than business. I took courses with Peter Drucker and William Gomberg in social systems, reading Marx, Schumpeter, Veblen, etc., and a course in America in the twentieth century with Thomas Cochran. Professor Cochran was primarily a business historian. He taught the history of science and economic history as well as foreign policy and the arts. I loved the class; he provided me with a role model. Suddenly I

saw that my background in business and science could help me understand history if it was taught from the cultural point of view, and I decided to go back to Penn and enter the American Civilization Department. I would become a historian of American culture like Professor Cochran. Thus perhaps it wasn't too late to begin a career which would allow me to understand the world around me and, since I had been trained from birth to be an American, to also understand myself.

As I was reading the Beats in my spare time, and was also interested in Zen Buddhism as portrayed by D. T. Suzuki, Alan Watts, and Kerouac in his portrayal of Gary Snyder in *The Dharma Bums,* I was curious about finding out what (if anything) would be left when I subtracted my cultural conditioning from my "self."

But first there was the draft notice to deal with. I had mixed feelings about the army. I wouldn't have called them if they hadn't called me, but I did have a residue of patriotic feeling left from World War II, when I saw the American army as defending me against the Nazis, and I felt the army would be a step toward my manhood and my Americanization.

Because of my Wharton MBA, I could receive a direct commission as an officer in the Medics if I signed up for three years. This suited me fine. I would be helping people rather than shooting them, and I could save up my officer's pay to finance my Ph.D. studies when I returned to Penn.

Charlotte came east in March of 1962, and we were married. I did my two months' orientation at Fort Sam Houston in San Antonio, Texas, once again finding myself in the now-familiar position of being with people who had already studied most of the material, since I was one of the few officers who had not had ROTC. The recruiter had assured me that I would not really need much army training, as I would probably be in a management position in a large hospital. I might not even have to wear a uniform, he said.

Wrong! In six weeks I found myself alone at night in Texas rattlesnake country, trying to make my way home by compass, and at Fort Devens in Massachusetts I quickly became troop commander of the base hospital, leading 180 men in a parade somehow. Fortunately, I had been a Boy Scout in the Bronx for six months. I pretended I was our Scout leader and shouted orders to the men, some of whom had fought at the Battle of the

Bulge. This made more for comedy than tragedy, but the older soldiers were good-natured about it; somehow I was now their superior and could put them in jail.

Virtually all the soldiers lived on the base or in the nearby towns of Ayer and Shirley. We lived about a half-hour away in Fitchburg, an interesting old mill town with a French-Canadian quarter that resembled a little Montreal, including Italians, Finns with public saunas, etc. Charlotte had feared going to school with East Coast kids, but the professors at little Fitchburg State were delighted to have this West Coast wild girl with the unkempt look who wrote English papers about her search for the meaning of life.

The professors at the college had no contact with the soldiers, but one English professor, Louis Shepard, and his wife, Ruth, were very kind to us. Louis was a brilliant madman with twelve unpublished novels, a wide range of knowledge about world lit, and a house filled with books from floor to ceiling, along with records, paintings, and grotesque little "gargoyles" by the dozens he bought at Woolworth's. Raised in hotels by his mother, an actress, Louis had a theatrical quality that was new to me. He gave winter clothing to his poor students and jogged along the country roads always carrying a loaded pistol. He

As a bat boy at the Polo Grounds,
New York, 1956

had evenings at home for us and our friend Richard DeLisle in which he would show long movies he had made from his car, at random, as he drove around, while plying us with gallons of cheap wine and playing loud Wagner and excitedly shouting, "It's great! This is really great!" at the appearance of every new gas station on the little screen. Once I went with him to the liquor store and was surprised to hear the clerks call him "Father." When we left, he explained: "Somehow they got the idea that I'm a priest, and I never saw fit to disabuse them of that notion because now they give me a clerical discount."

Louis was a tremendous influence on me. I had never known any professors as friends, much less an artist like himself, and I was amazed that he was interested in me. Just as I was fascinated by him, he seemed to admire the fact that I knew advanced calculus and relativity and somehow I had gone to Wharton and was now an army commander interested in pursuing the liberal arts. He helped me to see myself as someone who might be an interesting person in his own right, even though I felt I had always taken the safe route of ambition and security.

Charlotte was very happy at Fitchburg State, but I began to sink into suicidal despair. I had not realized the army would take so much time. Besides long daily hours on the job, I also was Officer of the Day once every eleven days, which meant a stretch of thirty-four hours of straight work, or twenty-four extra hours over the weekend. I was attempting to prepare for my future studies by getting the equivalent of a B.A. on my own in the few hours I could find to read. I read in every spare moment I could find, relentlessly, starting with the ancient Egyptians and Greeks and studying large texts on the history of art, literature, religion, politics, architecture, and filling myself in on the history of American culture alongside this, while reading spiritual writers and Russian novelists to attempt to save my soul and keep from killing myself. Then I would get desperately drunk with Gus K., a big guy who lived in the funky flat above ours. Gus drove a huge Lincoln and ran errands for the mob.

The army broke my heart. I had had an idealistic view of America. Lincoln's calling it the world's last best hope made perfect sense to me. Since the Holocaust and war I had been searching for a reason to believe in people and had projected my beliefs onto "America." I had wanted to believe in the army, but now I had found it to be not so different from the Bronx, but without the Jewish irony and sense of humor.

I had ideals of bravery and honor associated with the army in my mind, but I had found it to be merely the world's second-largest bureaucracy, not so far from the Soviet Union which it resembled. There were the deadly plutonium particles of bureaucracy always floating about, killing any signs of independent life. There was little patriotism and less intelligent consciousness, coupling an unearned arrogance with the most powerful weapons known to mankind, weapons developed by people like me, engineers.

This was a combustible mixture that terrified me, yet I could think of no alternative for myself. I became depressed, but I still attempted to hold on to my American values and ideals. I did not realize that what I was sensing was the nascent mentality and preconditions of Vietnam.

I felt completely isolated on the base. I thought the world was controlled by unconscious violent people. Just when I had finally found a direction in life, I was being forced to spend my days in meaningless activity. I felt my spirit was dying just as I sensed a new vision beginning to open up to me. Something was very wrong with everything, and I had to find out what it was before I got killed, or worse, killed someone else for the wrong reason. As the Vietnam War began to heat up, these became more than theoretical questions, matters which I felt endangered not only my life but my eternal soul.

Yet I couldn't let go of America or of my normal straight life. I began to act in a crazy manner. One day I left the fort and drove to nearby Concord, where I lay on Thoreau's grave to seek an answer but found none and fortunately was not arrested. Finally I determined to kill myself. I went with Charlotte to her Catholic church for mass as one of my last acts on Earth but was astonished to find that, as Paul Tillich said, God is who appears when you reach the place where you are absolutely certain there is no God. I attempted to die there in the church, to stop my heart from beating, but I was unable to do so. There was something in me, something larger than what I normally thought of as "I," that refused to let me die. Some hard shell of resistance broke inside me; I began to weep, statues moved, and I felt that Jesus authorized me to take communion, which I did. I felt reborn, though not as a Christian. I knew I was

at the beginning of a long and difficult road, but that it was not going to be a dead end.

My last year in the army was much easier. I no longer felt it necessary to follow the advice of my wife and my pal Marty and love my fellow officers. Once I stopped being a saint and became a Bronx street guy again, the army proved to be easy to get around. For example, I quickly became postal officer, so I could lock myself in the PO and read everyone's magazines. Charlotte taught high school English for a year in Leominster, and we moved onto Fort Devens. I continued my frantic studying and broke the national curve on the graduate record exam, finishing thirty points above the ninety-ninth percentile on the business and economics portion.

Then a series of ironies ensued to my benefit. I won a three-year, full-tuition National Defense Fellowship, worth tens of thousands of dollars, which paid me a stipend to go to Penn. I had not applied for the fellowship. It was given to the American Civilization Department because they were attempting to develop a mathematical method of studying history, which it was thought might somehow be of use to the Defense Department. I, as an army officer with a background in higher mathematics, was exactly the candidate they were looking for. I didn't know any of this. All I knew was that I had won a great prize. They didn't know that I was going back to college because I had had it with both the Defense Department and with science and math and I was surrendering to the enemy——the liberal arts.

I went back to Penn in the summer of 1965. I had constructed a liberal university world in my mind which was exactly the opposite of the army. My friend Bruce Kuklick writes amusingly and accurately about my appearance there in his memoir *The Pro-Vietcong Youth Club,* in which he shows me arriving, to the amazement of the students already there, expecting to find a kind of Platonic Academy where I would study great ideas at the feet of wise men and women. I was quickly disabused of this notion when I went with great anticipation to my first lecture by the dean of American literary historians, Robert Spiller, whose work I had been studying in the army. Professor Spiller immediately counted each of the 120 students present and found that he had only 119 IBM cards. I had not realized I had to bring mine. He asked me to leave. I explained my situation, but he wouldn't budge. I told him I had been studying for three years in the army for this opportunity and that everyone there knew me from other classes. He told me I had to leave. I refused. He refused to begin the class. Neither of us would yield. It looked like the police might have to be called. Finally the students in the back began to shout at him and he was forced to give in. This was what his reading of all twenty-eight novels by James Fenimore Cooper had led to.

My ideals were shattered, but I learned an enormous amount at Penn. I disagreed with Murray Murphey, who was in search of an objective method of history, but I learned from his brilliance, and from the passion of James Flink, and ultimately from the wide knowledge of Professor Spiller as well. I studied with Thomas Cochran, a great historian, and my aim was still to become a professor of history. Although I loved the literature classes taught by Neil Leonard and Robert Lucid, I felt it was already a stretch to attempt a history emphasis, relying upon my knowledge of science and economics to get me through. I didn't even consider a lit major. For my M.A. thesis I did original work on Frederick Winslow Taylor, the father of scientific management and the first efficiency expert. I was fascinated at the way he carried his ideas to mad extremes, even inventing, at the turn of the century, a more efficient tennis racket. This seemed completely crazy to me, but now it turns out he was simply ahead of his time.

My friends there included Bruce and Riki Kuklick, now both professors at Penn. The Kuklicks took me in hand, inviting me to their parties and generally looking out for me in the university. They were far ahead of me politically and introduced me to a politically radical group of students which included their friend Russ Stetler, who later became Bertrand Russell's secretary and a leading figure in the antiwar movement.

I was still supporting the war reluctantly because I did not like the bureaucracy and lack of freedom under communism; I thought of the United States as the better of two evils, much to the Kuklicks' dismay. Then Charlotte's brother Rod, a navy fighter pilot on the aircraft carrier *Independence,* was shot down and everything changed. Suddenly Rod, a nice guy whose position on the war had been much like mine, hesitantly trying to do his duty, was an MIA. (He still is.) This tore our family apart.

Charlotte and I began to attend teach-ins and to study the background of the war, to oppose it, and to try to bring Rod home, while her parents turned to the right, to "uphold the principles he had fought for."

Opposing the war was not easy if you were honest with yourself. There was a domino theory people spoke of which said if we didn't stop "them" in Vietnam we would have to stop them in San Francisco. This never made any sense to me since North Vietnam had no navy. I found it hard to imagine thousands of Vietnamese showing up under the Golden Gate Bridge, paddling in inner tubes with rifle straps in their mouths. But there was a certain ironic truth to the domino image—once your own support of the war collapsed, every other belief you had in the society and its institutions fell as well.

Somehow I had always been confused about the war. It seemed out of focus—I could never quite make sense of the data coming in, until I reversed my hypothesis and turned against the war. Suddenly everything made sense, and I let go of my old American values, or at least I attempted to save what I saw as the old American values. I had never been a moral relativist. Call me old-fashioned, but I did and still do believe it is wrong to be a Nazi. Now the American people were threatening to move into that same "Not-see" position I had opposed all my life.

Of course, the antiwar movement appealed to my hatred of authority and to my artistic imagination. At the first demonstration I went to at Independence Hall, on July 4, 1966, a young man chained himself to the Liberty Bell. This was such a beautiful symbolic act, and the police (i.e., my old nemesis, the "army" mentality) were so baffled about how to deal with this, they were frozen in place; I cheered until tears came into my eyes. These were my people. This was my kind of protest.

The American Civilization Department was conservative politically, but history professor Gabriel Kolko was a big influence on Bruce Kuklick and myself at this point. He taught us American foreign policy and the longtime connections between U.S. corporations and the government. I remember once, before a large planned demonstration, he advised the students against chaining the doors and locking the professors outside the building. He told the students to lock them *inside* the building.

Nonetheless, my principal energies at Penn were spent studying, and I had little time for anything else from 1965 through early 1967.

Serving as company commander, Fort Devens, Massachusetts, 1963

Charlotte had given up teaching after she volunteered to work in the Head Start Program, teaching preschoolers in the poorest black neighborhood in Philadelphia, and ran into trouble with the welfare mothers who complained that her clothes weren't neat enough. She began to work as a secretary in a mental hospital.

In January 1967 I learned that my father had been found dead in his liquor store. My mother planned to close the store, as it wasn't really worth anything, but I realized it was providing support to three Puerto Rican families and it might continue to do so, and help out my mother and myself as well, if I let the employees run it under my distant supervision. This idea worked. I came to Manhattan every weekend from Philadelphia to supervise the store and do the accounts; in the summer of 1967, when I had finished my class work, we moved to Greenwich Village, where I began the four crazy and wonderful years during which I wrote the Ph.D. dissertation for Penn, actively rioted against the war, ran a liquor store on the edge of Harlem, wrote *Blues for a Dying Nation,* and took advan-

tage of the education Manhattan offered at that time in foreign movies, music, museums, theater, street politics, etc.

Knowing nothing about academic politics and career tracks, I decided to write my dissertation in literature, although virtually all my classes had been in history. I came to feel that I would rather teach Herman Melville than Grover Cleveland. Working with Dr. Neil Leonard, a jazz historian as well as literary scholar, I wrote on black humor in the American novel, with emphasis on the works of James Purdy. I stressed the connections between the anti-liberal, anti-"white" (i.e., respectable "New Yorker") humor stance of the black humor novelists I loved, and the new left, which was also beyond trying to appease the middle-class liberals who had begun to look like conservatives with better PR men. Like the new left, black humor was consciously in bad taste and thus called into question the notion of good taste and who determines it. Pynchon, B. J. Friedman, Heller, Southern, and especially Purdy were my subjects.

During the writing, I got to know James Purdy, who lived in Brooklyn. He had someone interview me before he would grant rare permission to quote from his works, but then we became friendly, and though I only met him a couple of times, he called me often and wrote me excruciatingly funny letters about the decadence of the literary scene. I recall him saying to me once in his small, nasal, Ohio twangy voice, "Jerry, when you really start burning things down, tell your friends not to worry about the *New York Times.* I'll take care of that."

In the dissertation, which I finished in 1969, I also began to consider the connections between comic detachment and Buddhist nonattachment. I spoke about this later when I appeared at my first writers' conference, in Marin County in 1971, and met Gary Snyder and Allen Ginsberg. The first words Gary said to me were, "So you're the comic Buddhist I've been hearing about."

I had planned to teach when I finished with school, but life was very exciting, the liquor store was functioning, and I was learning so much every day in the Village that I decided to take a year for myself and write a novel. I had never really written anything like this before, never been published, never sent out a story or poem or taken a writing class or even really been an English major. But I had come to believe that I had something I needed to say.

The Ivy League dissertation had taught me a great deal, but it was a form that said, "I'm a tank. Fly me!" I was boiling with emotions I could barely contain. I never expected to get the book published, but I wanted, for once in my life, to follow my heart, to take the one leg I had always kept in the system and plant it outside. The good-boy, fast-track high achiever, who had made it through schools, universities, and the army, was cracking, and a new Jerry was trying to break out and be born. I didn't want to reach a cul-de-sac, like my hardworking, "good" father did.

I sat down in the fall of 1969 and decided: "These pages are mine. For once in my life I will try to please no one but myself, and I will say exactly what I feel, even if I have to trash my public persona in the process." Six weeks later, I rose from the desk with the first five-hundred-page draft of *Blues for a Dying Nation* completed.

After collapsing with exhaustion and flu for two weeks, I rewrote the book in eight weeks. During this period the Kuklicks introduced me to their friend Elizabeth Long. She worked for Knopf and asked if she might take a look at it when I finished. I knew no one in publishing, so I was delighted to give her the manuscript, although I was not sure how one packaged the pages. I bought a metal file box and laid the pages in it. They swooned and sagged into the lower corner like a fish, but I knew of no alternative.

A couple months later, I received a call from Robert Gottlieb, the editor in chief of Knopf, the future editor of the *New Yorker,* and possibly the most powerful person in publishing in the world. He told me he liked the book and that Joe had it. "Joe?" I said. "Yes, Joe Heller. He likes it too. Can you come up and see me?"

My first dilemma as a writer was whether I should call Joseph Heller "Joe." Heller was one of my idols. In the army, when I had thought I was crazy because it seemed to me that all the twelve thousand other people on the base were crazy, I read *Catch-22* and found the "friend" I had been looking for. I realized that everyone else *was* crazy. In *Blues,* I wrote that one person who thinks differently is crazy. Two people who think differently are the beginning of a counter-culture.

Because of my own experiences as a reader, I have always seen the novel as a life-rope thrown to a sinking person. I have never been ashamed of the fact that I write books to try to do what I can to change the world, raise consciousness, and help people. Of course, the best way to do this is to do a good job, to focus on the craft.

As I had no riots scheduled that week, I went up to Gottlieb's office, which was larger than our entire apartment (sixty-five dollars a month, with the shower in the kitchen, on Grove Street). Robert Gottlieb was very bright and honest, but he wanted me to reorganize the novel. To make it into "a real novel." My question was, "Who determines what a novel is?" He said he would not publish the book in its present form, but he could think of several editors who would. I realized what I was sacrificing by giving up a chance to work with such a gifted and important editor, and with a possible endorsement from Joseph Heller, but I could no longer compromise. I walked out of the office determined to find one of the editors who he had said would publish the book as I had written it.

It didn't take long. A young editor at Dial Press, Karen Kennerly (now executive director of PEN), said to me, "Let's do it. Let's leave it the way it is and get even crazier." Karen lived in Miles Davis's house, and we worked on the book there. Miles, Joe Heller, these had been my idols. I had passed through the looking glass into another world, one from which I could never return.

One trail that led to *Blues* began at the attack on the Pentagon in October of 1967. I had never been much of a joiner. I saw clubs as things they hit you with. I went to the Pentagon by myself. I had become accustomed to a state of living in which I had lots of friends but felt alienated at the core. But that day changed my life. This was really the first major East Coast protest. I had expected a couple thousand demonstrators at most, but when I saw sixty thousand young people with the courage to face paratroopers with M16s and bayonets, I realized that a dream that I had given up on was suddenly coming true. I was no longer alienated.

I marched with the writers. I had not written anything myself, but somehow I felt at home there. Norman Mailer had spoken out bravely against the war and made himself a possible target when we encountered the opposition on the Virginia side of the Potomac. The American Nazis were located in Virginia, and I wanted to be beside him to fight in case he was attacked. As it turned out, the march itself was peaceful and Mailer was quickly arrested at the Pentagon itself. I joined

Ed Sanders and the East Village hippies to "levitate the Pentagon." We danced around and chanted, and I was on national TV wearing my army fatigue shirt and hat and carrying a skull on a pole that I had bought in New York at a Halloween display.

The paratroopers were stationed at the top of the steps of the Pentagon with rifles and bayonets pointed down at us. Choppers flew overhead, and sharpshooters were stationed on the roof. I walked up to the troops and realized I could not be afraid of them, as I had recently been commanding troops just like them. The silver bar on my cap protected me like an amulet.

I was proud of the students, especially the women, who were not just making coffee but were on the front lines with the guys, in a life-threatening situation, although it was the guys whose bodies were really on the line in the draft. I felt I understood the situation very well, having been on both sides of the conflict, and it astonished me that some of the students actually believed that we might get into the Pentagon and destroy computers. There was even a debate right on the steps about whether to charge the troops. I took the bullhorn and shouted, frantically, "Do you think this is a college football rally? We're here because these people are murderers. This is the Mafia. They'll kill you. If you want to charge, go home and get guns. Haven't you seen the Odessa steps in Eisenstein's *Potemkin?* Don't charge *up* steps!"

I saw, at that moment, that the government would eventually shoot down innocent students. This was where the theme of games versus reality in *Blues* came from. One of my favorite sentences in the book is "When the gun goes off, the game is over." That is, the difference between games and reality is the presence of death. One of the reasons I wrote *Blues* was to warn the students, but by the time it was published the Kent State and Jackson State shootings had already occurred. I was outraged when I heard the news, but not surprised. I quickly made speeches against the war at New York University and Columbia, and then ended the day in a comic-tragedy when I retreated to the Medieval Art room at the Metropolitan Museum and was escorted out by the police.

The primary emotion in *Blues* is rage. Hence the outrageous tenor of the humor. I even insult the reader at the conclusion of the book. At the time, I said that I wished I could actually throw the book at the reader. *Blues* is written

in the collage form. I was influenced in this by Dos Passos and Brecht. I feared that TV had rendered the novel impotent. Thus I set the book in the form of a televised football game with quarters instead of chapters, as if to co-opt some of TV's power and influence. The novel had commercials, but for the government, which is the way I see the evening news. Following the early collage artists like Picasso and Bracque, I actually pasted newspaper articles into the text from the *New York Times.* Just as you are about to say that an event in the book couldn't happen in reality, I stick in a clipping that is even crazier, thus jarring your sense that you know what is real and imaginary.

I wanted the book to reach out to the world, not to be powerlessly isolated. The sixties were a time when all the lines and boundaries and binary opposites that make a culture, that tell us what is true, real, and good, had to be attacked. Thus in theater the artificial boundary of the proscenium arch was violated by having actors go into the audience and begin to remove the spectators' clothes. This kind of theater was not merely a safe place for doctors and lawyers to sleep of an evening. But how to bring this vitality to the novel?

The collage form reached out of its element both by being in a third dimension (actually physically reaching out of the frame) and by using newspapers, i.e., content from outside the imaginary realm. I chose newspaper filler pieces on the grounds that the real disintegration of the culture was pictured there, while the drama of the world leaders on the front page was a kind of mythology to portray the culture as still functioning coherently. I chose pieces whose content resonated with the themes of the novel.

I also interrupted the narrative for "camera angles," with each camera signifying a different tense—close-ups for present tense, etc. One device I invented was not noticed by anyone but it worked. Namely, I timed the interruptions to the text so that the reader's experience in reading would parallel the narrator's experiences in the book. For example, about two-thirds of the way through the book, as the narrator becomes overwhelmed by the amount of new information he has to process, the interruptions to the text come more quickly, so the reader too is being assaulted rapidly from all sides with more incoherent information than he can digest. As the narrator struggles to keep from becoming involved in the action, the reader finds it difficult to get involved

Eve Rosen and Charlie Rosenberg's wedding, 1970: (left to right) brother, Mark Rosen;
Duane and Rozi Dobbs; the bride and groom; the author's first wife, Charlotte;
Mark's wife, Lucy Blau Rosen; and the author.

in the story because the text is continually being interrupted and fragmented and thus pushes him out.

Many readers said they became deeply involved in the story at the end, when the narrator becomes involved in the revolution; they didn't notice, however, that at that point in the text, exactly when I ask the reader to become involved himself by finding an absurd newspaper article and pasting it into the blank page provided in the book, the interruptions to the text cease. This has the effect of a play in which the curtain suddenly stops being closed and opened and the viewer's frustrated urge to suspend disbelief and become involved is given free rein.

The story itself was based on the radical saying that the bombs we dropped in Vietnam exploded in the United States. It seemed to me that the Vietnam War was destroying an entire country—ours. So it seemed sensible to explore why our leaders might want to destroy our country. In the novel, a senile general, who believes we are still fighting the Japanese in World War II, runs a base in Massachusetts. (I only recently noticed that my own holding of World War II values in 1965 was unconsciously parodied here.) Control of the base is seized by the commander of the hospital, who bombs the surrounding area, believing it has been infiltrated by Communists. He then provides the many casualties with the best medical care. Everyone accepts this except the young people who dress up as American Indians and attack the fort. (I was referring here to my own view of Vietnam as the last of the American Indian wars.) The young people are slaughtered mercilessly by the army troops led by the physician commander.

Much of the absurd humor of the book was based on true events. The doctors and the surgeons at Fort Devens Hospital did quarrel bitterly over the green versus the red identity pins. (Both sides wanted the red.) And the hospital *was* run by the colonel's elderly mother, but from the ward, not from his bathroom, as I had it in the book.

In 1970 my mother married Charlie Rosenberg. In April of 1971, they decided to take back the liquor store from me. I had been running it "with my left hand," as Gurdieff puts it, but I had kept it open for four years, making a steady profit for all concerned. I got along with the customers. I gave the employees responsibility, and they responded to my trust. They knew that whenever they were jailed or incarcerated in the mental ward at Bellevue, they would have a job waiting when they were released.

One point of friction arose around the matter of their having a gun in the store, which I would not permit, but this finally resolved itself in a forced compromise when we all realized I could not stop them from bringing bayonets to work.

My parents decided to run the store in a more businesslike manner. In a year the store was bankrupt. By then, I was in northern California. I had been ready to leave New York in any case. In fact, I was ready to leave the entire culture. Nixon was president. The war continued with no end in sight. The Ivy League professors whom I had imagined as the antithesis of the army were now running the army.

One possible way out of the culture for many writers at the time was to experiment with LSD, which seemed to block the cultural learning part of one's brain. Because I had already had a religious experience, I looked with some amusement on the idea of "God for a dime" from a pill. Nonetheless, I felt it a moral duty in a time of cultural collapse for writers to go to the frontier, so I tried it, and to my surprise, in one hour, I was right back in the same magical, sacred space I had entered in Massachusetts, and in another hour I entered realms which I had never dreamed possible.

I had expected a light show, but LSD is much more powerful than one might imagine—there is a reason why people take it twice, although it is difficult to imagine this if one reads the popular accounts of bad trips, etc. The history of wars is written by the victors. It wasn't the Aztecs who told us the story of the Spanish Catholic conquest of Mexico. But LSD is, in fact, an artificial version of the sacrament of many cultures' religions (e.g., the Huichols in Mexico), and I think anyone who believes in postmodern tolerance and multiculturalism has a duty to respect this. These American Indians were not fools.

The true power of LSD lies in making you believe that what we call reality is actually a dream and the LSD vision is real. All this might seem impossible, but then, so did the results of the Michelson-Morley experiment which led to relativity seem incredible (to everyone but Einstein). With all adult authority collapsed, it was hard to find any grounds to resist these visions of eternal love and spiritual hope without appealing to the traditional culture which had turned murderous and which we had vowed to escape.

All this was very disorienting, to say the least. Western religion was not much help, especially at a time when one could view the war in Vietnam as Catholics attacking Buddhists. But Eastern religions spoke exactly to this puzzling experience. The world was *maya*—the veil of illusion. I became an unaffiliated Hindu/Buddhist in the manner of Aldous Huxley. I now understood what the great Chinese sage Chuang Tsu was referring to when he said, "How do I know whether I am Chuang Tsu who dreamt he was a butterfly last night, or a butterfly now dreaming he is Chuang Tsu?"

But it was time to really leave. "Back to the country." In April 1971, we moved in with our friends Jim Saunt and Paulette Perone, who lived in Marin County, just north of San Francisco, with their three-year-old son, Claudio, and their huge German shepherd, Bela Bartok. Jim's sister Hani, formerly a nice Jewish girl from Shaker Heights, Ohio, was now a popular teacher in San Francisco's Latino Mission District. She traveled with a bodyguard of Brown Berets, and they often camped in our backyard. Paulette's twenty-year-old brother, Rocco Perone, lived up the street in a garage with his girlfriend Thais from Chicago. Their landlord's daughter lived above them in a geodesic dome in a tree. Paulette's youngest brother, Perry Perone, who was sixteen, showed up and moved in with Claudio. He became a follower of Sri Chinmoy and wore a large white turban. He then moved into a Hindu commune in San Francisco and became a cook in Carlos Santana's vegetarian restaurant.

Our next-door neighbor, who lived on fruits and nuts, returned from a two-month vigil in the desert and threw a two-week party for all the residents of the town of Fairfax, whether clothed or unclothed, living in a house or in the town park, but on the sixth day the party came to an end when two purses were stolen and our neighbor burned his sauna down. Life at our communal house seemed like a continuing party that

"Escape to California," Marin County, 1971

glowed and then flared up from time to time but was never actually extinguished. Charlotte and I found that we needed solitude as well as fellowship, so after I took a part-time teaching job at Sonoma State University, we moved up to Sonoma County in October, renting a tiny shack in an old African American farming community on a large plain west of Santa Rosa.

Sonoma State University was a kind of "Berkeley North" at this time, located in the area of the big hippy communes. On the day I interviewed for my job, four bands were playing on the campus. I loved going to work each day. You never knew what might occur. On one occasion a student, Brant Secunda, who had gone off to study with the Huichols in the Mexican mountains, showed up at my office so I could meet his new teacher. Don José was 102 years old. He was about four feet tall, with a withered arm. He wore the handmade Huichol clothing and was traveling around California with this young American, sleeping on people's floors. He had no English, but his smile spoke volumes.

I was staying away from political action, as it was making me sick, but when the United States invaded Cambodia, I couldn't resist driving down to Berkeley and helping to chop up with axes the parking lot which had covered People's Park.

In June of 1972, Charlotte and I bought a little old house in the apple orchards of nearby Sebastopol, where we lived across the street from my good friends poet David Bromige and novelist Sherril Jaffe. For twenty-two years, David and I ran the small but highly regarded and successful creative writing program in the English Department at Sonoma State, where I chose to be a part-timer for the first fourteen years, turning down offers of a possible tenure-track position. I learned much from David about language, literature, and London.

In the fall, Charlotte and I adopted a baby, Jesse, who now is twenty-five years old and lives with his wife, Kari, and daughter, Hannah, in Ohio, where he makes welded iron furniture.

Blues for a Dying Nation, published in February 1972, was a controversial and well-received book. It was given a full-page review in the *New York Times,* which called it "an honorable attempt at the Great American Novel." I was very proud of this since no one I had known growing up had read the *Times,* as it has little gossip, few pictures, and no comics. My parents were proud but not happy that my picture showed me with uncut hair and an Indian headband. The *Milwaukee Journal* said it was the best novel of its kind in several years, and it was cited in six major newspapers as one of the ten best books of the year.

This was a difficult time for me, as the sixties were clearly coming to an end and McGovern's decisive defeat in 1972 made it harder to deny this. How were we to come down and reenter the culture? I was teaching extra classes to fill in for a professor who died and thus I was teaching courses I had never taken and had to stay a day ahead of the students. At the same time, I was working on a novel which was the product of my desperation. Called *Farouk University,* this novel told the story of a brother and sister in despair with the culture who follow a swami who claims to be fake and who establishes a fake university. The protagonists want to go beneath their cultural conditioning, so they move into their own world of LSD and incest. The book insulted the publishing world and academia, and it could not be published in that time of retreat.

The sixties floated many people who would have drowned earlier. The path back was difficult for many, easier for some. Charlotte and I and Jesse moved to San Francisco. Rocco Perone, whose beautiful soul shone through his guitar playing, turned to heroin for a while and then drank himself to death. Hani Saunt moved to Israel and started a family. Perry Perone gave up his turban for a Harvard/Berkeley Ph.D. in economics and is now an official of the International Monetary Fund. My good friend Paulette married a musician who played in a band for a singer named Vice-Grip who slept in a coffin. Fifteen years later, she married Shep Pollack, former president of Philip Morris, and became a painter and honored patron of the arts. Little Claudio took degrees in history from Columbia, Oxford, and Duke and now teaches at Columbia.

Charlotte and I broke up in 1975. The parameters of marriage in the sixties were ambiguous. What was the place of fidelity and sobriety in a world in which the Blakean view prevailed? The equation had seemed clear: repression equaled unconsciousness and aggression. But what did an unrepressed marriage mean?

Charlotte married Jim Saunt, and they took Jesse back with them to Jim's hometown of Cleveland. She converted to Conservative Judaism. I wound up in a roach-infested flat in San Francisco, wondering how I was to proceed now that I had no publisher, no security in my part-time job, and no family. I began to date the wrong kind of women for me—the Bad and the Beautiful. One day my current date, a bright poet, soon to be the successful author of erotic grammar books, ran off and married a rich guy who wrote jokes for the *Hollywood Squares* TV show. I decided to change my life. I knew how to die—I had lived for years with the knowledge of the impermanence of our life here on Earth always at the front of my mind. But I had not paid much attention to how to earn a living. What had happened to the side of me that had earned a Wharton MBA? I cut off my hair, which I hadn't clipped for eight years, and went off to buy a piece of cheese, vowing to find a nice woman who was right for me—the Good and the Beautiful.

At the cheese store, a Dutch woman behind the counter turned to me and said, "Yes?" and as I looked into her bright, honest, vibrant eyes, I thought, "Oh, there she is." This was Marijke Wittkampf. We have been together for twenty-one years. (We were married in 1981.)

But before I met Marijke, in 1975, when I was living by myself in the roach motel, I was feeling very low. It seemed to me that I had lost everything in my life. One day I sat on the floor in the Buddha pose, and I said, "What would the Buddha say about this?" Immediately the answer appeared: "If you have nothing, at least you will have nothing to keep you from seeing clearly." I knew it was time to write another book.

I wrote *The Carmen Miranda Memorial Flagpole* from the point of view of an accountant, a Sancho Panza who has a wild Don Quixote novelist brother with high ideals and no grounding. *Carmen* exists at the node where the Jewish novel, the Beat novel, and the sixties anti-novel conjoin. It is a kind of Jewish-comic *On the Road* as written by Miguel de Cervantes. It was difficult to move the wisecracking Jewish tone into the sixties, as it seems more at home in the fifties, but I wanted a novel that came at you immediately on every page, BAM BAM BAM, like rock music, not a traditional novel which builds slowly in the manner of "classical music," so I wrote a tragedy composed of one-line jokes.

After I had published *Blues,* I noticed that people would come up to me and talk obliquely, slightly off the mark. I finally realized they were talking to the hero of my novel. (It was as if people were confusing me with an identical twin. I interviewed twins and found that I had an understanding of what their lives were like.) Americans generally find it difficult to believe that novels exist in the realm of the imagination and one doesn't simply write one's autobiography and call the book a novel to avoid getting sued.

This distinction was especially important in the sixties, when our overall aim was to point out that not only novels but all forms of the culture, even "reality" itself, were products of the collective imagination and thus capable of being reimagined. Karl Marx had warned us that people in power would attempt to confuse the social with the natural, making the world seem given and unchangeable rather than constructed by people. Novelists were certainly required to be in the forefront of this battle to control the cultural story. One had to reveal the arbitrary nature of the culture's concepts and assumptions, or the battle was lost before it was begun.

So I decided to attack these assumptions. I wrote about twins. An accountant and a novelist. But I allowed the accountant to tell the story. I gave my own name, Jerry Rosen, to him rather than to the writer. "Now, dear reader, figure out who is 'really' me," I thought.

I went further. I had an imaginary shrink write an introduction to the book declaring that I was a novelist who had come to believe that I was an accountant. I let Jerry Rosen counter this by saying that he, the accountant, had made up the shrink as a joke and the shrink didn't exist. The shrink objected, of course. (This had repercussions later in Cleveland during my national TV tour when one station hesitated to have me on, thinking I was an escaped mental patient.)

There was a debate in fiction writing at the time, which paralleled the debate in painting one hundred years before, about painting the real world or freeing painting from the "real." The French New Novel, in its attempts to abandon character and psychology, and the novels of the Fiction Collective, with their use of self-reflective and self-reflexive techniques, were often interesting but only in a very intellectual way, like fleshed-out ideas. In *Carmen and Dr. Ebenezer's Book and Liquor Store,* which followed, I tried to point to the artificiality of the novel, to foreground the author, and to make fun of the conventions of the novel, while still creating characters that the reader could identify with and feel deeply for.

I thought that if an electron could be both a particle and a wave, which by definition are mutually exclusive, why couldn't a novel be self-reflexive and deeply moving at the same time? Like Cézanne, whose paintings rise to the surface and point to their two-dimensionality and abstraction and yet are deeply moving and beautiful. As the Italian critic Franco Minganti said about my novels, "they have a depth of surface."

The public and critics quickly responded to *Carmen.* The *New York Times* placed it at the top of its "new and recommended" list and wrote, "Gerald Rosen has written a terrific book . . . a book which is deeply rooted in American popular culture, a book that reveals a remarkably acute understanding of both New York and California, a book that is both hilarious and devastating . . . an exceptional novel." The *Berkeley Barb* wrote, "Rosen is the happy blend of Tom Robbins, Joseph Heller, Mark Twain and Ken Kesey . . . a master of comedy." The novel was selected by the Quality Paperback Book Club and optioned for the movies by two Academy Award–nominated filmmakers who planned to do it for Francis Ford Coppola's Zoetrope Studio, which unfortunately ran into financial problems before the screenplay they wrote could be filmed. The Avon paperback edition brought the book to audiences around the world.

Carmen mirrors the path of the sixties in that it tells the story of two brothers who come to California with high ideals and jokes and have a great time until suddenly the wave moves out and they're left lying stunned amidst the wreckage on the beach. *Dr. Ebenezer* is a companion to *Carmen.* I wanted to write a novel with a happy ending. This is difficult to do because to avoid sentimentality you must earn the ending by first showing that you understand the cost of living in the world.

Dr. Ebenezer is a nuclear physicist who drops out and opens a book and liquor store in San Francisco's Mission District. He calls them knowledge and compassion. He says that if you separate these two qualities, you end up at Hiroshima. His guilt feelings lead him to an attraction to Japanese culture. This allowed me to express my own love of Japanese Zen Buddhist parables and *koans* and my affection for the films of Yasujiro Ozo, etc.

The book is a love story. He meets Wendy Oshima, a Japanese American. Her father, scarred by the American internment camps, has tried to turn her against America, but she rebels against his wishes and tries to be as American as possible, though, of course, she is still very Japanese in spite of herself. This makes her meeting with Dr. Ebenezer doubly ironical but filled with love.

For many people, this book is their favorite among my works, but 1980 was not a good time to publish a book about the sixties, and the novel was not printed in paperback, so it is my beloved stepchild that never was afforded its proper chance. The characters here also talk in one-line jokes, a device that brings the novel to the surface and points to its artificiality but allowed me to experiment in delineating the characters by the kind of jokes they tell. Jokes tend to be for and against something. Thus, if Treena says Ezra Pound was like a cracked bell, this little one-liner reveals her intellectuality and her knowledge of poetry, comments on both Pound's madness and his powers to sing as a poet, and, because of Pound's fascism, tells us that Treena is the kind of person who puts aesthetics before ethics. Also, like a metaphor, it brings to mind an image of the Liberty Bell and thereby comments on Pound's rebellious American roots, all in a single, casually tossed-off little one-liner that helps to explain Treena's attractiveness to intelligent men.

The *San Francisco Bay Guardian* called me a "poet of the one-liner" after this book, an honorific which I accepted with pride. In a way, *Dr. Ebenezer* is a kind of sitcom in which the characters joke about the Buddha, Freud, Jung, Darwin, Marx, Einstein, and Heisenberg. Jerome Klinkowitz (perhaps the best American critic of his generation) wrote, "I am now convinced more than ever that Gerald Rosen is one of the few original talents to have emerged from the American 1970s." *Dr. Ebenezer* was optioned by Phil Catalfo of New Dimensions Radio Network for a possible weekly nationwide series on National Public Radio, to be directed by David Ossman of the Firesign Theater; three shows were made, but the series was never funded as such. New Dimensions has 250 stations, and I have served as a kind of "novelist in residence" for them, appearing from time to time for an hour to talk about my work and about creativity (with Gabrielle Rico), and they tell me the tapes of these shows, which they sell, have been quite well received.

In 1984 I wrote a story called "Cause and Effect" which won the Cecil M. Hackney Award— First Prize—National Short Story. This story is about a novelist trying to figure out how to write a Buddhist story in which cause does not necessarily lead to effect—that is, there is always some freedom of response to one's situation. The story itself attempts to solve this by showing the novelist on a terrible day in which everything goes wrong. He finally winds up alone in bed in the silence and darkness of a citywide power failure, and yet he finds that he feels wonderful.

Another work I wrote from a Buddhist angle was *Zen in the Art of J. D. Salinger*, my only nonfiction book. Mary Lou and Barry Gifford are among my closest friends; when Barry was editor for Creative Arts Books in Berkeley, he asked me to extend a scholarly article I wrote for *American Quarterly* into a book on Salinger. The article was a seminal essay, "*The Catcher in the Rye* after Twenty-five Years," the first detailed and knowledgeable analysis of Eastern thought in Salinger's work. It opened up a new field of scholarly study and has since been included in several anthologies, including one in a series edited by Harold Bloom of Yale. The book was very well received; it sold out two printings, and today, twenty years later, it is still considered by many to be the best introduction to Salinger's work.

In 1984 I published (with North Atlantic Books, a great American independent publisher run by Richard Grossinger and Lindy Hough) my fourth novel, *Growing up Bronx* ("a humorous and touching novel," said the *New York Times*). North Atlan-

Charlotte and Gerald Rosen's son, Jesse, in Schiedam, South Holland, Netherlands, 1989

Rosen with second wife, Marijke Wittkampf, and Italian critic Franco Minganti,
Ravenna, Northern Italy, 1984

tic followed this with a sequel, *Mahatma Gandhi in a Cadillac* (nominated for the America Award in Literature—Best American Novel of 1995). In the late seventies, some of the anti-novelists were making extreme statements like, "Time and space, causality, and the self, do not exist." I noticed that they never said that the National Endowment for the Arts didn't exist, as it was supporting their musings. But seriously, I felt that this was mere intellectualizing, not grounded in existential truth, for if this were true for them, they could take LSD without any effect and they could not write such excellent grant applications. I had lived in a realm in which these ultimate truths were real, but I knew that now we were back in the world of the culture, which, though impermanent and ultimately to be revealed as an illusion, was for the time being real enough to cause pain and suffering. So I determined to go back to the culture in my writing as well as in my life and to try to speak in as simple a manner as possible about the path of my life here on Earth. The Belgian critic Paul Thiher, in his book on

postmodern narrative, wrote that when I returned to "reality" the anti-novelists quickly followed.

Among my books, *Growing up Bronx* was the one which the greatest percentage of people could read and identify with and enjoy. Besides the story of failure in America, a kind of reverse Horatio Alger story, it was also about transcending the search for a father. *Mahatma Gandhi in a Cadillac* tells the story of two young people in 1961 who are trying to find a path with meaning in a materialistic society. When I went to RPI, besides a career I was also looking for the truth, and this book traces the beginning of my sense that ultimately science was just another narrative, and thus, for me, the path with the most integrity would involve writing fiction, a medium in which one admits at the start that he is writing his own narrative and makes no claims on generally applicable objective reality.

I have been very fortunate over the past twenty-one years to have shared my path with a wise person, my partner Marijke. To my own spacey, idealistic, often intellectualized consciousness, Marijke has brought a Dutch common sense which does not sacrifice the spiritual sense of things but keeps it grounded in the reality of the everyday suffering world. (Someone has to watch the dikes.) When she studied with the late Chogyam Trungpa, he gave her a Tibetan name, "Star Lake of Liberation," and that is certainly what she has been to me. Marijke is a psychiatric nurse, and she knows that people go crazy on holidays and weekends. Thus she has missed many social gatherings and events but quietly goes about her business, bringing sanity into a vexatious environment at a difficult time for the healing professions. She has also brought me the joy of good Dutch friends, a large and generous extended family in Holland, and a country to root for in the World Cup. (Aanvallen Oranje!)

In the last ten years, it has been my pleasure to see my work accepted in Europe, where four university dissertations have been written about my books. In particular, the group of students and scholars around the noted Italian critic Professor Franco La Polla at the University of Bologna have been supportive and understanding about my work. I have published work in quarterlies in Ravenna, Florence, and Rome and have gone to Europe several times to speak about my path as a writer, lecturing at universities in Bologna, Lisbon, Amsterdam, Nijmegen, and Groningen. My work is taught at the Sorbonne and universities in Eastern Europe, and I have written two essays about the Beats, one for the Beat generation festival in the city of Cessana, Italy (1994), and the other, a major essay commissioned by the Venice Film Festival in 1996, on the Beats as renegade Ivy Leaguers.

In America my work has been taught at major universities such as Yale, Columbia, Penn, and Berkeley; Jerome Klinkowitz began his book *The Practice of American Fiction* with Nathaniel Hawthorne and ended it with a discussion of my work as an example of the continued health of the American novel.

In closing, I would like to thank my friends among the writers of California for their comradeship and support over the years. I met many of them at the Foothill Writers' Conference, where I have been invited back as a guest author by Richard Maxwell and Kim Wolterbeek each summer for twenty years. I would also like to thank Karen Kennerly, Sara Bershtel, Lindy Hough, and Rebecca Spalten for their help in editing my books,

and my old RPI friends, who have followed me through many peregrinations, among them my former roommates and oldest pals Harvey and Sue Braun, and Tom Baruch and Johanna Immerman, and my dear friends Serge and Judy Abend, Ed Segal and Lynn Newhouse, Mike and Karen Herman, Harvey and Betsey Eidinoff, and Lori Samet and Charles Davis.

I envy writers like Tolstoy and Dostoyevsky who still had a living spiritual tradition in which to plant themselves when encountering the modern secular world (whose invisible assumptions are rooted in us like a hypnosis). I set off on a search for certainty through science and wound up immersed in a world of mysteries within mysteries, but a world that is not meaningless. I began in the Bronx, but I entered realms that are beyond language to describe, places that are so beautiful and filled with kindness that when you get there you forgive God for everything you have been through in this terrible century—the wars, the Holocaust, all of it—and the thousand little hurts and humiliations which have been inflicted on you every day, and which you have inflicted on others, simply drop away like a heavy old robe on the beach, and you move forward toward the gorgeous and infinitely merciful light. You just do it. There isn't even a question about it.

And you realize that, in some part of yourself, you knew that this was how it was going to end all the time.

BIBLIOGRAPHY

Fiction:

Blues for a Dying Nation, Dial, 1972.

The Carmen Miranda Memorial Flagpole, Presidio, 1977.

Dr. Ebenezer's Book and Liquor Store, St. Martin's, 1980.

Growing up Bronx, North Atlantic Books, 1984.

Mahatma Gandhi in a Cadillac, North Atlantic Books-Frog Ltd., 1995.

Nonfiction:

Zen in the Art of J. D. Salinger, Creative Arts Books, 1977.

Stephen Sandy

1934-

MANIFESTATIONS

The record: I was born in Minneapolis at Abbott Hospital near Loring Park on August 2, 1934. I was educated in public and private schools on the south side of the city, first at John Burroughs and Robert Fulton Elementary Schools, then at the Blake School in Hopkins, outside the city. After a brief stint on active duty in the navy, I entered Yale College in the fall of 1951. I joined the NROTC; I left it by transferring to the AFROTC; I had grown passionate about my education and soon dropped AFROTC as well.

I graduated with a B.A. in English in June 1955 and was drafted by the army on September 12, 1955. After basic training, I went to signal school where I was trained as a radio operator. I was then stationed at Fort Meade, Maryland, where I worked for the newspaper at Headquarters Second Army. The editor of the newspaper allowed a month's leave, and I hopped flights to Morocco to visit my brother in April 1957. In July 1957 I received a direct commission as second lieutenant, Artillery, and was discharged to continue my education under the terms of a remote provision in Army Regulations.

I studied German at Harvard Summer School and in September 1957 entered the Harvard Graduate School in English, earning an M.A. in 1959 and a Ph.D. in 1963. While a graduate student, I attended Robert Lowell's poetry workshop at Boston University; later I worked with Archibald MacLeish. My dissertation, directed by Jerome Buckley and Harold Martin, was on the development of the English novel. I taught as tutor and General Education instructor while a student myself; in 1963 I joined the faculty as a full-time instructor in English. In 1967 I went to Japan as a Fulbright Lecturer at the University of Tokyo and returned a year later to a position on the English faculty of Brown University. Before going to To-

Stephen Sandy, 1997

kyo I had met Virginia Scoville in Cambridge. In 1969 we were married and we moved to Bennington, Vermont, where I would teach at Bennington College. A daughter, Clare, was born in 1976 when we lived in White Creek, New York, and a son, Nathaniel, in 1980 when we had returned to Bennington.

I spent time at Yaddo, where I first went in 1963, where for the next few years I worked as a sort of night clerk in the summers, and where this narrative was written. Since 1967 I have published seven volumes of poetry, a critical study, *The Raveling of the Novel*, translations of Seneca and Aeschylus, and miscellaneous criticism.

Perspectives

I was born at five o'clock; my mother never could remember whether it was five in the morning or five in the afternoon—a failure of memory that suggests other preoccupations on her part—and has made it impossible to get a good horoscope from the more principled astrologers.

Eric Schroeder, most discerning of historical horoscopists in the 1960s, affirmed that he could do nothing for me without the precise hour of my birth, regardless of knowing the latitude and longitude of my birthing to the closest degrees. In a way this confusion about the hour of my coming into the world stands

Stephen at six, Minneapolis

at the gateway as a token of my inability to get to first base in discovering a theological, arcane, or mystical explanation for my nature—its quiddities, strengths and errors, my failure to gain much clarity when I tried to understand my moral, intellectual, or spiritual nature.

When I was eighteen I found myself on a Holland-America Lines steamer creaking across the Atlantic for a summer in France. I was not only at sea for the first time but also in the middle of a severe adolescent religious crisis, desperate to pin down my relation to the probable propinquity of my maker. I was reading a paperback copy of *Portrait of the Artist as a Young Man*—rather hot I was to forge the uncreated conscience of my race, or at least of my family—and had grown friendly with a Catholic priest, a dark kindly handsome father chaperoning a platoon of teenagers. One night with a couple of beers between us, a storm raging on deck, I asked him not what I should do to be saved, but if I might join the church. He asked me if I had read the Bible from cover to cover. I had not. He told me to throw Joyce overboard and read the Bible through. I did neither.

My biological father could do nothing for us as to the hour of my birth, for that gentle and susceptible man was suffering pains of his own, an instinctive *couvade* during his wife's three labors to bring forth first my brother, eighteen months later myself, and in four years my sister. Alan's sympathetic agonies at the last stages of Evelyn's pregnancies sent him to bed in marvels of distress for a week or two, according to my grandmother Clara, and my mother always held that the strain of giving birth had made him suffer more than she had.

There were difficulties getting started. From age four I wore glasses, until I was ten. I have no memory, if I ever knew, of the precise nature of my vision problem. There was a wandering eye, however, and I was counseled to work on that with exercises from the age of four and for forty years thereafter. The muscles of the left eye were weak; it wandered and went out of focus, with the result that the right eye grew stronger. I went to the university for batteries of tests: psychological, IQ, optical, anything available. I was volunteered for a group experimental project, and Mother drove me over monthly for tests for so long I came to accept it as a part of my life. I felt special. When the results of the IQ test came back, Mother seemed both dissatisfied and impressed. I had a terrible stutter and this along with my odd ways perhaps gave her an idea that I was a genius, whatever that meant to her. I did not come up to the mark. But the results of the tests at least were not utterly disquieting.

My stutter made it hard to articulate thoughts. I tended to keep them to myself. Fortunately a kind and adept speech teacher, Mrs. Noonan, helped me at the Blake School. All had to take public speaking through the six years of upper school, and this weekly chore helped. (Classes were held in chapel; students had to memorize a prose piece such as "The Gettysburg Address" or a poem such as "The Maid of Dee," to deliver to the class. I delivered both of these texts.) Public speaking at Blake culminated in a five-minute speech to the assembled populace of the school, masters and students, in daily chapel. Two such performances were required, one in junior year, one somewhat longer in senior year. For years I recalled seniors chiefly by their chapel speeches. Some went through frenzied agonies. I remember when one or another student collapsed and Headmaster Alder rose from his thronelike armchair to assist the poor boy down from the dais. Such sights helped to make the prospect of addressing the school dreadful, enforcing my terrors but also strengthening my resolve. Strangely, the stutter vanished when I spoke. By college age it had all but disappeared; yet even now when I am with someone who stammers or stutters, like my friend Edward Hoagland, I may involuntarily produce sympathetic stumbling. I have had to tell a stuttering stranger that I am not making fun of his impediment but haplessly recalling my own.

In the thirties, as ever, parents tried to bring up their children according to the latest theories. Along with treating them to what must have been alarming doses of infantile theological discourse, I was a bad thumb sucker. Thumb sucking was viewed with shame and alarm. Eventually I was saddled with a leather hand harness that connected to a wire cage strapped onto the preferred right hand. The thumb was inaccessible, as well as almost anything I tried to pick up with the hand.

My odd ways amused my folks at first, then I think worried them. From the earliest age there was no doubt in my mind that we hapless mortals were but the function of higher or deeper powers. Spirits that informed my world and guided my actions stood by. The hand of God was undoubted and steady. I know I instructed my mother, father, and grandmother as to the nature of a great chain of being and hierarchies of divine forces as I understood them at the time. I discoursed on these matters, especially in the car when we were driving somewhere. I would stand in the back just behind the front seats, to be closer to my parents, and preach to them. When we drove past the cemetery on the way downtown, I informed them about what went on in the mausolea and that—before I came to be their son—I had long lived in (a particularly grand) one.

I cannot remember details of the cosmology I found or that found me. I believe, however, that children naturally have such thoughts, however unorganized; at least my own have told me of their metaphysical understandings. Somewhere are notes I took when Clare explained the theocentric cosmology she knew about one morning as I drove her to the Early Childhood Center. Years later, driving my son, age four, to the same school—and this without benefit of Sunday school—he suddenly announced: "You know, God is the king of nature. He lives up in the sky in the *Cloud Tower*. There is—he had a *queen of nature*—and there is a princess and a prince. If there are any bad angels or bad clouds they are killed with God's power. *By* his power" (emphasis his). I suspect all children have religious insights and concoct theological frameworks to explain their angle of vision on an otherwise arbitrary or fearful existence; whether they inherit these, remember them, or make them up, I cannot say.

My attraction to China was another matter. From earliest days I was obsessed with China. Father joked that I had been a "Chinaman" in a previous existence, but I have come to believe that if reincarnation is an option, he may well have been right. Mother used to wonder where this fascination came from; periodically she would announce that we did not know any Chinese people and that I had never met one. Nevertheless, they kindly brought me back books about China from New York. William Cohn's Phaidon volume, *Chinese Painting*, was a kind of visual bible for me. The classical landscape paintings of figures crossing a bridge that led up to mountains then to clouds, to retreats higher and higher among trees, meant

Father, Alan Francis Sandy, fishing in northern Minnesota, about 1925

a world to me. Some inarticulate urge in me responded to these images of seclusion, of withdrawal into a silent solitude—in a convenient hermitage just waiting (the traveler, to be sure, conveniently followed by a servant carrying baggage and a lute).

It is also possible that some of the attraction of these landscapes lay in their graphic depictions of variety, an inviting antipodes of my surroundings. I never saw a hill higher than three hundred feet, let alone a mountain, until I was thirteen. Growing up on the plains, where the sky is so very big and blank because the surrounding horizon is so low, calls forth a response, a knowledge of regular, unvarying, uninterrupted flatlands.

What were the Twin Cities when I was growing up? Under a thin veneer of gentility and

a park system designed by Frederick Law Olmsted, Minneapolis was still a boomtown, a station for gathering in the wealth of the frontier and the rich prairies. The state capital and a river port, St. Paul appeared to languish across the Mississippi now that the railroads had superseded river steamers.

Because they were first on the scene—after the rail tycoon James J. Hill—the lumber families were so august that they seemed almost to have faded into a celestial abode, a commercial glory, where what they had been "in" no longer mattered. Though it was dimly recognized, for example, that the Walker fortune came from lumber and the forest lands where the timber had stood, the family had long been chiefly philanthropists and art collectors, founding the Walker Art Center, commissioning modern houses to hold their collections of jade, precious rocks largely inherited from the founding chief of the tribe, T. B. Walker.

That art-loving lumber baron fancied old masters, but without a Berenson to pick them, going his own way, he ended with a multitude of fakes, which he housed in the Walker Art Gallery, the museum he built opposite Loring Park when the Minneapolis Art Institute turned down his offer to build a wing—a wing for his collections only and with his name over the door. Doubtless the institute knew about the fakes, a rabble of religious compositions which in my boyhood were divvied up among local churches when the heirs turned the Art Gallery into the Art Center, reinventing it as a modern art museum—the second or third in the country after MOMA and the Whitney. Its ornate Venetian palazzo by the Loring ponds got a face-lift. An architect stripped off one garment and fitted on another; it was transmogrified into a stolid but daring Bauhaus limestone box of windowless simplicity.

The prime reason for St. Paul being there was that it was just below St. Anthony Falls, thus the head of navigation on the Mississippi; and the prime reason for Minneapolis being there was St. Anthony Falls, which provided power for the mills. The milling district, a bastion of elevators and silos, might have been an architectural fantasy strung for a mile along the banks of the river. It was like an ancient city, battlements like the ramparts of a Midwestern Troy, as painted perhaps by Erastus Field. Against the level landscape of the Midwest the towers looked gargantuan, half threatening, improbable;

mysterious emblems of the land that held the produce of the land.

Presences

Alan Sandy, my father, was born in 1892 in St. Paul, Minnesota, to parents of Irish descent. The first Sandy in America apparently was one Thomas, a potato-famine refugee who settled in Pennsylvania and served in the Civil War. By the last quarter of the century the family had moved west to what had only recently been frontier. (For Minnesota the Civil War had been largely a military pacification operation within its own recently drawn borders; the official history of Minnesota during this period was titled *Minnesota in the Civil and Indian War.* One of my forebears had been a sentry on picket duty and alerted his battalion to an imminent ambush at the battle of Birch Coulee in 1863.) The young state then enjoyed a boom economy as it opened up the agricultural, timber, and mining riches of the upper Midwest and the Northwest Territory beyond.

The Sandy house was a modest one on Audubon Street, under the hill where fashionable folk lived. It was at river level, down from the mansion of James J. Hill, "the Empire Builder," at the head of Summit Avenue. (Summit was famous as the avenue Scott Fitzgerald lived too far down to be counted in the world he desired.) In 1898, the family moved to Minneapolis; Alan went to Emerson School, where J. Paul Getty was in the same class, through the eighth grade (1906, the end of his formal education). At this time, Alan's father Joseph lost his own and his parents' savings; the little bank paid the suspiciously high interest rate of 7 percent. Joseph repaid the debt by turning over his paycheck to his mother for years. So the family was secure, since Joseph was employed, but continually strapped for funds. Thus when Alan won the Northwest Junior Speed Skating championship, he did so on borrowed skates.

In 1907, the family moved to Portland, Oregon, for three years. (The eldest child, Irene, went to Los Angeles instead. The Sandys held that in a man's world the daughter ought to be helped. They gave her a start; the boys could fend for themselves. Irene did well; she bought real estate. She was a smart, cynical, presuming woman, something of a miser. When

I visited Irene on Country Club Lane in Long Beach in the sixties, where her garden bordered a fairway, she averred that she disliked people who hit golf balls onto her property. "They come over here wanting their *balls*, but I don't give 'em back. They put 'em on *my property*!" How much was a golf ball worth? I named a figure out of my head; Irene took me to her two-car garage; it was wall-to-wall pails, full of golf balls.)

In Portland, Alan got work as a "roustabout" in a wholesale house and attended night school. In 1908, back in Minneapolis, he worked as a stock clerk in a hardware store and started a garage in a barn on Lyndale Avenue, servicing cars for people who lived at fashionable addresses nearby. By 1915 Alan was traveling for an auto supply company; in 1917 he enlisted in the navy, where his savvy about cars landed him the job of chauffeur for the base commander of Cape May. After the war he returned to Minneapolis for more night school and work at Dayton's department store.

My brother was called Joe after our grandfather Joseph. Joe recalls Alan telling about his own father: a silent man, one who seldom displayed emotion. He would startle the family now and then by a dramatic gesture. He was an athlete, and once when Alan and friends were practicing acrobatics in the front yard, Joseph returned home in his suit with its gold watch and chain, looked once at the boys practicing their stunts, removed his coat and watch and, saying "can you do this?," turned a double back somersault, after which he silently put back his watch, put on his coat, and walked up the steps into the house.

Alan's mother, Alice, was known for her stories and jokes told in a strong Irish accent. Tales featuring anti-church themes couched in a now-amusing brogue signaled the gradual separation of the family from Catholicism and Ireland as they merged with the secular world of America, in which an ethnic heritage was celebrated and remembered, even as it was congenially abridged.

Joseph was, with his brother Art, a railroad engineer; this was the job most sought after—our father recalled—by men who had little education in those days. Joseph was a romantic figure for us, an engineer who famously—highballing home from Milwaukee to St. Paul one night—found only too late the body bound to the tracks at a curve he sped around and ran the hapless person over. Such were delights for little boys, but he was no hero when we met him at last, in 1938. Paralysed from a stroke, he returned from the coast in the care of his eldest son, Bill. They lived in the Majestic on Sixth Street, a threadbare place with an odor of scarcely genteel poverty. But the residential hotel was around the corner from my father's factory, where he would employ Bill as a one-man support staff, first in the front office and then, after some falling out, in the shipping room.

Evelyn, my mother, was born in 1901, in Charles City, Iowa. Her father, Eugene Martin, a doctor, died in 1912 of a stroke, only a month after his own father had died. Her mother Clara was proud of her New England Puritan heritage; she loved family history and saved boxes of midnineteenth-century letters—for example, those of my mother's aunt, Abbie Merrill Walker. Abbie had married Benjamin Walker, a geologist from Vermont who went to Iowa, then proceeded to Colorado, where he soon ran a mine at Cripple Creek, outside Colorado Springs, and where he acquired other mining interests. Eventually Abbie joined him, and his business world as well, for she became the first (and reputedly only) female member of the Colorado Springs Stock Exchange. It was money made in mining investments that provided for the widow Clara Martin and eventually passed to her daughter.

When Evelyn was twelve, her mother took her to San Francisco for a year. Soon they moved to Long Beach and lived with "Aunt Maud." They returned to Osage, Iowa, where the Merrills lived. Evelyn continued her schooling there, and they began going to Colorado Springs in the summers. In 1919, at Aunt Maud's insistence, all three went to Chicago to find first-class music and dancing lessons for Evelyn. Though she had whistled since five or six, she had no professional training; now they rented an apartment in Hyde Park and searched the music schools for whistling teachers and found one in "Professor" Leslie Groth. Aunt Maud loved Evelyn's whistling, but when Professor Groth told Clara he "could fit Evelyn for the stage in two or three months," Clara declined.

"I'm sorry but she has to go to college," she replied, and in 1919 Evelyn entered the University of Minnesota. She majored in anthropology. Dr. Jenks, a locally famous archeologist, invited her to go on a dig in New Mexico, but Clara scotched that. "She never wanted me to do anything," Evelyn told my brother. "I wanted to go to New York from college. But she didn't want me to go, so I didn't." Evelyn graduated *magna cum laude* in 1923; she observed that she might easily have graduated *summa*, but it was fashionable not to do too well. She went to work for the Minneapolis Board of Education, teaching foreign-born adults; worked below the bridge leading from Minneapolis's Seven Corners to the university, an area known as the Bohemian Flats (where John Berryman would jump to his death); became principal of a night school. In June 1928, after a long courtship, Alan and Evelyn were married; they lived in a succession of apartments with Evelyn's mother, but, with the arrival of the first child, they bought a larger place, a house at 5019 Colfax.

After my mother and father, the only family I knew were Grandmother Clara and Uncle Bill. Uncle Bill led a hapless but (apparently) happy life of missed opportunities and seemingly endless wanderings. He was a gifted entertainer, who had something of his mother's gusto in telling stories; more saliently for me, he had been a professional piano player. He would tell me how he had played on a Mississippi riverboat. He played ragtime in a day when no one did. He recalled when he was a friend of Scott Joplin, from whom he had learned "Maple Leaf Rag." Bill first taught me how to play "Maple Leaf Rag," so genetically my rendition stemmed from the composer himself. Uncle Bill had once married but was soon separated; he traveled around, played the piano. In 1927 my father wired him to come back at the founding of the Vanity Dress Company (perhaps feeling he needed fraternal support, with partner Sam Kahn bringing in *his* brother, Izzie). Uncle Bill then was living in Des Moines, Iowa, and he didn't come back. By the mid-thirties he had settled in Los Angeles near Irene, caring for their father; he worked in the sound studio of Metro Goldwyn Meyer. He would not go to work for my father until 1939, when he returned with Joseph to Minneapolis.

Bill would have agreed with Dr. Johnson that life holds little to be enjoyed and much to be endured. He appeared to accept his life which, to anyone not in the family, would appear a botched one, a wreck. His sweetness barely covered his gnarled manner; he seemed

Mother, Evelyn Martin Sandy

to have accepted failure. He used to smoke a cigar down to the butt. The acrid odor of his spittle mixed with tobacco and smoke is with me now, the cigar butt resting in an ashtray on the piano by the keyboard.

His easy affability made him a friend of many. John's Place, a Chinese restaurant on the second floor next door to the Majestic, was a favorite haunt. That old-fashioned place had floors of tiny hexagonal tiles, but everything else was Chinese: black nineteenth-century export furniture, booths made of carved wood, chairs with mother-of-pearl inlay, high tables with marble slabs set in them. Once Bill took me there for lunch the day after his birthday. John had thrown him a party; the tables were still joined, his place at the head of the

table was still set. Bill was invited to sit in it again. It must have been a big party, for they were still far from cleaned up.

By the fifties the distance between my family and Bill was growing wide; now he rarely came to dinner; at last, only at Christmas. When he retired, my father bought him a cottage at Lake Minnetonka in Wayzata on Park Lane, a little back road lined with cabins that the wealthy of posh Wayzata doubtless never knew existed. There, at the beginning of the TV era, he went out to wade one summer afternoon and sank beneath the waters. He had walked out on a dock; he disappeared; he could not swim. Neighbors missed him, called for help. Back in Minneapolis I saw with astonishment the failed rescue scene, William Sandy's name announced, the view of the dock he fell from, the absence of a body. But then . . . true to the errant comedy of his life, he walked on screen, having seen the drowning story on his own TV. The neighbor's Labrador had seen him in the water, dived in after him, dragged him to shore, whence they both went to his cottage to dry off. Bill had lit a cigar and given the dog something to eat when he found his moment of fame on the tube and ambled out to report, like Twain and Robert Graves, that reports of his death had been greatly exaggerated.

In 1956 he wrote me, "Lonesome onesome. No dough, no doe. Anyway I like me, and the feeling is mutual. I, I, I, Ay, Ay, Ay, (So. Am.) Oi, oi, oi (Irish); Oi, and put a *u* in it, and you get oui. Oui. That's we. Yes. . . ." Like a Greek wail of grief the succession of vowels echoes, a cry from a disconnected life.

Grandmother Clara lived with us always. She paid some of the bills and every day sat in her room to read the *Wall Street Journal, Time,* and *Foreign Affairs,* and her favorite, Walter Lippmann. She managed her own stock portfolio from the death of Eugene in 1912 to her own in 1957. How on earth did she do it, off there on our windy hill, year after year, reading those papers and journals cover to cover beside the lace curtains of the big window in her room on the northwest corner of the house, her great polished walnut marriage bed nearby, and the brass intaglios of Gibson girls in oak frames on the walls of flowered wallpaper, blue and rose?

Clara and her lifelong friend Maud Williams went to Cornell College Academy for four years before continuing on at Cornell College

(Iowa) for four more years. She was a remarkable woman: Clara, or Caddie, as we called her, was proud, soft-spoken but strong-willed, and overprotective—even for those strict days—of her daughter. When my mother entered the University of Minnesota and joined a sorority, Caddie moved in as the housemother. (It was amusing to learn years later that the house on University Avenue that the Kappa sorority owned had been the childhood home of another dignified Minneapolitan, Elizabeth Ames, the longtime director of Yaddo.)

Very early she acquired a reputation for her commanding bearing and soft voice, her intellectual grasp, wide reading, and august public manner. In college, appropriately, she played Antonio in *The Merchant of Venice*. During the war when I attended Robert Fulton Elementary, one day I went home early out of the principal's fulsome respect for my grandmother. It was an important day; the wife of an English lord was in town and coming to our house for tea! Her friend Rewey Belle Inglis wrote: "In 1942 our branch [of the AAUW] had the privilege of entertaining Lady Halifax during her goodwill tour of the United States. In the absence of our president . . . Clara Martin was chosen to introduce Lady Halifax and act as her personal hostess, as she did with the poise and graciousness always at her command."

But earlier—in the thirties—in the compact gray stucco house on Colfax Avenue, a number of people lived: my parents, brother, self, grandmother, and Esther, our housekeeper. In those Depression days, live-in help was almost hard to avoid if one *had* help, though where the bedrooms for all of us were it's hard to imagine. They must have been small. Esther lived with us until the number of children forced her to commute.

When my mother was in the hospital giving birth to me, my brother was scarcely a toddler yet able to cruise along the furniture, which he did, moving into the kitchen, where Esther failed to see him when he approached the gas stove. He reached up and spilled a pan of boiling water on himself—second- and third-degree burns over a quarter of his body put him in hospital as well. The guilt my mother must have felt may have had much to do with her blanking out when it came to remembering the hour of my birth. Though he recovered fully and all but the most severely burned

skin healed, my brother still bears a spread of scars and lesions on his right shoulder and breast.

Though of course I grew up accustomed to Joe's scars, I never learned of the coincidence of my birth and the accident until I was in my thirties. That my parents concealed the connection between me and my brother's burn and what they must have viewed as their own culpability suggests how deeply concerned they were not to let their sense of inadvertent transgression spill over to me. No vengeance took place; their affection for Esther must have been great, for they did not fire her. She was there when my sister came home from the hospital four years later.

In September 1937 my brother and I played on the front lawn, hoping to bury a red trike under gathered leaves, when the family Buick rolled up the drive and my sister appeared in the arms of a nurse, "red as a Red Indian," I am told I remarked. This was an intersection in my life, though I did not know it, for the baby was put in my room, a little blue room with chambray curtains printed with elephants and balloons; and I was moved into the bedroom of my brother. We would share a bedroom until I was fifteen and was allowed to move to the third floor of a much larger house near Lake Harriet. Our light-filled sleeping porch faced east, and one winterish day when we were both in bed with colds or flu, my mother announced that there was a surprise, and the Raggedy Andy book she had been reading us was set down; Esther brought in a mousetrap with the mouse it had caught for us to inspect. Though it looked broken, it did not look dead to me; I was restrained from petting it with my finger.

My brother's burn was not his only medical problem. When he was an infant, the doctor, on a house call, broke three needles in his arm during a failed attempt at inoculation; my father all but broke the drug-addicted pediatrician's arm—and replaced him with the sober but fanatical Dr. Robb. Joe, or Jody, had a terrible ear condition. Dr. Robb made house calls and scoured out Jody's right ear with a long pick; it pained him greatly and—surely—did no good. When he was six he had a mastoidectomy; there were no antibiotics, no medicines but aspirin ground up in a spoonful of jelly. He might spend a week in bed with inexplicable unending ear aches. Jody was to bear the brunt of early challenges with bravery, in his twenties conquering his ills and subduing nature by becoming a jet fighter pilot in the air force.

How did this ongoing suffering in my brother affect me? How did I think about it? Did I imagine myself as privileged not to endure it? Undoubtedly, I did. But I repressed all of it but the bare facts, some of them filled in later, years later.

The house on Colfax had been built about 1915 among similar houses, set back at a uniform distance from the Minneapolis street which, like nearly every other in town, was straight as a bore and planted with American elms at sixty-foot intervals on a strip—"boulevard" it was called—of grass eight feet wide between the curbstone and the concrete walk. The limit of my trike-traveled world on the west was Fiftieth Street, a major artery with a streetcar line. One way down Fiftieth was John Burroughs grade school; three blocks the other way was the neighborhood drugstore and filling station. To the south, a block and a half away, loomed the Minnehaha Creek bed, a deep shady glen with a little stream ambling at its bottom that debouched, a few miles hence, into the Mississippi. My brother and I were forbidden to enter this vale of danger—though a few times we dared—presumably because my parents feared some Huck Finn-like decampment. At any rate, *Tom Sawyer* was read to us, but never *Huckleberry Finn;* there was not even a copy in the house. Even then I did not care for the fussiness of *Tom Sawyer;* it was not until I was in graduate school that I read *Huckleberry Finn.*

There were shelves full of books, however; chiefly those of my grandmother, her rose and gilt set of Schiller, her father's calf-bound volumes of *Harper's Magazine,* Dickens. On the upper shelves were art objects, ceramics chiefly, an Imperial-yellow bowl of paper-thin Ruskin ware, a pitcher with a tiny spout my father had won as a child from his mother in a game of pinochle. In the sunroom beyond the living room stood an upright piano; on top were busts of composers, Mozart on the left, Beethoven on the right—and between them a Swiss barometer in the form of a chalet from whose doors would glide one figure if it were to be warm, another if cold. There was little enough Mozart, though perhaps my mother played "Für Elise" and other learner pieces she was even then

trying to remember from her girlhood musical training.

Downtown, business flourished, but the partner, Sam Kahn, wanted a business for himself. Sam was the patternmaker, a first-rate one; a good patternmaker is indispensible. Soon Sam and his friend Davidson, the head cutter, left Father and formed their own company, though they had little capital. The replacement Father found could not make patterns, and Sam Kahn couldn't sell dresses; so they joined forces again. Reorganized in 1928, the Vanity Dress Company began business in 1929 and immediately "went to town," in my father's phrase. The Crash didn't hurt them at all. The early thirties were good to my parents; they entertained their growing circle of friends and began to have the family they wanted. They liked to entertain and demonstrate that they were beginning to do well indeed.

I woke (about three years old) one night and crept downstairs into the midst of a party to find some mother comfort; I found a room blue with smoke, faces I would later recognise as Jess and Bob Hartzell, Dane and Tommy Donovan, others. My father took me upstairs, and I urinated as he, kneeling, held me at the toilet. In the light from the hall, his smooth black hair glistened and I stroked it before he took me back to bed.

Yet my earliest memory in that house is of lying by the dining table, in a carriage, at breakfast, while others ate. Mesmerized, I watched the sunlight through lilac branches at the French doors brushing across the curtain stays of cut glass, little rainbow shards of colored light flashing into the room where the voices of those who cared for me spoke desultorily on, waking to their day together, saying things I could not understand.

Banked Fires

In October 1938, we moved to a large new house. It stood above Lake Harriet, the largest glacial scoop of blue water among the twenty-two lakes of the Twin Cities. The house was expensive, yet like many others at the tag end of the Depression, it had been long on the market. Father was doing well in his business; he could afford to buy and, over the next decade, fit the place up freshly and add a two-storey addition with a three-car garage. Too old to be drafted—and his sons too young—the war years were good to him. Afterward, he understood the postwar need for a new look of luxury and hit the ground running when Dior's "New Look" was shown in Paris: the forties were to be his best decade for making money.

Inspired by the "sweater girls" in an Eddie Cantor show on a buying trip to New York in the 1920s (he was working for Dayton's as a buyer in the women's clothing department, run by his friend Dane Donovan), Father began with Donovan to manufacture form-fitting sweaters for women. A family tradition held that his company had been the first to market such sweaters—generally chorus line garb before—to the public. The business grew to include the manufacture of a general line of women's ready-to-wear. The Vanity Dress Company, with its Perry Brown label, was making a lot of money by World War II. Ever the puritan in bringing up his children, my father taught the habit of industry; I found myself sweeping floors or working in the shipping department on Saturday mornings, and doing the same as a summer job later on.

I liked the cutters, the operators, the designers, and at least they pretended to like me. Out on the floor there was an ethnic mix: the men, the professional cutters, were Jews except for one Dane; the "girls," women of every age, were Northern European, Scandinavian, Finnish, or perhaps German, reflecting the ethnic makeup of the town. One day after the war, three Black women wandered in past the punch-in clock; looking for work they had entered by the wrong door. Everyone in the shop stopped work; the operators stood up from their machines. The floor made a fairly happy family, but it was not—yet—for Blacks. Finkelstein, the union boss, took care of it.

It was an odd business to thrive in Minneapolis, so far from Seventh Avenue. Even so, most of my father's colleagues in the business (above the level of sewing machine operator) and in the Midwest garment industry generally were Jewish; I remember still the affection my father always showed for Abe Finkelstein, the chief bargainer for the ILGWU, and meeting this lanky man with a New York accent who seemed to be such a pal of my dad. It is still amusing to friends in the East to hear that a Midwestern boy grew up in the rag trade.

Our new home, 4815 Sheridan, had been built by an eccentric businessman, Robert Wetmore, general manager of a lumber company, in the teens; he filled the twenty-room colonial revival house—abounding with nooks and crannies and a stack of winterized porches—with the most modern conveniences. It had been the featured house in the summer 1919 *House Beautiful* ("Western Number"), replete with photos of elaborate woodwork and the "electrically equipped" laundry with its power mangle and huge gas dryer for sheets (a wonderful recess to climb in when no one was looking). Wetmore, a bachelor, built the house for himself and two spinster sisters. The rooms were appropriate settings for his antique furniture and boasted remarkable detail everywhere. The architrave and entablature of the front door were modeled by an uncle in Vermont; a large gilt eagle atop the entablature was from the roof tree of an eighteenth-century mansion on Cape Cod.

The top floor had six rooms lined with endless shelves and banks of dark paneled cupboards. They concealed a secret room behind a sliding panel of cupboards. Though my parents kept the secret even from their children, I found it one day. Attempting to hide a dime in a crack in the paneling of the room I played in and called my own, the dime disappeared, the paneling I jostled began to move, and the jig was up. Why was the room there? My aunt's silver from Long Beach spent the war there, safe from the Japanese, who it seemed would invade California with the sole purpose of looting her trove of silver. But what had it been built for in the first place? A space for a cache of liquor seemed the best answer.

There was a secret wine cellar as well, no doubt in case of a raid during Prohibition, and it was local lore that Wetmore had run liquor, moreover that large squads of friends bunked in the barrack-like sleeping porches, large enough to house a platoon. Gold eagle over the front door, shutters at the windows with silhouettes of eagles cut into each one, eagles carved into the architrave of the front door, big brass eagle of a door knocker—this panoply of patriotism took on a different meaning when I imagined Mr. Wetmore's nefarious side. What if the whole façade was a front to draw off the Feds? It was rumored in our new neighborhood, as well, that Wetmore's visitors were more than business acquaintances; they were young men who did not look as if they were employed—even if they did have fancy cars laden with booze.

I grew up in the secure farmland folds of a region that never mentioned—and seemed not even to know of—the trenches of World War I, flame throwers on Tarawa dropping snipers from the palms, the Final Solution.

Time magazine did color covers of the heroic leaders of the war; I collected them. The Axis leaders, cartoon visages of violent but incompetent power—from Hitler and Rommel to Tojo and Hirohito—grimaced and snarled.

Our own generals were benign and somehow friendly, noncombatant; I studied the bland ineffective looks of a Marshall or an Ike—and then the faces of the Allies: Marshal Tito; those Russians, General Zhukov, Stalin. They were hard to read—they smiled little and were cold, strong, dull. Were they good guys, or . . . ? When I was about ten, I asked Father what the word *dictatorship* meant. There might, he said, be a phone box in front of each house on the street, and if you wanted to go into your house, you would have to get permission.

Nearly half a lifetime before that, I stood with my mother and grandmother in the vestibule; through the wide open door, afternoon sun fell through maple branches dappling the light on the white enamel of Mr. Wetmore's Georgian woodwork. It was the first week of September. The *Star Journal* had just arrived, as it did always around 4 P.M., before Father got back from the office. Mother and Caddie both held the paper; they were hyperventilating and remained at the door—we never stayed but a minute in the vestibule. Something momentous had happened and had entered our home that warm September afternoon of 1939. Hitler had invaded Poland. They did not know how to answer when I wanted to know. "Something very sad has happened," my mother explained. And Caddie: "But it's very far away."

My parents' Minneapolis was a part of 1920s America that Edmund Wilson described as "a world dominated by salesmen and brokers." Through the first decades of the century, in spite of some stability from the Colorado mines, the family—on both sides, as their restless traversings of the country suggest—was seeking a niche, trying to gain a foothold in middle-class society that would afford them financial security and social respectability. By the midtwenties they had married, Father was supporting the family, they had begun to find a place. Though they were proud, they would have

Stephen, age four, with older brother, Alan

blanched at the idea of status. Pride manifested itself as discretion; modesty masked a strongly felt superiority; climbing socially was and would remain abhorrent to them.

In a Midwestern city where anyone might try to make it quick and big, everyone strove for wealth and even a grain of recognition to counter the poverty and anonymity from which most came. The majority were first- or second-generation families of Scandinavian or German descent; WASP families that had come from Victorian New England stirred the melting pot. So being able to think of oneself as WASP gave more than a dollop of glamor and respectability. At least I knew who my New England forebears were, and the table talk that taught us "who we were" listed heavily toward the maternal, Yankee side of the family.

The solidity of being a working part of the free enterprise system yet holding a pedigree must have given critical support to a family in the heady years before—and the hard years after—the Crash. It was as if Caddie's endless anecdotes of family history ("the worst crime committed by anyone in our family was in the seventeenth century when your ancestor, Hepsibah Hubbard, was fined for picking peas on Sunday"), her presidency of the local chapter of the Daughters of the American Colonists—her Grant Wood demeanour and patriotism—offered a useful, welcome ingredient to the family enterprise, to which Father contributed the equally important ingredient of entrepreneurial resolve.

The contemporary pejorative sense of "hustler" was unknown to him. His was a Horatio Alger vision. All his days he worked hard. "Labor is life," wrote Carlyle, and the last words Father spoke to me, when he was dying in 1987, were: "All I want is to be able to get out of here and go back to work." One of his favorite morsels of advice to his boys was: "You have to get out there and hustle." It was a life of innocence in which if you worked hard the pleasures and rewards of success would somehow come to you (even if they had not come to Uncle Bill).

My parents enjoyed their lives. They still liked to entertain, though not in the presence of their children. How this was accomplished is not clear to me, whether they now partied more at the Minnikahda Club, a swank place my family was invited to join after the war, or sent us to the movies in the care of Caddie. Of course there was the occasional great bash after the war, drinks and buffet dinner with a strolling accordionist for seventy, when I helped serve drinks and empty ashtrays. Earlier, against war shortages, they had laid in a large supply—several cases—of "French 75" (named after a First World War artillery piece) magnums in a room off the laundry, a treasured concoction of champagne laced with brandy. Today it sounds fatal; their supply dwindled slowly but steadily until the last bottle was gone sometime around VJ Day. One might have thought this cache belonged in the locked and hidden wine cellar, but when hostilities began, Caddie—firmly convinced that invading Germans and Japanese would meet at the Mississippi—had commandeered all spare rooms to secretly hoard the paper goods that were in short supply. The wine cellar was stuffed to the ceiling with cartons of toilet paper that would not get used up until the Korean War began.

Alan and Evelyn loved to sing and dance. They harmonized singing the popular songs.

Alan might have been a professional tap dancer and took his tap shoes to parties. He was famous among his friends (though not his children, who didn't hear of it until years later) for his dance performances on tabletops joined together after dinner on New Year's Eve at the club. (His final illness, at ninety-three, was precipitated by tap dancing at Christmas on his cousin Janet Aby's kitchen floor—kitchen floors were firm and acoustically good for tap.)

Vacations were largely car trips to northern Minnesota, when we would make a circuit of lakes and put up at resorts, always looking for where the best fishing was. We would move about like Gypsies, Father asking gas station attendants, guides, women who ran roadside "rest cabins," where the bass were striking. One such excursion in 1946 ended at Hamilton Lodge near Grand Rapids. Father and Joe and Susan went fishing in a rented rowboat powered by Father's ten-horse outboard Johnson Seahorse. Mother and I hiked along the shore trail amid the wind-tossed Douglas firs; auburn needles with their remote exotic scent floated down. We made our way out to the end of Chase Point Trail, and there, to my astonishment, we saw Father, Joe, and Sue in the boat not far below us. It must have been a long enough morning out on the lake for Susan (then only eight) at least, because when Father put ashore she and Joe got out and walked back with us to the lodge for lunch. Was the surprise Mother showed at finding Father's boat so near the end of Chase Point feigned? Was Father's being there below us part of their plan to give Sue and Joe free rein for adventure but, concerned for their safety, to get them out of the sun after a good taste of piscatorial endeavor? I think so now.

It was a life of innocence but not bigotry. My parents shared the prejudices of their class and time. They at once looked down upon and feared outsiders, newcomers, strangers, or those they viewed as such. After all, persons who didn't fit the mold of WASP American might by the way also offer stiff competition in the marketplace. My father trailed a thread of anti-Semitic prejudice in which he thoughtlessly joined in the sentiments of his day; yet he chose to spend the better part of his business career in the daily company of Jews. His partner had been Dane Donovan. It became Sam Kahn: they made a lot of money together—and they also dined at each other's homes.

When we drove north for a vacation, to Park Rapids near the White Earth Indian Reservation or to Bemidji, we would spot Chippewa shacks and even birch bark hogans in the clearings beside the road. From cords strung between trees hung little birch bark canoes and teepees—souvenirs for sale. Mother, the anthropology major who had taught foreign-born adults for years and worked in the immigrant ghetto of the Bohemian Flats, would point out these suffering, marginal lives. In her usual phrase—it's hard to convey how innocent it was, less condescending than scholarly in a vague anthropological way—she would say: "See? That is typical. That is very typical." This was the extent of her disdain for anyone alive, an embryonic recognition that others might possibly have ethnic identities (and sufferings) of their own.

The Midwest was so anti-German that teaching the German language had been made illegal in Iowa during World War I and remained so for decades. My grandmother, who had majored in German literature at Cornell College, kept her twelve-volume set of Schiller as a ladylike token of urbanity and defiance on the living room bookshelves, not far from the thirty years of calf-bound *Harper's* and her signed Burwash edition of the complete works of Kipling. In the middle of the war, a new maid named Edith arrived; merely for something to do while minding us afternoons when my mother was working for the Red Cross, Edith began to teach us how to count to ten in German. *Eins, zwei, drei. . . .* Needless to report, when my brother and I proudly said our lessons to our startled parents (our first foreign language training!) that was the end of Edith.

But the aversion to Germans was as a reed compared to the stout trunk of the demonization of Jews, unquestioned and firm; a rock, a shelter to come to when things did not go in the world the way they should have, or had in the past. The Other could be blamed, and was. In second grade during a recess tussle, my friend pushed me against a pipe of iron railing and I chipped a front tooth. The monitor grabbed the boy and took him to the principal, Mrs. Coleman. Alan, the boy, was sent home. When my father heard of it, he murmured the deed might as well have been part of a plot, at least an example of "pushy" Jewish behavior.

The first time a boy growing up in Minneapolis heard the word *holocaust,* it had nothing to do with Dachau or Treblinka; knowledge of these horrors was still far in the future. Rather, it was holocaust in a grain elevator. "$2,000,000 Fire Sweeps Elevator," read the headline in the *Minneapolis Sunday Tribune,* December 1946; "12 Escape as Explosion Sets off Holocaust."

Some years later I found two or three anti-Semitic pamphlets on one of the bookshelves that housed unused books, a late Victorian miscellany not for the front rooms, forsaken titles like *David Harum* and *Ben Hur;* in our house books were never discarded. There, between *Elbert Hubbard's Scrapbook* and volumes of Will Carleton's *Country Ballads* and *City Ballads,* some anti-Jewish handouts were stuffed along with some pulp cant out of Kansas from the crude press of Haldeman Julius. By now I was old enough to know this was wrong, and it was a surprise, like accidentally coming upon some secret kinky thing like the bullwhip hidden in my father's wardrobe. I took these to Mother, who professed ignorance—since she never looked at that dusty bookcase, I'm sure she was truly amazed. She had no idea where they had come from. I heard her muttering that these were "something your father probably brought back long ago from New York" as she whisked the forbidden sheets away. However in remission, the disease of racism had touched our house.

There was additional embarrassment about some of the reading material lying around. Certain books were not for children—or teenagers. At twelve I had heard of Proust. I was fascinated, as one will be at that age, by the challenge of the longest book in sight; I took down Moncrieff's two-volume translation, *Remembrance of Things Past,* and immediately fell to it, totally absorbed. *Swann's Way* was a revelation, the language, the sinuous sentences, the elegantly printed pages introduced me to a thrilling (if obscure) vision of what writing might be. But I had scarcely finished "Combray" before I was detected. My parents admitted that it was a good book and I had taste in taking it down, but that it was not for youngsters, this sort of book. It was a book Caddie had bought; not for us. Perhaps in a few years.

At about this time Mother and Father called me into the living room for a talk. They were sitting side by side on the red Hepplewhite sofa, shades drawn against full afternoon sun that made the window on either side of the sofa an oblong of bright luminous white. They had concluded, they informed me, that I was—there was a pause—that I was an *intellectual.* I scarcely knew what that meant. I thought perhaps it was a disease or disability. It was indeed a handicap for growing up in Minneapolis, where *art* was a four-letter word. They said they accepted me for who I was, and I could read as much or little as I wanted, but I had to get outside and exercise. It was then I agreed with my father to ride my bike around Lake Harriet every day, rain or shine. The lake was little more than four miles around, so it was not such a draconian measure. I quickly grew proud of my prowess, the independence of going so far, the calf muscles I was acquiring *solo* in the open air beside the lake.

After the war, a traveling exhibit of old master paintings came to the Art Institute on "loan" from museums of overrun (and overrunning) European countries. Half the museum was emptied to hold the Rembrandts, Titians, Guardis, Van Eycks. I asked, or at least thought, "Why can't we keep these?" Dr. Plimpton, the director, was upset after the show left because far more people than ever before had thronged the museum, so many that the floors had to be refinished. It seemed most everyone in town had visited, but they were not appreciating art (as subsequent attendance showed), they were gloating.

In the 1950s things fell apart. The spoils and triumphs of victory caught in the toils of the Cold War and Korea. Things had not been as they seemed to be; realities hid behind euphemisms. Poland and Belgium were not conquered countries, they were "overrun countries." In Korea, the war was a "conflict." The invincible Americans were not being defeated; they made "strategic withdrawals." Yanks died in thousands; the thirty-eighth parallel was either a last-ditch line of defense or a stalemate Washington called a compromise. The draft was reinstated.

There was no time now for Proust or for swimming at the club. I had been convinced to join the Naval Reserve and enter a basic training program, one summer long; it would be like summer camp. After graduation in June 1951, less than three months before taking the train for Yale College, I reported to the Naval Air Station on the outskirts of Minneapolis.

Private Stephen Sandy, 1955

Boot camp did not turn out like camp. There I was—on a navy base, imprisoned behind a fence, in my hometown. We learned to play at the rudiments of soldiering—or sailoring—and to accept, through dozens of films and lectures, the game of industrialized killing that played such an important part in the larger world of the century's first half. Silly brutalizings like buzz haircuts; the loss of clothes one never considered as conferring identity; the wimp picked out for hazing, maybe even on the crowded bus to the training station; bathrooms without stalls so that men might bond by sharing in the act of shitting. The VD films made more than one recruit vomit, sometimes on the recruit in front of him. I learned correct naval behavior, sacred General Orders, how to dress, how to salute, the mysteries of applying rubber de-icers to the fore edges of fighter wings—tucking them under an aluminum flange and sealing them with screws turned with a Phillips screwdriver, hour after hour, by hand.

Later, I saw that I had been too young, too innocent, for this navy experience to be a good one. Though I had marched with the others in the Minneapolis Aquatennial parade that July and afterward played Scott Joplin on an upright in a beer hall—with my fellows, given a night out—other hours held on more strongly in memory: in the sick bay, while in formation waiting to get shots, watching operations or a man getting a spinal tap. The pitiful populace of the brig at that little naval air station stained the whole community of greenhorn gobs, twice each day, by sharing the mess hall with them. At their table smack in the middle of the mess hall, once a hangar, the guards made prisoners brace through meals, and with the butts of their M-1s prodded and bullied them as they marched in lockstep away. Surely, I thought, the wrongdoers starved before they learned to obey the SPs perfectly?

On the home front the center had not held. Sam Kahn wanted a business for his sons; postwar prosperity found him backers; he proposed buying out my father's share; instead Father bought out Sam's smaller one. Sam and his cohorts left and formed the Kahn Dress Company. Father, addicted to Cokes and smokes, became a chain smoker and was drinking a dozen bottles of Coke a day. At Perry Brown, the designs, the "numbers," the efficiency were not coming. Father's star salesmen, Julian Bagby and Otto Fittings, from whose prowess in the field the success of any season hung, deserted. Father's boys had left as well: Joe for Amherst, me for Yale.

I knew Father was desperate. If I could help, I would feel loyal, empowered, independent. Father sent boxes of samples to me, an uncertain freshman in New Haven, offering the usual salesman's commission and addresses of shops that hadn't carried Perry Brown for years—and some that no longer existed. Mother was alarmed at our confusion about my role and my unreadiness as a college freshman—but went along with the scheme. I cooled my heels in a number of showrooms. The shops I gamely visited were slow, uncomprehending, polite. I didn't open a single account. A sense of shame and failure, and desertion, lurked in the wings of my feelings. But I had my classes to worry about.

Those were heady days. In the dress business, as the adage went, either you were making a lot of money or you were losing a lot of it. Our factory, the huge eighth floor of the Produce Exchange Building, had fewer and fewer operators at machines. Home for vacation, I went in to help. Father was closeted in his office now, where he had never spent time before—out on "the floor" was where he worked. His was the corner office on the top floor of the building, only recently redecorated by Levoy's. In the pattern room next door, I set a chair up on a cutting table. I climbed up in silence and peered over the transom into his private retreat. Head in hands at the big desk, he wept. Quickly I climbed down, ashamed at what I had done, appalled at what I had seen. The factory soon was silent. His business closed.

He had gotten a hole-in-one—certified by the PGA—in a golf tourney in 1948. Now he resigned from the club. He spent the better part of a year in bed—reading Winston Churchill (the novelist, not the statesman), the *Saturday Evening Post,* and *Police Gazette.* His doctor made house calls. Caddie footed college bills. 4815 was on the market. But who would want to buy so large a house, now a little run-down, with almost an acre of lawn and garden running from one avenue through to the next?

Long since, I had mailed the samples back; because of Caddie's help Yale turned down my request for financial aid. Another bid for independence had failed. I tightened my belt—no more trips to Northampton or dinner and theater parties in New York, carousing on the NYNH&H Railroad. And yet Caddie wanted to cheer me up and sophomore year bought me a Ming scroll at Mathias Komor, the Manhattan antiquities dealer, for my room in Pierson College. In junior year, 4815 was unexpectedly sold; we moved to a far smaller house in—I thought—a better neighborhood. 2011 James was in the heart of Kenwood, the old established Upper East Side (could there have been one) of Minneapolis. The house was roomy in ways that counted. Now Father stopped smoking completely ("they don't know if it harms you, but they do know it doesn't do you any *good*") and began selling cars.

Friends offered to stake him to a dealership, but he turned it down; high stakes gambling and running a business were not to be a part of this stage of his life, and Mother agreed. At 2011 they both seemed to lighten up. Father still had his 1934 Rolls, which he now kept in a garage on the other side of town except for a month in the summer. In a far less showy way, they prospered and manifested delight. Even Father's machinations, getting me into the navy (and its macho life) and keeping me out of Korea, one may judge, had worked. Though I would be drafted, it would be into the peacetime army.

Out of the army, back home studying Latin for graduate school, I built a walled garden for my parents in a corner between a wing of 2011 and the garage. Father and I drove round town at night lifting old eighteen-inch hexagons of dark cement, antique sidewalk pieces torn up to be replaced by strips of concrete, for a patio. And we lifted granite cobbles for garden borders from the sides of the streets the stones had been imported to pave in the nineteenth century. They were being torn up as the city laid down concrete or blacktop. We copped trunk after trunk load of the heavy stones, smooth and rounded on the top like loaves of bread from decades of wear by wagon wheels, horseshoes, and auto tires. A bashed lead Mercury lugged from 4815 stood on tiptoe in the center bed. Come fall, locked in hay mulch and rose stalks, he raised his dented blue arm, fending off the snow.

Mother planted roses, blue lobelia, maidenhair fern, exotic castor beans, tuberous begonias. Father grew so enamoured of the begonias he tended them daily, making sure of a lush display in the raised cobblestone beds all summer. Mother planned her mornings around having coffee in the garden. She loved its privacy so much, she would ask friends over for brunch to enjoy the privacy with her. There was bird song here, too, in the branches of the tall elms above us, and occasionally a cardinal for her to whistle with. That year my father sold more Studebakers than the rest of the salesmen in Hennepin County combined. His reading now was Dickens and Shakespeare.

Caddie still tended to business but was growing dotty. She possessed a pearl-handled pistol her husband had given her back in Iowa for self-protection when he was not at home. She still kept it, and bullets, in her bedside table. Discreetly, Father removed the bullets when Caddie took to kneeling at the front window of her bedroom and aiming the weapon out the window at strangers. She even mimicked the kick of the weapon as it fired, long-term memory calling up some youthful experience of firearms. When a passerby noticed a pistol barrel trained on him from a bedroom window, he came up to the front door and rang the bell. At last Father took the pistol from his mother-in-law. He was scared to death of violence and sold the piece to a dealer downtown. Caddie died quietly in her sleep in 1958.

Books

I was educated in public and private schools, first at John Burroughs and Robert Fulton Elementary Schools, then at the Blake School in Hopkins, outside the city. My teacher in kindergarten was Miss Easthagen (later she hanged herself); in first grade, Mrs. Knight, whose husband worked for the newspaper; in second, Mrs. Gittens; in third, Mrs. Kennedy in gray cardigan, a famous tyrant who made an example of me for bad penmanship as we learned cursive because I had mistakenly thought the words as well as the letters were joined; in fourth, Mrs. Paul, red hair, perfume, a big bosom swathed in green; in fifth, Mrs. Wrennie . . . they are as vivid as neighbors next door.

Blake School in Hopkins was a private school; the masters gave a firm if narrow education. In the sixth grade my class of twenty-five began to study the mysteries of algebra, ancient history, English. For three years there were fat mimeographed spiral-bound grammar texts. One master, "Chief" Wonson, had been a pitcher for the Minneapolis Millers. His chalk tray was full of tennis balls, and any rambunctious student would get one pitched at his head. Wonson had acute aim, but we had lift-top desks. If the culprit was fast enough, he could throw up his desk lid, and the tennis ball would fly back toward the front of the classroom. We loved Wonson, his athlete's chic and grace; he made being there unthreatening, nearly fun. He taught English; it was a relaxed, romantic literary study: we read Howard Pyle's *Men of Iron* and capped that with *Ivanhoe*.

Another master, Noah Foss, the head Latin teacher, was famous for a kind of makeshift stocks; he would close the window sash on an ill-prepared student, head and shoulders out in the cold. A classmate of my brother often spent the period bent over this way; he stammered, and later we learned that, born left-handed, he had had a slow time of it adjusting to the right-handedness he was made to adopt as a child. When he was left alone and allowed to return to being a lefty, he stopped stammering and improved his grades splendidly

With his mother in the garden he built at 2011 James Avenue, Minneapolis, 1955

by senior year. Blake life was full of the drill, a proto-military training: the playing fields had to merge with the *campus martius.* We learned to play. Play was obligatory. Everyone hurled himself against another because everyone had to play football, no excuse, no exception. The poet Allen Grossman, a year ahead of me, met this requirement by being manager of the football team. I edited the school paper and yearbook and found such escape routes as I could. At last came the respite of senior year, when things let up a bit.

After graduation, I felt bold enough to get in the car with my parents and drive to Noah Foss's house to thank him for his help over the years. He was, after all, an excellent teacher, if stuffy—always wearing high collar, tightly knotted necktie, navy blue suit and vest. None of this sartorial armor was an impediment, however, when he pursued and invariably overtook bad boys attempting to run away from some prank or simple malfeasance. I liked it that he always carried a Vicks inhaler and would loudly and continually use it when monitoring study halls, as if he were snorting delicious, indispensable fumes. In my doubtless limited view, he was thus wit, scholar, jock; a sketch and a noble eccentric.

He lived out of town on a few acres of orchard in a small house with his partner. We pulled up and got out, but, even though we had phoned ahead, there was no one in sight. Suddenly Foss dropped out of an apple tree beside us, landing agilely, extending a hand in greeting. He wore only shorts and sneakers, a collar of white hair circled his bald crown which, like his fit body, was tanned nut-brown. Even so, I recall that he was wearing his small-lens steel-rimmed spectacles. I stammered some thanks as did my father and mother; we drove away declining the proffered Coke. Probably we were upended by the Edenic manner of his arrival and his astonishing dishabille.

After my brief stint on active duty, I entered Yale College in the fall of 1951. To escape Korea, I joined the NROTC; Pete Wilson, a classmate, later governor of California, was in my company. He stayed on and became a marine officer, but I got out, transferring to the AFROTC, and became a student. I had grown passionate about literature and East Asian studies and soon dropped the air force as well.

I was an undecided boy from the uncouth Midwest, a proto-naval officer, a proto-poet, an awestruck stranger gawking at the windowless façades of senior society tombs or the fantasy-gothic skyscraper of Harkness Tower—and a dress salesman. I tried to keep these parts of me secret. In those days, there was more than a grain of truth in Kingman Brewster's remark that Yale was "a finishing school on Long Island Sound." I was delighted to be a member of the Silent Generation, partly because I had so many things to be silent about. I tried with the last jot of manner I could muster not to act like a weenie—the cant label applied to those who were so out of it they did not know they were out of it—harboring all the while fears that I might be exposed, through some clumsiness or sartorial slip, as a member of this untouchable caste. When I was one of the sophomores elected to the Elizabethan Club, I felt my fears begin to dissipate as confidence grew, sitting at the big table in the tea room at the end of an afternoon listening to Bernard Knox, Evelyn Hutchinson, Frederick Watkins, and other mighty professors reminisce, gossip, and banter; by junior year I had begun to join the conversations.

I didn't have much time or means for dating girls. Occasional weekend dates were obligatory, and I found them at Mount Holyoke and Smith and Vassar through kind roommates. But none was as beautiful and exotic as Virginia Woolf, with whom I fell in love during sophomore year after reading *To the Lighthouse* and mooning over her photo in Bennett's book on Woolf. One girl especially gave sexual experience. Ivy League girls of course would never go the whole way. However, I met one from Albertus Magnus, a local college, not a posh one. This meeting came about through a Dwight Hall dance. Dwight Hall dances were definitely not chic, not "shoe" as Yalies would have said. You would never get a trophy date at a church social. But I was shy, more so than I let on. I went to church every day, or nearly so, through the first two years of Yale. The most important part of my day was chapel at noon in the little gothic church in Dwight Hall on the Old Campus, and the wonderful part of it was, no one need know about it, since my devotions were completed on the way to lunch.

I grew increasingly involved in the poetry I had been writing now for a decade. In sophomore year I "went out for," in the phrase of the day, the *Yale Literary Magazine;* I made the board, and soon a poem was accepted. The crew at the *Lit* were very advanced. Morton Lebeck and friends would go down to visit Pound in St. Elizabeth's on weekends. David Slavitt even wrote an introduction to Pound's poetry, a sort of primer, which the magazine pompously published. On the board was Richard Sassoon, a friend; we had already met bureaucratically, so to speak, because our names were next to each other on college lists. Sassoon was a dark, quiet, scrawny little guy who smirked at college requirements. I liked that and him and saw something of him now and then through senior year. But I had no idea that he ever dated Sylvia Plath, in the same class year up at Smith, that he was her first (and later famous) demon lover with a dark sadistic streak. This view of Sassoon seems Plath's fantasy, but how could I know?

Through those literary, would-be-writer students, I met Russell Thomas and Peter Stansky; in junior year they urged me—required me— to go to the reading by Wallace Stevens in Strathcona Hall. It was a very crowded, hot afternoon in 1953, the last reading Stevens would give in New Haven. I recall, from my station high in the peanut gallery, the large dark-suited form of the man, his white hair, his almost indecipherable delivery. But I had attended the occasion, and that pleased Russell Thomas. Being there was the important thing. Those were heady days.

Doubtless I met Dick Sassoon at required phys ed in freshman year, since all Yale men— in alphabetical order—endured a posture exam and remedial training in erect and correct bearing, if need be. This was one of the wackier of Yale's antics; as freshmen we had to learn all about kypholordosis and other clear and present dangers to our well being. In a complementary moment at the end of my college career, I took another physical exam. In this case my approved Yale posture mattered not a whit. Now eligible for the draft, but with the menace of Korea luckily fading from the horizon, I still had to appear for my government draft physical. This I took in downtown New Haven; the room had many Yalies in it as well as townies. A classmate, the splendidly built and alarmingly fit heavyweight captain of the Yale wrestling team, was instantly given a 4-F and went his way because of a trick knee he had acquired, no doubt in some crafty fall he had learned on the mat. He smiled at me as he walked past where I stood in line, waving his canceled induction papers in farewell. I of course was found to be in 1-A shape.

I graduated with a B.A. in English in June 1955 and was drafted by the army in September. After another boot camp—in this case an easy and relaxing one—I was sent to Fort Meade, Maryland, to the 69th Signal Battalion, where I was trained to be a radio operator. After graduating signal school, and since there was little to do and no equipment to speak of at Battalion, I worked in Supply where an unconvincing ROTC lieutenant pretended to run the show while Sergeant Delmar silently managed everything. Soon orders came down transferring me to Headquarters Fort Meade, where I would work for the newspaper at Headquarters Second Army. The editor of the newspaper, Fred Eastham, allowed a full month's leave and I was able to hop flights, at length reaching Morocco where I visited my brother and his wife in April 1957. In July 1957 I received a direct commission as second lieutenant, Artillery, and was discharged to continue my education under the terms of a remote provision in Regulations that my editor pointed out to me.

Having done so well in Senior Generals before graduating from Yale, Talbot Donaldson, begrudgingly, admitted me to the Yale graduate English program. He opined that I would never become a scholar (he was, as ever, correct), but in the face of my ranking second among 155 English majors, he had no choice. (Fred Crews was number one.) But I had decided it would be best to change universities and applied to Harvard. I studied German (maid Edith, bless her soul, long forgotten) at Harvard Summer School and in September 1957 entered Harvard University Graduate School in the English department, earning an M.A. in 1959 and a Ph.D. in 1963. I studied with Douglas Bush, Archibald MacLeish, Albert J. Guerard, Wendell Clausen, Eric Havelock, Bob O' Clair, B. J. Whiting, Howard Jones, and Walter Jackson Bate. William Alfred was my mentor.

While a graduate student at Harvard I would attend Robert Lowell's poetry workshop at Boston University. There I would meet Anne Sexton and George Starbuck. Starbuck would write poems into the small hours at the Hayes Bickford in Harvard Square, where I also went for late hours to work on Virgil, Old English, or Shakespeare. We talked of many things: poetry and Lowell, Virgil, the poem he was working on at the moment—"A Tapestry for Bayeux" was wholly written in Hayes Bickford—though never his beloved Anne or his job at Houghton Mifflin. I spent an afternoon talking about Katherine Anne Porter's *Ship of Fools* with Anne and Maxine Kumin and their friends in Newton. Anne read my poems and liked "March Drive" best. I did not run with a literary crowd except for those I met at the Signet Society, such as Nemerov or Ustinov, and where later on I did meet Porter. I was surprised to find how finicky and nervous she seemed, as though the largely male audience she spoke to after the Signet dinner did not treat her with altogether the adulation she deserved. I ran into Eliot, quite literally, one rainy afternoon when I was leaving the Mount Auburn Street Post Office. A large man rushed up the stairs to the shelter of the portico; his umbrella was still aloft and its point impaled my coat. The umbrella instantly closed to reveal T. S. Eliot, natty and peering up at me. He said, "Beg pardon! I hope I have not injured you or unduly inconvenienced you." I said, "Mr. Eliot, my pleasure."

English studies weighed on me. The mysteries of Old English even under the obscure if amusing ministrations of the legendary F. P. Magoun were a burden. He looked like the cartoon figure Mr. Magoo (the story ran among graduate students that he was indeed the original). He was erudite beyond measure, but in Harvard's customary manner, the oblivious Magoun addressed the room rather than the students. Francis Peabody Magoun carried his books in a green cloth book bag much as everyone did. He would begin to lecture in an offhand way; heaving his green book bag off his shoulder, his face (and voice) disappearing into the green bag as he looked for a book or paper. The class might as well not have been there. Toward the end of the hour, he would pack up the bag, continue talking as he ambled toward the door and rest his hand on the doorknob, making remarks such as "Remember *trolls*. Trolls are interesting fellows. Trolls like to live under bridges." Then, without ceasing to speak, he would open the door and continue lecturing as he walked down the hall of Sever. Serious students scurried after him to catch the master's words. Others giggled and took more time. Later, on the steps of Sever, there he would be with a cigarette, still talking—not to anyone, but spouting his great knowledge to Memorial Quadrangle.

By the spring of my second year, money and dedication ran low; my wallet and my muse were sad. I applied to Iowa's master of fine arts program and was accepted. The idea of returning to the Mississippi basin, after I had gotten so far clear of it, was abhorrent; but it looked like the best choice. I did two things first, however. I went to see Bill Alfred, a jovial and devout English professor; he had read my poems and we had talked over martinis about writing while in graduate school. He was more sympathetic than any man in town; he had been a graduate student not long before and was writing his own plays and translations. I could not forget his couplet (out of Greek), "What makes us princes is that war in us / Of who we are and what we want to be." Alfred arranged for me to meet Robert Lowell and thence to join his workshop at Boston University.

It was a long trip by subway and trolley; the distance evaporated the exhausted formalities of Harvard. The ambience of Lowell's classroom—relaxed intensity—meant a refuge that was faintly exotic and very welcome. Casual reflections on class poems were buttressed by comparisons with earlier poems, obscure or great, recalled by Lowell, smoking cigarettes at all times, gesturing above the poems he addressed. He singled out individual lines to dissect; to excoriate and often then, surprisingly, to praise—almost in the same breath. The tone of those hours was set, dominated by Lowell's soft, tentative voice with its educated Boston vowels skewed by the Southern drawl and punctuated by periods of thoughtful stillness.

Penniless, I was initially concerned as to cost; my first chat with Lowell was on that score. He solved my ignorance of these matters explaining that he let anyone he chose visit at any time, and I was free to come as I liked. Cal, peering down at me in the late afternoon sunlight outside the classroom, seemed barely able to embrace the idea (in 1959) that a poet should be a Harvard English graduate student. Because of the arrangement with Boston University, workshop population varied from week to week—now a Harvard law student, now another guest from an earlier year. The writers whose work I knew were Anne Sexton, a regular, and George Starbuck, rare visitor because he worked at Houghton Mifflin.

Lowell instantly spotted mannerisms and derided affectations that yielded false sentiment. He fancied daring similes and approved some that to my eye were farfetched; yet his way was to cut through dross and dallying so that the text would reveal its central trope and drift of meaning. I was writing a suite of poems set in Boston, portraits and cityscapes set in the North End; Cal liked some of these (his favorite was "Her River"). But he asked where I was from; surely I was not from Boston. He looked off, intently yet vaguely studying some point in space as if trying to discern wherever it was I *had* come from. My poems did not *feel* like New England poems. I did not *speak* like a New Englander (all this in his hesitant high-pitched drawl). I confessed; the truth was out. Cal pronounced sentence: I must write about the Midwest; out of my roots. O no, I thought; not that! Soon I was writing the suite that became "Hiawatha."

It is midday, bright and warm, early May 1960. Today the class meets in a room facing the Charles; Cal sits in front of the high window, his hulking silhouette a dark outline against blue sky beyond. He has been asked to read a poem at the Boston Arts Festival in June; though he dislikes commission work and is diffident about what he has done, he has a poem that he would like to get our views on. It is about to go into the *Atlantic,* and final changes must be made. He passes duplicated copies of a four-page text around the table; for an hour we make comments (mostly from Sexton on my left) but largely listen to Cal read and then talk about what he is trying to do in "Col. Shaw and the Massachusetts 54th." We agree that the title is too topical and specific, going along with Cal's worry as to its "footnote-ishness." By fall the poem will be called "For the Union Dead."

Running a close second as sympathetic counselor was Jack Bate. Walter Jackson Bate, the chair of the English department, was finishing his great biography of Keats and as ever teaching Dr. Johnson. One afternoon that spring I went to see him; I thought I owed it to him to tell him I was leaving and why. His office was in Warren House, a luxurious, eccentric nineteenth-century maze of a house, once the home of Henry Warren, which housed the English department. Bate's secretary, Pauline Matthews, ran Harvard interference for him: Bate was not in. But I had just seen him close his door. Well then, why do you want to see him? I was resigning. How long would it take? Five minutes, tops. She disappeared. In two minutes she returned. I could see Professor Bate for *five minutes* and not a *second longer*; after five minutes she was coming in after me.

I entered the sanctum, a large room with a table in the center surrounded by chairs. Bate was sitting up on the table, rather like the Cheshire cat on his branch in *Alice.* We talked. He asked where I was from. I was from Minnesota. He noted that he was from Minnesota. Later, he lay down on the table and did leg lifts in the late afternoon sun. I stayed for two hours. When I left I was a graduate student once again, to the core; my Old English requirement had been waived, and Bate was willing to let me do whatever I wanted.

One thing I wanted to do was to study with Archibald MacLeish. He was a barrel-chested man (though surprisingly short when you met him at last), a man with a rich, carefully modulated voice, a manner of sweet bravado: a canny Scots courage veiling a hint of sentimentality. When he chatted with you, walking up Plympton Street, his brisk greetings to others and the pauses, gesturing with his hands while he chose a phrase, let you know that the sweetness of manner masked a steely core and a Highland (or Chicago) temper.

May 1962 was the month of MacLeish's departure. (We did not speak of retirement, but of departure.) MacLeish stood in the candle-lit upstairs banquet room of the Signet Society. Fifty men in evening clothes (and his wife) sat around him. He sang out an indictment of America in choice phrases, a stinging accusation of American selfishness. It was deeply meant and deeply moving. A standing ovation followed. Candles wavered in the air moved by hands clapping. Everyone stood, except for one, roundly against anybody who praised Henry Miller's patriotism. Then MacLeish talked about Hemingway; he said that he probably knew Hemingway as well as he had known anyone, "excepting my wife, of course." The crowd drew its breath and forgot to fidget. He read his poem for Hemingway, "The gun between the teeth explains. / The shattered mouth foretells the singing boy." And he explained the image of the film rewinding.

MacLeish, the Boylston professor, was preparing to leave the world for Conway and Antigua; he was leaving his last office. "When I left Washington," Archie told me, "I went to my farm, out in Conway." We were sitting by the window in his Widener office on a rainy afternoon. Archie gestured, as if Conway were just outside. "The weather was cold, it sank into you, a damp wind streaming down from the Berkshires. I tried to light a fire outside, but the wood was wet and would only smoke and sputter. I sat there on the ground and thought, 'It's just like me, I'm that way inside; I just won't burn inside.'" We looked onto a gray Harvard Yard. I told him I too was depressed from time to time. He gave me a brief hard look and said, "just wait." He went to a bookshelf and took down a seashell. He said that Elizabeth Bishop had given it to him long ago. It was for me. "I know it gets pretty damp in Cambridge; the shell may remind you of the sun and the sea."

The writer whose influence was the greatest on my Harvard years was Yeats. I took John Kelleher's graduate seminar in Yeats, a term spent reading his works in the upstairs parlor of Warren House. I was enthralled and read Yeats avidly and constantly so that other course work suffered. We read all of Yeats; I scoured Boston bookshops, Goodspeed's Milk Street especially, for old copies of his essays, fiction, and plays. Kelleher was not like the other great professors. He did not write critical tomes and articles; he taught. He had five daughters and the most debilitating stammer I had ever witnessed. He sat at the head of the table, a handsome man with a tall Irish face and a shock of white hair. The pace of the class was slow because he had trouble getting words out; he stumbled again and again, the Adam's apple rose and sank, the tongue protruded as he formed a syllable. As another student, Nora Sayre, remembers, it was difficult to believe anyone's tongue could come so far out of his mouth.

Yet nothing mattered but Yeats; Kelleher permanently imprinted Yeats in my mind. From my seat on Kelleher's left, I could see across from me one of two tiled fireplaces in the paneled room. Each old tile pictured a peacock; in the afternoon sun first one then another gleamed green and blue and red, and it

Drawing by Hyde Solomon, Yaddo, 1964

seemed that the setting of *Rosa Alchemica* had sprung to life. Kelleher had known Yeats, and the presence of the master lived in the room when John sang Yeats's poems in his beautiful voice—with never a stumble—or when he passed around snapshots of Yeats. One photo from the thirties, for example, showed the "gland old man" (he had had the Steinach surgery) reeling through a doorway on the arm of Lady Wellesley.

Standing By

After my orals one winter day, I limped toward Grays Hall Middle; Jack Bate caught up with me and we walked together. "I hear they opened a good vein and you bled well" was his comment about my performance. That May he offered me a job in the department to begin in two years, but I would have to get my thesis finished and have the Ph.D. beforehand. I had to promise that—if I wanted the job. My dissertation, directed by Jerome Buckley and Harold Martin, was on the development of the English novel. I did the work and received my terminal degree the following June.

Teaching at Harvard was a pleasure but also a great amount of work. I became assistant senior tutor of Dunster House (shortly before Al Gore was there) and then went back to live in the Yard again in Grays Hall. Teaching at Harvard required most of one's time—and considerable intrepidity, since many of the students were smart, quick, and ambitious, and would soon, I knew, outdistance their instructor. The students were rewarding, all of them, and included—among hundreds more—Heather McHugh, Francine Prose, Willard Spiegelman, Ann Douglas, Dennis Nurkse, Chris Cerf.

The Harvard appointment would end in 1967. I was ready to leave. After all, hadn't Jack Bate said that to stay under the wing of Mother Harvard too long would ruin my chances of becoming a poet, and wasn't he right? Late in 1966 I applied for a Fulbright lectureship to the United Arab Republic. I had always wanted to see the pyramids and mess about in the sand looking for amulets. I was invited to teach at the University of Alexandria. My courses were sent in for the catalog, someone found me an apartment, even hired a fatima to take care of it. I had packed at least my mental bags, and then the Six-Day War occurred. I got a wire

from Washington saying the lectureship was off and suggesting that I resume my previous position. I called back to tell them that I was, more or less, on the runway: everything in storage, I no longer had an apartment or a job, and the Fulbright people must take care of me.

A Mrs. Hatch phoned me and agreed to help, asking where in the world would I like to go? Of course—without thinking—I said I wanted very much to go to—Mainland China. Silence ensued on the other end of the line. This was years before Kissinger—still only two blocks away from where I spoke in Grays Hall, at the Institute for International Studies—had arranged the rapprochement; before Nixon had gone to China. It was an odd request, even a subversive one. Mrs. Hatch would see what she could do. A few days went by; she called back to say that no one could go to China, but they had an extremely attractive opening, with many perks, nearby. Politely but firmly and without a second thought I turned down the University of Saigon. Mrs. Hatch went back to the drawing board and later phoned to offer a position in Japan, which I quickly accepted. I would leave for Tokyo in July. I cleared out of Grays Hall and spent some days with Grey and Bingo Gowrie on Sparks Street before final departure.

Somewhere along the line I had met Fanny Howe; it may well have been through Grey Gowrie. Fanny was a delightful and strong-willed woman; her sense of humor and mine meshed, and we went together toward the close of my Harvard career. A gifted writer and a combative, loving, generous person, Fan meant a lot to me. Fanny's parents were Mark, a professor at the law school and historian (called by some "the last Puritan"), and Molly, the guiding genius of the Poets Theatre. They lived up on Highland Avenue, but Fan had an apartment out on Walden Street at some distance from the off-Brattle Street neighborhood where her parents and the Gowries lived.

At this time Grey Gowrie was very close to Robert Lowell, who that spring was in McLean (the hospital in Belmont) resting up after one of his manic-depressive bouts. Grey was allowed to sign Cal out from McLean because Cal always did what Grey said. (We assumed this obedience came from Lowell's regard for the dignity of rank; Grey was an English Lord, a peer of the realm, and aside from being good friends, Cal was moved by this aristocratic connection.) Fan and I had a party for Cal and Grey (and one or two others) at her apartment. It was only a spaghetti dinner, but the wine was ample. At this time, Cal had to be kept from making phone calls, but the merriment was general and no one noticed him quietly on the phone in the corner. When Cal raised his voice in a brief but commanding bellow, Grey jumped up and put the phone on the receiver. Lowell had put through a call to Jackie Kennedy again. Cal wanted to "get together" with Jackie; if they got married, "with her connections and my talent, why, we could rule the universe." This crisis safely over, we turned to gossip, politics, and laughter, until it was time for Lord Gowrie to take Robert Lowell back to McLean. I admired the genius of Lowell; his defects were only those of his period.

One morning I returned to Grays Hall to get ready for classes. The phone rang, and it was Fan saying that her father had died during the night. I cut my class short and went out to Highland Avenue. Fan and her mother, soon her sister Susan and David von Schlegel and a few law professors began to arrive overseen by Paul Freund, distinguished professor of Constitutional law and Mark's friend, who had taken charge of the first floor. It was a slow and painful time. Mark had been at the height of his powers and influence and was not old. Mark's death triggered a series of fallings away which, with my impending departure, signaled the end of the affair, and also the final chapter of my decade in Cambridge.

Arriving at Haneda airport outside Tokyo just after sundown, I was soon swept up into the slow whirl and languid bustle of the capital city, in the sixties probably the most cosmopolitan place on earth. (As well as newspapers in every language I had heard of, there were *six* English language papers.) In a few days I had attended a party—given by a Ghanaian at the Mexican Embassy for French, German, and American friends, as well as Japanese diplomats and a bevy of Tokyo starlets—and found Minnesotans like Bob Cote and the Meeches. At that time Minneapolis was on the great circle route to the Orient; business and pleasure both passed through Minneapolis from New York on the way to Asia. It may well have been that so many Japanese connections thrived in Minneapolis because everyone met on North-west Airlines, the Minneapolis airline and the shortest way to Eastern Asia.

The Meeches were friends of my parents from Minneapolis. Charlie Meech ran the American side of Yamatake Honeywell; his wife, Nuci, was the doyenne of American society in Tokyo—with a couple of other elegant competitors, to be sure, at her heels. They entertained often and lavishly in their Roppongi home. The Japanese side of Honeywell was headed by one Yamanishi, a highly cultivated man who spoke courtly English, a man so aware of American culture that, when he learned I was a writer, asked me about the current state of Provincetown Playhouse. He had gone to Amherst years before the war (where he was still a trustee) and had been a friend of Catherine Huntington, a patron of the playhouse. The relations between Japanese and Americans at Honeywell were so close that, I was surprised to learn, the Tokyo office of Honeywell never closed its doors during the Pacific war.

This was the land of Zen; in the noise and smoke of the metropolis, it was hard to believe. I sought out repositories of Buddhist art like the Nara Museum in Ueno Park and important hidden destinations such as the garden of Rikugi-en. I practiced *zazen*, such meditation as I had been taught in the States. On a visit to Kyoto with Julia Meech, I, Julia, Dick Baker, and Philip Whalen went to see the head abbot of Daitokuji. Baker was head of the Zen Center in San Francisco that owed allegiance to Rinzai; Daitokuji was the apex of the Rinzai sect; its abbot, the patriarch, and Baker sought an audience to get permission for American Zen adherents with bad backs or other physical ailments to perform *zazen* seated in a chair rather than on the floor. Baker wore his robes, for he was an ordained Buddhist priest by now, as we walked through Kita-ku from Gary Snyder's house; he attracted stares. Safely within the monastery complex, the cordial abbot, in an urbane Oxford English, invited us to join him for tea.

We sat at a heavy Chinese blackwood table; a famous Zen garden of sand and rock lay just beyond the shaded loggia where we talked. The garden had been designed by Kobori Enshu in the seventeenth century; the present abbot was his direct descendant. He spoke of *zazen* as the indispensible path to enlightenment, and of a boy of nine who had been sent by his family to train in the abbot's house. The boy did his zazen and performed his duties for three years before he went home for a visit. There he went skiing and hurt his back. He could no longer sit *zazen* properly. Baker asked, "And how did you handle it? What did you do for the boy?" "Naturally," replied the abbot in his quiet but lofty Oxford accent, "I had to send him home. He could no longer pursue his Buddhist studies if he could not perform zazen as it is required."

The boy's religious vocation had been canceled by back trouble. He could never become a Rinzai priest. This was the answer Baker received. Whalen went to look at the garden. He was more a Shingon sect Buddhist anyway, but clearly pained by the rigid dictate of this cultured man. On the way out of the great Daitokuji we saw a sign that said, "Want to learn about zen? Help accepted: wood to chop, floors to wash." Everywhere works seemed to take precedence over faith. To the Japanese, work *was* religious experience, and too often, as far as I could make out, of a simply grueling, mundane order. It was some time after my visit to the abbot of Daitokuji that I stopped sitting zazen.

Teaching took scant time, partly because student riots closed down the Hongo campus of Tokyo Daigaku; I also went once a week to the Tokyo University of Foreign Studies and to another campus of Todai in the suburbs. Getting to these sites took far longer, an hour and a half, than the teaching did, and I prepared for classes on the Yamate circle line, opening my books and spreading out as I headed for these classrooms. I did not stand out with my books, except as a *gaijin,* an outsider: everyone read on public transportation.

The trains and subways were all but silent, yet friendly, even sociable. Strangers offered to help you find your way. Everyone read except at rush hours, when the cars were too jammed. In the packed cars the polite reserve of the Japanese often melted away; men and women would jostle, fondle, even grope each other (compare Mishima's *Forbidden Colors*). The day that news of Robert Kennedy's death came, however, Armed Forces Radio, a sort of NPR from the military for English-speaking residents, told us to stay off the streets; no one knew what the Japanese reaction to this American violence might be. Kennedy was wildly popular in Japan. He had recently visited and had climbed Mount Fuji—a sort of patrician and

politic pilgrimage, and very welcome to the Japanese. I had been invited to a dinner party in Ikebukuro and was not staying put. The trains were quiet. On the way home, a Shinto priest in his robes saw me from down the aisle. He recognised an American and came up, knelt, salaamed, and commenced to pray for me—a mourning fellow citizen of Bobby Kennedy. Other passengers were a bit startled by this behavior and initially started to prevent him, but then nodded, agreed, watched. I did not dare to move.

The next morning it seemed that every window in downtown Tokyo displayed a poster-size photo of Bobby. How did they do it? How could they have prepared so completely? The Japanese were a mystery. The longer one stayed the less one understood. Nevertheless, I found myself intoxicated with Nippon (to translate their phrase for it), in some superficial way wanting to become Japanese. So when the Fulbright Commission offered me another year, I panicked. Doubtless I should have stayed, but if I did I would sink into a stupor of involvement with this sublime culture, like Peter Brogren and others at the Foreign Press Club, a hangout for the bibulous dispossessed. Before leaving the States, I had arranged for a job at Brown so that I would not end "on the beach"—unemployed—when I returned. I made up my mind to honor the commitment I had made to Edwin Honig, the Brown English department chair, and I came back on schedule.

Moreover, there was someone I wanted to see. Besides corresponding with Fan (who was moving toward marriage now) while I was in Tokyo, I also wrote to Ginny Scoville, whom I'd met shortly before leaving at the Cambridge home of the Moviuses where, up from New York, she was spending a weekend. I was feeling more and more drawn to the States, as if it were a rock in a storm of alien affections, a safe tree to come to for shelter, even if it didn't have a culture in the sense that Japan had one. Virginia was somehow convolved with this feeling; she was a spirit at the core—which she might be, since as yet we hardly knew each other. It fell out that her uncle Charlie lived about six blocks from my place in Shinjuku. It was one chance in ten million; this proximity seemed preordained. Going to dinner at the home of that charming man and his lovely lady (whom Ginny's mother called "Madame Butterfly") helped to cement proleptically a relation-

With his wife, Virginia, White Creek, 1975

ship with the Scoville clan that had scarcely begun.

At Brown I knew almost no one, and I went up to Cambridge to renew old ties. On a slushy March day in 1969, I went to Lowell's workshop, now at Harvard, in an Adams House basement, a ceiling all heat pipes and light fixtures. Cal was disturbed, manic; waving an arm, he talked about Churchill and Hitler. How there might have been no war had they gotten together—and why? Because "they were both painters." Cal had Churchill's *The Gathering Storm* with him and held it up. Bill Byrom complained. He lashed out at Bill, accusing him of knowing nothing—worse, coming from "a red brick university." (In fact Byrom was an Oxford graduate who soon became a fellow of Exeter College.) "Unlike the Earl of Gowrie here," Cal continued, pointing to Grey, "who understands these matters—and went to Oxford."

The last workshop I visited was in the Loeb Drama Center. Students and visitors packed the room; five times as many as there had been ten years earlier at Boston University. I didn't know a soul. Now all awaited the entrance of Lowell as if attending an audience. Cal came in, towering, bowed, dishevelled, a Rip Van Winkle figure, exhausted menace in his bearing. He carried an armful of mimeo sheets, the thickness of several phone books. He passed out a poem to discuss; quite before it had gotten around the room he was asking for responses. A student complained that he had not had the chance to read the text. Lowell removed his glasses, stared at him, then turned to the next student. Silence. Lowell began to speak, the courtly Southern drawl and Brahmin poise asserted. He talked about the text; he quoted Dante, Anthony Hecht. He praised the author—and reached for another text from the pile at his elbow. It was a different time, I saw, and whatever bond there had been between us was growing slack.

We spoke last in a Quincy House guest suite where Cal lay beached on a double bed. He asked what *one* modern Japanese novel he should read; I told him to read *The Makioka Sisters,* Tanizaki's masterpiece. He asked what I was writing. Had I written a book of poems about Japan? I admitted that I had been trying but had not yet. He chuckled—and pounced: "If you don't write a book about Japan, I think I'll go over there and write one myself—after I've finished with Israel. So you had better get to work, Stephen."

The year at Brown went fast. Honig was on sabbatical, and clearly the present chairman had no use for me. Yet I was the Phi Beta Kappa poet that spring. After the dinner and ceremonies, the pundits and grand Phi-Bet' wallahs went off together, doubtless to the Danforths or one of the other elegant mansions abutting Brown's campus. Ray Hefner, president of the university, had not been asked,

nor had I. The evening was an emblem of the social world of Providence, which stood in stark contrast to the vast hospitalities of Tokyo. English teachers by trade, the president of Brown and I walked back over the campus under the May moon, he to the president's house, I to my apartment. Hefner limped, and we walked slowly. It was a meditative hour. When I told him I was leaving, he said he wished he could as well. But it would be a year or two before his plans for reorganizing the curriculum could be fully implemented. Then he would resign and go back to Iowa—fast.

As for me, I was about to go to Vermont to teach at Bennington College and to marry. One stage, a peripatetic stage, of my life was over.

One way to divide the world is to put parents on one side, nonparents on the other. Parents seem to rush frustrated down their path

At the old Bennington: (from left) Arturo Vivante, Sandy, Linda Pastan, Peter Pastan, Maxine Kumin, Nicholas Delbanco, Ben Belitt," 1983

shouting, "You'll see," at the same time cooing about that "greatest joy." The intense abiding command of the tribe to be father thus might mean to enter one's share of the "great joy" or might be an urge to level, drafting one into that grousing sodality, that I might suffer as they did. Tension between those in the stockade of parenthood and those on the outside was hidden but no less there for that. My friends took an *unreasonable* delight or shock to learn of my expectant fatherhood. Decades later, I still find the divide an operative border. There is always in each new face I meet a look of either dismay or relief upon learning I am not childless.

Two is about to become three at White Creek. We move, it seems, in the sedate joy of impending grace. A stitch in Ginny's side; a hard lump the size of a pecan like a knot under her skin. The child is swimming about, moving up, West, new territory. She says, "The frontier is being pushed back, out toward Montana." "Tell it to stay out of South Dakota," I reply, "where there are badlands. To say nothing of Mount Rushmore." White Creek fills with a zany euphoria. *Plenum mobile.* "Space is up." Our child is on her way.

The presence of my parents, both in time and in cross-country distance, had imperceptibly, languidly, become an absence. The house in White Creek, New York, a brittle cottage nestled in a mossy cove of limestone rock, lost its Wordsworthian charm when, scarcely a half mile down the road, the Owlkill Rod and Gun Club first set up a skeet shoot, then a rifle range, and presently a Sherman tank, moved up from Hoosick Falls. One Sunday morning I drove downhill and saw its cannon raised, aimed toward Vermont, the barrel oiled and glistening in the sun. Our time had come.

By this stage I had become a member, and soon a senior one, of the Bennington College faculty. The days of learning as a pupil became days of learning as a teacher. It was my privilege to be a part of that clan: colleague and thus—at Bennington—friend of Bernard Malamud, Georges Guy, Phebe Chao, Ben Belitt, Arturo Vivante, Claude Fredericks, John Gardner, Philippe Denis, Nick Delbanco, George Garrett, Harry Mathews, and many more. Their collegial manner was informal, warm, serious.

For example, the Malamuds were beyond compare. He was both a very precise man and an amicable one. Bern and Ann's hospitality was warm and frequent. Alan Cheuse's wedding to Marjorie Pryse took place in their living room overlooking the Bennington valley at twilight. Robert Pinsky read Sidney. The Malamud children, Jana and Paul, looked on from their portraits by Rosemarie Beck on the blue walls. Ann served a splendid buffet; there was always plenty to drink. But Bern was precise; he invited guests for, say, 6:30. If you came a minute before, he would open the door saying, "You're early!" And if you arrived at 6:35 he opened the door saying, "You're late!" The circular drive before their house on Catamount Lane would fill up with guests checking their watches and then marching down to the front door en masse when it appeared to be the exact moment of which the invitation spoke.

Before long, when the college disposed of some property, we bought a house and an acre of land. It was at some distance from the campus, and a bargain. Van Ben is a compact Greek Revival farmhouse with a marble-floored porch across the road from the holiday mansion of the family that had bankrolled the college I worked at. Here our daughter Clare and son Nathaniel, born in 1980, were raised. The childhood I lived out for many years gave way to fatherhood. Enough of fathers—and father figures; it was time to be a father myself! The new house had room for the four of us: it had been two buildings, joined together in the twenties. The join leaked in the winters, but the discreet façade (small half in front) masked a roomy interior, the way I had come to think a home, or a life, should be: unassuming, even slight, at first glance, but spacious on further acquaintance.

Before the Civil War, Van Ben—at least the earlier, front half—had been the residence of Nathaniel Hall, whose farm extended in every direction, until the Hall-Park-McCullough family, rich from California gold, bought the fields and turned them into a park and built their high Victorian folly. Our house had been a part of the estate; our home and land were, by comparison, tiny; they were quiet and rural, yet near the schools Clare and Nat would attend.

Like Yeats's midforties, mine were a dry time; unlike Yeats I lacked even a publisher. But in the eighties, however it came about, I began to write again with a fresh lease on my vocation and a new access to my muse. The publisher Alfred A. Knopf took me on and

Speaking at Harvard's 350th Anniversary celebration: Derek Brewer, Master of Emmanuel College, Cambridge; the author; Archibald Cox; and Robert Runcie, the Archbishop of Canterbury, 1986

eventually published three books. At the college, I taught English and American literature, Chinese literature in translation, Latin. It had never been a school sponsoring narrow academic specializations. At Bennington one could teach anything—and was frequently asked to do so. Visions of Blake and Noah Foss rose before me when I began to give Latin tutorials, which served to refresh my Latin not only for teaching Virgil but also for translating Seneca's *Hercules Oetaeus* for *The Johns Hopkins Complete Roman Drama*.

But a detailed account of the decades at Bennington College must await another occasion—if indeed it deserves one, for the life of a sedentary poet and teacher stationed in the remote reaches of New England offers little to notice and less to celebrate, for all its minor contact with the world.

Coming Across

At the rail, I see the Last Supper carved in wood. The tablecloth is bisected into neat rectangles where it has been ironed and pressed. All the best for Christ, whose arms stretch above the tablecloth. It comes to me that in the time of Jesus, among poor Palestinians, no one would have had a great linen tablecloth, let alone an iron to give it such crisp divisions. Then I saw that the folds were there to give structure and pattern to a large otherwise empty space. They gave definition to emptiness even as they took away the vacuum. I thought, this is what Yeats meant by the image and the mask. And what Kenneth Clark meant when he wrote of the cords and ridges at groin and thigh in Classical sculptures of a man's body. You see, it's largely artificial to demarcate areas of the body, its parts, because there's really only one long constant soft expanse of flesh there. But the eye of the beholder yearns. It yearns to see the members distinct, to be able to see that this is where the arm stops, attaches to the breast; there is where the leg ceases, and how the trunk involves it. So with the Last Supper. We give it edges and sections, and draw lines through it so that we can know it. And we do know it as a complete thing, by its creases, divisions, folds.

*

A spring afternoon. Since I am in first grade, I am home by lunch time. Puttering about upstairs while my mother prepares for guests; three ladies coming for lunch and a hand of bridge. Snooping soon in the Shaker boxes atop my father's curly maple Empire bureau. Finding a little folder of what looked like pale balloons in a colorful packet saying Peacock Brand. I have no idea what their purpose is. Going to the bath to test one by filling it with water. What fun, throwing it out the window, the window just above the front door. The balloon, splattering at the feet of the three ladies being met by Mother. The water spilling across the brick, the balloon shriveling to reveal a broken condom. Three ladies in hats looking up. My mother on the stairs.

Sunday afternoon in winter I go with Father in the black 1939 Buick sedan to the drugstore at 50th and Penn for ice cream. Father avidly listens to the radio. The news is coming in that Pearl Harbor is being attacked. I ask what is Pearl Harbor, what the news means. Father is agitated and drives fast around corners, rocking me in the front seat against the gearshift and his overcoat. "Maybe war," he says.

*

4815, a perfect house for children who want places to play hide-and-seek. At the summit, a

secret room. Beyond, the neighborhood and the streets named in alphabetical order: Oliver, Penn, Queen, Russell, Sheridan, Thomas, Upton, Vincent, Washburn—site of Robert Fulton grade school—Xerxes. I walk from Sheridan to school, past a ginkgo sapling on Forty-ninth just past Wayne Blomgren's house. During the war, Raggedy Andy, our unkempt rattail spaniel, follows me to school; Miss Easthagen welcomes him in the kindergarten, though dogs are not allowed. Mrs. Sandy, after all, is president of the PTA. Raggedy Andy tips garbage cans in alleyways for smaller dogs; at a family council we must decide what to do. We all love the dog so; at length, he is enlisted in the K9 Corps, from which—after guard training—he will never be allowed to return; from which, after VJ Day, my father receives a canine commendation.

*

Wayne (how many boys named Wayne lived in that neighborhood?) Andrews, the aggressive boy across the street, older and bigger, climbs and lurks in trees of the vacant lots of woods by his house. He likes to wait for little boys and peer hawkishly, silently down at them. In that wood we play fort and dig pits. But if Wayne catches a stray boy alone in the wood, he ties him to a tree and leaves him there. That prehension is more embarrassing than painful at first, a kind of game in which punishment plays a part, until you get scared and feel forgotten, and Wayne's cords begin to hurt.

One cloudy afternoon I leave school to walk up Forty-ninth Street home. On the corner of Washburn a featureless stucco house stands on a rise of lawn worn bald as first base by kids running over it after school; a girl in my class lives there. Behind the house, a garage. My friend David runs down the driveway, telling me to come; leads me to the garage, where a knot of boys, some from his class some from fifth grade, have gathered. The father would have had the car at work. A sixth-grade boy is the center of the motionless gang; then I see the girl, whose home it is. . . . It is my first sexual encounter, wholly visual—and olfactory—in the breathless garage. The smell of gas and oil and dead grass in the garage seem to grow loud. I flee.

*

Little flashes in a larger world, like distant lightning, the hot afternoon of a Midwestern growing up. The usual toy soldiers. Acorn fights. Pictures from the *National Geographic* of a Ubangi woman with coils about her neck and heavy discs pulling at her lips, her eyes staring, possibly she smiles; a naked African youth, his muscular frame covered with ashes, rides on the shoulders of another giant he has just defeated in a wrestling match. What is exciting is the blank, careless, even stupefied look on both their faces.

*

Also from the *Geographic,* color photos of tantric Buddhist tangkas showing couples locked in strange embraces, pages I tape around the bedroom walls along with my handwritten enlargement of a phrase from the article, "Carnal Knowledge." Perhaps I think "carnal knowledge" means religious experience. But Mother is shocked, and down they come. She finds me in my room and questions me. "Do you know what carnal knowledge is?" Then more loudly, "You don't know what carnal knowledge is!" I cower on my bed.

*

Aspects. Jupiter (in Sagittarius) square Neptune (in Virgo): This aspect suggests emotional excesses and a craving for exotic experiences. There will be a great deal of wandering, either physically or mentally. Jupiter in Sagittarius indicates a love of philosophy, education, travel, and foreign cultures. You have far-reaching metaphysical thoughts. You wish to know the purpose of the individual in the universe, and what is the ultimate creative force behind the evolutionary process. There is also a deep interest in the social and philosophical ideas that have shaped history. Neptune in Virgo can manifest itself as a tendency to excessive emotional preoccupations; unwise dietary habits are typical for the Neptune in Virgo generation.

*

Mother in the garden tending the peonies, hosta, petunias; lithrum and Cleome out toward the lake beyond the garden. Petunias for "splashy" pinks. Her favorite, peonies, for the scent. Standing there motionless, white globes or pink, watching them. Or on the dining room porch, whistling to the cardinals in the elms beyond. The cardinals calling back to her. For long minutes, their ornithological converse.

*

Walking, because no transport is available, to church to serve at eight o'clock communion. The rector of St. Luke's is an austere Englishman, Norman Burgomaster, lately from assignment among the Eskimos, who looks like a Titian. Three-and-a-half miles to St. Luke's, starting at seven to be on time; the craggy visage of Burgomaster as I pour the water over his hands. Walking back, pheasants reconnoitering in the bushes by the banks of Lake Harriet.

*

My parents, next door at our neighbors' annual party for the Metropolitan Opera cast. Going to sleep, or not going to sleep, listening to Patrice Munsel sing the count, her role in *Die Fledermaus,* on the terrace. The next day Mother telling that she has talked with Nathaniel Merrill and concluded that he is a cousin.

*

Aspects. Mercury conjunct Venus in Leo: This gives you grace of expression in speech and writing. It produces literary talent and poetic ability. Often mental endeavors are carried on in partnerships. The mind is turned toward thoughts of love and you bear goodwill toward your fellows. Mercury in Leo gives mental self-confidence and positiveness in solving problems.

*

It is the middle of the night. I am in my lower bunk, asleep in the barracks at the naval air station outside Minneapolis. My body feels a warmth on the legs and suddenly I am wide awake. By the side of the bunk a gross sailor, totally plastered, weaves slightly back and forth, pissing on my bed. Slowly I raise my leg, cock it back, and give him an enormous kick. He hurtles back, across the aisle in front of the row of bunks, and with a loud crash that terrifies me clatters into the row of wall lockers. He sprawls on the floor and all is silent. At reveille the next morning he lies there still.

*

My father at 2011 in the yard getting the leaves up, slightly bowed over his rake, collecting silence. Later, madly dancing for his grown-up children, doing his mimic of a model showing a frock on the runway, in Mother's clothes.

The prefab huts at the Cascades, near White Creek, like the cells of hermits. The Cascades, in shadow and chiaroscuro of rock outcroppings capped in snow, lit now by concealed, "artful"

spots. Mist roiling up from tumbling waters. Could I really be "the madman of Shu" in such a cell? I say at once, I could never work there. And would rather have a Muromachi scroll of a vale on my wall. That chasm is too "romantic," picturesque. Perfection in nature is a heavy distraction.

*

Our son at five: "Everyone knows that the world does not end, but the world does end. Mom, does the world end? Are you just like mud when you're dead?"

*

Aspects. Moon (in Capricorn) sextile Saturn (in Pisces): this gives patience and practicality in professional and domestic matters. It indi-

Sandy with his son, Nathaniel, and daughter, Clare, 1997

cates good organization, frugality, and integrity. Saturn in Pisces is a difficult position because it causes you to become trapped in memories. It is difficult for you to deal with the demands of the present.

Moon (in Capricorn) opposition Mars (in Cancer): This indicates a volatile, emotional nature. You can lose your temper over petty annoyances, particularly domestic ones.

Note: You may possibly have your moon in Aquarius rather than Capricorn if you were born late in the day. I cannot do your houses or angles without knowing your birth time. You have no air signs. . . .

My father dying of a slow stroke in Northwestern Hospital: "Don't ever educate your children. They'll leave you forever."

*

The Anatomy of Melancholy, as first printed: the dreaming in the center, the learning at the margins, decorating, buttressing, refracting, "tucking in" the text.

*

In a long perspective, the situation does not matter, the telos only does, and that is the enduring trade. Think of a man in his study, surrounded by his books, looking at them— like a cat with unfocused stare crouched under a peony bush—wondering whatever had they meant to him, things he once read, loved ones, loved things and days, and what he had been about. At the bottom of the garden of years, what is time? What matters but a few facts and loved ones held; or a mind, on the long frayed track of memory, running in the dark?

BIBLIOGRAPHY

Poetry:

Stresses in the Peaceable Kingdom, Houghton Mifflin, 1967.

Roofs, Houghton Mifflin, 1971.

Riding to Greylock, Knopf, 1983.

Man in the Open Air, Knopf, 1988.

Thanksgiving Over the Water, Knopf, 1992.

The Thread: New and Selected Poems, Louisiana State University Press, 1998.

Chapbooks:

Caroms, Groton School Press, 1960.

Mary Baldwin: Poems, Dolmen Press, 1962.

The Destruction of Bulfinch's House, Identity Press, 1963.

Wild Ducks, Ferguson Press, 1965.

Japanese Room, Hellcoal Press, 1969.

The Difficulty, Burning Deck, 1975.

Landscapes, White Creek Press, 1975.

End of the Picaro, Banyan Press, 1977.

The Hawthorne Effect, Tansy Press, 1980.

Flight of Steps, Bellevue Press, 1982.

To a Mantis, Plinth Press, 1987.

The Epoch, Plinth Press, 1990.

Vale of Academe, Holocene, 1996.

Marrow Spoon, Garlic Mouth, 1997.

Nonfiction:

The Raveling of the Novel: Studies in Romantic Fiction from Walpole to Scott (criticism), Arno, 1980.

Contributor to anthologies:

Best Poems of 1960: Borestone Mountain Poetry Awards, 1961, Pacific Books, 1962.

Jonathan D. Cutler, editor, *"Harvard Advocate" Centennial Anthology,* Schenkman, 1966.

The "New Yorker" Book of Poems, Viking, 1969.

Arnold Adoff, editor, *City in All Directions,* Macmillan, 1969.

X. J. Kennedy, editor, *Messages: A Thematic Anthology of Poetry*, Little, Brown, 1973.

The New Yorker Book of Poems, Morrow, 1974.

Daryl Hine and Joseph Parisi, editors, *The "Poetry" Anthology, 1912-1977: Sixty-Five Years of America's Most Distinguished Verse Magazine*, Houghton, 1978.

Literature and America III, Nan-un-do, 1980.

Poems on My Mind, Longman-Cheshire, 1981.

A Century in Two Decades, Burning Deck, 1982.

An Anthology of Magazine Verse and Yearbook of American Poetry, Monitor Book, 1985.

Donald Parker and Warren Herendeen, editors, *The Visionary Company, Special Malcolm Cowley Issue*, Dobbs Ferry, 1987.

Paul Ruffin, editor, *Contemporary New England Poetry: A Sampler*, Volume II, Texas Review Press, 1987.

Michael Klein, editor, *Poets for Life: Seventy-Six Poets Respond to AIDS*, Crown, 1989.

Laurence Goldstein, editor, *Season Performances*, University of Michigan Press, 1990.

Richard Nunley, editor, *The Berkshire Reader: Writings from New England's "Secluded Paradise," 1676-1990*, Stockbridge Berkshire House, 1992.

Thomas E. Foster and Elizabeth Clark Guthrie, editors, *A Year in Poetry*, Crown, 1995.

John Hollander and David Lehman, editors, *The Best American Poetry 1998*, Scribner, 1998.

Translator of "A Cloak for Hercules," verse translation of Lucius Annaeus Senecca, in *The Tragedies*, Volume II, Johns Hopkins University Press, 1995; "Quis Multa Gracilis," verse translation of Horace, in *Norton Treasury of World Poetry*, Norton, 1998; *Seven Against Thebes*, verse translation of Aeschylus, University of Pennsylvania Press, 1998.

Also author of text of "Vita de Sancto Hieronymo," an antiphonal cantata with music by Henry Brant, MCA Music, 1973, and *The Austin Tower*, 1976. Author of musical settings, including (all music by Richard Wilson, except as noted; all published by G. Schirmer, except as noted): *A Dissolve*, 1970; *Light in Spring Poplars*, 1971; *Soaking*, 1971; *Home from the Range*, 1971; *Elegy*, 1972; *Can*, Belwin-Mills Publishing, 1973; *The Breakers Pound*, music by Dan Locklair, Kerby Ltd., 1989; "The Second Law" in *The Aids Quilt Songbook*, Boosey and Hawkes, 1993.

Contributor of poems, articles, and reviews to periodicals, including *Agenda, Atlantic, APR, Boston Review, Boulevard, Chelsea, Grand Street, Harvard Magazine, Harper's, Kenyon Review, Nation, New Republic, New Yorker, New York Times, Paris Review, Partisan Review, Poetry, Salmagundi, Southwest Quarterly, Virginia Quarterly, Yale Review*, and others.

Barry Silesky

1949-

Barry Silesky, building a vision in northern Wisconsin, 1976

Thor's Helper

They're cutting out the stump now,
    the saw's hum drifting
through city walls, carving another
    world. Cut oak
amid smells of pine, smoke from the first
    fires. Split and stacked,

in a year the oak would be dried to warm us.
    Enough for a few November days
still lies in back of the old house we built.
    Almost
        deer season, long-necked geese swoop in
and out of the swamps, rough barks gather at
    sunset
        on the way up, as the ragged V's

head out. Next week, the last trip north
    to that house. I hauled the chimney
cement block by block to the roof, only
    dropped the last eighty pound block near
the top. Made it all the way the second try.
    Stood in snow waist deep to cut wood,

split out back stripped to a shirt in zero
    degrees.
        I loved the sweat, the climb
to the roof to clean the chimney, check
    shingles,
        any reason. Sharon and Joyce lay naked
on the deck below the day I vented the roof
    the way I should have at first. I had to

build that deck twice. And once, shelves, each
    wall,
        screen porch, every inch. It's not true
ash, that tree they're finishing off. It stood a
    long time.
        Seventy feet high, four feet across,
older than four wars, six presidents, houses
    on either side, this one.

"Thor's helper," from the rose family, the
    mountain ash
        was known to ward off evil, pieces
to stop any disaster. We were going to live
    there
        for good. So Clark drank too much,
talked too much the more he drank. So I fell
    in love
        with Lynne, who lived with him,

and she half with me. So I drove the van
    into a ditch after a long shot of whiskey
the night my wife left the message
    she couldn't resist
that sailor. I can still see
    the white snow in the headlights, my hands

clenched on the wheel. The house is finally
    sold. Lynne married Dave. The wife
I had is gone. Dick and Denise
    divorced. We planted
two birch, a white pine, vegetables, peonies, iris.
    The bugs were impossible.

In the old countries, they'd carry twigs, splinters
    of that ash for luck. It was another
age. I'd have tried it if I'd known. They're
    going to build
        an apartment building in that yard.
Those winters would never end. Two hours,
    and the tree's done.

All the poems, stories, sentences, lead back and forth, crossing and recrossing trails, and the whole's not anywhere; but this poem is where I have to start. I watched that tree come down through the kitchen window of the Chicago two-flat that's been home for the last dozen years, the sound of the chainsaw bringing back again the country I left, and as I felt the loss again—both the tree and the country—I thought again, even as most of me knew better, that I'd somehow gone "fundamentally wrong" (as an old landlord liked to put it, about the whole progress of civilization) in settling in this city.

I know that at any given time part of me always wants to get out of wherever I am. And in this case, the roots of the two sides, the rural north and the urban midwest, run deep. The only important figure not in the poem is Paul; but then, he is, underneath, for once not visible, but present as ever. Nearly twenty years after I've moved back to the city, he's still there in the middle. And so, maybe because he's *not* in the poem by name, the place to start:

A little more than six feet tall, and thin, with a dark, full beard, Levi jacket buttoned up, standard jeans, and Sorrel boots, he's coming up the trail over a crust of snow, through oak and jackpine and hazelbrush. Actually, I'm pretty sure the day he appeared at the edge of the clearing was a little earlier—late October I think—but the early winter picture is more accurate in texture and feel—"truer" (and isn't the function of autobiography to tell the truth?), despite my ongoing argument with a journalist friend who insists the truth is only in verifiable fact.

I do remember that the cold came early that year, even for northern Wisconsin, so maybe there was snow. And I was outside, splitting or stacking firewood, or working on the outside of the geodesic dome my wife Loren and I were getting ready for winter. The friend who had initiated the project had come up to Minneapolis with his wife a year before to get his Ph.D. in "Future Studies," and they'd bought ten acres of these woods, an hour and a half north of the city. The idea was to build a weekend retreat, a sort of communal version inspired by reading the ecologist, architect, and thinker Buckminister Fuller. The dome would shed snow and rain, be simple to heat, and provide a gathering place to foster communal

"Playing guitar on the porch of my house, with a friend," near Grantsburg, Wisconsin, 1977

relations. In exchange for making it habitable for the winter, we would have a place to live for the season. We had been traveling since late spring, living in our van, and the dome seemed the perfect stop on our way to—what? Enlightenment? Some future, at least, that had nothing to do with the world we'd grown up with and left in Chicago. Left, we were sure, for good.

Paul was moving up from Minneapolis with his girlfriend and building an A-frame just around the corner, only a few hundred yards away, really, through the woods. He'd had the basement poured and the block laid by a contractor, but he was doing the carpentry himself, with sporadic help from friends. He was also sleeping on a plywood slab in his basement, next to a new woodstove where he was burning fresh green oak from the trees cleared for his house, not realizing how little heat the logs would give as the sap sizzled away. His roof was the subfloor above.

We didn't say much then besides acknowledging that we'd be neighbors, and it wasn't until I left some three years later that something in my nostalgia, and his own wider reaching out, really drew us close. At times he could be almost gregarious, and from the beginning I was attracted to his delicious irreverence, his brash humor. We also had the same taste in rock 'n' roll (an important consideration in those days), and roughly the same inexperience in building and living in the woods. But there was clearly something apart in him, and his girlfriend, as well.

I remember him telling me how he went out to the swamp early one morning at the beginning of duck hunting season, listened to the silence, spotted the hunters out in their boats, waiting, and started screaming at them:

Go home! You've killed them all! Nothing out here anymore!

And his story of finding a pile of trash in the woods nearby, and an envelope in it with a local address—then taking the trash to that address, ringing the bell and telling the woman who answered that she'd forgotten something as he handed her the bag.

It's the righteous outlaw—brash, intemperate, outrageous (the archetypal American hero?)—that he stirs up for me. I guess it's one of the parts of myself I've most liked since childhood. Though in the same breath (a short detour, here?) I must confess that the rebelliousness that attracts me, that in no small way got me out of Chicago and up there in the first place, that is such a cornerstone of my generation (of America itself?), was never strong enough to draw me into real disobedience, either as a child or teenager or adult.

Okay, I did push a kid down my front hill in third grade, making him break his arm; I did throw a few snowballs at cars coming down the block, and tomatoes at other cars on the freeway one night in sixth grade (I didn't hit any); I joined a demonstration against George Wallace's speech at the University of Minnesota with my junior high politics club in 1964. And yes, I smoked marijuana in my college dorm and many other places, and tried a good variety of the requisite illegal psychedelics of my time. And I did get tear-gassed in Washington, D.C., in a 1969 antiwar demonstration, and helped tear down the fences to block the state highway through my college campus during 1970 demonstrations. And a few years ago I spent a couple hours in the neighborhood police station lockup when I was arrested for scalping baseball tickets.

But for me, this all comes more under a heading my wife would label "passive-aggressive"; maybe they're skeletons that would make a political career impossible, but hardly the record of a desperado. Perhaps more to the point is that urge to walk the boundary, to push at the limits of the acceptable, yet retain access to both sides. I don't have to squint too hard

to see it in my poems and fiction, if not the biography I wrote of Ferlinghetti, another literary figure who also remained mostly within accepted borders, at the same time flirting with the edge.

And so: how did it happen?

I knew almost nothing about building when I started working on the dome, though I remember my grandfather (my mother's father) doing a lot of handyman work when I visited, and doing some on visits to our house as well. On the other hand, I don't remember my father even mowing the lawn. I think my parents viewed physical labor as something for lower classes. But it was 1976 when I began working on the dome, I was 27, and I had seen several of my peers, college educated, give up the intellectual ambitions they had been raised with to take up physical work, those skills being somehow more elemental, more in tune with essential rhythms. Another close friend had given up teaching for carpentry in the previous years. Friends in Colorado had quit college and were living for free in abandoned cabins they'd found in the mountains and fixed up. It made so much more sense than doing the alienating work of the mind. And maybe just because I was so unprepared, because I am physically small and not especially dexterous, I was attracted to the challenge.

During the winter Loren and I spent in the dome, we decided we liked it up there, and in the spring we bought ten acres on a nearby corner to build a place of our own. Not a dome, we both agreed—there were problems with insulation and water leakage, and not enough privacy—but an actual house. Or more accurately in my view, a cabin: one or two rooms, maybe three, but small. The idea was simplicity and self-sufficiency—the currency of the time.

Loren on the other hand wanted a larger, more conventional house. And so, we argued. As we'd argued about the Montessori school she set up and ran in the city, about leaving it, about where to go next, about plants and furniture and people. Later, friends would remember us arguing incessantly, though at the same time, they were surprised when we did finally get divorced. Despite the arguments, we seemed to have such understanding and sympathy; and so we did. More evidence, I suppose, of the truth that the workings of men and women are basically indecipherable to all but the principals.

Either way, our compromise was finally much closer to her vision—a twenty by twenty-four (smaller than she wanted) frame house on a basement (which I agreed was a good idea) with a gambrel roof so we could finish the second storey (much more space and work than I wanted). A quarter of the second floor would be open both for the look and so the wood heat from the basement would rise easily. By March, we were assembling what we could from farm auctions and newspaper ads—lumber and paneling, a ladder, a wheelbarrow, tools—I took down trees to widen a clearing, we hired an excavator to dig the hole for the basement, then took one last vacation trip back to Chicago to visit friends before the project began.

It was harder than anything I'd ever imagined. I still remember the day I came home from helping a neighbor shingle a steep roof and stared at the hole in our woods. It was a gaping maw that looked ready to swallow me instantly. I remember the day I cleaned off the tools and wheelbarrow and collapsed against the concrete block wall the mason we'd hired had set up while draining cans of beer as we mixed and wheeled mortar until I wasn't sure I'd ever move again. And the day I stared at the first wall I had spent the morning carefully measuring and cutting and nailing together from rough cut two-by-fours, complete with two windows, and realized with the force of a fist

*"This is the house I built
with my ex-wife, Loren,"* 1978

in my stomach that I'd built the whole thing a foot short. And the day I stepped on a nail through my tennis shoes and spent the afternoon waiting for a tetanus shot. And the day I hauled the last chimney block up the ladder on my shoulder to the roof, and six rungs from the top, dropped it.

But I also remember making it all the way up after a ten-minute break and setting that block on top. And the sound and flash of rose-breasted grosbeaks, and scarlet tanagers, and endless blue sky that grew over me the day I climbed out of the basement, where a neighboring farmer and a few friends had just helped us pour the cement floor. And swimming naked in the Saint Croix River after impossibly hard work, and nothing but green and blue everywhere. And the stairway downstairs, and the tight, turned stairway upstairs that Loren built by herself. And the shingle pallet that she turned into a kitchen frame to hang utensils. And her on the heavy other end of countless objects and tools. I said it many times then and it is no less certain now—from the ground to the chimney, that house was as much her work as mine. Probably more, considering her drive to begin it and carry it through.

For the worst part for me may have been my total inability, despite my spiritual ambitions, to fathom the mental discipline the project required. I'm embarrassed now to think of the times I swore the outcome couldn't be worth the uncertainties, the arguments, the work. I remember another weekend neighbor couple somewhere in late middle age saying we were such nice people, she hoped the house wouldn't be the end of us—because building projects had a way of doing that. And though I've long said that it wasn't the building that undid our marriage, it certainly sharpened differences that were always there.

Still, twenty years later I take as much pride in having built that house, and in the physical work I did in the three years I lived there, than in any of the books or poems, the magazine I edit, my teaching, anything of the "intellectual" work I've done. Somehow that work was expected, at least by me. But this other, that's the wild card, the odd seed that more than anything makes me. And so, when I think about those years, I'm still prone to wonder, as I did when I watched the mountain ash come down, whether I was wrong to leave. This, despite the unavoidable conclusion, every time

I think it through completely, that living here in the city has been a fine choice. For regardless of my accomplishments there, I learned also that I'm not really a builder; in the end, I don't have the patience, the gifts of physical dexterity, or the "figure-it-out" instincts the job requires. In the end, what I've really wanted to do is mainly what I'm doing, and I suspect the regret I feel is mostly a product of my inability to accept the limitations of the human—the mind wanting everything—all the good stuff, that is—all the time.

Still, the whole experience of living there, of building, remains at the center both of who I am, as well as how I write. For it is exactly the problem of how things fit together that is at the roots of the poems and stories, if not the biography as well. And so, from the time it became clear that I finally ought to sell the place, that the roof and ceiling hadn't been built right, and that it was too much work to keep up and too far from where I'd come to live:

Rural Particles

Asters, yarrow, an enormous oak at the edge of the bank leading down to the river. Each leaf, each blade of grass is part of the force a man's trying to measure as he walks toward the water. And they're strong; they hold him here with this arrangement of particles: the blue house, a crane, a handful of blackberries—but they're hard to figure. As soon as he gets an idea, a pipe starts leaking and the whole equation changes. He thinks there's a way to understand it so he keeps reading: up, down, strange; hard to believe this is science. It's something he takes on faith—a voice on the phone, a rocket past the moon—then a woman walks through the door announcing the African drought, kids out of the question, and he's up half the night with her. Where's the chapter that tells what to name this? The formula for its vector?

So he's put the place up for sale. If someone's buying, it could be a chance to start over, or at least continue with new luggage these pieces might fit into. If he keeps shuffling the figures, he thinks the new particles these weak interactions bring in and out of the problem—the job in the city, the woman, the moon—might coalesce into a sequence that points the way. He thinks: I can quit smoking for good, cut

off my beard. It's been years since I've been to the mountains. But when the offer comes, he can't bring himself to take it. The pages go by so fast the woods blur as the fall's first storm moves out the summer. Then the wood chips fly as he piles the oak for another winter he won't be there to see, and it's time to go. It doesn't make sense at all. It's something he understands.

What led to the house most directly, and the life it promised, was the Valley. So I have to go back a little further.

The floor of the San Luis Valley in south central Colorado is some eight thousand feet high and nearly a hundred miles long as it widens from Poncha Pass toward Alamosa, with the Sangre de Cristo mountains towering on the east and the San Juans on the west. To say it's breathtaking doesn't begin to explain. I see those peaks again as I write this, the Sangres's jagged scrawl at the top of their steep black wall; the way the clear morning sky gives way to clouds in the summer afternoons; the way cars and buildings are tiny insects spreading south as you watch from the base of the mountain; the way the shadows carve their way across the valley floor, and the sunsets glow and shimmer red and orange as the sun falls behind the San Juans.

I remember following the directions my old high school friend Dan sent to Chicago in the early summer of 1974, and driving the dirt road up from the Valley floor. After negotiating our way through cattle gates and up the rocky trail, we found the old, one-room log cabin, and I remember the slight chill of thunder clouds rolling in over the sun. I remember sitting out back one night with him and his girlfriend Barb, and Doug and Sue, playing guitars, watching stars, and smoke, and ghosts of lightblinks on the Valley floor. I remember all six of us naked and stoned in Doug and Sue's farm garden, Loren hugging their goat around its neck. And all of us soaking in a cold spring pool just up the hill. And sitting in the cool shade of their kitchen. Most I remember the smell, the dry earth, not green, but no less fetid, and rich, a smell I've known nowhere else, that will put me back there in an instant.

That first summer, we only visited a few days on the way to California. Loren had never been west, and I was heady with the privilege of showing her the way. We went on to California, and I remember driving across the Salt Flats, stopping in Reno and winning a few dollars at blackjack, hiking above Lake Tahoe, and sleeping on the beach at Bolinas after a drive from Truckee for a rock concert at the Oakland Coliseum. But when I came back to Chicago, I only wanted to live in the Valley. For me, its smells and views and people, its pure physicality, were simply magic.

So the next summer, after I'd finished my first year in graduate school (the Writing Program at the University of Illinois-Chicago), we went out there again, planning to stay until we had to come back again for school. Dan and Barb had set up a tepee a few yards from the cabin, and had been living in it since fall. Life in a tepee, he said, was closer to the elements, to the land, to the ineffable spiritual center. And it was much easier to keep warm in winter.

Except, he wasn't there. We were greeted instead by my sister, whom I'd told about the place after our visit the previous year. She had left Minneapolis on her own odyssey, and now she was living in the tepee. Meantime, Dan and his wife had separated after the winter, she going off with another man, he with Gina, a woman he'd met over the winter and who was living with her young son in another cabin across the valley. Now she and Dan were in California on their spiritual journey.

So Loren and I stayed in the Valley. We hiked to the top of the mountains, took baths in the hot springs on the Valley floor. We visited the "Lightning Bar" (named after the Arlo Guthrie song) in the high country across the valley where people who had owned the first music and head shop in Minneapolis had bought land and built cabins. We listened to Jane play guitar, and Doug, and all of us together. And lay in the hot springs on the Valley floor, staring at the mountain peaks. And ate mushroom soup made from what other friends had gathered by the river that flowed down from the mountains. And drove to the Great Sand Dunes an hour further south and climbed to the top of one, then raced back down, and drank water, and drank, and drank. And rode back from a day in the town an hour away in the bed of Doug's pickup, watching mountains and stars revolve around us.

But after a few weeks we got restless. We had an address for Dan in Mill Valley, and we decided to go.

He had hitchhiked to Mount Shasta by himself, he had meditated, and prayed, and he was staying now in a house with two other men. Gina had been there with him, but the spirit had sent her to live in a tent with her son in Inverness.

The night we got to the Mill Valley house, Dan was there by himself. So we spent a day or two, and Dan decided to come with us back to the Valley. We went to see Gina, then drove. Two days after we were back, Gina arrived, announcing that she hadn't intended to come, but the spirit insisted; if the injunction wasn't divine, its mystical clarity couldn't be denied. Such was the world we lived in.

And so I remember the August night we drove back into Chicago, how the city and its smells seemed literally to emerge from Dante's *Inferno*. And when we got to our apartment, it was piled with new cabinets and furniture; the landlord had decided to remodel the kitchen, and all we could do was stay out of the way. Loren hated that homecoming as much as I, and agreed we had to get out. She would sell the Montessori school she had run for a year and search with me for something else. We didn't know what, but it wouldn't be in a city. We moved to another apartment for the last year, and when I finished my master's degree, we sold off and stored all that we owned, packed the rest into a new Ford van we had equipped with a bench and foam pads to sleep on with the help of another friend, and left Chicago for the great blank.

In most ways it was a great trip. We spent a month or so visiting my mother and stepfather in suburban St. Paul, my grandparents and great-aunt up in Superior, Wisconsin, storing our things, getting ready to go further. We drove to the San Luis Valley. What we found, of course, is what most find who go off into nothing: you take your geography with you. The anxieties and upsets and problems are no more than temporarily relieved by changing location. We stayed for a week or so, then went further west. In Santa Barbara, we stayed with another old friend, traveled with him and his girlfriend to San Francisco, met other friends and went up to Eugene, Oregon, to see another friend. It was late September then, and time to settle, at least for a while. We talked, we looked for signs, we threw the I Ching. Loren wanted to go back to live in Santa Barbara; I wanted to go to the Valley. In the end, we thought of Wisconsin and the dome.

Perhaps that complex is the center. But of course, it's not the beginning.

Monday

Simple as this garage, wrapped & shingled at
   the end
of an uncut lawn. It was dark when the drive
   began.
It took a long time. Green thick
with the last of summer, all the lines
are gone from the clothespole, its shadow
a broken cross against the wall, an echo
of this church, school attached, children
sent for something better than the
   neighborhood public,
though they don't know. Simply, it's what they
   do:
here's the first letter. Plywood's nailed over
to keep that garage from breaking open,
   anyone
from breaking in. Three strands of rusted
   barbed wire
top the chain link against the alley. A man
and a woman, dirty t-shirts, jeans, slouch by.
Summer strokes the back of the throat, and
   that house
is my grandfather's, far north, on a street
of peeling houses, where a lost train's whining
some impossible distance. He's been dead five
   years.
It's another state. Two mourning doves
hop in the overgrown apple tree on the other
   side
of the yard, ripe fruit hanging way too high
to gather. "You'd better sit down young man,"
comes through a window, then the movie
   soundtrack,
the narrator's voice static and drone. I take
a breath, shut my eyes and hold it. The bell
   rings.

*

Inside, sweat & mumble, and I'm supposed to
tell them something to help. My first teacher's
quiet voice, gray hair tied to a perfect oval
made her Grandma. She played piano.
The climbing gym sat on the green linoleum
in the next room. We lay on our rugs for nap,
though I never slept. When water pooled
about the girl in the circle who couldn't
hold it until her turn, of course we laughed.
Of course she cried. Miss Hawn cleaned her
   up,
took her to the office and she went home.
When it was my turn for a birthday party,

I got sick. Joy taught me to tie my shoes.
From the second storey window, I could see
over the maple in the front yard.

*

Is this still the "magnificent adolescence"
Ortega y Gasset proclaimed the day I was born,
the America "capable of digesting" politicians'
mistakes? Hiss was on trial. Judith Coplon
got three to ten years for passing secrets to
   Russia.
Hordes of grasshoppers flooded the ranges,
   eating
the cattle feed. Kate Smith sang on the radio.
It was 94 degrees. Now it thunders.
Rains. My hand's paralysis left since winter
could be a warning, but it hasn't gotten worse.
Refugee camps overflow, but in another
   continent.
The president swears he'll make schools better.
"Discover Columbia, Chicago!" the poster
on the window says. This must be it.

The poem is always metaphoric, but as with any poem, it also touches the actual. In this case, the touch is more than glancing. Since 1983, I've earned part of my living teaching poetry writing in public schools, and this poem begins on the steps behind a classroom in a far north Chicago suburb. The incidents from the last strophe all come from the newspaper on the day I was born. It would have been *The Minneapolis Tribune* if my mother read it, though I doubt that she had the time or in-

With Loren, at my sister's wedding, 1976

terest that day. She was hot and uncomfortable, there was no air conditioning. She was twenty-six, and about to deliver her first child. I was told that as soon as she was released from the hospital, she took me north to her parents' house just off the Lake Superior shore to escape the summer heat. For a few weeks then, my father drove up the three and a half hours on weekends.

Her parents lived in the smallish two-storey, three-bedroom frame house they had built when they were married. They'd raised her and her younger brother in it, on the same lot where my grandmother's father had his house. My great-grandfather had come from Russia as a young man in the 1880s, after serving in the czar's army, though how he made his way to Superior, Wisconsin, is another lost immigrant story I can't guess. I know he was a plumber, and successful enough to buy the lot and first house to go with it, and raise six children, two of whom became doctors in Buffalo, New York. My grandmother was the oldest, and just three when they came to America. Zeda retired from his plumbing shop after a robbery and beating when he must have been in his seventies, and I remember him only as an elderly shadow when we came to visit. By the time of my birth, only two of his children—my grandmother and my aunt—remained in Superior, my aunt and her husband in that same house she grew up in, still with her parents; my grandparents right next door.

My grandfather came from New York as a small child, but how he got there, and then to Superior, is also a mystery. What I do know is that as I get older, see the adult man I've become, it is his breath that I feel more and more in my cells. One of my sons is named after him. Half the house I live in is a result of money he earned. He was the self-made man of his time. When his own father died in 1915, my grandfather was nineteen and had three younger sisters and two younger brothers. There was no Social Security of course, and few women worked outside their home, so family support was his responsibility. He gained his accounting degree through correspondence, joined the army to fight in World War I, and served under a lieutenant who went on to become a wealthy financier after the war. My grandfather worked as his assistant as he got rich, but he lost his fortune in the 1929 stock market crash, and so during the Depression Grandpa work-

ed as a secretary, a court reporter, whatever he had to. After the Second World War, he rose to become secretary-treasurer of the local bus company, and by the time he died at age ninety, he had amassed nearly a million dollars. He was an athlete (the fastest sprinter in town races when he was young, a baseball player, a skater—my grandmother told of pleading with him to quit skating in his seventies when he went out for a leisurely turn or two at a local rink and couldn't resist keeping up and then racing with men thirty and forty years younger), a serious bridge player, a respected leader in his small religious community. He was a handyman extraordinaire, and a patriarch in the old sense. He had a fierce and terrifying temper (my mother remembers him teaching her to drive, screaming at one point, "I could teach a monkey to drive easier than I can teach you!"), and in the family his word was law.

His temper had calmed a good deal by the time I knew him, and I remember him as a mostly wonderful grandpa. When we were in elementary school, my sister and I used to visit for a week or two by ourselves, and he'd give us new coins, buy us trinkets at Woolworth's, take us to his office on Saturday mornings to play with the machines, show me how to help with the yard- and housework. But at the same time I remember him cursing FDR, and embarrassing me when I visited in high school in the sixties with friends by raging that they should "string up those niggers" who were demonstrating and teach 'em all a lesson. And as an adult, I still remember him at the bridge table the first time my new wife made a hand, shaking his head and growling that "luck is better than brains anytime."

I also remember sitting in the upstairs closet of the bedroom my sister slept in during our visits there as children. There was an old Underwood typewriter and a chair, and on it I began my first novel—a "real" baseball story—like the ones I'd read, but without the silly romance and "human interest" that just got in the way of the good stuff about who got the big hits and how the runs were scored. In between chapters I wrote sports articles—accounts of whatever game I watched on TV. And I remember reading—*Hardy Boys* mysteries bought for a dollar each from the shelf at the back of Roth's Department Store; Reader's Digest Condensed Books (*The Year the Yankees Lost the*

Pennant, A Nun's Story, I Lived Three Lives, The Three Faces of Eve); and beautiful leather-bound volumes from the shelves on either side of the TV in the small den off the living room (works of Poe, Dickens, Twain; books which I have now in my house and which my own children have begun reading).

Altogether, then, I suspect that I owe the roots of whatever my accomplishments, in both writing and building, more to my grandfather, and my visits to his house in Superior, than to anything else.

Still, the father is the figure by whom sons know themselves, and with whom they must struggle throughout their lives. I'll accept the conventional wisdom, though my father's hand is much less apparent to me. Not that he was entirely absent in the ways some fathers are, leaving a palpable hole their sons must find a way to fill; and I am aware of important parts of my temperament that he bequeathed me. But my father was not a great part of my world, and his presence seems much more to one side.

His mother had a heart attack that interrupted my parents' honeymoon, and she died a few months before I was born, so I never knew her. Her husband lived until I was eight, so I knew my Grandpa Ike, though not well. I was told that his father came from Manitoba to Wisconsin in a covered wagon, and that my grandfather went up from Eau Claire to Hayward to manage the store there when some relative died; but more is lost to me. I remember him making pancakes for us some mornings, and taking me out early in the morning to the shed by the lake cabin he'd had built near the northern town of Hayward, where my father grew up, and lifting me up to start the pump. But the memory's pure sepia.

My father was their only son and third child, though the one before him died in childbirth (or early infancy, I haven't found out which for certain). And by smalltown standards, the family was prosperous. His father was manager of the main department store in Hayward, Wisconsin (pop. 1,000 or less then). As an apparent result of this background, my father was indulged, and never felt the need to work much to get material things, for which he never wanted. Through my own youth, then, I had the sense that work and material success weren't really important.

On the other hand, he was an ace cardplayer and golfer—competitive, and a winner. He played on the town's small course and became expert (he scored a hole in one on the course in my mother's town shortly after he'd married her), though he wasn't otherwise physically active in the least. I don't think I ever saw him with a tool in his hand, or even mowing the lawn, or doing much besides a little bowling and golf and bridge.

I know that partly this was due to a heart condition connected with high blood pressure; when I was five, and he thirty-nine, he suffered a heart attack no doubt resulting from the condition that had first been diagnosed at his World War II army exit exam, and the treatment of the time prescribed avoidance of physical activity. Though he hadn't been in combat in the war, he'd been a lieutenant in charge of loading and unloading bombs, which must have caused serious tension, and by the time the war was over, his blood pressure had shot up. Like most soldiers, though, he was eager to get home when the war was over, and so declined more testing and treatment, thus bypassing the chance for a lifetime disability pension which could have eased the financial pressures he never saw coming.

But his business career is another story. He never participated in the postwar economic boom of the fifties—neither his job for his ambitious and successful brother-in-law, nor his small retail business ever generated much, the last ending in bankruptcy. Still, from all I know, he was much happier anyway to sit in a chair and sip his martini.

Perhaps more to the point, like most fathers of his time, he was not much interested in the lives of his children. Mostly I remember him sitting in front of the TV when he was home. I remember him playing catch with me exactly once. I remember him playing nine holes of golf with me once for my birthday. I remember him taking me to a handful of baseball games—the local minor league team a couple times, then the major league Twins once or twice, after they came to Minneapolis-St. Paul from Washington, D.C., in 1961. (Once was to a sold-out Yankees game with a friend of his and his friend's son; when we got there, he sold off two of the four "obstructed view" bleacher seats he had behind the chain-link fence, bought two better seats from scalpers, and took off with his friend and the better tickets, leaving the other son and I with a distant view of Mickey Mantle's back and instructions where to meet them after the game.) And my sister shares my memory of our only family picnic. It ended with me throwing up a banana split I was allowed to have, and so ate, mainly because I was stunned that I was allowed to have it.

I was also told that he had a terrible temper as a child, but as an adult, he was always very mild and contained, and very well-liked by his peers. He grew to be president of his college fraternity at the University of Minnesota. But he quit three credits short of graduation. Those last two facts may comprise the essence. That, along with the fact that my mother adored him. He was nine years older than she, and when at twenty-five she met him, she already felt on the old side to be unmarried, so was enthralled by the attentions of this sophisticated, handsome older man. Thus, all the time of my youth, my parents seemed deeply in love.

I remember them doing dishes after supper one night and suddenly breaking off and chasing each other through the house, my father waving a dishtowel while both laughed hysterically. I remember my mother nestling against his neck on the couch. I remember her saying often that it was vital that the marriage came first, before the children. I remember only one argument between them, when

"With my sister, Barbara, in our living room: first photo evidence of my real self-image"

my father had caused the family to be late to religious services. The argument ended with my father simply saying to my mother's complaints, that was enough. And so it was.

I grew up then in a family which felt rock stable, and in which there was no question that my father was its head, and a sort of demigod from my mother's point of view. I can see several lessons gleaned from this model. First, of course, I felt no particular need as I grew up to work hard to achieve what didn't come by gift. Whatever I managed I was sure was enough. And partly as a result of my father's model as someone who got along socially with everyone, I also seem to have inherited an ease with a wide variety of people (which is no doubt one factor that helped me research a biography).

The nature of roots are always multiple, however, and the older I get, the less sure I am that "normal" has any meaning outside the general realm of collective statistics. In my case, the term lost its currency when I was fourteen. It was the year Kennedy was shot, and I remember details of the day, and seeing Oswald killed on TV the following Sunday morning. For me the events didn't change anything, though; they were only interesting splashes in a fairly predictable current.

The day I remember was in March, Friday the thirteenth in fact (though I've never been at all superstitious), and the memory doesn't really kick in until afternoon. There was a faculty-student all-star basketball game that had the school's attention, and I'd arranged to do a "play by play" into a tape recorder from the gym teacher's office above the court (another example of my manipulation for notice in the world?). Afterward, I took the bus downtown to get my braces adjusted, then came back, had a quick dinner (we had barbecued chicken most Fridays, it seems to me), and went off to the Kenny Carnival. Sister Elizabeth Kenny was the elementary school I'd attended, and some of my friends had formed a dixieland band to play as one of the attractions at the annual fund-raising bazaar. I was to be the carny barker, calling the crowd in to hear them. At the end, not surprisingly, there was a party that I was told about, to go on in someone's basement. I was delighted to be invited, and hoped against hope that my father would let me go, though he was notoriously restrictive about his children—in retrospect I suppose it was the concern most parents feel about their adolescent children out in the world, in his case heightened by the sixties' turmoil beginning to heat up, and his own smalltown background against the temptations of the larger city. When I asked him if I could go, his "no" was pretty expected. Still, I was hurt and angry, and pleaded a little, though there was no real chance he'd change his mind.

He dropped my sister and me off at home and picked up my mother to go have coffee with her at a diner a few blocks away. They would be back in an hour or so, and I remember sitting on the fading red couch, looking at the newspaper an hour or so later, my sister in the kitchen, an idle moment's wondering why my parents weren't back yet, and the doorbell ringing. When I went to answer it, I remember my mother's face crumpled like old paper in the narrow window, and the enormous policeman behind her. When I opened the door, she staggered inside and collapsed on the floor.

On the way home from the coffee shop my father had said he had a terrible headache, then stopped the car and slumped against the wheel. He was dead of a cerebral hemorrhage. He'd turned forty-nine the previous November; my mother was forty.

M uch in the days that followed remains clear, and will—coming downstairs the next morning to see my mother sitting on the couch exactly where she'd been sitting all night, with a friend of hers keeping her company; the house filled with relatives; the funeral; the Hebrew Kaddish that I said every day at afternoon services for the next month.

My mother remembers me as an unusually compassionate teenager, but my own sense is that I was as purely self-interested as anyone at age fourteen. While the rooms were filled with mourners upstairs, I was playing my own version of basketball with myself in the basement, wondering when I could go back to school, hoping I wouldn't be embarrassed by the "gift" the teacher would force everyone to contribute to, and doing my best to make life ordinary.

Even then, amid the sense of loss and grief, I think I realized that there would be more room for me. And it's certainly clear now that was so—that had my father lived, there would have been years of hurt feelings, silence, and fights, fueled by my coming of age, and values honed in the sixties. But because my mother

"With Barbara, on the steps of our grandparents' house," Superior, Wisconsin, 1974

always deferred to him—as a woman of her time, brought up to defer to men—after he died, that deference fell in part to me. The result was an immeasurably larger field to explore.

So, my senior year in high school, there was Naomi: dusty blonde, a bit ungraceful, eccentric, definitely an attention-getter, even popular among a certain group. She was elected "Daisy-Mae" at the "Li'l Abner" dance; she was a hit as a mock Cher in the high school talent show; she'd written poems that her teacher praised; she was an editor of the school newspaper and the head of the annual literary magazine. She borrowed her about-to-be-ex-boyfriend's Mustang convertible to drive the two of us to the homecoming football game. She was my first real girlfriend. She let me kiss her. And more.

Not least, she was a good four inches taller than I was, and for a teenage boy who'd always had to look up at the girls his age, that was a very big deal. Our alliance lasted throughout that senior year and pretty much banished the self-consciousness I had about being the world's shortest boy. But my relations with her also led me to poetry and prism glasses and darkened rooms and Bob Dylan and high school

The author's second wife, fiction writer Sharon Solwitz, "a few months pregnant," 1986

existential crises, and to others of the "artsy-intellectual" crowd.

I had always assumed that after high school, I'd go on to the University of Minnesota, like most everyone else I knew, then to law school there. (Ever since getting hooked on TV's *Perry Mason* when I was nine or ten, I was sure I wanted to be a lawyer). But some of my new friends were going to colleges named Smith and Dartmouth and Stanford. I don't remember why Northwestern occurred to me, except that it wasn't too far from Minneapolis, it was supposed to have a good law school (I thought then that it'd somehow be an important advantage to have gone to an undergraduate school with a good law school), and in the previous few years a good football team. When I went in to see my counselor about college, however, whatever he said discouraged me from thinking I could get in there. But his very skepticism pushed me; I took the requisite entrance exams, applied, and was accepted. Even then though, I was far from persuaded. I didn't even

know where Evanston was—somewhere near Chicago, I knew, but where? And where, really was Chicago? Much better, and more sensible, to stay in Minneapolis with friends and girlfriend and what I knew.

On the other hand, I was awarded enough scholarship money to make Northwestern just barely affordable. So here was a chance to do something else. I could always come back after a year—even less—if I hated it.

I still remember the first months as among the most lonely and difficult I'd gone through; but by the end of the first year, not surprisingly, I was eager to go back. For it was there that I learned to play bridge, and drink Budweiser, and love Dylan Thomas and Yeats and Nabokov and Dave Van Ronk. I spent the first two summers working at some relatives' artificial flower emporium in Minneapolis, a couple of August weeks in 1969 by myself, in charge of a branch in Rochester, about sixty miles away. One of those mornings, I stood at the front counter and read a small inside-page article in the local paper about Woodstock, and I remember promising myself never again to miss that kind of massive celebration.

That November, then, I gave up tickets to a Rolling Stones concert to ride with a carful to an antiwar moratorium in Washington, D.C., where with nearly a half million others (according to one paper's estimate), I was initiated into tear gas and riot-helmeted police. Then, in the spring of 1970, when the school shut down in the wave of student strikes that followed Nixon's invasion of Cambodia and the subsequent killing of Kent State students by National Guardsmen, I boarded a bus to Washington, D.C., with other students to lobby congressmen for an antiwar bill.

I remember listening at meetings with several senators and representatives. I remember Marlowe Cook, the Kentucky senator whose daughter I'd gone out with a couple of times. And Walter Mondale, the Minnesota senator, whom I got to meet in his office with only one or two others. I remember both Cook and Mondale saying they would in fact support the antiwar bill, then being shocked to find a week later that Cook voted against it. He was a Republican, of course, so the only real surprise was that I heard whatever he said as being support for the Democratic amendment, though such support was no doubt "deniable" in the fashion of politicians. For me, the event is worth mentioning only because it was my first close brush with hypocrisy at that level.

More important personally, was that on the bus I met Loren. I guess it was her vibrancy and high energy that attracted me. I remember her in the darkness of that Greyhound, talking and listening intently in the group of men surrounding her, then on the way back, sitting with her, and just the two of us talking. Tied to the handle of my overnight bag was the strip of red curtain she'd helped tear from her sorority house curtains to make the armbands we wore to signify our participation in the strike and the movement.

Then that summer I hitchhiked to D.C. and surprised her where she was staying in a large suburban house with several others. I stayed there with her for a week or so, and tried to persuade her to come with me to the west coast, which she finally wanted to do. But she felt she had to get her father's permission, and she wouldn't go against his no. Still, it was a good trip. I got a ride all the way to Los Angeles, where I stayed with some older cousins of my mother's and their family. I remember that I tried to visit Disneyland once, but they turned me away at the gate because I had long hair, and a few days earlier some "hippies" had caused a disturbance that made the "magic kingdom" somehow less magical. After a couple of days I hitchhiked up to Santa Barbara, then on to San Francisco, where I walked around the ruins of Haight-Ashbury, and Ferlinghetti's City Lights, among other attractions. Finally I flew back to Minneapolis.

I f it's true that we all marry some version of our opposite-sex parents, both Loren and my present wife provide evidence. Above all, my mother is an energetic, gregarious woman, though she carefully follows the etiquette of her social class. She worked as an executive secretary from the time my father died until her own retirement twenty-one years later, and I've come to realize that it is her devotion to work and her absolute adherence to prescribed social forms that have borne her through the difficulties of outliving both my father and her subsequent husband (whom she married in 1969).

Like my mother, Loren was energetic and outspoken and a hedonist of sorts. Though the variations are always key. Much more than my mother, she was an experimenter, and drawn to adventure, if—again like my mother—within conventional borders. She was also quick to change direction when she got bored, while my mother has essentially stayed with what she knew since moving to Minneapolis after college.

Mainly I think I wanted to marry her because I hadn't done such a thing—it seemed the imprimatur of adulthood and offered a solid touchstone in an uncertain stage of life. In the end, though, whether it was her volatility against my "staidness" in wanting to live quietly in the rural midwest, or differences in temperament exaggerated by the proximity of building a house together, or something I've never understood, after about seven years together, the last three up north, she'd had enough. She spent more and more time other places, and just before Christmas in 1979, she moved to California.

The friendships I made in the Wisconsin country were intense, and when she left I couldn't imagine following, or not staying in the house we'd built, where I was sure I'd found

"Twin sons, Jesse and Seth, on the steps of our home in Chicago," 1990

my real home. But when she did her final packing, winter had barely begun, and the winters were long. In those final weeks, I remember drinking Cabin Still bourbon, wallowing in country music, seeing everything at the distant end of a long tunnel. At the very end, some friends came up to visit with whom I'd decided to at least go back to Chicago for a break—a few weeks at least, maybe until spring. And I remember driving back and literally feeling the weight lift with each mile. I was sure I'd be back up north, but it was just as clear that I'd never go back to Loren.

At first I lived with the woman who had come up to visit, and with whom I'd gone back to Chicago. She'd just ended a romance, and within days we were a couple. I did some sheet rocking and carpentry, some office work, and landed a writing project, visiting homemade candy and ice cream stores for a family guidebook. (One I remember was a small store on the south side of Chicago where the owner offered me one of the first new ice cream bars he'd just invented, and went on about his plans to make them a national product—which plans I filed in the usual back brain with the millions of great ideas you never hear about again. "What do you think?" he said. "We're calling them 'Dove Bars.'") I persuaded the publisher to let me produce a similar guidebook about the Minneapolis-St. Paul area, and so went back up there in summer to set up shop, spending long weekends in the Wisconsin house. At the end of the summer, though, when that project was finished, I felt back to zero again, with no good idea what to do. Then I got an invitation to come back to Chicago and teach composition at the college here where I had earned my writing degree.

It was during the orientation meeting there that I met Sharon.

Chosen

Bell bottoms under her chador, long red hair, she's walking the desert market live from another planet. They spit on her clothes, steal her knife, raise the price of the horse, the cooking pots. She's on the way to God, whatever Its name. She may not be sure, but Donnie is, and she's proud to follow. Tonight three men rape her friend. She rides her horse to the border, climbs the mountain, listens.

Then she's walking uphill, star smear, nail of moon, lighting the way her feet know, back to where she will find him. She's been alone, loading bananas for months, cooking on the kibbutz, and she's home. She looks in the one window of the yurt they built, and there he is, sleeping. Next to his head, a pile of blonde hair.

She sits on a blanket on a street in the city they left, easel and charcoal sign saying I'll draw you, pay what you want. She's following the line of a nose. She's carrying food at a restaurant smiling "welcome to RJ's." She's in a circle, the leader's asking questions, and they're taking turns explaining their trouble. She's naked and breathing yes. Each time he is the one.

It's from a story, in the ongoing urge to understand what happened, and the names, as they say, are changed; but this time most of it's true: she'd lived on a commune, gone to Nepal, to Israel, divorced, settled in her ex-husband's hometown, worked as a waitress, took therapy, and finally had begun to write the stories she'd always wanted to.

The first years we were together stand to this day as the best I've known—both money and time enough, and the element you can only get somewhere before forty—the idea that things will get better. Not that they've gone bad. But as she reached the end of her childbearing years, like many women her age and station, she decided that a child was the main thing she wanted. And when she finally got pregnant, they were twins.

I've more than offended most everyone who'll listen by whining about the hardship children have meant, especially those first half-dozen years, and though I may someday revise that view, that someday is still in a future I can't imagine. For some of the very things that most drew me to my wife are exactly the things that have made being a modern parent with her so difficult—particularly against the background of my own parents' model—that she's as committed to her work as I am; that she wants as much freedom as I do, that she is as entitled. Suffice it to say that for those first half-dozen years, I was tired, and sick, about three-quarters of the time.

Okay, I know I complain too much. But for me, my children are the absolute physical manifestation of ambivalence. On the one hand, I know well that what I have is pretty much

Center stage at a poetry reading, Navy Pier, Chicago, 1991

what I always wanted, and enviable in many quarters. I manage to make a living writing and teaching, which is work I love, and as I write this last, my boys have blissfully passed those terrible early years so that I've actually been experiencing some of the clichés about the pleasures of parenthood. I should say a few words then about how wonderful I think my boys are—and I do think they are, but I really don't have good words to describe that—the physical shock of their presence, from touch to smell to look to sound, is beyond anything I could have imagined.

On the other hand, they're at their first overnight camp as I write this, and the sudden freedom I feel at a week without them is almost as equally stunning.

And on yet another hand, I'll never hike miles in the mountains with them, or by myself; I'll never run with them.

The "hand's paralysis" noted in the "Monday" poem never has gotten better, and the thing of which it is symptom casts a long shadow.

It actually began in the late fall of 1973, though there was nothing wrong with my hand then. Rather, I woke to an inexplicable numbness on one side of my face that just didn't go away. I went up to visit family in Minneapolis for Thanksgiving and stayed to have tests—a spinal tap, an EEG, and then I saw a doctor back in Chicago. He told me the tests showed a syndrome often related to stress, especially occurring after its release. It often disappeared after an illness—he knew one old doctor who used to inject patients who had this condition with a few drops of milk from his lunch, the alien protein stimulating a fever. But if the condition persisted, or worsened, it was multiple sclerosis. Only a few days after that appointment, I came down with a flu, and I was on my back for about ten days. When I recovered, the numbness was gone, and I felt perfectly normal.

Then in January 1991, when my children were almost four, we were in south Florida, at my in-laws' condominium there, and I woke up one morning with a tingling numbness in my legs, and in my right hand. I'd been jogging the day before, as I did through most of my thirties, but this was a complete mystery. When I got back to Chicago, the numbness slowly began to recede, eventually leaving my legs completely, though not my hand. I made doctor's appointments, went through tests. The diagnosis then was clearly M.S., probably triggered, according to some current theory, by an immune system reaction to the flu shot I'd had about six weeks earlier.

So far, the doctors tell me I'm lucky. So far. If I tell someone I've got the condition, there's a sort of shock; but my case was and has been relatively mild. There's permanent numbness in my right hand, I can't walk far before my right leg gets too weak to go on, and my balance isn't always the mindless simplicity of normal—but I can button my shirts, ride my bike six miles along the lakefront downtown, work out at a health club. I can climb a ladder, shoot a few baskets. I can walk and hike a little—if not the miles I wish, I still managed to go some five miles with my family in the high Cascades this summer—though I had to stop and rest every few hundred yards the last couple miles, and hope the nerves would work again, and enough strength come back so I could go on. I can still type, if a shade less accurately and quickly than before.

And so I do. Mainly I try to ignore the condition, as impossible as that often is, and simply go on. In some basic way, I guess I still don't quite accept that the situation is permanent, that I'm just not going to get better. Still, just as strong is the need I feel to face what's there: I know what I have to live with. Perhaps the whole problem is simply my personal version of having to accept the physical losses that are the human con-dition.

And then? An end, of course, that somehow connects with the beginning, completes a circle, leaves everyone with the exhale of relief, though we know that any autobiography can only be a progress report:

One Bird

after "Crow on a Sunny Branch"—color wood block print by Ohara Shoson, 1911-1915

Hand's bleeding almost stopped, the broken
glass shattered in the sink is cleaned now.

The picture on the shelf above reminds me
there's always just one thing, two sides.
I should write back to the woman who sent it.
Aren't we finally old enough to not be

upset by such attention—your old boyfriends,
ex-husband, etc., ringing the doorbell,

while the women I loved fade with the flesh,
cells gone to memory? Touch me, here,

I used to think, not understanding
desire's real point. I put salsa on everything

these days, trying to feel it, while my finger
is numb to her breast. Some theories claim

this disease is another virus, and maybe
the drug to cure it is on the way. Doctors

test my balance as I listen for the music
I always loved, stumble into the street.

BIBLIOGRAPHY

In the Ruins (prose poems), Center Press, 1983.

Ferlinghetti: The Artist in His Time, Warner Books, 1990.

The New Tenants (poems), Eye of the Comet Press, 1991.

One Thing that Can Save Us (prose poems), Coffee House Press, 1994.

Also editor of *Another Chicago Magazine*.

Ron Silliman

1946-

UNDER *ALBANY*

For Colin and Jesse,
Later

Ron Silliman

If the function of writing is to "express the world."

Jon Arnold looks out over the straw-haired sea of fifth-graders directly into the dark eyes of Susan Hughes. Behind him, cordoned by both the furniture and the authority of the instructor's desk, Vance Teague, then in his sixth year of teaching at Marin Elementary, observes the latest in his unending string of small pedagogical experiments. Unlike dividing the classroom into teams and having them compete for grades, this one shows promise. Each Wednesday, students will be given one sheet of lined paper and a ballpoint pen—industrial strength, the point never retracting, virtually impossible to open, snap or chew through. The students are allotted one hour to write whatever they wish, whatever they might. There are no rules, and that *is* the rule.

On the following Wednesday, just before "writing hour," Teague, who had first met Arnold and myself while student-teaching kindergarten under the creaking but benevolent mentorship of Mrs. Seager, will select a handful of students whose writing in some fashion has "excelled," having them read their works aloud to the class. This will be my first experience of The Reading.

Arnold, a sharp kid who frightened me because he was constantly pushing me and our mutual friend Timmy Johnson toward further and further transgressions of adult authority, stares into the intense smile of the partly Native American girl whose dark hair and faintly olive skin makes the pale northern European tones of the classroom visible to all. He begins to read. The subject of Arnold's paper—*how would a ten-year-old think of this?*—is the reaction of students hearing him (already typecast as one of the "wild kids") read aloud. Arnold's paper, which may have been shorter than this comment upon it forty years later, is a Swiftian satire on class relations . . . in all senses of that phrase. The students get the joke instantly. There is a lot of wincing and laughter and, at the end (and for the only time all school year), applause. I remember the humor as terrific, although cruel.[1]

---

[1]While Arnold told me, when I ran into him at a reading of Kit Robinson's and Rae Armantrout's at San Francisco State in 1992, that "I was so in love with Susan

I am transfixed. So much so, in fact, that I am unable to write a coherent sentence in the following hour that day and turn in a blank sheet of paper. A week later, I use the "free writing" period to attempt a piece that tries to switch literary genres sentence by sentence, essay one moment, science fiction the next. My effort disintegrates into garble. (Although in retrospect I realize that I somehow already knew what a genre was and that there were differences between them.) Teague is concerned. Within a matter of weeks, I am writing "novels," though, sitting on my narrow bed in the small room I shared with my younger brother, Cliff, longhand tales scrawled into thick notebooks ("the assassination of Hitler," "manned rocket flies behind moon only to disappear"). Within a year, I discover that I can get out of almost any unpleasant school assignment other than math or wood shop by merely offering to write a five- or ten- or twenty-page paper on the topic. I never seriously heed a teacher's syllabus again.[2]

I veered away from Arnold by the time high school arrived, his outsiderness reaching regular truancy. With my home life, school presented itself as an alternate society (if not reality), an utter necessity. Arnold got a job after school working for the local hospital, but rumor had it that he'd been fired for taking an amputated arm home instead of following proper procedures for its disposal. Soon after, he joined the military. A few years later, the *Albany Times* noted that he was a part of the honor guard at some major state function, perhaps Nixon's inauguration. Once in the very early '70s, I ran into him wearing full leather biker drag in Moe's Books in Berkeley. When I saw him at State nearly twenty years later (it was he who recognized me), the narrative of clothing was aging beach boy, his torso and limbs, every visible inch, covered with tattoos. He had come to study writing.

The "average" sentence in "Albany" is 6.94 words long.

My father withheld child support, forcing my mother to live with her parents, my brother and me to be raised together in a small room.

At night we would lie in our two single beds across from one another and I would tell Cliff, two years, seven months younger, long stories, the sort of gothic horror only a nine-year-old could envision. He would tell me to stop and start to whimper and finally begin crying so that eventually my mother would burst in to tell us to be quiet. This went on for years, until I was old enough to get a crystal radio set and flashlight, and could hide under the covers, listening to the all-news station and reading Steinbeck novels until I fell asleep.

The cruelty of my behavior is evident. It's not an excuse to say that I was nine years old, or twelve. What motivated me? Over forty years later, it is still unclear to me whether I was driven out of a confused sense that my brother's arrival shortly after the disappearance of my father had been, in some vague way, the cause of that man's abandonment, or whether the practice of emotional terrorism (modeled with such artistry by my grandmother) was simply the only form of autonomy I understood.

. . .

I can't afford an automobile.

At first, the long ride out on the bus from San Francisco to San Rafael was a luxury. Prohibited by Selective Service regulation from earning a living wage at my conscientious objector's "alternative service" job, I worked for the Committee for Prisoner Humanity and Justice (CPHJ) for the first year at no salary, the second year at just $125 per month. To survive, I found a part-time night job doing lay-out and paste-up with the Kalendar, a first-generation gay bar newspaper whose editor and publisher harbored dim fantasies of develop-ing an empire of alternative media if he could just meet this week's payroll. With

---

Hughes," his text described her as picking at the hair on her arms, a comment that must have radiated with the gender and racial anxieties of the 1950s in a working-class suburb that actively sought to keep ethnic minorities out.

[2]I never thanked Vance Teague for the gift of this lesson (although I have Arnold), other than by way of a brief note on the website for Albany High alumni. According to Al Nielsen, my sixth grade teacher, Teague retired after suffering a heart attack several years later.

Metalanguage: Susan Hughes, Jon Arnold, Tim Johnson, and Ron Silliman in sixth grade at Marin Elementary School (Hughes is in the third row, second from the right; Arnold is immediately to her right; Johnson is immediately below Arnold; Silliman is on the bottom row, third from the right)

barely enough money to afford my $50-per-month rent in a large communal flat opposite the Panhandle in the Haight, I often hitchhiked the seventeen miles north over the Golden Gate Bridge to work and back. Later, as funds became more plentiful and my need to be reasonably on time grew, I chose to ride the Golden Gate Transit buses[3] out, hitching back in the evening rush.

The Golden Gate system was notably different from both the San Francisco Municipal Railway (the "Muni") or my earlier experiences

with AC Transit in the East Bay. I would board the bus on Van Ness and after only a couple more stops in San Francisco, the bus tended only to lose passengers as it traveled north through Marin County. This meant that if I picked my seating with a little luck and care, I could sit without a rider next to me for the entire thirty-minute ride, an unusually smooth journey given the state of the then-new buses and the fact that our journey was against commute traffic on the freeway. If other transit systems were carnivals of human interaction, filled with the racial and class conflicts that find themselves funneled into public space, the Golden Gate buses were a refuge. Often the bus was quieter and more private than my home. I would

---

[3]The Marin-Sonoma suburban system that came into being the week I started my job at CPHJ in February, 1972, replacing a previous Greyhound system.

read or stare out the window and increasingly I began to use the time in order to write.[4]

Far across the calm bay stood a complex of long yellow buildings, a prison.

Because the hill sloped away from the rear of the house, the modest five-step red cement front porch was counterbalanced by a long rickety wooden stairway leading down to the yard in the rear. There was room enough at the top of that splintery deck for no more than one adult to stand (the only one who ever did, really, was my grandmother, reaching into the clothespin bin that my grandfather must have built into the railing, hanging clothes on a line nearly twenty feet over the yard). I would spend hours up there, looking out over the minuscule expanse that was our backyard, with its lone tree next to our small sway-back garage, a hydrangea bush in the near corner, a few straggles of berry bushes against the chain-link fence that separated our yard from that of an old woman who lived by herself on the next block over. On a clear day, I could see beyond Albany hill all the way across the bay to Mount Tamalpais and, further to the north, right at the water's edge, San Quentin. Who did I think lived there? Doing what?

My grandfather's one real friend from the Pabco plant was jailed for vehicular manslaughter and sent to "Tamal."[5] One summer day, my grandparents, my brother and I rode the Richmond-San Rafael ferry—we were headed for a week's vacation along the Russian River—and stopped in the parking lot of the prison. My grandfather got out of the pale '51 Pontiac and walked up to and eventually through the entrance of the medieval-looking structure, disappearing inside for a visit that lasted at least

Jessie Aileen Coates on the day of her wedding to Arthur Tansley, Silliman's grandfather, in 1920

an hour while the rest of us waited in the summer sun. What did I think this meant?

Who was this man? He was a figure of conversation from time to time at home, but as was true for everyone but immediate relatives and a few members of my grandmother's VFW Ladies Auxiliary branch, he never set foot in our house. I never once saw the man. Having served his term, he returned to his job in Emeryville, retiring a year ahead of my grandfather. Within a week of his retirement party, he committed suicide.

A line is the distance between.

I'm waiting in a long queue to register for classes at San Francisco State. The fellow in front of me, wiry and lively-eyed David Perry, turns out to be a writing major likewise, a grad student by way of Bard. I quickly blurt (brag?) that I'm "in correspondence" with Robert Kelly, with whom he's studied. It turns out that there are other Kelly students in the area, at Berke-

---

[4]Although I write significant portions of Ketjak in transit, the first poem I will complete entirely on the bus is Sitting Up, Standing, Taking Steps. The Chinese Notebook was also written entirely on Golden Gate Transit. By 1976, just two years after I first begin writing daily on transit, I write Bart, a work premised entirely on the transit system upon which it was penned. After I leave CPHJ in the fall of '76, my writing again becomes more varied in terms of the circumstances of its composition, although I continue to use transit regularly through 1986 (when I finally learn to drive).

[5]The name the U.S. Post Office gives to San Quentin.

ley—Harvey Bialy, a microbiologist/poet married to a slender, intense exotic dancer named Timotha, and John Gorham, a graduate student in English and possibly the finest natural lyric poet I would ever meet.

Bialy is giving a reading soon thereafter in Albany in the same two-room public library where, just three years earlier, I'd first discovered Williams's *The Desert Music* and seen in an instant how poetry could be put to non-narrative purposes. Bialy's poetry is spare and intellectual in a way that doesn't tell me anything other than that it wants to be known as such. I much prefer Bialy's reading mate, a Canadian graduate student at Berkeley named David Bromige. Paul Mariah, a poet I've known slightly through the open readings at the Rambam Bookstore in Berkeley, does the introductions.

To get home afterwards, I thumb a ride. A car stops immediately, the driver a slightly older fellow—he's twenty-nine, I'm twenty-one—I'd seen in the back of the crowd at the reading. In the time it takes him to drive me back to my apartment in the Adams Point neighborhood of Oakland (I don't realize for some time just how far out of his way he has gone), we discover not only an affinity to the poetics of Bromige, but that we shared a strong sense of Robert Duncan's importance, an interest in Zukofsky and Ashbery, and even a friend, one of my early publishers, Iven Lourie of the *Chicago Review,* having been the driver's roommate for a time back at the University of Chicago. The driver introduces himself as David Melnick, and he turns out to be a shy, witty, brilliant person, deeply insecure. One of the three most intelligent people I will ever meet, we instantly become friends for life.

Through these people (especially Melnick and Gorham and Bromige) I will gradually get to know firsthand a much broader community, including Ken Irby, Tom Meyer, Jonathan Williams, Sherril Jaffe, Jack Shoemaker, David Sandberg, d alexander, Joanne Kyger, and Jerome Rothenberg. These poets are, with only the exception of Perry and Gorham, older, more confident, more widely published. There are only a couple with whom I feel comfortable enough even to speak as a possible equal. (Melnick and Bromige, democrats both, pretend not to notice, coaxing me, prodding.)

Beyond Ashbery, Zukofsky and Duncan, Melnick's favorite poet is David Shapiro, whose early success with trade publishers intimidates

me. I also don't know how to take the casual sense of form practiced by the New York School in general. I'm reading Olson's Maximus poems, all of Blackburn, anything I can get by Whalen, Duncan's Passages as they appear. I'm still trying to figure out how to write The Poem. I still envision it as a distinct formed object, perfect for publication in a magazine.

In 1968, the problem of form is the problem of the line. It, I decide, is the question that nobody, not even Olson, knows how to answer.[6] What, in free verse, does it mean? Olson's answer, more rigorous and less mushily metaphysical than Williams's, is nonetheless filled with gaps and contradictions. Yet even an O'Hara and a Ginsberg seem to acknowledge it. Without ever having read a word of Derrida, I distrust the essentialism of speech Olson's projective verse appears to propose (later I will realize that I've turned Olson's poetry into a straw man, his position in my head far more extreme than any he ever took in life, and only after that, a good while after that, will I come to recognize how useful this process had been).

By 1969, I'm also reading modernist fiction. In a notebook, I try over and over to craft out a "perfect paragraph," with the opening sentence of Faulkner's *Sound and the Fury* as my model. The only part that will survive is "the garbage barge at the bridge." The origin of the sentence in my work is a reaction to the Faulkner, to the Joyce of *Ulysses,* the Kerouac of *Visions of Cody,* Stein everywhere. I sit on the roof of an apartment house now at the edge of the rad lab woods just north of the UC campus, watching the sun set into the high rises of San Francisco, reworking the passage endlessly. One model in my mind, at some point, was Ponge's *Notebook of the Pine Woods,* a journal of the author's stay in hiding from the Nazis during which he attempts a single sonnet. Writing and rewriting my paragraph, I escape any concern that I'm merely imitating Creeley, Olson, Williams, Duncan, Kelly or Eshleman in this poem or that. It also allows me a strategy for literature without progress. I use everything I ever learned about the line, but without ever having to decide what precisely this was. It will be another five years before I actually start to write poetry in prose.

---

[6]In retrospect, I realize just how few of even these poets would have agreed with me then.

The "problem" with the line may be, ultimately, that there is no problem.

They circled the seafood restaurant, singing "We shall not be moved."

By the time I was a senior in high school, I was already participating in the picket lines of the Congress of Racial Equality, mostly at Jack London Square in downtown Oakland, careful not to tell my mother or grandparents where I was going. I knew hardly anyone—they were all college age and older and seemed infinitely more worldly—but I wanted to know them all—that may have been the point—but I was too timid to speak to anyone beyond the singing and chanting that ran as a constant soundtrack to these events. These were the first interracial crowds in which I'd ever found myself. They represented some utopian possibility, a voluntary association that existed solely through action and driven by desire and honor and a sense of justice. The contrast with my family, claustrophobic and seethingly dysfunctional as it was, could not have been more striking.

At some of these pickets in early '65, I began to notice one woman, a few years older than myself, with thick black bangs, intense brown eyes and a sharp, ready laugh, a natural leader. She was one of the very few people who would make eye contact with me, and one day at an afternoon demonstration at Spenger's in Berkeley I recall her coming up to me to ask why people seemed so upset. "Malcolm X was murdered this morning," I replied. This was how I first spoke with Rochelle Nameroff, who would become my first wife.

My turn to cook.

In the 1960s, mixed vegetables stir-fried in a wok, tossed over brown rice.

In the '90s, poached salmon, just barely cooked. Broccoli, steamed but still crisp. Couscous, which few people seem to realize is actually a pasta, the world's oldest.

It was hard to adjust my sleeping to those hours when the sun was up.

The buses had not yet begun running when my shift was over, so I walked up Main Street from Paul's Pies, then over toward our apartment at the edge of the park. How was I going to do this when winter arrived, with the lake effect snow that invariably hit Buffalo? The entrance to our apartment was up the rear stairs, and we couldn't afford real curtains so there was no way to keep the sun out as I tossed and turned and tried to sleep.

The event was nothing like their report of it.

Working all day as a shipping clerk for PG&E in Emeryville, I was unable to get to the UC administrative building in which the students were holding their sit-in before the campus police locked the building at 5 p.m. For hours, I and several thousand other people milled around the building, singing songs from the civil rights movement along with the several hundred students indoors. People brought newly purchased plastic garbage cans filled with hot coffee, plus small buckets filled with birth control pills for the women now locked in. These were sent up ropes to the second-floor balconies while film crews in the building's lobby turned their kliegs on us. The entire plaza had the air of a festival about it, with the very serious undertext of the presence of the police.

I stayed until midnight, then headed home as I had another long day at work the following morning, so was not around when, at 4:00 a.m., Governor Pat Brown (at the urging of local officials who claimed that the offices were being trashed by demonstrators, which was not true) sent in the cops and over 450 students were arrested.

The next evening, Brown was quoted by Walter Cronkite on the CBS Evening News as declaring that students had been misled by outside agitators. To illustrate the concept, the screen showed the images of us on the building's steps outside, carefully raising buckets and cans up the ladders. I was on screen for all of five seconds.

The following morning, when I reported for work, I was told that my position as stock clerk was "no longer needed."

. . .

Mondale's speech was drowned by jeers.

Dianne Feinstein, recognizing that her chances of being nominated as his running mate were fading in front of her eyes, leaned into the microphone and scolded the crowd at Justin Herman Plaza, which only booed more vigorously.

Ye wretched.

The smallest fragment of song, if it is the right song, can ignite what Proust rightly called the involuntary memory. *The Internationale* will ring in my ears as coins are being placed upon my eyes. In much the same way as my grandmother always broke down weeping whenever she heard a solo bugle play *Taps*. Similarly, the receptors in my body cued for acid and speed reawaken now decades later at any tune from *Highway 61 Revisited*. When Peggy left, virtually without warning, for India in 1975, I realized that playing the music of Marvin Gaye over and over might provide short term solace, but would ultimately make it impossible for me to listen to that music in the future. And it has.

. . .

Yet his best friend was Hispanic.

What I know of my grandfather's family is almost entirely hearsay, although I never once in the fifteen years I lived with the man heard him speak of them. His mother was "a monster," "a terror," "cold," and "mean." On that my mother and grandmother both agreed. (I should be suspicious. This is the exact story I hear about my father and his family from my maternal grandmother.) His own father, grandson of the British naval explorer Sir John Franklin, had been killed by a car on Thanksgiving Day sometime around 1910. One brother moved to Lodi, a farm town in the central valley, changing his first name to Frank to the bafflement of all. Another, Charles Tansley, stayed in the Berkeley area, but the only times I ever saw him was at a small service station on Monterey where he would sit on an overturned drum spitting into the grease, trading lies with his friends.[7] There was a sister whom I never recall having met.

My grandmother's first memory of him came from an event in the combined fifth-sixth grade class at LeConte School they attended. A fellow student had had a seizure and my grandfather, following the recommended practice of the day, had inserted his belt into the boy's mouth to keep him from swallowing his tongue. While my grandmother, the youngest of eleven surviving children in a single-parent household, only made it to ninth grade, my grandfather graduated from Oakland Technical High School and worked briefly for Santa Fe railroad before joining the army and shipping off to Paris to load taxis with munitions during the First World War. Returning, he took a job with what was then called the Paraffin Company in Emeryville where he worked from 1919 until 1961.

Aside from my grandfather's jail acquaintance, they had no apparent friends other than the chapter members of the Berkeley Veterans of Foreign Wars which, in the 1950s and '60s, actively supported the work of the House Un-American Activities Committee. In retrospect this seems odd, given their consistent support of the Democratic Party and rather intense dislike of Richard Nixon. In a house in which there were virtually no books other than Reader's Digest condensed novels, my grandfather was a news junky. He read the *Oakland Tribune* end to end every evening, watched John Cameron Swazee and later Huntley and Brinkley with a predictability Spinoza would have understood, riding around with the car radio invariably tuned to news. It was his bulky black Royal typewriter, purchased in order to carry out his duties in the VFW, which, in my later years in high school, I would carry from its perch on a small table in the dining room and set up in the kitchen, typing away novels, school papers, and my first attempts at poetry.

He taught me how to bat, taking me to Bushrod Field in North Oakland where he'd first learned to play. When it came time, in my teen years, to teach me how to tie a tie, he did so grudgingly. Our relationship was already strained and ties were, for him, something he wore only a few days each year. He tried once or twice to teach me how to drive, but began shouting whenever I made a mistake.

I decided not to escape to Canada.

Functionally, I was an idiot, appealing my draft status without benefit of a lawyer. In 1964,

---

[7] In the last years I lived in Berkeley, Krishna and I would meet people at Cafe Roma in that same location. Our behavior with our friends over upscale pastries differed from my great uncle's principally in style.

when I first registered and applied for conscientious objector's status, the standard measurement was a demonstrable family commitment to pacifism within a clearly defined religious framework. I was the son of an ex-cop and navy veteran with a bad (and documented) habit of assaulting people and the guys on this board *knew him*. I cited passages of Kerouac and mumbled some argument about an indigenous mode of Zen Buddhism. My rejection reached appeal sometime around 1967 and the board examiner wrote mostly about my showing up to the hearing in a surplus-store Army jacket. I may have been the only person ever denied for reasons of style.

Showing the file to a draft counselor at UC Berkeley, he got on the phone to Ann Fagan Ginger, a lawyer who ran the Meiklejohn Civil Liberties Institute, an anti-draft legal assistance project, out of her garage in Berkeley. Later that same day, she read the files as I sat silently in front of her and, without even asking me, picked up the phone and called the ACLU.

Revenue enhancement.

I do not recall a time in which I was not the absolutely poorest kid in my class.

Competition and spectacle, kinds of drugs.

In the early 1970s, the *Poetry Project Newsletter* would dutifully list all of the contributors to current magazines except for myself, Watten, Andrews, and a few others the editor felt certain were part of this bad new nameless thing.

In 1978, the Art Institute auditorium, as Barrett began to draw an analogy between Zukofsky's poetry and a scientific concept, Robert Duncan, who had already finished speaking, went ballistic, leaping up, flapping his arms like a crow, yelling, "No, no, no. Zukofsky was all about life, all about song"—a conception of song that would have made any twentieth-century composer cringe (and which, at least at that early moment, Watten had never denied). If this was to be an Oedipal moment, Duncan understood the role assigned to him and so determined to slay the threat before it did him.

What Tom Clark objected to most was not our poetics, but the simple fact that, insofar

as we did not fit any of the previous aesthetic buckets, we changed an invisible internal balance of the larger whole, and it was that whole to which he had committed his life, his desire, his imagination.

If it demonstrates form some people won't read it.

Form proposes its telos: "I know just how many lines this sonnet will take." In 1981, when I wrote "Albany," there was still significant controversy over the deliberately "inorganic" elements of my poetry, especially the use of repetition in *Ketjak* and the Fibonacci number system in *Tjanting*. Poetic fashion has changed and changed again since then, and it most certainly will continue to do so.

Was I "betraying" my literary ancestors (and in what sense did I admit their paternity)? In a sense that both Olson and Duncan would have understood, it has all always been one poem. The one shown on the opposite page, to be exact.

When I look at this chart, which I've been using for several years now,[8] what it tells me is that to work, to maintain the sense of balance that seems to govern my intuition of what goes where and to what degree, is first of all a sense of the size and scope of the next level of the work: it must roughly equal all that has gone before. Roughly is a very general term: *The Alphabet* is nearly twice the length of all the other works on this chart. Combined.

What the chart doesn't show is how, or when, or why, there has been a shift in the work from structures that carried forward a formal concept as a mechanism for breaking up the habits of perception and those that tend to define a form and in the process to seek mechanisms of sub- and di- version. It begins in *The Alphabet* very early. I can find its traces already in the first section I ever wrote for *The Alphabet*, "Force," written a year before "Albany."

In fact, far from being the apotheosis of exoskeletal determinism in poetry, as I've sometimes been portrayed, I find that I've spent seventeen of the last twenty-four years actively

---

[8]Several of the sections that were merely guessed at or barely sketched out when the chart was drafted have now been completed or are nearing completion, and "Y" has become You.

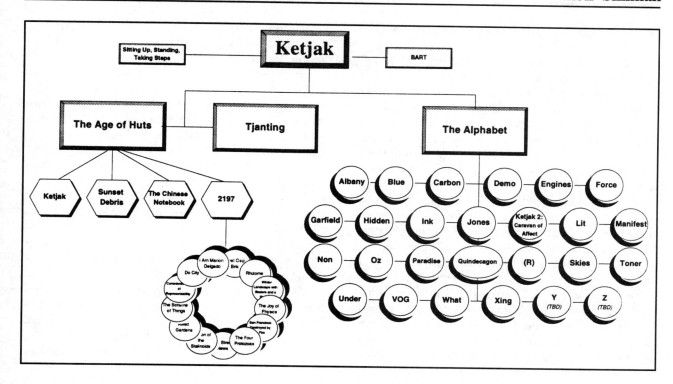

undercutting expectations within form, compared with the seven-year stretch that begins with *Ketjak* and proceeds through *Tjanting*.

This thought makes me wonder if I shouldn't think now of proceeding in yet another way.

Television unifies conversation.

Our next-door neighbors, the Pruters, were the first ones on the block to own a set, a large box with a small blue round screen. A year later, when we first bought ours, we would turn it on at 5:00 p.m. every day, letting it warm up for a half hour against one of the test patterns that was on before the arrival of the first broadcast, *Howdy Doody.*

Died in action.

Chris Martinez is a superb infielder and your basically happy kid. His house, right on the corner of Nielson and Marin, is covered with foliage, as if vegetation would protect the family from the fast, heavy traffic of Marin. We play pickup games of baseball in the elementary school playground hour after hour.

Whenever Chris plays, I shift to the outfield, because he's the better second baseman. He and his best friend, Ray Nottingham, always show up and leave together. They are in our minds a unit. Since they are both one year younger, I don't see them socially once we get past the age of pickup hardball.

Later, Ray's dad sits on the local Selective Service board and takes the role of my inquisitor. Do I think all violence is bad? What would I do if I discovered Adolf Hitler attacking my mother? The two other panel members, one on either side, stare at me, silent. I am terrified of them. This panel is my nightmare of older male authority. I feel powerless and threatened.

Decades later, on the wall in the mall in Washington, it only takes a few minutes to find Chris's name.

If a man is a player, he will have no job.

Around were not a few, but dozens of young writers who seemed content to work at the most minimal part-time positions in order to free up time to write. I was always showing up at readings late and exhausted, having just gotten in off a bus from Sacramento or San Rafael. I never "couldn't find the time to write."

Becoming prepared to live with less space.

After nearly three years during which I'd had only one roommate at a time, I wanted a larger number of people to bounce off of, less of the immediate competition one got (*I* got) over the tightly rationed physical resources of a flat. I also was worried about money. Rents in San Francisco had risen much faster than my ability to earn a living in the prison movement.

At a natural food store on Clement, I saw an ad for a room in a seven-bedroom house on California, right at the edge of Pacific Heights. The people, all of whom were younger than I, seemed friendly, intelligent, straightforward. I was pleased that there had been no turnover in the apartment in the preceding two years. But a gay man, a filmmaker, had just moved out after the one couple in the house had given birth to a young boy, Alyosha. What I didn't realize at the time (although possibly I should have) was what a transformative, even explosive, event that child was to "communal" life.

My room was to be a closed-in back porch, no more than 12 x 12, but it opened onto a large, almost cavernous room that I was told I could make my own, but had to leave open as it was the sole "public" pathway to the downstairs john. I painted the room a deep yellow, almost a goldenrod, and Elliot Helfer, a roommate of mine from a few years before, contributed some furniture—a dining-room table and Morris chair that he had built himself. I set up bricks and boards in the yellow room and mounted the first truly serious bookcase I'd ever managed.

The day I moved in, one of my new roommates wandered about the downstairs naked all afternoon (I think this was a test). She was getting ready to go to Stanford, which had already accepted her, but before she'd moved into the house on California Street, she'd been in the county jail for boosting checkbooks and credit cards from people's mailboxes. At the time I knew her, she was a bartender in the Tenderloin (although, still working in the prison movement, I didn't yet know what that might involve).

Her boyfriend carried a sullen macho act to an extreme. One night, sitting on the front porch, she sighed that she wished that street lamp wasn't glaring down at them. He took a pistol out and shot the light out. The bullet ricocheted through the room in which Alyosha and his parents were trying to sleep. Their reaction was to move.

It rapidly became evident that this beautiful and entirely harmless infant had set off a chain of events and, within six weeks, I found myself the last remaining member of the household. I called the lady, an ill-tempered, horrible German woman who lived in the Sunset, and arranged to take over responsibility for 3028 California Street. I then put signs—3 x 5 cards really—up at the San Francisco Art Institute and in the laundromats, bookstores, and natural food stores in town.

My idea was that I would pick the first of my six new roommates, then she or he and I would then pick the second one, then the three of us the next, and so on until we had filled the house. Because of my finances, I needed to accomplish this quickly. I couldn't afford more than a single month of the rent for the entire seven-bedroom home—$350. But I couldn't decide who, precisely, should be that critical first roommate. One fellow I liked a lot was a tall, laconic painting student at the Art Institute, Mel Laubach. Another was a hippie nurse by the name of Peggy. Finally, almost at the last moment (both had virtually given up on me), I settled on Mel and persuaded him to interview Peggy. She had only a day left in her flat in the Mission when we called to invite her to join us. The next person to join us was Richie Jenkins, a country rock guitarist who'd once played in a band at Queens College called the Bankers, fronted by lead singer Lorenzo Thomas.[9] He was followed by Liz, a grad student at San Francisco State who was studying for a special ed teaching certificate. We then picked on an extraordinarily quiet and shy nutritionist and a tiny young woman who was a hotwalk at a local racetrack.

Having arrived at six, we were unable to agree on the final person. We'd interviewed maybe fifty people over two weeks and everybody was tired and exhausted and disgusted. None of the people we'd met had been able to muster up more than two positive votes for admission. It looked bleak and we held a house meeting one evening (we were waiting for the fifty-first interviewing victim to arrive). Instead

---

[9]As it turned out, although I didn't realize this for almost a year, Richie was also the kid brother of playwright and novelist Len Jenkins.

of looking for what we wanted in an ideal roommate, we concluded, we should instead identify in advance what we *didn't* want. Even here we found ourselves hopelessly vague. All we could agree on was that we didn't want a rock drummer—that would be just hopelessly noisy.

Soon after, the doorbell rang and in walked Frank India. He was, he explained, a rock drummer. He laughed when we explained our collective (and massive) groan, and described how drummers used practice pads. We took it as a sign and he moved in almost immediately. This combination of roommates lasted without change for maybe eighteen months.

As I had to catch the bus seventeen miles out to CPHJ in San Rafael every morning (except for the days I had to catch a Greyhound 90 miles to Sacramento), I was the early riser in the group. Since Peggy usually worked the night shift, first at Children's Hospital (six blocks west of the house) and later at Mount Zion (six blocks east), we'd often pass at the kitchen table. We had long quiet conversations every morning for months and I gradually got so I couldn't hear the thick Carolina accent anymore.

This house turned out to be the perfect collective living situation. We'd all spontaneously troop over to the local ice cream parlor after dinner, a virtual party in motion, or else all catch the bus (none of us owned a car) down to Chinatown to catch a double bill for 99 cents at the Times Theater, or possibly to see the Cockettes. Richie's band played down off of Union Street and had a single forthcoming from Fantasy Records. Lizzie decided to translate some of *Ketjak* into American Sign Language for a class she was doing, and Mel decided to turn this into a performance for one of his classes, held in this instance at the downtown Museum of Modern Art on Van Ness.

It was the kind of house where I could bring home a rotting bear rug that I'd found literally in a dumpster around the corner and put it into the middle of the living-room floor and everybody declared they loved it, so that it stayed for months, even though you could smell the faint, sweet odor of mold.

We also had great parties, with everyone taking seriously the lone rule that you had to invite at least twelve people each. Beer and grass and red wine and amyl nitrate flowed freely. Everyone thought of it as *style*.

My one sexual relationship at the time I first moved to California Street was a casual

affair I'd been having with a married friend. Casual in the sense that it had no narrative—it was literally, and by design, not going anywhere. It was a relationship I'd begun in college when I was still married to Rochelle, who had first introduced us. Off and on, it continued on a sexual level for over a decade. A brilliant artist in her own right, this woman was/is, more than anything, a dear friend, which gave our sex a sense of play (and occasionally even incestuousness). We never planned anything. The sex was spontaneous and the situation carried its own sense of risk. Never once did she lead me to believe that she ever intended to leave her husband, whom she clearly loved. What she was looking for in this has never been clear to me, especially when she got involved with other people, both men and women. What I seemed to be looking for, and this is hindsight, was to understand the infinite depths of friendship. We would have long, casual discussions about everything in the world, her own edge-of-lumpen origins a perspective remarkably close to my own. Next to David Melnick, she was the second person in my life to see and unconditionally accept me for who I was, a gift that I think may be the most difficult to give.[10]

The only one of my roommates who ever openly disapproved of this arrangement was Peggy, who at the time declared that she was attempting to swear off men and sex altogether, attending meetings of followers of the original "Don't Worry, Be Happy" guru, Meher Baba. Peg told me, in a nonaccusative way, that I was involved because the sex was safe. Nobody was asking for any sort of commitment from me and the highly variable nature of the relationship (we could go for months between assignations) didn't get in the way of my work.

One night everyone in the house, plus a few folks who more or less happened to be sitting around the kitchen table, decided to head over to a restaurant on 24th Street. Over dinner, we agreed to head back across town to the Presidio Theatre, which was then showing the Erotic Film Festival. The films were all shorts, mostly student works, only a small portion of which could ever have been called hardcore

---

[10]Eventually it would be her desire for children that would move our relationship to another level. She wanted to be certain that her husband was the father.

porn. One consisted entirely of a person eating slices of an orange in extreme close-up.

After the films, Peggy brought one of the guests (a poet and friend of mine) back home. I realized that her "anti-sex" rap had its limits, or at least its exceptions. Even more importantly, I felt crushed. It made me realize that I had begun to think of her as something other (and more) than "just a roommate."

Some weeks later, after a long Saturday on which Elliot Helfer and I had gone hiking in Tilden only to get lost amid a dense forest of brambles, I had to rush to the First Unitarian Church as CPHJ was holding a film benefit on which I'd promised to work. As I was heading through the kitchen on my way out, Peggy said that she wanted to see the movie, an ancient black-and-white chain-gang classic. She grabbed her purse and came along. Afterwards, we took the 38 Geary back, walking the last half-mile down Presidio to California, when I leaned over and kissed her. This led to a series of questions that lasted off and on for two days. What was I looking for? Would I be willing to take responsibility for birth control? Was I going to try and change her spirituality?

I must have answered adequately, since late one evening the following week, when I'd found myself nodding off during conversation in the living room with the rest of the gang and had excused myself and gone to bed, Peggy came into my room, slipped out of her jeans, climbing under the covers. "Okay. Here I am," she said.

Nora the nutritionist had seen Peggy slip into my room, not to return. By the time we got up the following morning, the entire house knew what had happened. There was a lot of eye-rolling and a few jokes in modestly bad taste. At least a couple of people were upset— one woman who'd decided that she was going to seduce me and the live-in (non-rent paying) beau of one of the other women who viewed Peg with more than a little interest— although it would be weeks before we would figure this out.

For a couple of months, life seemed perfect. I was in the middle of writing *The Age of Huts* and felt my poetry was really breaking into new territory. Every time I opened the notebook I got excited. Barrett Watten had promised to bring *Ketjak* as a book out soon. It was gradually becoming evident that Califor-

nia would soon pass a bill eliminating the indeterminate sentence, the only question was when and with what kind of terms to replace it (I was hard at work answering that latter question). Living in a large collective household with my lover seemed like just the right balance of privacy and intimacy.

One evening I was standing in the living room talking with Richie. In the kitchen, I could hear Peggy talking with Mel. I hear her say, "I've decided I'm moving to India and I think I'm going to stay." It was the first I'd even heard of this idea, but (as I wander in dumbfounded to the next room) she's already bought the ticket. Six weeks later, she's gone.

As it happened, she didn't stay forever, but by the time she returned, I'd given up and was seeing other women. We tried, off and on for the next three years, to re-establish the spark our affair had had those first few months, but one of us was always desperately seeking out the other, whose head was for the moment someplace else. It devolved into an adolescent break-up and make-up pattern.

In late 1977, she'd gone back to North Carolina for a few months when the members of the household (which had gone through an almost complete recycling of roommates after Peg departed for India) voted to go on rent strike as the landlord refused to do repairs. The landlord sued and people began abandoning the house for better quarters. I moved to a flat in the Haight and put Peg's stuff into cartons in his garage. When she returned, we took over an old apartment on San Jose Avenue and tried living together as a couple. After six months, we both knew it wasn't working. She moved out and eventually returned to the Carolinas.

Live ammunition.

The windows of the Main Library seemed to implode and the small "bookmobile" by the entrance rocked as its walls freckled with gunshot. We'd locked the door of our second-floor classroom in Wheeler but were unable to keep ourselves from peeking out the window in horror as the deputy sheriff raised a shotgun and fired into the Rare Books Room across the path. Nobody said a word.

Secondary boycott.

By the mid-1980s, the political activists I hang out with are beginning to confront the same set of questions facing my poet friends—how, in one's mid-life, to move from transitory inadequate jobs to some sense of continuity as a life, which means a sense of career that may (or may not) be related directly to writing or activism. In the DSA office, national political director Jim Shoch complains that it's impossible to have an "interesting" conversation with members of this same organization Jim has spent fifteen years building. He's already applied to graduate school.

My crime is parole violation.

The joint has a discourse and logic that took years to learn. There are a variety of ways people can avoid telling you what exactly they've done to warrant incarceration. Even harder for an outsider to fathom is the sense of time as urgency without future. The sense was not the continuous present of modernism, but rather a perpetual one in which every moment was new, in formation. This proved ultimately to be a more important lesson than anything I had learned in college. Twenty-one years after leaving CPHJ, it still governs the function of time in my writing.

Now that the piecards have control.

What was the moment in which any hope for the Left's ability to form a majority coalition that could genuinely govern in the U.S. was truly lost? Was it as late as 1968? Or did it occur earlier? When the labor movement broke off from socialism? When unions stopped being activist and became service organizations?

Rubin feared McClure would read Ghost Tantras at the teach-in.

Jerry Rubin was, I immediately surmised, a jerk. But this woman who was volunteering as his secretary was not. With her dark bangs, long flowing hair, intense brown eyes and sharp, almost explosive laugh, she was entirely unlike anyone I'd ever met in my Waspy world before. I was apparently the only person they'd found who had any idea how to contact Dave Van Ronk (and my thought was merely to phone Izzy Young at Folk City in New York), but this made me a sort of resource. Shortly thereafter, I ran into her again at Pepe's, the pizza parlor of choice for Telegraph Avenue street people in 1965. She was hunting for a mutual friend in search of some grass. I was reading either *Naked Lunch* or *Last Exit to Brooklyn* and it occurred to her that I was literary. She asked me what I knew of Yeats, but, knowing nothing, I was derisive. She'd just come from the opening performance of the film *Help,* which she gushed over. Since I considered the Beatles a commercial rip-off, I was even more derisive. She challenged me to see the film with her the next day, which I did, interpreting it as a series of psychedelic drug jokes. Had she ever taken acid? She had not. So the following night we saw the film again (skipping the second feature, Glenn Ford or someone like that in *The Love Boat*), stopping at the drinking fountain on the way in to wash down some commercially produced Sandoz. After the film was over, she went into the women's restroom and didn't return for nearly an hour. She'd been, she told me, watching the walls. Over the course of the next week I also introduced her to DMT, which at the moment was what a friend and I were trying without great success to introduce into the Berkeley market. It had few of the psychological effects associated with acid and lasted for only a very brief period, less than an hour, but the visual hallucinations were far more intense and one felt as if one's limbs had been rendered into some soft and pliable material.

One night after a party, we returned to Rubin's office above some stores at the corner of Telegraph and Dwight, where the organizing committee permitted her to sleep. On Rubin's couch in that dark office, I lost my virginity to Rochelle Nameroff who, on Halloween just two months later, I would marry.

This form is the study group.

College is a process that takes bright young people and renders them illiterate. None more so than the professors who are forced to remain within the confines of this institution, replicating the cycle over and over. My teachers at Berkeley, at San Francisco State, at Merritt College had perfect contempt for one another and none of them—with the exceptions of Bob Grenier and Ed van Aelstyn (one of the founders of *Coyote's Journal* who briefly taught linguistics at SF State)—could have ever read the work of someone such as Jackson Mac Low.

For me, very early on, perhaps because I was publishing and going to readings and giving readings before I really went to college, the community of the poem, of the reading scenes and small presses, with always that concentrating, centering fact of the text, any text, at hand, in front of one's eyes, words forming in the mind from the muteness of letters clustered along invisible lines—the community of the poem was (and remains) the center around which learning in my life can occur.

I dedicate poems precisely because I want to invoke this community, to say its real name(s).

The Sparts are impeccable, though filled with deceit.

The long crowd milled into the auditorium to hear the panel and its lead speaker, the head of the FMLN, while outside members of the Sparticist League not only waved banners denouncing him as a traitor to the Left, but brought their own spotlights in hopes of attracting some TV time.

As early as high school, Trotskyism had been attractive to me because it was the only tendency visible on the Left (I knew nothing at the time of the Frankfurt School) that always articulated, at once, both the value of Marxist analysis and the horrific depredations that were Stalinism. Any history of the United States in the twentieth century that does not attempt to comprehend the trajectory and fate of the various Trot tendencies is useless.

A benefit reading.

I had never put on a reading before, but thought I could get Bob Creeley, then living in Bolinas, Joanne Kyger (ditto), and Edward Dorn, who was staying that year in the Sunset District, to agree. I sent each a letter, explaining what CPHJ was, its relation to the California prison movement, the movement's general direction, what the location for the reading was like (the First Unitarian Church on Franklin in San Francisco), etc. My co-workers were supportive, but probably more bemused than any-

thing—why rent such a large room for a poetry reading? Who were *these* people (none of my co-workers had ever heard of any of them)? Before I could even follow up with phone calls, Dorn called and asked me to come see him. I left work early, hitched (my characteristic mode of transportation in the 1970s) down to the city and caught a bus out past Golden Gate Park and took the long walk uphill to a small white stucco dwelling on a block crammed with little single-family homes (the walls, like so much of San Francisco, nearly touching). Dorn's house was chaotic, an ironing board dominating the middle of the living room, his wife and a young woman who was introduced cursorily as "the nanny" chasing after kids. "Nobody told me about the fog in the summer out here," he said, waving me over to a round dining-room table.

"The idea of twelve months of indoor behavior is intolerable." He wanted to know in great detail about the CPHJ (Creeley and Kyger both later agreed without a single question about the group or its work or the movement in general), how was it funded, did we serve all kinds of prisoners and not just the media "stars," what was San Quentin like, what was my relation to the group, etc. As we talked he reached into an open bowl on the table and began to roll a joint the size of a small cigar. He passed it over and I took a deep first breath, my lungs and throat clinching tight to avoid coughing. It was harsh weed, the strongest I had ever smoked. Dorn finally had one condition, that he be allowed to go on last so that he could arrive at the last moment and not have to deal with either Creeley or Kyger. I agreed, which was how it finally occurred.

On the night of the event itself, during the intermission, Opal Nations, new at the time to the United States, came up to say that he had never been at a reading with 400 people before. I had, but I certainly had never tried to set something up like that. It had been (in retrospect) remarkably easy.

Among the attendees, although I would not know this for years, was a San Francisco poet who hung out with the Auerhahn Press people, Geoffrey Brown, and his girlfriend at the time, Krishna Evans.

He seduced me.

"Each year, I pick a student to be my lover," he said. The small basement apartment in the

Haight was dark not because the sun was already setting, but because so little light could get between the buildings of San Francisco. He talked incessantly, at least partly out of nervousness. I hardly knew which story to believe. He claimed to have been illiterate until he was in his teens, later to have become a lawyer. He spoke of being the reincarnation of Jack Spicer, who'd been dead just two years.

Thirty years later, the smell of scotch still repels me.

AFT, local 1352.

The faculty union chapter at San Francisco State in 1981.

Enslavement is permitted as punishment for crime.

Rebecca's husband was the sergeant in charge of security at the Federal Correctional Institution in Pleasanton. They lived in a trailer home in a "residential" section of the facility, housing in the area generally costing more than guards could afford. We rarely spoke about what I knew about what their lives might be like. After Rebecca was "riffed" by ComputerLand, Gaylynn would drop off her child at the prison each morning for daycare.

Her husband broke both of her eardrums.

This woman was a co-worker, a nurse at Hospitality House, but it could have been Marti with her out-of-control stalker cop ex-husband, or Mrs. Rodriguez, bleeding to death on her front porch just doors up the street from my own house or any of several other women I've known. Having been raised primarily by women, the ongoing battle between the sexes has always seemed anything but metaphoric.

I used my grant to fix my teeth.

Eating a biscuit in Perkos's cafe on Henderson in Porterville, 1997, I break yet another tooth.

Rochelle Nameroff, early 1966

They speak in Farsi at the corner store.

The town of Albany was separated from the Scottish northwest corner of Berkeley when the latter was incorporated shortly after the turn of the century because the owners of the Hercules Powder Plant, manufacturers of dynamite, were afraid of the constraints on their business a local governing board might put into place. Later, after the plant had blown up for the last time and the company relocated north of Richmond to a site on which it constructed its own town, Hercules, Ocean Vista, as Albany was briefly known[11] used its geographic linkage and legal separation to create a new community of small, single-family homes, most of them constructed in the 1920s.

---

[11]It has no vistas and you cannot see the ocean even from the peak of its lone hill.

Many of the early families worked either in the industrial plants that lay close by the bay in Berkeley and Emeryville, dumping raw sewage directly into the waters, or else were the shopkeepers who serviced the people of Berkeley. As the university began to take on an identity as early as the 1930s as a site for such suspect activities as folk music, race mixing, and even communism, the natural town-gown distinctions of any college burg were accentuated by the legal divide between the two communities. Albany, by the 1950s, was as much a *not-Berkeley* as it was anything in its own right.

This was reinforced still further by the local clique of Solano and San Pablo Avenue shop owners and realtors who literally governed the place (one of whom was a cousin through marriage to one of my grandfather's nieces). Within walking distance of the University of California campus was a city of 17,000 that was thoroughly red-lined, that housed the northern California headquarters operations for right-wing cabals such as the John Birch Society and the Minutemen. In school, there was a Japanese student in one class, three Hispanics, a Jew, and an African American in others, but there proved so few of any single group that each individual was forced to stand for all Others in the school. In Spanish class, our teacher insisted that we speak as she alleged people spoke in Spain and not as they did in Mexico or only a few blocks beyond the border of town, a dialect she no doubt thought of as an Indian mongrelization of a great European tongue.

YPSL.

With the exception of the CP and the larger Trotskyist tendencies, the 1960s rolled over the Left formations of the 1950s like a tidal wave over so many sand castles. Unprepared to deal with a popular rebellion to its Left and with none of its regard for McCarthy-era caution, an organization like the Young People's Socialist League was rapidly reduced to the alphabet soup of history.

The national question.

The war at home was not an object, but a process, one that reached an apotheosis in the weeks immediately following the murders at Kent and Jackson state universities. At Berkeley, we simply stopped going to classes. At first, everyone stopped going to class. Instead we worked eighteen- to twenty-hour days organizing canvassing projects throughout the entire East Bay. For a time, we literally stole resources from the buildings—entire printing presses—carrying them to a house north of campus that a handful of English majors shared. After we realized that the "reconstitution" was so total that the regents and school administration simply planned to do nothing in response, no arrests for theft, no lockouts of the now empty buildings, we returned and turned the campus into an anti-war operation the size of the Rouge Plant. Thousands of students participated every day. I ran a silk-screen poster operation out of what had been a classroom in Wheeler Hall, an endless stream of boxy prints that read "Another Home for Peace." The smell of the paint and the curious feeling of participating, being, if not in control, at least active in my own destiny was intoxicating. Even then, I think I must have realized that I had a penchant for infrastructural projects, as I spent much more time helping groups to go out into the community than I ever did canvassing myself. Once a week, however, I would get out and go door-to-door, usually in the outer reaches of Contra Costa county. Invariably, I would run across some kid who'd failed to report for induction, but who didn't know that resources existed to contest the draft. We'd stand in the shadows of a porch as he would explain that he was frightened, but that he'd already figured out that whatever the consequences might be, the worst alternative surely was to submit to the draft. I would hand out brochures, explain why I and other students felt it necessary to oppose American intervention in a land that held no strategic value to the United States.

The war itself would continue for another five years, but after the middle of 1970 the question was not one of the outcome, but of the conditions of the American defeat. Although thousands of Americans and millions of Indochinese were still to die, and although the largest marches were still to come, from this point forward everything began to have the air of the foregone conclusion.

Already the Left was splintering. As early as 1966, Rochelle and I stood in the front yard of our North Oakland cottage and watched the

Black Panthers two doors down practicing close order drills, more like a junior high school traffic squad than a military unit. There was, it seemed apparent, no room for us in that world, so how then did our Left fit together with it?

Even in the 1960s, one segment of the anti-war movement based their arguments not on the stupidity, cruelty, or arrogance of U.S. policy, but on the inherent rights of the Vietnamese, Laotians, Thais, and Cambodians, an implicit essentialism of habitation that always made me nervous. The idea that a given people "owned" a particular territory in perpetuity seemed to ignore everything I knew about human migration. The concept even of continental stability seemed only to demonstrate that people could not subjectively experience or recognize geologic time. Within that tendency, there were always some who would portray this or that or another group, first in Indochina, then later in Central and South American, Africa, and the Middle East, in beatific terms. I would run into this same tendency again in an even more virulent form, in the prison movement.

Gradually, I began to realize that with all of the good reasons for political action in the world, even good reasons for supporting the indigenous efforts of local groups in the so-called developing countries, the Left would be motivated and even to some degree directed by individuals driven by needs of any entirely different order as well.

I look forward to old age with some excitement.

Sixteen years later, I am writing from room 218 in the Motel 6 of Porterville, in the Sierra foothills north of Bakersfield. My nephew, Stephen Matthew Silliman, is just four days old. Allen Ginsberg has been dead for thirteen days. Their worlds never crossed, just as mine never crossed Gertrude Stein's. But I know people who have slept with people who have slept with people who slept with Walt Whitman. At ninety-four, Carl Rakosi's mind is clear as a bell. Others at twenty-four, hopelessly muddied and muddled. Once, walking on the beach at Stinson with Rae Armantrout during our student days at Berkeley, I knelt to pick up a beautifully pocked smooth gray stone (I still have it). She asked me what I was doing. "Looking for the good ones," I replied.

Ron Silliman, Nielson Street, Albany, California, about 1950

42 years for Fibreboard Products.

He was first-line management all the years I was growing up, a foreman in the newspaper pulping operation. Once, sometime in the early '50s, he'd been standing on a four-story-high stack of papers when the water boom swung and hit him from the rear. He called home to say he'd be "a little late" for dinner, having broken both wrists and ankles. Later, as his hearing declined, he refused to see a doctor or consider a hearing aid, fearing that they would use this as an excuse to fire him immediately before his retirement. As it happened, he spent the entire last year on the job working to avoid just that result.

Although we drove right past the plant every time we took 80 through Emeryville (there's a tall dark high-rise apartment complex there just east of the freeway now), he never took either my brother or me to the job. I never once heard him speak of his work with satisfaction or pleasure.

Food is a weapon.

Nothing in the global marketplace more accurately depicts the pathology of capital than

Prison movement activists after a panel at Santa Rosa Junior College, about 1974: (from left)
Popeye Jackson (UPU), Alva D'orgeaux (CPHJ), Silliman (CPHJ), Bill Hamilton (CPHJ),
unidentified UPU member, Carol Parker (Connections)

the distribution of survival. This sentence is for Corrine Dufka of Nairobi, Kenya.

. . .

Music is essential.

It was a bookish kid's way to discover the world. At sixteen, a reference in the liner notes to a Kingston Trio album led me to buy a record of someone I'd never heard, or heard of, before—Pete Seeger, which in turn led to Leadbelly, Woody Guthrie, the Weavers, which in turn. . . .

The cops wear shields that serve as masks.

The one time I was injured in the hundreds of demonstrations in which I took part

was, in 1970, one of the rare times when I'd decided not to be involved, so was merely milling around the outskirts of an audience of several thousand, listening to the speakers, when the cops rushed the crowd from behind. I didn't even notice them until the baton rapped me across the back, sending me stumbling right through a line of cops. I kept running and got free, but the next morning couldn't get out of bed for the pain. Rochelle called John Gorham, who drove me to Herrick Hospital where X-rays suggested a bruised kidney.

Her lungs heavy with asbestos.

Evelyn Schaaf was short, heavy, almost always angry and abrasive. She also had a quick sense of humor and the second loudest laugh in the world. Her husband, Valmar, a civil engineer who financed her political activities and usually served as the president of the board of whatever nonprofit they were running at the time, still liked to identify himself as a "union thug." His laugh is louder.[12]

When, over the phone, I'd first asked her what CPHJ was, she laughed and responded "Two fat ladies!" In fact, there was a core of around a dozen volunteers, most of them older women, all but two widowed or divorced, who'd been galvanized around the death in San Quentin of a young man by the name of Fred Billingslea, an African American who'd suffered a psychotic break in prison—not such an unusual occurrence—and had been screaming in his cell, smearing feces on the wall until the guards came up and fired tear gas canisters into it with shotguns. One canister hit him in the throat and he went down instantly. They moved him unconscious to the prison hospital by dragging him down several flights of stairs by his ankle, his head hitting the concrete and metal steps again and again.

What made CPHJ possible as "alternative military service" was the presence of certain names on the letterhead, U.S. Senator John Tunney, plus Congressmen Leo Ryan and Ron Dellums.

My first day on the job, I opened perhaps a hundred letters that had come in the mail from different prisoners, their friends and family, learning the complex code by which these letters were used to document complaints, problems, practices. At the end of the day, I was given a key to the office and told to open it up the next morning and start with the mail as soon as it arrived. But when I got to the office on the second floor of an old legal building on Fourth Street in San Rafael across from the absent original civic center, a nervous man in his mid-forties was literally cowering in the doorway. He was, he said, an escaped prisoner, at least technically. He'd been released to a

halfway house at the edge of San Quentin to work for a few months prior to his parole and had obtained work in a local body shop. The boss, thinking he was doing the man a favor, told no one on the staff of the man's situation and one of the administrative workers had invited him home, first for dinner and then to spend the night. After several years away from even the sight of women, the offer proved impossible to decline. But now, with dawn, he realized he'd be reported missing and that the police would be looking for him. "Escape" in those days tended to carry a five-year term.

I opened the office, let him in (I was probably harboring a fugitive), then called Evelyn at home, who suggested a lawyer to call. I did, explaining the situation, and he agreed to phone the prison and arrange a "surrender" if they would agree not to prosecute. They consented and all that remained was to transport the man to the lawyer's office without him getting picked up or arrested in the meantime. So I walked down the hall to the office of Sally Soladay, another lawyer who had been instrumental in the formation of CPHJ (she was the lawyer handling the Billingslea wrongful death action for his family), explaining the circumstances all over again and they agreed that a lawyer should act as his chauffeur. One did. This was my second morning on the job.

Two weeks too old to collect orphan's benefits.

We'd gone into the city to the Haight where Bill said he could score some acid, something I'd been wanting to try for weeks, maybe months. I had no idea what to expect at all—everybody had said the drug was/would be "incredible" but no one had said how exactly, in what fashion. Of the four of us, only Bill had taken it before and he only once. In Chinatown, as the visual elements of the early high began to emerge, my teeth chattering compulsively, I sat cross-legged on Grant Street and watched catfish through the window of a market as they gradually turned into dragons. Every Disney character then in existence was milling around the crowded intersection of Columbus and Grant. We didn't *do* anything—we wandered about, giggly and amazed. Later, after midnight, as the visuals calmed down, we drove back to Berkeley where I decided not to crash on David's

[12]In the late '40s, when it was already apparent just how debased the Communist Party had become, Ev and Val had been infatuated with Mao, some of whose ideas still wafted through the air of the office, the entire idea of a project of recreating consciousness, "socialist man." By 1971, when I first met her, they'd decided to focus specifically on local issues and had spent most of the previous decade running the United Farm Worker support organization in Marin County. They'd met sometime around, perhaps during, the Oakland general strike in the 1940s. She'd spent the war "double-bottoming" boats with asbestos insulation, protecting them in theory from torpedoes.

couch but instead had Bill drive over to Solano in Albany to the newish apartment complex where my mother now had an apartment.

As I wandered up the stairway, I began to realize that I was still too high to deal with my mom, who might still be awake. Since I stayed at the apartment maybe three or four times per week, it wasn't as though she expected me, or at least this was how I envisioned it. Instead, I took the small door that led up to the roof, looking out over the small town in which I'd grown up, thinking big, vague thoughts. The sense of height and breadth on the rooftop was very close to flying and I recall looking down at the street for a long time, trying to understand why flight had been denied to humans as a species. It seemed so unfair.

At one point, I noticed the television antenna for the complex. I had never realized the sculptural qualities of this wire construction before. It seemed anthropomorphic and very inviting. I sat in front of it and examined it slowly and carefully, and then began methodically to disassemble it, looking at each section of aluminum with a sense of wonder. What *was* aluminum? How could a metal seem so "made" and yet so insubstantial. There was a spiritual quality to the transitory nature of industrial process that I'd never appreciated before. Aluminum clearly was alive—it had an intelligence that took exactly the shape of its being.

For reasons I will never understand, I began singing to myself. I don't recall what, other than that it was a Sinatra tune (although if you'd asked me in 1964 what I thought of Sinatra I would have said that I despised him). I was still humming this as I wandered downstairs and turned the key to the apartment. Inside, the light to the living room was still on, my mother sitting on the couch, looking angrily at me. She accused me of being drunk and reminded me that I wasn't old enough yet to drink. I said nothing since this was a better impression I imagined than telling her the truth. Had she even heard of LSD?

Then she added, almost in the same breath, before I could decide whether or not to trust myself to say anything at all, that she'd gotten a phone call from my uncle in Pasco. My father had been in an accident somewhere in South Carolina. After several days, he'd died. I still didn't say anything, nor did she. I went to the room that was nominally mine and lay

on the bed I'd grown up with—the "cottage cheese" stucco and asbestos walls pulsated every shade of the rainbow. I don't recall what I thought—I don't even recall thinking—but I remember looking inside myself, imagining that I should find an emotion somewhere, puzzled a little that I seemed to find none.

This was August 21, 1965. On this same day in San Francisco (although I would not realize this for years), Jack Spicer died. In Mount Pleasant, South Carolina, it was the tenth birthday of Nancy Silliman.

A woman on the train asks Angela Davis for an autograph.

Some of the passengers on the BART (Bay Area Rapid Transit) car look up, trying to figure out who the "famous" woman is. I'm sitting half a car away, jotting in a notebook.

You get read your Miranda.

Autobiographer's motto: *You have a right to remain silent.*

As if a correct line would somehow solve the future.

My brother had invited Barbara and me to the Christian commune where he now lived, on the edge of Petaluma. The group was learning how to farm, but at the time (1972) was relatively incompetent at it. City kids, playing country. Barbara, the quintessential suburban princess, had to show someone how to cut off the head of a chicken, which she did quickly, irritated at their lack of understanding of their own actions. Later, during a house meeting, we saw and heard several of the group's members talking in tongues.

Talking with my brother during his early years as a "born again" Christian often felt eerily similar to conversations I had had elsewhere with friends who'd gotten involved with one or another ultraleftist political cult. In each instance, the unassailability of the logic was taken by the speaker as a given, regardless of just how loopy any of the individual statements that followed might be. (The leader of the Sparts, for example, once called the Albanian CP a bunch of "goat fuckers," which gave the Socialist Workers Party—by comparison a "centrist" Trotskyist tendency in those days—occasion to blast the Sparts for ethnic bias, to which the Sparts responded, "well, the Albanians are a peasant people and obviously the SWP doesn't understand peasant life, being just a bunch of petite bourgeois deviationists.")

My brother's sense of my Marxism was never informed by having read much political theory or history. Once, when I was working in the prison movement, he told me that he'd been reading Solzhenitsyn's *Gulag Archipelago*. Wasn't communism a repressive system?

Certainly Stalinism was, I replied. For example, look at Castro outlawing homosexuality in Cuba. My brother, who at this stage of his life was still literally leading book-burning demonstrations in front of the Theosophy Book Store in San Francisco, was soon defending Castro. Leucretia, his wife at the time, glowered at me.

They murdered his parents just to make the point.

No week ever went by during my childhood in which my grandmother did not tell me how my father had "ruined" my mother's life.

Long before I ever met Robby or Michael Meeropol, I took the execution of Julius and Ethel Rosenberg as an emblem for cruelty.

It's not easy if your audience doesn't identify themselves as readers.

What I desire in poetry, my own and that of others, is that everyone work as hard as possible, the sort of labor that is indistinguishable from the best play, the most passionate lovemaking, the most intense experience of music or painting or cinema. I am perpetually startled, stunned even, not simply that this desire is not universally shared, but by the degree of hostility with which it is so often met.

Mastectomies are done by men.

Cancer has its politics. In the years since I wrote this sentence, I have come to know hundreds of people attacked by the cells of their own bodies. Jerry Estrin never stood a chance.

Our pets live at whim.

I grew up with cats and for years tended to adopt strays, named variously Useless, Topaz, Alto.[13] The cool, dispassionate consideration of an alien species seems to me often the perfect perspective from which to view the human. What I discovered as an adult, however, was that my obsessive self-centeredness didn't translate well to ongoing care of others. Without exception, my cats found neighbors who voluntarily fed them on the back porches and decided that this would become home.

Net income is down 13%.

One's relation to a statistic is invariably both personal and dissociated. At the time I wrote this sentence I was about to leave Hospitality House, where I had worked for five years, to try and live for a year on part-time teaching jobs at San Francisco State and UC San Diego, making ends meet with the money I had saved from my 1979 NEA grant.

> Those distant sirens down in the valley signal great hinges in the lives of strangers.

August 18, 1965: three men are working in a small brick building, little more than a room. One of them (my father?) flicks on a switch when he shouldn't. 23,000 volts flail through the air, setting off an explosion so intense that the piping on the wall melts. My father gets up and staggers outside, eventually into an ambulance, third-degree burns over 80 percent of his body. It's the toxins in his blood from all the burned tissue that kills him three days later, kidney failure. "He kissed me good-bye, went to work, and never came home," says Buddy, the half brother I won't meet even by telephone for another thirty-one years.

A phone tree.

The ability to differentiate and to organize that differentiation is the essence of politics as a practice. We'd borrow the law offices of friends,

---

[13]To whom *Garfield* is dedicated.

bring in some pizzas and Cokes, and hit the phones from 6:00 until 9:00, night after night. The list in front of us might include every "high probability voter" registered as a Democrat in a multi-unit building (and therefore a renter) in a middle- or lower-income neighborhood. (In the "better" neighborhoods, we'd run into tenants who identified as *future* owners and who were therefore much less apt to vote for their own immediate self-interest.)

The landlord's control of terror is implicit.

As a member of the Arson Task Force of the San Francisco Fire Department, I helped to construct a list of landlords whose "problem" tenants always seemed to have fires, so that hence forward any fire in one of their buildings would automatically initiate an arson investigation. My own landlord showed up on the list.

Not just a party but a culture.

A quotation of Jim Shoch (citing perhaps Stanley Aronowitz) on why the American Communist Party had a lasting impact where other radical organizations did not (especially notable when one considers the deformed nature of the revolution that the CP was forced to support). This principle is also why an internationalist poetry of urban centers—the essence of the avant-garde tradition—holds such a strong attraction for me.

Copayment.

Telephone message, Friday, June 6, 1997: "Hello. You may not know me, but my name is Ron Silliman. If you are the Glenn Silliman who is the son of Glenn Sherman Silliman, born in Prosser, Washington, and who died in Mount Pleasant in August of 1965, then I am your older brother." Within forty-eight hours, Buddy's sister (I did not know for certain that she was his full sister, that he even knew her, that she was still alive, even what her last name might be), *my* sister, reaches Jenny, my brother Cliff's wife, in Springville, California: "Hello. My name is Nancy Silliman Bryant and I am not a crackpot."

Only known photograph of Ron Silliman with his father, Glenn Sherman Silliman, early 1947

He held the Magnum with both hands and ordered me to stop.

I did and immediately he spread-eagled me against a pastel sedan parked at the curb, crooking his neck just slightly to talk into a speaker mounted on his epaulet: "Got him."

This soon produced two men in their early thirties who looked as if they had just come from a golf course. They identified themselves as members of the FBI and asked me where I had stashed the gun and the money. I stammered my reply in the form of a question—*what gun, what money?* From the bank, one of them replied, nodding back toward Solano, the commercial strip a block north. There was a Wells Fargo at the end of the block.

By now a police car had arrived and those neighbors of mine who were already home from work began milling on their porches. We'd only been living in the house across the street for a few weeks and had been anxious, as the first student household in a notably middle-class neighborhood, to make a good impression. I'd been on my way to meet Rochelle and her friend Brandi for dinner and had thought to bring a joint with me as a gift for the meal. Now I was relieved that I'd decided against it. I denied everything and they told me not to be a smart ass.

The original officer who stopped me, a light-skinned African American somewhat smaller than myself, was on his radio again, trying to convince a bank officer to walk a single block to make the positive i.d. before they took me downtown. Apparently the manager was reluctant because the officer was explaining that he understood that it was after hours and that the day had been harrowing enough with the robbery. The FBI twins were pawing through my wallet. I was sweating and shaking like a leaf, but I wasn't handcuffed or spread-eagled anymore. I explained who I was and where I lived and what I was doing and asked why they thought I would be dumb enough to rob the bank on my own block. Because you go to UC, the second agent sneered.

Finally an older man in a cheap dark suit arrived, the branch manager. "Yes, I said the robber had long blond hair," he sneered, visibly upset, "but I also said it was a woman." Even after he left, they kept me on the corner for another twenty minutes while they checked to see if I had any outstanding problems with the draft.

The garden is a luxury (a civilization of snail and spider).

At dawn or maybe even a little before, I sit on a chair out on the porch, watching woodpeckers hop up and down the bark of the black oak, the trees beginning to fill with the songs of birds. A hawk's silhouette is visible on a branch further down the hill. In the distance behind me, barely audible, is the clickety rattle of a train heading to Harrisburg.

They call their clubs batons.

Prior to swarming onto campus, the cops and deputy sheriffs would cluster around behind the administration building, swinging their clubs idly, like baseball players preparing to bat. The element of sport was visible in the air.

They call their committees clubs.

The Communist Party by the 1970s was a pathetic thing, at its core a collection of seniors with relatively little capacity left for direct political organizing, still ignoring the crimes of Stalinism and deeply committed to a politics of duplicity. Around these old Lincoln Brigade vets were a younger circle of African American activists—Angela Davis is the name everyone recognizes—actually attempting to use the resources of this ancient organization. Characteristically, every Left movement in the Bay Area had one or two CP members whose job it was to be supportive of the movement and report back to the organization on our "progress" in on-the-ground socialism. There was always a limit to how much we would trust the obvious CP member, who would never, of course, admit that this was his or her role. Their behavior was very much like that of police infiltrators but without the crazed provocatism. From some of them, I gradually got an image of what a lifetime committed to the Left might look like.

Her friendships with women are different.

I've come to appreciate this even more over time. When we moved to Pennsylvania in 1995, I had my job as ready social net into which I could fit. Being a poet also provides one with a sense of a community in many different cities. In addition to Bob and Francie, whom we knew from Berkeley, and Howie who'd been on the *Socialist Review* editorial collective and his wife Debbie, who'd worked at Hospitality House, there were Gil and Julia and Rachel and Eli. I also used e-mail a lot, and could walk to the Paoli Amtrak station and find myself in midtown Manhattan with no difficulty.

In the twenty years I've known Krishna she's made only two new close friendships. To be physically removed from most of her close friends is for her a serious dislocation in a way that is completely unlike anything I've ever experienced.

Talking so much is oppressive.

I get loud when I get anxious. Later I wish I hadn't.

Outplacement.

Everyone has figured out a theory by which they won't be the individual laid off, even as they understand that cuts are coming and that this round will be steep. After they learn, a few go around saying good-bye to the survivors while others clear their desks out almost instantly, as if shamed. Tauscher, the bulky CEO of Vanstar, loved to use the phrase "by the end of the day" to punctuate his speeches, even after it got to be a joke with the staffers who had seen over fifty vice-presidents "churn" over less than seven years. "By the end of the day, we'll all be riffed," said Kit, making a verb of the acronym for Reduction in Force. And eventually he was.

A shadowy locked facility using drugs and double-celling (a rest home).

The woman in the next room moaned endlessly, unconscious even of her moaning. My grandmother, who had known her for decades, seldom even referred to her now. Her eyes darted around the room even as they failed to see all but a few peripheral shadows and bursts of light. On the far side of her own room sat her older sister, who from time to time would burst out with a question—"Who is that?"—which my grandmother would answer only by scolding her, "Oh, you know who this is!" or "I've already told you a dozen times!" I would sit quietly. On a few occasions, I would read to her from a book about a cat detective.

That was the Sunday Henry's father murdered his wife on the front porch.

For this he received six months in prison and was soon back at the same factory as my grandfather, where he worked as a janitor. The explanation was that the boys were not his children and for her to threaten to walk out and to leave them behind had been unthinkable. Patiently, my brother tried to teach Henry to read, using adventure comic books. Later, Henry and his brother sodomized the boy next door to us with a wooden board. The last I heard of him, a year or two after high school, the Hell's Angels were looking for him: he'd knocked a member's eye out with a hammer.

If it demonstrates form they can't read it.

The reception of my writing can be divided easily into two periods—before the publication of *Ketjak* in 1978 and after. I'd been toying with the idea of a larger prose poem and the idea of something programmatic. I wanted to attack what I saw as the *sweetness* of Stein and Mac Low's dependency upon restricted vocabularies (as in, say, an insurance tract—*Stanzas for Iris Lezak* was still a new publication in 1974). The problem was how to begin.

One evening, Barry and I went to the Asian Art Museum in Golden Gate Park to hear a concert in its auditorium, the West Coast debut of Steve Reich's *Drumming.* It was the third Reich performance I'd attended, the others being Paul Zukofsky's performance of *Violin Phase* on my twenty-first birthday on the UC campus (several listeners walked out, led by, of all people, Mario Savio) and a "tape performance" of several loops (including *Come Out,* the work of his I'd first discovered on a record) at the newly opened University Art Museum in Berkeley.

As *Drumming* began and proceeded (augmented by the room's almost perfect acoustics), I began to sense, for the first time, exactly what the formal structure of *Ketjak* would be. Within a week I was beginning to scribble out ideas and, finally, on my way to meet my ex-wife Rochelle (we were to meet on the steps of the Bank of America headquarters), I began to write in a cheap notebook, my first sentence inspired by the B of A's architecture, "Revolving door."

If it demonstrates mercy they have something worse in mind.

Unquestionably, the key word in "Albany" is "if." Every one of the sentences around which the work is organized begins with this word.

Twice, carelessness has led to abortion.

She's talking to me on the telephone from Ashville, explaining matter-of-factly that she's heading tomorrow for Atlanta, where the procedure can be performed legally and safely, her voice drained of any emotion, and I realize, three thousand miles to the west, that we will never be a couple again, that it has never even occurred to her to ask me what I think.

To own a basement.

After high school, I would pile into a car with some friends at least once or twice a week and we'd cruise up into the Berkeley hills to look at the houses that we declared we would own once we grew up. These homes ranged from the utterly middle class to faux mansions, many of them in 1920s Craftsman style, in contrast with which the small thousand-square-foot house I shared with four members of three separate generations felt like a shoebox. Or worse. The idea of a basement when I wrote this sentence maybe twelve years later was that of a completely inessential element of housing. Since so many of the people I knew at that point in San Francisco were crammed into shared living arrangements, the idea of owning something that could include the inessential seemed unfathomable.

I am writing at this moment in the finished basement of a split level house with 2600 square feet (not counting a two-car garage) on a half acre of land in the outer Philadelphia suburbs.

Nor is the sky any less constructed.

As simple as the recognition that neither the sun nor moon ever really "rises" or "sets." The idea of "constellations." How quickly we forget how the city lights erase so many stars even on the clearest of nights.

The design of a department store is intended to leave you fragmented, off-balance.

David Antin has compared this to the new sentence. But retail design is an art. A department store is an elaborately spatialized narrative—the last sentence is always the same: *you buy.*

A lit drop.

On Saturday mornings throughout the late 1970s, I would spend three or four hours with between twenty and fifty like-minded souls walking San Francisco precincts for the New American

Movement. More often than not, the operation was contributed to another group: a labor union, a political candidate, the coalition supporting or opposing some measure on the ballot. With San Francisco's local elections in odd years and California's general tendency toward propositions at all levels, there was literally always something to be contested. Rent control, district election of county supervisors and homophobic (or otherwise reactionary) state measures seemed constant.

The New American Movement (NAM) had been started earlier in the seventies by former members of SDS. Having for the most part dropped out of school to take activist jobs in the cities, they found themselves first without the grounding orientation of campus life itself and then without the more immediate context that an organization like SDS had provided.

But SDS had never played a significant role in the Bay Area, largely because the 1960s Left had grown up around the anti-HUAC[14] demonstrations of 1960, the CORE integration actions of the early sixties, the Free Speech Movement at Berkeley in 1964 and the first Vietnam Day Teach-In a year later. With no particular need for SDS to serve as a catalyst for political revolt—the role it played in so many other cities and campuses—the organization had little real focus in the Bay Area and became instead a front for the local branch of the pseudo-Maoist Progressive Labor Party.

Still, by the early 1970s, the diaspora of campus politicos had taken effect in the Bay Area as well. While the prison movement was somewhat unusual in that its activists tended not to have come from the campuses, but rather tended to be homegrown (*organic,* in Gramsci's terms), the tenants movement and others were filled with former students who both wanted a means of looking at their own daily work critically while connecting up the many small Left-leaning organizations into something we all still fantasized as a mass phenomenon.

While working in the prison movement, I'd attended some of the local preformation meetings of NAM, but was still wary of any organizations with a specific ideological line as I'd always felt such groups, almost irregardless of what the line might have been, to be manipulative in their use of people and issues almost

---

[14]House Un-American Activities Committee.

invariably counterproductive to the building of a larger Left coalition. The presence of people I'd long since learned to distrust at Berkeley, such as Michael Lerner, put me off even further. Working sixty- and seventy-hour weeks, plus the long bus rides either to San Rafael or Sacramento from the city on a daily basis made it easy just to ignore the idea.

But after I'd taken a year off and then gone to work at Hospitality House in the Tenderloin, at first with an ostensibly nonpolitical job working on a neighborhood ethnography, I'd begun to wonder what the connection between my job, the obvious social needs of the people in whose neighborhood I spent eight to ten hours every day, my writing, and a larger sense of meaning, I began to look around for something that could tie these diverse aspects of my self back together. Several of the young lawyers who were active in the housing movement (conversion of residential hotels into tourist use was a burning issue in 1978) were members of NAM as was the newly hired political organizer for the local chapter of the Gray Panthers, Jim Shoch.

Shoch was someone I'd heard about over the years. He'd been tossed out of Stanford for his involvement in Bruce Franklin's Venceremos Brigade, the same group (yet another variation on Maoism) that had adopted Popeye Jackson's United Prisoners Union. Later I'd see his name in connection with a left-wing newspaper in San Francisco that had more or less plagiarized some of my writing on prisons verbatim. Since the purpose of those pieces was to create direct political pressure, I'd not been offended.

The potential of placing as many as fifty volunteers for a lit drop week in and week out put NAM almost on a par with any labor union in the city as far as most liberal politicians were concerned. A significant portion of the local pols would join just before election, as they did the various gay, Asian, African American, and Latino Democratic Clubs. Others, including Barbara Boxer, were happy to have the support on the weekends, but made it manifestly clear that they never wanted NAM's endorsement or to be associated formally with something that looked like a socialist organization.

On Saturdays we'd walk precincts, starting off with a forty-five minute or so milling around and orientation over coffee and donuts. Then,

in pairs, we'd pick a precinct and get whatever the week's flyers or brochures were and head out, sometimes by car, often by bus. On a couple of Sunday evenings each month, NAM would have a chapter meeting, where as many as sixty members would gather, usually at the Socialist School offices in the Mission, to debate topics, discuss a possible merger with Michael Harrington's Democratic Socialist Organizing Committee (DSOC), and occasionally to endorse candidates or propositions for a forthcoming ballot. It was an easy schedule for a single person to fall into, although it was a curiously male world.[15]

One day sometime around 1978, Walter Park, a DSOC activist and single parent, got himself a small computer kit (probably a Heath Kit). As primitive as this pre-DOS machine was, it enabled Park to develop specialized mailing lists without having to type names over and over on photocopying labels. Households with Spanish surnames, households in which all registered voters were male (or female), households in multi-unit buildings.

Within eighteen months, Park was the county chair of the Jimmy Carter re-election campaign (San Francisco being one of the few districts Carter would carry in that election) and the frequency of lit drops began to decline, replaced by direct mail and the phone bank.

I left Hospitality House in 1981 in order to teach for a year (first at San Francisco State, later at UC San Diego). When I came back, I spent about four months looking for a new job and began to work again with the newly merged Democratic Socialists of America that now combined NAM and DSOC. When Shoch or perhaps Mitch Omerberg announced that they needed a volunteer to handle the mailing list and that the list was on Park's computer in the offices of the Independent Housing Service (a group that located, tracked and otherwise promoted wheelchair accessible apartments) in the Tenderloin, but could only be used after hours, I volunteered on the spot. Computers, I had decided, were something that I needed

---

[15]With the exception of a couple of dates early in my career in the prison movement, I never got involved with women I met through my political work, in part because there were so few. But also because even as I worked long hours every day in that world for years, I was always, first and foremost, a poet. It was to my life and needs as a writer to which any woman would eventually have to adjust.

to understand. I had already seen them transform the structure of Left political activity in San Francisco. At the time, the IBM PC and the Apple Macintosh were each less than two years old.

They photograph Habermas to hide the hairlip.

We *improve* our heroes out of no need of their own. This is why, at least in part, the reaction to any statement that seems to attack this defended image is met with such fierce opposition.

The verb to be *admits the assertion.*

"Use active language" is precisely the kind of bad advice creative writing programs still shovel out with no shame and even less contemplation. That single verb form that invokes the passive tense acknowledges the presence of a writing mind.

It was Grenier's intransigence, his absolute horror at the conventionally literary that made me realize that I would not become a serious or mature writer in any fashion until I was ready to embrace everything I had ever been warned against.

The body is a prison, a garden.

Should you someday die of a "natural" cause, then that which will kill you is present already within your system. Once each year I pass, without celebrating, the anniversary of my death.

In kind.

In 1972, I lived on less than $150 per month, the following year barely any more.[16] My third

year out of college and in the prison movement saw my wages nearly double—to $250 per month. By the time I left CPHJ in 1977, I was earning all of $450, more than some of the lawyers in the political collectives around town, but barely anything to live on as San Francisco rents skyrocketed.

This only deepened the irrational feelings (the inability of the starving person to ever feel full at a banquet) I carried with me from my childhood. I felt exploited and angry because my comrades at CPHJ, most of whom (and all those in positions of power) either had independent sources of income themselves or were married to men who paid all the bills while they carried on the "good fight" as volunteers, never moved to raise a single cent unless and until the organization was on the brink of collapse for want of it. I was, with less than a dozen other people, rewriting the entire sentencing section of the California penal code, worrying every day about the consequences of the slightest rewording of a paragraph on hundreds of lives, men and women and their families who would all have to live with the consequences of our work. But often at the end of a long day in Sacramento, walking back to the Greyhound Station for the two-hour ride to San Francisco, I found myself barely able to get a taco in a fast-food joint.

I get back to the city too late to go to a reading, too poor to buy a new book, and often feeling totally disconnected from my roommates, none of whom (with the two notable exceptions of Elliot Helfer and Barrett Watten) ever seemed to realize the psychic weight I carried around with me.

At Hospitality House, the dynamics had been fairly similar. The board was willing to work to raise enough funding to pay the staff whatever the minimum was that would keep them coming back to keep the agency running. Barely making the minimum wage, these were the hardest working and smartest co-workers I would ever have. In five years at HH, as the staff always called it, I worked on a small coalition that saved over 10,000 units of low-income housing.

After I left Hospitality House to teach for a year, I made a decision that whatever job I returned to in the non-profit world would have a significant fundraising element. I was no longer going to leave it to others to determine whether or not I had enough money to go the dentist

---

[16]By now at least, having been "freed" of my alternative service obligation by virtue of the fact that I, and every other conscientious objector of that same period, had been "drafted" and inducted unlawfully, at a time when others were not being called, CPHJ now took it upon itself to pay this directly, where the previous year I'd worked nights doing layout and paste-up and miscellaneous writing for a small gay bar paper in San Francisco.

or a movie or eat fish. This was how I ended up as the director of development for a graduate school focusing on East-West religions, the California Institute of Integral Studies, and how I came to meet Hank Rosso, the man who professionalized nonprofit fundraising in America and who, in his own quiet way, taught me almost everything I would ever know about marketing.

Client populations (cross the tundra).

Once known as Saint Anne's Valley, a residential district in which Robert Frost, Isadora Duncan, and Alice B. Toklas had been born, the presence of brothels had given the Tenderloin its name by the 1890s. In the 1930s, the TL was the first gay neighborhood, as such, in the United States. In the 1950s and '60s, as the merchant marine district South of Market[17] was plowed under and increasingly fewer men were able to get jobs at sea, the TL became an overflow receptacle for these mostly alcoholic drifters just a few blocks north of their old homes. Also in the 1950s, senior citizens began to arrive, unwilling to move about with their children as the post-war economic boom all but erased the three- and four-generation household. Later in the '60s, as the Haight filled beyond capacity with suburban youth and a brief 1966 riot at the corner of Divisadero and McAllister led San Francisco to "redevelop" the Fillmore district as they had SOMA, African Americans and the more isolated hippies began to fill the community. In the 1970s, as Ronald Reagan and Jerry Brown emptied the state's mental hospitals,[18] the neighborhood changed again. By the end of the decade, Indochinese refugees began to slowly fill the residential hotels and apartment buildings. A family of nine, each receiving funds from the Indochinese Resettlement Assistance Program, could pay considerably more for a one-bedroom apartment than the single psychotic. But if the social ecology of the neighborhood was fragile, some portion of each group lingered on until the human texture of these 44 city blocks and 19,000 people became as rich a soil as I have

ever seen. Before a new hotel went in kitty-corner from the 5th and Market BART station, there was a tavern that catered exclusively to transvestites and transsexuals of color, and the men who loved them. The corner of Leavenworth and Eddy was devoted almost exclusively to the pursuit of heroin. Streetwalkers generally worked east of Leavenworth because the far side of that street marked the boundary of the northern precinct, whose cops had a bad reputation for "bruising the merchandise." The mob ran a couple of bars and eateries by the hotels, but was more visible around the porn shops and massage parlors. The homeless began to multiply toward the end of the Carter regime.

.   .   .

Off the books.

The idea of poetry as a "career" in a society that doesn't value literacy is an inherent contradiction. I have worked as an encyclopedia salesman (I quit after two weeks, having sold none, after a lawyer I knew showed me how the pitch I was trained to give "mooches" was a modest form of fraud), a shipping clerk, an accounting clerk, a mail sorter, an amanuensis for blind graduate students, a janitor for Giant Hamburgers (I wouldn't eat hamburgers for years after), a reader for a junior college anthropology course, a case worker and then lobbyist for the prison movement, an editor, production person, occasional writer and even astrologer for an early gay bar paper ("Now is the weather for leather"), a newspaper editor, housing activist, writing teacher, director of development and college administrator, editor of the *Socialist Review,* and finally marketeer and analyst in the computer services industry.

The whole neighborhood is empty in the daytime.

At the time I wrote this, I understood this sentence as a comment on the social uses of urban space. With hindsight, I see it now also as a remark on class. The suburbs are full in the middle of the day in ways that an urban working-class neighborhood like Bernal Heights in San Francisco is not.

---

[17]The Moscone Center, hotels, and museums dominate the neighborhood today.

[18]The community services that were supposed to supplant them were never funded. Whoever imagined that they would be?

Children form lines at the end of each recess.

Many of my memories of elementary school in the 1950s are tinged with a sense of the implicit *militarism* of daily life. The junior crossing guard squad of which I was so briefly a member spent half of its time mimicking military drill teams.[19] The scouts, which I shunned at every level, seemed to me a paramilitary organization. Even Little League seemed to me totalitarian (although, ultimately, what kept me from it was the sense I always had around games of angry fathers directing everything—the idea of a father of any sort, especially furious and browbeating, totally intimidated me).

Eminent domain.

After the episode in which my grandmother came after me with a knife, I left for New York and my mother and brother finally did what should have been done a decade earlier—moved to an apartment of their own. It was an incredibly small and dark place that was literally the rear of a mom-and-pop store a block from the El Cerrito Plaza and had already been marked for demolition in order for the BART tracks to go up. Living there, however fitfully, after I got back from the East was the strangest experience. The family that owned the little store had already moved and were permitting their stock gradually to run down, restocking a little less each week. In some sense, the store had already become a kind of ghost. Immediately out back were the Santa Fe tracks and, once I learned how slowly the trains moved past the plaza, I started hopping them for the two-mile ride to University Avenue.

Rotating chair.

I receive a photocopy of a letter today, angry, accusative, directed not at me but at Charles Bernstein for having somehow traded on a friendship with Robert Creeley to obtain a job at SUNY Buffalo. Inside the envelope is the fragment of another envelope addressed to "Professor Ron Silliman, Dept. of English, University of Pennsylvania," over which in pencil has been written "Unknown/Not at this address." On the flip side of this scrap of envelope is typed "If not at UPenn, what are you doing living at the end of the 'Main Line'?"

Something like this happens two or three times each year—absolute paranoia combined with a sense of outrage, entirely innocent of the facts. The author of this screed has actually published well over a dozen books, several with major trade and university presses, but he is convinced that I (and no doubt others, many others) have obtained something that he cannot and that this must have been done through some underhanded, conspiratorial fashion.

The history of Poland in 90 seconds.

My brother and I would sit in the rear of the Pontiac as my grandfather drove around,

Ron Silliman, about 1977

---

[19]I was expelled from the squad after I'd locked a seventh grade bully, John Crewdson, later a Pulitzer Prize-winning journalist, into a school locker.

Ron Silliman in the office of The Tenderloin Times, *1980*

doing chores. He very seldom would talk to us, listening instead to one of the AM radio stations that focused on news. (FM was still an oddity that we didn't have until 1958.) As the days wore on, I grew used to the rhythm of hearing minimalist updates of this or that story. I recall being riveted by the contest between Estes Kefauver and Hubert Humphrey at the 1956 Democratic Convention, at the death of Pope Pius XII and the selection of his successor, at the arrival of Castro victorious in Havana (reported at first with some sympathy since he was thought of then as a "reformer" and

not a "Marxist"—even the *Reader's Digest* ran a friendly interview). I was in the gradual process of becoming not only a news junky, as I remain to this day, but also of listening to the rhythms of a particular narrative style.

Flaming Pintos.

A sentence without apparent context is difficult to place, difficult to weigh. A sentence without a verb even more so. In the context of the poem, this fragment seems to be about the lethal nature of corporate irresponsibility, about the automobile as an icon, and the possibility of some sort of ironic twist in the trivialization that occurs by making the phenomenon plural. What motivated the sentence was a discussion I had at a party with Mark Dowie, the journalist who first reported the Pinto's problem with exploding gas tanks. The scion of a liquor fortune with Robert Redford rugged blond good looks, Mark had been the very timid and tentative compiler of a pamphlet on community resources for ex-prisoners and I had given him some advice on the project. His presentation of self changed dramatically after his research into the depredations of Ford received national attention, rending him the opportunity to bring his upbringing to bear in the new role of Expert. Soon, though, it became apparent that instead of being characterized as a new heavyweight journalist, he would be known instead as the "guy who broke the Pinto story," regardless of how much good effort he put into anything else. This sentence is, in fact, what Mark told me would eventually be engraved on his tombstone.

There is no such place as the economy, the self.

If a lion could speak, it would talk very slowly. Civilization constructed of complex nouns for which no exact equivalent in nature can be found. Identity is composed of our response, passionate or ambivalent, to exactly such muddy notions. Reading *Poetry Flash* with the photograph of Barrett looking boyish and introspective, I remember someone (Kit? Alan? Steve?) saying aloud, "It looks like we've been named."

That bird demonstrates the sky.

One way to view nature that incorporates both chance and change. Define the trail by that which is transient. Also, it's something Krishna and I both enjoy and at which neither (for once) is an expert. What is better than a northern flicker at the suet cake? The Virginia rail, perfectly still in the muddy reeds. The long parsed tail of the tropic bird. Once in a bed-and-breakfast, exhausted after a long day of seeking the worm-eating warbler in a vacant lot in Davenport, Krishna had an ec-

topic pregnancy, the fallopian tube literally exploding, and nearly died.

Our home, we were told, had been broken, but who were these people we lived with?

My grandparents had no idea that they would ever be asked to raise a second family and my grandfather's lapsed Catholicism turned his own guilt into open disapproval at my mother's failed marriage. Also, he'd never raised boys and as the youngest in his own family, did not understand how one might nurture anyone younger. Eleven hundred square feet and two bedrooms did not divide easily into five people and three generations. As his hearing declined, he became quieter and quieter, a simmering, seething presence that never quite managed to erupt. My last two years of high school, I probably said less than one hundred words to the man. Six weeks after graduation, I was gone.

Clubbed in the stomach, she miscarried.

The whim of existence: my grandmother was the youngest of thirteen. Two years later, her father was dead. My parents would never have met without the geographic and social dislocations created by the Second World War. They almost certainly would not have married without the mutually damaged home situations each was escaping. My brother and I were each the result of failed birth control. Had my father remained at home, it is unlikely that I ever would have gone to college. Had my father remained at home, I would have learned to love camping and become good with weapons. If I had not grown up on the fringes of Berkeley, it is unlikely that I would have ever stumbled across William Carlos Williams (most Americans never do). Had it not been Berkeley, Rochelle would never have arrived in search of a student movement. Had I not turned on the television, would I ever have discovered Zukofsky? Had I not been in New York on the literal day of the Gulf of Tonkin incident, would I have thought to have gotten a draft counselor early enough to have made a difference? Had I not been reading to the blind, would I have stopped in the classroom doorway at Boalt to listen to Fay Stender talking about the San Quentin Six case and would I, six months later, have thought to have sought my conscientious objector's slot with a prison movement group? Had I not had to take the bus to Sacramento so many early mornings, would I have ever walked past Hospitality House and stared in at its windows filled with street people artwork and thought, years after, to have sought a CETA job there? What if I had not stopped drinking? *What if Jon Arnold had not invented metalanguage in front of me, a ten-year-old boy, as though on his own?*

I wrote this sentence thinking of David Mandel's sister-in-law, beaten at the Oakland Induction Center. Today I read the same sentence inside out.

There were bayonets on campus, cows in India, people shoplifting books.

One night, as the cops were approaching slowly in a vehicle that somehow spewed pep-

per fog, a particularly acrid and painful form of tear gas, as I was rushing with others to drag some saw horses from a nearby construction sight to create a blockade on Bancroft, I looked up to see that the person who was lifting the other end of the wooden beast was a fellow I'd known as a bully in high school (he'd once, in a fit of anger—I'd let a teacher who was a friend know that some students had obtained a copy of a forthcoming test—shoved me literally down a flight of stairs). Our eyes locked briefly and the air seemed full of the sounds of sirens, breaking glass, shouting people, rocks bouncing off all manner of surfaces and, more distant, the bullhorn of the first prowl car intoning that "this is an illegal assembly." We stared just long enough to realize what we were doing and who we were, then we rushed with the sawhorse (its yellow blinker flashing all the while) and hurled it atop the mounting pile of other debris. As the car approached, we could begin to smell the fog and dashed

Crossing guards—Ron Silliman (third row, second from the right), Tim Johnson (top row, second from the right), Chris Martinez (bottom row, far right), John Crewdson (holding up flag to the right)

with the rest of the crowd back down the side street to the next instant of engagement. I never saw him again.

I just want to make it to lunch time.

A typical day at the office: I arrive a few minutes after the designated hour of eight, plug in my ThinkPad, unlock one or two of the eleven filing cabinets I use on a daily basis, and log on to one of two e-mail systems. The first, a mainframe system called PROFS, also connects me to internal postings from a wide range of other IBM divisions and subsidiaries. If one or two postings from the hundred or so I will scan seems pertinent to our division, I will download it. After PROFS and Lotus Notes, I log onto the Internet and scan headlines from a variety of news sources, including the *New York Times, Washington Post, BusinessWire, Reuters* and several computing journals (with special attention to *Computer Reseller News* and *Information Week*). By 10:00 or 10:30, I will have scanned between 500 and 700 articles, maybe taking note of six or eight. On some days at this point, I will begin (or continue) to work on a periodic e-mail publication I write. On others, I will turn to research one of the inquiries I've received from other departments, executives, sales reps, and managers in the field. An inquiry can take anywhere between five minutes and two weeks to complete. As details emerge during the day from these sources, I may update a series of ongoing presentation files.[20] Most often I use lunch to look at my hardcopy mail—computer magazines, research reports, direct mail for events, the occasional invoice. The further each day proceeds, the more apt I am to be pulled into meetings, to conduct consultations for various departments, to embark on "out of the ordinary" projects. At least one hour over the day is given to talking to reps, managers, and industry analysts about various "issues." There are always between six and ten of these in an ongoing state at any given moment. By 4:00, I begin to sense whether one or another will lend itself to a concentrated effort in the early evening, once the secretaries and hourly workers depart around 5:30. If so, I plot it out and work until 7:00.

Uncritical of nationalist movements in the Third World.

The world is a system, complete.[21] In spite of Marx's comments about the impossibility of socialism in one country, the Left has repeatedly rallied around attempts to set up just such a logical contradiction. Invariably these attempts fail—capital demonstrates its power to undermine any local effort, regardless of how well intentioned it might be. During the Cold War, the U.S. posture of isolating and threatening pockets of resistance, particularly those within what it imagined grandiosely to have been its own sphere of influence, Asia and the Pacific, forced the smaller power to over-militarize. The most militaristic and least democratic groups within that nation were thus rewarded, promoted, reinforced.[22] The impact on the civilian populace was (also invariably) predictable. Instead of critiquing these deformations and supporting what were now dissident forces within these tiny countries, the U.S. Left, stuck on a simplistic the-enemy-of-my-enemy kind of thinking, tended to excuse the excesses (the North Vietnamese hunt down and execute Trotskyists), even to imitate them at home.

Letting the dishes sit for a week.

I was raised in a world in which the dinner was always on time and always predicted: on Friday there would be fish sticks. Even now, over thirty years after leaving home, I am torn—always—by the desire for intense order and its exact opposite.

Macho culture of convicts.

Because her former husband, a San Francisco beat cop, had on more than one occasion tailed her off-duty and at least once come

---

[20]An example: every Tuesday afternoon I update a series of charts that track the stock performance of several companies that perform desktop services.

[21]As has been increasingly evident, the state itself is merely a convenience. Capital and its latest expression, "information," are more powerful and fundamentally stateless phenomena. The creation of the European Union is itself a desperate attempt for several governments, formerly "world powers," to reimagine themselves as relevant.

[22]The same strategy domestically was carried out under the banner of Cointelpro.

to her job to ask her supervisor if they knew that she was involved with "revolutionaries," Marti's gone to court to get a restraining order. The irony was that her fling with Wilbur "Popeye" Jackson, the head of the nominally Maoist United Prisoners Union (UPU), had been short-lived. What lasted was her distrust of the police, which Jackson shared but hardly had created.

The UPU had splintered off from the larger Prisoners Union in 1970 after a meeting to which, it was rumored, both sides brought guns. The Prisoners Union's goals were clear, defined, and in retrospect relatively modest. It did not seek an end to prisons, nor critique the social concept of incarceration, but wanted to define and defend the civil rights of prisoners both in the joint and afterward. Focusing on eliminating the Byzantine vagaries of the indeterminate sentence as a primary goal, the Prisoners Union was largely composed of white ex-cons, led by Willie Holder, a classic Okie robber who looked and sounded like a wizened version of the musician Willie Nelson. Also around were John Irwin, a '50s era robber who'd gone on to become a sociology professor at San Francisco State; Frank Smith, a literate one-time drug dealer and kidnapper—surprisingly gentle and good-willed given his biker-qua-mountain-man persona; and Roney Nunes, who'd served time in the Midwest for a crime that he'd later proven he had not committed only to pull off a bungled robbery in California for which he'd done a few years. Other than Willie's wife Patty, the Union in the early '70s had almost no women in positions of authority. Deftly using the credibility of Irwin, the persistence of Holder, and the reasoning skills of Smith, the Prisoners Union had gotten the ear of several legislators, some lawyers (notably Jim Smith and Michael Snedecker), and had received the gift of a large but rundown building on San Francisco's Potrero Hill from an elderly sympathizer. Holder and his wife lived upstairs (always with a few recent parolees and occasionally someone like Snedecker whose choices as a lawyer kept him as close to a street person as a practicing advocate could be).

The UPU stood in sharp contrast with its leadership focused entirely on the charismatic nature of Jackson, an African American from rural Louisiana with the thickest accent I'd ever heard. Off the record, the Prisoners Union's rap on Jackson was that he'd been a snitch in the joint and was an empty-headed idiot interested only in sex with white women and ripping off the Stanford students of the Venceremos Brigade who helped to fund his organization. The UPU's position on the Prisoners Union was that it was run by hillbilly white racists, one step removed from the Aryan Brotherhood[23], who were using their connections to liberal politicians to angle for grants. The UPU argued that all felons were involved in class war whether they understood it as such or not and that band-aid measures like administrative due process in internal disciplinary procedures or the replacement of the indeterminate sentence by a more systematic (and thereby more "fair") structure of penalties for crimes only served to strengthen the system and slow the progress toward a necessary revolution that would be led not by college-trained leftists, but by former prisoners who had had direct experience within "the belly of the beast."

I had friends in both organizations although relatively few seemed to understand what I thought I was doing working in the prison movement. (In 1976, Holder, who by then had known me for five years, asked me "well, just what did you serve time for?") In 1972, when I began working with CPHJ, it had been clear to me for at least two years that no revolution was even remotely in the offing in the United States and I had no illusions that the working-class people of Concord or Alamo or anywhere were about to follow somebody whose greatest accomplishment may have been a bungled liquor store robbery.

Still, it was (and is) true that economic crime carries within it a domain of the irrational that was and always will be about class. The women around the UPU were not only neither idiots nor dupes, but were some of the most intelligent people I would ever meet in the prison movement. For the most part they all came from the very lowest fringes of the working class—a position with which I immediately identified—and some would go on to significant careers as lawyers and private eyes.

Popeye was another matter. A shrewd political thinker with a mercurial temper, he played all sides against one another, even within his own organization, which recycled people in purges and counter-purges. One time Marti asked me

---

[23]One or two of the ex-cons who cycled briefly through the Prisoners Union went on to people local Klan groups.

to help her move from her apartment in the Mission, a move dictated by Popeye after it had been decided that there must be FBI infiltrators in the group.[24]

Each of the collective houses and apartments that UPU members shared were to be broken up as they were to find housing with people outside the movement altogether. When I arrived at Marti's apartment, there were guns on the kitchen table, set there just so people would feel comfortable enough to cooperate in getting a couch down a flight of stairs.

Marti soon left not only the organization but the Bay Area, settling in the Sierra foothills in hopes that her husband would not find her. Two years later, Popeye Jackson was murdered in the front seat of his car, parked in front of his apartment on Albion Street in San Francisco. Shot alongside him was a young schoolteacher from the Contra Costa suburbs who'd been active with the UPU for only a few weeks.

Ron (left) and his brother, Cliff Silliman, about 1954

With a shotgun and "in defense" the officer shot him in the face.

If one has a shotgun, defenses purposes do not require you to aim at the head of the other party. This was the report given in the media concerning the capture of a bank robber, treated as though without question or controversy.

Here, for a moment, we are joined.

It took me, it seems, forever to reach out to your mother. Peggy had moved out of the flat on San Jose Avenue in the Mission District some six months before, after which I'd had a short and profoundly unfulfilling relationship with an Australian painter and performance artist.

I had worked for a year on an ethnography of the Tenderloin for Central City Hospitality House. The project team needed an administrator, having hired one only to have him quit in a huff and hurry, so were delighted

when I literally walked in one day, able to handle that work, edit the final report and interview the one neighborhood group the two primary researchers, Toby Marotta and Clark Taylor, felt nervous about—ex-felons. Marotta and Taylor were interested in the Tenderloin's gay history, but it was the entire community that was to be described by the project. By design, two members of the team were neighborhood residents, one of whom, Dorothy Rutherford, a one-time fashion model and one of the last true hippies, had promptly moved herself and her four-year-old son out to Bernal Heights where she shared a flat with two other women who worked at the agency, Kathy Ryan and Krishna Evans. At the time, Ms. Evans directed the arts program on the agency's main floor, a large open studio crafts and fine arts workshop that funded itself by asking participants to make two of anything they worked on and to donate one item for sale through a "store" that consisted of the agency's Leavenworth Street windows.

She had impossibly thick, long black hair with just the slightest threading of silver, which she wore pulled back in a failed attempt to look plain. She wore oversized army pants and tank top t-shirts, never with a bra. More important, she had (has) the most complete smile

[24]This was absolutely the case. Sara Jane Moore was revealed as an informant after her attempted assassination of Gerald Ford. The FBI wanted to know why my phone number at CPHJ was in her address book.

I have ever seen.[25] Although our programs only occasionally had direct business with one another, it was evident that she was a passionate administrator who cared deeply about her students and took her job with absolute seriousness. She was capable of great theater in staff meetings, raging out, slamming the door behind her. Once, the director of the drop-in center upstairs, a man who often came to work smelling of wine, pawed a high school coed who was interning in the arts program. Krishna walked up to him, flattened him with a single punch (several metal folding chairs crashing out of the way as he fell backward). She stormed upstairs to the executive director's office and got the man fired on the spot.

Because Hospitality House defined itself as a place open to anyone, regardless of how marginal, the various floors were always full of street people, runaways, ex-cons, drag queens, psychotics, confused post-docs, alcoholics, junkies, the works. For awhile, our receptionist was Jerry-Diane, a pre-op transsexual whose goal in life was to become a lesbian. It was, and I mean this literally, the finest working environment I have ever had, can ever imagine having.

Early on in my tenure with the ethnographic project, Peg and I had been invited over for brunch to the house on Bernal Heights, along with several other HH staffers. The house on Winfield Street was a rambling Victorian, set high into the hillside. I remember the weather that day as perfect and a sense of life there as almost utopian. In retrospect, I'm sure what that meant was that I was attracted to all three of the women who lived there. It was already apparent to both Peggy and me that this latest attempt to construct a relationship was proving a disaster.

Once or twice a week after work, Dorothy, Krishna, and I, occasionally with one or two other members of the staff, would head over to Harrington's, a cavernous Irish pub only a block from HH, where we'd sit, drinking watery draft beer or gin and tonics, eating hot dogs and popcorn, talking office politics for hours. Dorothy, who'd lived for several years in Spain and had several full-grown sons there, often brought along her four-year-old boy, Jose.

Ron Silliman, high school senior, 1964

Once, at an agency picnic, I sat on the grass and Krishna (without asking, without being asked) lay back to put her head in my lap. My heart raced a million miles. Another time, one of the neighborhood men, Eugeia Shaw, celebrated his twenty-fifth birthday at a Castro Street pizza parlor, after which Krishna and I took the longest of walks back through the mission. She pointed out Hungadunga, which had been the leading commune in the free-food family and where she'd had several friends and a few lovers.

I had a prohibition in my head about sleeping with my co-workers. I was insecure enough about employment generally to feel that some crossing of the boundaries like that would certainly make life crazy. Although I'd had more than a few unrequited crushes on women in other organizations of the prison movement, I'd virtually fled the apartment of a young single mother who volunteered for CPHJ, not because I wasn't attracted, but because I was.

---

[25]This same smile, Colin, appears miraculously on your own shining face.

When the ethnographic project came to an end with the publication of "TERP Report," the five of us on the project were duly laid off. I'd already proposed to Claudia Viek, the executive director of Hospitality House, that what the neighborhood needed, more than anything else, was a positive self-image. Some of the folks in the upstairs drop-in center had started a mimeographed publication called the *Tenderloin Times*. They'd published three issues with runs of about 150 each, until somebody on the board discovered a recipe for mistletoe tea and had flipped at the idea of the toxic possibilities. I'd suggested that I could take over the paper, turn it into a real neighborhood paper just like the *Bernal Journal* or *Potrero View,* and sell enough advertising to cover the printing costs. Since that wouldn't provide enough work (or cash) to make a real job out of the position, I suggested that I run a writers workshop, trying to get funding from the California Arts Council for that, and that I also work on housing issues in the neighborhood with funding from the agency itself.

I felt ambivalent about the idea. Krishna had given me several hints that, if she ever broke up with her current boyfriend, an itinerant and seldom-employed rock musician who periodically went by the name Random Chance, she'd be available and was interested. We'd ride buses to the Haight after work, she on her way to class at USF, me on my way to the Grand Piano, and increasingly our conversations turned to relationships and what each of us was seeking. We never actually said out loud that it was each other we were talking about.

It was apparent that this woman was brilliant, beautiful, had a sense of the arts (she'd studied ballet with Balanchine and Cunningham), was committed to her work and the people of the neighborhood she served. A cousin of hers, Julie Garrett, was visiting San Francisco and would come to the Writers Workshop, hanging around afterwards to ride on the Mission Street bus with me. Julie would tell me, at length, that Krishna was interested in me, but was afraid that I might be too intellectual. At other times, Dorothy and Steve Brady also dropped similar hints.

Peggy had long since returned from Georgia and the abortion, moving to an apartment directly across the street from the one we'd shared on San Jose Avenue. "If I'm the one who moves," she said, "I won't feel like I was the one who was dumped." I moped around for a few weeks, then, at a music performance at Mills, I ran into an Australian artist whom I knew very slightly. She and I talked and later I ran into her again after a performance in the city. We got involved soon after, although it devolved almost instantly. I was looking for a relationship and she seemed absolutely terrified by the idea. I was restless.

A month after the job at the Ethnographic Project ended, one of the administrators at HH quit, leaving a small, part-time salary. Claudia called and asked me to start work on the new position, waiting until we heard from the Arts Council to pick up the other segments. The truth was, I hadn't even begun to look for another job yet. Instead, I'd spent the month watching the relationship with Jill devolve, had done a performance I'd been thinking about for a year at least, reading all of *Ketjak* aloud on the steps of the Bank of America branch at Powell and Market Streets, three days after which I had had a tooth extracted. The oral surgeon had told me I would need a ride home afterwards, so I'd asked Dorothy, one of the few people I knew who owned a car (a clunker that cost maybe $200). As I'd woken groggy from the anesthesia, Krishna stood over me, explaining ex post facto that she thought it would be "fun to help."

I accepted the position.

One evening six weeks later, on my way to Bruce Boone's for a meeting of the Marxist study group that we were in together, a young woman next to me on the Mission Street bus asked about the book I was reading, Georg Lukács's *History and Class Consciousness.* I'd been writing notes in the margins and underlining passages in several different colors of ink.[26] She nodded as I explained what I was doing, asked who Lukács was, and, after she "debused," suddenly ran back up to my window shouting her phone number. I called the next day and we went to lunch at Knight's on Golden Gate Avenue, a giant old-style cafeteria that catered to the City Hall and lawyer set. Laura was working as a legal secretary for Charles Garry, a criminal defense specialist I knew slightly from

---

[26]Looking at the book today, I see, on the inside front cover, in a black box, "Opacity 159." In orange, above, "Art begets dialects begets history 137-145." In red, below, "The production of new needs = the accumulation of SURPLUS VALUE 180!" In blue, to the right, "Aura as a bourgeois (unmediated) element in art 158!"

my work at CPHJ, but thought of herself as a folk singer between gigs. "Before gigs," she corrected herself, laughing.

As we ate and I slowly began to realize that the excitement of a chance encounter on the bus hadn't led to any sort of miracle, in walked Dan White with a couple of his aides. White had just resigned from his position as a San Francisco County Supervisor, unable to make ends meet on his $9,000 a year salary—I could hardly blame him—but had just changed his mind and was trying in vain to convince Mayor Moscone to reappoint him to his same old seat. White had been in the headlines for weeks and I was surprised that Laura didn't seem to know who he was.

It was only a day or so later that, as I attended a political conference at Horace Mann School in the Mission, I first heard of the massacre at Jonestown. Garry was down in Guyana representing Jim Jones, the charismatic San Francisco preacher who'd become increasingly paranoid and hostile, leading his congregation literally into the jungle. He'd arranged for a visit by Leo Ryan, a Congressman from San Mateo County and a former paper member of the CPHJ board. Among Ryan's entourage was a photographer from the *San Francisco Examiner,* Greg Robinson, who'd recently finished doing a feature on Krishna's program at HH. Both Ryan and Robinson were killed in the attack on the visitors at the airstrip as they'd attempted to depart. As Jones and his followers began to drink poisoned Kool-Aid, Garry slipped into the woods to hide. In a matter of an hour, over 900 people were dead.

I felt sick the minute I heard the first details. Like anyone on the Left in San Francisco, I'd run into People's Temple members dozens, perhaps hundreds of times, usually helping out with the Saturday precinct work alongside the New American Movement, DSOC and the unions. Ryan, a former schoolteacher who'd once spent a week "undercover" in prison just to get a feel for the environment (and not part as a media grandstanding stunt), was that rare individual, someone motivated into electoral politics by the idea of accomplishing something.

The next week was Thanksgiving. I found myself in that tortured state of needing to read every word in the media about Jonestown, feeling increasingly nauseated the more I read. On Monday or Tuesday, Dorothy, who was again

temping at HH, came down to my office to say that she, Krishna, and Kathy were going to have a meal of Thanksgiving leftovers on Friday and did I want to join them? She may have invited me to Thanksgiving itself, but I was already committed to my mother's. A day later, Dorothy again dropped by to say that she and Kathy were planning to go to the movies later that night "so that it will just be you and Krishna, if that's okay." More than a little amused by the transparency of this set-up, I accepted.

The next two days gave me time to think. I'd had what seemed excellent reasons not to get involved with Krishna. There was the work taboo. She was, she said, still involved to some degree with this musician, although she'd also hinted on several occasions that she was looking to move on. As it stood, our relationship wasn't predicated on my life as a poet. Peg

Krishna Evans at the Esmerelda Steps, November, 1978

had been the first woman in my life for whom that had not been, if not the paramount fact about me, at least an important one. And Peg had been jealous of my writing in a way that had surprised me. If Barbara had been merely envious of the relative success I'd had publishing, a competitive envy, Peggy saw my writing as a relationship in itself, one that would prevent her from ever establishing the sort of balance between us she imagined herself to be seeking. It was impossible to know in advance how Krishna would feel about that. There was no question that I found Krishna desirable and fabulous, but there was also a side of me so anxious I could (rather like a cat) spit. I'd seen her at work under the hectic and often harsh conditions of that environment, dealing with crazies, street people, seniors, city bureaucrats, inept board members, the corporate types on the United Way review committee. On one occasion a client tried to kill her, attempting to ram her with a ladder—she remained magically calm under the threat, turned by the event into pure concentration itself, never once allowing her assaulter to imagine himself in control, talking him into a form of submission while I and an art teacher physically stopped the ladder each time this speed-crazed young man roared forward.[27] I'd also seen a harder side at work also, the flashing temper and take-no-prisoners insistence on honesty. Unlike my situation with Jill, where I'd hopped into bed with no hesitation, knowing that there would be few lasting consequences if it didn't work out,[28] I could sense that Krishna would be exactly the

opposite. If I got involved, it would have to be all the way.

On Friday at dusk, I walked the mile from the apartment I now shared with Fred Glass over to Krishna's. An index of my anxiety and sense of anticipation that evening is that I can still recall the precise quality of twilight along Mission as I walked, stopping once or twice to write down sentences in a notebook that would later find their way into *Tjanting*. It was a beautiful clear evening, oddly balmy for San Francisco in November. The steep climb up Virginia Street to Winfield, and the ever steeper climb up Winfield, seemed to stretch out forever (I'd only made the trip once or twice before, so wasn't yet familiar with every step).

Dorothy and Kathy wolfed down their dinners, a moist and well-stuffed turkey, and started to head out the door to a movie. But there was a catch—cousin Julie, who had become a semi-permanent house guest, staying in a room nominally devoted to weaving equipment, decided (I forget why) not to go along, even though Dorothy and Kathy offered to pay her way. Given the layout of the house, two tiny bedrooms by the front door, beyond which was a huge, central kitchen, with a dark, windowless alcove that nominally served as the living room, stairs up to an attic-like loft that was Dorothy's space, and on the other side the room that had become Julie's space all focused around a large, round kitchen table, there was virtually no way to be in the house without being in Julie's presence, unless Krishna and I were to retire to her bedroom (too loaded with anticipation, lust, and symbolism) or Julie were to retire to hers (too clueless to figure this out).[29] So we sat around the table and talked for several hours. I have no memory whatsoever what about.

At midnight, I noted the time and Krishna suggested that the two of us walk around the top of Bernal Hill, a rare blister of open space in San Francisco, topped with a huge microwave dish for the phone company. Although three of the most economically depressed housing projects are within a short walk of this mile-long unlit, half-paved circular road, we thought nothing of heading off into the darkness on that warm night and found only two or three

---

[27]What had set Eric, an unemployed African American with a family crammed into a small hotel room on Mason Street, off was another HH client who'd called him nigger. The staff in the upstairs drop-in center had rescued that idiot, but had done so by diverting Eric, who was literally exploding with anger and methamphetamine, down to the arts floor where he'd gone after the first white person he saw, Krishna. As fifty or so people surrounded us, it was evident that Eric was, in the eyes of many, the victim in this scenario, so that Krishna, John and I all understood that we needed to resolve the circumstance not only without anyone getting hurt, but without Eric getting arrested either. Around the corner, out of sight, the SF police waited it out, which took a good two hours. They thought we were crazy. But it ended with Eric going out with John and me for a cup of coffee to talk about why anger and speed mixed badly.

[28]It would be another three-plus years before city housing specialist Dick Gamble, the first AIDS victim in my circle, began to grow thin and pale.

[29]Worse yet, there was a downstairs apartment, a small separate unit, in which the erstwhile-musician/boyfriend lived!

Silliman with his wife and children: Ron, Jesse, Krishna, and Colin, Bay of Fundy, Nova Scotia, 1997

cars with teenage couples parked overlooking the Mission. We walked slowly and talked, although even at this point we did not touch. I could sense from Krishna's body language that she wanted me to reach over to her, but that she wouldn't or couldn't do that herself. My mind was racing a million miles an hour as I remembered every reason why I did or didn't want to act. Eventually we got back to her front stairs, where we paused silently for what seemed like minutes.

"Would you like to come in for tea?"

"Why not?" Trying to sound casual. In fact, it is only now that I realize I've decided, not so much that I've made a decision but rather that I recognize a decision I've arrived at on some level almost inaccessible to me.

Inside again, I'm immediately relieved to discover that Julie has finally gone to bed. Kathy and Dorothy are still out, but for how long? For the moment at least, we're alone in the kitchen. Krishna moves to brush past me to put a kettle on for tea and I reach out my arms, palms up. She takes my hands and without the slightest hesitation sits in my lap, which surprises me but feels wonderful. We kiss.

"So what are your intentions?"

"Why don't we discuss this in your bedroom?"

Eventually, that is exactly what we do, another long conversation, only now at least it is Krishna who is being infinitely cautious, hesitant about going forward. Her reaction to my reaching out seems more one of relief than desire. I'm trying very hard to understand and read these subtle signs. Already we've crossed over emotional boundaries we won't ever be able to re-erect. I want to make love, but she's not ready, she says. "Lets just sleep." So we do.

At dawn or just before, I wake and lean over and kiss her gently. She's awake also, although maybe I don't realize this at first. Without a word, she slowly rises and stands over me on the narrow bed, removing her clothes. This is the closest thing to a vision I will ever have.

We make love twice, taking almost until noon to finish. When we finally stumble toward the kitchen, Kathy and Dorothy are at the table, laughing that they'd gotten up in the morning, realized I must still be there, and had headed out of the house to give us privacy. They've returned hours later post-brunch and we're still in bed and they'd begun to wonder if we would ever rise. We eat a cursory breakfast and say very little. We're exhausted and shy and exhilarated. I feel as though I've used a lifetime of adrenaline—it would be easy to hallucinate. After the meal settles us down somewhat, we walk very casually back to my apartment on San Jose where we spend the afternoon in bed.

It is only because I've promised to attend a book party at Geoff Young's in Berkeley that I ever really rise at all that day, at dusk, because Tom Mandel's coming by to give me a ride. Krishna and I dress and we sit on my minuscule back porch overlooking the minuscule Poplar Alley until the bell rings. As Krishna says good-bye and heads up the hill, Tom looks at my poor dazed expression and says, "What hit you?"

It would make sense, narratively, to stop right here, but life is not a plot. On Monday morning, I wake and rise at Krishna's. We decide (or maybe it's Krishna who decided this) that she should go into work first and that we shouldn't arrive together. Later, as I'm riding the Mission bus down past DuBoce, somebody who's been playing a boom box turns the volume full blast. I hear the words "Mayor Moscone and Supervisor Harvey Milk have been shot and are presumed dead this morning at City Hall," and then the sound is turned back down again. No further explanation. The words sound completely foreign and meaningless at first. I've known George Moscone since I first worked for CPHJ and he sat on the Senate Judiciary Committee. I've known Harvey Milk because everyone in San Francisco knew Harvey Milk. In a moment the bus turns onto Van Ness and when it reaches City Hall, I get off. I walk inside past no security whatsoever and see Bill Kraus, Harvey's aide and a DSOC activist, red-eyed, talking to a crowd. Rudy Nothenberg, one of Moscone's assistants, is running full tilt

up the broad stairs. Police are everywhere. TV cameras are everywhere. Why am I here?

I walk outside again, down Golden Gate Avenue two blocks and the one block up Leavenworth to Hospitality House. As always, the step from the brilliant sunlight of the street (made all the more stark by these treeless Tenderloin stucco facades) into the shadows of the arts center is almost blinding. I wait for my eyes to adjust to the dark. Nobody's working—everyone is just standing around, talking. They've already heard. I remembered seeing flowers already sprinkled on the steps of City Hall as I'd left and I suggest that we should buy some also and take them there. Several of us head out to purchase roses from a street vendor near Harrington's. By now City Hall is secured and closed, so we stand around the broad stairs, Krishna and I and Dorothy and Spider and I don't remember who else. It's a beautiful sunny afternoon. It's a terrible day. The headlines in the newspaper boxes are still filled with Jonestown.

Krishna had already planned to leave the following weekend for Baltimore and Virginia where a sister is getting married. It feels as if we spend the week itself attending one memorial service after another. It's an insane time and I feel wildly out of sync to be so intensely aroused and pleased every single minute of it. The morning she flies off we stand at the top of the Esmerelda Steps, one of the great secret views of the city, not long after sunrise, talking about how we'll write to one another.[30] We already know (have known for months) that talk, casual, intimate, intelligent conversation, will be an important form for us. It will be a long time before many other important things occur. Over four years, for example, before either one of us really settles into monogamy. Another six before I stop drinking. Eight before we marry. Eleven before Krishna nearly dies from an ectopic pregnancy. Twelve before I begin to go blind from cataracts. Thirteen before you are born. Sixteen before we all move to Pennsylvania. But in more ways than an individual could hope to understand, the logic that leads through each of those events was already implicit (though not inherent) the in-

---

[30]I will send her a letter that takes up the whole of a Chinese notebook, a favorite form of mine in the mid-'70s, which she still has somewhere. She writes me a long detailed description of the wedding.

stant I said yes to a cup of tea. I crossed a line in my life from which I have never stepped back.

This, in a sense, is the exact opposite of telos, but rather a recognition that choice is central to freedom. With both its intended and unintended consequences.

I remember a day fourteen years earlier when, seventeen years old, my high school flattop just starting to grow out, I was walking through Newport, Rhode Island, wondering what to do in the next forty-eight hours when the annual folk festival would begin and my room at the local "Y" would go instead to someone with a reservation. I looked to the left as I crossed the intersection, noticed a small coffeehouse and thought to walk in. Asking to speak to the manager, I inquired if they needed any assistance for the festival week and that I'd happily accept meals and a place to sleep. Can you perform, I was asked. I lied, saying that I could do stand-up comedy. I only had to do one set during the week, possibly because I was dreadful at it.[31] But this was enough not only to give me shelter, literally a pallet on the floor, but also access to some backstage parties connected to the festival. Which was how I found myself sitting next to Bob Dylan on a couch one night as he and Paul Stookey and Sebastian Dangerfield improvised a version of "King Bee." I'd never heard of the British rock group whose record Buffy Sainte-Marie told me this song had been found on, but sensed that I was being given the most privileged of "inside" information. What if, I thought to myself, I hadn't looked to the left when I'd crossed that street?

That night in 1978, with Krishna already thousands of miles away, I'm walking alone through a human sea of candles in the shabby urban park in front of City Hall, hyperconscious in this first separation that the same dynamics are now being played out in my life on a whole other scale. I'm overwhelmed by all of the visible grief I see around me in this memorial rally held both for the assassinations and the mass suicide in Guyana. And I'm overwhelmed by the vertigo of love. I understand already that I'm involved far more than I've ever been before, that I've arrived at a whole new level of risk. So the same thought recurs: *What if?*

---

[31]I plagiarized my material from the dim memory of an old Alan Sherman record.

And, *How much courage will I have to see this through?* On a stage mounted over the City Hall steps, Joan Baez is singing *Amazing Grace*.

The want ads lie strewn on the table.

It is not possible to "describe a life."

From *ABC* (Berkeley: Tuumba 46, 1983). "Albany" first appeared in *Ironwood* 20 (Tucson: Fall 1982), vol. 10, no. 2, pp. 112-113.

BIBLIOGRAPHY

Poetry:

Crow, Ithaca House (Ithaca, NY), 1971.

Mohawk, Doones Press, 1973.

Nox, Burning Deck (Providence, RI), 1974.

Sitting Up, Standing, Taking Steps, Tuumba Press (Berkeley, CA), 1978.

Ketjak, THIS (San Francisco, CA), 1978.

Tjanting, Figures (Berkeley, CA), 1981.

Bart, Potes & Poets Press (Elmwood, CT), 1982.

ABC, Tuumba Press, 1983.

Paradise, Burning Deck, 1985.

The Age of Huts, Roof (New York, NY), 1986.

LIT, Potes & Poets Press, 1987.

What, The Figures, 1988.

Toner, Potes & Poets Press, 1992.

Demo to Ink, Chax Press (Tucson, AZ), 1992.

Jones, Generator Press, 1993.

N/O, Roof, 1994.

Other:

(Editor) *In the American Tree* (poetry anthology), National Poetry Foundation, University of Maine at Orono, 1986.

The New Sentence, Roof, 1987.

Also author of *Beyond Prisons,* a screenplay for KQED-Television, 1973.

Editor of *A Symposium on Clark Coolidge,* 1978. Contributor to numerous journals in Canada, England, Mexico, and the United States, including *Arts in Society, Caterpillar, Chicago Review, Poetry, Rolling Stone, Southern Review, This,* and *Tri-Quarterly.* Editor of *Tottel's,* 1970-81, and newsletter of Committee for Prisoner Humanity and Justice; executive editor of *Socialist Review,* 1986-89, member of editorial collective, 1986-91.

Bernard Weiner

1940-

This world is not enough; behind/beyond this reality are the hidden worlds of meaning, connections, subtext, sub-subtext, the cosmic link, the mystery realm, the deeper level, the divine, call it what you will—you know what I mean. Voyaging into those mysterious, redolent areas is the journey we're on—in addition to doing the grocery shopping and taking out the garbage.

There are an infinite number of ways into these deeper levels. Some enter through religion or philosophy or golf or scuba-diving or nature-walks. My primary method of entry is through the arts—art being for me a kind of decoder, stop-timer, puzzle key to help me better understand myself and the world, the processes of life, the magical mystery tour, how I might fit into the ongoing flow.

I don't remember when I might first have harbored such thoughts about art or flow, even unconsciously. We moved to Florida from Pittsburgh, Pennsylvania—where I was born, on February 9, 1940—when I was five. Growing up in Miami, I was a fairly normal child: playing outdoors most of the time, engaging in raucous games with my friends, participating in organized sports, carrying out minor—and not-so-minor—mischiefs.

The "not-so-minor" refers to that period, around ages six to ten or so, when I was deeply troubled and acted out by shoplifting, getting into gang fights, torturing animals, and setting fires to abandoned lots and buildings; clearly, among other reasons for my wild behavior, in my new environment I was asking for more attention and affection from my busy, burdened parents. Later, as an adolescent, I came to realize that one could obtain attention and affection—which I took to be pretty much the same thing—from a wide variety of people, in more socially acceptable, less personally dangerous ways: through the exercise of leadership and through the arts.

I always possessed a vibrant imagination—in my young-boy period, in the early 1950s, I read at least a half-dozen fiction books each week—but I suspect that my transferring imagination to the page was aided by several key events:

Bernard Weiner, "meditating" for the camera from an Anasazi lookout cave in New Mexico, 1996

My grandmother, who lived with us, died when I was seven; not much was said about her disappearance from our lives. My best friend died a year or two later; nobody talked about his death either, neither my parents nor his, and so I was left, once again, to puzzle out the nature of death and its effects on the living—a major bit of shadow matter that I'm sure worked its imaginative magic on my young child's mind. (In later years, two of my best friends also died, and I'm still dealing with those losses.)

Also around this same time, when I was about ten, my father was hospitalized for stomach-ulcer problems, and, in addition to worrying about his chances for survival, for several months I had to go to work (after school and on weekends) with my mother to help keep our family's little grocery store in operation.

This seminal event in our family's otherwise fairly normal life—my dad in crisis in hospital and then his recuperation period, the necessity for me to work to take up some of the slack—forced me to "grow up" fast, assuming a responsibility not shared by many children my age. (My older sister, Roberta, in some ways was similarly speeded into adult concerns: she already was launched on an operatic singing career by age twelve; my younger sister, Linda, was only six or so.) But even while working, I still was a kid: on my work-breaks, I made my way up a tall tree outside the store—climbing perhaps twenty feet high into the branches, there to soar (along with my real, and often imaginary, playmates) into the adventurous ether of fantasy.

My parents were proud of the way I had come through in a familial pinch, helping them out

Florence Neil and Daniel Weiner on their wedding day, 1933

in the store; consequently, the image I had of myself was improved. I stopped setting fires.

My father recovered and I quickly evolved into an ordinary mid-'50s adolescent/teenager: rhythm and blues, rock and roll, friendships, dating, school activities, tennis and basketball, formal dances, delivering newspapers on my bicycle—these were my main concerns. (There also was social/political involvement, but I'll get to that below.) In high school, I continued working part-time at my family's new, larger grocery store—as a paid employee rather than as a for-free family member.

During all my public-school period, I was a fairly good student, with a high grade-point average, usually obtained either by my ability to charm the teachers with my poetic/artistic patter, or by last-minute cramming, mixed with the store of information amassed through my voluminous reading.

From the age of ten until my bar mitzvah at thirteen, I also attended Hebrew high school at the neighborhood Orthodox synagogue after my regular public-school day; because of my penchant for philosophical thinking and because I had a talent for cantorial singing, it seemed I was being groomed for the rabbinate. Shortly after my bar mitzvah, I rebelled and went out to play baseball, rarely to return; the "real world" at that point meant more to me than the spiritual world—a position that reversed as I grew older.

The first poem I can recall writing was composed probably around age eleven or twelve; it was inspired by listening to the gentle Southern rain outside my window, and was about a drop of water sliding down the petals of a flower into the center of existence. It probably was a terribly gauche poem, but the fact that I was able to put these thoughts into form on paper opened a door of perception for me: one could reach the important, could convey feeling and meaning, could access the inaffable through the affable, through those imperfect but vital human tools—words. And, emotionally, I felt better, more complete, more myself, more whole, after having, with my words, contacted that mystery realm, however tentatively.

When I was about fourteen or fifteen, my mother (who, in her day, turned out some clever rhyming verse) took me to her nighttime creative-writing class at the University of Miami; the professor allowed me to contribute some examples of my own attempts at poetry and prose. The positive feedback I got from him, and from the other adults, encouraged me as a teenager to continue this attempt at deep understanding and human communication via words. And I'm still doing it nearly forty-five years later. As a matter of fact, as you may have noticed, I'm doing it right now.

In "Invitation to a Dance," the introductory poem to my first collection, I noted that I am "always pregnant with myself"; with my poetry, "this wild pulse of freedombirth,/I keep time with my life./Catch me if you can." (From *Selected Poems*.) In other words, poetry for me always has been a kind of journal-keeping: each poem is dated, with the place noted where written. One speaks to one's soul first; then, and only then, is the invitation given to those who may wish to join the dance, the hunt for personal and metaphorical meaning.

Now, having said this, having noted how fidelity to my personal muse is what happens when writing a poem, I must confess that, at some point (usually in the editing room, so to speak), I know I also am writing potentially for a public and thus must not get too arcane and self-involved or nobody else will be able to, or will want to, follow.

I suspect that this desire to communicate came not only because I always have been a fairly social being—while also recognizing how vital solitude is to my mental health—but also because I grew irritated when I read poems that allowed for no way into the private universe of the author. I wanted my work to reflect my highly personal searches and journeys and speculations, but in a way that invited others into the "conspiracy" of meaning and the enjoyment of sound and wordplay.

If my trees fell in a forest, I wanted ears there to hear the sound. It was a social as well as an artistic gesture.

On the other hand, I did not want my poems (and plays and stories) to travel so far along the accessibility route that they would become over-simplistic and just ordinary and shallow. So, to this day, I struggle with walking the fine line in my art between being accessible and being appropriately complex. I find that the more self-involved and involuted my writings are, the least successful they are as works of art. I continue to compose such "inner" works, usually for therapeutic reasons, but they either lie fallow, never to be taken up again, or serve as rough drafts for more accessible public works that will follow.

Using the writing facility I was beginning to develop, I went into journalism as a teenager, as an editor of my high school newspaper and later as editor-in-chief of the university paper. The

Bernard, flanked by his sisters, Roberta (left) and Linda, 1947

essence of journalism is the composition of highly readable prose, instantly understandable to others. Was journalism the chicken or the egg: i.e., did I enter journalism because I already was bitten by the "accessibility" bug or did journalism lead me to the necessity for writing clearly and accessibly, in both poetry and prose?

There are important similarities about journalism and poetry that drew me to both: not only does each bring a kind of order to the chaos of the world (and my mind), but each permits me to experience the world intensely though at arm's length. I think I was an infinitely curious but fairly fearful young man, anxious to meet the world straight-on and taste it fully yet at the same time nervous about the consequences of so doing. Journalism permitted me a bit of both: one could experience the world in all its variety but in a sanctioned, protected way. As a journalist—as a reporter, columnist, critic, or editor—I could move in the world as an institutionalized observer, asking questions and seeking information that otherwise might be denied to someone considered merely "nosy." Writing criticism, which I began while at university—plays, films, dance, jazz, opera, books, cultural essays, etc.—flowed from some of the same impulses of enjoying that arm's-length approach to reality.

Poetry was much the same. I both experienced something—an event, an emotion—and then, from some distance, explored through words its meanings. Sometimes, I even would be aware as I was living an event or emotion that I was poeming it in my mind (or shortly would be putting it on paper). That overlap was psychologically disturbing during my youth: i.e., how could I be fully in the moment if at the same time I was aware of being in the moment?

That Zen-like conundrum fascinates me even today, but at the time, especially while at college, I thought I must be going crazy, and went to the campus counseling clinic to try to figure out how to encompass both parts of my self in my Self. (I was much taken with Dostoevsky's "Underground Man," who noted that "acute self-consciousness is a disease." I felt thus diseased, and needed help in figuring out how to lower the level of such self-consciousness and/or grow to accept such bifurcation as a natural part of who I was. Years later, I came to appreciate this ability to operate on several levels at the same time as a gift. How slowly we learn!)

I began acting as a young child, performing in plays and musicals with my older, professional-singing sister Roberta, and on my own. However, in high school, I became afflicted with a debilitating case of teenage embarrassment and would not go on the stage. But I loved the artificial world of the theater—which in many ways seemed more real and interesting than the normal life I was living in Miami in the '50s—and so I began to write plays. Though I wouldn't have articulated it in these terms, on some level I believed then, as I do now, that in addition to providing a personal outlet, the theater is a unique cultural crucible in which society can explore its demons and its epiphanies.

My first effort, written around 1959, was a stodgy bit of existential philosophizing, *'Til the End of Time*; in its metaphysical speculations, it was so unlike the light comedies and kitchen-sink dramas my contemporaries were fooling around with that the university literary magazine felt compelled to publish it. The next summer, based on this script, I was accepted into the Harvard playwriting program.

My next few forays into playwriting in the '50s and early '60s were somewhat in the spirit of the early Dadaists/Surrealists and the modern breakthroughs made by Samuel Beckett and Eugene Ionesco in Europe (along with a bit of Pirandello): *The Fourth Monkey*, about a trio of scary clowns who see no evil, speak no evil, hear no evil, and do no evil—or good; *When in the Farce of Human Events It Becomes Necessary*, a weird comedy that concluded with two characters coming onstage and just silently sitting there, facing the

seats—leaving it up to the audience each night to determine how the show ended; *The Usual*, subtitled *Hommage et Réponse à Samuel Beckett*, involved two guys drinking in a cafe and telling jokes.

I was, as you can see, heavily influenced by the European Absurdist playwrights—at least stylistically, though my plays often had a more activist thrust than those of Beckett, Ionesco, Pinter, et al. In an author's program note at the time, I wrote: The world may or may not be Absurd in any metaphysical sense, but it certainly seems that way when you read the evening paper. The well-ordered theater of days gone by, the well-made play of tradition, simply doesn't correspond with the lunacy and unpredictability of the real world. . . . To the early Absurdists, unexplainable lunacy was not mutant behavior, not an exception to the rule, but rather the true explanation of the non-laws of the universe . . . I do not share many of the metaphysical assumptions of the Absurdists, but I do admire their craft, their humor, their insights, their ability to create life in a basically moribund theatrical tradition.

I was directing and writing plays in college (and I even got back onstage as an actor in university productions) and beginning to review shows as well, including productions directed by my professors and featuring actresses I was dating. Obviously, I had to make a moral decision: do I tell the truth about their work, which could contain negative assessments as well as positive, or do I fudge a bit? I chose telling the truth, and learned a hard one: friendships, love relationships, etc., are virtually impossible when the power balance is so out of whack between critics and those they review.

In my fiction writing at the time, I was heavily influenced by the spare, tough styling of Ernest Hemingway—I even headed off to Pamplona to run with the bulls—and by such imitators as Vance Bourjaily (*Confessions of a Spent Youth* was one of my favorites). In nonfiction writing, I was a great admirer of the likes of C. Wright Mills, Vance Packard, David Reisman, Paul Goodman, Dwight Macdonald, Robert Warshow, I. F. Stone, Harvey Swados. (For the most part, interest in female and nonwhite fiction/nonfiction writers—such as the African-American authors listed below—didn't come until later.)

Throughout my life, I have always felt that I've been a decade or more behind my chronological age. For example, in my late twenties, I felt as if I were still a teenager, emotionally and in terms of life-experience—which may help explain some of my wild, adolescent-style behavior in the tumultuous 1960s, and the ways I chose to attack society's major institutions.

I suspect that in addition to the fact that those institutions were greatly in need of a major shakeup, sexual ignorance and repression in my teenage years had something to do with those desire-for-liberation feelings, as well as a kind of natural rebelliousness of second-generation Americans to their more traditional first-generation-immigrant parents with their conservative "old world" ways.

My parents, Daniel Weiner and Florence Neil Weiner—Russian/Polish Jews from the Eastern European *shtetels*—arrived in America as children, but they still carried many of their old values, and anxieties, with them into adulthood. I think I inherited their dedication, hard work—starting from nothing, eventually they were able to send their three children to college—and sense of morality. I think they also inculcated in me many of their fears and anxieties.

I think of "The Sixties"—for me, maybe 1962-74, although I was involved in the Civil Rights Movement in my native South in the late '50s as well—as the forge that helped "fire" my personality, and politics, and probably a lot of my aesthetics. Again, it's the chicken-and-egg conundrum: Did I enter that tumultuous period already pretty well formed in those three areas of personality/politics/aesthetics and merely solidify my stances, or was I indelibly stamped by the tumultuous events of that era, shaped as I went along?

Which brings us to the early political activism I promised I'd talk about: I became politically aware and engaged as a teenager by: 1) simply looking around at the world of South Florida—racially segregated, with African-Americans and Seminoles always on the short end of the stick and the long end of poverty and repression; 2) coming into contact with two adult mentors in the B'nai B'rith Youth Organization—I was a member of a BBYO boys' fraternity—who helped educate me in the ways of understanding social/political contexts; and 3) beginning to discern the behind-the-scenes realities of American political life that were being revealed in the '50s and early '60s, usually locally but on rare occasions also on the national stage: the Army/McCarthy hearings, the Cuban missile crisis, CIA machinations in Guatemala, Iran, Indochina, etc.

At Miami Senior High School (where I was student body vice president), my school political activities were fairly lightweight. The world changed drastically in the next few years: much was revealed and there was more willingness on the part of young people to deal with the revelations. At college, I was significantly *engagé*, both actively and journalistically; for example, in 1961, as editor of the University of Miami student newspaper, I launched a campaign for racial desegregation of the university—which earned me serious death threats and at least one thwarted attempt on my life—and I used my bully-pulpit to ally the campus movement for desegregation to the African-American push for desegregating lunch counters and swimming pools and other municipal facilities in the apartheid South.

My political heroes at the time were India's Mahatma Gandhi and Florida's Governor LeRoy Collins, the latter of whom courageously spoke from his Christian heart about how segregation had to go. (He was not reelected; Florida was as racist as they come—it had been the second state to secede from the Union.) Later, I would come to admire Martin Luther King, Jr., Cesar Chavez, the later Robert Kennedy, Fannie Lou Hamer, Robert Moses, Saul Alinsky, Dorothy Day, and others, who were willing to lay their bodies on the line for their beliefs—and writers like Ralph Ellison, James Baldwin, Lorraine Hansberry, Langston Hughes, Zora Neale Hurston, William E.B. DuBois, and others, who so powerfully captured the black pain I could see around me each day. And, of course, I was deep into jazz and R & B; my heroes were not only the godparents of soul—Billie, Bessie, Duke, et al.—but also those who were capturing the hearts of the young, black and white: Bo Diddley, Fats Domino, Chuck Berry, Ray Charles, Little Richard, Leadbelly, and such gospel greats as Mahalia Jackson and the Staple Singers, especially Mavis.

Growing up in the segregated South—with parents who, despite their own histories of having been persecuted as Jews, shared many of the racist sentiments of the time (calling grown black men "boys," for example)—was a troubling experience for me, who so admired and identified with the black culture of music and outsider survival-wit.

Though I certainly was part of the folk music/coffeehouse scene in the late '50s and early '60s—a scene that was almost totally white—I found myself gravitating to the few nightclubs in the ghetto sections of Miami where whites and blacks could mix socially and listen to jazz and R&B. I thought it criminally stupid for the white culture to deny itself the chance to experience what the black culture so vibrantly had to offer. Well, that's philosophy from a later adult perspective; at the time I probably just liked the music, liked the "underground" nature of the experience, and especially liked being "cool" and Beat-rebellious—I used to wear my shades all the time, even in dimly lit clubs. (Of course, I had white music heroes as well in the '50s: the Weavers, Joan Baez, Pete Seeger, Fred Neil, et al.)

I joined the Congress of Racial Equality, the Fellowship of Reconciliation, the War Resisters League, and so on, but those were distant, national organizations. As an activist/journalist, however, I could work in my local area for social justice and to help break down barriers between the two cultures. Again, sometimes this was accomplished as an activist but usually it happened in my capacity as journalist, using words as tools, always in the service of deeper understandings; often I took to wearing both hats: once, all it took to get major, immediate change was a letter from me as editor of the university newspaper to Miami's mayor, threatening to organize mass picketing and boycotts unless the downtown department stores desegregated their lunch counters. The city fathers, eager to maintain the tourist trade, discerned the potential for bad publicity, and moved quickly to do what was right.

While attending college—on a four-year scholarship from Sigma Delta Chi, the professional journalism society—I worked on the copy staff of the *Miami Herald*, and later joined the *Miami News* as a cub reporter and copy editor. After four years at the University of Miami, majoring in government—my minors were in English, psychology, sociology, and journalism—I was ready and eager for graduate school. I was accepted by Harvard (where I had attended summer session), Chicago, Columbia, and Claremont, but only the last-named offered me a fellowship, so in 1962, finances dictated that I head off to Southern California. I was eager to go: I had had enough of Miami, which at that time remained a backwater Southern town, with enough traces of New York and Havana to make it bearable. I felt stifled there, encased in a world that I characterized in the poem "My American Dream" where the prevailing iconic image was "cheese dip and a satisfied smile." (From *Selected Poems*.)

Separated by 3,000 miles from my old life—parents, friends, geography, etc.—I felt absolutely liberated, as I had felt previously when studying

Weiner in his "writing incubator": one of the Balafi towers in Ibiza, Spain, 1963

at Harvard (where I had taken a playwriting class from Robert Chapman and an international politics course from Hans Morgenthau.) Intellectually, I took off in my Claremont classwork, glorying in the ideas we played with in the special unit of which I was a part: the Intercollegiate Program of Graduate Studies. I had been in the Honors Program at the University of Miami—an elite curriculum designed to protect us from the mass of the student body, or perhaps it was the other way around—but, as much as I had enjoyed that undergraduate experience, the IPGS was a much more meaningful eye- and mind-opener, using faculty members from all six of the Claremont Colleges in our seminars. For example, a group of fourteen of us students might be reading Joyce's *Ulysses* or Ellison's *Invisible Man* and leading the seminar discussions would be five professors: a philosopher from the Graduate School of Theology, a literature professor from Pomona College, a marine biologist from Scripps, a mathematician from Harvey Mudd, and a sociologist from Pitzer.

The montage of ideas and analyses was, to say the least, rich and fascinating. I've always been a dilettante—an epithet in which I take pride, since I'm fascinated by so many things and like to dance amongst them all—and this type of education was perfect for me, allowing me to exercise my brain-muscles in ways not always permitted in more traditional kinds of education.

My area of study in graduate school was government and international relations. I was fascinated by politics, nationally and globally—interested in how society worked and where political action could make a difference in people's lives—but I think there was a deeper motivation. The arts is where my heart and soul resided, and where my spiritual side could flower, but I always felt I could get lost in that heady ether, could disconnect from the world in which most people lived most of the time, could become an artist unfeeling about the world because ignorant of its realities; my interest in government tied me to the world as it is, forced me to meld the ethereal and artistic insights I gained through my writing and reading with the mundane, quotidian realities affecting ordinary people. The mix of politics and the arts was the way I balanced myself in the world.

I had located my study carrel in the literature section of the campus library, and, when I grew bored with my government studies, I simply would lean over and grab a novel to read. My papers on the American Constitution or Maoist China might well be framed within a discussion of Dostoevsky or Beckett or Borges or Naipaul. This cultural amalgam tended to puzzle my professors but since my writing was interesting, they indulged me.

Figuring I would never make my way through the Ph.D. grind, I stopped in 1964 to get a master's degree; my thesis was on the World War II-era Greek Civil War. Surprising even myself—well, maybe not that surprising, as I didn't want to get drafted—I slogged on and completed my Ph.D. dissertation in 1966, on the Truman Doctrine. My aim was to show how a distorted cold war mentality in the mid-1940s led inexorably to a misguided Vietnam War twenty years later.

In addition to intellectual "liberation" in Claremont, I also felt liberated culturally and sexually. For reasons far too convoluted psychologically to go into, I was still technically a virgin at age twenty-two. I set about to make up for lost time in singing the body electric.

This breakout from sexual repression on my horny part just happened to coincide with the advent of the birth-control pill and other inducements to sexual liberation for women. I was having a grand old time—but made sure I didn't commit myself to matrimony. In truth, I was terrified of the idea of marriage, since my parents'

marriage was a grand failure, composed of so much disappointment, bitterness, and resentment that our family home was filled with a constant, corrosive tension. I loved my parents deeply, and was saddened by the fact that they couldn't love each other. (As it turned out, it was during this liberated period in Claremont that I met Heidi Linsmayer, who fourteen years later would become my wife and soul-partner.)

Part of that liberation process involved foreign travel. Somehow, I was able to save up enough money every three years from 1963 to 1975 to fly off to Europe. I traveled and wrote in a variety of countries, but mostly the magic happened in Spain, especially in the interior of the island of Ibiza, where, with a friend, I rented a place—no electricity, no toilet, no running water—that seemed to serve as a remarkable creative incubator. ("Time,/Passing through long ago,/took a liking to the place,/and decided to stay," I wrote in the poem "San Lorenzo" in *Selected Poems.*) Poems and articles and stories flowed out of me, including one of the few stories I've ever written that has never been published, a novella entitled *Notes from an Ibizan Journal, 1963.* Going to different parts of the world stirred up things in me that resulted in productive creative work— and a broader perspective of the socially possible.

Catching the Wave

The pale, prim housewife from San
  Bernardino,
In her unsexy onepiece bathing suit,
Takes her daughter's rented boogy-board
Into the water at Brennecke's Beach
And tries out a few kiddie waves.
I look elsewhere for adventure.

When I next see her,
She's graduated to medium-sized waves,
And her approach, while still somewhat
  tentative,
Is fun to watch.

Her face is a big grin of accomplishment.
You can almost see her shedding some of her
  fears
And prissy behavior patterns
When she returns to her mainland life.

Later that day, I see her again.
Now she's riding the waves, not just floating
  with them;
She knows how and when to catch the crest.
She's ecstatic.

She's discovered the power.
Her life is enlarged.
She is connecting, and knows
She can connect.
The power of being in the flow can be hers.

God help her and those around her.
Their lives are no longer the same.

Kauai, Hawaii: August 1992
(From *Songs of Non-Enlightenment*)

As had been the case in college, where I had acted in University of Miami productions and reviewed plays and films for the campus newspaper, I continued in graduate school to write and direct plays and to work as a film/drama critic for the local paper, the *Claremont Courier.* I had had several plays produced and published while in college and the pattern deepened in graduate school. Using a pseudonym, I submitted *When in the Farce of Human Events It Becomes Necessary* and *The Usual* to the Claremont College's play-writing contest, won first prize two years in a row and had the works performed (and one published). I also had my first poetry book released, the aforementioned *Selected Poems,* in 1965.

While I was completing my dissertation at Claremont, I obtained a one-year assignment teaching American government at San Diego State College. Here, in 1965, at the age of twenty-five, the two major tributaries of my life—art/imagination and government/social action—joined in a major flow. I was writing a lot: plays, poetry, short stories, film reviews for *San Diego Magazine;* I also was organizing against the slowly evolving Vietnam War, leading "teach-ins," giving talks, circulating petitions. I also had my first psychedelic drug experience, with Sandoz Laboratories-obtained LSD, which freed up my consciousness in profound ways. In short, "The Sixties"—the war, mind-expanding drugs, political and cultural organizing, etc.—were beginning to flow through me, and out from me.

The following year, having obtained my Ph.D., I joined the faculty at Western Washington State College, teaching government and international politics. The Bellingham campus in 1966 was a quiet, backwater institution in a small, quiet, somewhat isolated Northwest town. I was not quiet, nor was I used to swimming in backwaters. I had arrived from Southern California, where things were starting to pop, culturally and politically.

I found myself in 1966 in the unsolicited role of advance scout for The Sixties "revolution," and suffered the consequence of being out there pretty much on my own: within three months of my appearance on campus, my department chairman announced that I would not be rehired. He felt threatened by my unorthodox "style"—bright paisley ties, public antiwar organizing, siding with student demands for educational reform, odd teaching methods (lecturing on the lawn on non-rainy days, holding mock war-crimes tribunals, etc.), and, above all, my willingness to question his authoritarian decision-making—and I was to be booted out. I filed a grievance, since the chairman had not followed proper procedures, and he was warned not to do that again. So I was back for another year.

By 1967, The Sixties had reached even sleepy little Bellingham in a major way. Antiwar activity was at a fever pitch—I was deeply engaged in trying to stop the bloodshed, which was tearing the country (and Bellingham) apart in a kind of cultural/generational civil war—and the scene was so bubbly that the following felt obliged to come and check it out: Ken Kesey & The Merry Pranksters on the Bus, Neil Cassidy, Allen Ginsberg, Timothy Leary, Kurt Vonnegut, the Jefferson Airplane, et al. Having earned a reputation the previous year as an *agent provocateur* from the revolutionary forces in California, I was at the heart of a lot of this countercultural activity—firing up antiwar crowds with forceful speeches, organizing mass marches to protest the war, driving draft resisters across the border into Canada, leading discussions about the possible benefits (as well as the potential dangers) of psychedelic substances, supporting rebellious students in their quest for more meaningful, "relevant" classes—and thus was not long for future employment in my department. The chairman followed enough of the procedures this time and I was out.

I could have left Bellingham, defeated and dispirited, but I decided to stay—a decision made easier by the fact that I wasn't having any success in locating another teaching position, colleges being loathe to hire a young "radical" professor at a time when campuses were exploding in antiwar/educational reform ferment all across the country. In truth, I wasn't all that radical; by instinct, temperament, and age—being just five years or so older than the students I was teaching—I found myself more in the position of being a mediating force between competing interests and groups and generations. But certainly I was regarded as "radical" by my sixty-five-year-old department chairman—especially when I urged mass rallies of students to "be in the system but not of it," i.e., work the system, figure out how to negotiate within it, but don't give your soul to it. (The chairman and I met twenty years later; I apologized for driving him up a wall, sometimes deliberately, by my behavior, and he, eighty-five years old, confessed that he had been ill-equipped emotionally to deal with change and so responded the only way he knew, with repressive measures.)

A Hippie on Vietnam

" . . . better to live out one's own absurdity than to die for that of others."
                    —Ralph Ellison, *Invisible Man*

You suck
The gun, conformity's child,
Marching off to where,
And try to yank
Me with you.
But, man, there's a draft
In here,
And I ain't about to spread
Your Death-
Of-a-cold, daddy.

I've got planes to fly in my brains,
And trains to drive in my veins;
Got junk to flush through my trunk,
And mud to swirl through my blood.
Colors to blow your mind,
Speed to leave you behind.

I've got seeds to chew,
And glue to sniff,
Buttons to pop
And acid to drop;

I've got beans to stuff up my nose,
And three lids of grass in my toes,
And I'm a mighty fine rose.

Get found!

Bellingham, Wa.: April 1967
(From *The Bellingham Poems*)

Another reason to stay in Bellingham was my close identification with many of the budding counter-cultural institutions in the area: alternative schools, a food co-op, a free university, hippie back-to-the-land communes, the antiwar move-ment, a laid-back drug scene, a thriving arts colony (for which I was writing and directing plays), and, most important to me, a wonderful alternative newspaper for which I had been contributing film and drama reviews. As I later noted in the introduction to *The Bellingham Poems*, Bellingham at that time was "the perfect artists' colony precisely because we weren't aware that we were."

While serving as the founding administrator of Northwest Free University—a kind of alternative college that offered classes for both townsfolk and campus types—I also volunteered more of my time to the newspaper, *Northwest Passage*. This publication had begun its life as an "underground" hippie rag but slowly evolved into an above-ground "journal of politics, the arts and good, healthy livin'," with an emphasis on protecting the environment of the gorgeous Pacific Northwest.

During my tenure as editor, the collectively produced, biweekly paper—which circulated mainly in the Seattle/Bellingham/Vancouver area—became even more of a political and environmental force, and a kind of communications bridge between the warring generations; politically, though the paper clearly was antiwar and left-leaning, my aim was to aid in developing alliances across many barriers (age, race, political affiliation, etc.) in the service of community-building, and I think, to a certain extent, the paper was successful in doing that. We knew we were effective because politicians and corporations were subscribing, so as to figure out how to combat our influence.

I was living a penurious life, sponging meals off old faculty friends, living in the parish house of the Unitarian Fellowship for $35 per month, dipping into my meager savings to stay afloat. I was also something of a sexual neurotic at this point, flagrantly promiscuous in my loneliness; given the aphrodisiac associated with power (and given my notoriety in the community), I was not lacking in willing partners. But even I knew that was not a satisfying existence.

Connecting Bedrooms

The girl living upstairs from me
Thinks I love her.
You can see it in the way
She asks to use the phone
Or borrow a bottle-opener.

She's let me know
That she can hear the squeakings of my
 springs

And the grunts and cries of delight
When I'm with someone.

And she's jealous.
I can tell.

Too tired to fight honesty,
I accept her vision,
And so I love her.

Now I can hear *her*
Writhings and groanings
Through the ceiling separating our
  bedrooms.
She thinks I'm jealous.

        Bellingham, Wa.: Winter 1969
        (From *The Bellingham Poems*)

Liberation

Appetite-eyes then:
    candlelight, incense,
    rushing talk,
    soft caresses,
    then hot handling,
    hot blood,
    clothes floating to the floor,
    bed knocking the history of the wall—
Exploring our newness, our boundaries.

Later, after months of yes,
And hurt,
I go to Spain
To serve my American time.

When I return,
I learn my postcards reached you at a
  hippie commune, late.
So I travel out, eager in memory's mouth,
For our reunion
In the pure, greentipped air.

You're galloping your horse into the yard,
We merge with a slow-motion hug,
Slightly off-track,
Then talk of separate summers:
Chronologies, names, places.
Something is wrong.

We walk to your unheated room
(In this house that has no hot water),
Passing jam-printed guitars
Lying half-loved on the stairs,
And I ask if you'd like to visit some
  friends.
You say yes, but you want to change first.

Shall I leave? turn my back? pretend to
  look out the window? simply stand?
There's no need to wonder:
You undress casually before me,
Your breasts as uninterested as the flaking
  grey wall.

        Maple Falls, Wa.: November 1969
        (From *The Bellingham Poems*)

To "June," After a Separation

Soft rain slowly peels
Winter's white membrane
Off the sleeping earth.

My dog charges outside
To run the green
And smell the secret
Months of snow
Have kept from her nose.

It does no good for me
To tell her
This is not the same earth,
She is not the same dog,
One can't go home again,
And dark snowclouds will return:
She's rolling on her back,
Laughing at the rain!

So, seeing you again,
I take off my shoes
And run my heart through
The almost-Spring
Of happy illusion.

        Bellingham, Wa.: February 1969
        (From *The Bellingham Poems*)

After several years of this semi-hippie life, isolated from the urban realities and feeling awful as a result of a romantic breakup (mostly occasioned by my unwillingness/inability to commit emotionally to my partner, whom I genuinely loved, this at the same time I was leading "encounter groups" to help people open themselves up), I wanted, needed, to leave Bellingham. I searched for jobs in newspaper or broadcast journalism and, lo and behold, found the *San Francisco Chronicle* nibbling at my bait. In 1971, the *Chronicle* hired me as a critic-in-waiting, and assigned me to work as a subeditor in the meantime.

I enjoyed the work, but editing other people's copy was not my idea of creative employment.

Besides, I was writing up a storm: finishing a novel (*A Novel Project*), completing *The Bellingham Poems*, doing film commentary, reviews, and articles for, among others, *Sight & Sound* (England), *Take One* (Canada), *Jump Cut, Film Quarterly, Overseas Weekly, Village Voice, The Nation, The Progressive*, the Sunday *Chronicle*. In addition, under the title "From the Belly of the Beast," I was sending back political and cultural columns to *Northwest Passage*: dispatches from the "front" to my cultural-revolutionary comrades.

In 1974, the *Chronicle*'s chief drama critic resigned and I was moved into the job. I was thirty-four years old, single, and infused with an enormous reserve of energy and enthusiasm, which I utilized in covering the exploding theater scene in the Bay Area. Naively, I assumed that I would be filling this critic's role for a few years or so—five years at the outside—and then would return to my own playwriting, directing, poetry, novels, political activism, etc. Sixteen years later, I finally was able to engineer an exit.

What kept me going during those sixteen years—or at least for about ten years, from, say, 1974 to 1984—was the exciting, exceptional quality of the work I was reviewing. The Bay Area was in the midst of a golden decade of brilliant theater—especially of the more experimental variety, which forms excited and challenged me—and I felt like a kid in a candy shop.

I also enjoyed the opportunity, through my writing, to help publicize these major artists and thus to help shape Bay Area theater—and even beyond, to a certain extent, both because many of the artists I championed had been on, or were about to move onto, the national and international scene (Bill Irwin, Whoopi Goldberg, Sam Shepard, George Coates, Robin Williams, Lily Tomlin, Danny Glover, the San Francisco Mime Troupe, John O'Keefe, Geoff Hoyle, Leonard Pitt, Paul Dresher, Snake Theater of Chris Hardman & Laura Farabough, Soon 3 of Alan Finneran, Winston Tong, et al.), and because I worked for many summers as a master critic at the National Critics Institute at the Eugene O'Neill Theater Center in Waterford, Connecticut, helping train a new generation of young reviewers.

At the O'Neill, teaching was up-front. But I've always thought of myself as a teacher—and a student—when writing as a critic. The world of the theater was a rich, exciting way for me to learn more about life, about history, about the complexities of personality, about almost everything. I soaked it all up. Then, adding insights from

Weiner, the radical young professor, addresses an antiwar rally at Western Washington State College, 1968

my own life, in my reviews I spoke not only of what I had seen the previous night onstage but revealed (subtly, I hope) the gradual shaping of a world-view. A sharp reader of criticism reads the critic, not the review, and I think I provided a solid philosophical touchstone for my readers—about a half-million a day and a million on Sundays—to react to.

In *The Cambridge Guide to American Theater* (Cambridge University Press), the entry on criticism says: "Over the past two decades . . . with decentralization of the American theater and the demise of major newspapers nationwide, critics for dominant papers in major markets have gained immense power over theater in their areas. Dan Sullivan and Sylvie Drake in Los Angeles, Richard Christiansen in Chicago, Kevin Kelly in Boston, and Bernard Weiner in San Francisco, for example, have had real power to make reputations and close shows. And with local productions originating with an eye to Broadway, these local critics, indirectly, have gained power over

Weiner (second from left) interviewing playwright Sam Shepard (right) at San Francisco's Magic Theater, with artistic director John Lion between them, 1979

what is seen in New York." In the entry on me, the *Guide* noted more specifically that: "Weiner encouraged an explosion of new fringe theater activity and championed the work of visually-based experimental artists." I felt delighted that I was part of a movement to help keep as much shlock as possible out of the New York and national limelight, by celebrating and publicizing the true breakthrough artists who took theater to new creative levels.

The night-after-night reviewer's schedule—roughly, 250 shows per year, year in and year out—burned me out early. I took a semi-sabbatical—a half-year in London, complete with wife and young child—in 1980, and came back refreshed, a condition that lasted all of about two weeks when I jumped back on the treadmill in 1981. Things were still popping in Bay Area theater.

In 1988, I took another sabbatical, but by this time, several things had changed. First, the theater scene was providing me with fewer highs, more lows and a whole lot more mediocrity in the middle. The post-'60s burst of creativity (lasting roughly into the early '80s) had played itself out; there was less of quality and fewer aesthetic breakthroughs to gladden this critic's soul.

In addition, *I* had changed. First, my creative muscles were atrophying; I needed, desperately, to get back to my own literary and dramatic work. Eating off the plates of others was making me feel like a cultural parasite; I needed to get back into my own kitchen and begin cooking again. True, I had created and directed a few things during my *Chronicle* tenure—writing and staging an experimental piece at the Bay Area Playwrights Festival, directing the Northern California premiere of Joe Orton's *What the Butler Saw,* etc.—but these were few and far between, and were scrunched into a hectic work schedule. I felt that poems and plays and fiction were down there, somewhere, in my creative well, but the longer they stayed there the more chance they—I—would stagnate.

Then, too, I was now forty-eight years old, had a wife who was increasingly resentful of my nightly disappearing act, and two small boys who, in important ways, saw me as a somewhat marginal figure in their lives, especially at their all-important going-to-bed times. In effect, I found myself repeating my father's workaholic style that had isolated him from much of our family life.

I also had been longing for a return to work on spiritual development (devoid of drugs, which I rarely partook of anymore) and to my Tai Chi/ meditation practice. In my earlier years, I had been excited by the insights provided by such thinkers and writers as Houston Smith, Alan Watts, D. T. Suzuki, Walt Whitman, Yogananda, et al., and I wanted the freedom to explore my own thinking in the spiritual realm.

And so I used that 1988 sabbatical to figure out what to do. I think I had made up my mind to leave my job, but I couldn't even admit it openly to myself. Jumping back on the treadmill in 1989 helped me make the decision: I was tired, dispirited, and, if I didn't get out and soon, I might start taking out my frustrations not only at home but on those I was reviewing, and I didn't want either of those things to happen. And so, at age fifty, I simply turned in my resignation and departed, in effect leaping off a cliff, hoping there was water or something down there that would save me from total destruction.

The most important transition was becoming a full-time husband and father. It took a few years for me, for us, to make those individual and deep family connections work, but the payoff has been enormous, emotionally and in terms of freeing me to write more meaningfully.

Since leaving the safe, secure *Chronicle* job, I've enjoyed the precarious life of a part-time instructor (at various colleges and universities), writer/director/dramaturg—working in the Bay Area and, on occasion, around the country—and free-lance journalist. In addition, my poetry tap has begun to flow again: *Songs of Non-Enlightenment*, a collection of recently written poems, was published in chapbook form, and a new collection, *Deeper into Non-Enlightenment*, is in the works. In terms of plays, I helped found and run The Playwrights' Lab of Marin Theatre Company, outside San Francisco, and have had a number of works presented there: *Playing for Peace* (1998), *Somewhere between Purgatory & Nirvana* (1997), *Running*

in the Wake (1997), *Power Play* (1996), *Jack & Blewish* (1996), *2 X 4 Play* (1995-96), *The Other Side* (1994). I've also been getting back to short stories and novels—and a memoir. I continue to review on occasion, mostly books, and do some arts programming and producing/directing for KPFA (Pacifica Network).

Other things happened as well once I left the daily work grind. In 1990, my son Erik was on the cusp of turning thirteen; he didn't want a bar mitzvah, but I didn't want that important year—just prior to his beginning high school— to go unmarked. I thought about an alternative rite-of-passage and got together fathers of Erik's eighth-grade schoolmates to see if they were interested in joining me. They were indeed. Each of us had had much the same experience: no matter if we had been "initiated" through bar mitzvah, confirmation, Eagle Scout induction, or whatever, each of us had longed for something

The author, "a bit bemused," cradles his ten-day-old son Erik, 1977

"The family is complete: Mark is born," 1982

less generic, a more personal ritual that would tie us more meaningfully to our fathers, our parents, our culture.

So, over the course of the year, we fathers devised a coming-of-age ritual for our sons. (The mothers took part in the early planning, but then left us to our own devices, as they prepared their own letting-go ceremony.) The two-and-a-half-day weekend event took place on a twenty-five-acre plot of land, next to a river, in the Sierra foothills. As one might expect, given my background, the script I came up with included a lot of dramatic touches: a short play, puppet figures, masks, music, dancing, theatricalized rituals, etc.

The spiritual/psychological power of the event blew us dads away—and obviously affected the boys as well. As we told people about what we had carried out, interest seemed to grow, and we found ourselves serving as consultants for other fathers interested in doing something similar. Remembering that, when I was writing the script, I could find precious few antecedents in initiation literature—most of what's out there consists of scholarly exegesis, anthropological analysis, tribal studies, and the like—I decided to publish a report of what we had done, as a rough model for other dads: *Boy into Man: A Fathers' Guide to Initiation of Teenage Sons.*

With very little marketing, the book took off, and for the next several years, I was on the booktour and lecture circuit, and found myself regarded as an "expert" on adolescent initiation and the healing role of ritual in contemporary life. The book continues to sell, and I continue to serve as a consultant along these lines. I'm considering updating the book, because I've learned so much since it was published that should be in there, including what I picked up from doing an initiation for my second son, Mark, and his friends.

Both my sons, God help them, are actors. Erik is a sophomore at New York University's Tisch School of the Arts and already has performed in shows in Manhattan; Mark is a junior at San Francisco's High School of the Arts, and has performed professionally as well. My wife, Heidi, is a marvelously creative painter/sculptor—and a sensitive, loving being. Our household, to say the least, is an interesting one, with various aesthetic principles (and artistic egos) constantly bouncing off the walls.

We all are busy little beavers in our specialized areas. I find myself calmed usually by meditation, hiking and biking, spending time around large bodies of water, and writing poetry; perhaps some of that calmer attitude can be glimpsed in *Songs of Non-Enlightenment.*

Vipassana
(For Jack Kornfield)

Sometimes life goes by so fast,
My life goes by so fast,
That all I can catch is the blur
As I'm pushed forward,
Or as I go around in circles.

The fan whirls briskly on the ceiling
As I revel in its artificial breeze
In the heat of sweltering Poipu.

If I concentrate on the center of the fan,
All I see is the blur
Of motor, machinery, whipped air.
But if I focus on a single blade,
Following it around and around on its
 predetermined path,
I see the four propellers,
I see the mechanism of how it all works,
I see fanness.

I can do this best when the fan is at
 medium speed,
But the same principle of observation
 works at high speed as well.
You follow one propeller blade round
And the fan slows itself
Into its essential pattern.

So I try to look at my blur
In pieces now,
One day at a time,
One action at a time,
One feeling at a time . . .
One breath at a time.

Kauai, Hawaii: August 1992

Vibrations

It's quiet time, just before lights out.
My nine-year-old, in his pajamas,
Is reading his favorite story to me.
His head is resting on my foot, and my
 ankle
Becomes a magical resonator of his voice
 box.
Up my leg, into my chest and skull,
My ribs and head are slightly vibrating
To the sound of Matilda and her psychic
 powers.
His head is very heavy now on my foot,
And I want to shift.
But if I do, even a millimeter,

I know that I'll lose this intense physical
 connection.
I close my eyes and let my son's voice fill
 my bones.

I hike along the ridge, breathing the
 green,
Marveling at the milky seed-puffs in the
 summer sun.
My calves feel full, tested, awake to the
 challenge of the hike.
My lungs intake, hold, outgo, hold: I'm
 getting high on walking.
After an hour, I rest
And dig a sandwich and apple out of the
 backpack,
Then read some Rumi and hear Beethoven
 in the trees.
I lay my head on the earth, merging with
 the hum.

Olema, CA.: September 1991

Song of Non-Enlightenment

I'm not enlightened,
I just know a few things.

I know that if you look in a mirror
And see yourself,
You're mistaken.

I know that if you run fast,
You'll get ahead of yourself.

I know that if you look directly into the
 light,
You're not ready.

I know that if you think you can fly,
You are.

I know that if you're too cautious,
You'll go far—
But not far enough.

I know that if you're wild and crazy,
You need to.

I know that right angles do not always
 meet
Exactly.

I know that if your heart is open,
Your eyes are.

I know that helping others

Is a good prescription.

I know that spiritual masters are fakes—
And they know it, too,
Which is what gives them their authority.

I know that if you're aware of the
    blessing,
You're not really here.

I know that my body helps me understand.

I know that laughter is light.

I know that love doesn't make the world
    go around.
It is the world.

I know that hate feels good,
Really good . . .

I know that 2 + 2 doesn't equal 4.

I know that poetry is map-making.

I know that marriage is a prison
And that the convicts are free.

I know that joy is the best medicine
Even when there is no evident disease.

I know that learning is painful.

I know that everything is skin:
Semi-permeable.

I know that some people are annuals and
    some perennials.

I know that not enough can kill you
And too much can make you sick.

I know that fantasy,
Like reality,
Is a crutch.

Family portrait: Mark, Heidi, Bernie, and Erik, 1995

I know that babies are sacs of becoming,
Moving from pure Are.

I know that fear is a juice worth drinking.

I know that writing is a way in.

I know that anything is a way in.

I know that the truly enlightened
   understand the All.
(I'm not even on the outskirts of the
   particle.)

I am not enlightened,
I just know a few things.

I know that as long as I can keep this list
   going,
I'm heading in the right direction.

I know that I need to change direction.

                 Santa Cruz, CA.: October 1991

BIBLIOGRAPHY

Poetry:

Selected Poems, Graphic House Press, 1965.

Ten New Poems, CEE Press, 1968.

The Bellingham Poems, Goliards Press, 1973.

Songs of Non-Enlightenment, Transformation Press, 1995.

Plays—Published and Produced:

'Til the End of Time, Tempo, 1962.

When in the Farce of Human Events It Becomes Necessary, Claremont Quarterly, 1964.

The Film: A Monologue for Many, Horizont (Sweden), 1967.

Plays—Produced:

The Fourth Monkey, 1962.

The Usual, 1964.

Vietnam Play, 1968.

Shadows Cast No Bright, 1968.

The Other Side, 1994.

2 X 4 Play, 1995-96.

Jack & Blewish, 1996.

Power Play, 1996.

Running in the Wake, 1997.

Somewhere between Purgatory & Nirvana, 1997.

Playing for Peace, 1998.

Nonfiction:

Boy into Man: A Fathers' Guide to Initiation of Teenage Sons, Transformation Press, 1992.

Contributor to various collected works, including *California Theater Annual,* Performing Arts Network, 1982-83; *West Coast Plays 15-16,* California Theater Council, 1983; *Prima Facie 1986: An Anthology of New American Plays,* Denver Center Theater Company, 1986; *Burns Mantle Theatre Yearbook, 1989-90,* Applause Publishers, 1990; and *Around the Absurd: Essays on Modern and Postmodern Drama,* edited by Enoch Brater and Ruby Cohn, University of Michigan Press, 1990.

Also contributor of essays, reviews, and commentary to various periodicals, including: *The Drama Review, Yale/Theater, American Theater, Village Voice, The Nation, Tikkun, Film Quarterly, Take One (Canada), Sight & Sound (England), Jump Cut, Performing Arts Magazine, North American Review, Performing Arts Magazine, Los Angeles Times, Seattle Post-Intelligencer,* and *Western Political Quarterly.*

Cumulative Author List

CUMULATIVE AUTHOR LIST
Volumes 1-28

List is alphabetical, followed by the volume number in which autobiographical entries appear.

Cumulative Index

CUMULATIVE INDEX

The names of essayists who appear in the series are in boldface type. Subject references are followed by volume and page number(s). When a subject reference appears in more than one essay, names of the essayists are also provided.